AF371545

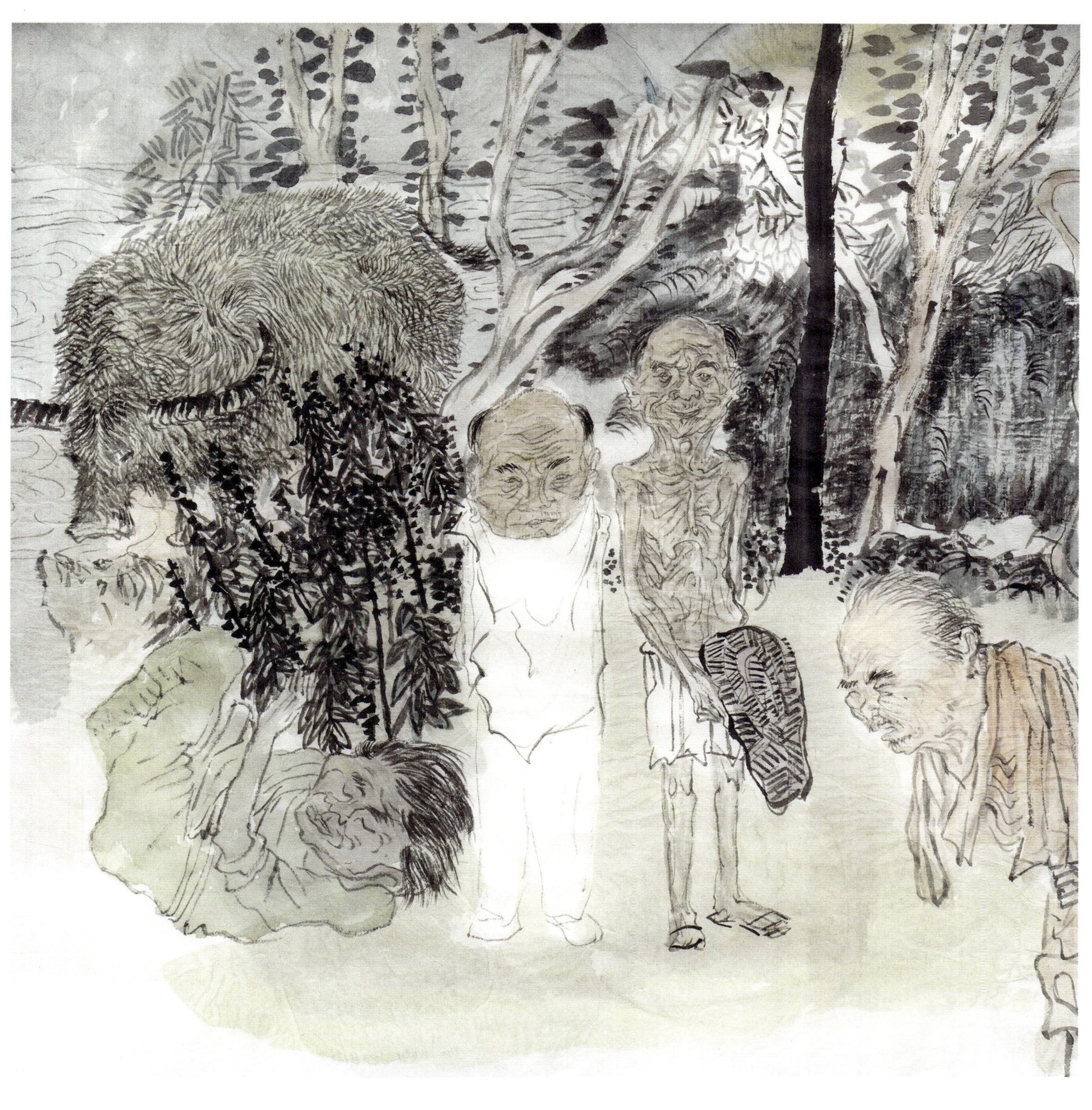

drawing people

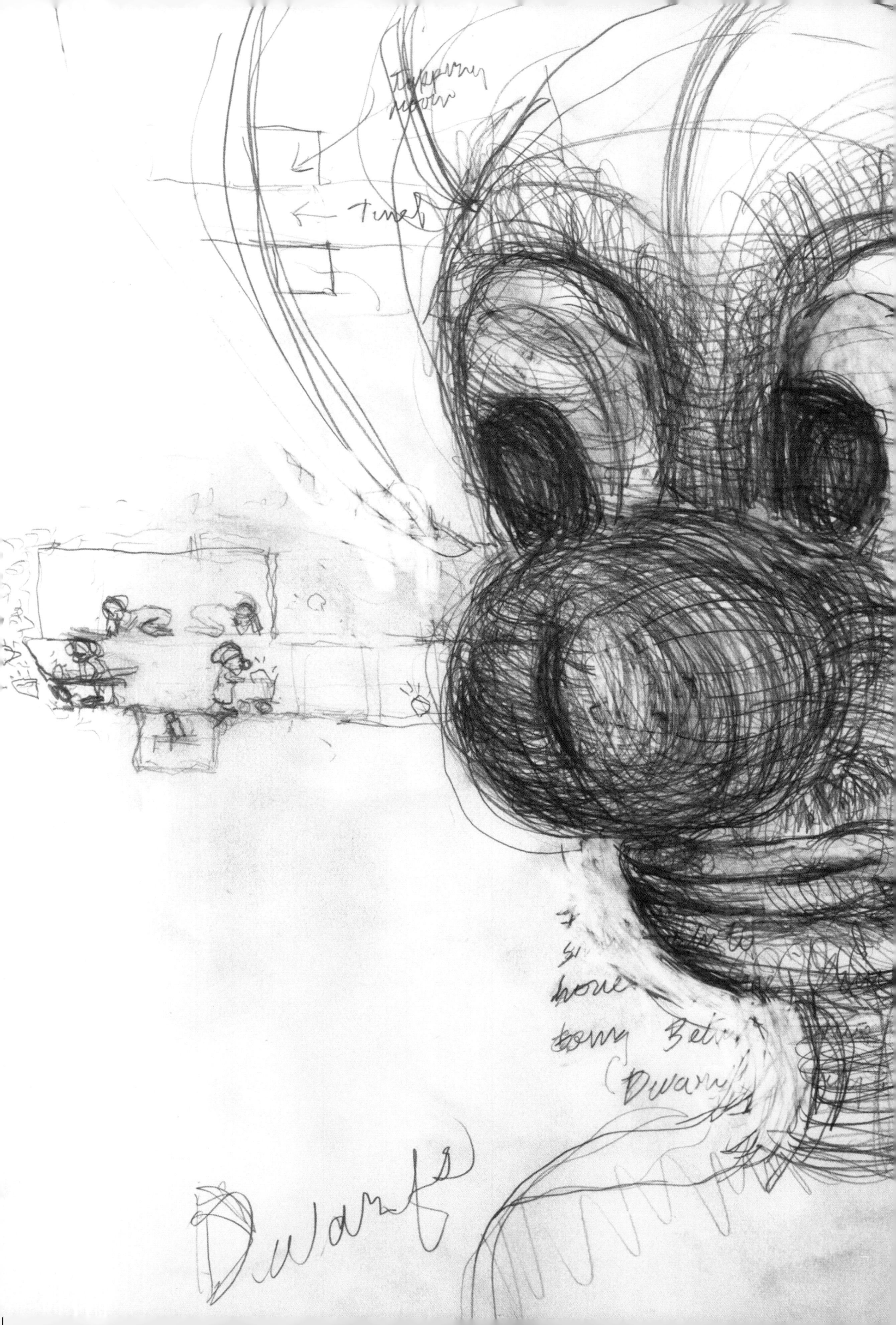
Tunnel
Dwarfs
Dwarfs

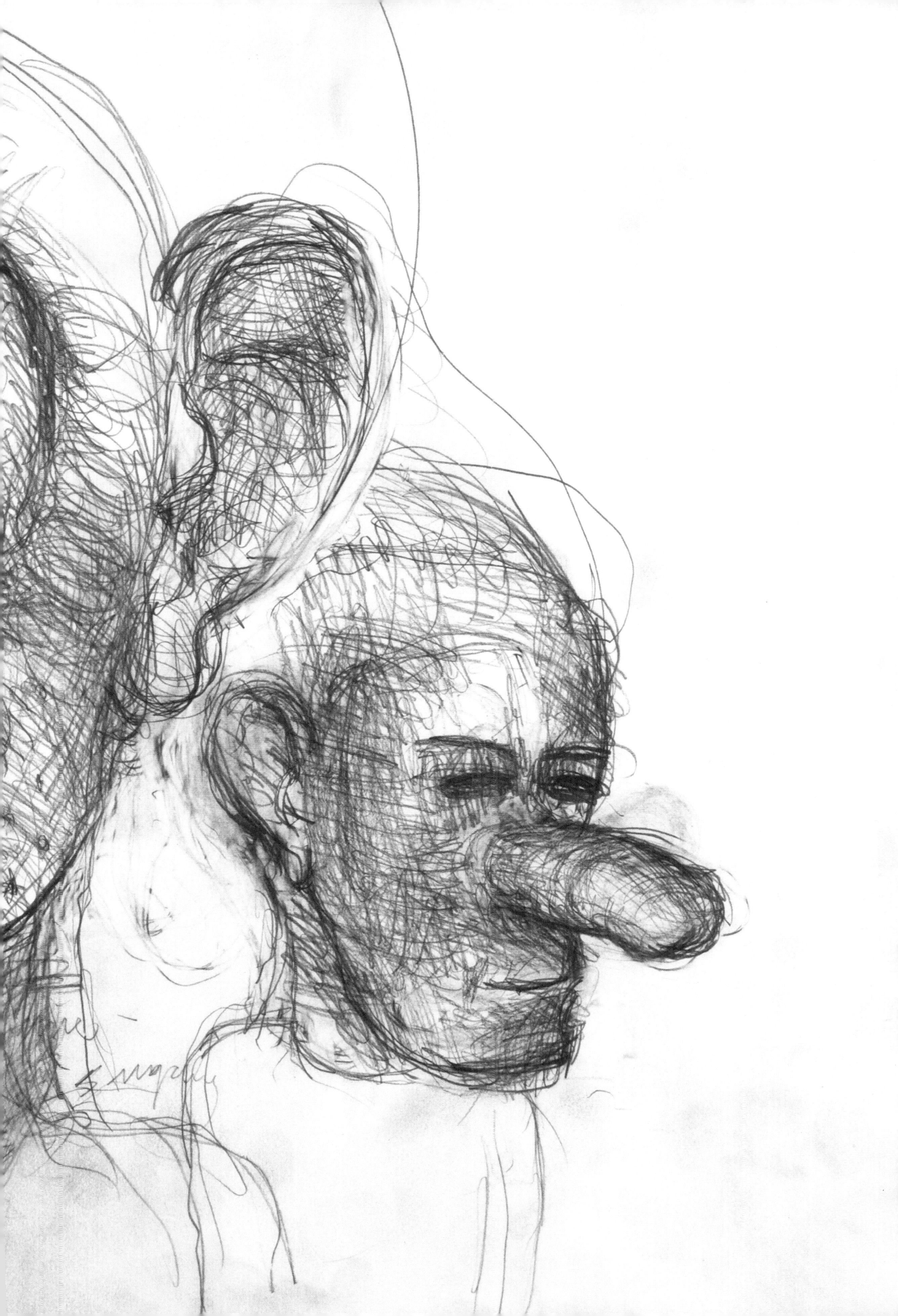

ROGER MALBERT

drawing people

THE HUMAN FIGURE IN CONTEMPORARY ART

With 318 illustrations, 246 in color

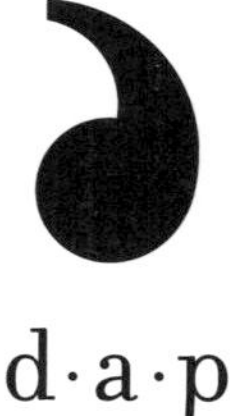

d·a·p

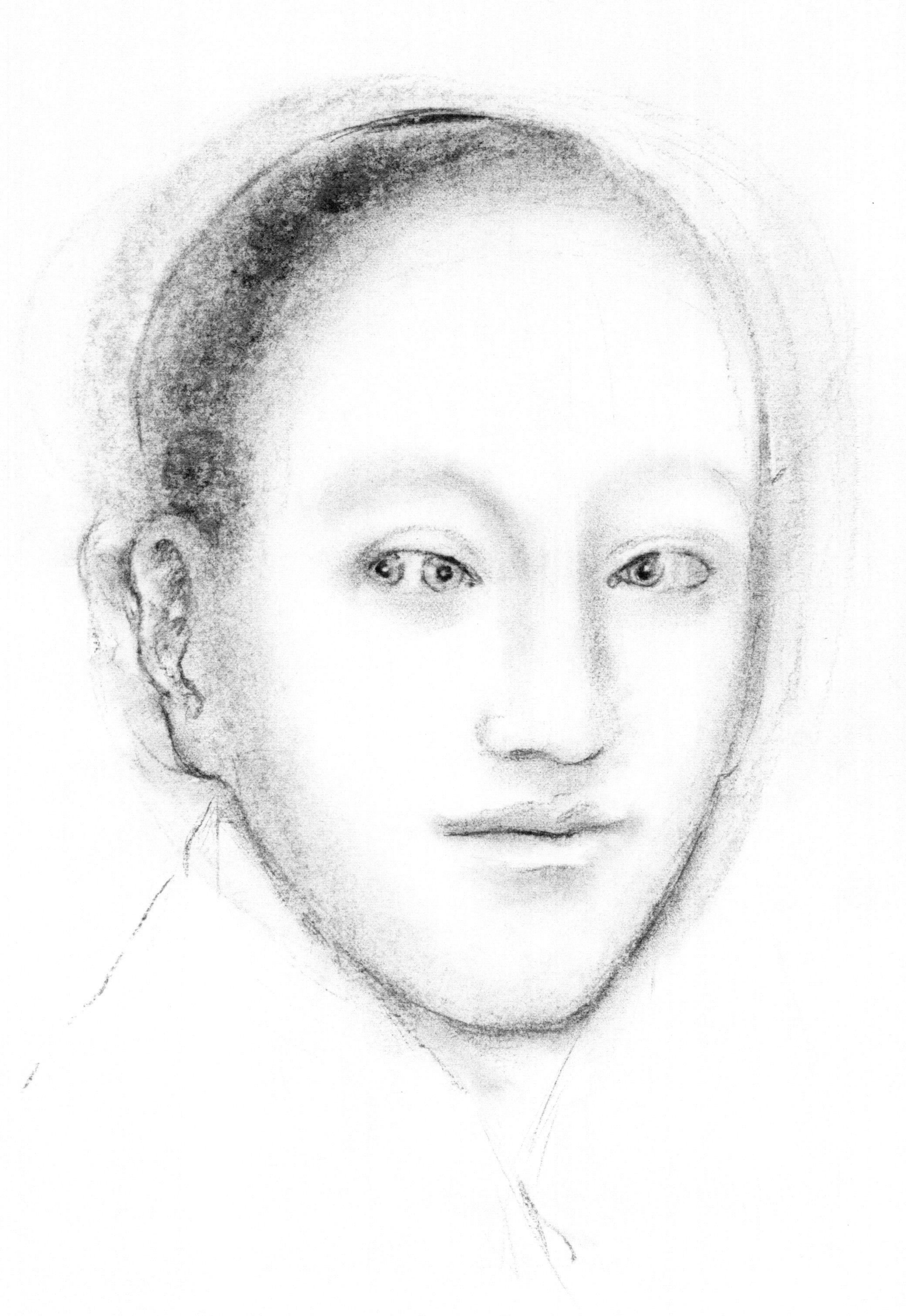

page 1
YUN-FEI JI, *The Water Buffalo*, 2006
Mineral pigment on rice paper, 33 × 32.8 cm (13 × 12 ⅞ in.)

pages 2–3
PAUL McCARTHY, *Dwarf Heads, Dwarf Mine*, 2008
Pencil on paper, 45.7 × 61 cm (18 × 24 in.)

page 5
JUUL KRAIJER, *Untitled*, 2002
Charcoal on paper, 70 × 50 cm (27 ½ × 19 ⅝ in.)

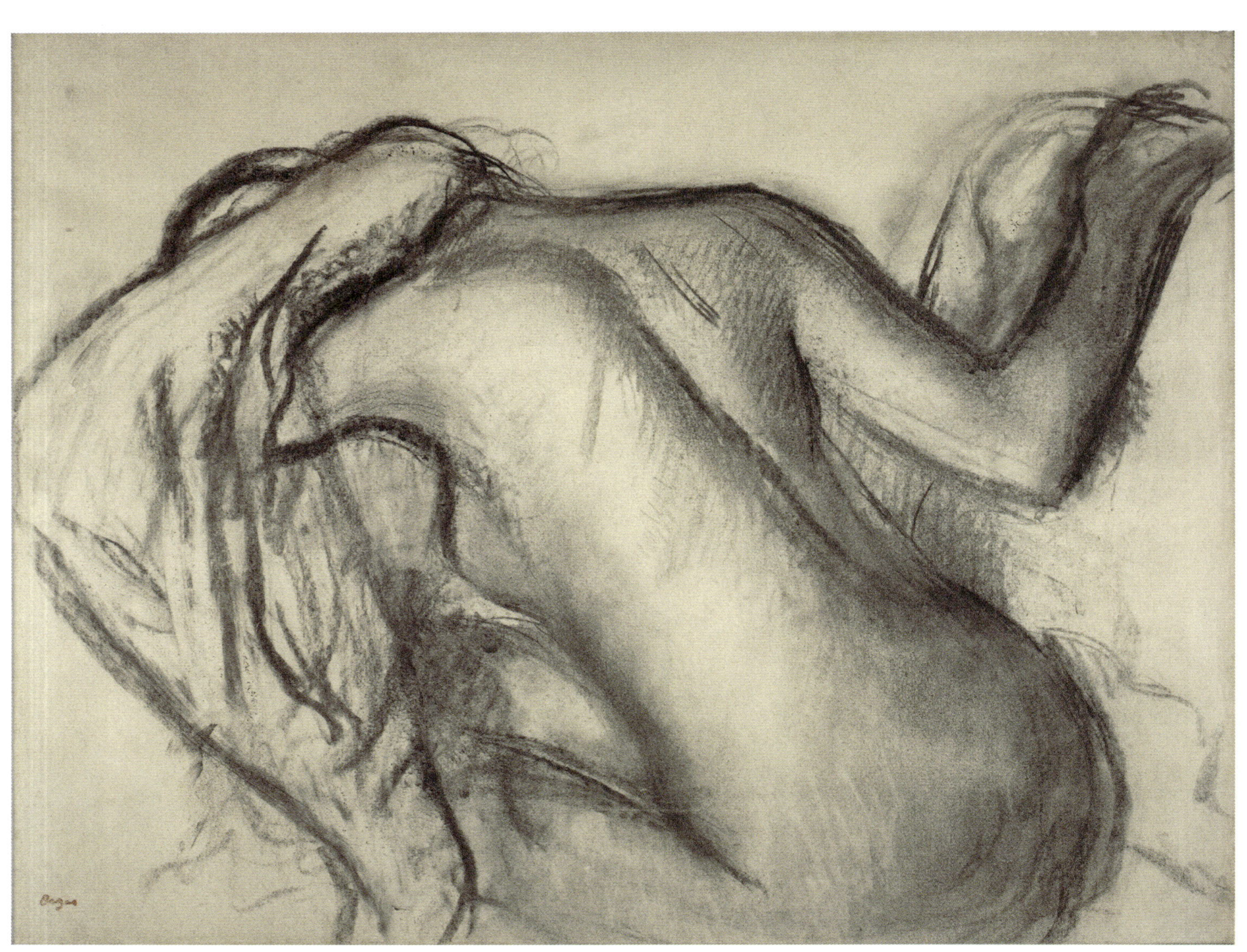

introduction: A UNIVERSAL LANGUAGE

Drawing is one of the most direct forms of visual expression.
It is where art begins, literally, both in human evolution and the
development of the individual. Before writing, there are images,
scratched onto a cave wall or scribbled in crayon on cheap paper.
And among the first subjects, along with animals and the sun,
is the human figure.

In Western academic art education, figurative drawing was until recently considered the foundation, the essential discipline underpinning all others. Although it is no longer a requisite skill for contemporary artists, a high proportion would still undoubtedly say that they first showed talent as a child through a precocious facility for drawing (a proclivity that may have been drummed out of them later at art school). To be 'good at drawing' can also be a redeeming quality in an unscholarly and rebellious pupil, an escape route to individual liberty, a declaration of future destiny, possibly a vocation. Drawing is more than simply a skill, like playing football or the saxophone, or sewing or mathematics. It is a path to self-discovery, revealing a cast of mind, an imaginative capacity and a mode of perception. Drawings give access to the obsessions, sense of humour, emotions and fantasies of their creator. This is not to say that the adolescent drawings of a future artist will necessarily display exceptional originality and sensitivity, but they often show signs of a distinct individuality, a personal vision that in retrospect can be seen to anticipate future creative preoccupations.

Of the many children and young people who draw obsessively and cleverly, only a few will aspire to become what we call fine artists. Many more will find outlets in illustration, graphic and digital art, fashion, comic books, cartooning or graffiti. It is not this book's intention to denigrate these other spheres of visual expression by their omission, nor to claim special status for the drawings that end up in galleries and museums. Yet when we consider the subject of drawings of people in a global context, we are presented with a field so vast that a narrowing of focus is necessary to contain it. This volume therefore focuses on drawing as a central practice in international contemporary art.

The 71 artists in this book are grouped in five chapters under broad thematic headings. Several of these themes are variations on conventional art genres. The first chapter, on the body, takes as its point of departure the traditional category of the nude, but gives it an anti-classical, anti-idealist twist: the body treated not as an object of curiosity or desire but as it may be experienced from within, through the senses or, as we generally perceive our own bodies, in parts. Chapter 2, 'Self', incorporates portraits and self-portraits, but with an emphasis on their metaphorical or psychological rather than objective representation.

< EDGAR DEGAS, *After the Bath, Woman Drying Her Hair*, c. 1893–98
Charcoal and brown chalk on pale pink wove paper,
49.7 × 64.4 cm (19 ⅝ × 25 ⅜ in.)

Chapter 3, 'Personal Lives', is also concerned with the self, but this time in a social sense: how we relate to others and to the world. The fourth chapter, 'Social Reality', ranges broadly over history and politics, looking at how artists use figurative drawing to satirize, comment on, or otherwise engage with these facets of experience. Finally, 'Fictions' covers a variety of imaginative compositions, some springing from observation or based on photography, others more fantastical or even visionary. These themes are by no means prescriptive, and readers will discover affinities between artists across chapters as well as within them.

DEFINITIONS

Drawing is not a watertight category absolutely distinct from painting, collage, photography and other media, and expanded definitions have loosened our ideas of what a drawing may be. Traditionally, drawing in the West has been identified primarily with works on paper created using a brush, pen, pencil, charcoal, crayon or other hand-held mark-making stick. Images on canvas are generally considered paintings, even when line predominates over colour. But you can draw in blood or with a tattooist's needle, or dribble saliva or coffee onto a flat surface, or spray-paint a figure onto a wall and call it a drawing. And of course you can draw on a computer screen. In this book, where the emphasis is on the subject – the human image – the majority of works were produced by relatively conventional means. But this is not to discount the value of less orthodox strategies or technological wizardry, of which several examples are included here. The back-to-basics approach is simply a starting point. Art stripped to its barest essentials is equivalent to the notion of a 'Poor Theatre', as the Polish Director Jerzi Grotowski defined it in the 1960s: with the 'superfluous' trappings of scenography, lighting, props, technology, costume and sound effects removed, Poor Theatre, like drawing, is reduced to the basic perceptual relationship between actor and spectator; it thus 'reveals the backbone of the medium, but also the deep riches which lie in the very nature of the art-form'.

The concept of 'international' contemporary drawing should also be qualified here: this is not a multi-authored survey and neither is its author a global explorer. The book is informed and enriched by my direct knowledge of many of the artists it features, encountered through exhibition and publication projects or connections made by friends and colleagues (my debt to advisers is acknowledged more fully on p. 250). Many, especially the younger generation, were discovered through online research. Drawing, always a relatively portable medium, is now instantly accessible via the internet, even if the originals should be experienced at first hand truly to be appreciated. This book, in bringing together examples of the medium's freshest work, offers insights into these artists' imaginative worlds through close engagement with drawings to which a computer screen could never do justice. As for the selection itself, my perspective is of course partial: this is not a neutral but a personal view, and there is an emphasis on realism and the grotesque, the capricious, the perverse and the satirical. The underlying premise is that there are things that can be said about the human condition in a drawing that cannot be expressed in any other way. Unembellished, unmediated and uncensored, drawing is a free zone, where artists may think and imagine whatever they like. This book celebrates that freedom and the skills with which it is earned.

ALBRECHT DÜRER, *The Artist's Mother*, 1514 >
Charcoal, 42.3 × 30.5 cm (16 ⅝ × 12 in.)
Inscription: 'This my pious Mother bore and brought up eighteen children; she often had the plague and many other severe and strange illnesses, and she suffered great poverty, scorn, contempt, mocking words, terrors, and great adversities. Yet she bore no malice.'

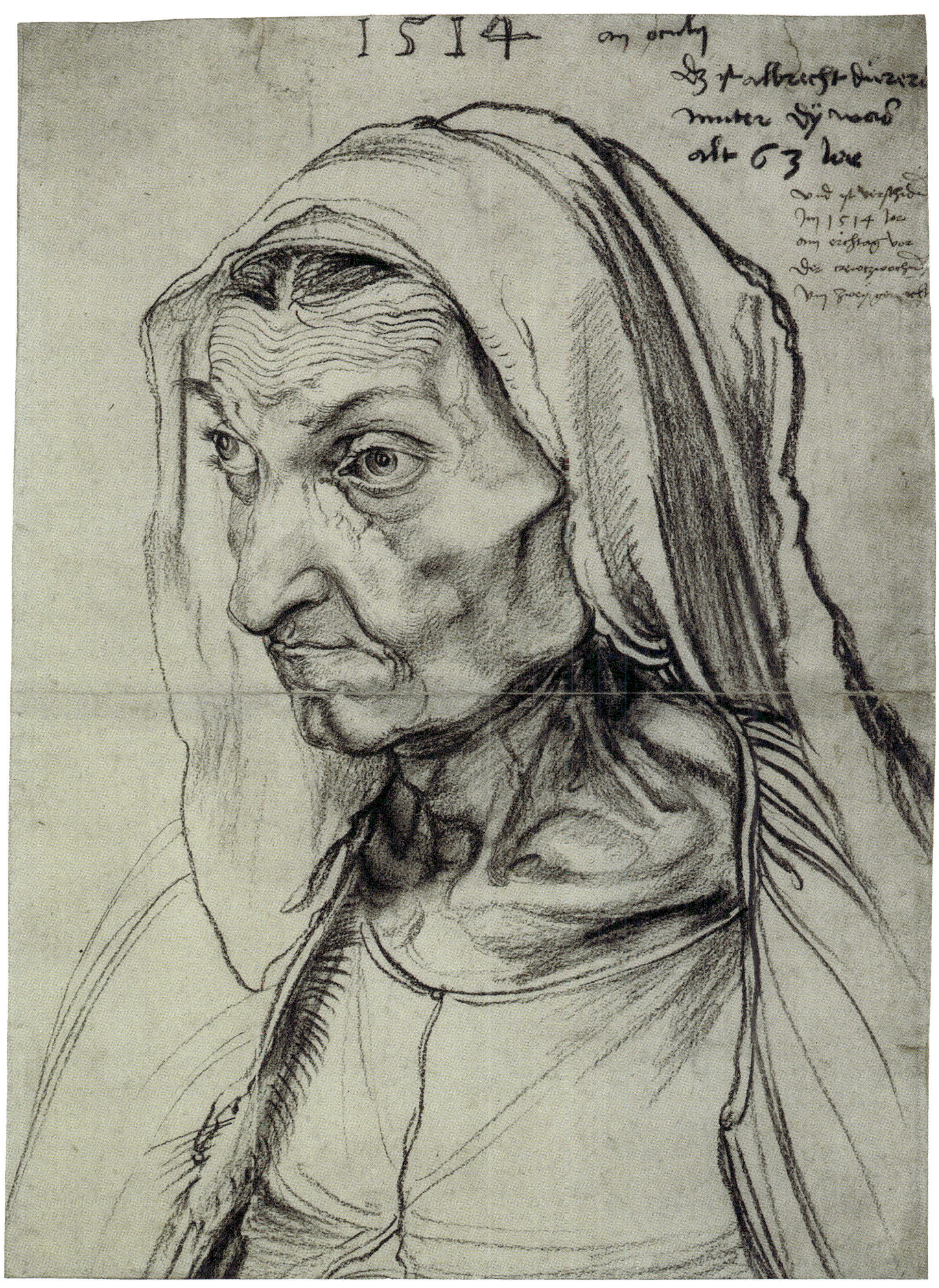

1514
Das ist albrecht dürers
muter dÿ woß
alt 63 Jor
vnd ist verschiden
Jm 1514 Jor
om erchtag vor
der crewtzwochen
vm zwey gekin in der nacht

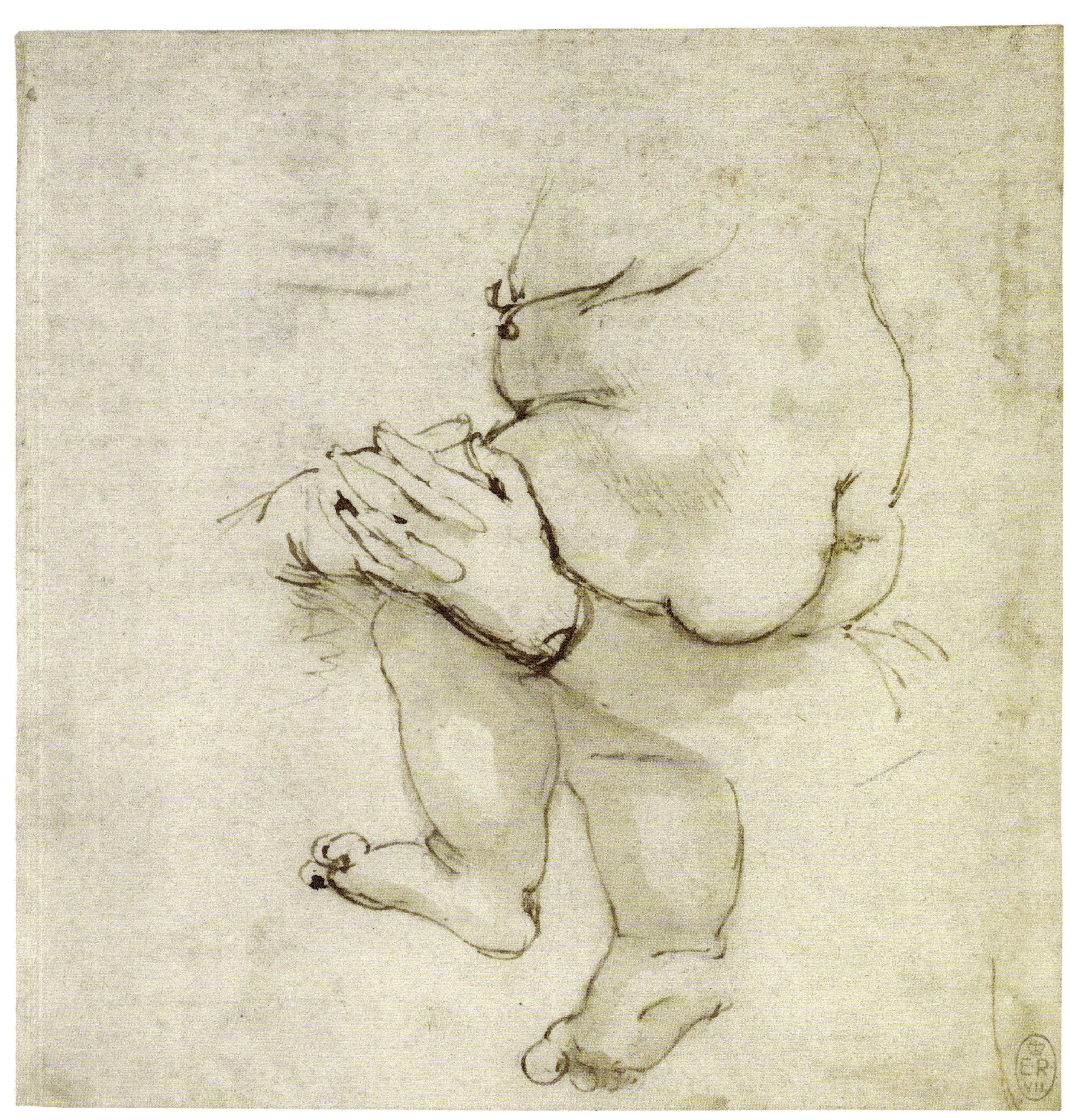

DRAWING AND LOOKING

Treatises about drawing conventionally start with perception: to draw is to look, and to discover, analyse and depict the objective world. Drawing from observation involves a triangular relationship between the eye, the hand and the object. Learning to draw begins with learning to observe, to notice and register sensations. Hand-eye coordination is acquired through practice until it becomes second nature. The realist artist and writer John Berger defines drawing as synonymous with looking: a life drawing is essentially an act of discovery. In the process of looking at and drawing a figure, we notice relationships between positive and negative space, the angle of the head, the folding of one hand over the other, the curl of hair over an ear, the turn of the mouth. The variations are infinite, which is why some artists continue to draw from the figure throughout their careers.

The idea of drawing from life seems so natural that it is easy to forget that it was not always so. When medieval artists needed figures for a composition, they would draw from copy or model books (like pattern books) filled with stock figures and poses, and studies of drapery and exotic animals, which were themselves derived from paintings or antique sculptures. These books were a rarity, being made of expensive parchment or vellum (calfskin), and were passed from artist to artist, becoming worn through frequent handling. The practice of drawing from a nude model did not develop until the mid-fifteenth century in Renaissance Florence, in the studio workshops of Filippo Lippi and Antonio del Pollaiolo. It coincided with the availability of cheap paper – manufactured in quantity to supply the newly invented printing presses – which allowed artists to sketch experimentally and make exploratory drawings. The sketchbook was a by-product of this period of industrial innovation.

< LEONARDO DA VINCI, *A Study of a Baby in its Mother's Arms*, c. 1478–80
Pen and wash, 13.3 × 13.0 cm (5 ¼ × 5 ⅛ in.)

Leonardo da Vinci was one of the first Renaissance artists to draw directly from life, not only in the studio but also in the street. He advised his fellow artists to be constantly alert to the world around them and always to carry a sketchbook: 'When you have learned perspective well... and have committed to memory the bodies of things and the parts thereof, you should take pleasure when you walk for recreation in seeing and considering the attitudes and actions of men in conversation, in quarrelling, or laughing, or fighting together, noting their gestures and those of the bystanders who intervene or look on in such cases. Make a note... with a few lines in your little book which you should always take with you. Its pages should be of coloured paper, so that you cannot rub your sketch out, but will have to change from an old page to a new one when the old one is filled. For these are not to be erased but preserved with great care, because these forms and actions are so infinite in number that the memory is not capable of retaining them, wherefore keep your sketches as your aids and teachers.'

It is astonishing to think that two of the greatest draughtsmen in the history of Western art, Leonardo (1452–1519) and Albrecht Dürer (1471–1528) were near-contemporaries and that both were devoted to the then-revolutionary practice of drawing empirically from nature. The humblest of subjects – a few tufts of grass, a hare, a baby's backside in the hammock of its mother's hands – was sufficient to inspire their curiosity. 'For truly art is hidden in Nature', wrote Dürer, three and a half centuries before Impressionism. 'Who can extract it, has it.' Dürer drew the earliest known self-portrait from the mirror in 1491, at the age of twenty, and much later, in 1514, he drew *The Artist's Mother*, one of the most profoundly realistic and moving portraits ever made in charcoal and one that remains a touchstone of the pathos that a great drawing can express. It shows his mother, haggard and worn, two months before her death at the age of 63. Dürer has been accused of displaying a lack of sympathy in this work, but no artist who has looked closely into the face of an old person would agree. After her death, he inscribed on the drawing, 'This my pious Mother bore and brought up eighteen children; she often had the plague and many other severe and strange illnesses, and she suffered great poverty, scorn, contempt, mocking words, terrors, and great adversities. Yet she bore no malice.'

No artist will ever surpass the subtlety and drama of the Old Masters' renderings of the human image in charcoal, chalk, silverpoint, graphite or ink. Yet there is no limit, in principle or in practice, to the variety of possible ways of drawing people, because the variety of human beings is infinite and so is the number of ways of being an artist. Technological innovation presents new possibilities, but it is striking how many artists today draw with the same primitive tools that Dürer used five hundred years ago. And this same medium, charcoal, was also available to the Palaeolithic artists who drew galloping bison with such incredible fluency in the caves of Lascaux in France thirty thousand years ago.

DRAWING FROM LIFE

Berger has said that there are three distinct ways in which drawings can function: to question and study the visible, to lay down and communicate ideas, and to draw from memory. For the realist, drawing is a discipline, a skill acquired through study and practice. It is not easy to learn to draw a convincing standing figure, with limbs in proportion and foreshortened as they appear to the eye, feet planted firmly on the ground, one hip tilted slightly to bear the body's weight, the eyes set naturally beneath the brows, the face expressing consciousness and personality. Most of us would be embarrassed by our efforts. Yet we observe people every day. Why should it be so difficult to render what we see? Instructional books advise the student to break it all down into cylinders, cones and spheres. Or we can learn to measure each distance and relationship with our thumb on the pencil, holding it at arm's length to ensure consistency, checking verticals against a doorway, correcting as we go along and always leaving traces of our changes, because, after all, this is a work in progress. Whole days can be devoted to this simple exercise and the result still full of visual problems – the greatest being that it can turn out to be inert, flat and uninteresting.

Alberto Giacometti, who dedicated his life to drawing and sculpting solitary figures in space, and who declared that 'drawing is all', describes an experience he had as a student in the 1920s after spending several days drawing a skull: 'One day, when I wanted to draw a girl, something struck me, which was that I suddenly saw that the only thing that stayed alive was her gaze. Everything else – the head turning into a skull – came to more or less the same thing as a dead man's skull. What made the difference between a dead man and the person was her gaze.' Giacometti's quest was an unending philosophical one: an enquiry into the nature of perception. In drawing from observation, the visible object, whether a figure or a tree or a chair, eludes capture, disappearing as soon as the artist looks away from it, the instant his eyes fall to the paper. It is only the 'residue of a vision' that he can attempt to preserve and represent.

Henri Matisse was similarly devoted to drawing from the model, but with an entirely different emphasis: not on analysing the phenomenology of perception, but rather on registering emotion. 'I have always seen drawing not as the exercise of a particular skill, but above all as a means of expression of ultimate feelings and states of mind... a means that is condensed in order to give more simplicity and spontaneity to the expression which should be conveyed directly to the spirit of the spectator.' When drawing from life as a student at the Académie Julian, he said, 'I did my utmost to depict the emotion that the sight of the female body gave me.'

Matisse's passionate response to the nude would have been anathema to his teacher, the academic painter William Bouguereau, who told Matisse that he would never learn to draw. The life class was meant purely for the study of the figure, a means of mastering perspective, proportion and foreshortening through careful calculation and measurement. The artist could then improve on nature by removing imperfections found in the actual model and adding a touch of classical grace. This stilted aesthetic, a corrupt descendant of the Italian academies of the

Renaissance, was famously loathed by the early avant-garde
– Kazimir Malevich described the life class as the 'death
sentence' – and academicism has generally been cast as the
enemy of modernism. Matisse, ironically, went on to run
his own art school for a while, where he employed some
of the same methods as the Académie – plumb lines and
plaster casts. But one of Matisse's most radical breaks from
tradition, his *Blue Nude* of 1907, came in precisely the same
year as Picasso's *Demoiselles d'Avignon* (discussed below)
and, like Picasso's painting, featured the naked female form
transported as far from classical ideals as could be imagined.

HENRI MATISSE, *Nude with Necklace Reclining
on Flowered Quilt*, 1935
Pen and ink on paper, 45 × 55 cm (17 ¾ × 21 ¾ in.)

15

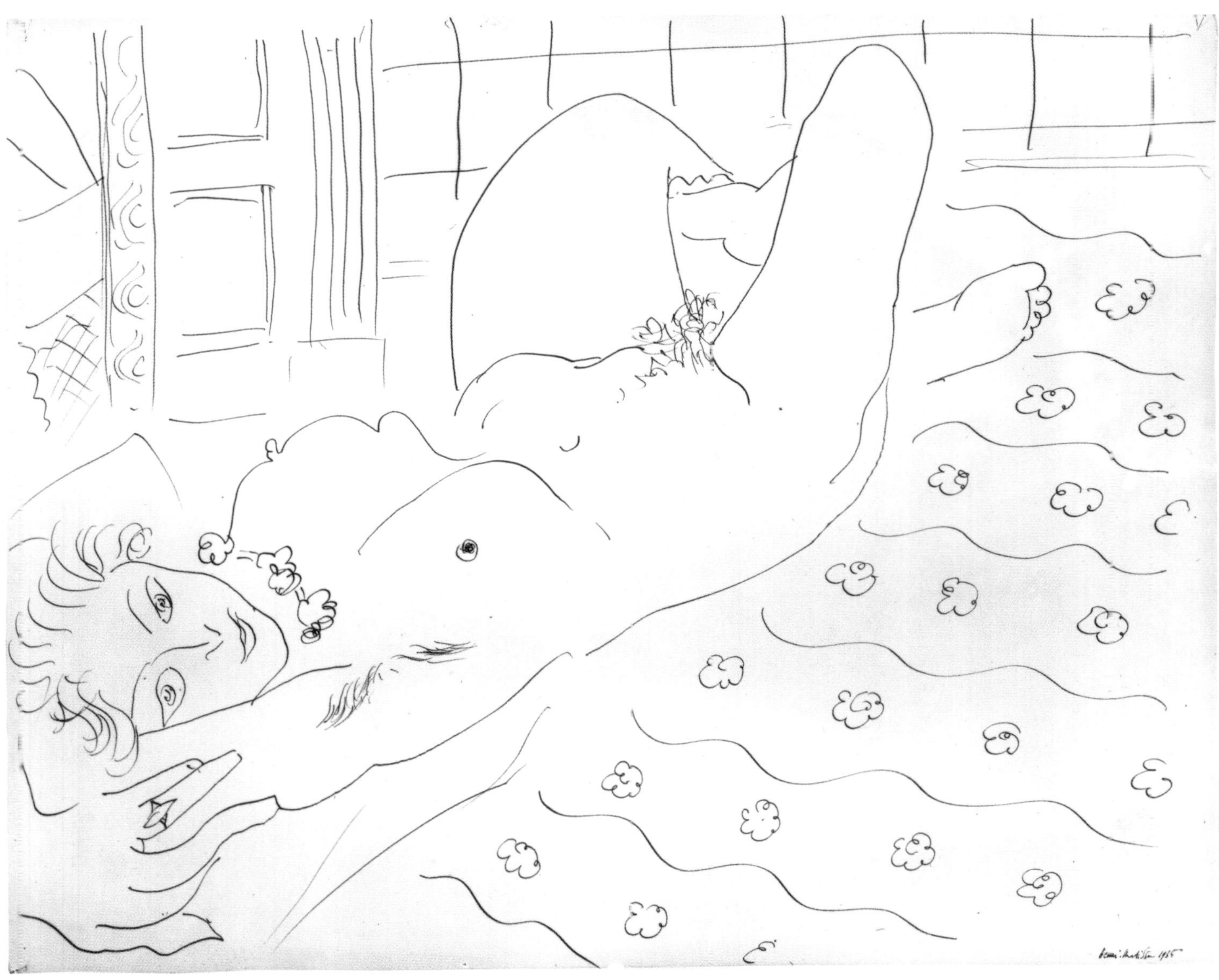

Life drawing went into what appeared to be terminal decline in the 1970s in many art schools. It was considered an anachronistic pursuit irrelevant to contemporary creative practice, and even an obstacle to artistic progress. From a strictly modernist perspective, the life class epitomizes everything that is moribund and oppressive about academic art. The class itself is not the liveliest of situations: ideas are rarely employed, the only obligation being to render what is set before one through obedient, repetitive exercises in looking. Politically, the life class is no less indefensible than it is aesthetically, for it can hardly withstand the critiques put forth by opponents of human objectification. Today, however, those polarized institutional and ideological debates have receded. Life drawing is more likely to be appreciated as an amateur pastime, a healthy antidote to the distractions of a hyperactive and superficial age, a slowed-down means of expression like acoustic music, creative writing or yoga. Drawing is a way of recovering one's senses, individuality and place in the world.

A fresh approach to life drawing was instigated in 2009 when the London-based contemporary art agency Artangel, together with the British artist Alan Kane, launched the project 'Life Class: Today's Nude'. This consisted of a series of drawing classes, broadcast on daytime television, as well as drop-in lunchtime classes in locations across London and other cities in the UK. Each of the five televised classes was taught by a different British artist – John Berger, Maggie Hambling, Gary Hume, Humphrey Ocean or Judy Purbeck – and the classes took place in a variety of settings, from municipal halls to the Royal Academy's eighteenth-century Life Room (which is designed like an operating or lecture theatre). The declared aim was to democratize art 'by taking the nude life class model out of the rarefied intimacy of the studio and transmitting it nationwide'. Television nudity tends to be self-consciously titillating, but these demonstration classes, in which the artist–presenters had the difficult task of giving a running commentary while drawing, were notably chaste, as life classes usually are. Another example of life drawing with a contemporary twist occurred

in New York at the Whitney Biennial in 2012, when the artist Nicole Eisenman set up a 'Figure Drawing Atelier' in the gallery and the public were invited to participate in a drawing session involving five nude models. This was inspired by Eisenman's practice of drawing with fellow artists, in which they would share the posing between them.

Perhaps in light of the chequered history of life drawing outlined above, few of the artists represented in this book draw directly from the model, and when they do it is rarely in the traditional manner. Amy Sillman's ink drawings are abstracted from drawings from life; Paula Rego creates compositions combining her favourite models and stuffed dummies; Kiki Smith draws friends, assistants and others she has invited to pose for her; Elizabeth Peyton draws both from photographs and from life. Peyton's experience of life drawing is far from the cold, impersonal atmosphere of the life class: she has spoken of the excitement, 'the pressure of being in a room with someone' and not knowing what will come of it. The more distinctively erotic charge of being with a naked model that Matisse invokes seems to have little appeal for contemporary artists, except, one could imagine, for Chris Ofili. And the idea of an existential encounter and dialectical exchange between artist and model, so strong a theme in the discourse of realism, has practically disappeared, dispelled by the seemingly ubiquitous presence of the camera.

FIGURATIVE DRAWING AND MODERNISM

A line drawn on the ground, ten metres long, may signify nothing but its own extent; or it may represent a border between two territories; or end with an arrow, in which case it becomes directional; or culminate in a circle punctuated with eyes, nose and mouth, making it a neck.

The grand narrative of post-War modernism is often presented as an inexorable march towards abstraction, minimalism and conceptualism. Figurative drawing has tended to be disparaged as retrograde, unless mediated through mass culture or otherwise

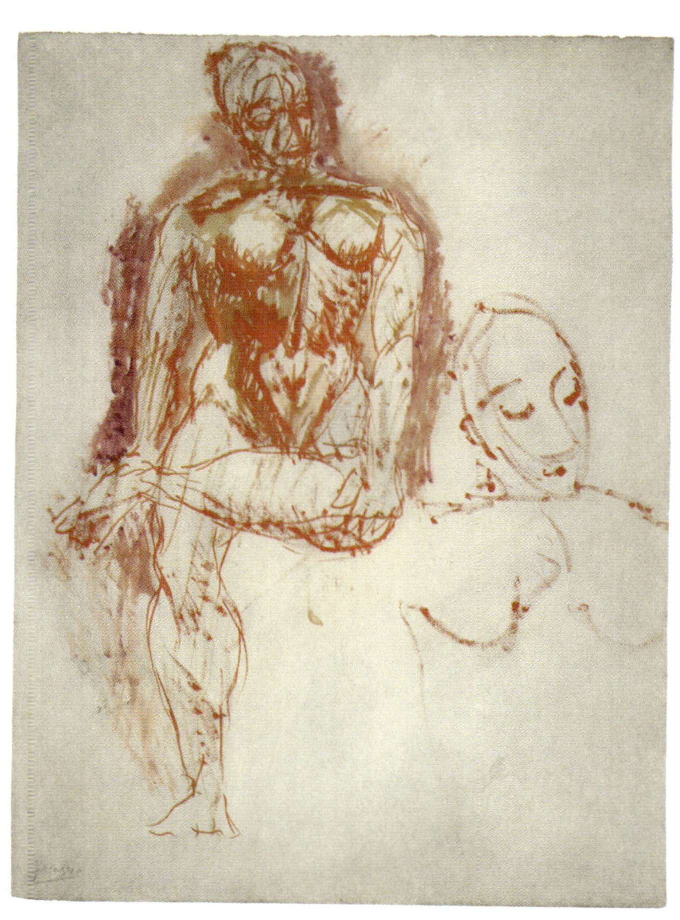

overlaid with self-reflexive irony. Those puritanical versions of art history that exclude the figure now seem outdated, but they still prevail in textbooks and are insufficiently contested. We have moved on, certainly, in terms of current artistic practice, from what might be described as the 'prohibition era' of the 1960s and '70s, when the human image was virtually taboo in many art schools (except in the largely ungovernable media of photography, film, video and performance). Pluralism is the now the order of the day. No ruling orthodoxy could dictate an artist's choice of subject. Yet drawing, usually marginalized in monolithic – masculinized and museum-orientated – histories of the major modernist art movements, is rarely given its due as a vital propelling force of experimentation and radical breakthrough. In fact, as a few examples will demonstrate, figurative drawing often played a seminal role in the most innovative art of modern times.

In early-twentieth-century Europe, Cubists, Futurists, Expressionists, Dadaists and Surrealists assaulted the human image in every conceivable way, fragmenting, distorting and flattening it, rendering it unrecognizable and incomprehensible to conventional minds. Many of the early modernists were supreme draughtsmen and it is natural that experiments in representation and its deconstruction were initially conducted in drawing. Picasso's sketchbook drawings of 1907 reveal his thinking, step by step, in preparation for the single most revolutionary painting of the modern era, *Les Demoiselles d'Avignon*. In hundreds of drawings in fifteen sketchbooks he rehearses the pose and expression of each individual, shaking up the composition and changing every aspect of every figure repeatedly. These drawings are not abstract art; nor do they appear to be travelling even remotely in the direction of abstraction. Their subject is the human body, physiognomy, character, sexuality, psychology, conflicting emotion and atmosphere. It was, Picasso said, his 'first exorcism painting'. He was exorcizing the spirit of academicism, the classical ideals of harmony and beauty that stifled the imagination. The strongest of the drawings are of far more than documentary interest; they are high-voltage and confrontational works of art in their own right.

17

Surrealism began as an experimental movement dedicated to exploring the irrational unconscious mind through writing and drawing. The Surrealists' use of the 'exquisite corpse' technique of constructing a drawing is a variation on the old parlour game of 'Consequences', where one player writes a line, folds over the paper and hands it to his or her neighbour, who adds another line without knowing what came before, resulting in an illuminatingly nonsensical narrative. Drawings composed in this collaborative way produced monstrous composite creatures, mixing species, sexes and body parts. Another Surrealist practice, automatism (the technique of free-association, allowing imagery to spring spontaneously from the unconscious without preconception), was more individualized – André Masson's automatist ink drawings, for example, all share an identifiable style – and the results are more revealing psychologically. Surrealism was defined by its founder, the French poet André Breton, in the first Surrealist Manifesto (1924) in primarily literary terms, as pure

'psychic automatism... by which one proposes to express – verbally, by means of the written word, or in any other manner – the actual functioning of thought... in the absence of any control exercised by reason, exempt from any aesthetic or moral concern.' In automatism, drawing and writing are contiguous and potentially interchangeable; the free flow of thought, of images and ideas, should be uninterrupted by mental or material constraints. Drawing's immediacy and fluency mean that it is much quicker and closer to the source of unconscious impulses than more complicated and cumbersome media. 'The Surrealist tradition has become the basis of many drawings,' remarked Marlene Dumas, 'without the urge towards revolution and madness. Or should I say that drawings have become the cartoons of our small dreams. Maybe drawing should never have become "art" after all.'

Another Surrealist exponent of automatism was the Chilean Roberto Matta, the artist who took this powerful imaginative tool to New York in 1939 and introduced it to Arshile Gorky

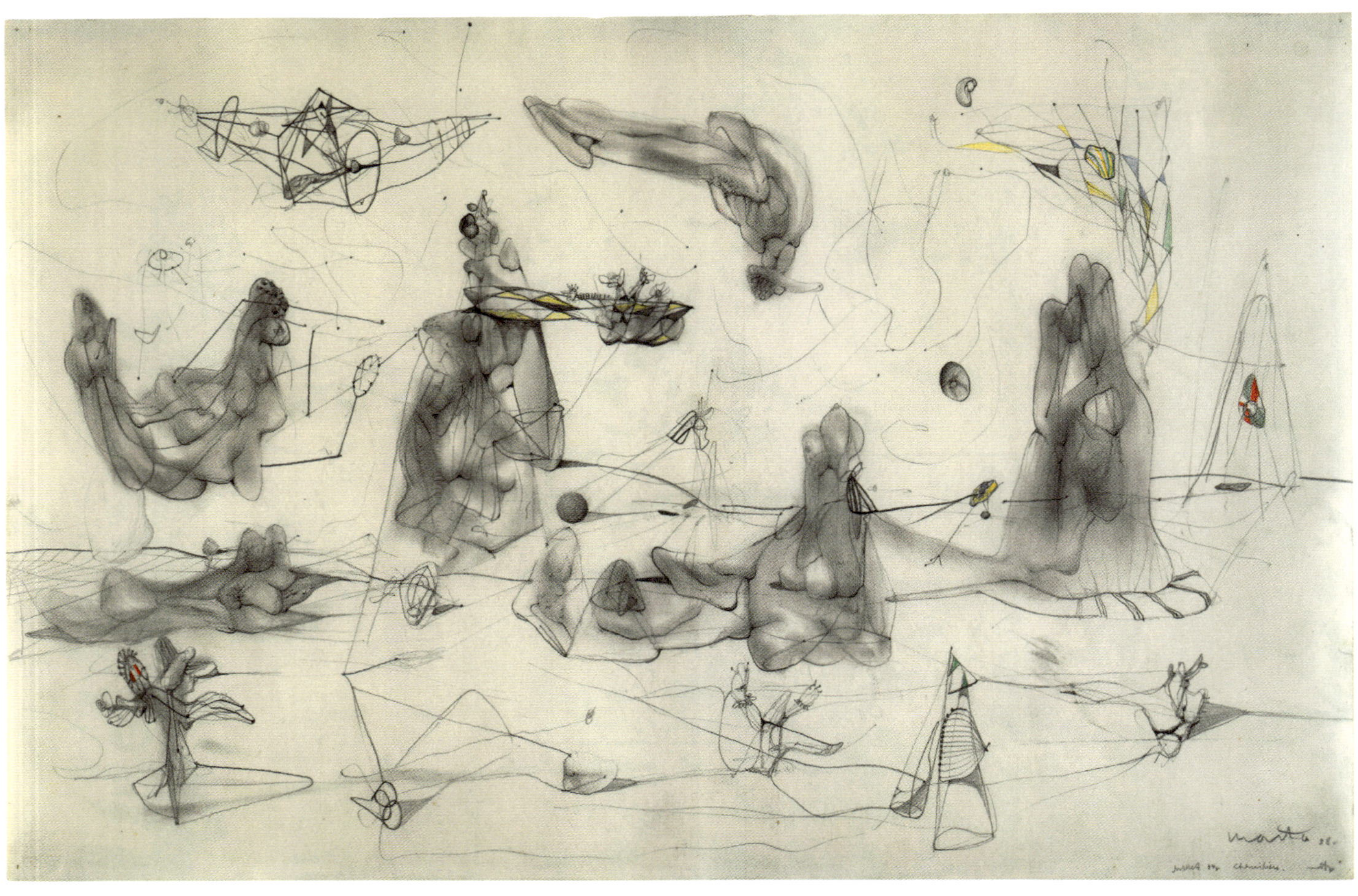

and Jackson Pollock. Matta's most original drawings of the 1930s and '40s include small exploratory works in pencil and crayon that he described as 'psychological morphologies', projections of inner psychic states that could only be grasped intuitively, by a mind open – like a scientist's or a poet's – to unexpected discovery. Hints of human shapes float into view in these drawings, but the artist drops them the instant they start to move beyond ambiguity. 'Automatism', he said 'is a method of reading "live" the actual function of thinking at the speed of events, to group unconscious material functioning in our memory with the tools at our disposal, with the language we possess, if possible grasping instantly, all at once.... Automatism means that both the irrational and the rational are running parallel and can send sparks into each other and light the common road.'

A highly political and contrarian artist, Matta held to his own pictorial principles of fierce figurative imagery and deep illusionistic space, against the grain of modernism's insistence

< ROBERTO MATTA, *Endless Nude*, 1938
Pencil and crayon on paper, 32.4 × 49.5 cm (12 ¾ × 19 ½ in.)

JACKSON POLLOCK, *Untitled*, c. 1952–56
Dripped ink on Howell paper, 46 × 55.6 cm (18 ⅛ × 21 ⅞ in.)

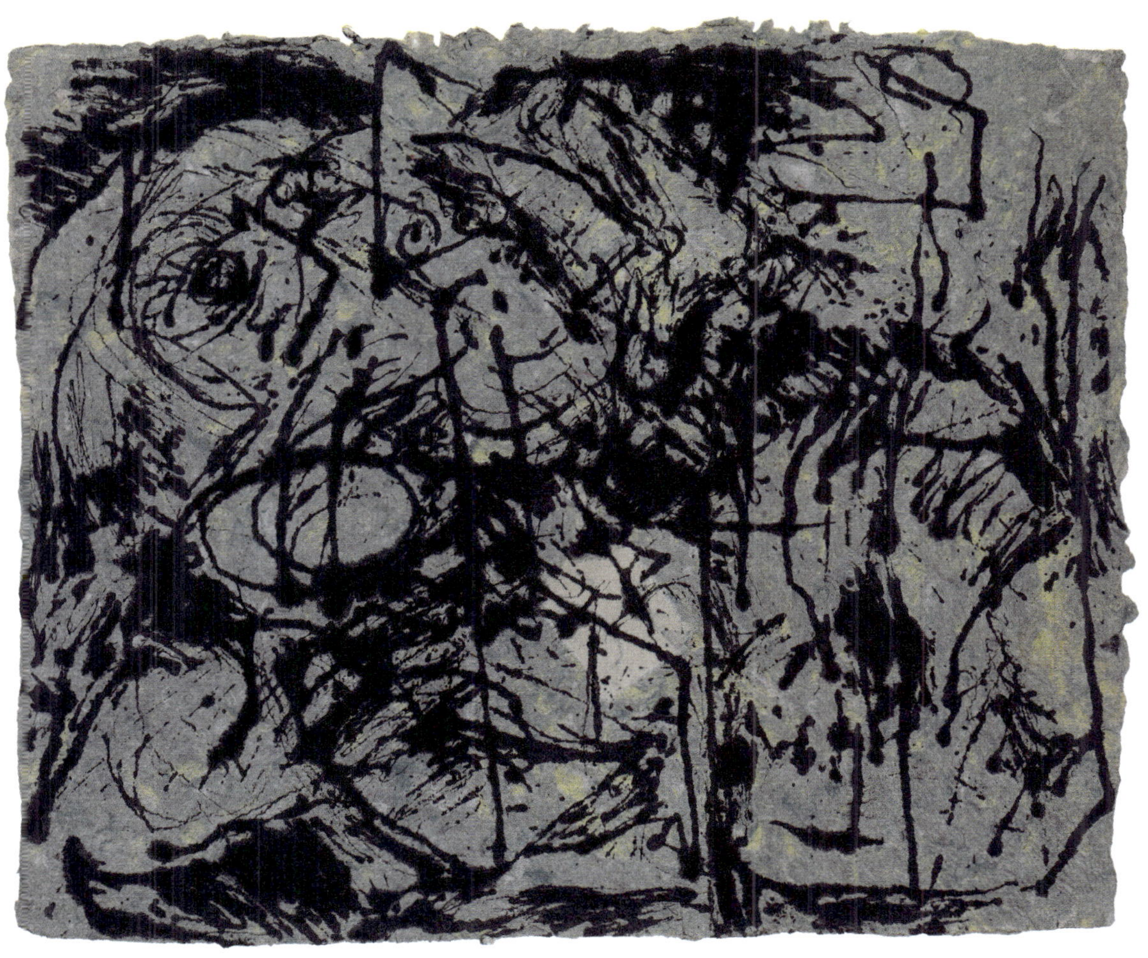

at the time on flatness and the elimination of meaning or representation. As a consequence, he has been sidelined in mainstream histories of post-War American art, although even among the artists who feature most prominently in those histories, there are some, such as the Abstract Expressionist Pollock, who had a deeply ambivalent relationship with figuration throughout their careers. Pollock famously declared that he chose to 'veil' his imagery, yet that repressed subject-matter returned persistently to haunt him: those distracting faces, eyes, dismembered limbs, totemic figures, moon women and self-portraits that continued to surface in his drawings and paintings until the end of his life. While Pollock wavered, fellow New York School painter Philip Guston made a conscious escape from abstraction. For two years, from 1967 to 1968, he abandoned painting and did nothing but draw. He was later to say, 'I cannot make a dot or a line which doesn't represent a known thing.' Thus, one of the most dramatic paradigm

PHILIP GUSTON, *Untitled*, 1975
Ink on paper, 45.4 × 61.9 cm (17 ⅞ × 24 ⅜ in.)

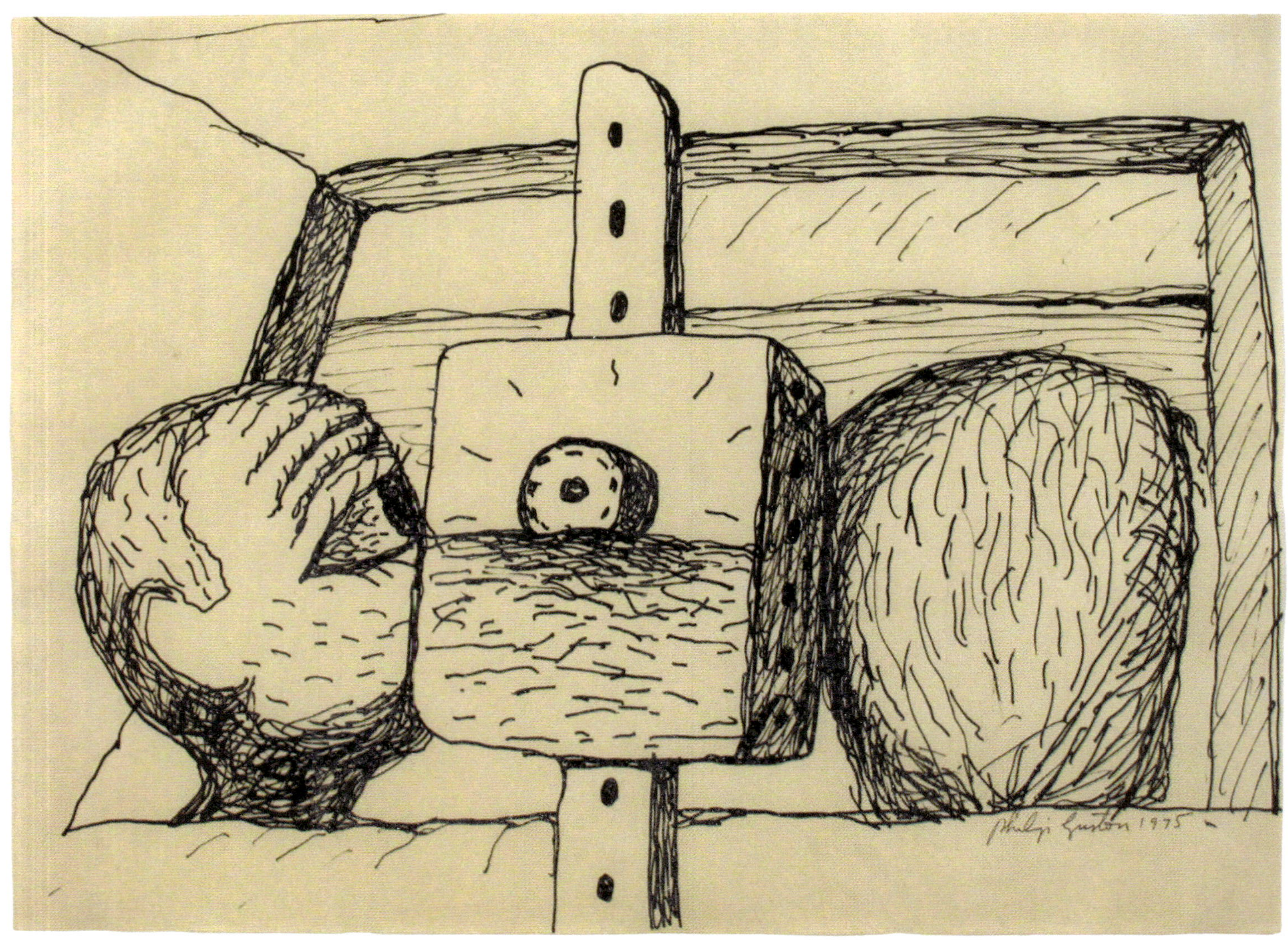

shifts in modern art – the return to figuration – was essentially accomplished through drawing. 'My strongest sensation at that time was a feeling of needing to start again with the simplest means to clear the decks', reflected Guston in 1974.

By coincidence, Guston and the underground cartoonist Robert Crumb were producing a similar species of cartoon imagery simultaneously, although neither was aware of the other – thus closing the gap between 'high' and 'low' that fine art had long attempted to widen. Guston's strong affection for comics was shared by other American artists of his generation, and Guston himself has described how comics led him into drawing in the first place: 'When I started I wanted to be a cartoonist, in fact. I like cartoons very much. Especially some of the older ones…. They were great draughtsmen. Herriman, you know, Krazy Kat?' His determination to stay grounded in 'mundane' reality and reject the aesthetics of the sublime is what makes his work continue to resonate in the twenty-first century – the age of disillusionment. 'Sometimes when my painting is getting too artistic, I'll say to myself, "What if the shoe salesman asked you to paint a shoe on his window?" Suddenly everything lightens. I feel not so responsible and paint directly what the thing is, including the necessary distortions.'

ART OR ILLUSTRATION?

Of the thousands of figurative drawings produced every day around the world, the vast majority, outside the life class, would be classed as illustrations. It may seem perverse in a book about drawing people to exclude *a priori* that very category in which the human image is most prevalent. There are accomplished illustrators, cartoonists, comic book artists, animators and graphic novelists whose stock-in-trade is the human image. They can draw brilliantly and depict the figure in every imaginable way: falling out of a window, slurping cereal at the breakfast table, wrestling with demons, dying in agony, driving, reading, rioting, philosophizing; whatever people do, there are skilful illustrators around who can

depict it. What distinguishes their drawings from those of authentic 'fine' artists who could, in theory, draw any one of these same subjects and call it art?

An illustration is often defined as an image made to accompany a text, or a drawing for reproduction. But that cuts out tattooists, sign painters and graffiti artists, and it doesn't allow for the fact that artists too produce books and printed matter, as well as animation, signs and T-shirts. When art school tutors speak disparagingly of 'mere' illustration, the implication is that something essential is missing. Is there some ineffable quality, a superior consciousness, a meta-awareness, that elevates the artist above the lowly domain of the illustrator? The art/illustration divide seems to be tantamount to a social class distinction. Art is the aristocrat: refined, high-minded, acutely conscious of its place in history and excessively attentive to its lineage. And art is expensive. Illustration is the menial labourer, working long hours for low pay. As Crumb has said, 'cartoons were very working class [in the US until the late twentieth century], cheap entertainment for the masses, like vaudeville, early movies, pulp magazines and so on.'

The border between art and illustration has become increasingly permeable, however. Crumb and other illustrators such as Art Spiegelman and Mœbius (Jean Giraud) have been honoured with retrospectives in major museums around the world; the graphic novel has risen to heights of inventiveness and sophistication almost equal to the American comic strips of the early twentieth century; manga and *bande dessinée* are fully assimilated into mainstream culture. The crossover operates in both directions. There are many artists in this book who engage creatively with genres of illustration, whether by appropriating illustration's language within a new conceptual frame, such as Raymond Pettibon or Francesc Ruiz; deploying a sequential narrative format, as is seen in the work of Emma Talbot, Chad McCail and Marcel van Eeden; applying techniques of illustration on an extravagant scale or taking them to fanatical extremes, as in Laurie Lipton, Erinc Seyman, Charles Avery and Makoto Aida's drawings; or, as Tabaimo has done, by entering wholeheartedly into the mode by collaborating with a writer and producing drawings for a newspaper serial.

DRAWING AND PHOTOGRAPHY

So intimately are drawing and photography related that the English pioneer of photography, Henry Fox Talbot, entitled his first books of photographs, published in 1844, 'The Pencil of Nature'. He described his pictures as 'Photogenic Drawings, without any aid whatsoever from the artist's pencil'. Photography's impact on art has been exhaustively debated for decades, and questions of their relative status and value are now more or less resolved. The camera long ago supplanted the pencil as a means of recording the empirical world – except, curiously, in such circumstances as English courts of law, where no photography, only an artist's impression drawn by hand from memory in an official, ham-fisted style, is permitted. In general, however, we no longer rely on drawing to provide evidence of what someone looks like; we are inundated from all directions by photographic impressions. From a utilitarian point of view, the camera has superseded the pencil as decisively as the car has the horse. People ride horses now mainly for pleasure, not in order to get around. And drawing from observation, as a contemplative practice, a mode of looking and registering sensation, is done today mostly for personal satisfaction or self-discovery.

A drawing is an expression of personality. It is never neutral or entirely objective, even if it assumes the manner of photographic accuracy and emotional detachment. Roland Barthes's famous definition of the difference between a photograph and other forms of representation, such as drawing, was first published in 1978, shortly before the beginning of the digital revolution that transformed humanity's relationship to visual imagery and the camera. Today, photography's claims to veracity have been undermined by digital manipulation. Nevertheless that basic ontological distinction between the mechanically produced photograph and the handmade image remains valid and useful as a starting point in considering the specific characteristics and appeal of drawing.

'What is the content of the photographic message?' wrote Barthes. 'What does the photograph transmit? By definition, the scene itself, the literal reality. From the object to its image there is of course a reduction – in proportion, perspective, colour – but at no time is this reduction a transformation (in the mathematical sense of the term). In order to move from the reality to its photograph... there is no necessity to set up a relay, that is to say a code, between the object and its image. Certainly the image is not the reality but at least it is its perfect *analogon* and it is exactly this analogical perfection which, to common sense, defines the photograph. Thus can be seen the special status of the photographic image: *it is a message without a code.*'

Barthes proceeds to contrast the photographic message with other 'analogical reproductions of reality', starting with drawing. In each of these, the manifest content is supplemented by another, connoted message (a suggested or implied message, as opposed to a *denoted* message which is one conveyed directly). 'There is no drawing,' said Barthes, 'no matter how exact, whose very exactitude is not turned into a style'.

What Barthes calls the 'analogical plenitude' of a photograph becomes the basis for his rich structural analysis of photographic meaning. Drawing lacks the same indexical relationship to empirical reality; it is always encoded. Every mark in a figurative drawing bears a double meaning, signifying the object depicted and also the artist's intention, sensibility and powers of depiction. However, this lack of factual authority is also an advantage. There is no longer any need for a drawing to fulfil the function of an objective record. It can be left to the camera to deal literally with the everyday world of appearances, in all its banality. Drawing is now autonomous: it does not depend for its existence on presenting the world

as it appears to the eye. The draughtsman or -woman is free
to invent an imaginary world according to his or her own
desires, with no obligation to include phenomena that are
irrelevant and uninteresting (although nothing is incapable
of being made interesting in the right hands). Drawing is
not subservient: it offers the possibility of an escape from
reality, as well as a means of representing it as truthfully or
as selectively as the artist cares to.

In some ways it is photography that is subservient to
drawing: artists have used photographic sources as the basis
of their work since Fox Talbot's time. Now, when a billion
images – photographs as well as paintings, drawings and
digitally concocted fantasies – are available at the click of
a button, these inevitably become an inescapable part of
the visual field, which the artist is free to appropriate and
reinterpret. It may seem ironic that so many artists today
draw directly from photographs, converting the mechanically
processed, ready-made – or 'pre-cooked' – image back into
the raw, rudimentary form of a handmade drawing, rendered
laboriously with charcoal, pencil, graphite or ink. The decline
of observational drawing coincides with this shift, although
the stalwarts who still draw from life would argue that there
is no comparison between the dialectical relationship of the
artist and his or her live subject, and the act of copying or
translating from a flat photographic image. These stalwarts
might compare this to the difference between travelling to
a distant place and watching a travelogue on television.

Yet this is not really an ethical or existential question:
the work of art is an artificial construct, and whether it
derives from an authentic experience or an imaginary one
is fundamentally of little consequence. Many of the artists
in this book use photographic sources, and each does so in
a different way: compare Jowhara AlSaud's manipulation
and erasure of parts of the image; David Haines's practice
of composing and drawing from his own photographs
based on found internet imagery; the compilation of a
repository of documentary photographs as a rapid means of
recovering – and skating over – history, in the work of Chen

Shaoxiong; Marc Brandenburg's technique of reversing the
image from black to white; and Richard Forster's practice
of meticulously re-drawing a distressed reproduction, and
in doing so creating an uncanny ghost of an image with
more physical presence than the original. Marlene Dumas,
one of several artists in this book to rely almost entirely on
photographs for her drawings, has said, 'Whether you start
with a photographic source or not, that doesn't change the
basic assumption that a (modern) painter is more interested
in images than in the actual living of modern life; and that
painters are more interested in their intentions than in their
subject matter.'

OFF THE PAGE: ANIMATION, WALL DRAWING AND INSTALLATION

Away from the context of reproductive media, drawing is
usually described in terms of materials – works on paper,
for instance, where the blank sheet is a void, an expanse of
emptiness before the first mark is applied, with that drama
being repeated with every new drawing on every fresh sheet.
A precarious, understated presence, like a delicate sound
on the edge of silence, is how drawing in its pure form is
generally characterized. Paper can fade or be ripped, stained
or burned, a drawing can be smudged or erased; as the
philosopher Alain Badiou observed: 'The fragility of drawing
is its essential feature.' Print and digital media blast away that
fragility, multiplying and disseminating the image to excess.
Yet while the unique hand-written or typewritten literary
manuscript may be a thing of the past, the unique original
drawing continues to have irreplaceable value and meaning.
All artists who love drawing hold to that value to a certain
extent, even those who apply their practice as draughtsmen
and -women in the continually expanded fields of shadow
play, video projection, animation and installation.

William Kentridge is one of the most influential artists to
have taken his drawing beyond the limitations of charcoal
on paper, turning the fragility and mutability of the medium

to his advantage. Kentridge's first animation, *Johannesburg, 2nd Greatest City After Paris* (1989) was initially entitled *Drawing for Projection*, and the artist has always insisted on the centrality of drawing to his practice: 'the starting point is always the desire to draw, an interest in seeing my drawings progress.' The animated films are 'a way of holding on to all the moments and possibilities of drawing.' He has described his method as 'stone age film-making', a term that incorporates his unique method of working and reworking the same sheet repeatedly, modifying the charcoal drawing by minuscule degrees and recording each phase of its evolution. The animation is a way of extending the temporal dimension of drawing; Kentridge's are not conventional drawings for animation, but rather a kind

WILLIAM KENTRIDGE, *The Refusal of Time*, 2012
5-channel video with sound, 30 min., with megaphones and breathing machine ('elephant'). A collaboration with Philip Miller, Catherine Meyburgh and Peter Galison. Collection of Ishikawa Collection (Okayama). Installation view, Parasophia: Kyoto International Festival of Contemporary Culture 2015 Prelude (exhibition: 'William Kentridge: The Refusal of Time'), former Rissei Elementary School, Kyoto, Japan, 2014

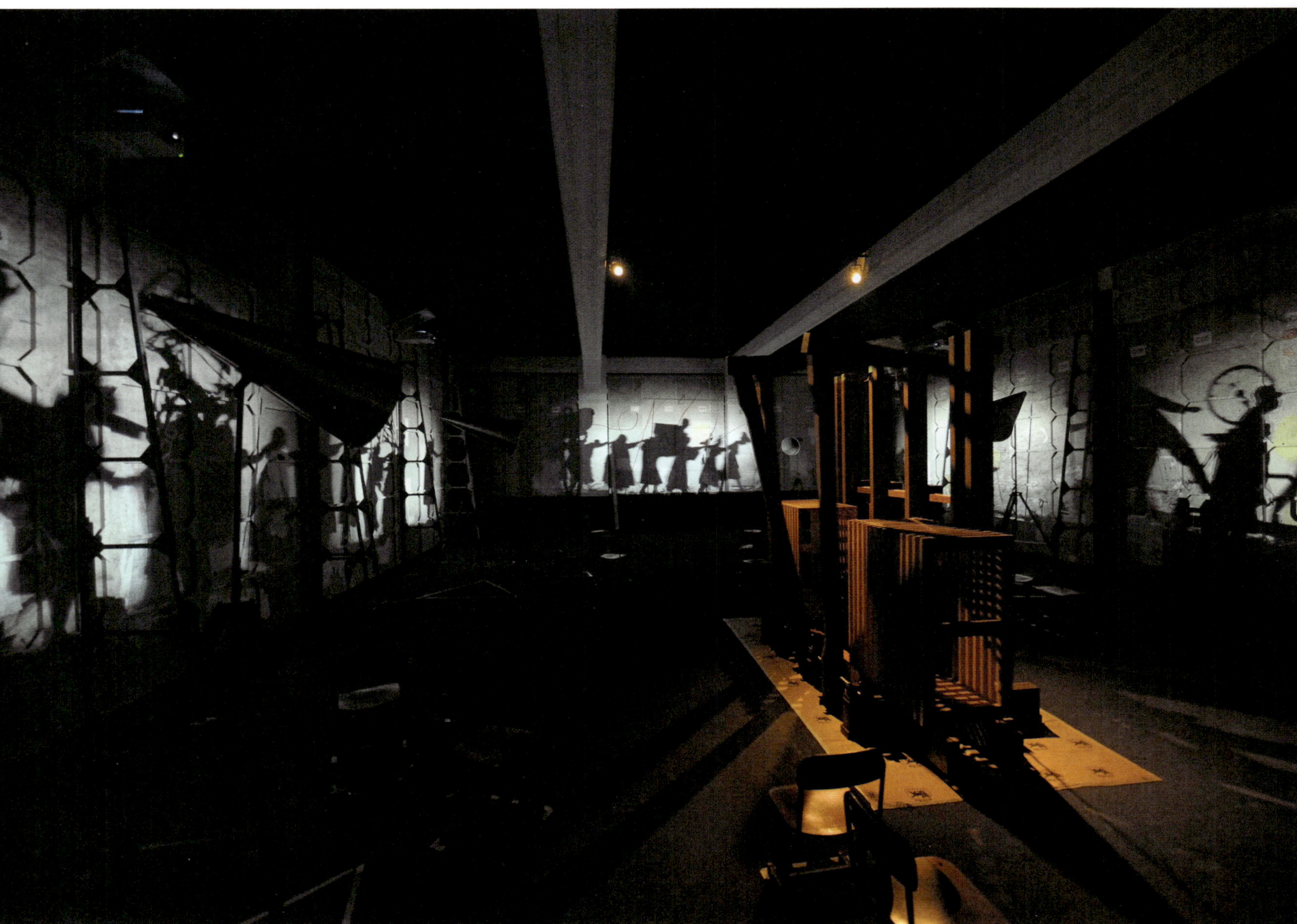

of motion-picture palimpsest, whereby the same drawing is shown at different stages, with earlier traces remaining visible.

Kentridge's skill and experience across the fields of drawing, printmaking, theatre, puppet theatre, film and opera crucially inform his way of exhibiting his animations as multi-screen installations. Music, too, plays a major role. His video installations were introduced to China at the Shanghai Biennial in 2000 and inspired young artists like Sun Xun – who similarly had a background in printmaking and drawing – to create animations fusing hand-drawn imagery in ink and charcoal with digital media. Sun now has his own animation studio, yet like Kentridge his emphasis is firmly on his drawings, which he creates meticulously, frame by frame. 'Animation is not in itself an important thing', says Sun. 'In a way it's like history – it only shows the most external things. In fact animation is always incomplete. Only by striving to break through the limitations in other media can I reach the most precious aspects of animation.' An example of the way in which Sun presses traditional media into service for radically new and apparently incongruous ends is his 2011 animated film *Some Actions Which Haven't Been Defined Yet in the Revolution*, which involved the use of 5000 individual woodblock prints, each one immaculately cut. His subjects are illusion, deception, alienation and the elusiveness of history – hefty metaphysical themes that call for complex modes of presentation. In common with many of his contemporaries, Sun often draws directly onto the gallery walls to create a total environment for his animations.

Another pioneering figure whose work is rooted in drawing, but who has expanded it into animated, kaleidoscopic installations, is the Indian artist Nalini Malani. Like Kentridge, with whom she is often compared, Malani creates dynamic, immersive environments that combine the technically simple devices of shadow play and light projection with multi-channel video and music to tell epic tales commenting powerfully on the moral and political crises she perceives in her society. Traditional folk tales, Greek and Hindu myths and vernacular imagery feed into her densely layered narratives, which play off the atmosphere of floating phantasmagoria: shadow play from revolving painted cylinders that are perpetually in motion.

The contemporary artists mentioned above are diverse, sophisticated, multi-talented and technologically versatile, yet drawing remains at the heart of their practice even while they extend its frames of reference and mix traditional modes with new media and other disciplines. Ironically, their attachment to simple tools, such as charcoal or brush and ink, is actually a stimulus to exploring new directions and establishing a dialectical exchange between old forms of image-making and digital media. In addition, they regularly dissolve the boundaries between visual art and theatre, film, literature, dance, music and performance. It is significant too that all of these artists are profoundly engaged with the issues of their time, philosophically, politically and aesthetically; their practice is flexible and capable of bearing complex, multiple meanings. The fact that it is based on drawing rather than photography ensures that their subjectivity is visibly invested in every project; their signature is always apparent.

Drawing magnified through projection, animated and enveloping, embracing or trapping the viewer in three-dimensional space: the strategies for maximizing the impact of imagery originated by simple hand-drawn means are immensely stimulating. They leave behind the idea of the small, flat image quietly contained on the printed page, or so it seems. Yet the pure act of drawing a human image, which precedes all of those variations and expansions, is far more easily translated into print; the scale and medium and relation to the hand – and the hand is as much involved in experiencing an illustrated book as is the eye – lend themselves to this form of reproduction. Time-based media are ephemeral, in that they can be switched off; projected images are immaterial. The hand-drawn image will last as long as people care to preserve it; it will stand the test of time. After the original, its reproduction in a book is the next best thing.

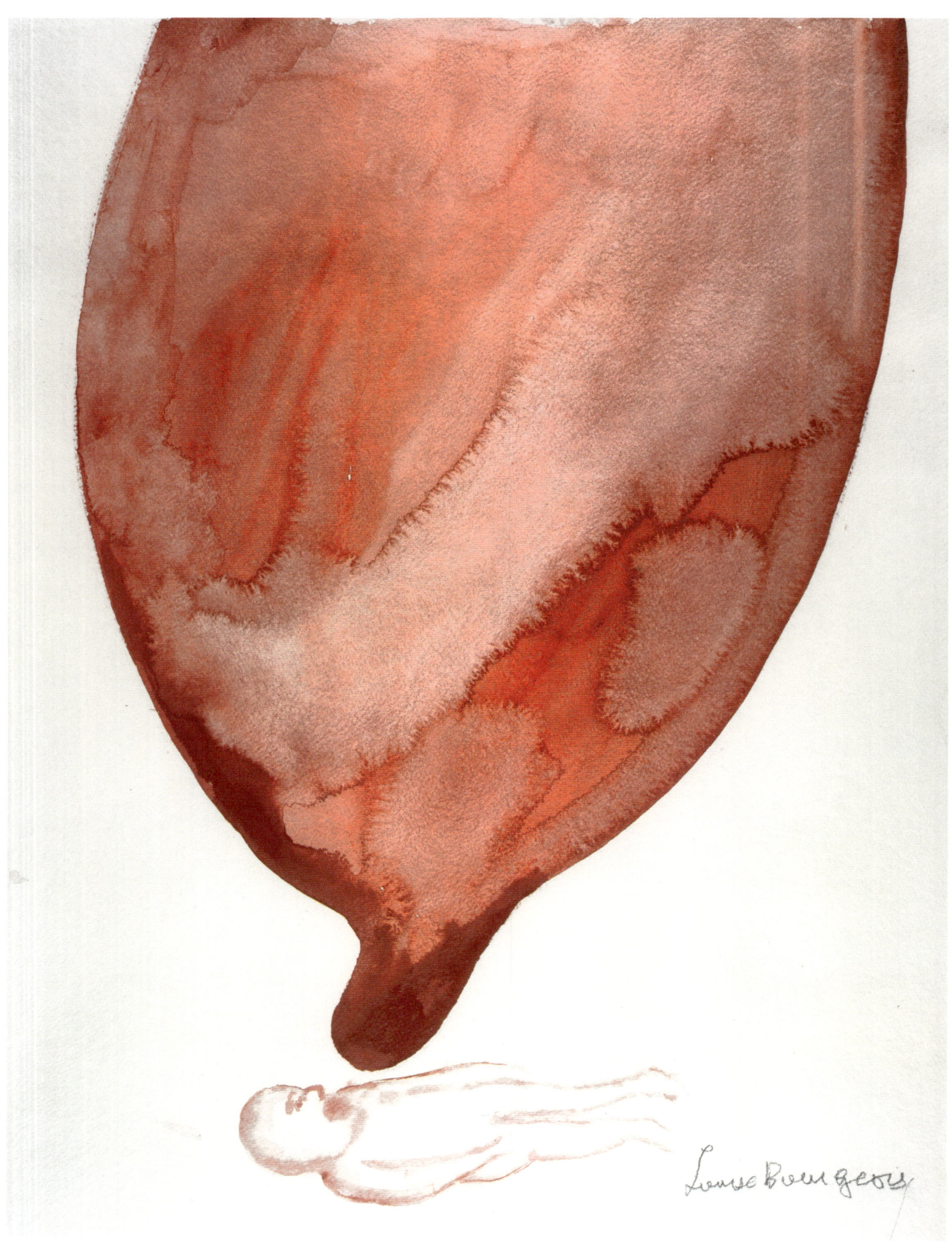

Louise Bourgeois

1

body

There is only convention in the 'realistic' depiction of the body. The body depicted always tends towards exaggeration, either in the convention of the grotesque or the convention of the ideal. There are few images less interesting than an exact anatomical drawing of the human form. This problem arises from the corresponding problem of the absence of stance. Grotesque realism is emblematic of the body's knowledge of itself, a knowledge of pieces and parts, of disassociated limbs and an absent centre. The realism of the ideal is emblematic of the body's knowledge of the other, a knowledge of facades, of two dimensions. Only in the embrace is the other's body known as one's own, in parts. Perhaps this is why the grotesque has become the domain of lived sexuality, while the ideal has tended toward the domain of the voyeur and the pornographer.

SUSAN STEWART *On Longing: Narratives of the Miniature, the Gigantic, the Souvenir, the Collection*, 1984

If it is true that no depiction of the body, to be interesting, can ever be entirely neutral and objective in the way that a depiction of a chair or a bicycle might be, then the body must be a uniquely revealing subject, telling us more about the sensibility, beliefs, motives and passions of the artist than any other. What does it mean to draw the body in the twenty-first century? The opposition that Susan Stewart describes between classical idealism and grotesque realism is a fundamental dialectic in the history of modern art. The drawn or painted image of the naked body was the locus of aesthetic struggle – formal and ideological – from Picasso and Matisse's revolutionary nudes of 1907 until academic painting went under in the latter half of the twentieth century. How to envisage the human form in contemporary times? Religion might have a say in that, if humanity is made in God's likeness, or indeed if any representation of the human image is forbidden. On the other hand, in the age of photography and the internet, it may seem quaintly irrelevant to consider the dangerous implications of drawing the body, as if anything were still at stake. Can a drawing shock? There is no drawing that can compete for transgression with the most banal pornographic image. Yet there are things that a drawing can convey that are beyond the reach of photography and digital media – just as there is no substitute for a handshake or a kiss.

With Stewart's argument as a point of departure, this chapter examines the ways in which contemporary artists' drawings can express 'the body's knowledge of itself' as distinct from – and often in opposition to – the classical tradition of objectification. Historically, the concept of grotesque realism derives from literary criticism, but it is easily applicable to visual art, where the contrast between classical ideals and low alternative genres, such as caricature and carnival, is immediately discernible in representations of the body.

< LOUISE BOURGEOIS *The Feeding*, 2007
Gouache on paper, 60 × 45.7 cm (23 ⅝ × 18 in.)

The Russian literary critic Mikhail Bakhtin, writing in
the 1930s against the grain of Socialist Realist orthodoxy,
expounded what was to become an immensely influential
theory of popular culture grounded in the medieval humour
of the market place and carnival, and exemplified by the
writings of François Rabelais. In *Rabelais and His World* (first
published in 1965), Bakhtin extols 'the boundless ocean of
grotesque bodily imagery' that exists across time and in all
cultures, with its emphasis always on humanity's animal nature
and not on the elevated spiritual and moral values that the
institutions of church and state traditionally required art to
affirm. 'The grotesque image displays not only the outward
but also the inner features of the body: blood, bowels, heart
and other organs.' Bakhtin writes: 'Wherever men laugh and
curse, particularly in a familiar environment, their speech is
filled with bodily images. The body copulates, overeats, and
men's speech is flooded with genitals, bellies, defecations,
urine, diseases, noses, mouths and dismembered parts.' In
contemporary art the spirit of this alternative canon can
be seen in the visceral excesses of Paul McCarthy and the
subterranean fantasies of Louise Bourgeois. These artists
exemplify two enduring variations on the historical avant-
garde's revolutionary longing to overturn conventional
values: McCarthy's is satirical, grossly offensive and anarchic,
attacking by ridicule, while Bourgeois's is introspective,
springing from Surrealism and psychoanalysis, uncovering
the hidden recesses of consciousness and the unspoken, and
often unspeakable, impulses rooted in bodily desires.

Bourgeois made it her lifelong mission to mine the depths
of her childhood emotions, to reach back from adulthood to
her earliest fierce feelings of jealousy, rage, attachment and
dependence. Her principal goal, she declared, was 'to relive
a past emotion'. What makes her obsessions so fascinating
and distinguishes her anxiety from that of the average
neurotic is that as an artist she was 'blessed with the ability
to sublimate' – to use her emotions as raw material which she
could calmly and selflessly convert into extraordinary images
with a universal force. Self-excavation was her creative mode
of work. Her regression was in the service of her art. The
drawings reproduced here, made when Bourgeois was in her
late nineties, show a naked expectant family and a giant breast
bearing down on a small person no longer an infant, and are
examples of the artist's irrepressible carnivalesque humour.

McCarthy's comic dwarfs mock Walt Disney's characters with
devastating veracity. They look like real individuals moulded
into shape and able to think – albeit primitively, perhaps like
their creators in Hollywood. A phallus in the centre of the face
is a perfect metaphor for rampant capitalist entertainment.
While the face is the body part with too many and confused
messages, the genitals are undisguised and unreflective – even
if at times they appear to have a mind of their own. McCarthy
dips into an ancient well for this displacement joke: comic
inversion, the substitution of bodily parts, is a traditional
trope in graphic humour. The mask conceals and parodies the
face; the body, unclothed, speaks for itself. When artists are
relieved of the obligation to admire, respect, pay homage to
or otherwise flatter their subject, and if sober realism is no
longer the aim, then the field is wide open for fantastical and
witty invention. The body cannot be unmasked like the face,
but it can be distorted, transformed, squashed or stretched,
its parts rearranged. Such pictorial liberties may be
condemned by puritans as violations of the sanctity of the
human image, offences against reason and the solemn belief
that the body is to be taken seriously. The body may well
be a serious subject in the real world, where it is exposed
to pleasure and pain, but if there is one place where it does
not matter what happens to it, it is on the page in a drawing.
There, anything can happen, without consequences.

An artist might treat the body not only as a physical object,
but also metaphorically, as a psychic entity whose outward
form expresses an inner condition. Think of an actor or
dancer's exaggerated expressions of emotion conveyed
through the body, convulsing it into distorted shapes, folded
or wracked or crucified; or imagine the body in space, perched
and commanding from a height or pinned cowering in
a corner, or deliberately hidden, or racing about the room.
Antony Gormley's chance-based ink drawings explore the
relationship of the body to the space it inhabits, invoking
what he calls 'relational fields', event-based phenomena that
he associates 'both with the origin of celestial bodies at the
beginning of things, and with the emanations that appear
in lucid dreaming'. The body asleep and dreaming exists only
notionally in space: its true life is occurring within (or seems
to be). And in dreams, the body can take on multiple forms
or become a single part, such as a giant breast, or wear a penis
for a nose. In art, as in psychoanalysis, only the exaggerations
are true, or at least interesting. Drawing the body without
exaggeration, as Stewart suggests, is simply boring. There
is no more appropriate and adaptable vehicle for the
representation of mental and emotional states than the
human form.

With the rise of women artists to prominence over the past
half-century, the terms in which the body is represented have
inevitably altered. An impatience with external appearances
– the routine exploitation of the female body as a perennial
signifier of erotic desire – is one sign of change; there is a shift
of emphasis towards more nuanced understandings of gender
and sexuality, and a greater awareness of the body's biological
processes and internal organs and of our existence in time
and in relation to others. For an artist like Nalini Malani, who
began her career with a spell as a medical illustrator, 'organs
and bodily fluids have a presence and identity of their own....
As I have grown older, I find that there are emotions attached
to organs. As you wake in the morning, as I lie down, I say,
"Well, what's my kidney saying to me? What is part of my
body saying to me?" And I think as women, there's always
this thing about, "What's happening to my breasts, what's
happening to my uterus, what's happening to every part?"'
In Malani's work the body becomes politicized, a site of
conflict, bearing the history of traumas inflicted by men in
periods of massive social upheaval – such as the Partition
of India, which resulted in tens of thousands of rapes and
abductions, a pattern often repeated where there is war and
civil conflict. We use the same word for the effects of those
atrocities – trauma – as we do for such psychological crises
as the infantile jealousies of Louise Bourgeois. Trauma leaves
a trace, on the mind and the body. Representing it visually
on the *imagined* body is a challenge for artists, since there
is no readily available language with which to talk about
these subjects.

Violence, of course, is easy to depict literally, like sex.
What is more difficult is to show the impressions of these
experiences as they endure in the memory, in the waking
and dreaming mind. Mithu Sen's drawings of the body
dissected with scalpel-like precision show pleasure and
pain overlapping; physical and mental realms merge,
coexisting in space, though not in time (these may be
bodies perceived over years, condensed into a single
image). Most contemporary artists draw without a model
for reference: the bodies they depict are known to them
intuitively or habitually; they are their own, or variations
on or extensions of themselves. The body experienced from
within, drawn with a trembling, roaming, self-pleasuring
hand, dissolves into skeletal form in Chloe Piene's melancholy
but voluptuous meditations on the frailty of fleshly
existence. Similarly, Ed Pien's grotesque bodies erupt from
a spontaneous process of automatism: drawing fast without

allowing the conscious mind to interrupt and define the
subject. Eventually, through repeated layering, the sheet
is densely crowded with figures that have a common shape,
belonging in their wiry entanglements to the same genus,
perhaps human, perhaps some other indeterminate mutation.

This fantastical aesthetic also underlies Wangechi Mutu's
hybrid prototypes. Mutu's sketches of nudes shown in this
chapter seem particularly stark when one knows how
sumptuously they would be dressed if featured in one
of Mutu's more characteristic watercolour collages. In the
drawings shown here, Mutu permits her figures to step out
in unadorned line drawings that express with brutal frankness
the themes of 'loss, desire, morbid fantasy and the injured
body' that she identifies in her work. These drawings, and
Mutu's images of mutilation, may answer the question as to
whether a drawing can still elicit shock in the contemporary age.

The artists represented in this section offer some
alternatives to the traditional idea of the naked body in art
as an object of aesthetic appreciation. The classical nude,
harmoniously composed with gracefully proportioned limbs,
arranged to delight the eye, is no longer an ideal to which
many artists would subscribe, unless laced with irony or
critique. Overuse has cheapened the thrill. Of course there are
political circumstances when social taboos give sensual and
erotic subjects a special charge, but outside of those culturally
repressive conditions, the simple affirmation of desire
in response to physical beauty is not enough. We need
some depth, an intimation of consciousness behind the
gorgeous exterior. Besides, the body is not simply an
instrument finely tuned for pleasure; it is also a medium of
discomfort, pain and ultimately death. Contemporary drawing
offers an element of realism that is necessary to register the
body's imperfections and conflicts, and to apprehend the
body's passage in time, rather than holding it suspended for
eternity in a realm of platonic perfection.

NALINI MALANI *Born 1946, Karachi, Pakistan. Lives and works in Mumbai, India*

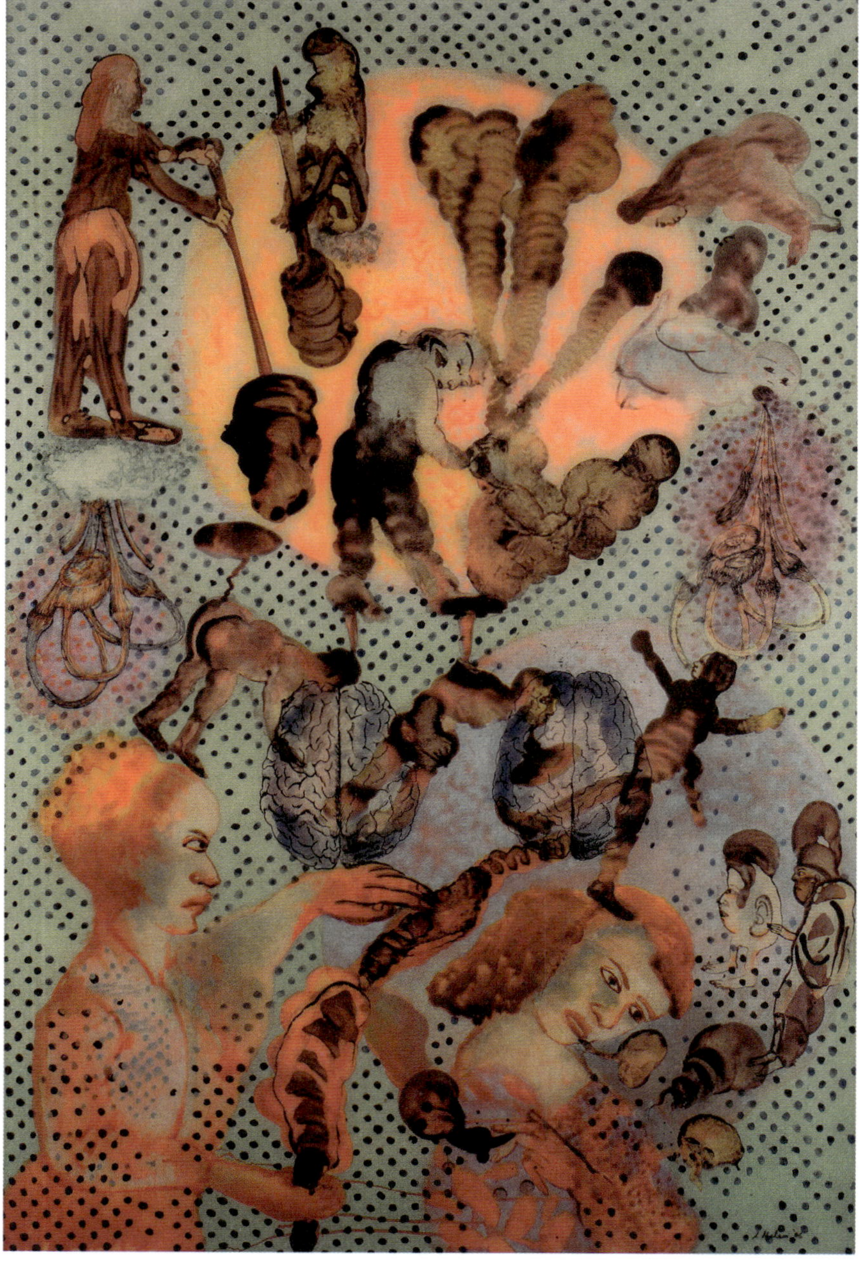

One of India's foremost contemporary artists, Nalini Malani began her career as a painter, was a pioneer of video art in the 1970s, and has worked in performance, theatre and film. Yet drawing is always her point of departure: 'I draw therefore I am', she has said. 'Drawing/painting helps me to dream, to free-associate… to compose ideas that can then engage to create works in other disciplines.' In the early 1990s Malani made immersive video installations that involved projecting light onto imagery drawn onto scrolls of a type of clear polyester called Mylar. Later, she drew onto the reverse of Mylar cylinders and displayed them rotating in the gallery space, so that the viewer became a participant in the resulting kaleidoscopic shadow play.

As a child of the traumas of the 1947 Partition of India, violence, sectarian hatred, fanaticism and the pain and degradation suffered by women have always preoccupied Malani. Her multi-layered allegorical drawings often deploy female figures from literature and mythology, such as the Hindu earth goddess Sita and the Greek heroine Medea, both of whom shared a similar fate: the abandonment or murder of their children. Malani's style of illustration borrows from the Indian vernacular Kalighat tradition, and combines free-floating figures with bodily imagery, including internal organs, bones and excrement, all leavened by jubilant colours.

Sita / Medea, 2006 >
Acrylic and enamel reverse painting on acrylic sheet
183 × 122 cm (72 × 48 in.)

(overleaf) *Akka, 2006*
Acrylic and enamel reverse painting on acrylic sheet
150 × 76 cm (59 × 29 ⅞ in.)

(page 33) *Nursery Tales I, 2008*
Acrylic, enamel and ink reverse painting on acrylic sheet
183 × 100 cm (72 × 39 ⅜ in.)

Medea III, 2006
Acrylic and enamel reverse painting on acrylic sheet
183 × 122 cm (72 × 48 in.)

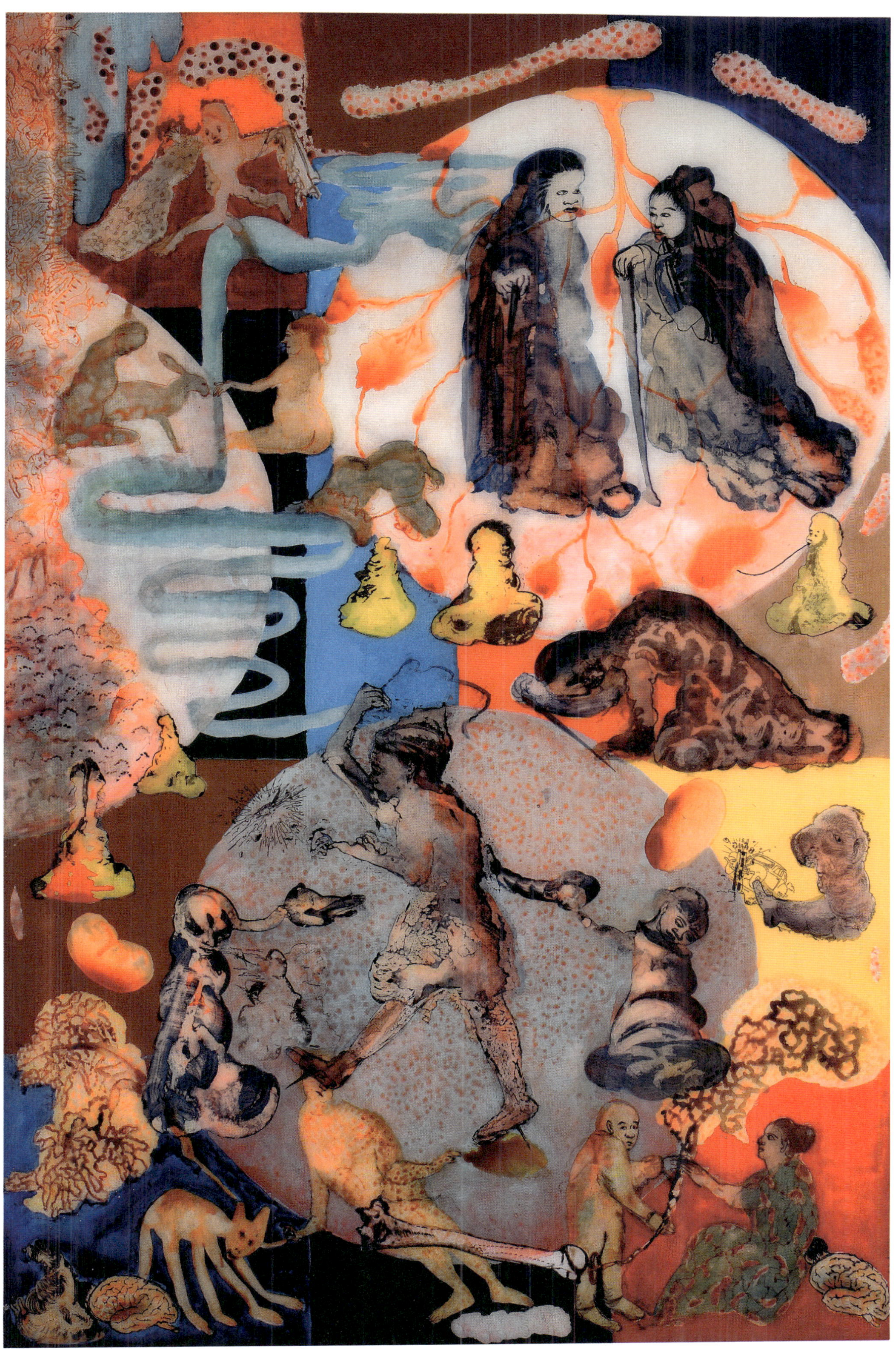

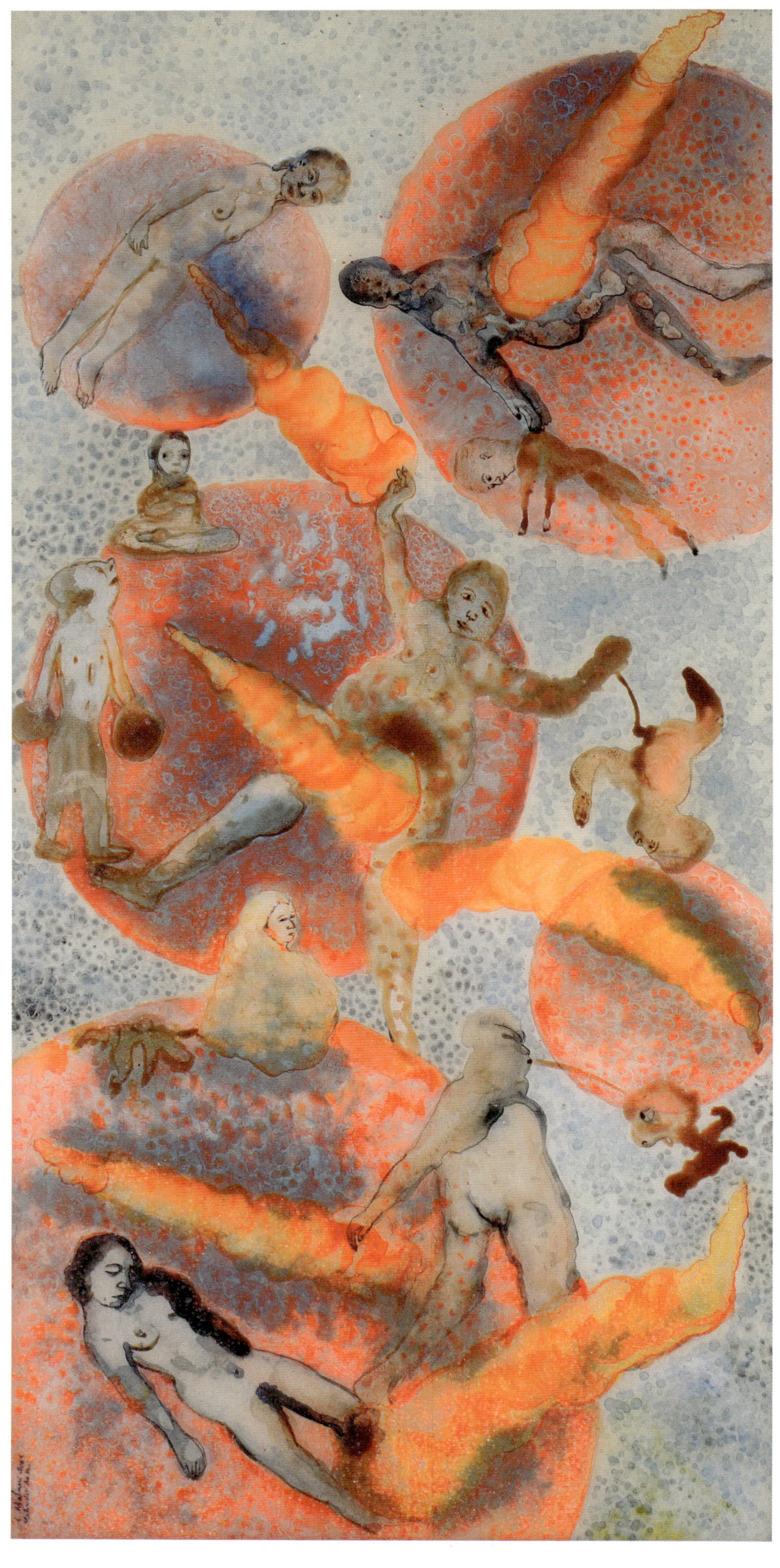

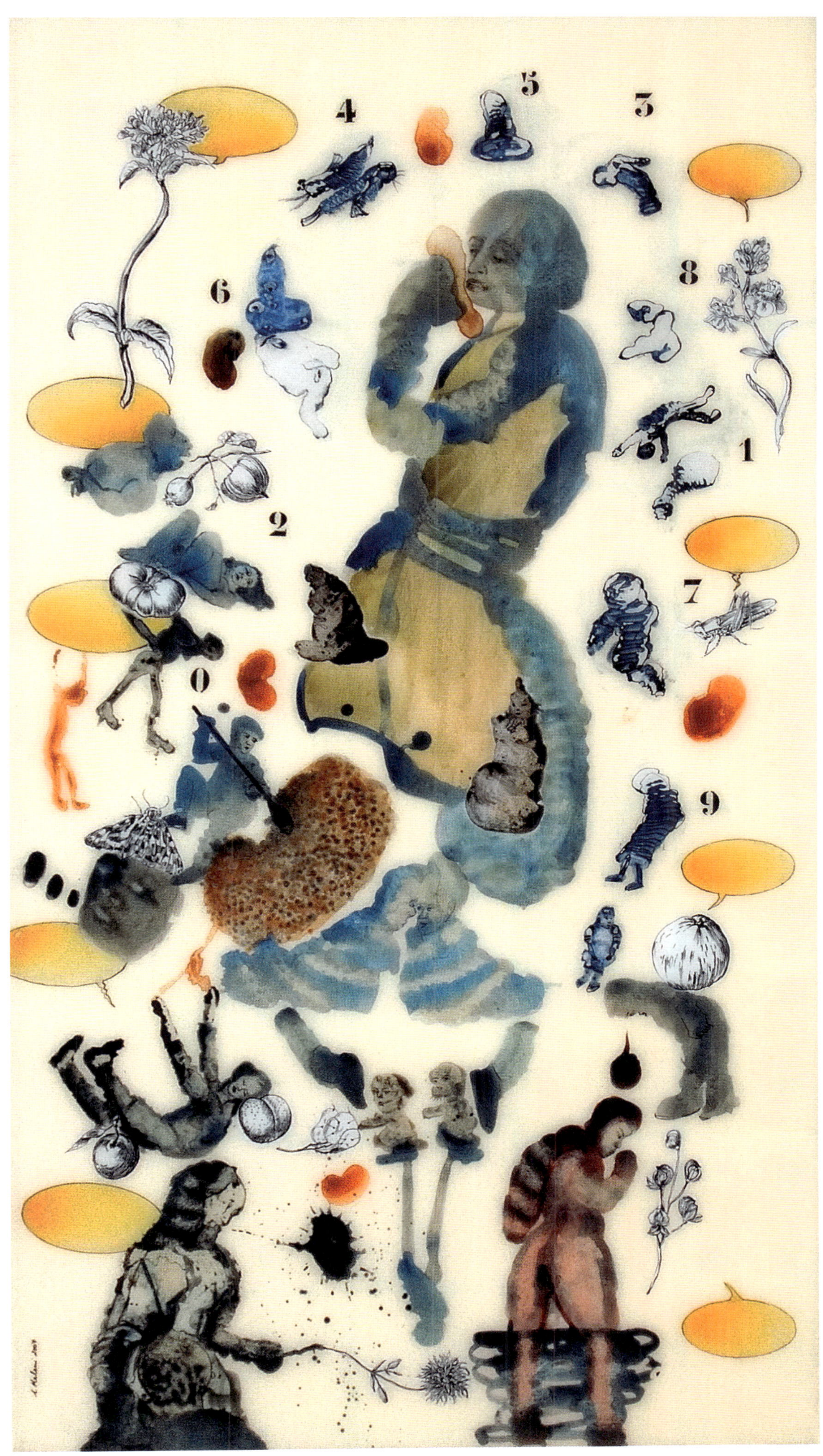

WANGECHI MUTU *Born 1972, Nairobi, Kenya. Lives and works in New York, USA*

Wangechi Mutu is celebrated for her voluptuous collages in watercolour. Taking her visual inspiration from magazines spanning fashion, travel, pornography, ethnography and mechanics, Mutu creates fantastical hybrid creatures; part-human, part-animal, -plant and -machine, they prance, crouch or recline provocatively in the twisting undergrowth, their skin mottled or spotted like that of a leopard or snake. The slender silhouette of a high-class model is often still discernable amid these deformations, giving sexual allure to images that are in other respects grotesquely mangled. This deliberate confusion of attraction and repulsion makes for an ambiguous message. There is a delicious atmosphere of excess that is perhaps too easily assimilated into the very culture of

luxury and privilege they seem to critique. This makes all the more interesting those drawings in which the imagery is seen raw – for instance in the sketchbook drawings reproduced here. Mutu showed her sketchbooks for the first time in her retrospective at the Brooklyn Museum in New York, USA, in 2013–14. 'The sketchbooks are a very private activity for me', she has said. 'I haven't shared my bare-bones drawings with the public before. I find them very revealing – they tap into my subconscious quite deeply. But what I love about the drawing is that it has this very pure aspect to it… because it's not fussy or overdone or overly layered. It sits on the paper for better or worse, super-visible.'

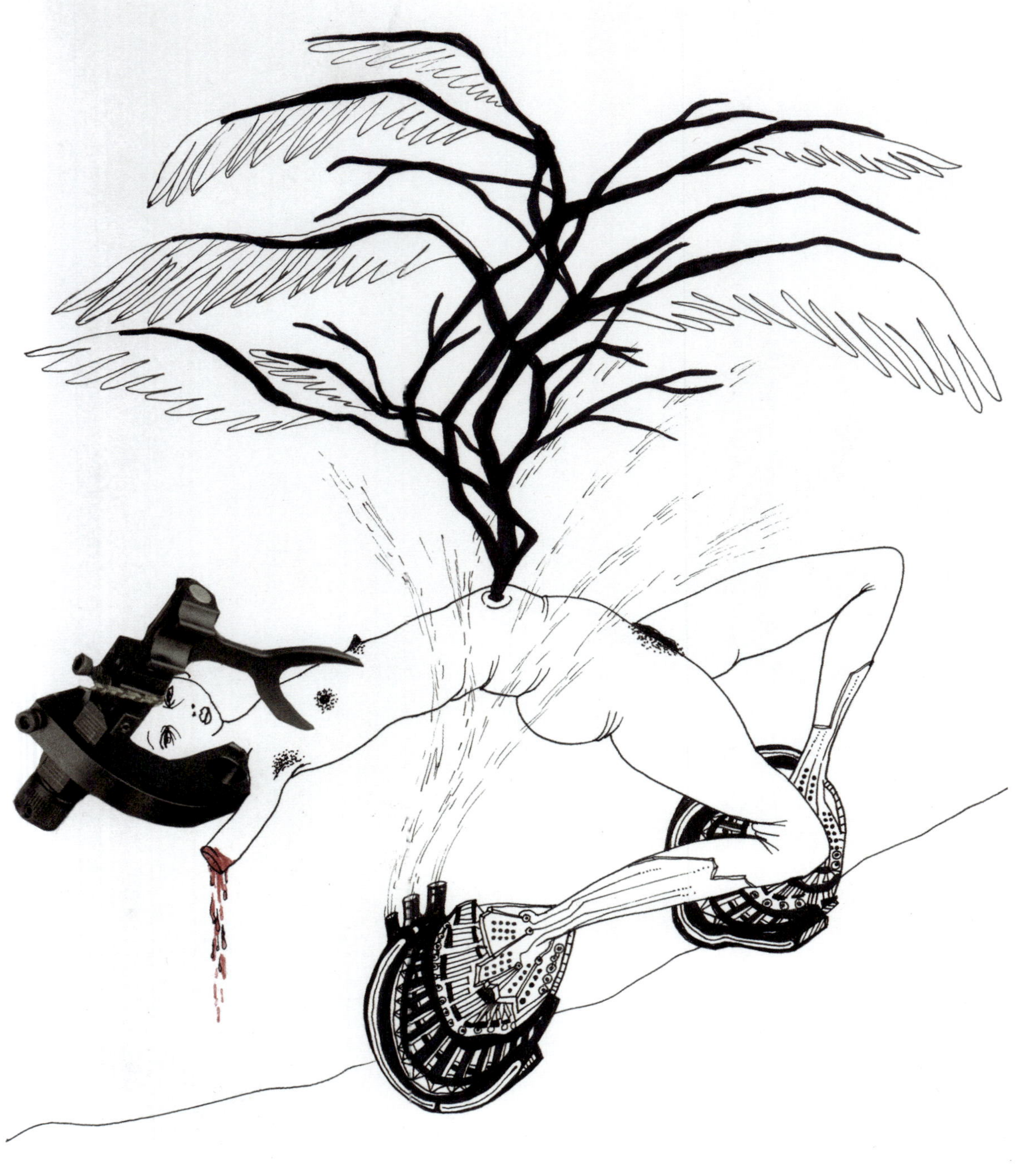

Sketchbook Drawing, 2011–12
Pen, ink and collage on paper
27.9 × 21.6 cm (11 × 8 ½ in.)

Sketchbook Drawing, 2010 >
Pen, ink, and collage on paper
19.7 × 27.3 cm (7 ¾ × 10 ¾ in.)

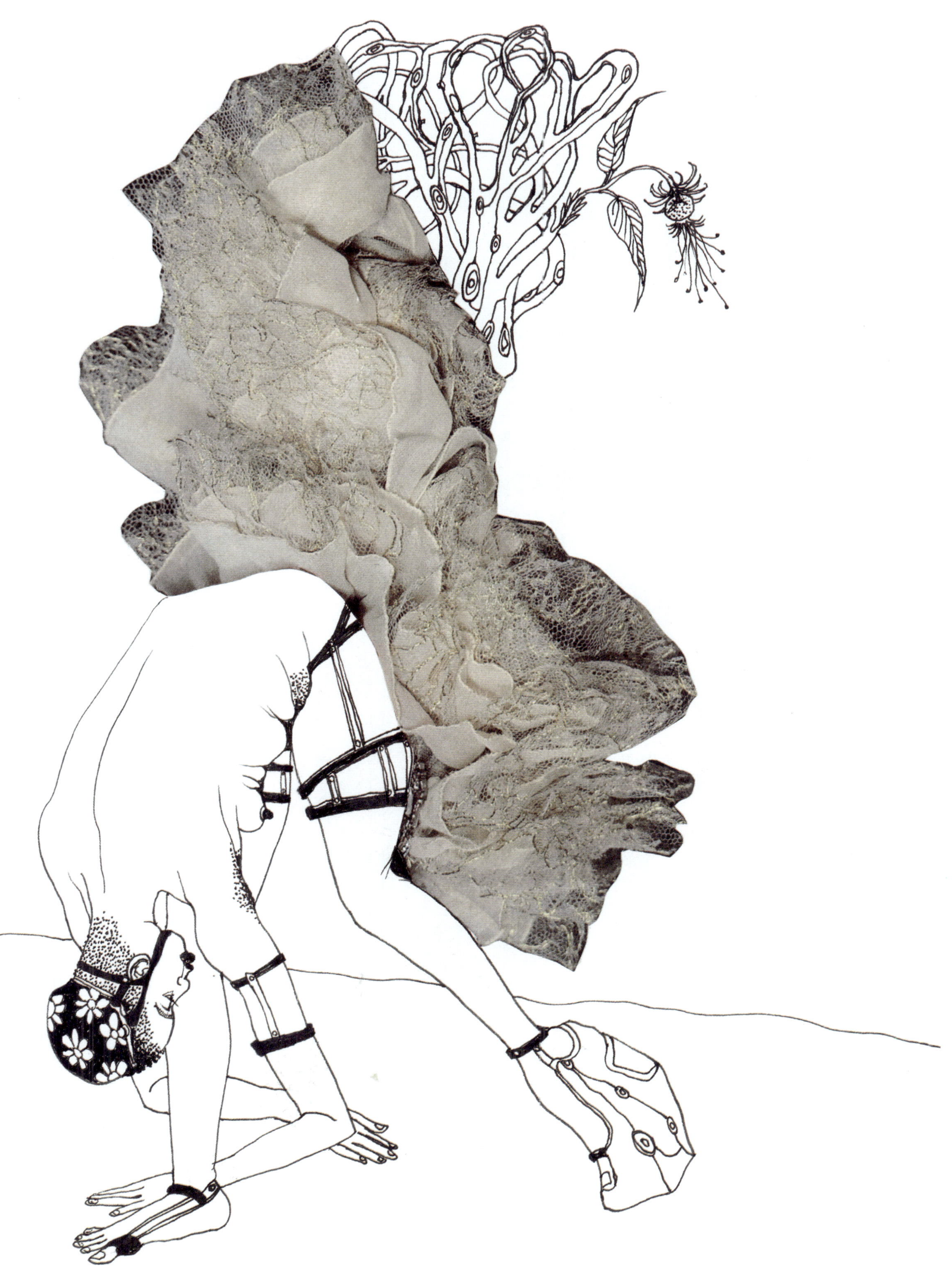

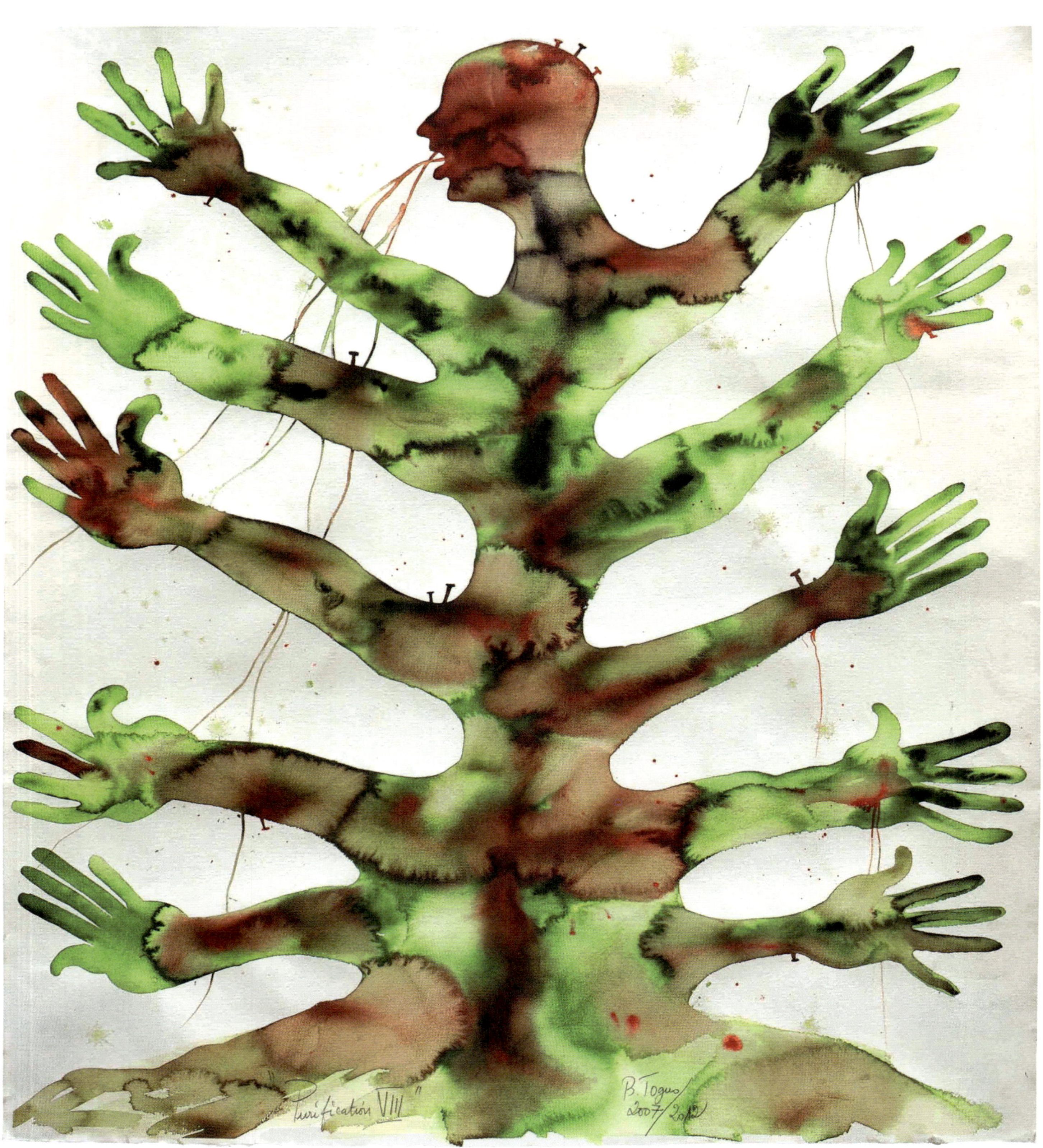
"Purification VIII"
B. Togus
2007/2012

BARTHÉLÉMY TOGUO *Born 1967, Mbalmayo, Cameroon. Lives and works in Paris, France, New York, USA, and Bandjoun, Cameroon*

Barthélémy Toguo is a humanist whose profound sympathy for mankind's predicament is manifested in each one of his diverse creative projects, which range from sculpture and performance to artist's books and drawing. Born in Cameroon, Toguo has travelled widely, resisting with subversive humour the stereotypes that an African can encounter when crossing European borders. In his performances, for instance, he has carried luggage hand-carved from solid blocks of wood through customs and travelled first class on a TGV train from Paris to Cologne while dressed as Parisian refuse collector. Toguo invests the income from his work in Bandjoun Station, a not-for-profit artists' centre in Cameroon that combines artistic and agricultural experimentation in order to make a 'strong political statement' on self-sufficiency.

In the context of his continual outpouring of watercolour drawings, Toguo shows the body as a biological entity linked to other beings by a network of roots, stems, sprouting leaves, bulbs and fruits; the head (usually in profile) vomiting or swallowing entrails; limbs, feet and hands splayed and pinned down with nails. Toguo applies the watercolour fluently, often wet-on-wet so that it spreads and dissolves, and his recurrent reds and greens are a code that signifies the pains and pleasures of mortal existence.

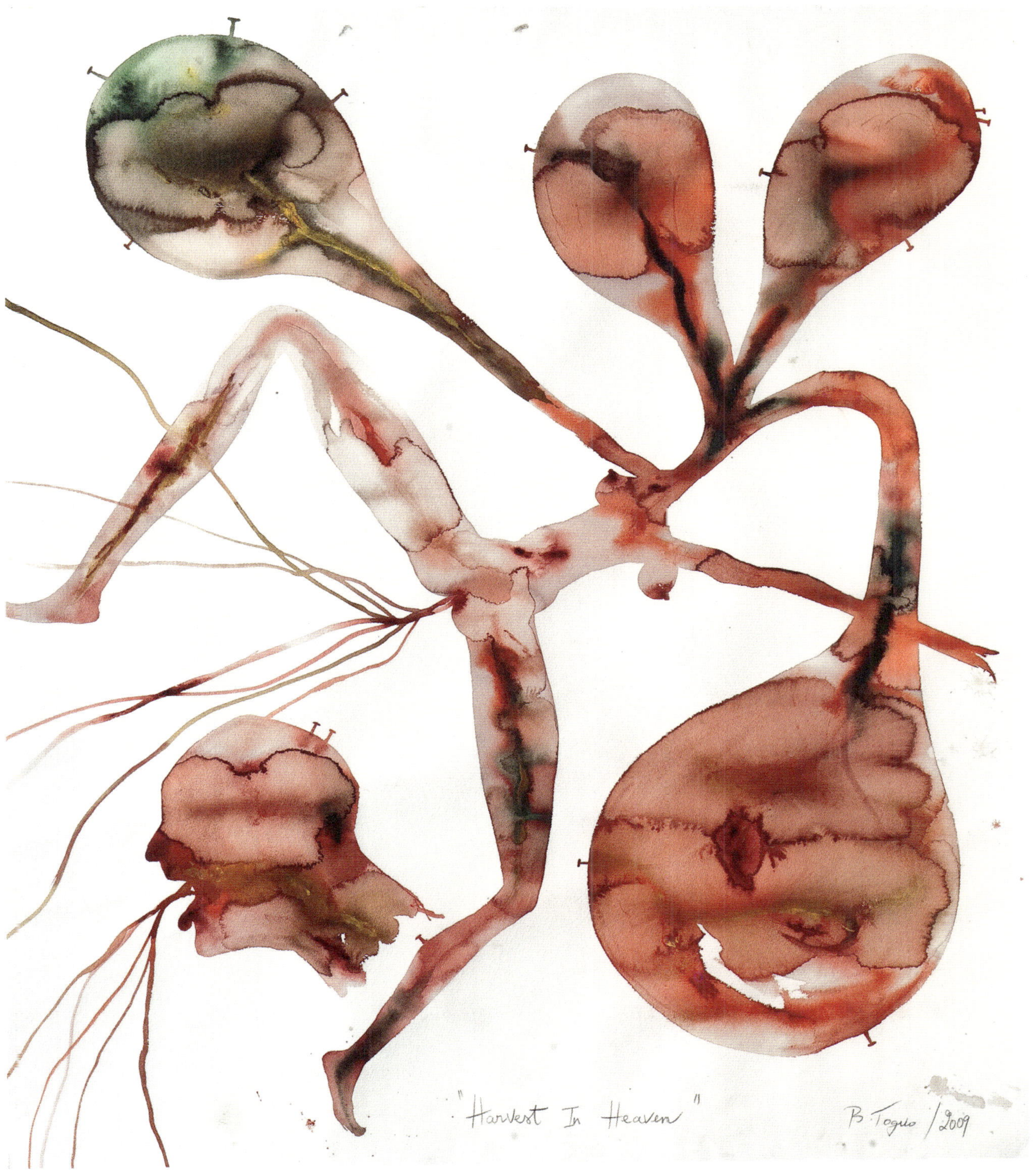

< *Purification: XXIII*, 2007
Watercolour on paper
105 × 105 cm (41 ⅜ × 41 ⅜ in.)

Harvest in Heaven, 2006
Watercolour on paper
113.5 × 100 cm (44 ⅝ × 39 ⅜ in.)

Ed Pien's drawings are generated through a process of fast gestural improvisation in brush and ink and acrylic on A4 sheets of paper, with each act of improvisation timed to take three minutes. The resulting drawings are pressed wet onto further sheets of paper, allowing accidental smears and blotches to interrupt the imagery, which has itself been produced spontaneously. The pieces of paper are then configured into larger compositions onto which Pien continues to draw repeatedly, so that the figures crowd, overlay and often obliterate one another. Despite the deliberate lack of planning, Pien's work regularly features similar figurative motifs: grotesque, hybrid creatures – part-human, part-animal – sporting multiple limbs and orifices.

The palimpsest effect that results from this time-governed process suggests that its narrative is potentially endless. The drawing is finished the moment the artist stops laying down marks, but it implies its own future expansion: the figures proliferating into infinity. The traces of past activity – the earliest stages of the drawings – are in some areas entirely eclipsed by subsequent drawings, while in other areas they remain visible on the surface. 'Using the trace as a metaphor,' Pien has said, 'I contemplate how a past or present action affects future events: through our actions, we become our own ghost that comes back to haunt us in the future.'

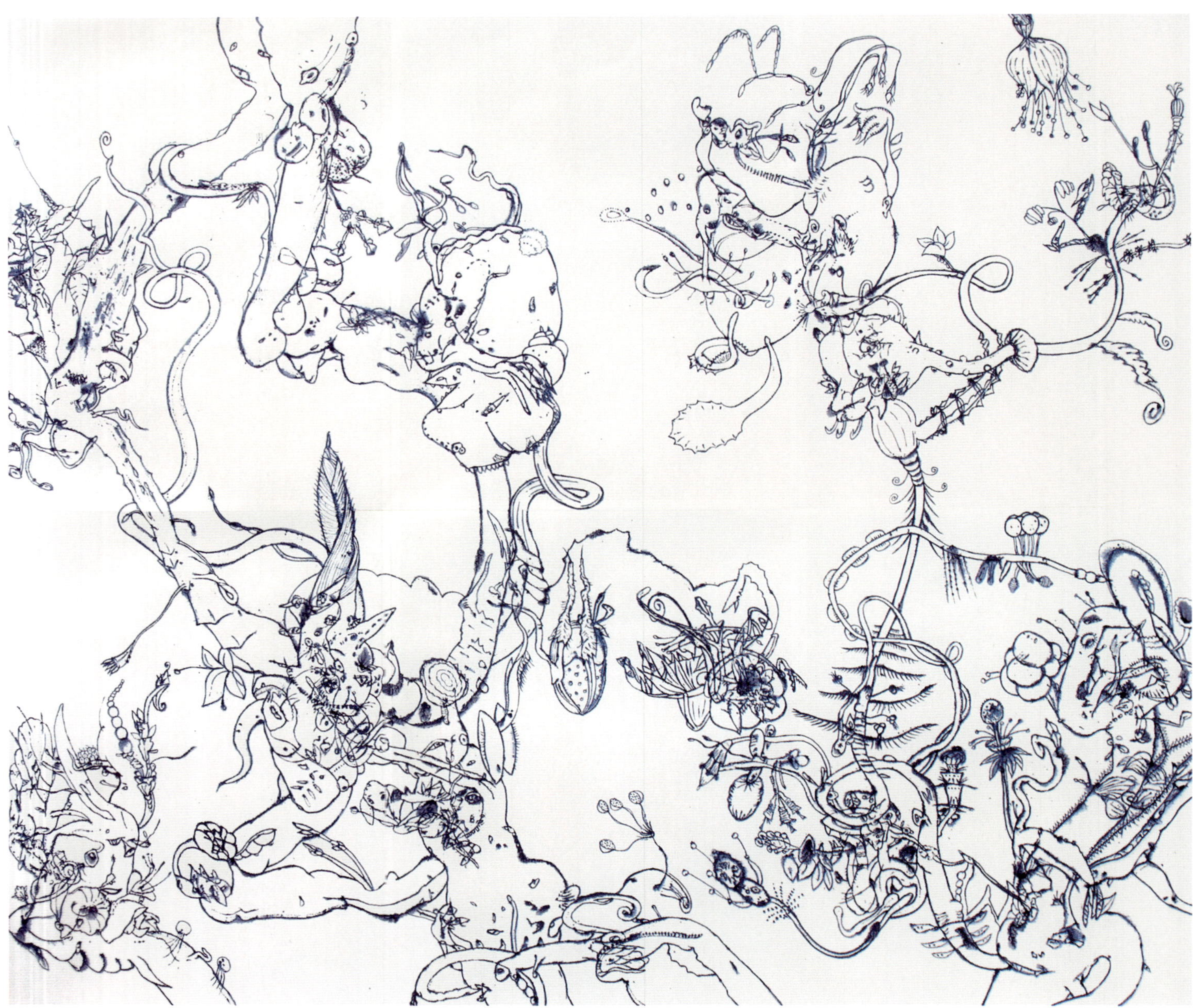

Blue Monkey and a Chinaman, 2009–10
Ink on sectioned paper
61 × 68.5 cm (24 × 27 in.)

HEX, 2013 >
Ink on black sectioned paper
46 × 76 cm (18 ⅛ × 29 ⅞ in.)

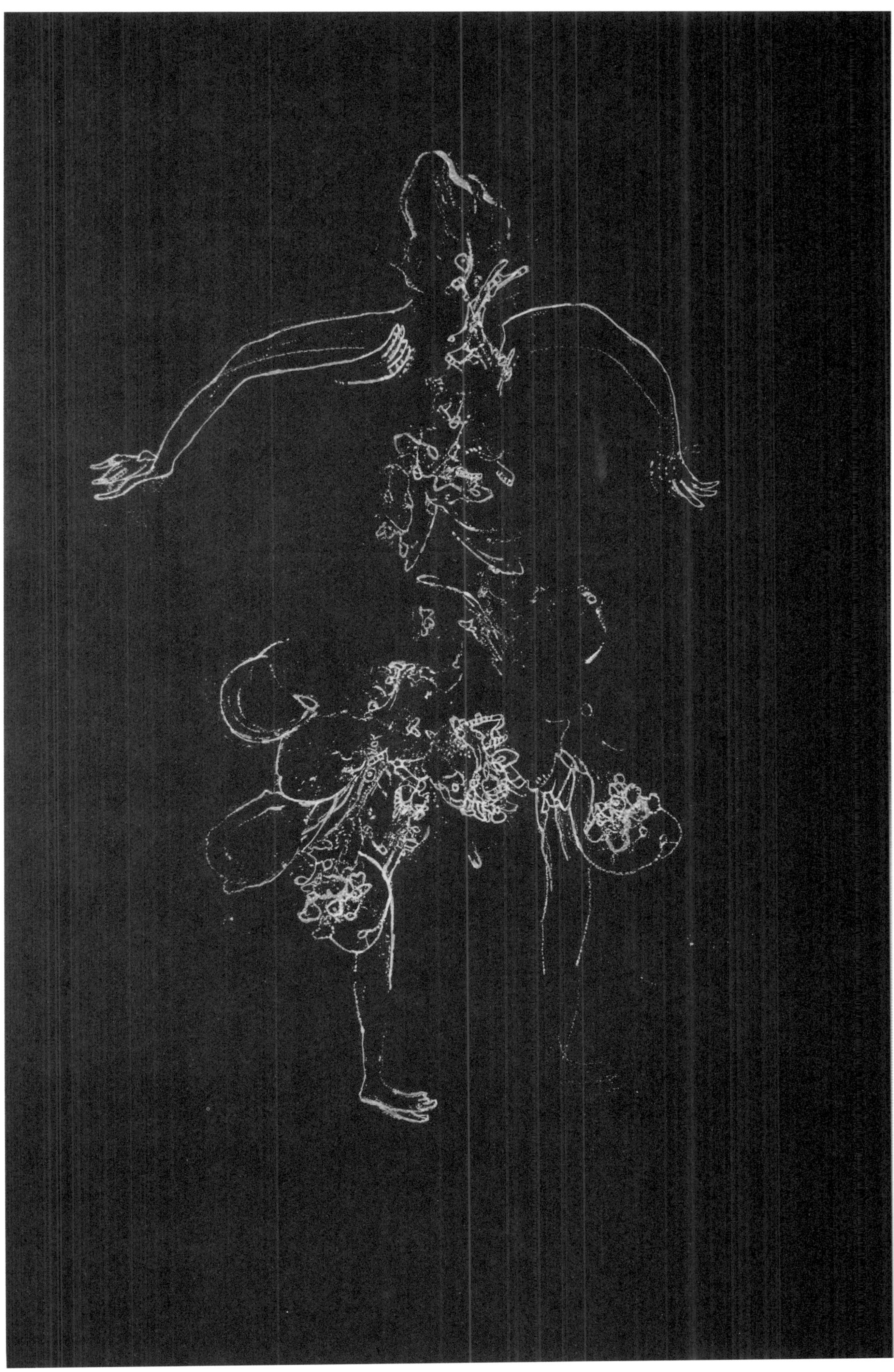

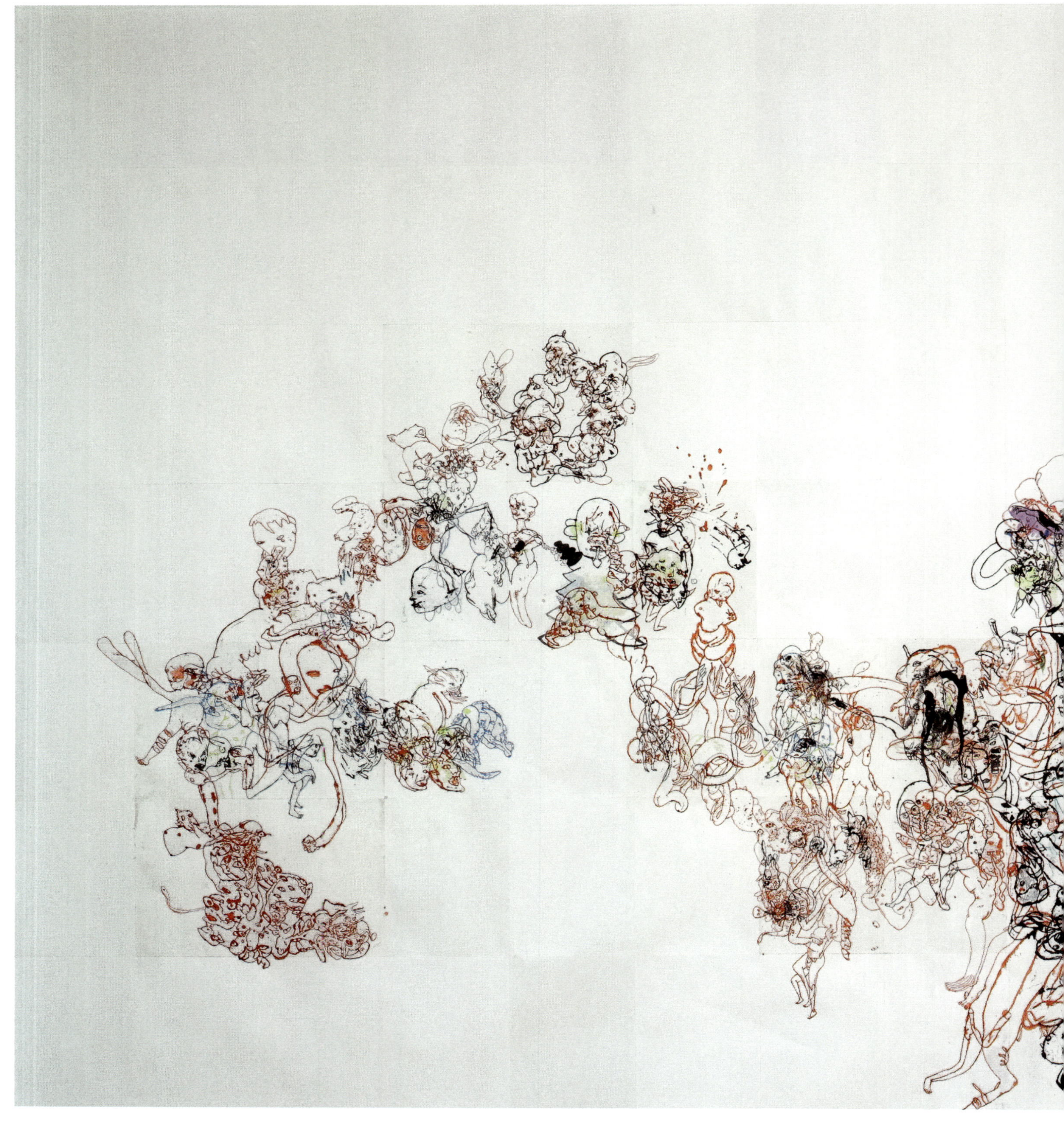

Ad Infinitum, 2010
Ink, Flashe and collage on sectioned paper
197 × 392 cm (77 $\frac{1}{2}$ × 154 $\frac{3}{8}$ in.)

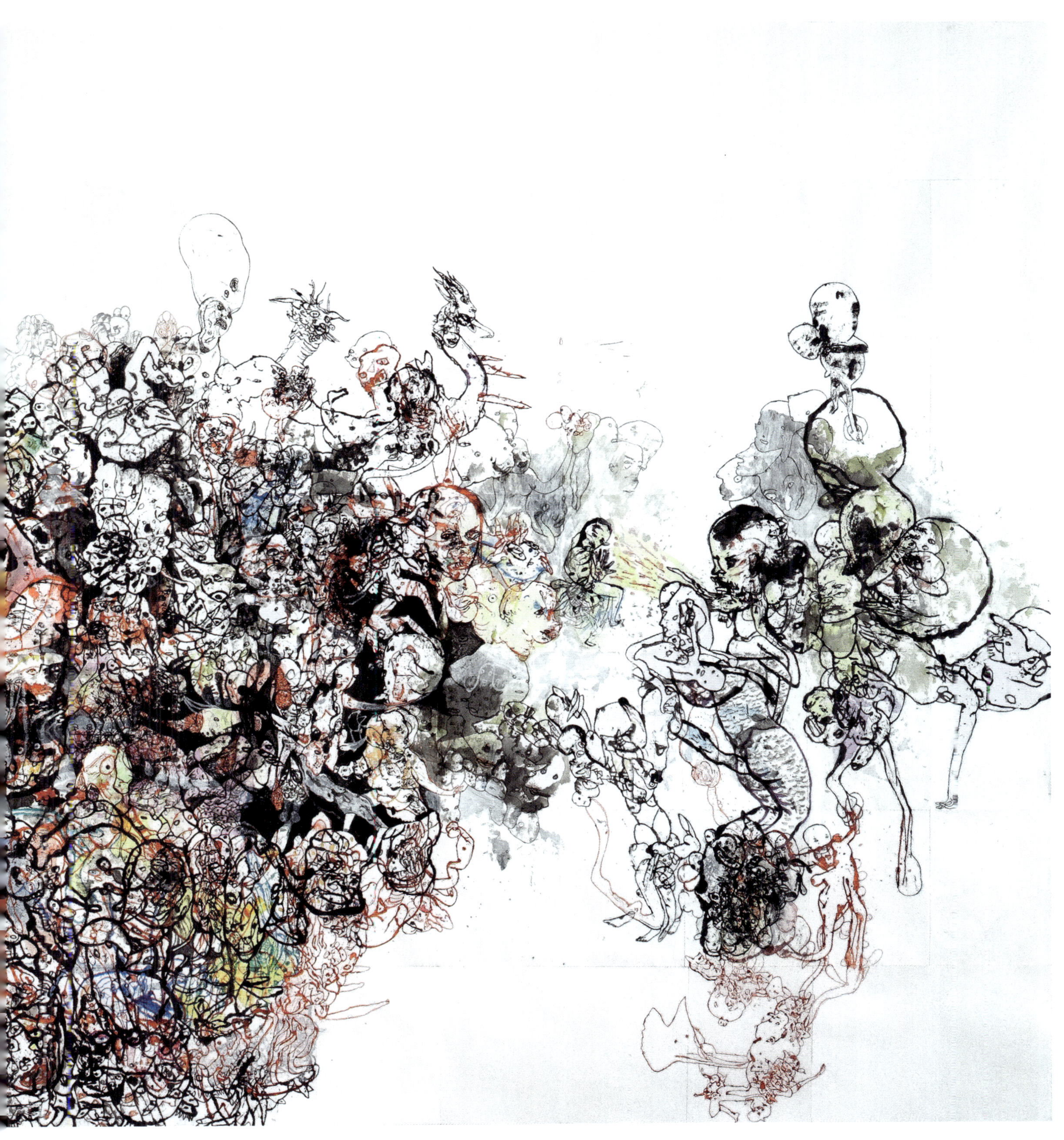

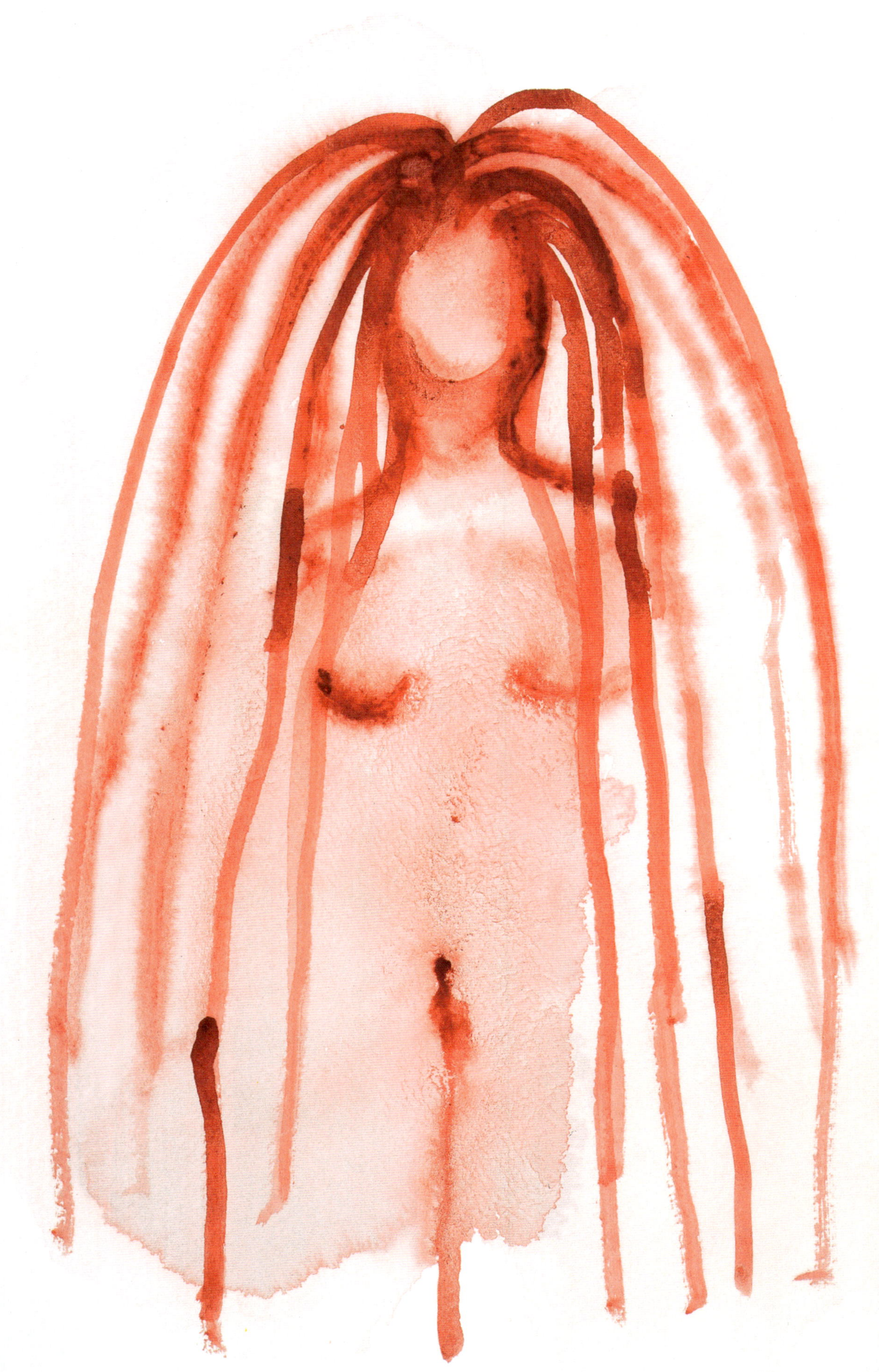

LOUISE BOURGEOIS *Born 1911, Paris, France. Died 2010 New York, USA*

Louise Bourgeois was an obsessive artist known for producing work steeped in psychoanalysis, inspired by dreams and childhood memories of family conflicts, and deeply attuned to the primal emotions of fear, rage and sexual jealousy. Her language was that of the body, as a whole or in parts, which she used as the source of psychologically charged imagery that had an unmistakably feminine thrust.

Bourgeois grew up in Paris, moving to New York in 1938, and although her work has affinities with Surrealism, she distanced herself from that group. Instead, she declared herself an Existentialist and thereby aligned herself with Alberto Giacometti, a sculptor who set immense store by

drawing. Bourgeois drew compulsively in journals, many of which remained hidden in boxes for decades until her death. She had studied mathematics and was always interested in abstraction, and first learned to draw while repairing tapestries at her parents' factory, such that for Bourgeois drawing was always associated with reparation. Her work is a form of autobiography: *The Insomnia Drawings*, made between 1994 and 1995, express her introspective, oneiric state; the spirals and mathematical patterns reveal her more meditative side, and were perhaps made as a way of calming herself. The drawings shown here are as vivacious, expressive and satirical as a young child's, despite being made when the artist was in her late nineties.

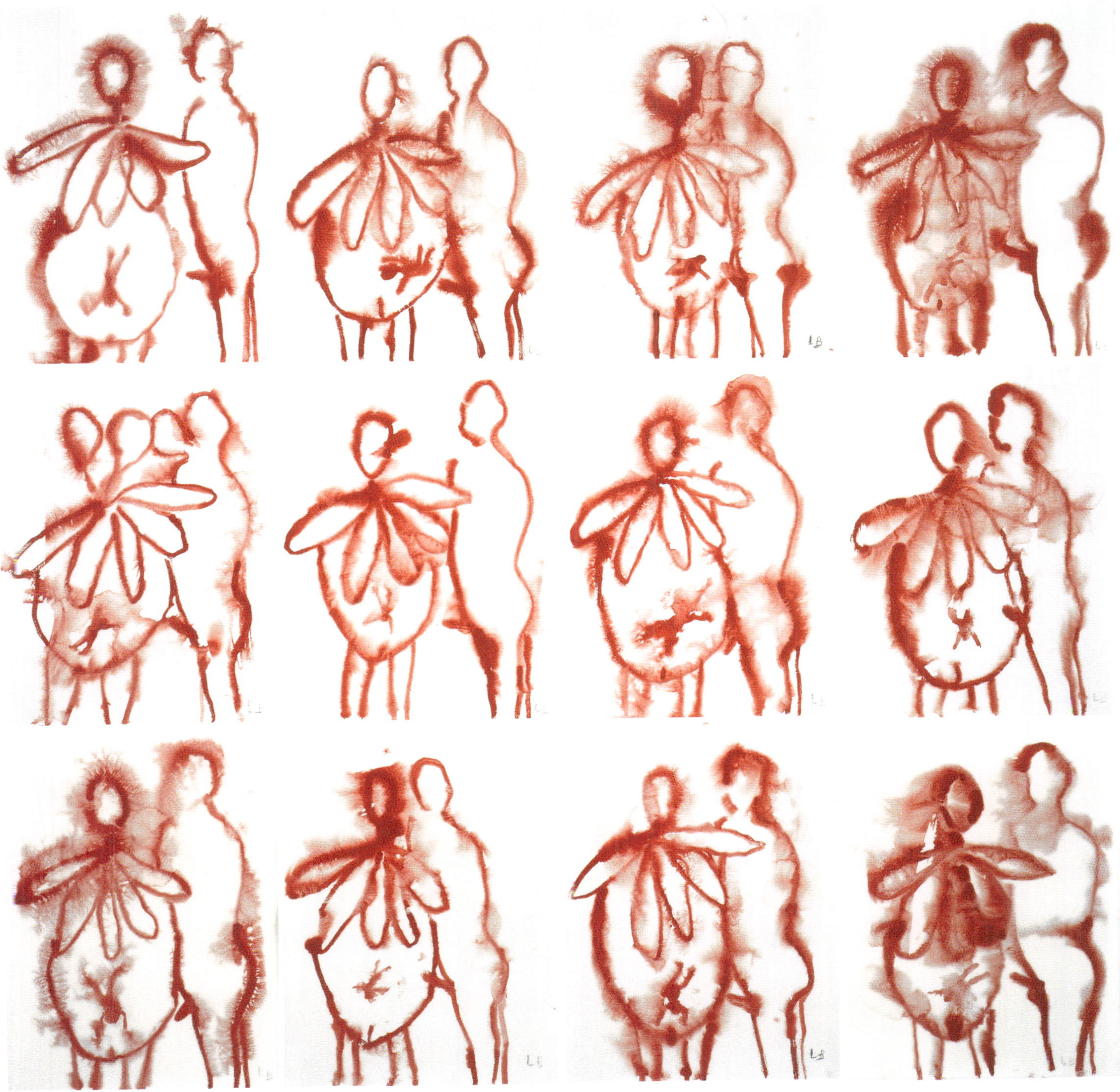

< *Femme*, 2007
Gouache on paper
37.1 × 27.9 cm (14 ^{5}⁄$_8$ × 11 in.)

The Family I, 2007
Series of 12, gouache on paper
Each: 59.7 × 45.7 cm (23 ^{1}⁄$_2$ × 18 in.)

44

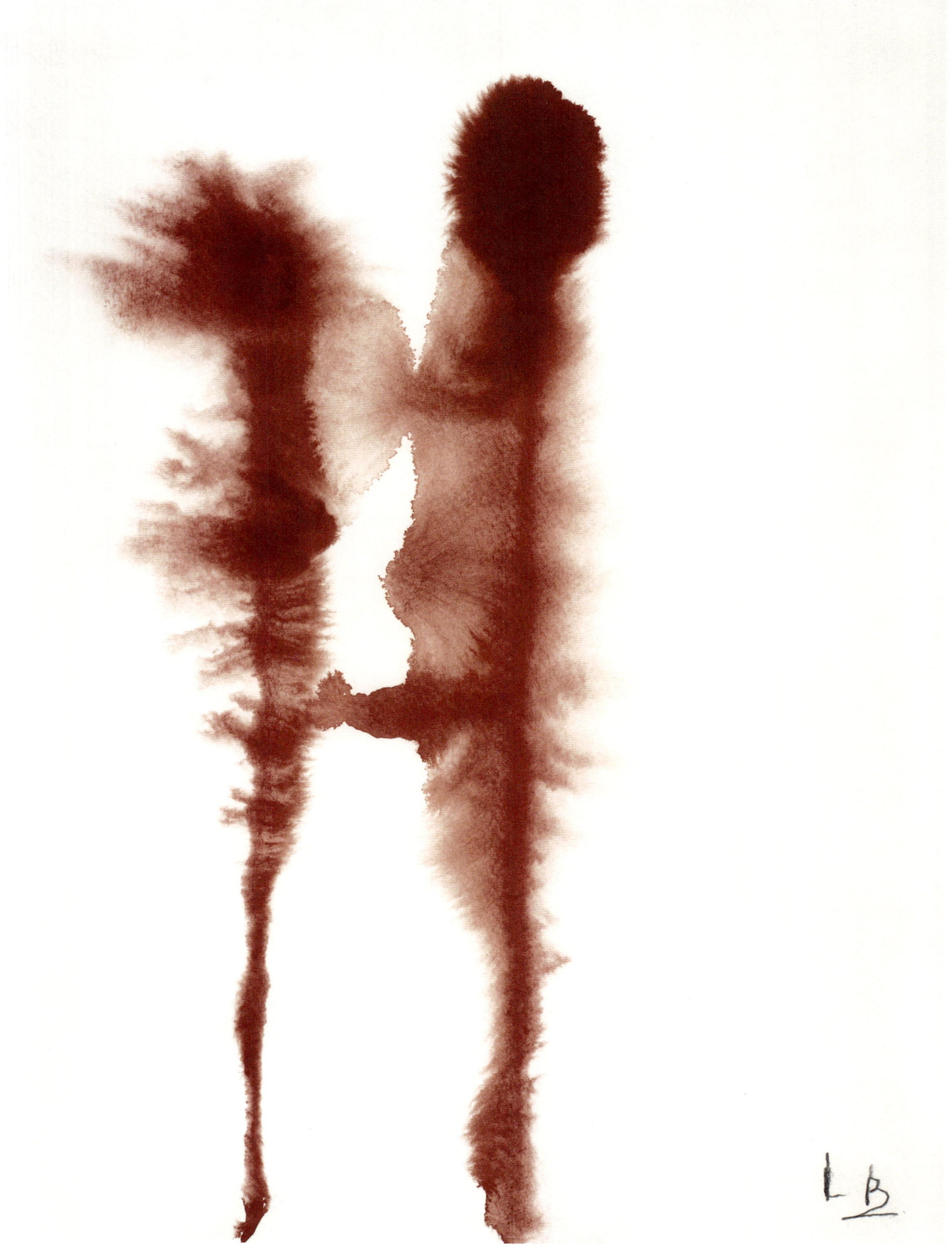

Couple, 2007
Gouache on paper
37.1 × 27.9 cm (14 ⅝ × 11 in.)

The Birth, 2007 >
Gouache on paper
60 × 45.7 cm (23 ⅝ × 18 in.)

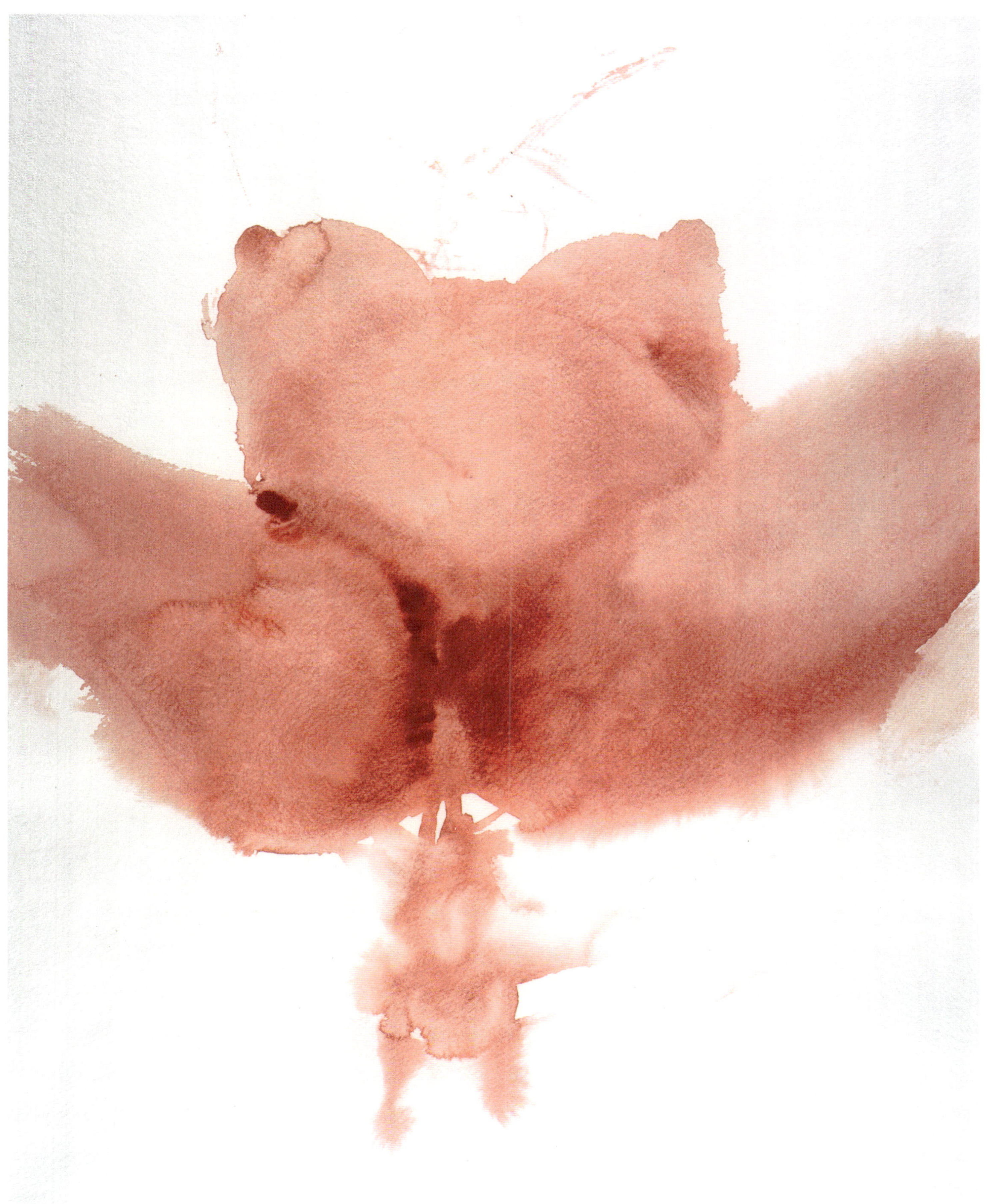

ULRIKE LIENBACHER *Born 1963, Oberndorf, Austria. Lives and works in Vienna and Salzburg, Austria*

'Drawing is a key medium for me in my work; it's my backbone. It is of the first order; it is neither a sketch nor a preliminary study. My drawing is the expression of a conceptual process, a process of construction. I never draw to capture impressions spontaneously. Drawing implies such "sparse" means that it demands reduction and precision.'

Ulrike Lienbacher's drawings and sculptures address related subjects: the human body (in the drawings, always female) in a culture obsessed with hygiene and health; the aesthetics of the gymnasium; the high value placed on youth and fitness; and the auto-erotic undercurrents in physical exercise. In her drawings of faceless young women working out, stretching, posing and performing ablutions, the precision and clarity of Lienbacher's line complies with the cool aesthetic of the gym, in which cleanliness and order prevail. In these drawings, the cult of fitness is linked to commodity fetishism. The impersonal, almost abstract, aesthetic of bodily perfection is epitomized by these uniformly trim young gymnasts. Impurity and disorder are an ever-present threat, showing up, for example, as stains on the soles of feet or dirty water in the basin. Hair is symbolically trained and controlled, as is seen in the drawings shown here, or occasionally allowed to fall loose – the one sign of freedom and individuality in an otherwise disciplined world.

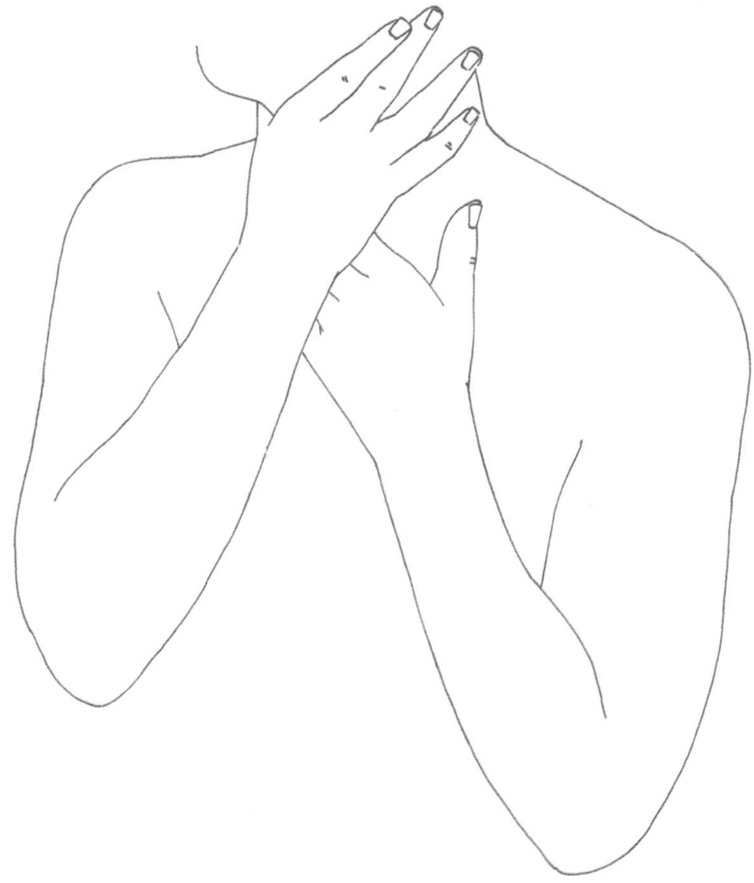

Untitled, 2001
Ink on paper
38.5 × 30 cm (15 ⅛ × 11 ¾ in.)

Untitled, 2002 >
Ink on paper
47 × 39.5 cm (18 ½ × 15 ½ in.)

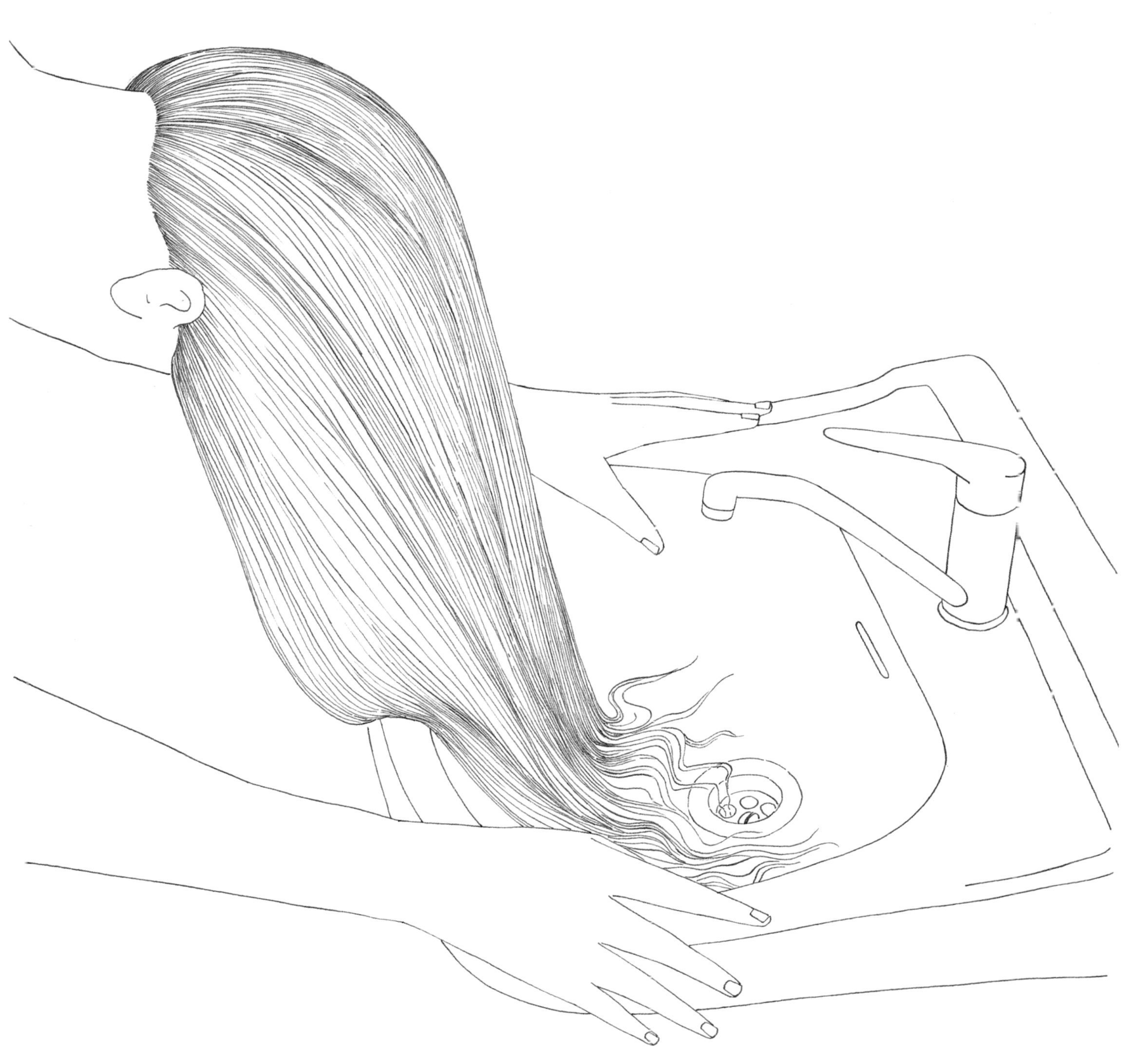

48

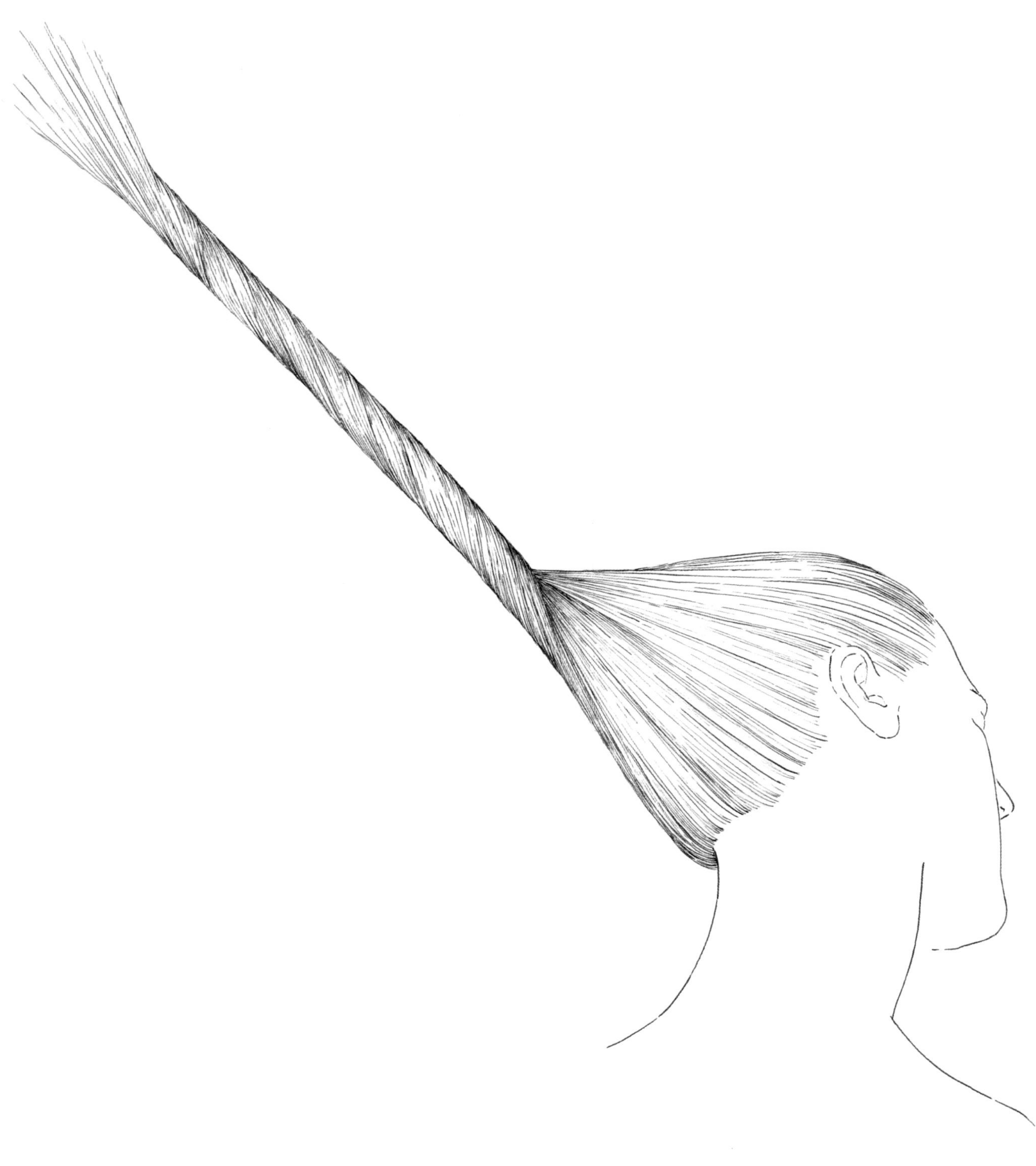

Untitled, 2010
Ink on paper
65 × 54.5 cm (25 ⅝ × 21 ½ in.)

Untitled, 2008 >
Ink on paper
106.5 × 76 cm (41 ⅞ × 29 ⅞ in.)

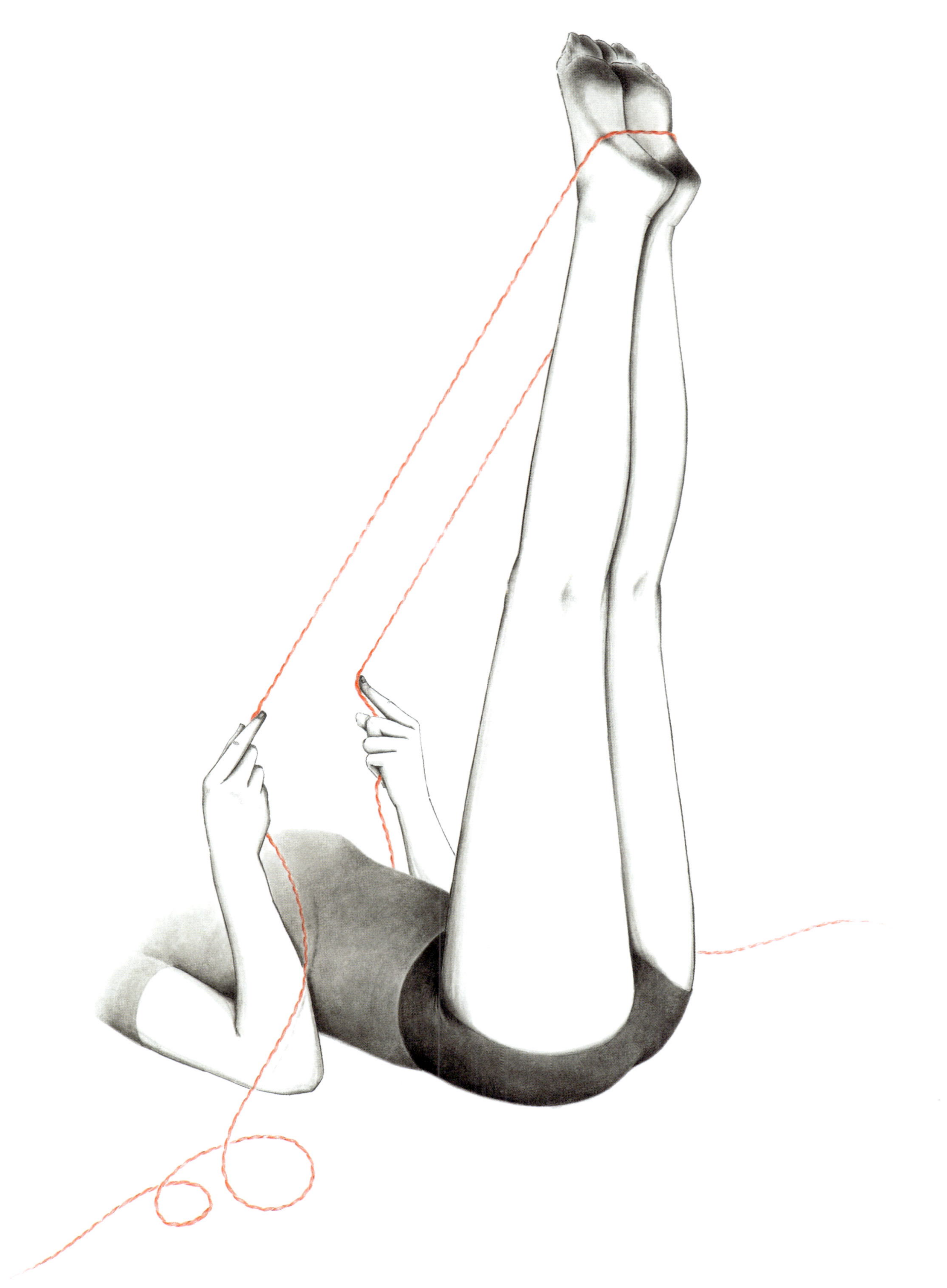

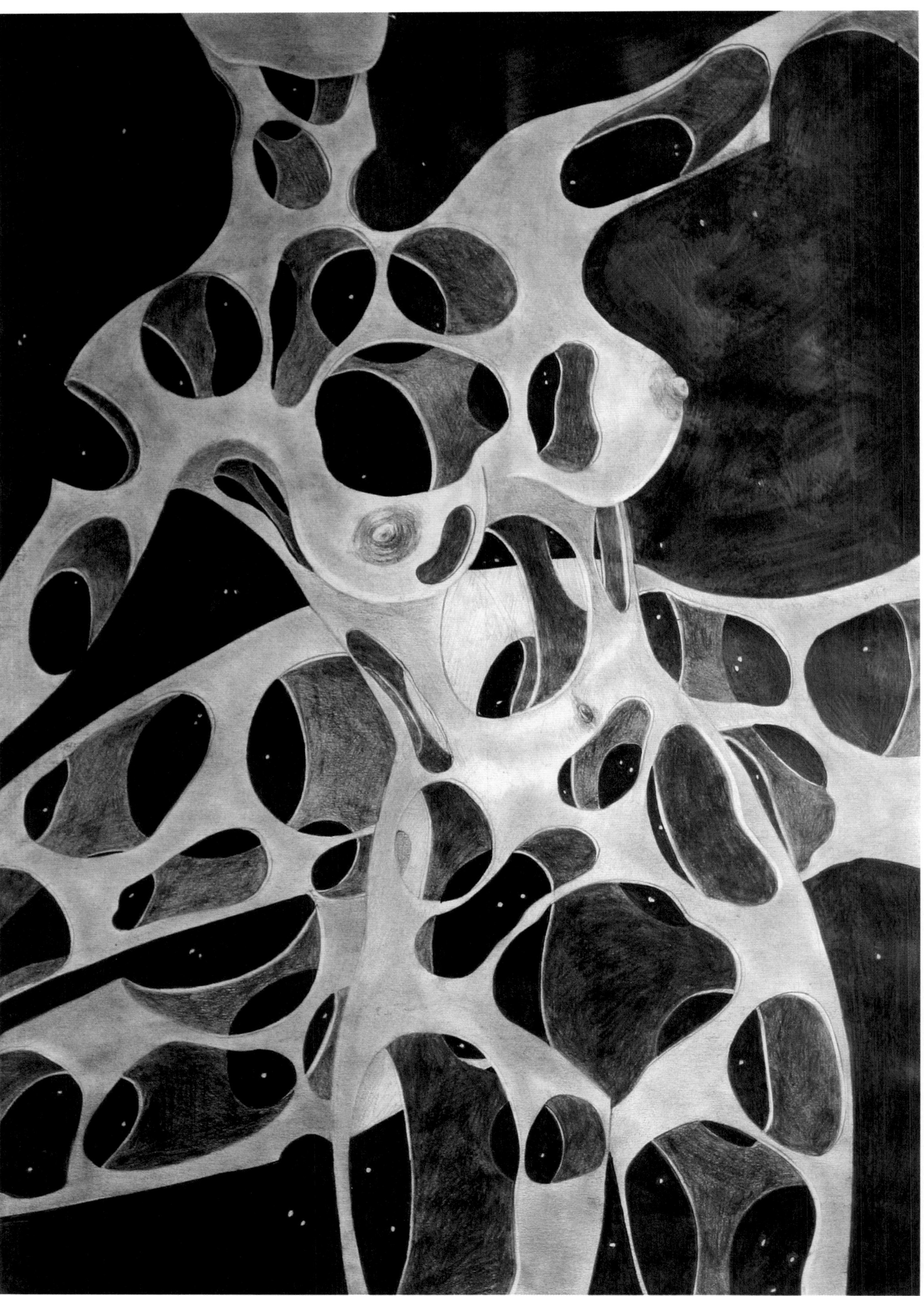

ODUN ORIMOLADE *Born 1976, Lagos, Nigeria. Lives and works in Lagos, Nigeria*

Odun Orimolade trained as a painter at Yaba College of Technology in Lagos, where she now teaches. She works in sculpture, installation and performance, and although she would not define herself as a one-medium artist, she has sought to condense her imaginative concerns in drawing, which for her is the most fluid and versatile medium ('all motion is drawing', she says).

Orimolade's drawings are a highly subjective means of self-excavation. She fuses a naturalistic figurative idiom with fantastical and biomorphic forms that emerge spontaneously, through a process that is part technical experimentation and part mystical reverie. An initial concept, usually inspired by Yoruba philosophy – such as the multiplicity of selves or facets of the psyche – generates imagery that hovers between solidity and flickering insubstantiality. The pulsating rhythms of the body in dance, the growth of natural forms such as plants and trees, the flow of water or the drift of smoke: all are evoked in the patterns that spread across Orimolade's pages. Her insistently volumetric handling lends the illusion of tangible reality to bodily and ornamental imagery, which floats in deep, seemingly infinite pictorial space. 'I am very interested in the idea of overlapping realities and seek that in most of my work', she says. 'I am also preoccupied with the idea of space. I cannot say why but I seem to be gravitating away from directly figurative work, though the idea of the living form is very present.'

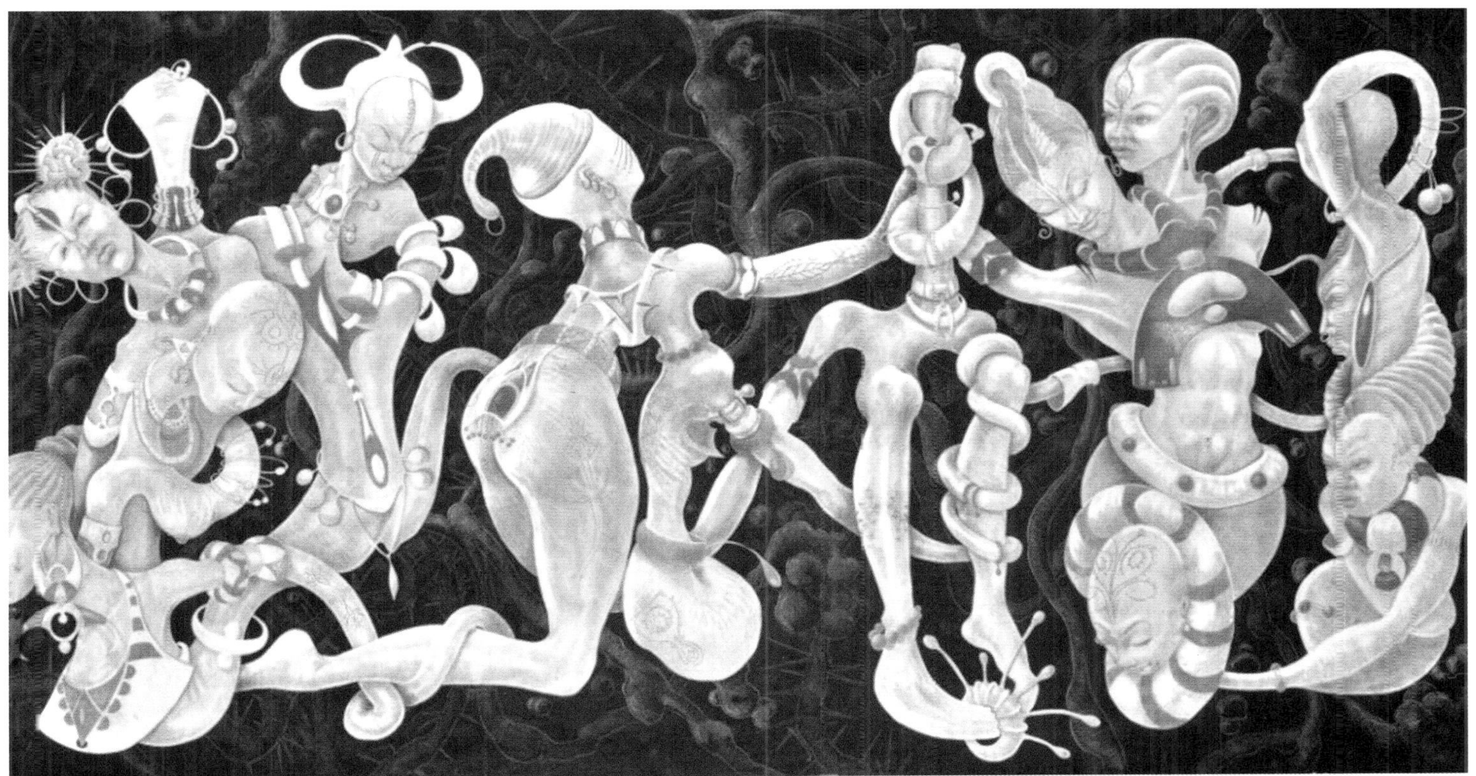

< *Clarity*, 2006
Graphite pencils on hot pressed paper
51 × 71 cm (20 ⅛ × 28 in.)

Multiplicity, 2012
Graphite, pastel pencils and ink on hot pressed paper
122 × 244 cm (48 × 96 ⅛ in.)

ANTONY GORMLEY *Born 1950, London, UK. Lives and works in London, UK*

Antony Gormley's *Body drawings* (2009–11) are a continuation of his series, begun in 1990, entitled *Body & Light*. Yet the *Body drawings* mark a shift in technique into water-based paint on a wet ground, with the paper laid flat. The medium used is carbon and casein – a highly saturated paint that disperses readily – and the drawings were made with a calligraphy brush using what Gormley describes as 'both rapid touch and staccato shakes'. He has written: 'For me drawing in its essence is *mediumistic:* it is both the evidence of a material event and the ground onto which the perceptions of the viewer and artist,

as equal partners, may project their thoughts and feelings. The arising of an image is literally an apparition: the appearance of something out of nothing.' Gormley has long been preoccupied with the relational field between body and space, and perceives his *Body* series as the result of an event-based phenomenon in which the body is felt 'not as a knowable object, but a subjective space of becoming'. The spread of paint takes on a life of its own beyond the control of the artist, yet produces expressive marks loaded with a sense of the uncanny: a fugitive image that evokes a human presence.

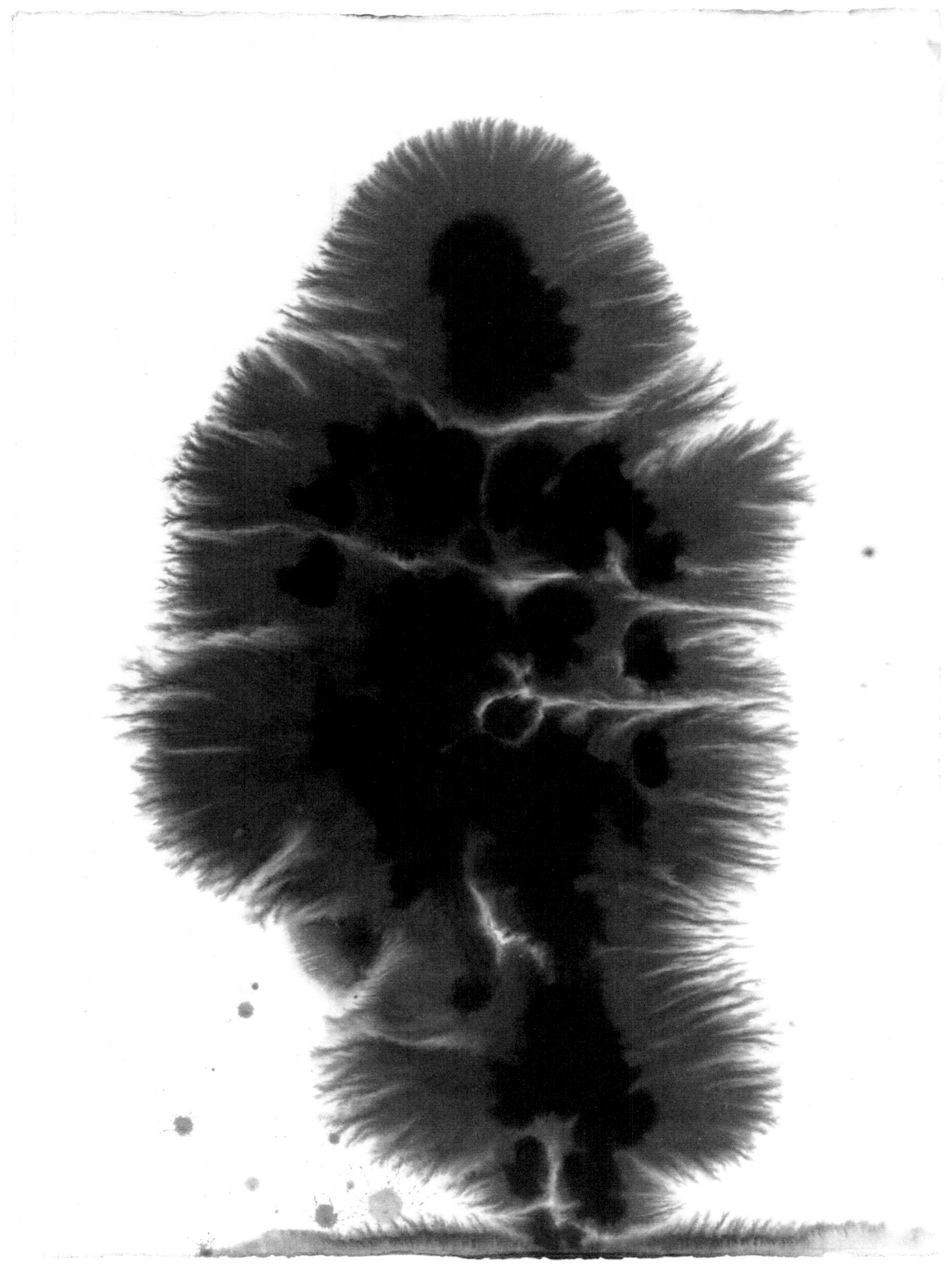

BODY XXXV, 2011
Carbon and casein on paper
75.5 × 55.5 cm (29 ¾ × 21 ⅞ in.)

BODY XXVI, 2010 >
Carbon and casein on paper
38 x 28 cm (15 x 11 in.)

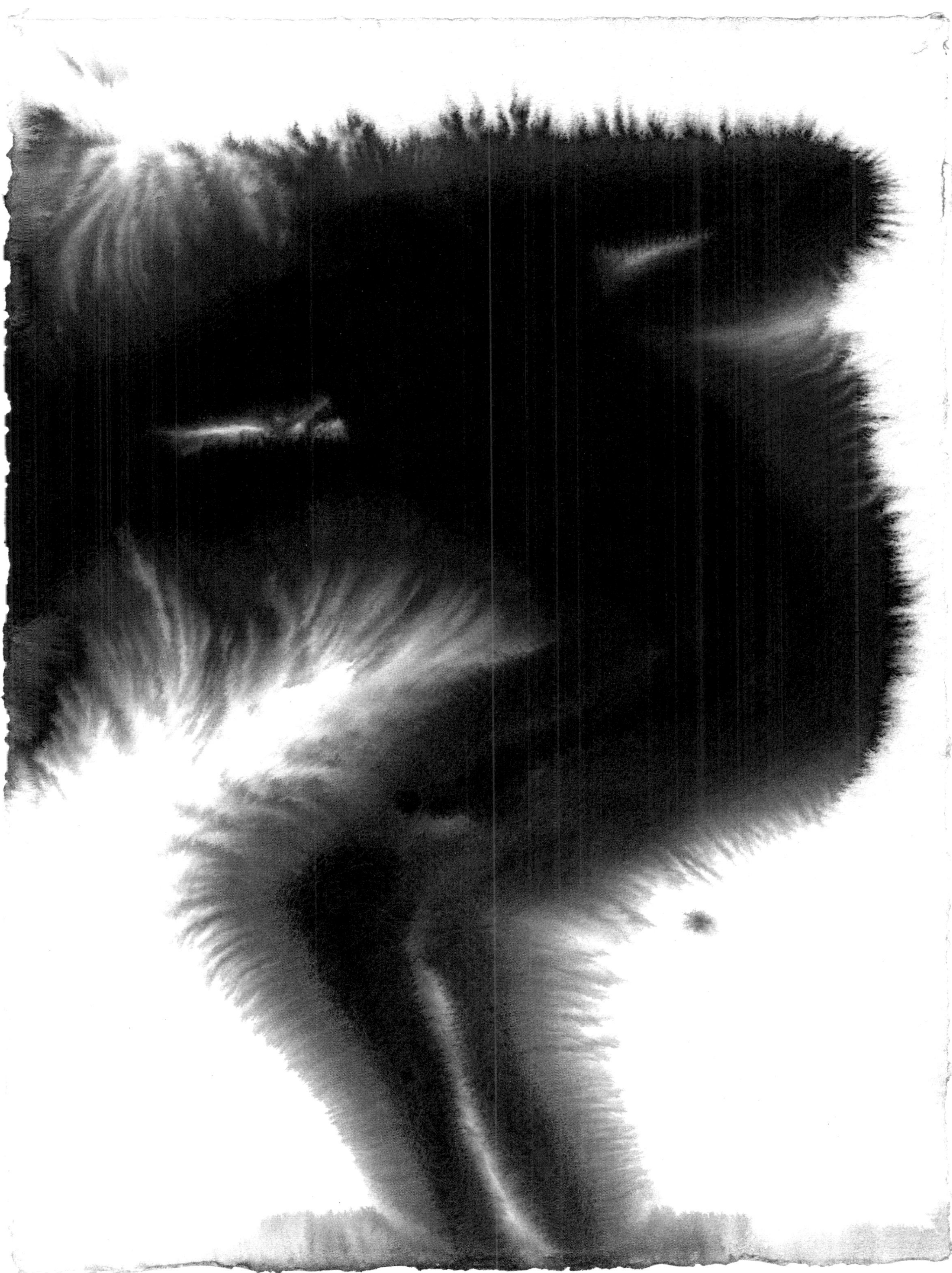

54

Mithu Sen is a multimedia artist and poet who places drawing at the centre of her practice, describing it as similar to 'pulling out' something from within herself. Sen's visceral, uninhibited exploration of her physical and emotional being – which encompasses her struggles with identity, creativity, pain and sexuality – is aptly expressed in her own words: 'A fresh bleeding scratch on my body / When dried, is the drawing for the next morning'.

In the 2010 installation *Black Candy (iforgotmypenisathome)*, the artist attempts to project herself empathetically into the minds of two gay men (the work is a tribute to the gay Indian artist Bhupen Khakhar, who died in 2003). Sen has scripted and recorded an imaginary dialogue between the couple ('not conjoined twins but gay lovers'), and draws them naked, flayed and androgynous, their animal and human selves entangled, their bodies' internal organs exposed. In one x-ray-style drawing, a man bears a foetus; in another he excretes; and in a third he is 'beheaded' by a prostate operation. According to Sen, the themes she addresses are in fact genderless: they are the crises of all human life, 'including confused emotional and sexual identity, fear and denial', all of which the artist manages to address with a combination of humanity and humour. When installed in the gallery, the drawings are shown on sliding screens so that viewers can rearrange their order, thus entering into the dialogue and creating their own narrative from it.

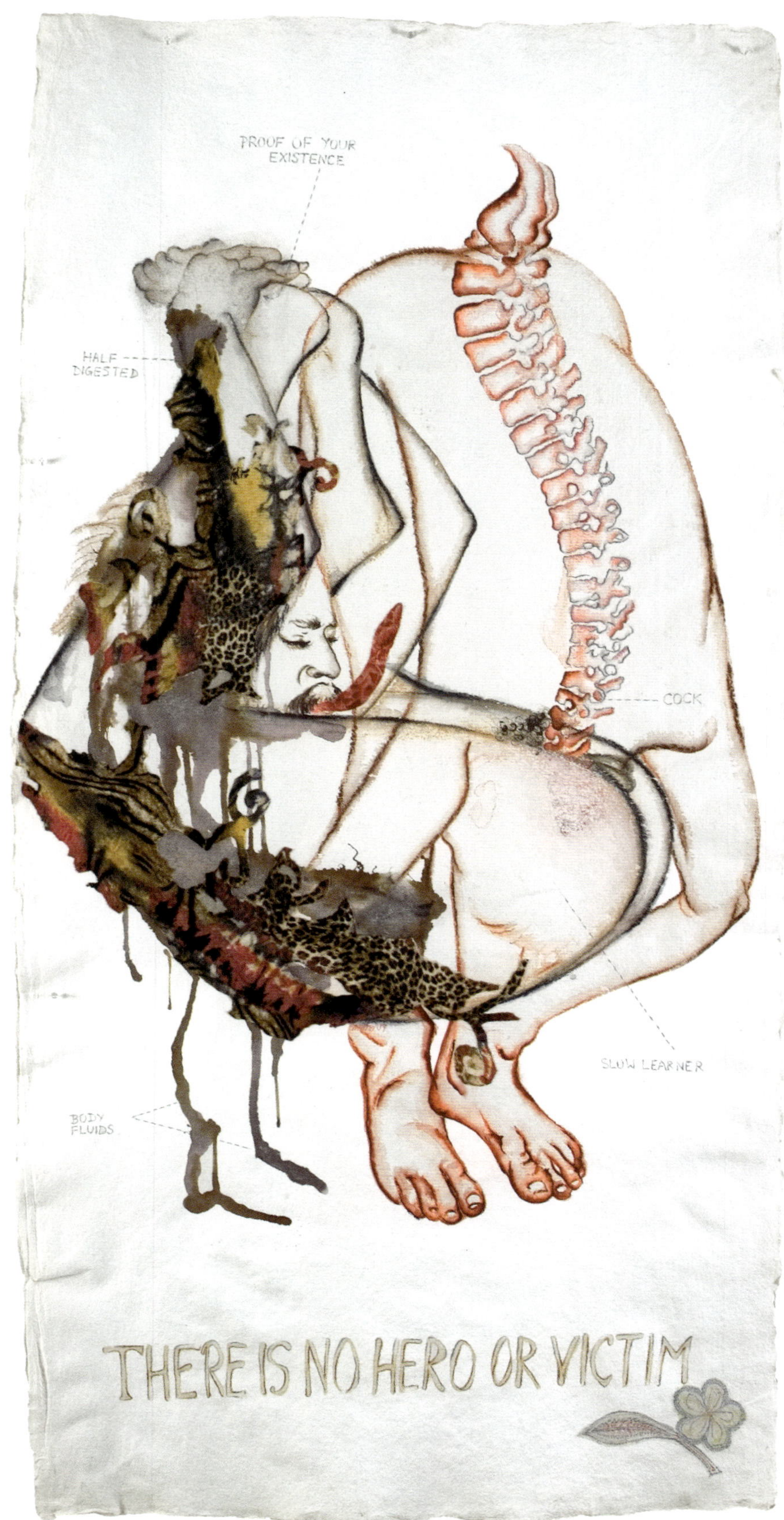

There is No Hero or Victim, 2009
Mixed media drawings on custom made handmade acid free paper
210.8 × 106.7 cm (83 × 42 in.)

Beheaded after Prostate Surgery, 2009 >
Mixed media drawings on custom made handmade acid free paper
210.8 × 106.7 cm (83 × 42 in.)

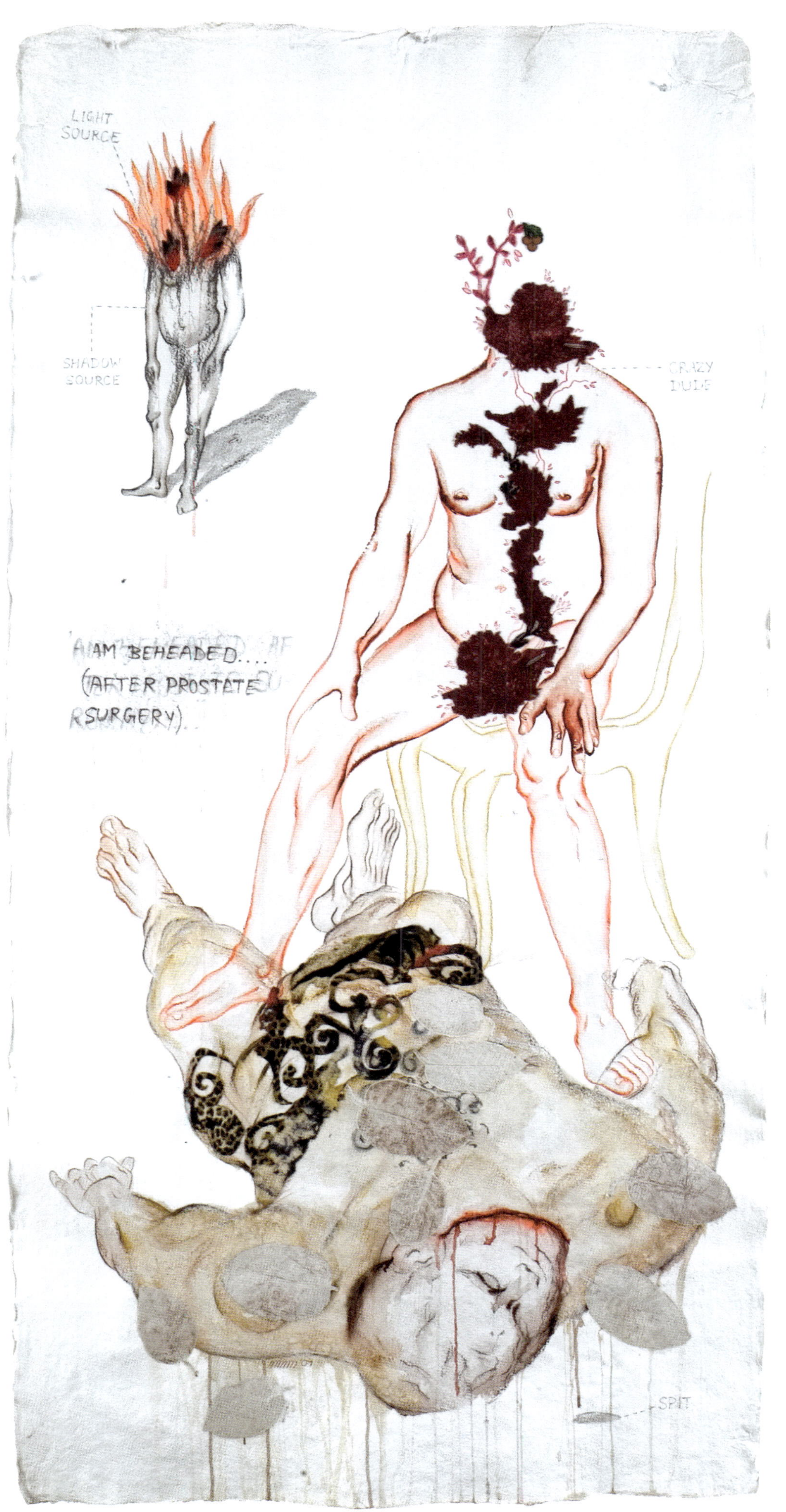

LIGHT SOURCE
SHADOW SOURCE
CRAZY DUDE
I AM BEHEADED....
(AFTER PROSTATE SURGERY).
SPIT

CHLOE PIENE *Born 1972, Stamford, Connecticut, USA. Lives and works in New York, USA*

Analogies abound in Chloe Piene's graphic works: between Eros and death, the human and the animal, and drawing and masturbation. Naked, skinny women – possibly self-portraits – recline or sprawl, isolated in space, the contours of their bodies traced in tremulous charcoal lines that sometimes digress to reveal the skeletal frame beneath the skin's surface. Skulls, grinning malevolently, are juxtaposed with rounded breasts, and bony fingers intimately caress flesh. This morbid meditation on death is evocative of the Mexican Day of the Dead and of the allegorical *danse macabre* or 'dance of death' of medieval Europe – in fact, it is the Northern European tradition with which the artist claims the closest artistic affinity. The themes are familiar, yet the bodies are sensitively and vivaciously drawn: a wavering line scoops up the contour of an arm and then floats away loosely into what may be a string of small bones, the beads of a necklace or pure abstraction. A recent exhibition has paired Piene's drawings with those of the German draughtsman, sculptor and photographer Hans Bellmer, and they are also reminiscent of the graphic work of Egon Schiele and Willem de Kooning. Like these twentieth-century artists, Piene makes drawings that are sexually charged and aggressive, and achieves maximum impact using the barest of means.

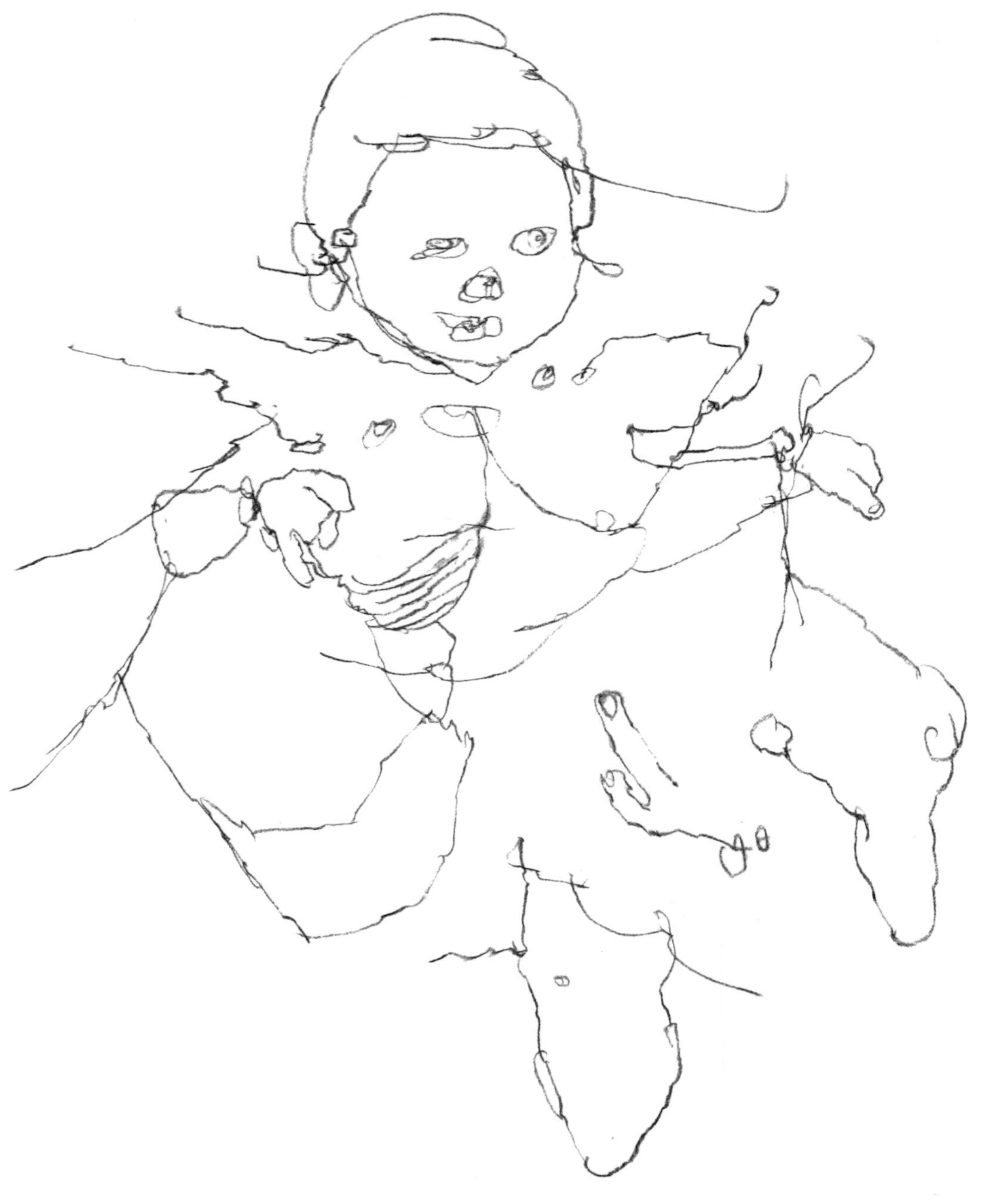

Funnybaby, 2007
Charcoal on unbleached paper
125.7 × 87.6 cm (49 ½ × 34 ½ in.)

Sleeper 02 (Vintage Hat), 2005 >
Charcoal on vellum
125.1 × 76.2 cm (49 ¼ × 30 in.)

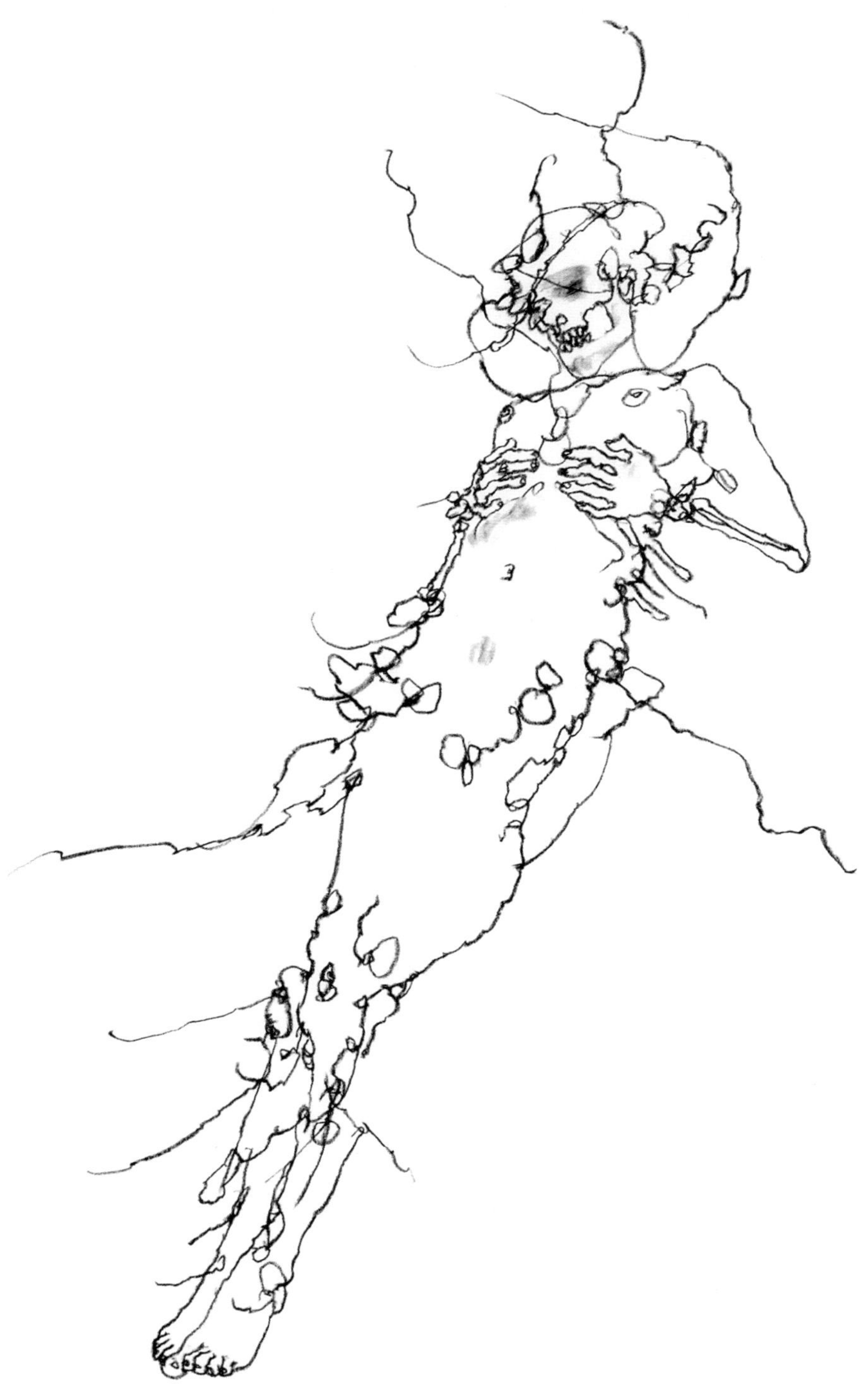

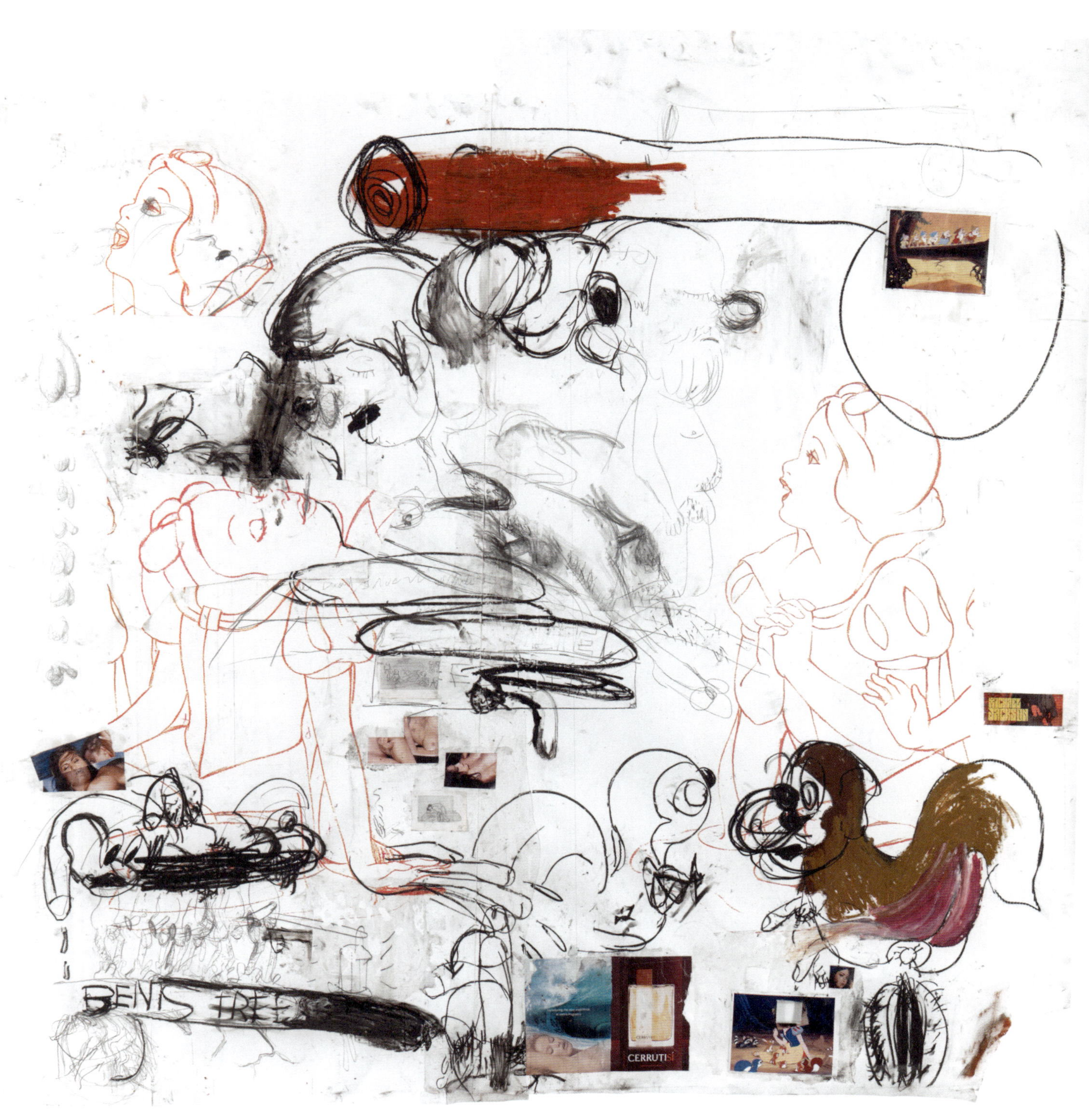

BENIS FREE
CERRUTI

PAUL McCARTHY *Born 1948, Salt Lake City, Utah, USA. Lives and works in Los Angeles, California, USA*

LA-based artist Paul McCarthy is renowned for his provocative video installations and sculptures, and his performances in which he enters into a regressive persona with shamanistic abandon. There is a carnivalesque humour in his visceral, obscene and scatological enactments of the obsessions of American consumer culture: food, sex and power. In these performances he is hilariously degraded, immersed not in blood and shit – as it may seem at first – but rather in tomato ketchup and chocolate. McCarthy is now in his late sixties, and his video productions have grown in scale and ambition throughout his career, particularly in their parodies of Hollywood B-movie and porn film sets.

McCarthy's 2013 performance piece *WS* is based on the German folk tale of *Snow White*, but filtered through the lens of Disney and spewed out again as a lurid parody of American kitsch and sexism. McCarthy first generates the imagery for productions such as *WS* in drawings in which he allows his unconscious to run riot. In the drawings shown here, for instance, Snow White's dwarfs are worked up into characters with their genitals on their faces, in an overt mockery of the phallocentricism of much of American mass culture. McCarthy regards his drawings as performative works in their own right, made 'in a sort of trance…. It's more about making than telling. Drawing is a form of analysis. I'm not controlling it, just allowing it to unfold. It's not about clarity, it's about each piece suggesting the next one in a continuum.'

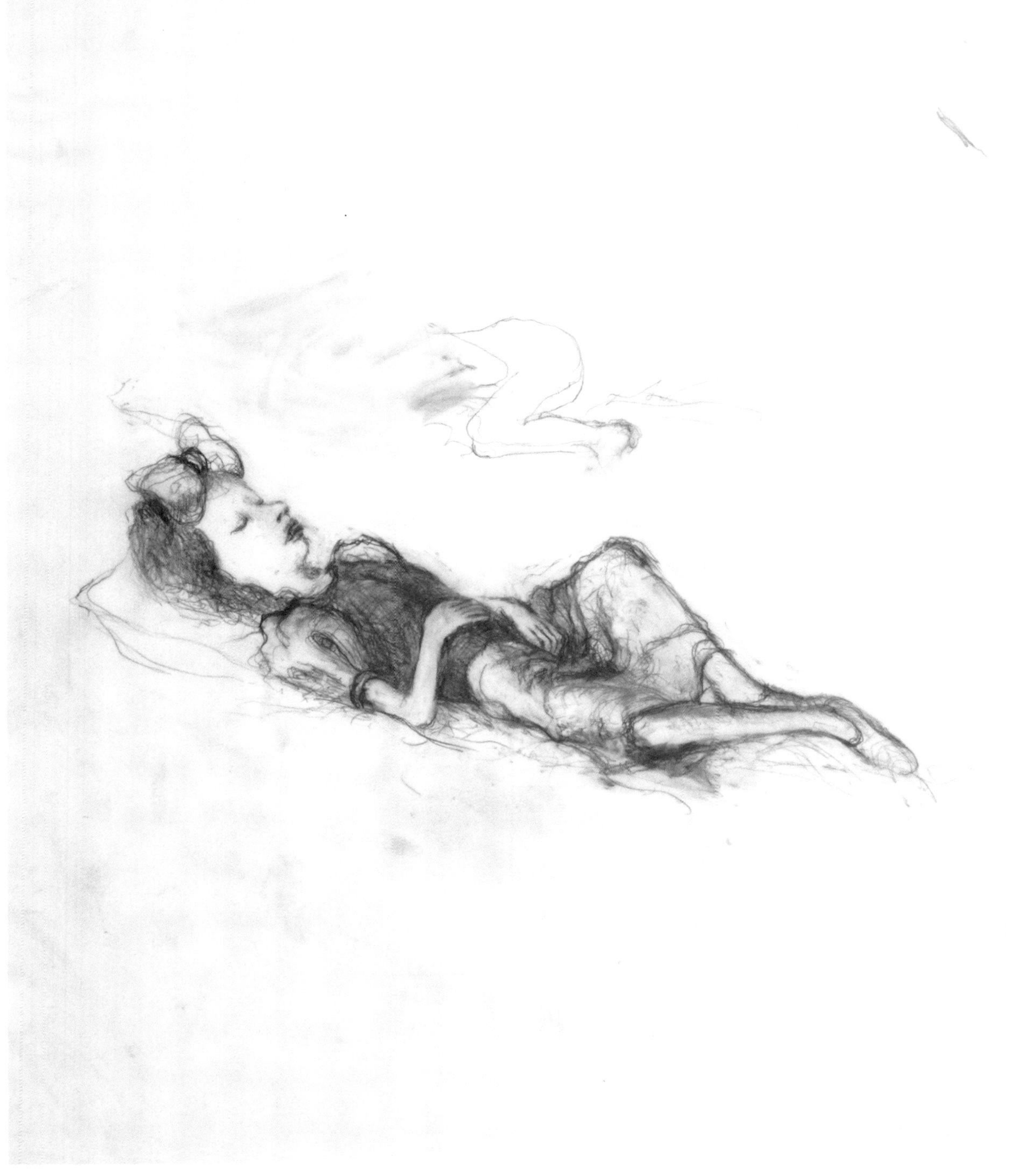

< *Michael Jackson*, 2009
Oil, charcoal and collage on inkjet print
276.9 × 274.3 cm (109 × 108 in.)

Group 2 (detail), 2008
Series of 7 drawings, pencil on vellum
47 × 268 cm (18 ½ × 105 ½ in.)

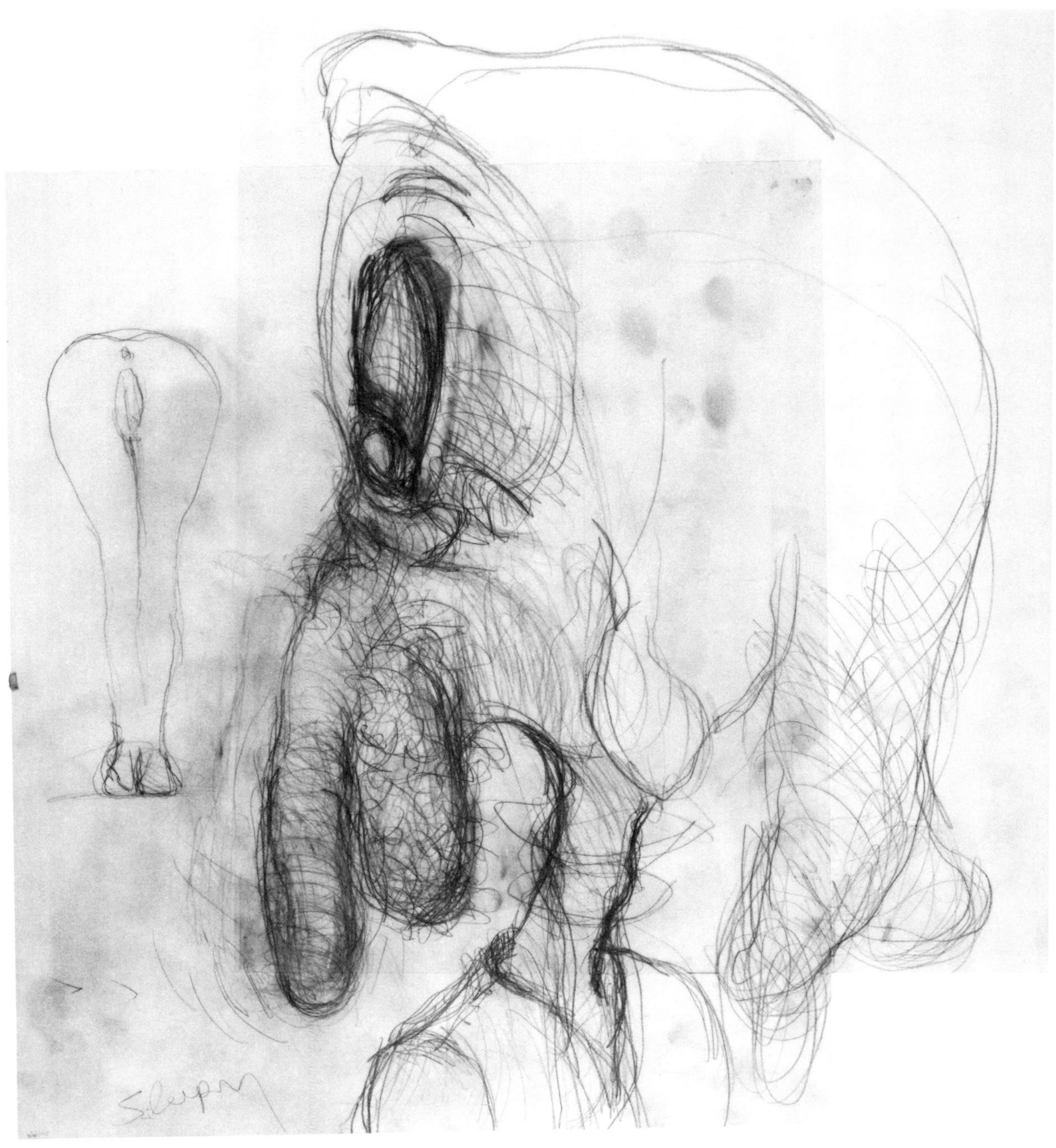

Dwarf Heads (detail), 2009
Series of 6 drawings, pencil on vellum, tape
Installed as an individually framed set: 61 × 433 × 3.5 cm
(170 ½ × 24 × 1 ⅜ in.)

323-825-0915 (Blockhead Drawing 2 of 4), 2000 >
Pencil on transparentized paper
61 × 47.9 cm (24 × 18 ⅞ in.)

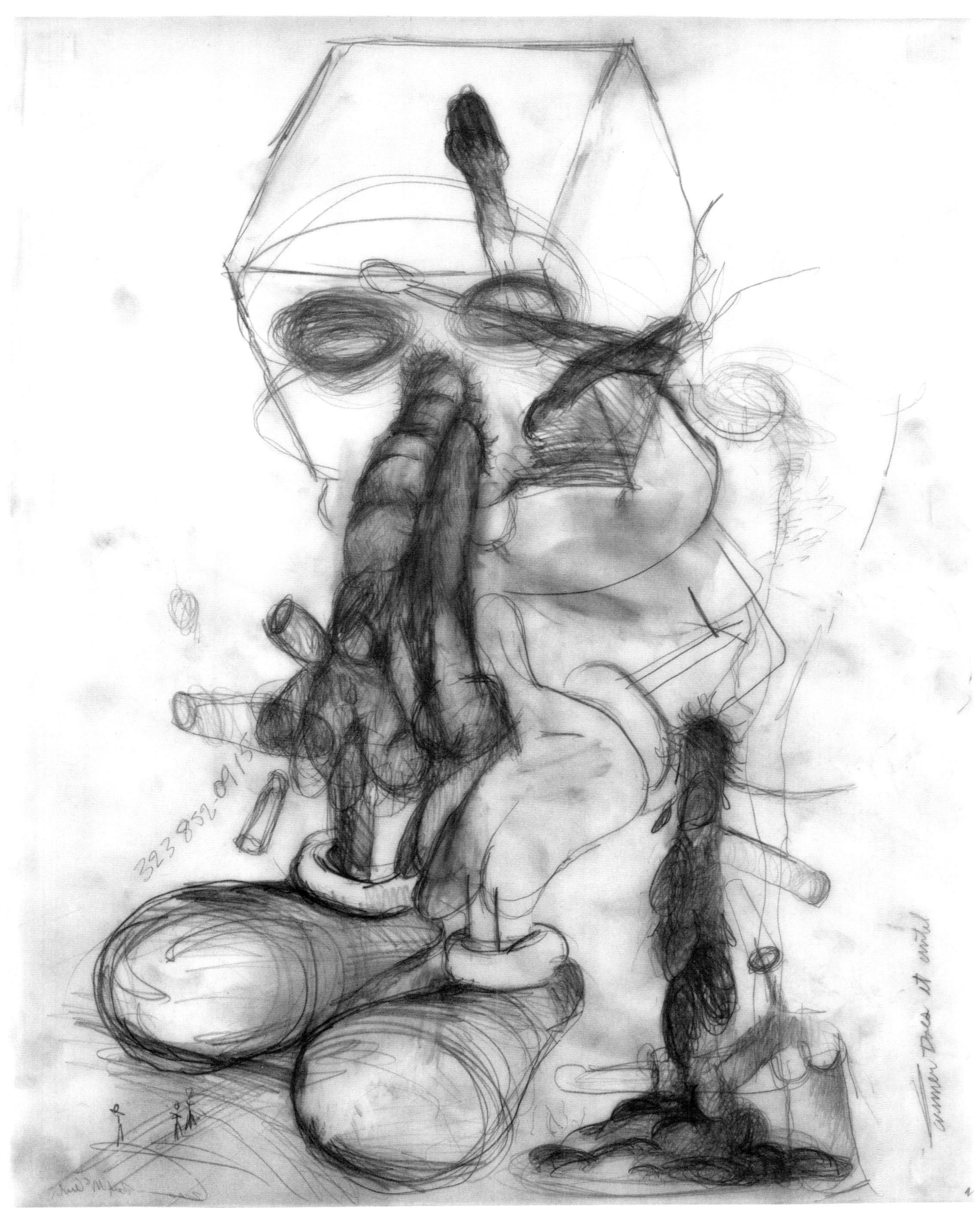

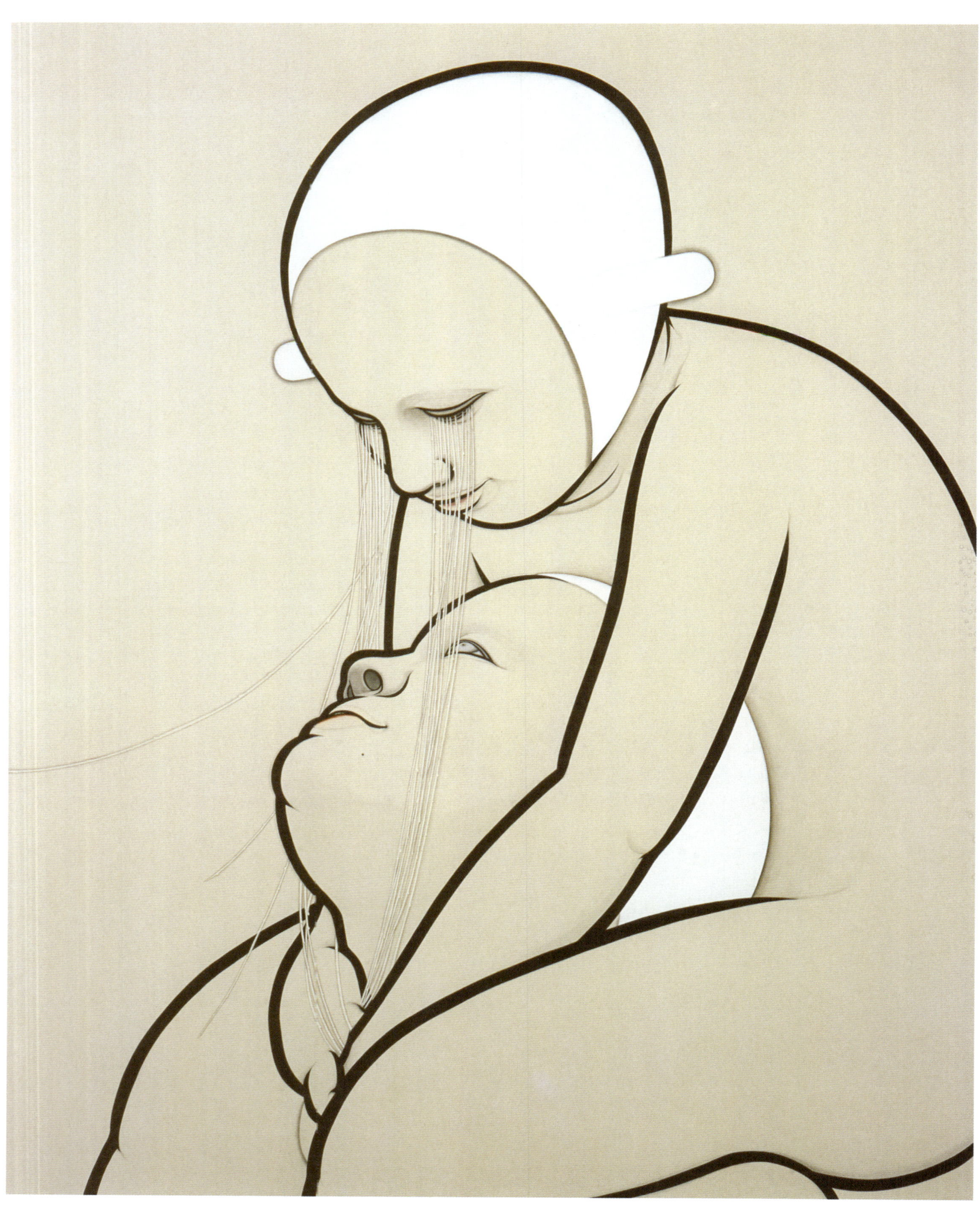

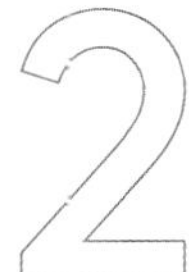

self

"Look, if you draw these lines the face turns sad." In what category does this sentence belong? How is it used? I once said that it was like a geometric proposition. But one could be of the opinion that it was a psychological, and therefore empirical, proposition. (Comparable, for example, to: If you add these ingredients, the substance turns yellow.)

LUDWIG WITTGENSTEIN *Last Writings on the Philosophy of Psychology, Vol. 1, 1949*

To start with the basic dialectic of vision: if we have sight, we see and we are seen. We are both perceiving subject and the object of the other's gaze, with all the intricacies of self-consciousness that this entails. We see others and we see ourselves in reflection, but we can never really know how we are perceived. Self-knowledge is thus circumscribed, its limits fixed at the interface between self and other, and we can only imagine how we appear to them, and guess how they appear to one another. We form our self-image by gauging our imagined place in the social scheme, and regard those around us with a sense of relative familiarity or strangeness. Familiar people can appear strange when perception is altered, in extreme emotional or psychotic states or under the influence of drugs, or when we look at someone especially closely – studying a face intently, for example, while drawing it. On the other hand, a total stranger can be brought up close in the act of drawing and seen as though known intimately for years.

One of art's functions is to defamiliarize everyday reality rendered dull by habit, and to reawaken the mind to the strangeness, as well as the beauty and ugliness, of the visible world. This requires a special alertness and self-awareness. If it is incumbent on the artist, like the philosopher and the poet, to seek self-knowledge more wholeheartedly than the average citizen, then one way of achieving this is through the self-portrait. The simple act of looking in the mirror removes the artist from the realm of pure subjectivity. As observer, he or she is split or doubled, is at once self and other. The usual intimate exchange between artist and model is condensed into self-scrutiny, with the potential prospect of self-revelation. The result may be self-aggrandisement, straightforward pride, confidence or vanity, cool self-analysis, self-parody, self-pity, lacerating self-loathing or self-abasement. The great self-portraits of the past seem to connect us directly with the soul of the artist; we feel we would know these individuals

< KUMI MACHIDA *Rocking Horse*, 2010
Sumi (blue and brown), pigments, mineral pigments and colour pencil
on kumohada linen paper, 140 × 113 cm (55 ⅛ × 44 ½ in.)

instantly if we encountered them, just as we would recognize our closest friends.

The uncanny doubling of consciousness involved in the self-portrait is what intrigued philosopher Jacques Derrida, who analysed it in 'Memoirs of the Blind: The Self-Portrait and Other Ruins', his 1991 essay on drawings selected from the collections of the Louvre in Paris. 'I have always experienced drawing as an infirmity,' he confesses disarmingly, 'even worse, as a culpable infirmity: to this day I still think that I will never know *either* how to draw *or* how to look at a drawing.' The type of drawing to which he is referring is mimetic – drawings made from life, where the model is the referent – and Derrida's implicit reproach is partly aimed at the draughtsman's (i.e. his own) ineptitude. Beyond the question of competence, however, Derrida identifies a theoretical paradox, an 'abyss', in the relationship between the drawing and the thing drawn, which he describes as a 'disappearing apparition'. 'How can we claim to look at both a model and the line that one jealously dedicates with one hand to the thing itself?' That logic of 'the invisible at the origin of drawing', in the gap between the artist's gaze and the hand's inscription, he likens to the hand of the blind, which 'ventures forth alone or disconnected.... It feels its way, it gropes, it caresses as much as it inscribes, trusting in the memory of signs and supplementing sight.'

Yet in the self-portrait, the artist's eye encounters itself – as Derrida puts it, the eye of the hunter meets the eye of the hunted. This existential drama underlies all self-portraits. Also present is an invisible screen that exists between the viewer and the artist – namely the mirror, where the viewer now replaces the artist's reflection with his or her own face and 'returns' the gaze in an imaginary encounter.

It is unusual for artists today to depict themselves in so traditional a way, but as an idea the self-portrait remains intriguing, one of the quintessential riddles of pictorial metaphysics, like the picture-within-a-picture and the devices of *trompe l'oeil*. Francesco Clemente, an artist whose limpid visage appears frequently in his paintings and watercolours, speaks of his 'self-portraits without a mirror'. The artist deploys his own appearance, for him the most commonplace of subjects, as a poetic manifestation of psychic states, a simple piece of iconography that because of its familiarity

is 'seductive' and 'easily shared' with the viewer. Yet the experience of the self is not a constant for Clemente; he conceives of it as being in continual flux. 'My ambition is that both my life and my work can be expressive of the acceptance of the continuity of discontinuity.... The moment you accept that there is no continuum, that there is no reality to a solid notion of self... the moment you accept this, you can be free.'

While Clemente's lyrical self-portraits radiate exuberance and sensuality, Kiki Smith's drawings of herself, her family and her friends are more reticent, but they too arise from an inner vision that is mystical and life-affirming. Most of the women Smith draws have a similar detached, impersonal expression; they gaze calmly, if not always serenely, out at the viewer. 'I don't like personality', the artist has explained of her work with the human form. 'I just want to talk about the generic experience of the body without its being specific to specific people.' Like Clemente, who has spoken of his wish as a young artist to participate in 'the renewal of consciousness' instigated by the radical counter-culture of the 1960s, Smith is suspicious of everyday capitalistic versions of subjectivity, which she sees as being 'owned' by commercial, political, institutional and mainstream religious ideologies. The assumption of a singular personal identity is questioned, then, by both artists, but from contrary standpoints – one polytheistic, envisaging a multiplicity of selves behind the mask; the other pantheistic, proposing an emptying out of personality through the contemplation of nature and the cosmos.

Juul Kraijer is another artist who implicitly repudiates empirical notions of personal identity. Her drawings of sightless subjects, with eyes closed or multiplied or erased, are not self-portraits but rather emblematic images of the 'everywoman', whose inwardness, worn like a death mask, removes her from the world of expression and individuality. She exists in a meditative state between sleeping and waking where the self is extinguished; she becomes a feminine archetype. The solitary, enigmatic female figures in Tomoko Kashiki's work are more specific in character: like Smith and Kraijer, Kashiki draws only women, but they inhabit a dream-like realm that it is hard to imagine another person intruding upon.

The antithesis of this rarefied atmosphere of silent
introspection is found in the drawings and paintings
of Marlene Dumas, whose work expresses a passionate
engagement with the world and the most emotionally direct
and empathetic response of an artist to her subjects. In
contrast to the neutral or universal features of those unearthly
souls portrayed by Kraijer, the people Dumas depicts are
distinctly individualized. Working from her vast archive of
photographs, Dumas relishes the infinite variety of human
characters, the unique particularity of each face. Of her
experience of working on her many series of portrait heads,
each in most cases a single face on a separate sheet of paper
or canvas, she has said, 'The groups of portrait heads are very
addictive. One can't stop once started. It's as if one wants
everyone you have ever met or seen, to be touched by your
hand. The dead and the living. Sometimes I get scared that it
can become too obsessive and that one can't get out of this
trance. Everyone is so different and yet quite similar.
All discrimination becomes senseless and useless.'

Dumas' big-hearted humanism is a rare phenomenon in
contemporary art, where a critical or ironic distance normally
detaches the artist from emotional subject matter. She
belongs to a grand tradition of realism that reaches back to
Rembrandt, Goya and Manet but falters in the Western art
of the twentieth century with the advent of abstraction and
conceptualism. Dumas's freedom from the aesthetic strictures
of her time may owe something to the fact that she grew up on
the periphery of the international art world, in South Africa,
where the human urgency and complexity of political life
under apartheid overshadowed the finessing of self-conscious
theoretical positions that absorbed artists in Europe and
North America. (The same applies to William Kentridge
who, like Dumas, takes ostensibly old-fashioned practices
of figuration and breathes new life into them.)

Paradoxically, for all her apparent identification with and
compassion for her subjects, Dumas works exclusively from
photographic sources, often with unknown origins. 'I am an
artist', she says, 'who uses second-hand images and first-hand
experiences.' She has spoken of the 'essential immorality
or indifference' of the photographic image when removed
from its original context. It might be argued that in her
work she recovers photography's conscience, reinstating

the psychological, moral and metaphysical implications of
the image, seizing her subjects as though she were the sole
witness to their essential humanity, their anguish or ecstasy,
which would otherwise be lost forever in a heartless universe.
And that tells us something about the theatricality of artistic
emotion. 'In art the world is flat', she says. 'It's still generally
believed that unreal situations created by art conjure up real
emotions in the art-lover, and that artistically minded people
are also automatically civilized people. But art-emotions are
ontologically different from everyday emotions.'

The chasm between art and life is both ontological and ethical,
for moral responses generally follow from emotional ones.
We tend to speak as though the human image in art has the
power to arouse the moral responses we feel – or should feel –
in our relations with real people. We identify emotionally, we
sympathize, with an image of suffering or despair, a mournful
face, as if it were real. But as Dumas says, in art the world is
flat – in drawings, literally two-dimensional. Those slight
adjustments that can make the difference between a happy
and an unhappy face, a line turned up rather than down, are
psychological devices. They can affect our reaction to that
image but not our actions in life.

TOMOKO KASHIKI *Born 1982, Kyoto City, Japan. Lives and works in Kyoto City, Japan*

Tomoko Kashiki's exquisitely crafted images are inspired by the traditional Japanese *bijinga* (images of beautiful women) featured in prints and paintings of the *ukiyo-e*, or Floating World. She depicts only women, usually solitary and introspective, in dreamlike spaces, often with a watery ethereal atmosphere: intimate interiors, bathrooms, swimming pools or misty gardens. Kashiki's women are not conventionally beautiful; their elongated, sinuous limbs often culminate in grotesque tangles of root-like fingers and toes. Her figures stretch, curl up or lie on the floor, fold themselves around columns, or crouch in corners, mysteriously suspended.

There is a tension in the air, as though these girl–women are anxious and existentially precarious and will never mature. Their bodies seem almost to dissolve into their surroundings: the swirling patterns in wooden floor tiles, the delicate fabrics or the gently billowing muslin curtains. Kashiki has described her personal approach to beauty: 'I have a clear vision of what beauty is for me. I can say that I draw and paint only to realize beauty.... My idea of beauty is a very fragile conviction... it changes and is transformed by my feelings.... Of course the actual feeling might change as time passes.... So, I try to think that time stops when I draw.'

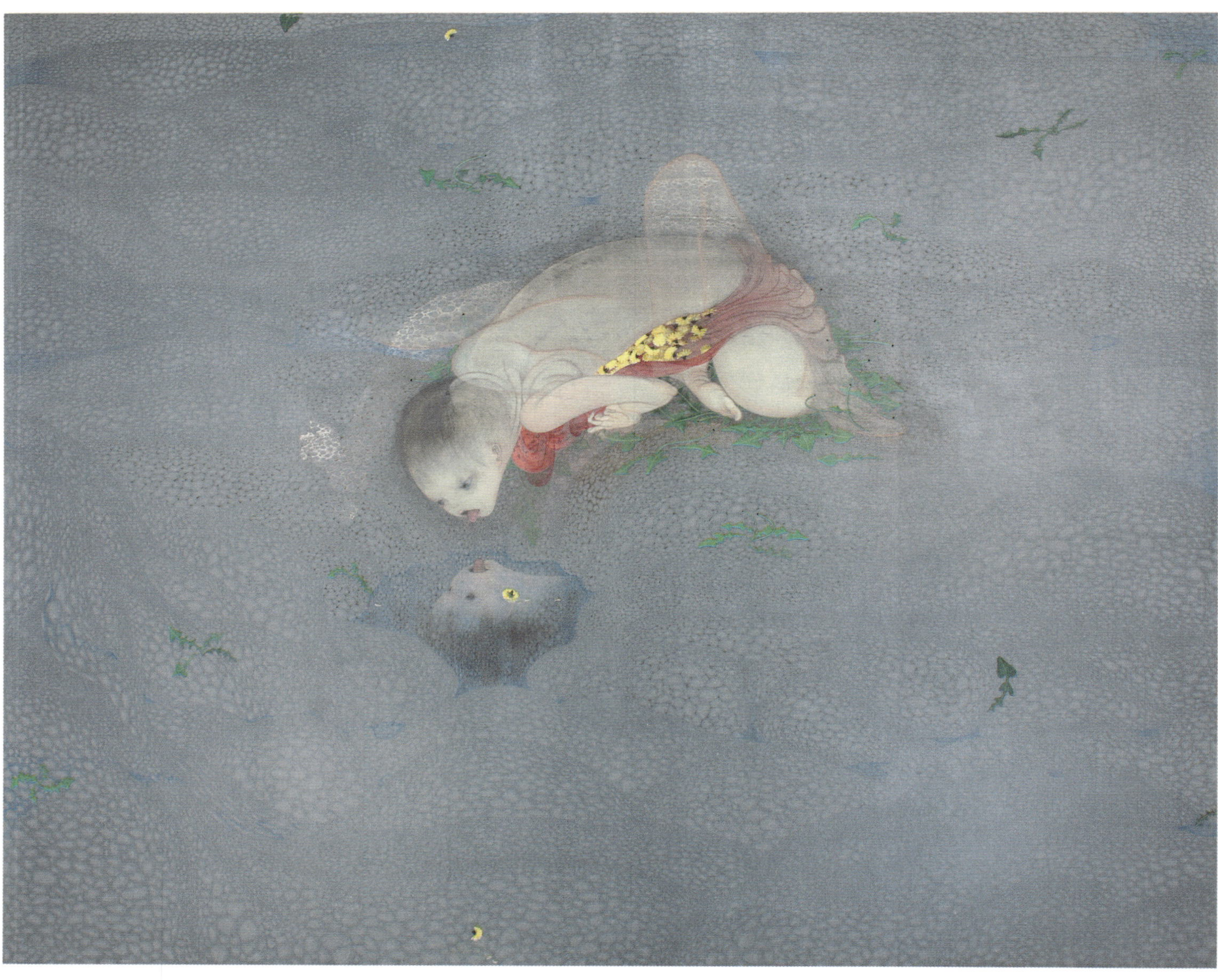

Dandelion, 2009
Acrylic, linen and wooden panel
130.3 × 162 cm (51 ¼ × 63 ¾ in.)

Draw, 2008 >
Acrylic, ink, pencil, cotton and wooden panel
130.3 × 162.1 cm (51 ¼ × 63 ⅞ in.)

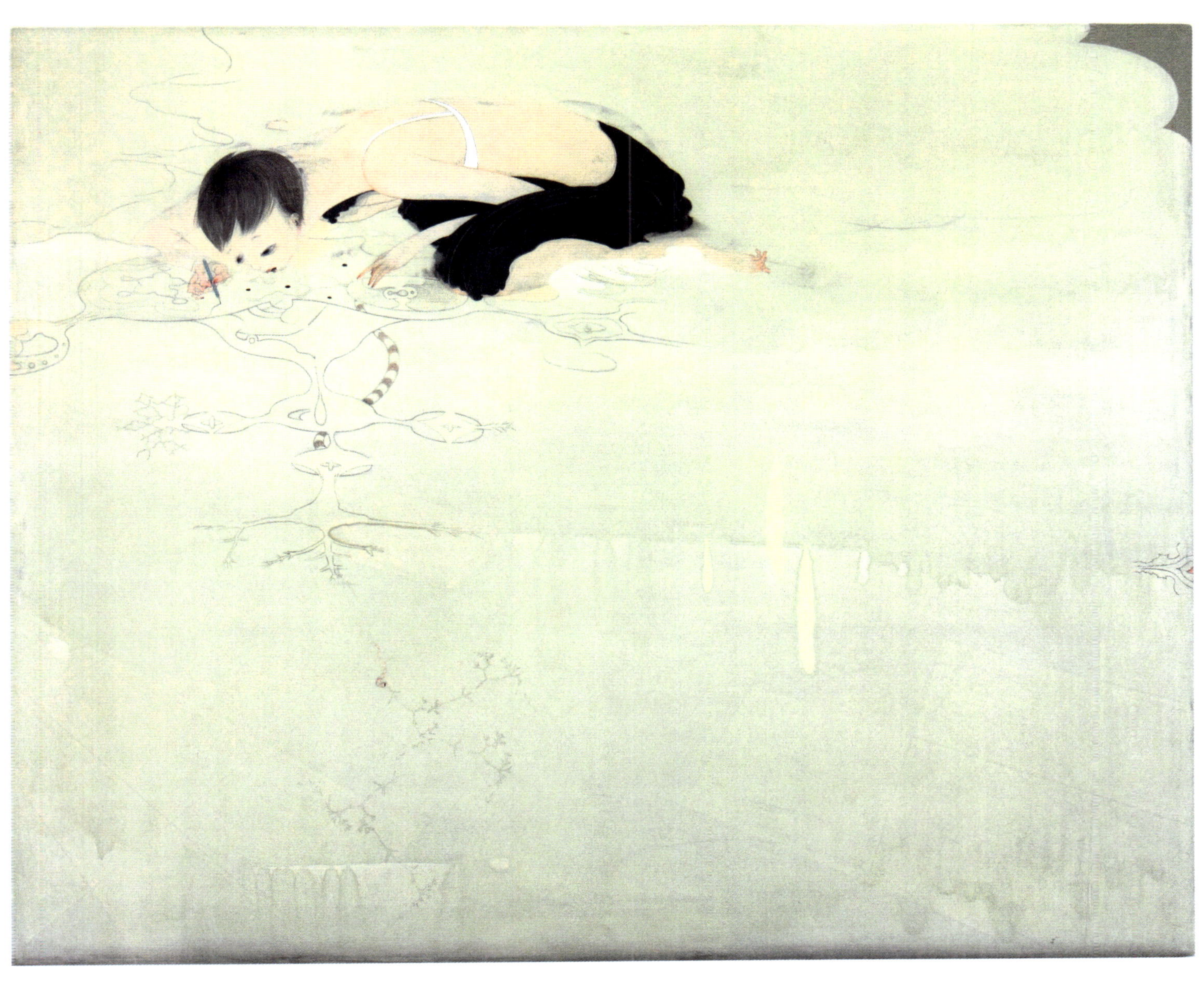

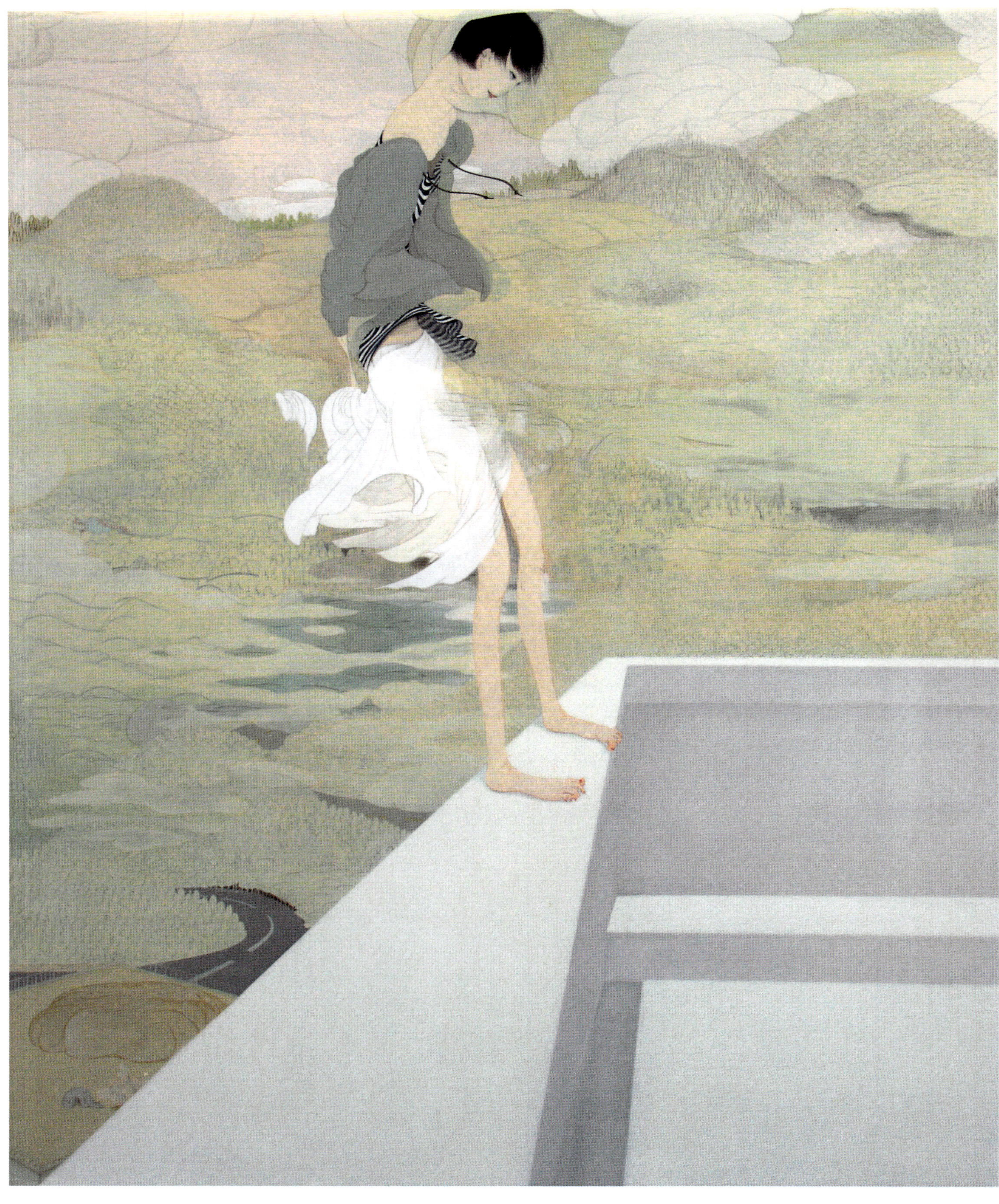

Roof Garden, 2008
Acrylic, pencil, tracing paper, carbon, cotton and wooden panel
225 × 183 cm (88 ⅝ × 72 in.)

Morning Glory, 2009 >
Acrylic, carbon, linen and wooden panel
227.3 × 181.8 cm (89 ½ × 71 ⅝ in.)

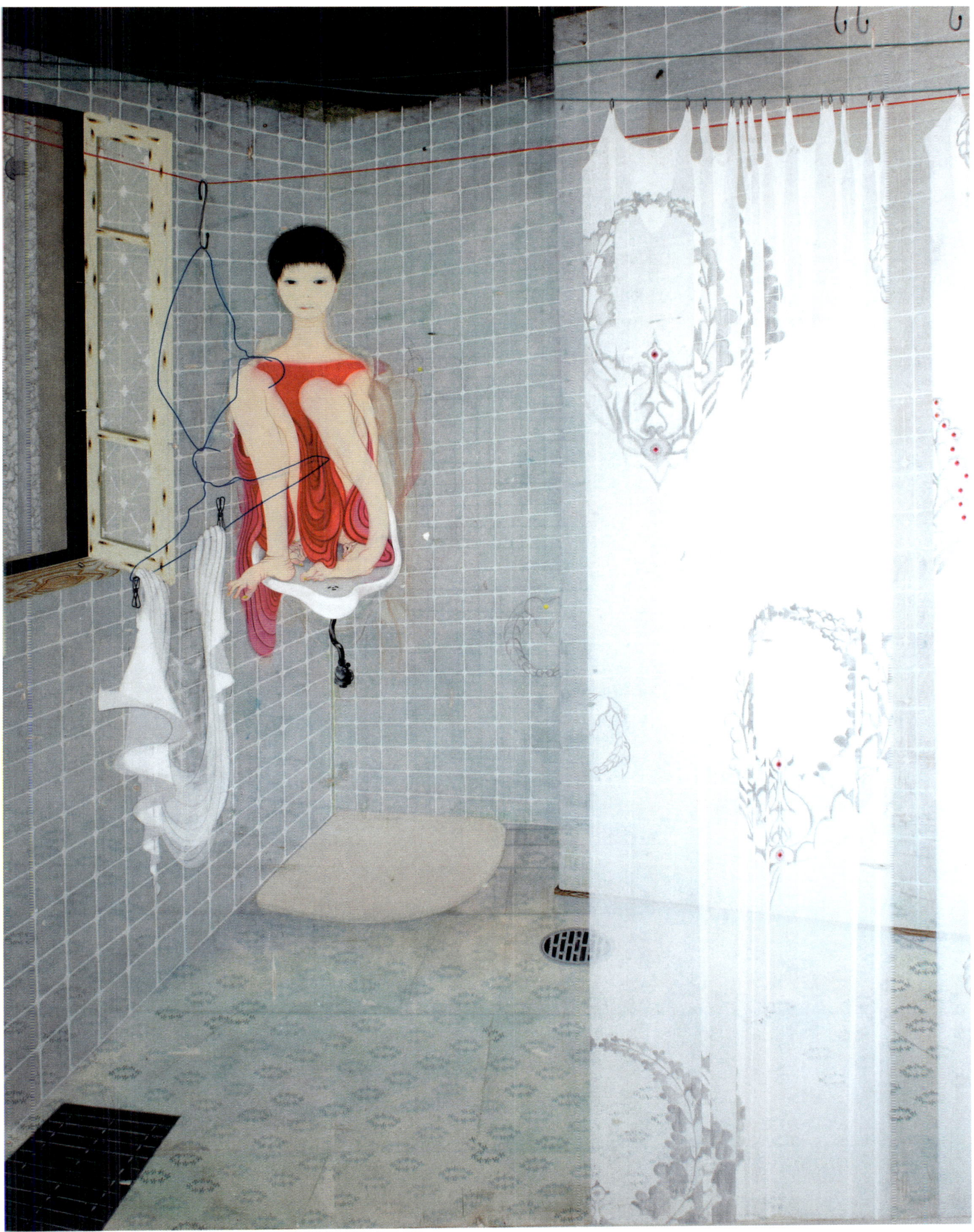

FRANCESCO CLEMENTE *Born 1952, Naples, Italy. Lives and works in New York, USA, and Varanasi, India*

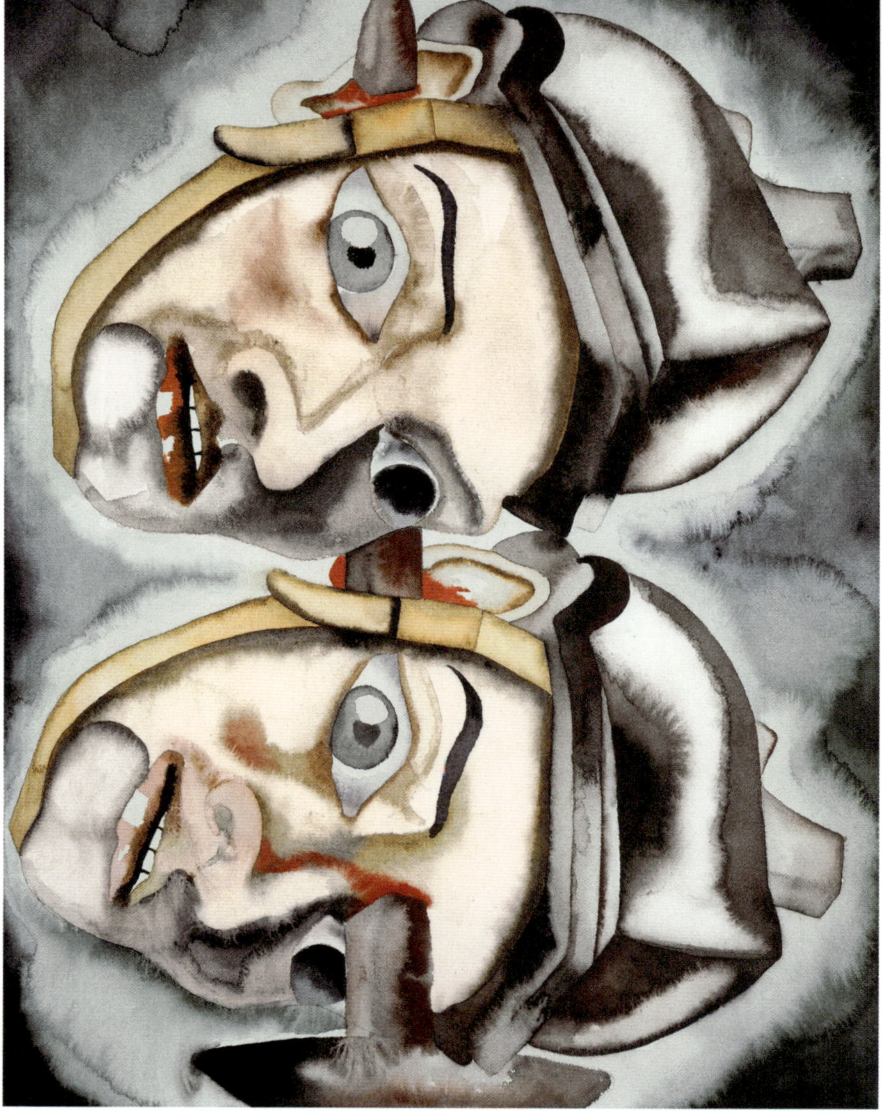

Francesco Clemente is a nomadic artist who has lived between India and New York for more than three decades. He underwent a classical education at school in Italy but as an artist is largely self-taught, drawing inspiration from the art and contemplative traditions of India and other non-Western cultures. A prolific painter and watercolourist, Clemente's vision is intuitive, poetic, erotic and his imagery ceaselessly inventive. Since the 1980s he has painted portraits of friends, mostly artists and poets. His watercolours on handmade Indian paper are often large in scale, giving them an imposing presence when viewed in person.

Between 2006 and 2008 Clemente took extensive trips to Brazil, and in Rio de Janiero and Bahia he made watercolours of the rituals and objects associated with Candomblé (meaning 'dance in honour of the gods'), an Afro-Brazilian syncretic religion combining elements of West African (mainly Yoruba) and Catholic traditions. Candomblé temples are known as Terreiros, and are host to spiritual performances or rituals that typically involve feasts, drumming, dance, animal sacrifice and spirit possession. Clemente's fascination with such cultures is based on the affinity he perceives between painting and 'the implements of rituals, which are mnemonic keys that you use to remind the viewer and yourself of a broader worldview… that we are told is no longer within our reach: the sense of the sacred.'

Actors of the Terreiro VII, 2006
Watercolour on paper
61 × 46 cm (24 × 18 in.)

Self-Portrait in White, Red and Black VI, 2008 >
Pastel on paper
102 × 66.5 cm (40 × 26 in.)

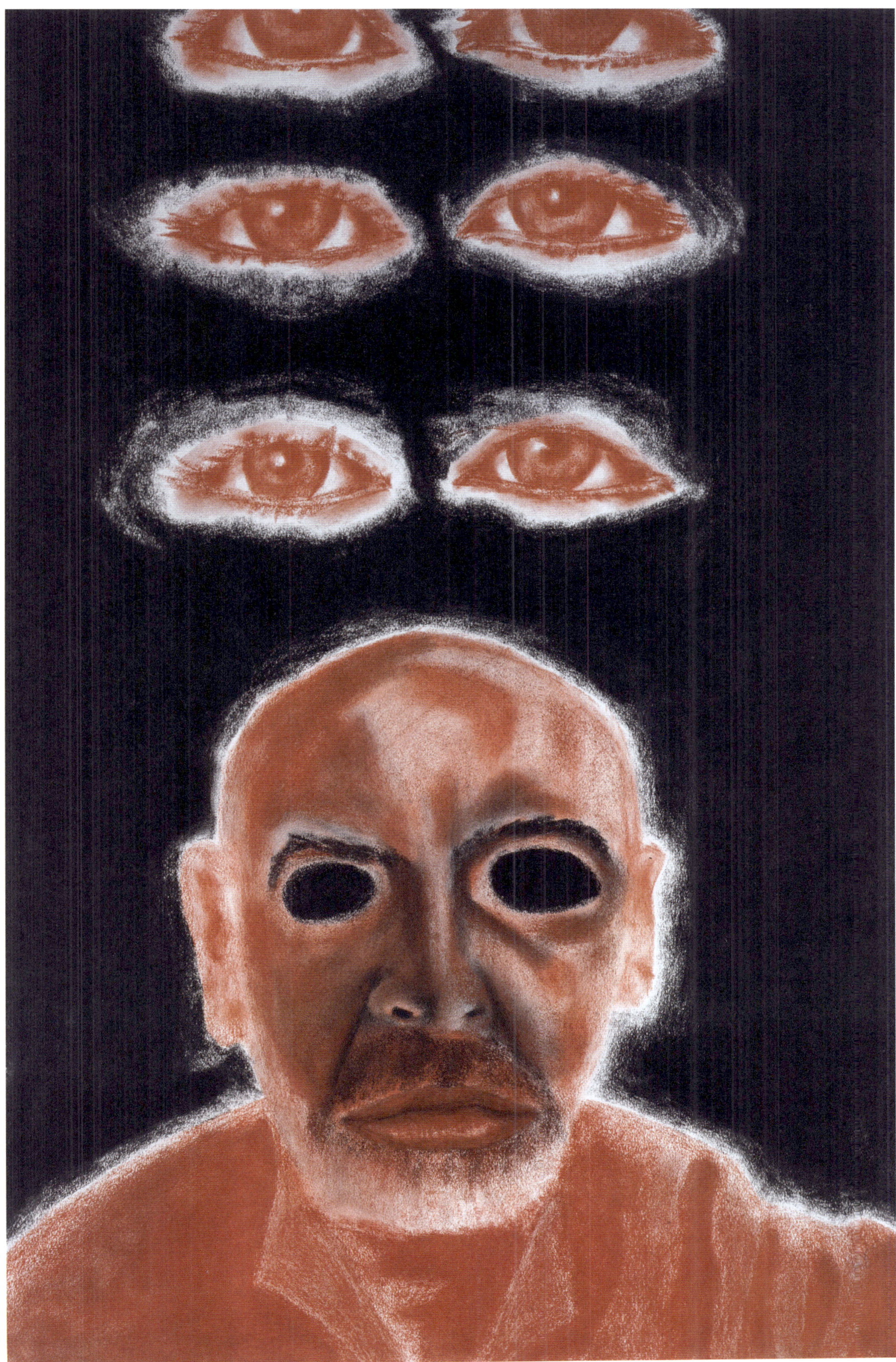

KIKI SMITH *Born 1954, Nuremberg, Germany. Lives and works in New York, USA*

As a sculptor Kiki Smith is renowned for her unconventional use of materials such as resin, wax, cloth, terracotta, gold, glass and paper. She is also an accomplished printmaker and there, too, has demonstrated exceptional versatility, reflecting her passion for craft and popular decorative traditions, a passion that is also manifested in her ink drawings and collages. Having been a proponent of feminism since the 1980s, Smith makes women her principal subject – their physical being and spiritual communion. She was brought up a Catholic, and there is a strong mystical strain discernible in her work: a desire to invest objects with symbolic meaning. At the same time, she has dwelt on the body and its abject and vulnerable aspects, specifically its internal organs, fluids and excretions, and the connection between animals and humans – or, as Smith puts it, 'nature and human nature'.

Smith's materials are rich in metaphorical significance: the Nepalese paper that she draws and prints onto, for instance, has also been used by the artist to make figurative sculptures. It seems fragile but is actually strong; its translucent, creased and wrinkled surface is like a skin that becomes coextensive with the skin of the figures portrayed. Smith often draws people from life, and her style is direct, almost naive, with a focus on the eyes – often regarded as windows to the soul – that brings out with intensity the presence of each individual.

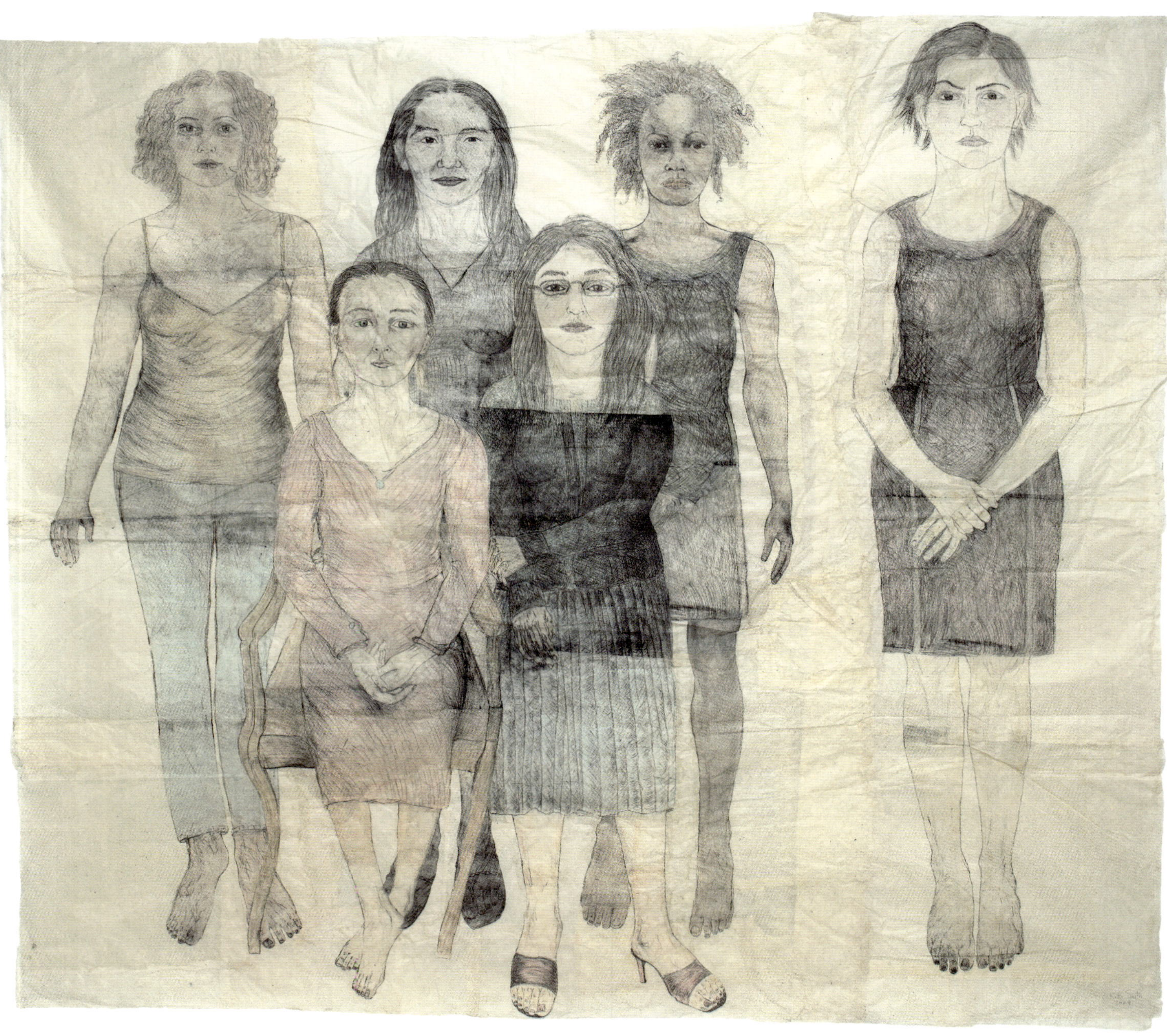

Assembly, 2009
Ink and coloured pencil on collaged Nepal paper
195.6 × 224.8 cm (77 × 88 ½ in.)

Coming Forth, 2008 >
Collage and ink on Nepal paper
250.2 × 207 cm (98 ½ × 81 ½ in.)

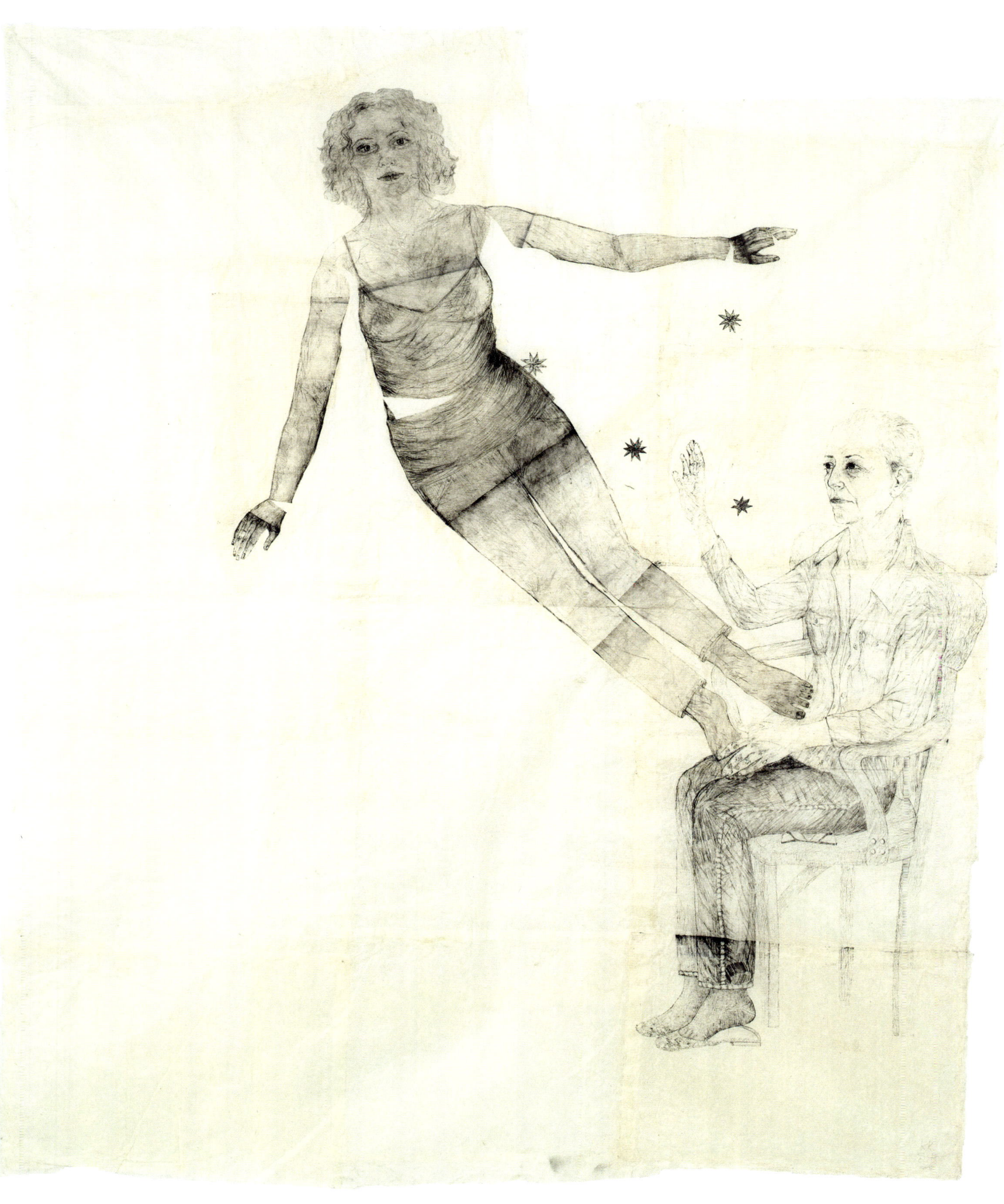

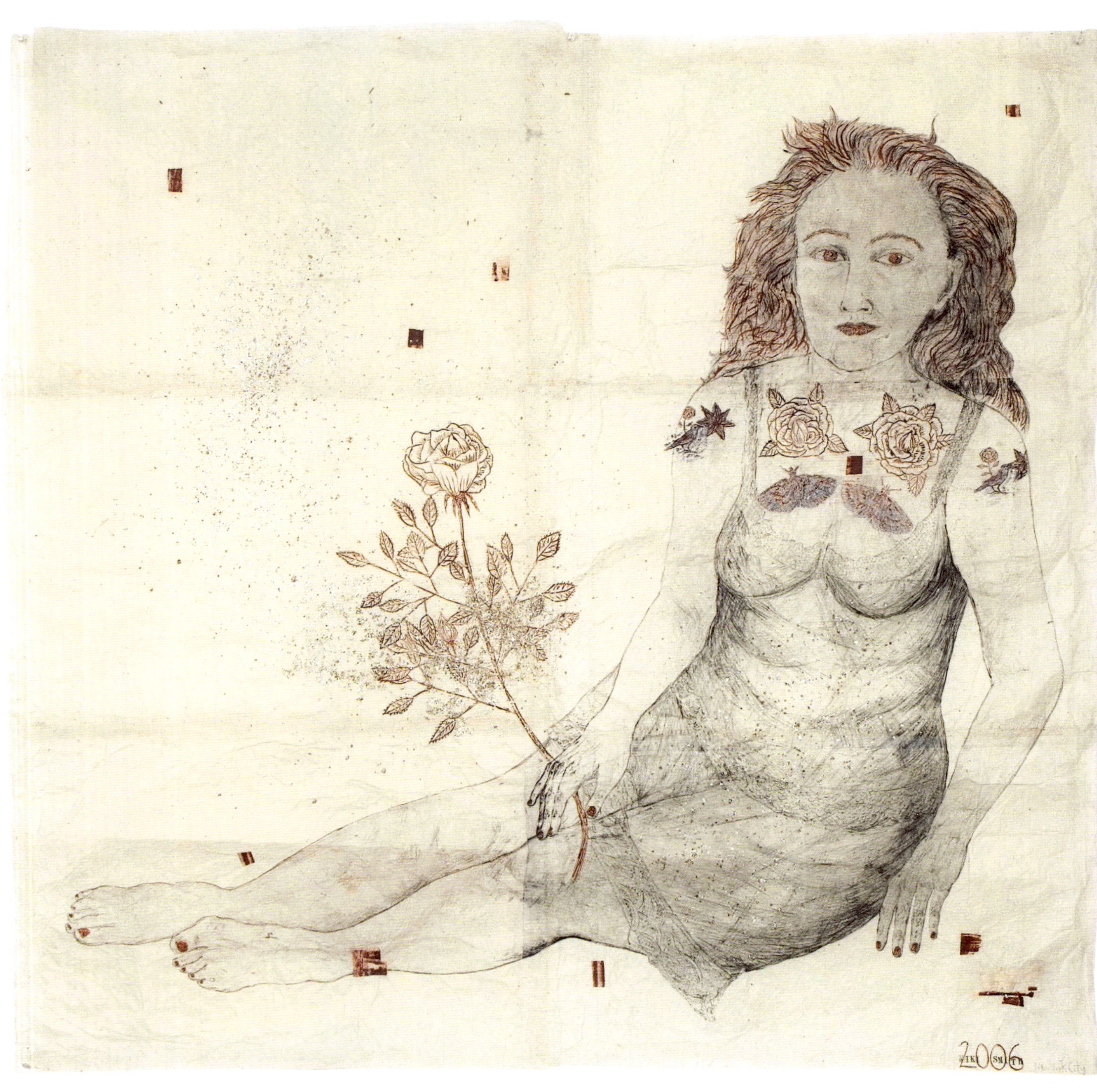

Kiki Smith in New York City, 2006
Pencil, red ink and glitter on Nepalese paper
143 x 143 cm (56 ¼ × 56 ¼ in.)

Pietà, 1999 >
Ink on Nepal paper
141 × 74.9 cm (55 ½ × 29 ½ in

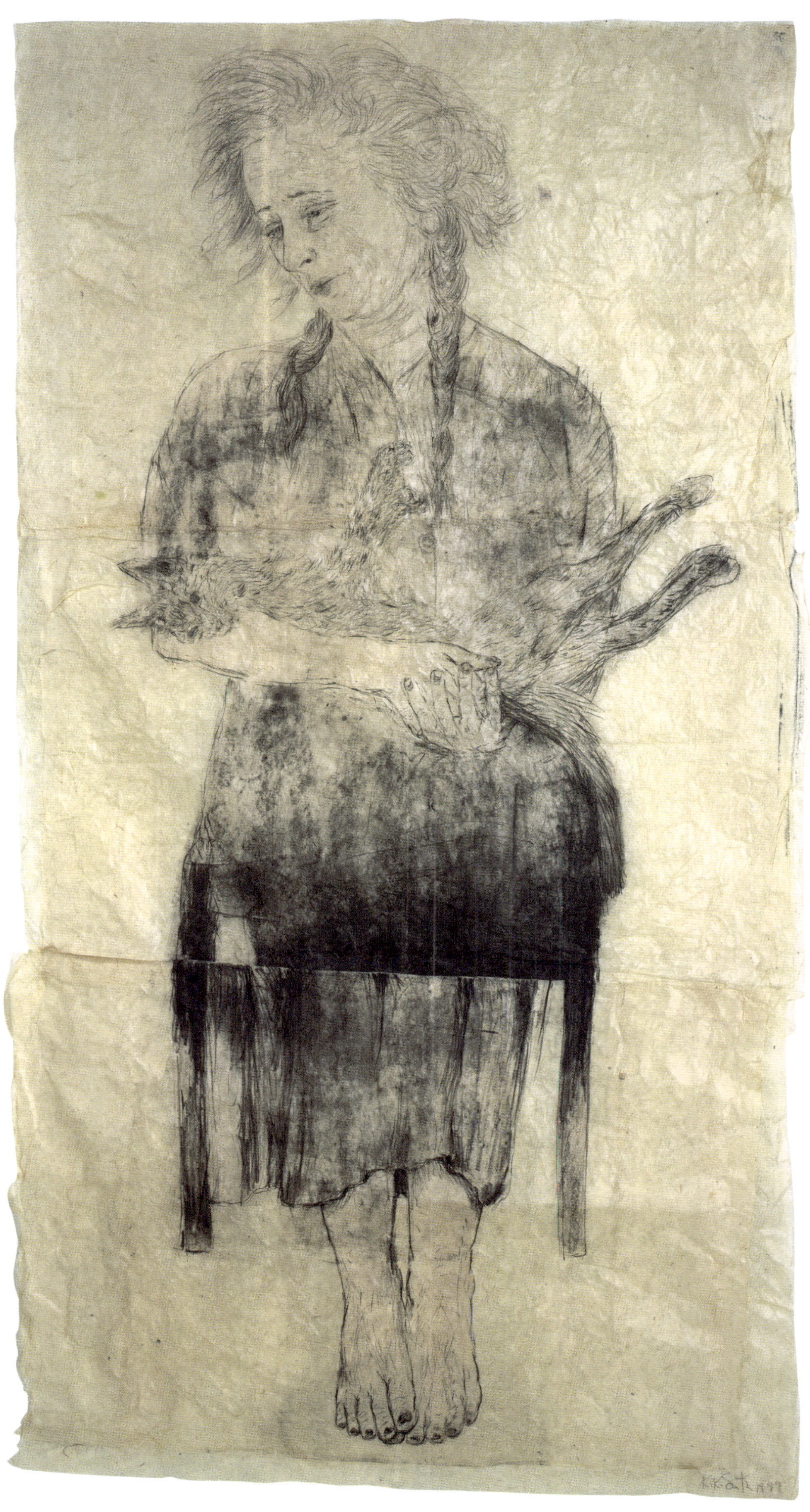

Marlene Dumas has drawn and painted many portraits, faces looking straight ahead and set against blank backgrounds like ID mugshots, each on a separate sheet of paper or canvas. Often these portraits are grouped together, stacked or lined up, suggesting an identity parade or an institutional system for 'processing' individuals. Dumas has depicted psychiatric patients, fashion models and black people in this way, with an acute sensitivity to the singularity of each face, its unique character and expression, as well as to the politics associated with grouping faces by social or racial type.

The faces in the series shown here – a group of men of Middle Eastern appearance – were drawn directly from news photographs and personal snapshots, and mix suicide bombers and jihadists with ordinary young men living in the artist's neighbourhood in Amsterdam. Deliberately uncaptioned, the drawings remind us how difficult it is to distinguish mass murderers from regular citizens. Our emotional response to a face is irrational; stereotypes are easily conjured up by the media, which aims to thrill and frighten as much as to inform. Dumas's drawings restore humanity to faces that are regularly objectified and even demonized in news photographs. Further, and perhaps more controversially, they highlight the way that media demonization can also lead to peaceful citizens being mistaken for violent ones. In the context of these drawings, however, Dumas's fluent, sensuous brushstrokes soften the features, eliciting empathy without discrimination.

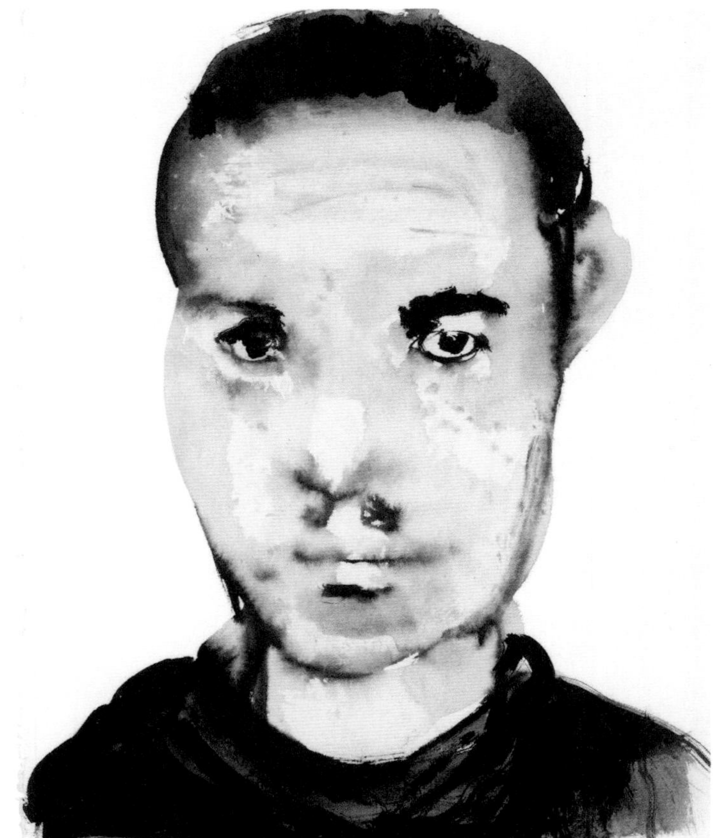

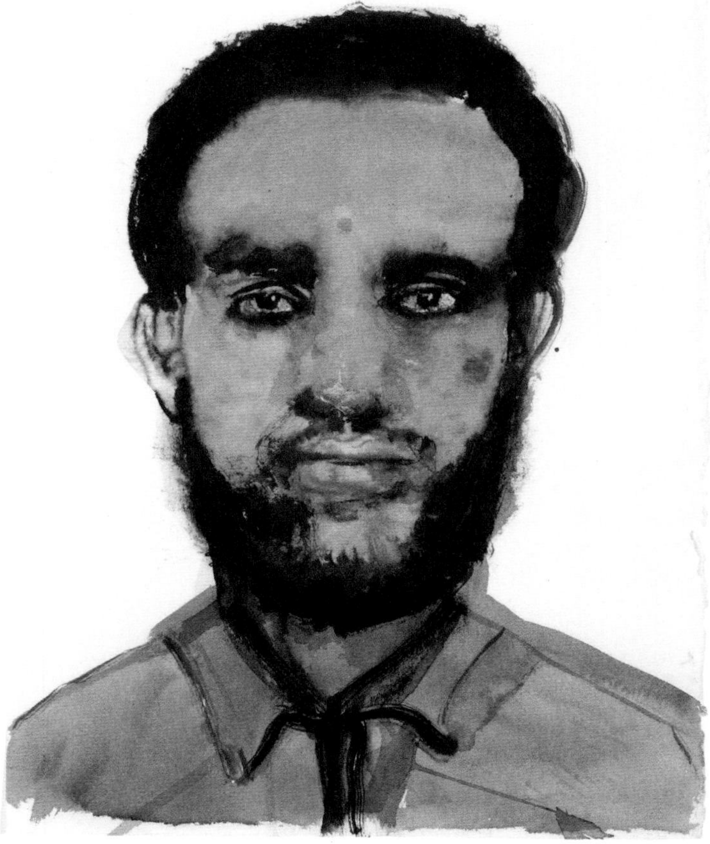

(this page, opposite and pages 78–79) *Young Men*, 2002–5
Series of 12 drawings, ink on paper
Each: 54 × 53 cm (21 ¼ × 20 ⅞ in.)

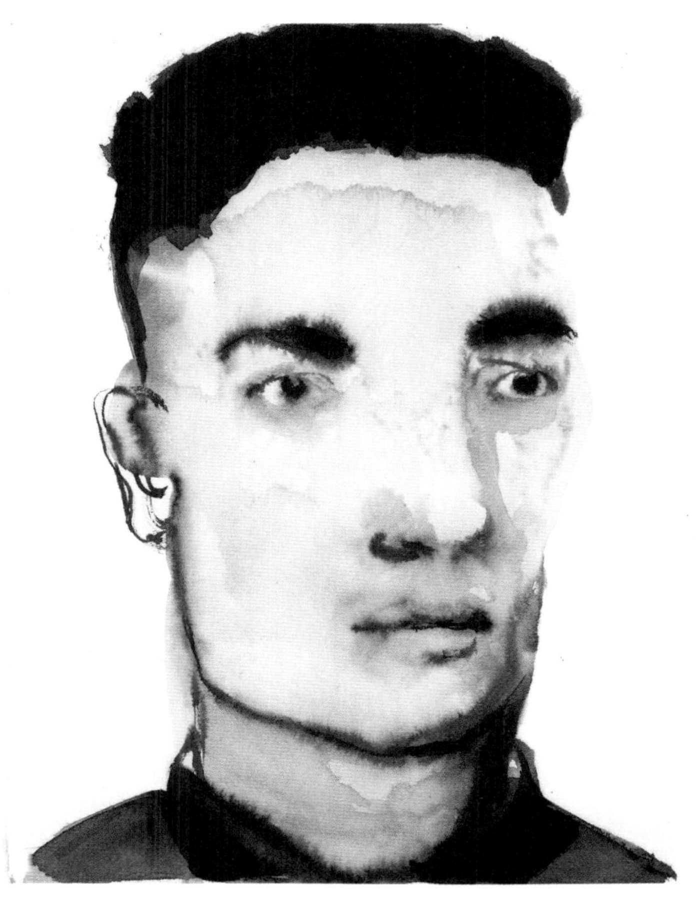
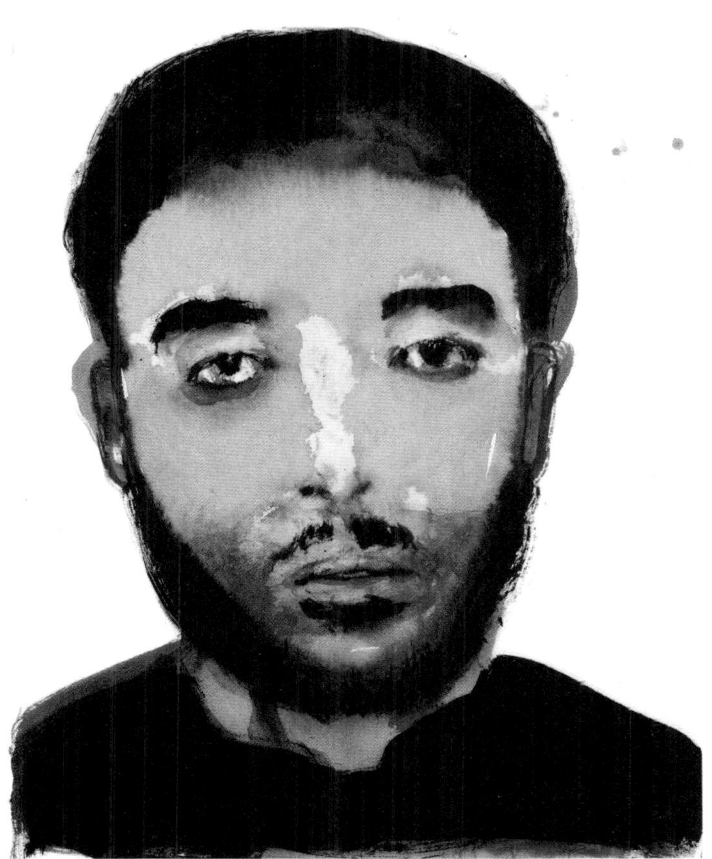
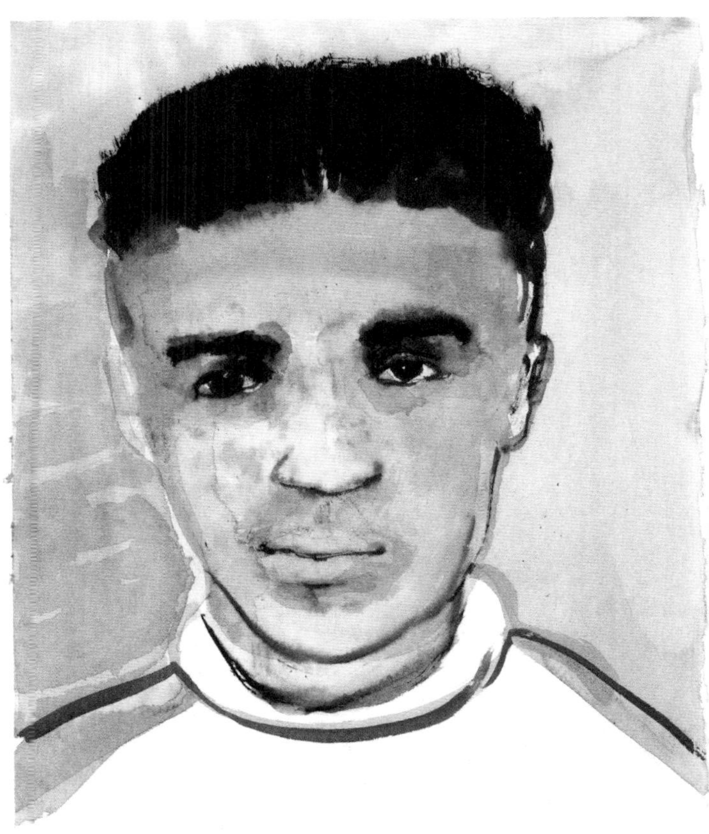
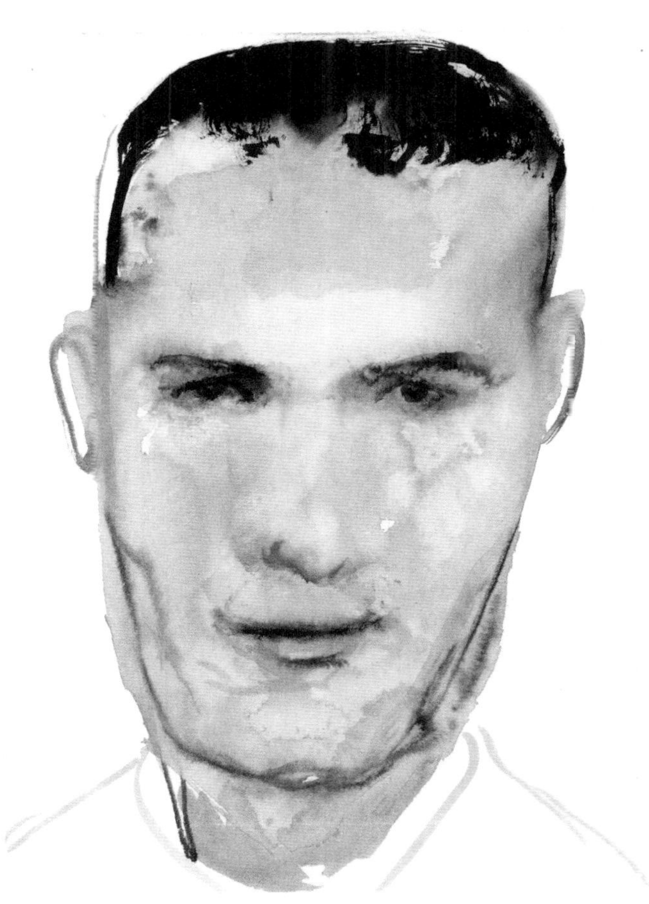

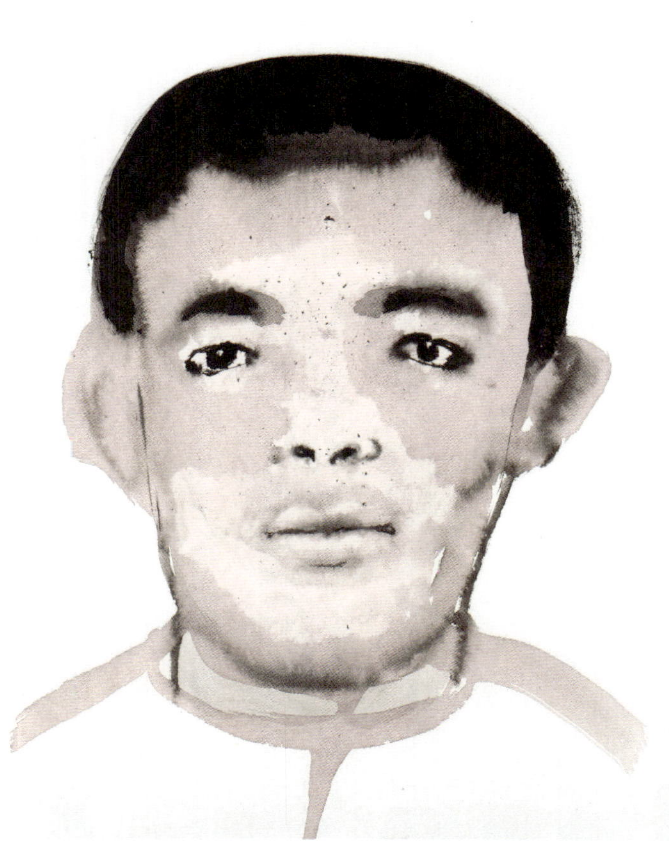
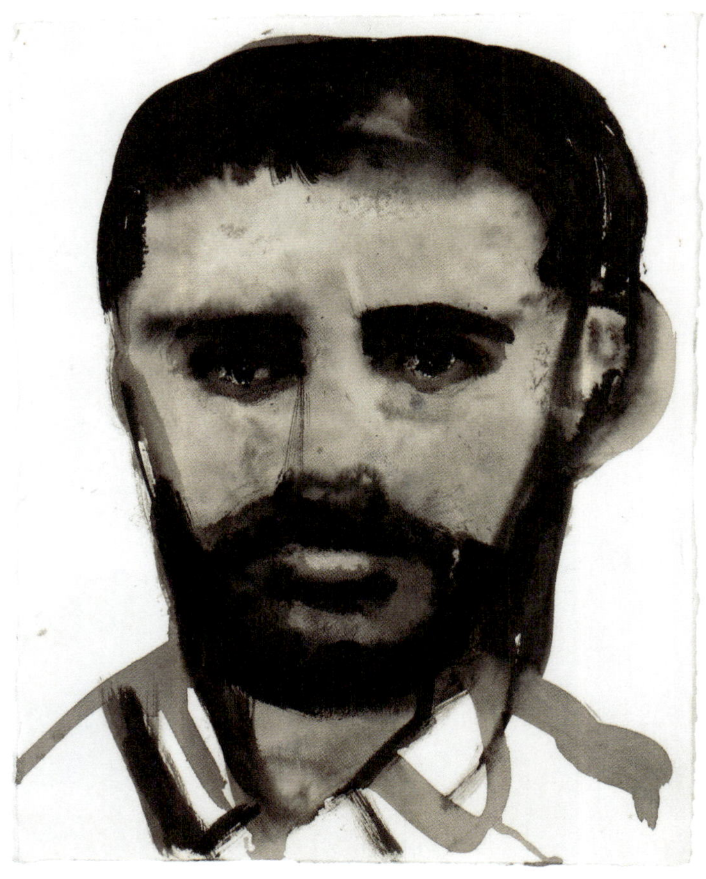
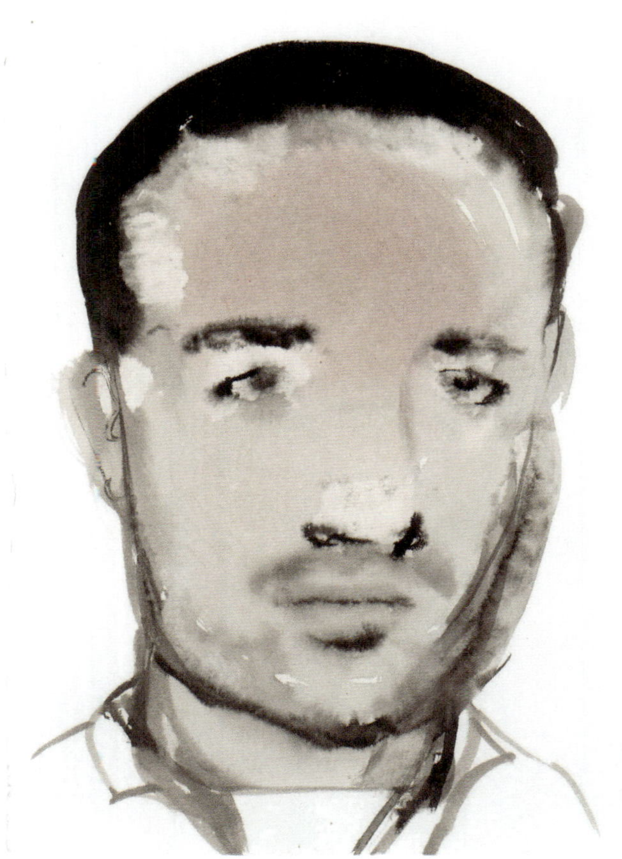
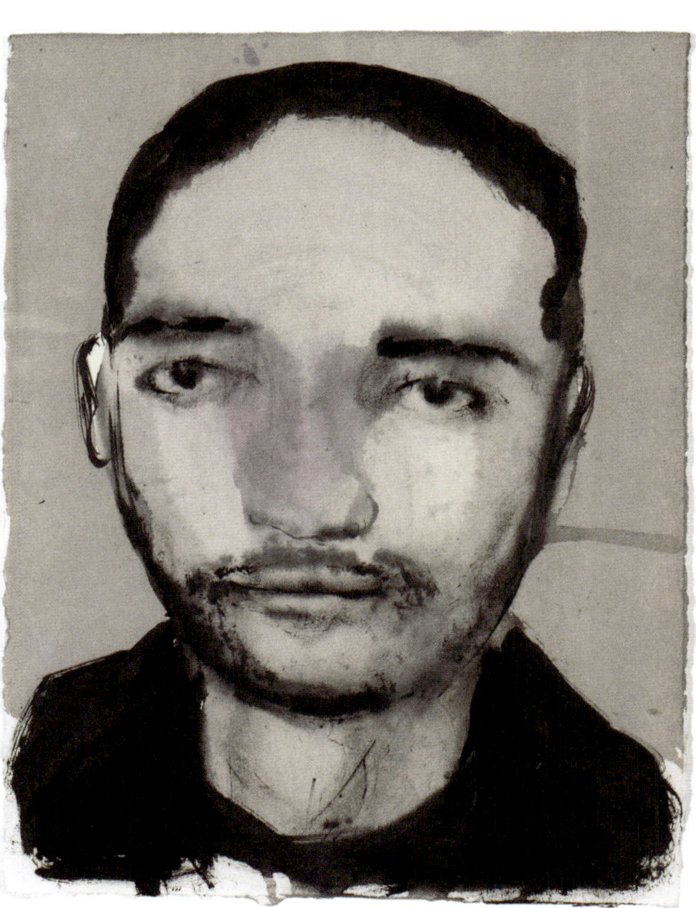

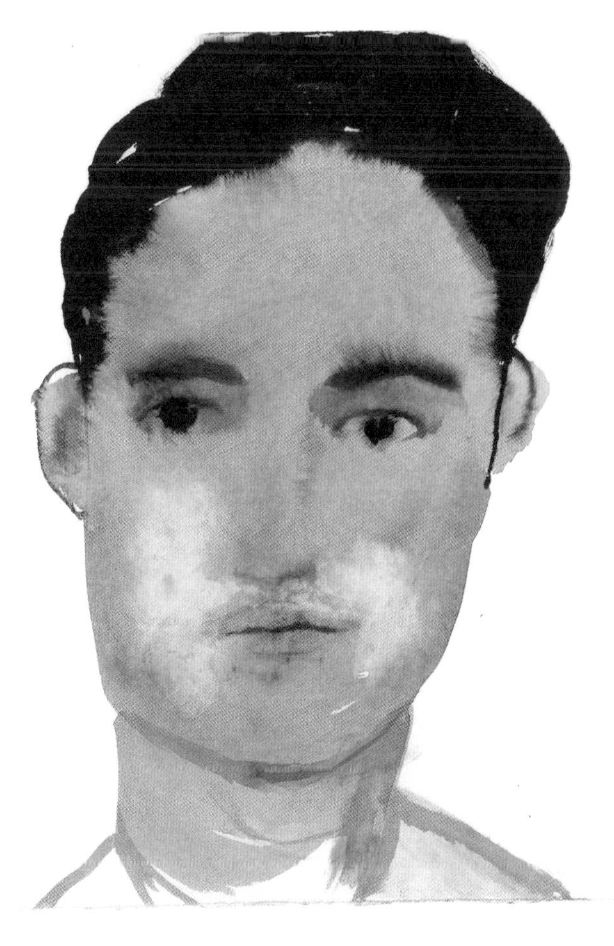

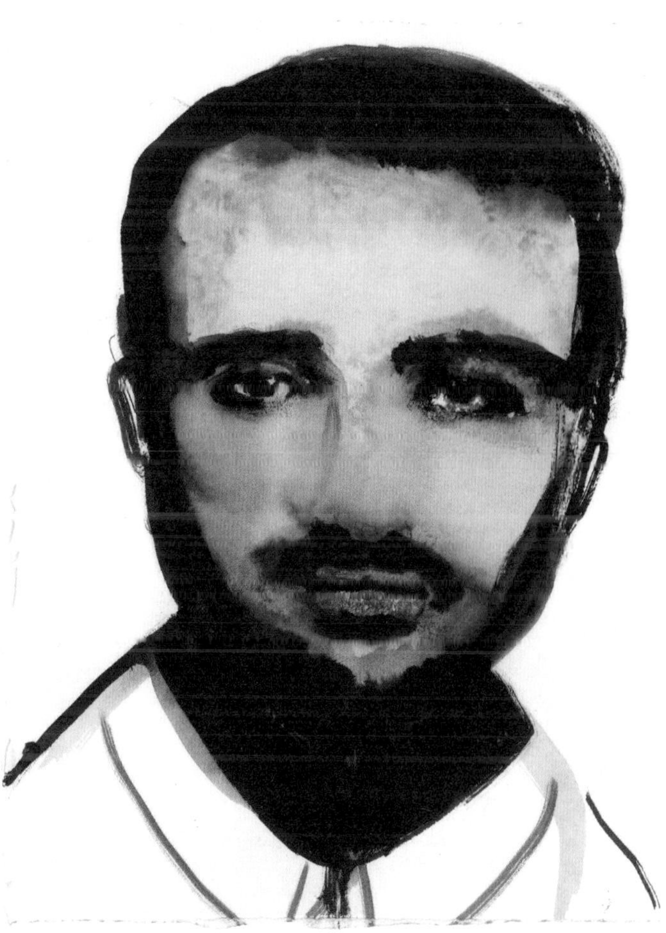

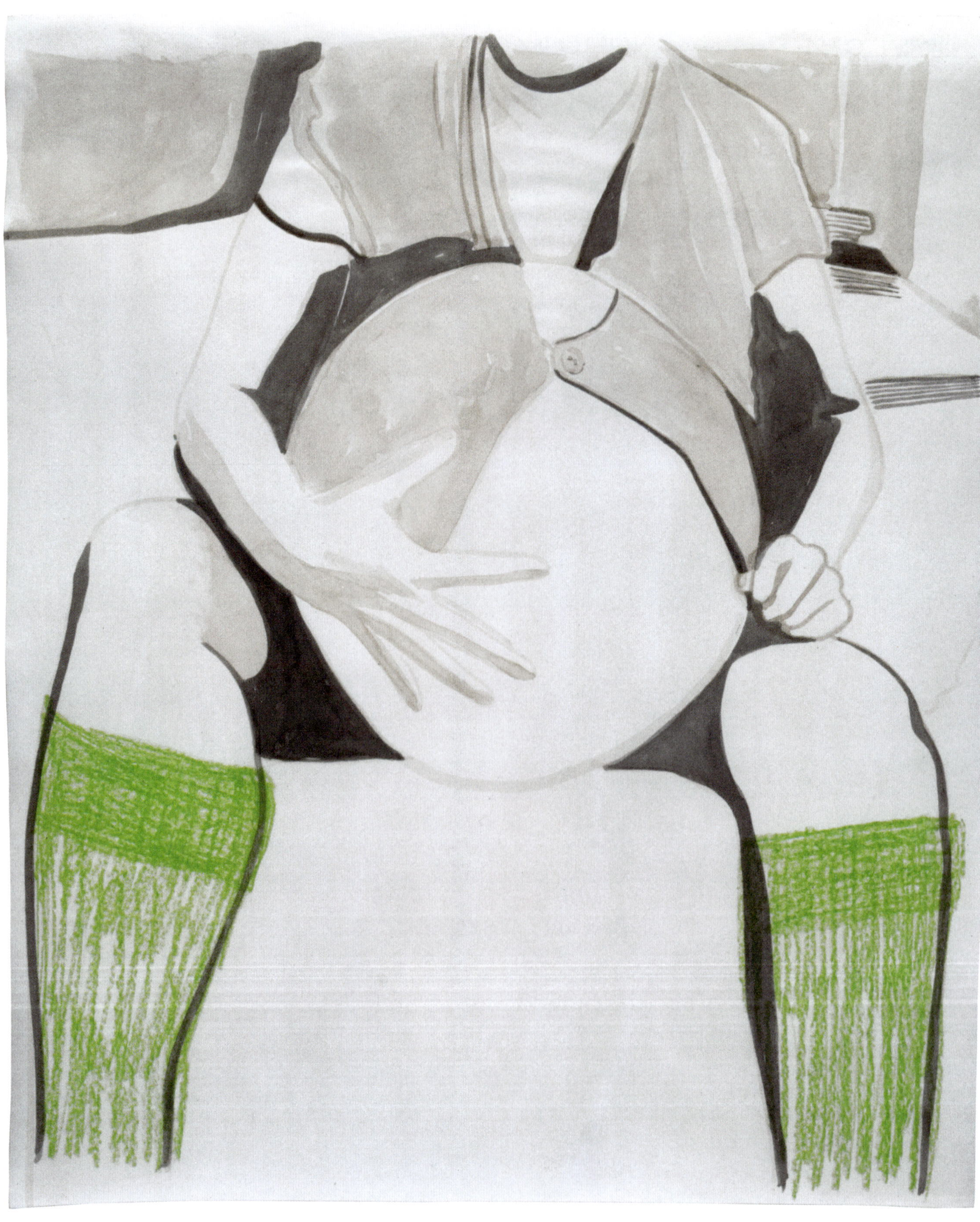

ROSEMARIE TROCKEL *Born 1952, Schwerte, Germany. Lives and works in Cologne, Germany*

An artist whose subtle strategies and fragmented practice elude easy categorization, Rosemarie Trockel is best known for her industrially knitted woollen pictures incorporating logos and symbols, as well as her wittily subversive sculptures, videos, books and collages. Yet drawing has always been central to Trockel's practice and she has produced more than 1,000 drawings during her career. Through this medium she has played with ideas of authorship and sexual identity using many different styles and techniques. She has drawn human, animal and chimerical heads, sketched designs for book covers, real

and imaginary, and experimented with various methods of mark-making and graphic notation. The two drawings shown here exemplify her skill as a draughtswoman. The headless figure cradling a ball in *Atlas* anticipates Trockel's video of 2003 entitled *Manus Spleen 3*, in which an apparently pregnant woman celebrating with a toast at her birthday party takes a pin and pops the balloon under her dress, revealing a phantom pregnancy. *Small Devil* is one of a series of drawings showing young people, mostly boys, sleeping open-mouthed, each rendered in a different graphic style.

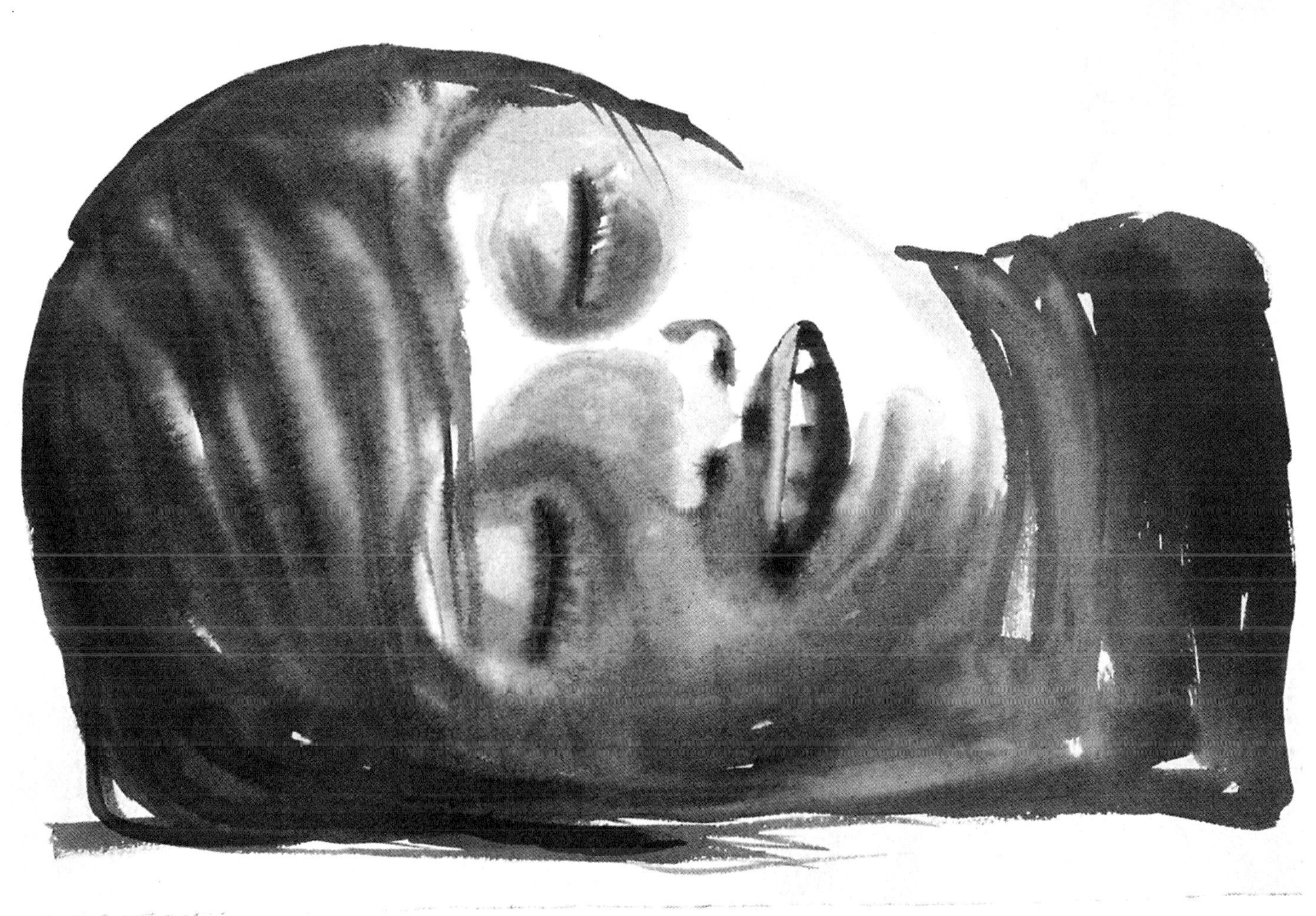

< *Atlas*, 2001
Acrylic and crayon on paper
58.4 × 49.8 cm (22 ¾ × 19 in.)

Small Devil, 2000
Acrylic on paper
30.9 × 41.4 cm (12 ¼ × 16 ¼ in.)

SEVDA CHKOUTOVA *Born 1978, Sofia, Bulgaria. Lives and works in Vienna, Austria*

In her large-format graphite drawings Sevda Chkoutova has traced the phases of a life, perhaps her own, from childhood, through puberty and adolescence, to adulthood, motherhood, maturity and beyond. Her style has altered with the progression of time; in the earlier drawings, such as those reproduced here, the figures are rendered tonally, in shadowy atmospheric spaces, with faces turned languidly or anxiously towards the viewer. In this adolescent moment, the spaces are often elaborately layered and theatrical, as if the world of décor and clothing offers infinite choices for self-invention. Chkoutova defines her subject in psychoanalytic terms: the interplay of the ego and the id determines the formation of the self. Costumed or naked, the children, girls and women in Chkoutova's drawings seem vulnerable and uncertain, suggesting that the beautiful, sensual dreams of youth are perhaps too fragile to endure. One series of drawings, produced around the same time as those illustrated here, is entitled *verblüht* – 'faded' – after a Bulgarian proverb the artist's mother used to tell her, warning that young girls fade at the first touch of a man.

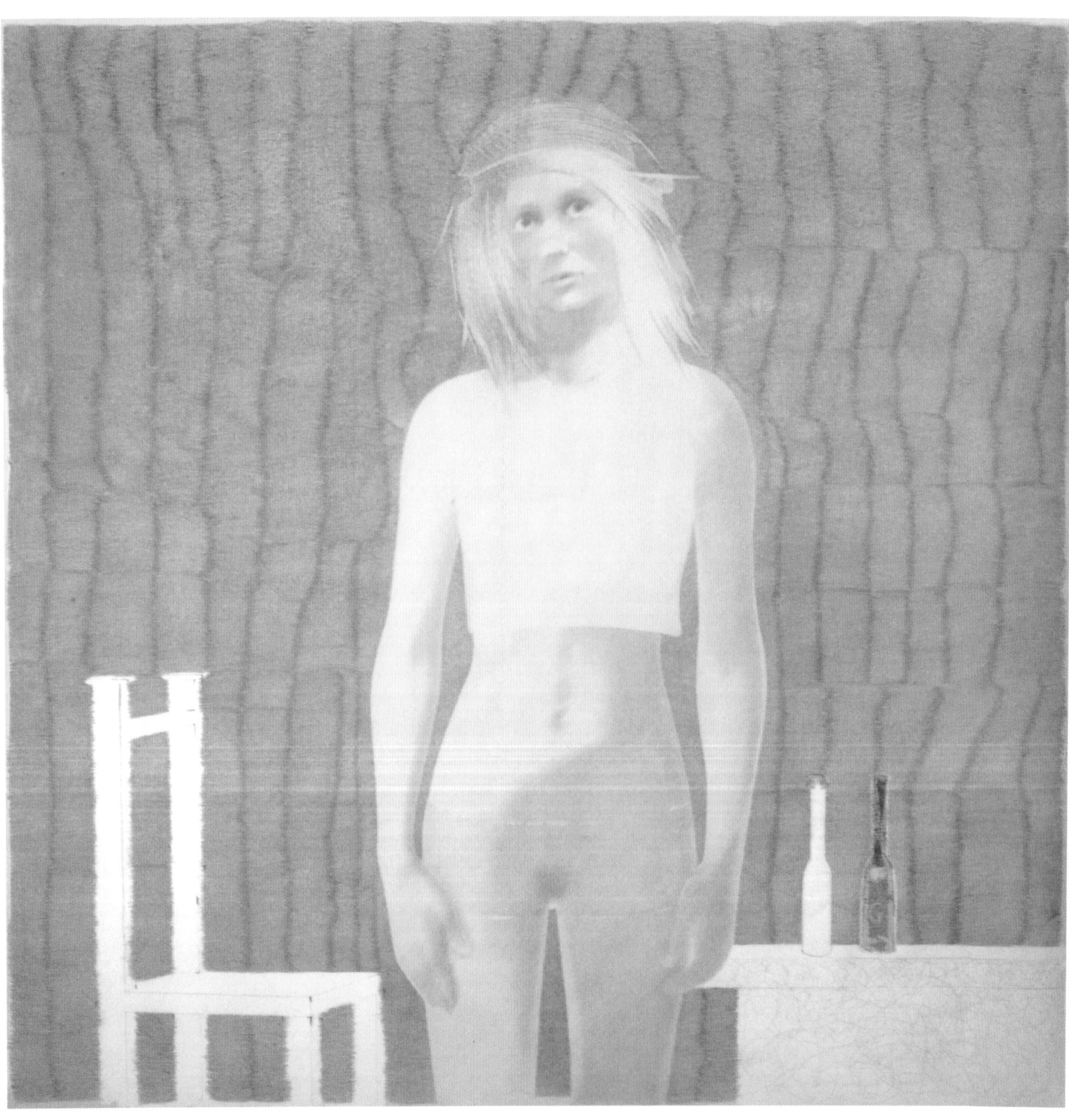

Karussell_05, 2007
Pencil on paper
150 × 150 cm (59 × 59 in.)

Narzisse_05, 2008 >
Pencil, colored pencil and crayon on paper
150 × 150 cm (59 × 59 in.)

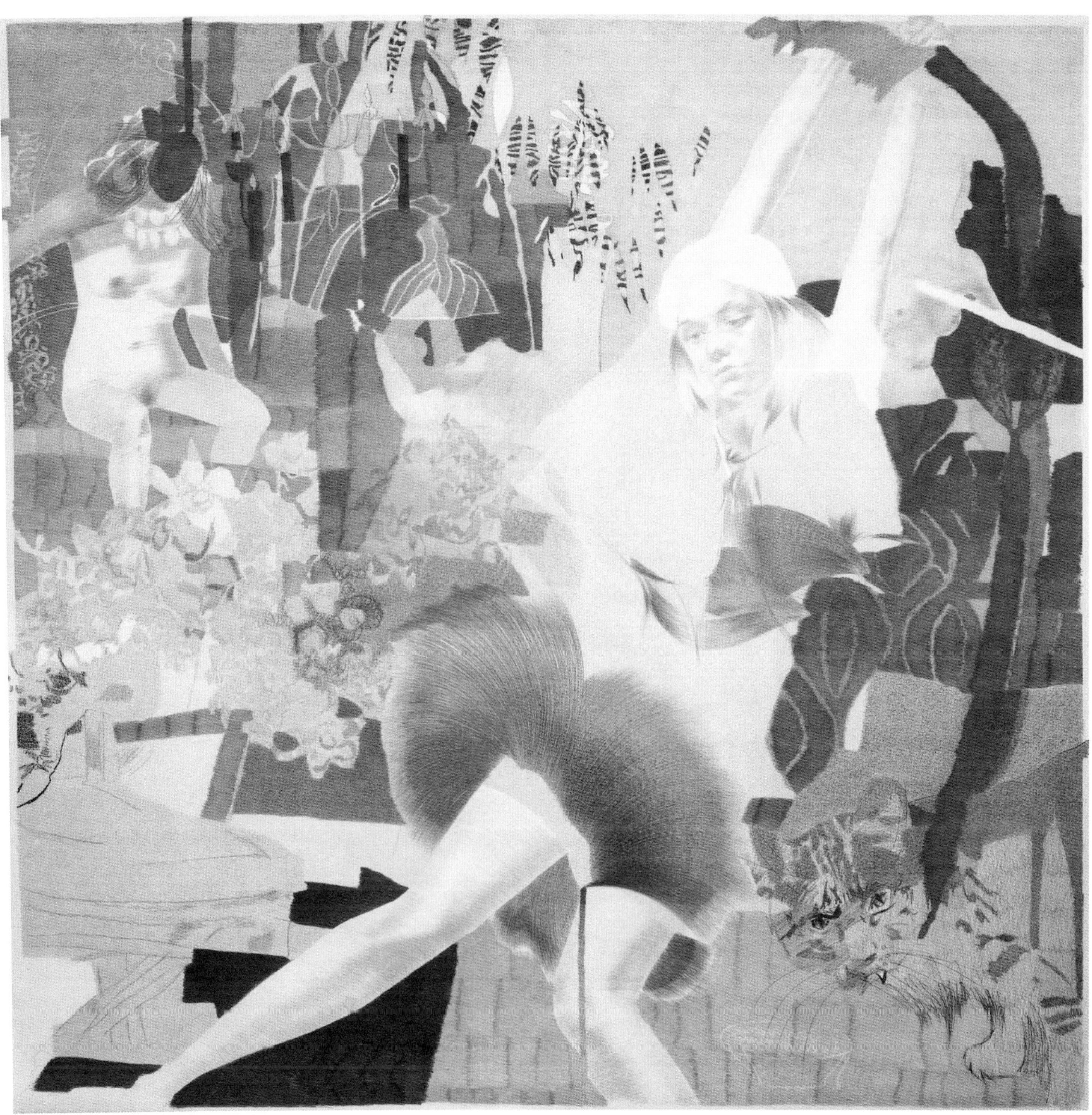

'My motifs are the human body and its mantling', Martin Assig has said. 'Most are headless figures. Sometimes the heads are concealed. This corresponds to personal experience. I perceive myself as headless unless I look in the mirror. I see bodies, arms, legs; the head is there in my senses and my imagination. Thus, in my pictures I come very close to personal body experience. The headless figures in my pictures are not an Other, but are vessels of feeling. The viewer can adopt the position of a figure.'

Assig's work is characterized by a stark existential intensity that is found both in his paintings in wax and his drawings in ink or charcoal. The body, usually female, is seen in isolation and close up, fragmented, often with a skirt acting as an enclosure or architectural form – a church, temple or sacred vessel. Medieval icons, religious reliquaries and *art brut* are among the artist's influences in his meditations on the universal themes of creation, existence and death.

84

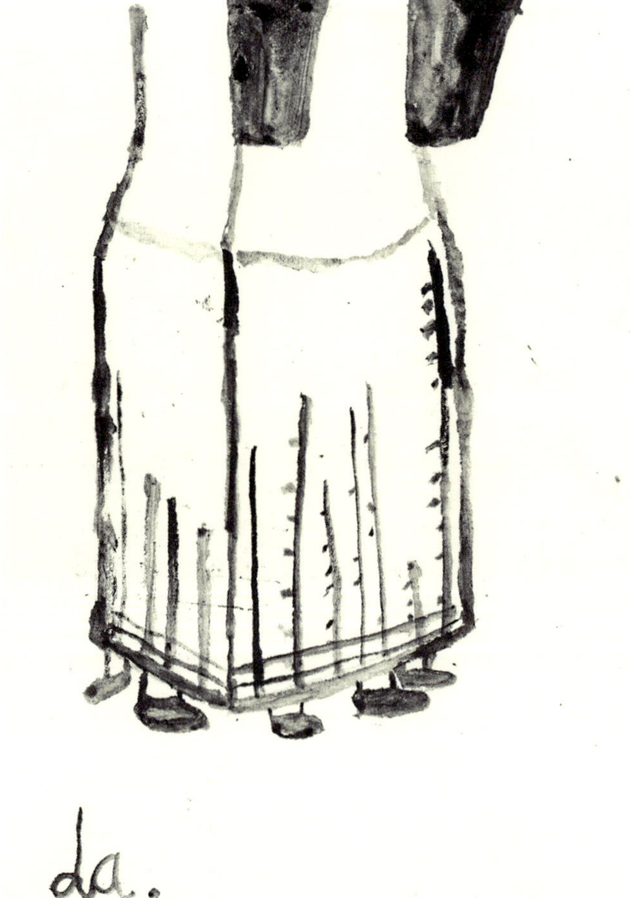

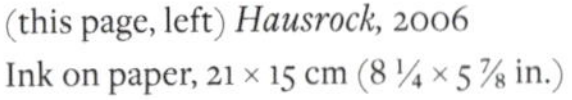

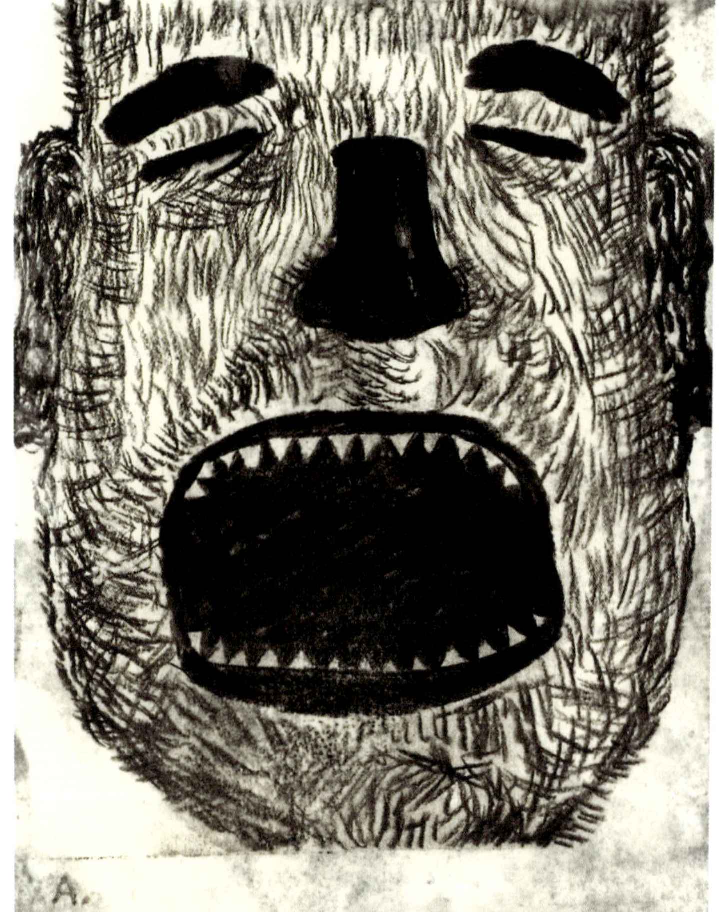

(this page, left) *Hausrock*, 2006
Ink on paper, 21 × 15 cm (8 ¼ × 5 ⅞ in.)

(this page, right) *Die Beute #114*, 2008
Wax and charcoal on paper, 30 × 23.5 cm (11 ¾ × 9 ¼ in.)

(opposite, top left) *Partisanin*, 2003
Ink on paper, 21 × 15 cm (8 ¼ × 5 ⅞ in.)

(opposite, top right) *Jenny*, 2011
Ink on paper, 24 × 17.5 cm (9 ½ × 6 ⅞ in.)

(opposite, below left) *Grundstein*, 2005
Ink on paper, 21.5 × 15.5 cm (8 ½ × 6 ⅛ in.)

(opposite, below right) *Alte Geschichte*, 2002
Ink on paper, 24 × 17.5 cm (9 ½ × 6 ⅞ in.)

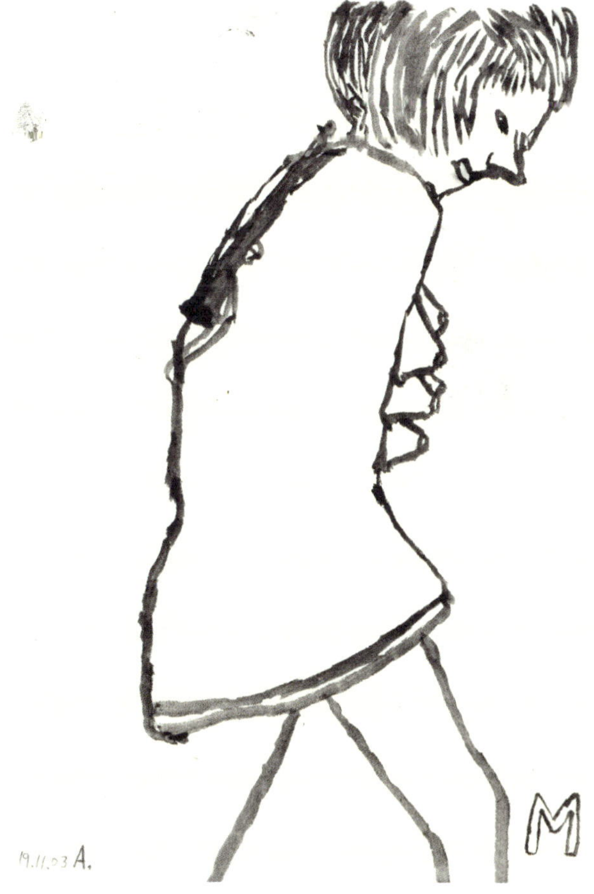

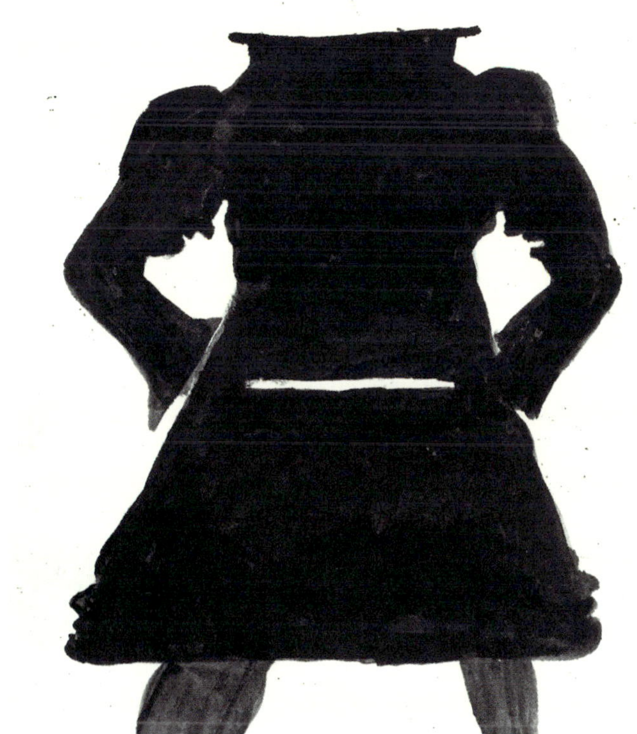

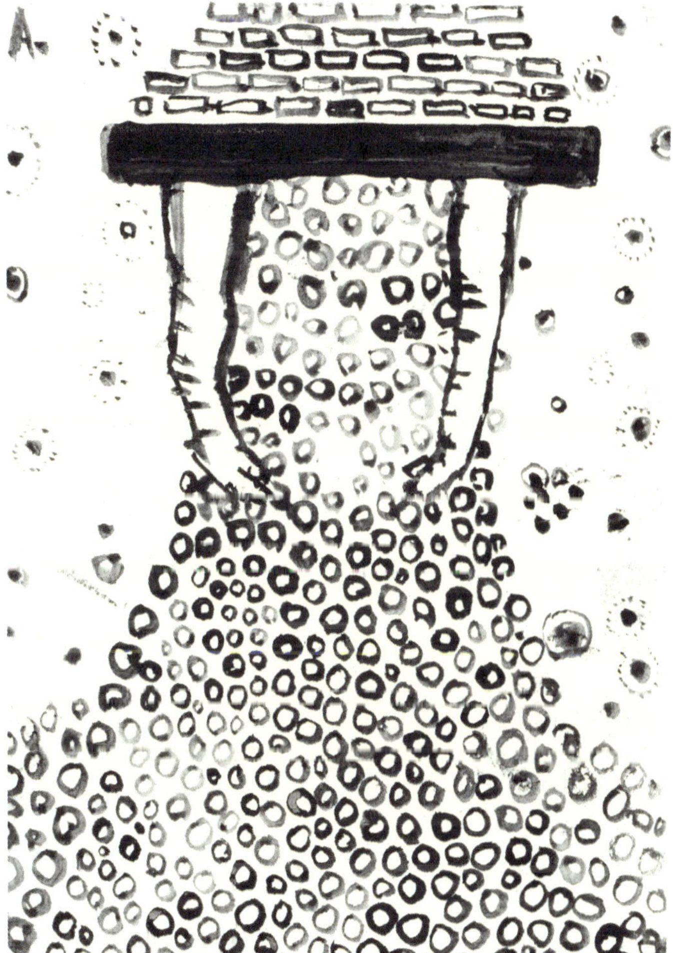

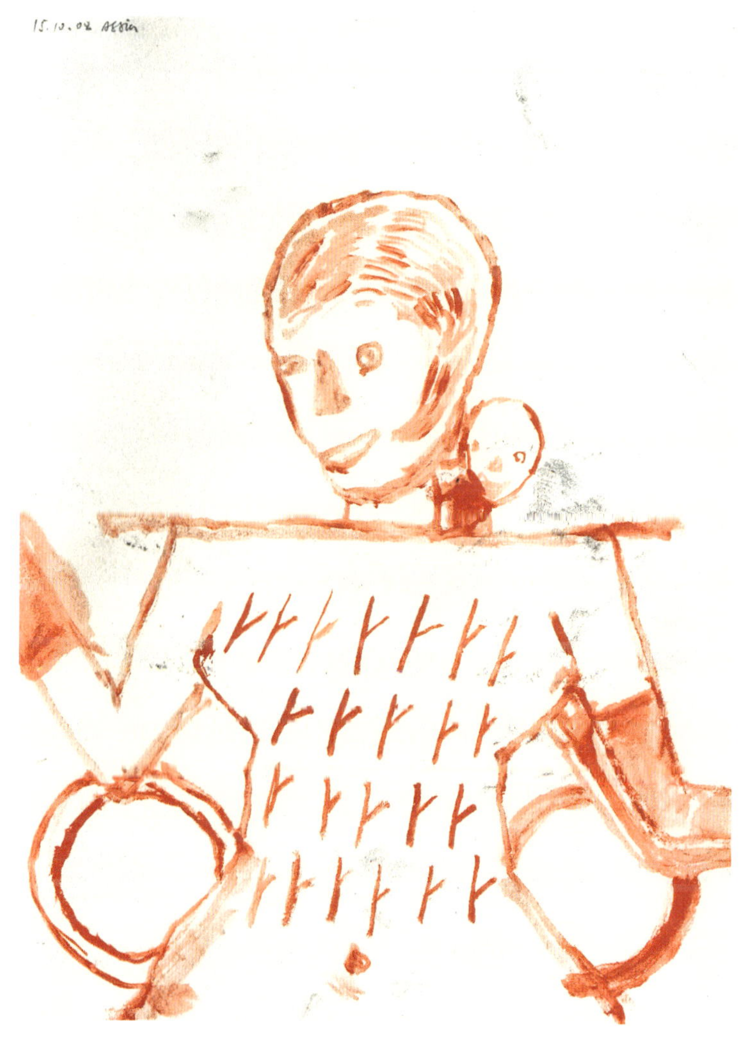

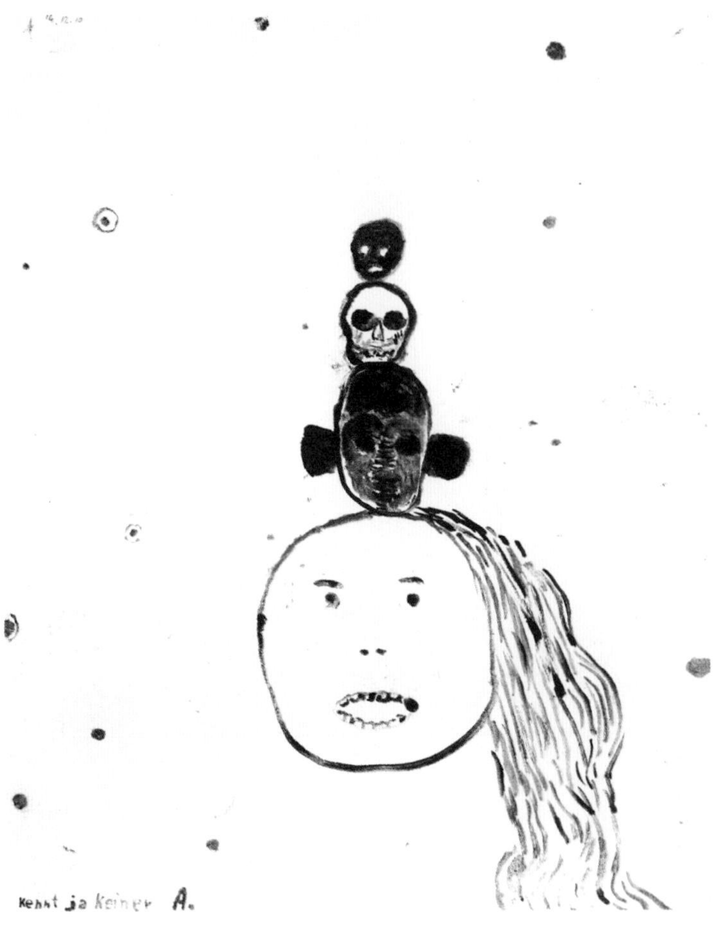

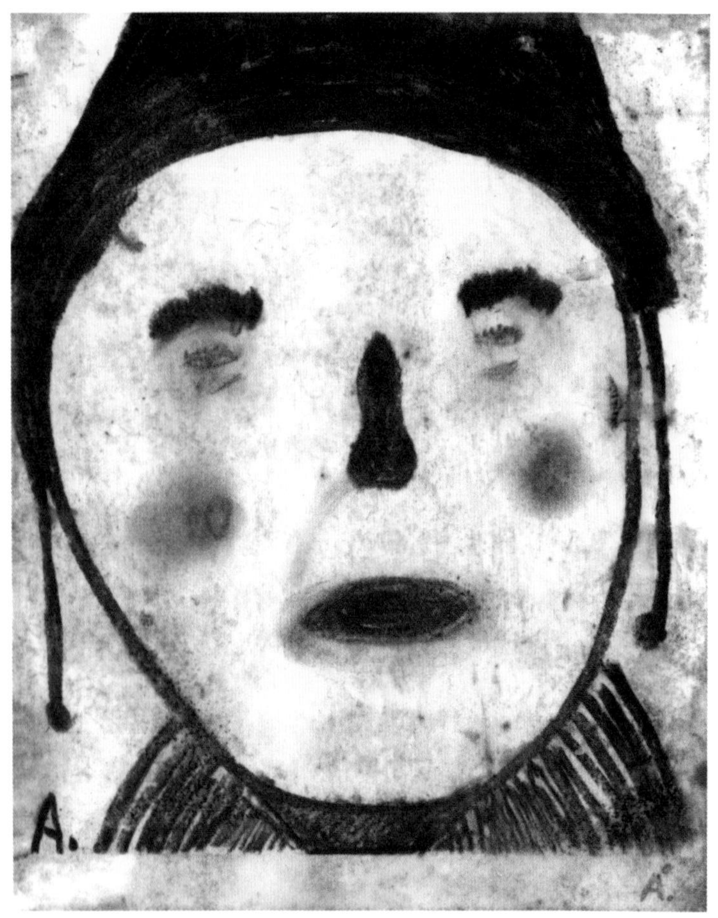

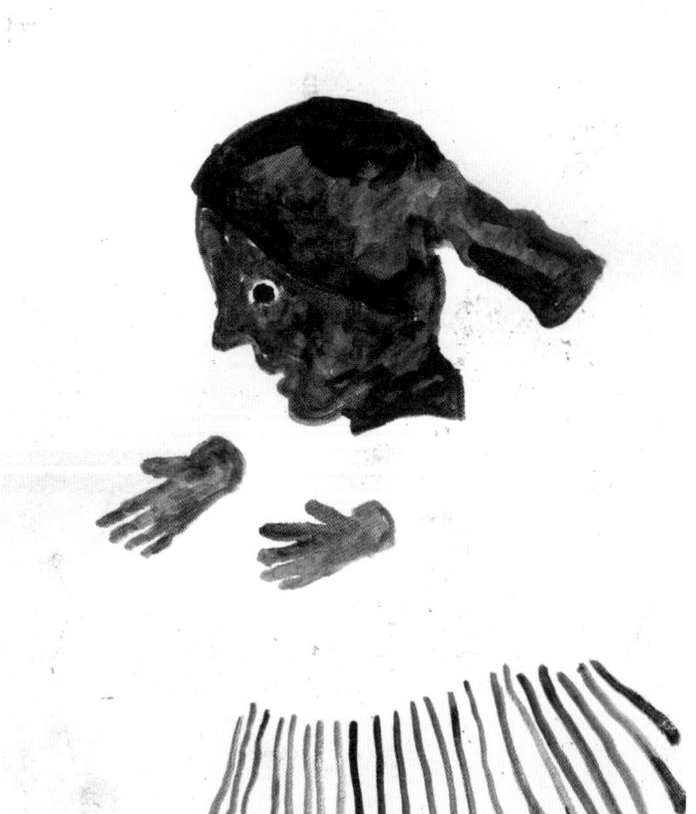

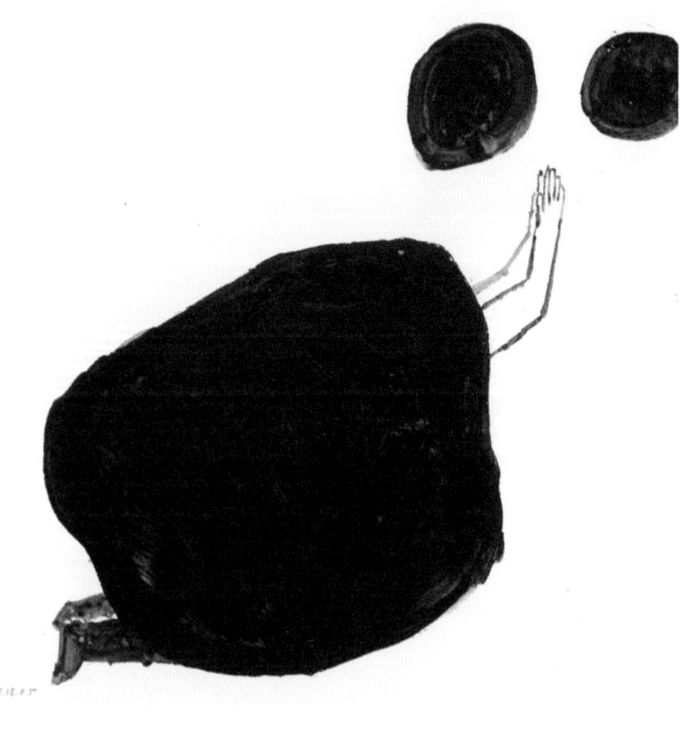

(top left) *Jongleurin,* 2010
Ink on paper, 24 × 19 cm (9 ½ × 7 ½ in.)

(below left) *Mariechen,* 2011
Ink on paper, 24 × 17.5 cm (9 ½ × 6 ⅞ in.)

(top right) *Die Beute #101,* 2008
Wax and charcoal on paper, 30 × 23.5 cm (11 ¾ × 9 ¼ in.)

(below right) *Nonne,* 2005
Ink on paper, 30.5 × 25 cm (12 × 9 ⅞ in.)

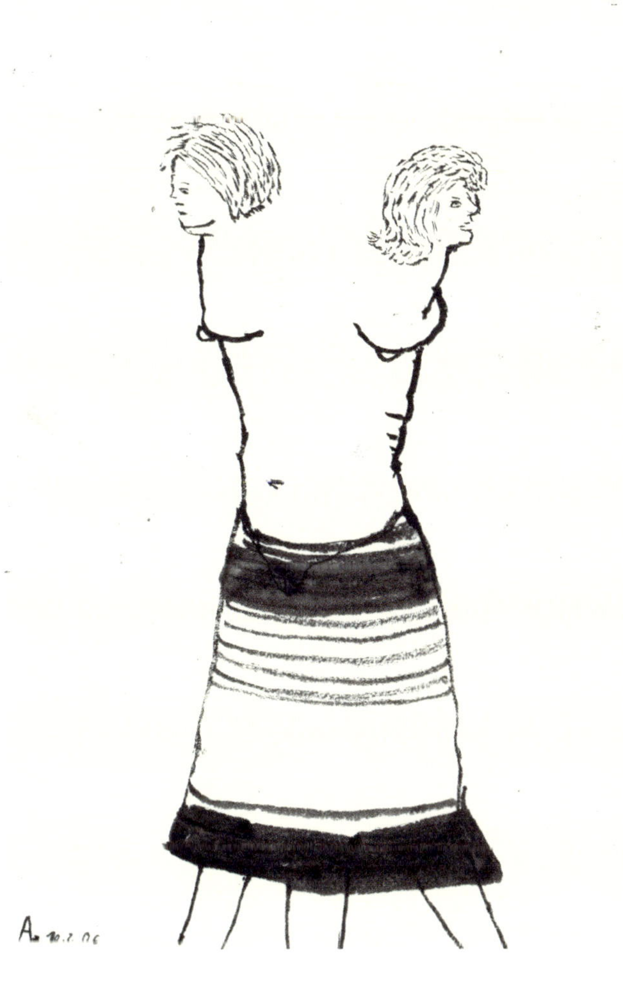

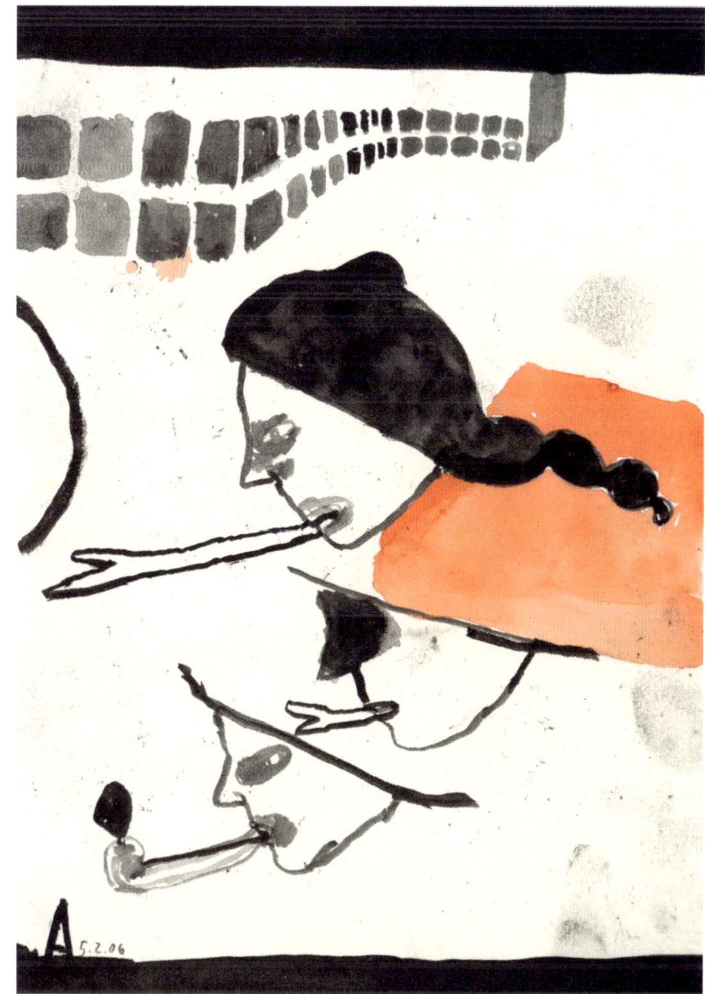

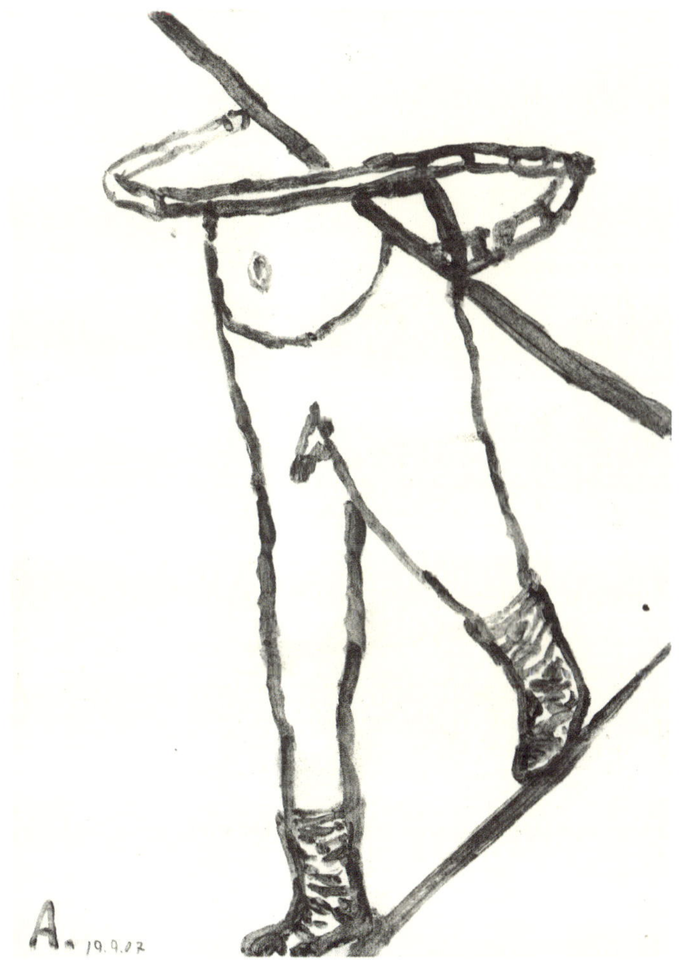

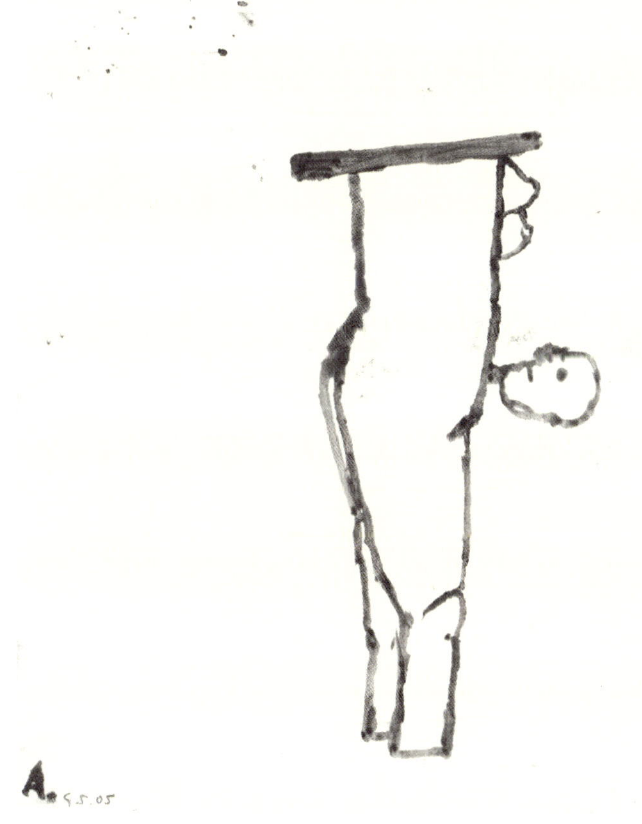

(top left) *Freundin,* 2006
Ink on paper, 21.5 × 15.5 cm (8 ½ × 6 ⅛ in.)

(below left) *Vordermann,* 2007
Ink on paper, 21.6 x 15.4 cm (8 ½ × 6 ⅛ in.)

(top right) *Rauchen,* 2006
Ink on paper, 21.5 × 15.5 cm (8 ½ × 6 ⅛ in.)

(below right) *Liebhaber, zwei,* 2005
Ink on paper, 21.5 × 15.5 cm (8 ½ × 6 ⅛ in.)

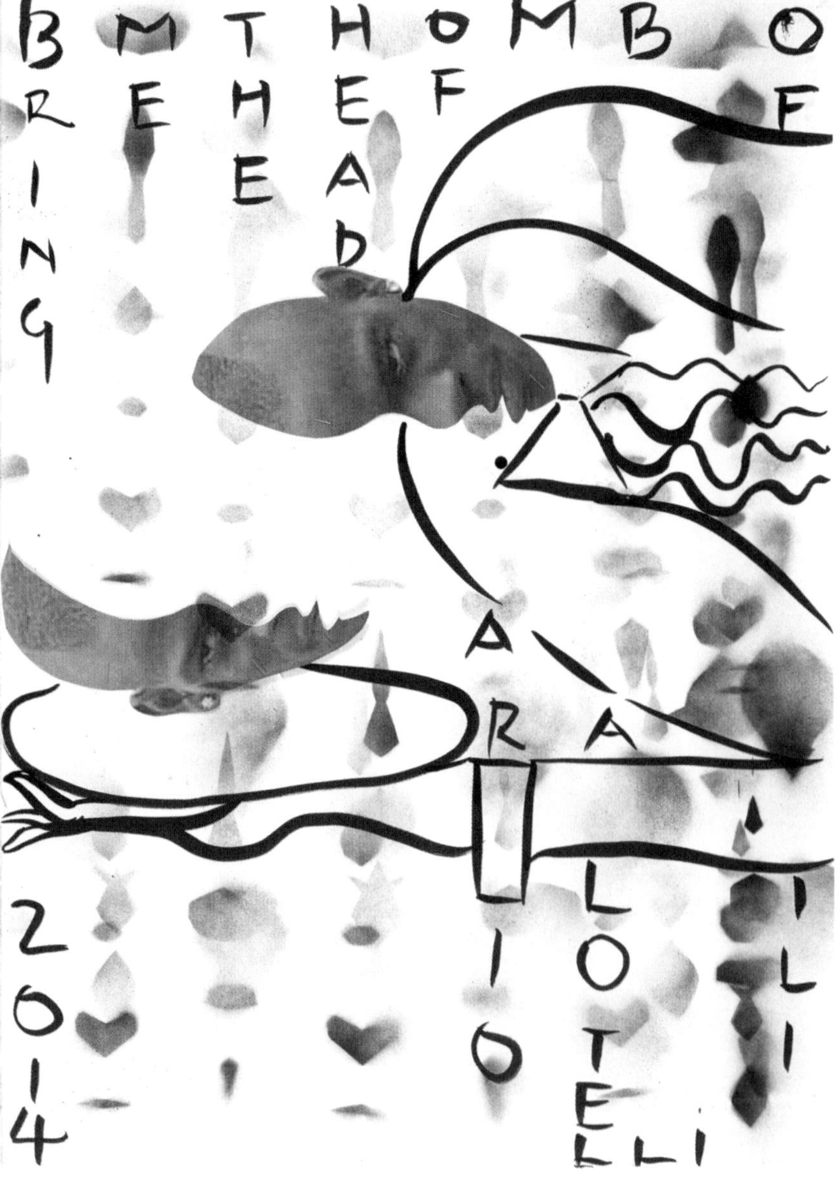

Since moving from London to Trinidad in 2005, Chris Ofili has relinquished the labour-intensive, intricately beaded surfaces for which he was well known – each one composed of multitudes of tiny painted spots and elephant dung – and has turned instead to a looser, more painterly handling. Yet the imagery in these more recent works is not so different; the earlier paintings were likewise anchored in drawing and Ofili has always been a fluent watercolourist and an exquisite draughtsman.

The Afro-muses, one of which is shown here, are silhouetted black and brown personages with the regal air of princesses and the loose-limbed, voluptuous bodies of goddesses, celebrating beauty and sensuality with uncomplicated assurance. Collage has been a subtle but significant ingredient in Ofili's paintings, which might be peppered with the disembodied heads of black heroes such as musicians, sometimes threaded together like beads on a necklace. The Italian–Ghanaian footballer Mario Balotelli (nicknamed Super Mario) is an iconic, almost mythical, larger-than-life personality; flamboyant, always in the news, often racially abused and regularly in trouble. Ofili's *The Baptist* creates a parody of this using the biblical story in which John the Baptist's head is offered to Herod the Great. Balotelli is represented as self-sacrificing, presenting half of his own head on a platter, adroitly split, profile and full-face combined.

The Baptist 2, 2014
Paper collage, ink, spray paint and staples on paper
76.5 × 56 cm (30 ⅛ × 22 ⅛ in.)

Untitled (Afronude), 2006 >
Watercolour and pencil on paper
Paper: 63.5 × 43.2 cm (25 × 17 in.), framed: 82 × 60.8 x 2 cm
(32 ¼ × 24 × ¾ in.)

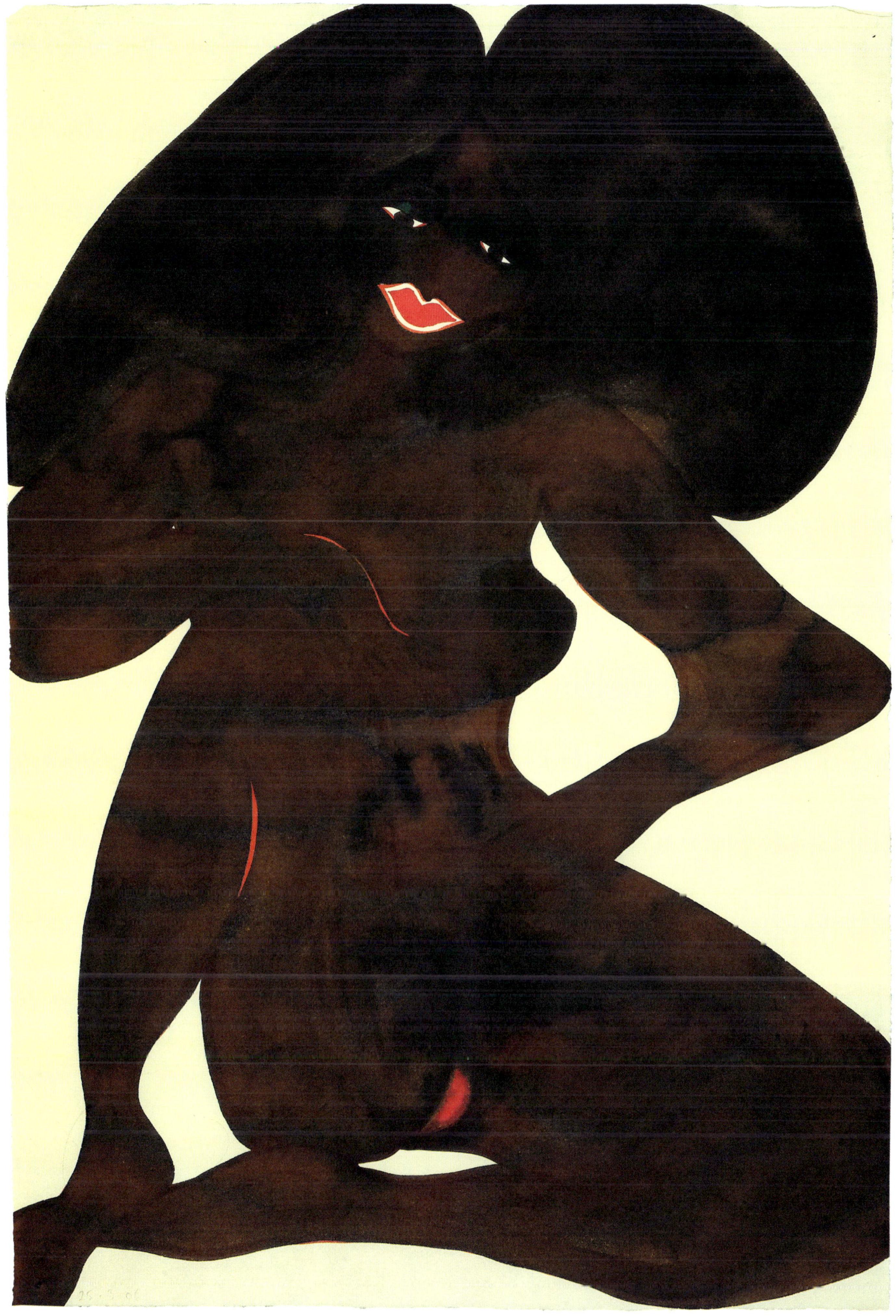

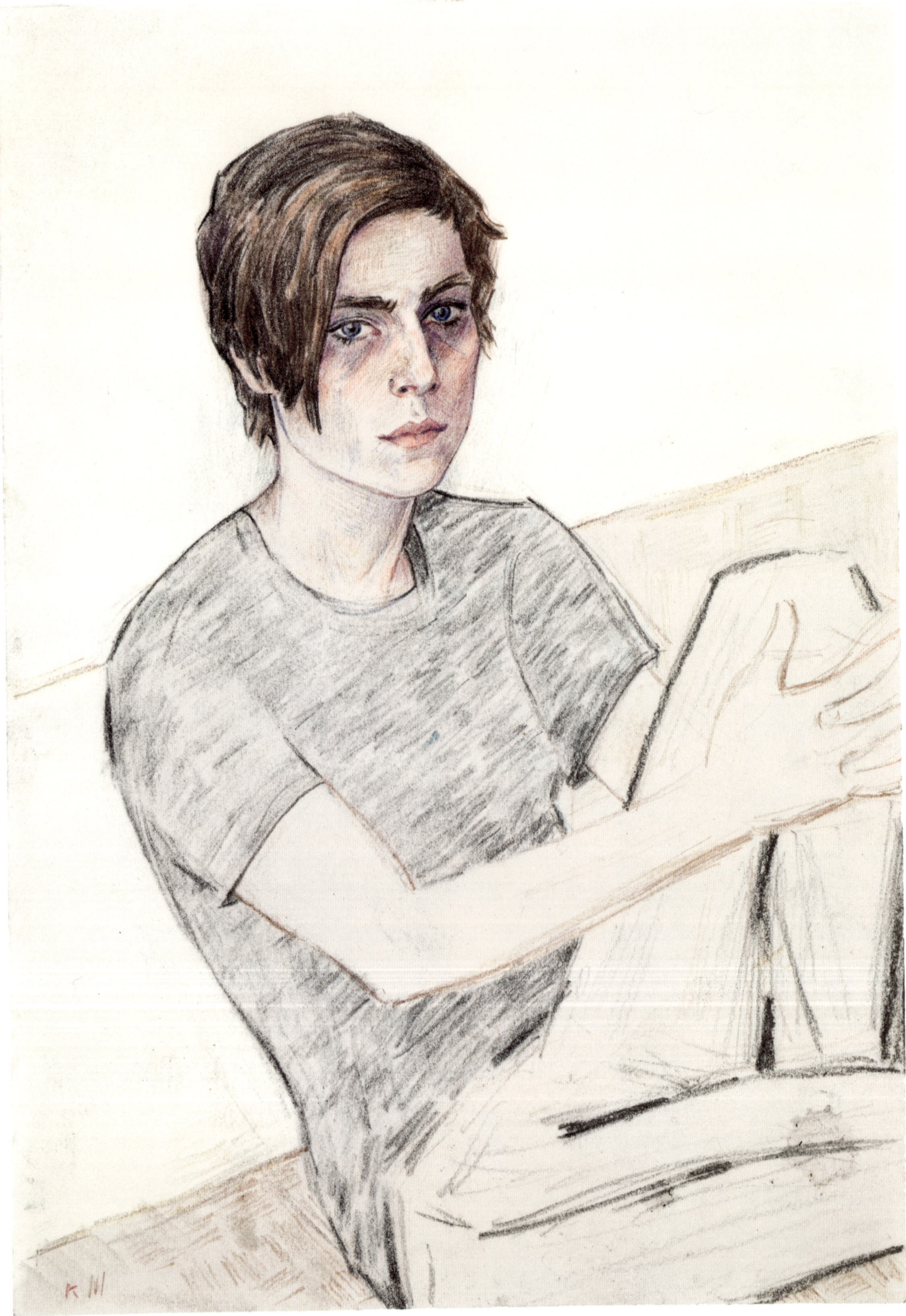

ELIZABETH PEYTON *Born 1965, Danbury, Connecticut, USA. Lives and works in New York, USA*

New York artist Elizabeth Peyton has been drawing and painting portraits since the mid-1990s, depicting subjects from her own life and beyond – from close friends and contemporary artists, musicians, actors and other celebrities to historical personages such as European monarchs and nineteenth-century writers. The portraits are subtle, intimate and romantic, and disarmingly small in scale. The subjects are depicted with affection, as they would wish to be seen. Desire tinged with pathos seems to permeate these images; they reflect a moment, fragile yet intense, tenderly observed by one who sympathizes

with – perhaps participates in – their dream of eternal life. Peyton's recent work has a more melancholy and distanced atmosphere, as if existence weighs more heavily with the passage of time. In her sensitive pencil study of the Swedish artist Klara Lidén, Peyton's subject looks up at the artist or viewer patiently, unguarded but alert, while the evanescent watercolour evokes the vulnerability and remoteness of a person in sleep. 'I think it's all in people's faces', Peyton says. 'They really are history. And it passes and they change, and that's it.'

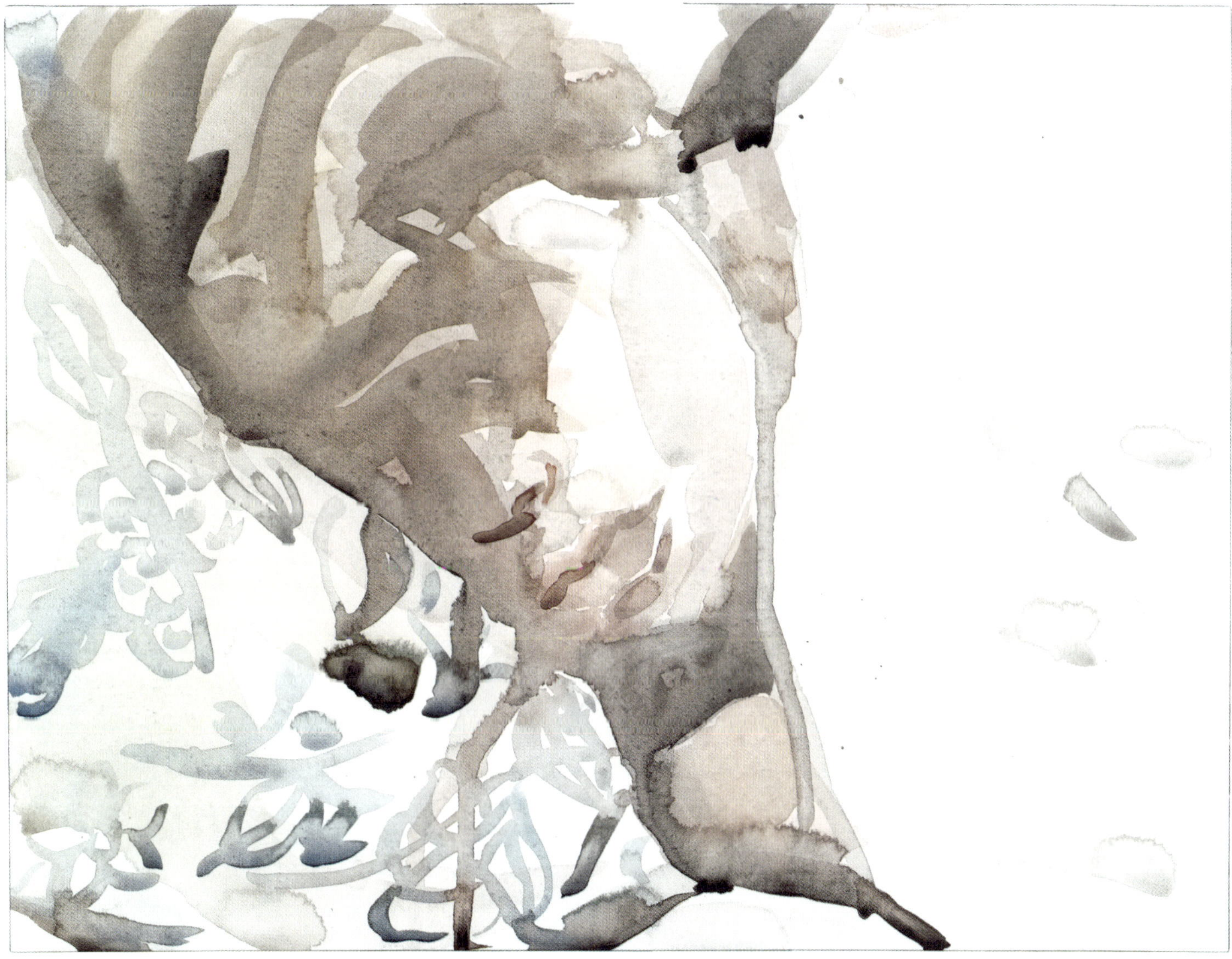

< *Klara (Klara Lidén) 10 October 2009 Berlin*, 2009
Coloured pencil on paper
21.9 × 15.2 cm (8 ⅝ × 6 in.)

Klara, 2010
Watercolour on paper
31.1 × 40.6 cm (12 ¼ × 16 in.)

Kumi Machida uses traditional Japanese pigments and handmade paper to achieve her own idiosyncratic ends. Her gracefully flowing lines, meticulously applied using fine brushes, describe forms that are comfortably smooth and rounded – babies' heads, children's toys and electrical appliances – yet with a surreal and unsettling twist, a hint of cruelty and manipulation. Her radically cropped images are also disorientating in their lack of scale. There is no background or context to which to refer: the babies might be giants, or prototypes for a newly manufactured species. Fingernails sprout thorns. A slot or eye in the back of a baby's head gives the game away: that perfect sphere with the hole in the top is designed to perfection. Helmets may be worn

for protection, or fixed permanently to skulls and engineered to expand with growth. Strange threads, whether of tears or mucous or hair extensions, extrude from the eyes – in one drawing they are draped over the baby's proud parent beneath. It is tempting to seek the meaning of these bizarre scenes in the artist's biography; Machida willingly describes her own feelings of estrangement when growing up, specifically her sense of being the wrong sex for her parents, and probably wrong in other respects also. These personal experiences work their way into her drawings, with each image seeming to encapsulate an intense emotion, a particular fear or some variation on the uncanny.

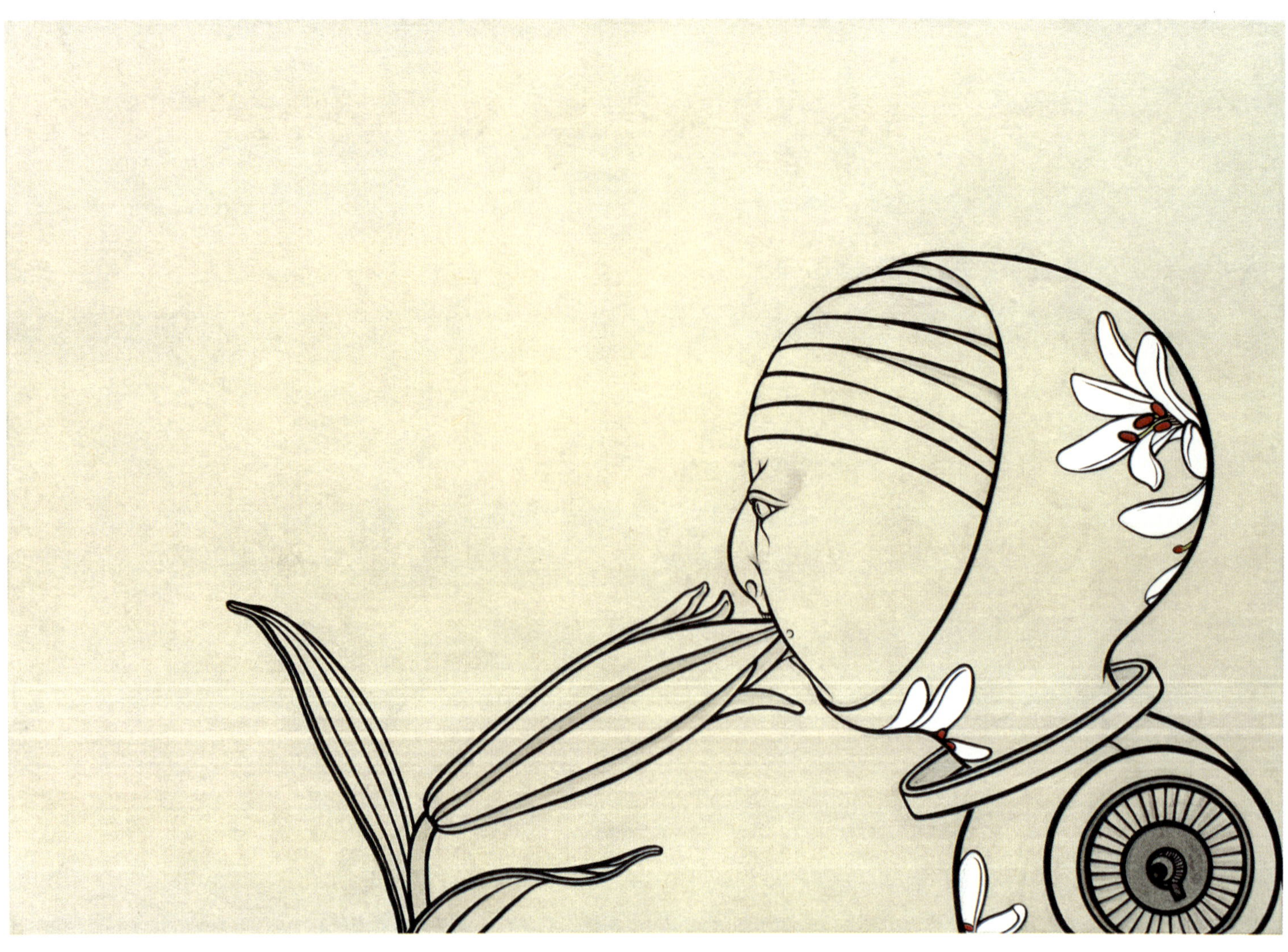

Ugliness, 2003
Sumi (blue), mineral pigments and gofun pigments
on kumohada linen paper
29.5 × 42 cm (11 ⅝ × 16 ½ in.)

Clothes, 2006 >
Sumi (blue and brown), pigments and mineral pigments
on kumohada linen paper
130.3 × 89.4 cm (51 ¼ × 35 ¼ in.)

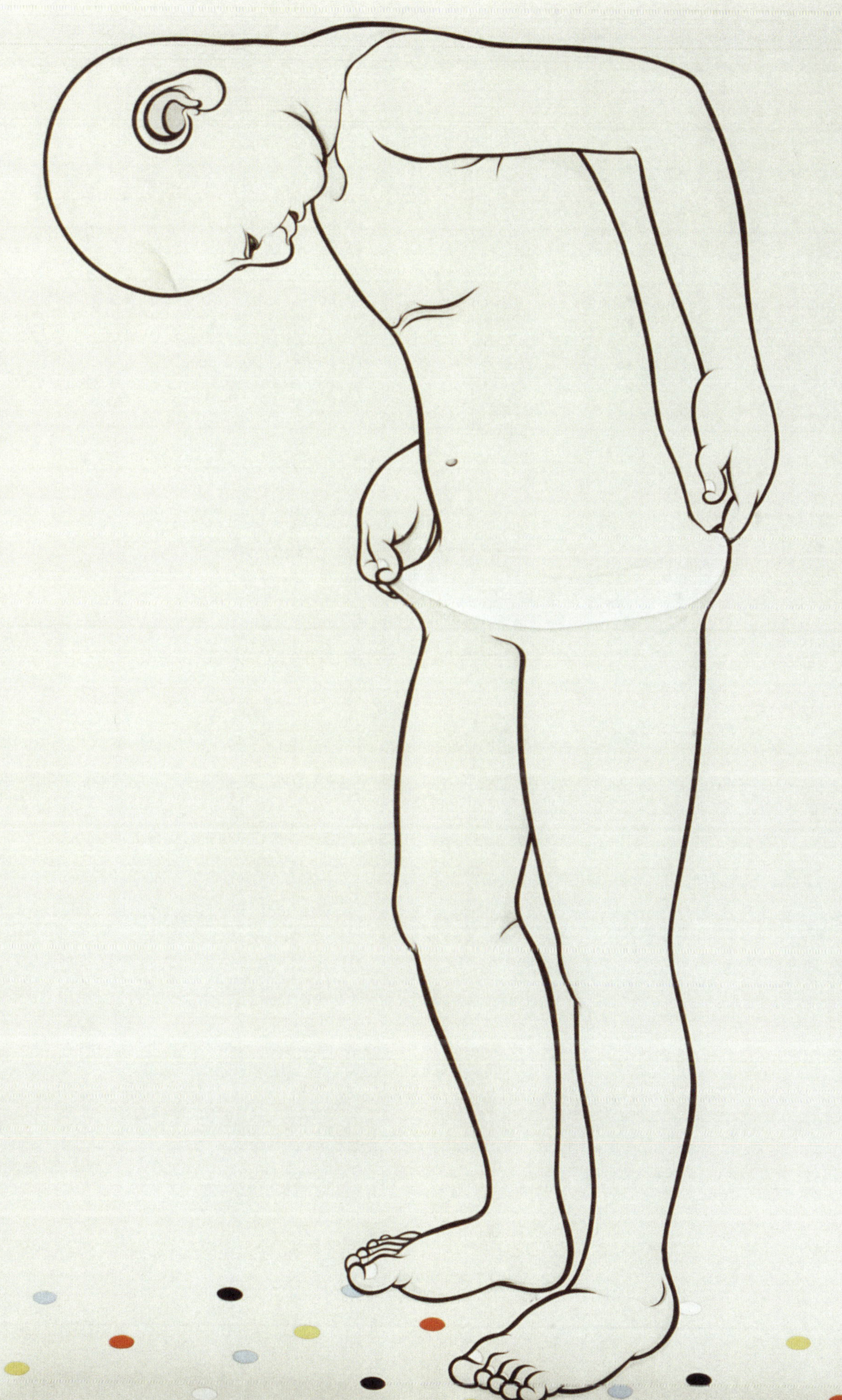

JINJU LEE *Born 1980, Busan, South Korea. Lives and works in Seoul, South Korea*

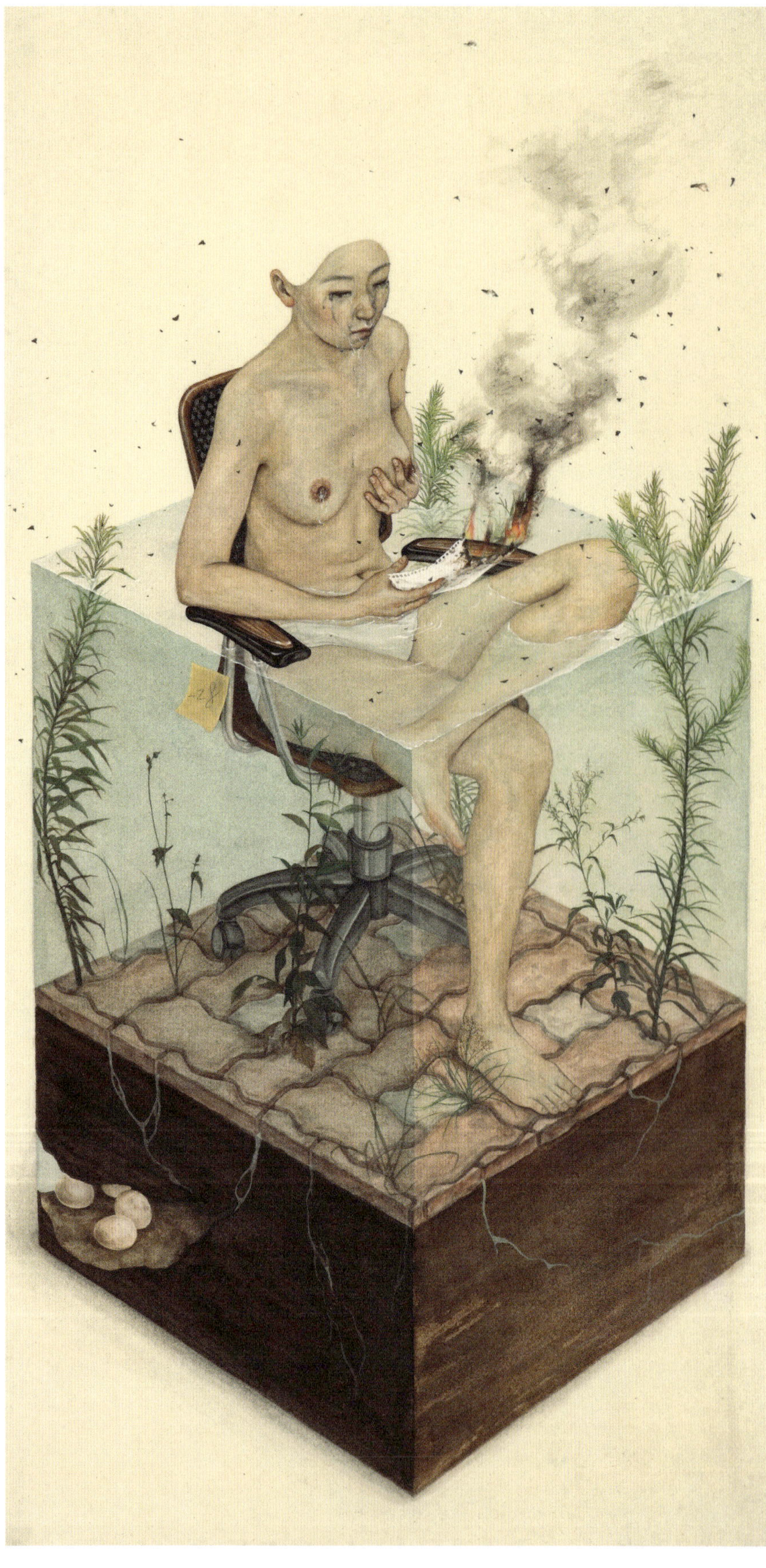

Memory is Jinju Lee's subject, in particular the unwanted recurrence of dark memories of early childhood. Why do memories persist in returning? French novelist Marcel Proust's explanation of the phenomenon of involuntary recollection, namely that it encapsulates the 'essence of the past' by virtue of its unexpected occurrence, prompted by trivial actions such as eating a piece of cake, is no doubt informed by that author's happy childhood. But what if our early memories are predominately negative, or at any rate, what if those negative experiences are the ones that continue to haunt us? Lee dissects and analyses dreams and memories – whether real or invented is unclear, and perhaps irrelevant – in precise, unsettling detail. She assembles objects, 'tiny useless daily things', and scatters them about like litter in the sections of landscape she composes. These landscapes resemble the small suburban gardens and public picnic areas of the real world, innocuous places rendered disturbing in their transformation into dreamscapes or memoryscapes. The female figures that populate them are anonymized through the removal of their hair, usually a conspicuous sign of feminine personality. The bleak, airless atmosphere of the spaces they inhabit is boxed in and flatly lit. Fire and water are mixed in this 'melancholic psychic field', as the artist describes it, as are memory, dream and reality.

Circulation, 2011
Korean colour on fabric
135 × 70 cm (53 ⅛ × 27 ½ in.)

The Last Winter, 2011 >
Korean colour on fabric
148 × 110 cm (58 ¼ × 43 ¼ in.)

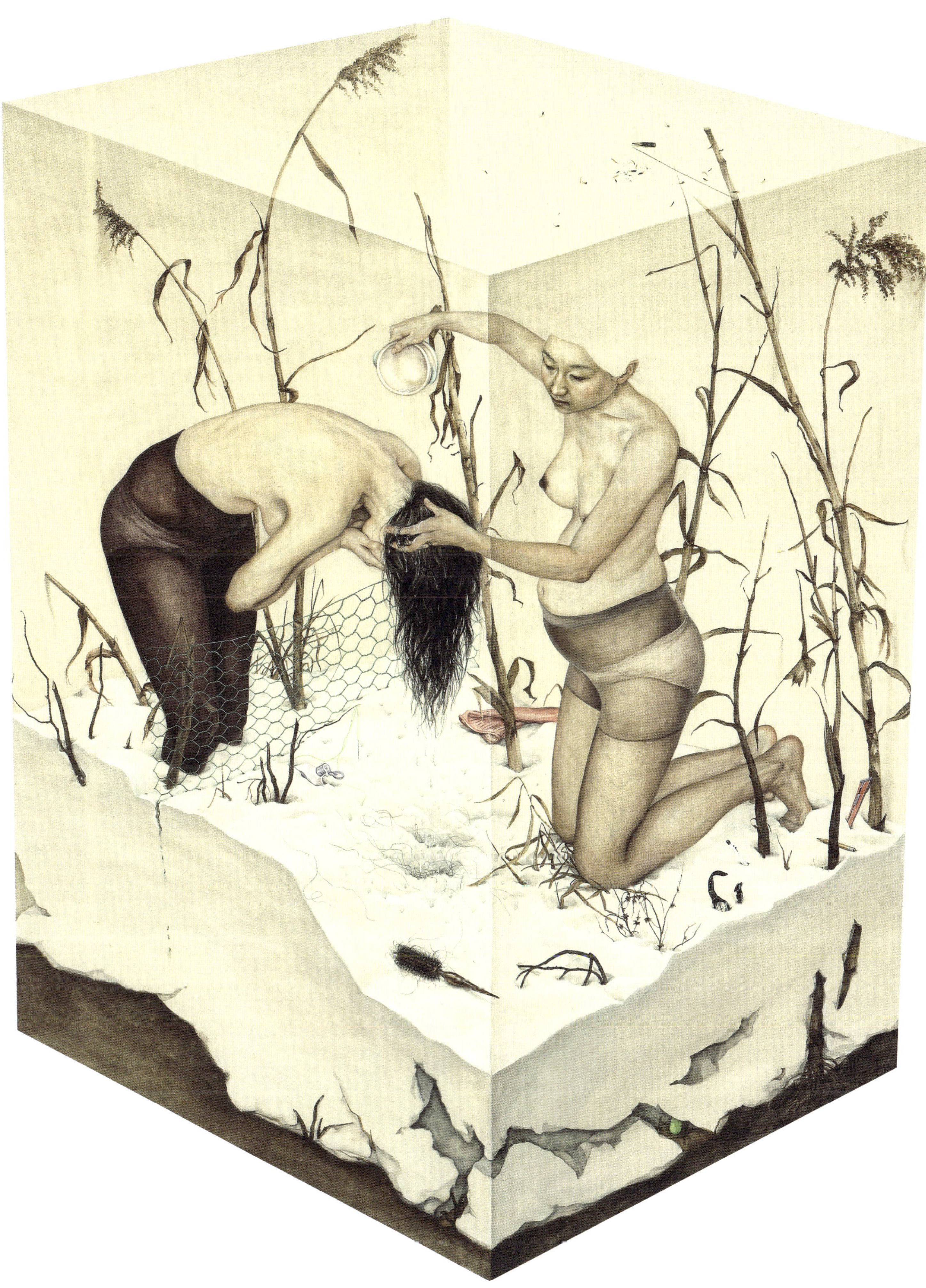

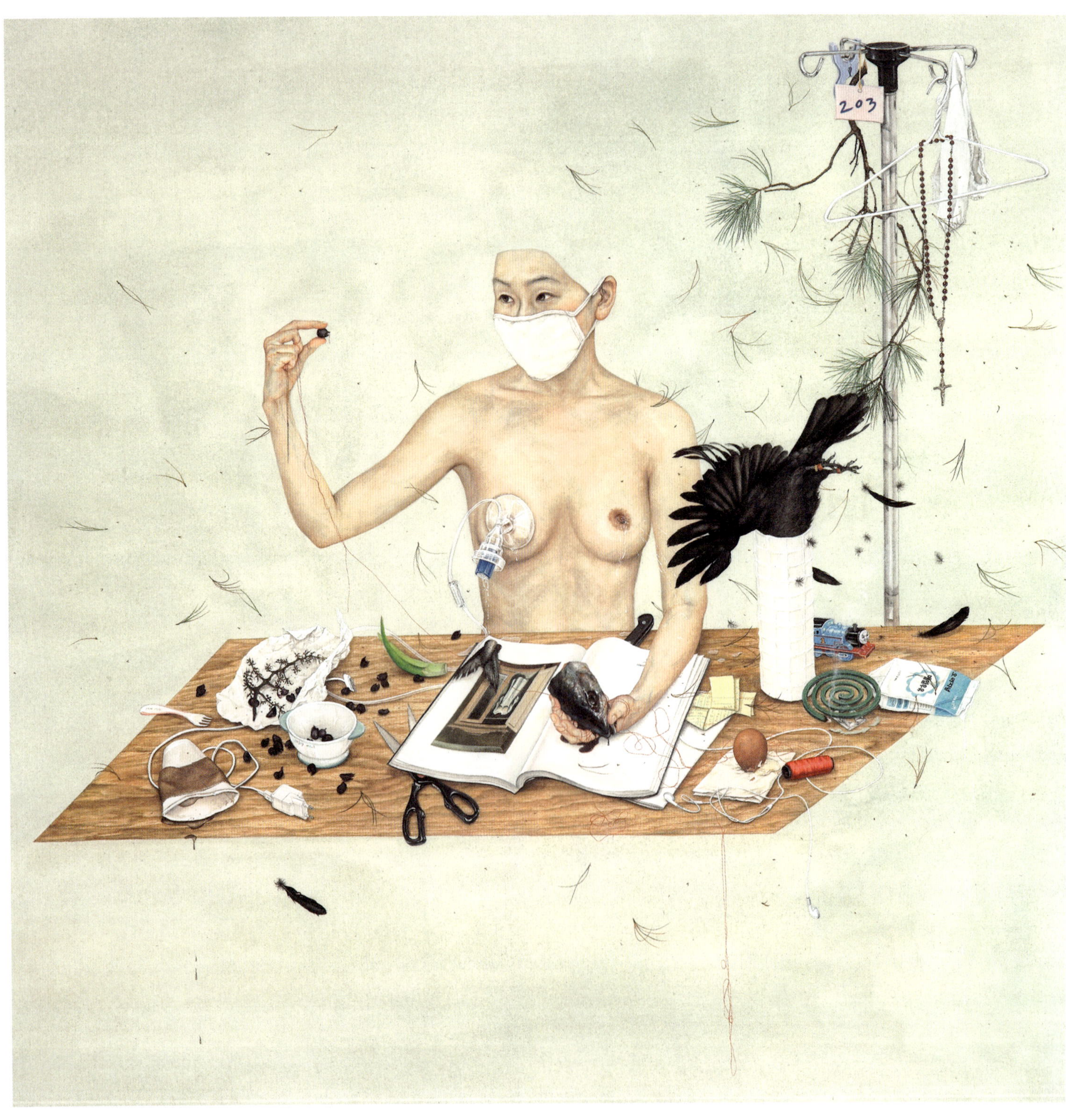

Restraints–Boundaries, 2012
Korean colour on fabric
104 × 117 cm (41 × 46 ⅛ in.)

The Material of Mind, 2010 >
Korean colour on fabric
150 × 150 cm (59 × 59 in.)

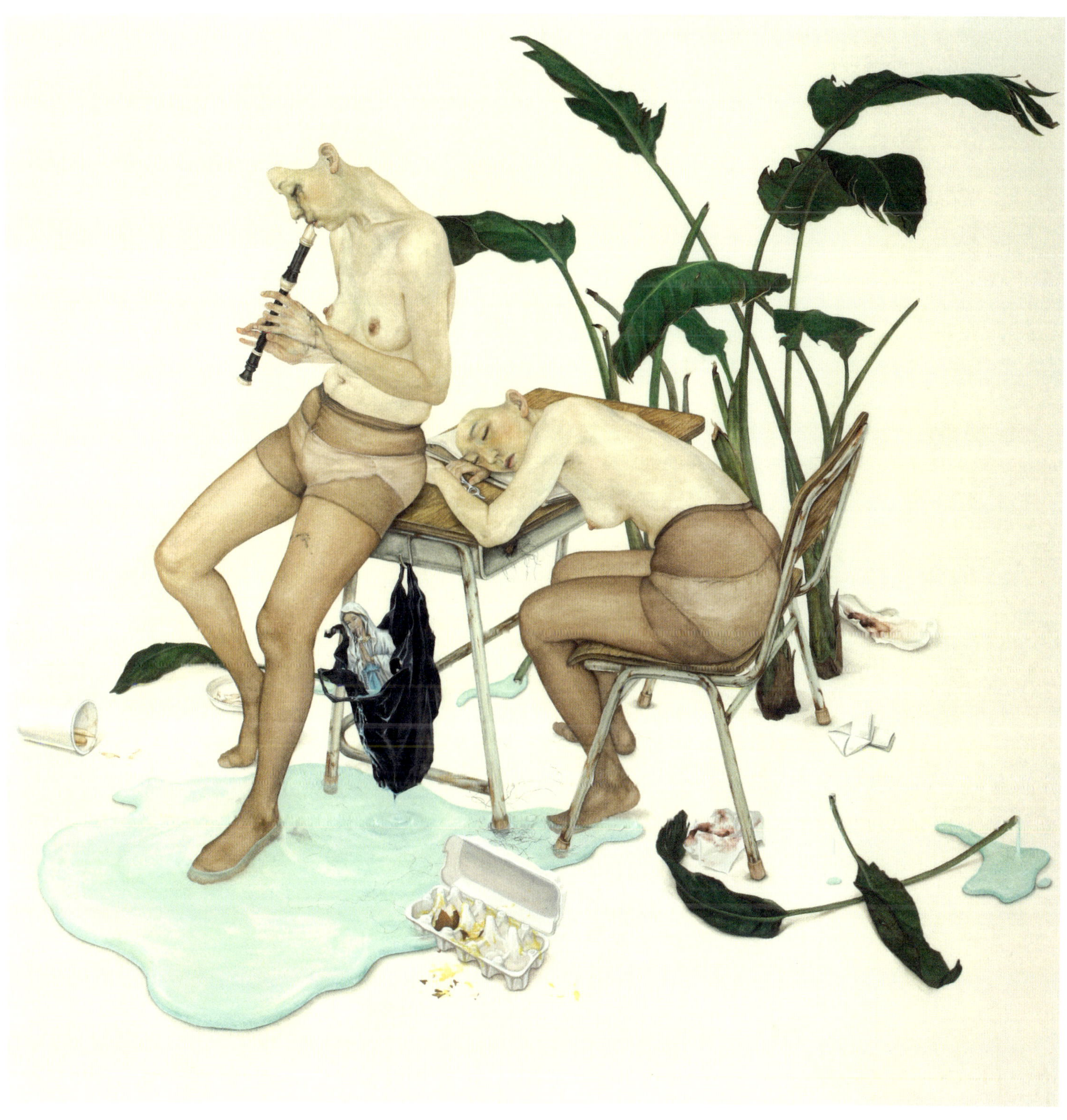

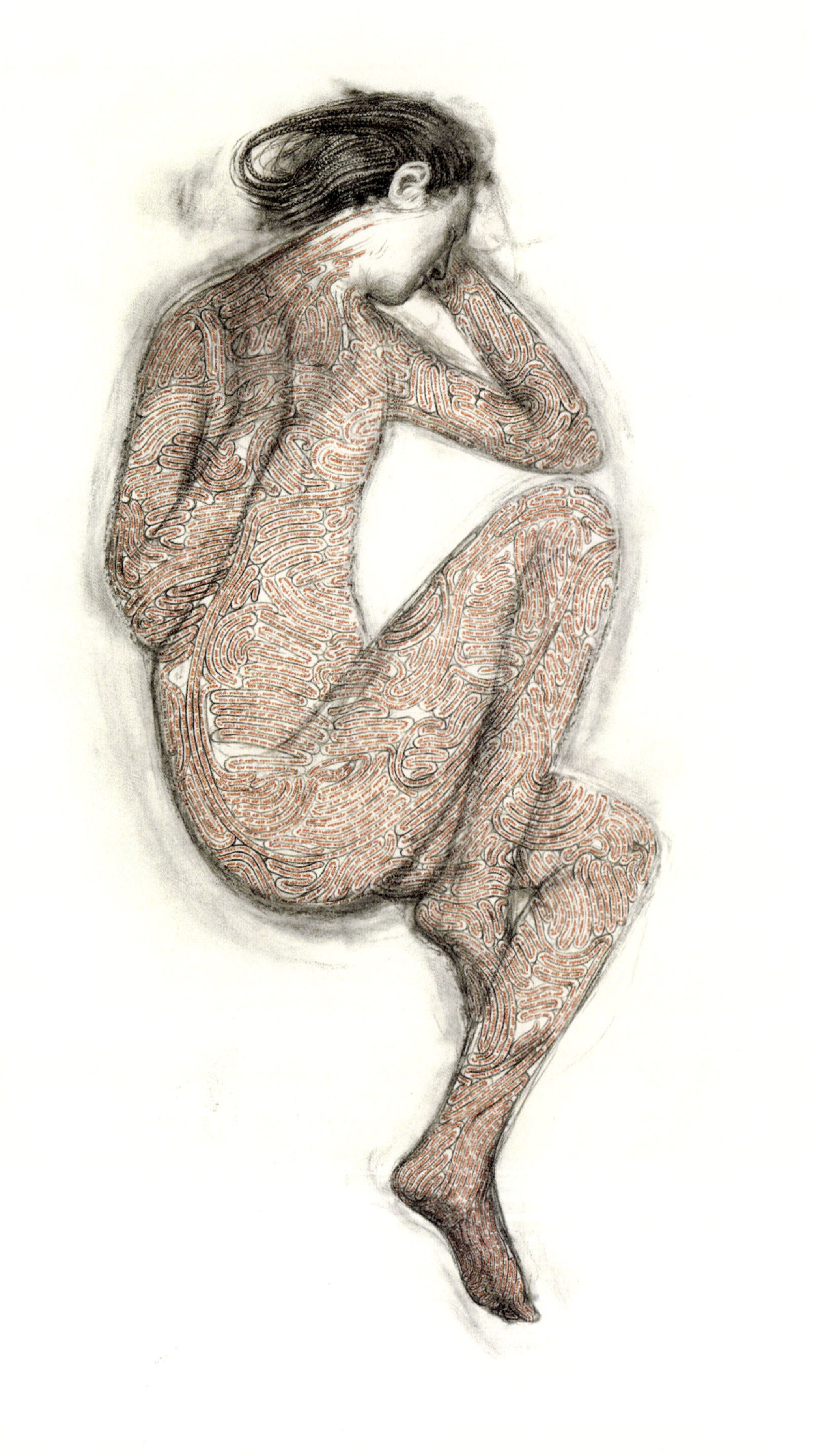

JUUL KRAIJER   *Born 1970, Assen, The Netherlands. Lives and works in Rotterdam, The Netherlands*

Juul Kraijer's subject is the same naked female figure she has drawn repeatedly for more than a decade, whose features she has universalized and pared down (removing the eyebrows, for instance) so that she becomes almost an archetype, an 'everywoman' or, as the artist describes her, an 'emblematic embodiment of states of mind'. The impassive visage, in a state of half-sleep, seems to exist at an interface between self-awareness and self-extinction. This 'everywoman' is a vessel for metamorphosis; the eyes closed or multiplied or transmuted into leaves or fish or moths. In one drawing, a disembodied face is cupped and lifted by a pair of hands, the fingertips defining its contours. Here, the vulnerability of the exposed face is conveyed in the fragile, smoky charcoal line that sits lightly on the surface of the paper, looking as if it could be brushed away with the sweep of a hand. A sense of touch is implicit in the medium of charcoal, the body's outlines subtly suggestive of physical sensation, as though the charcoal were an extension of the fingertips. As Kraijer has stated, 'Charcoal on paper verges on the immaterial. It is wafer-thin and scarcely affixes: just like the pattern on a butterfly wing'.

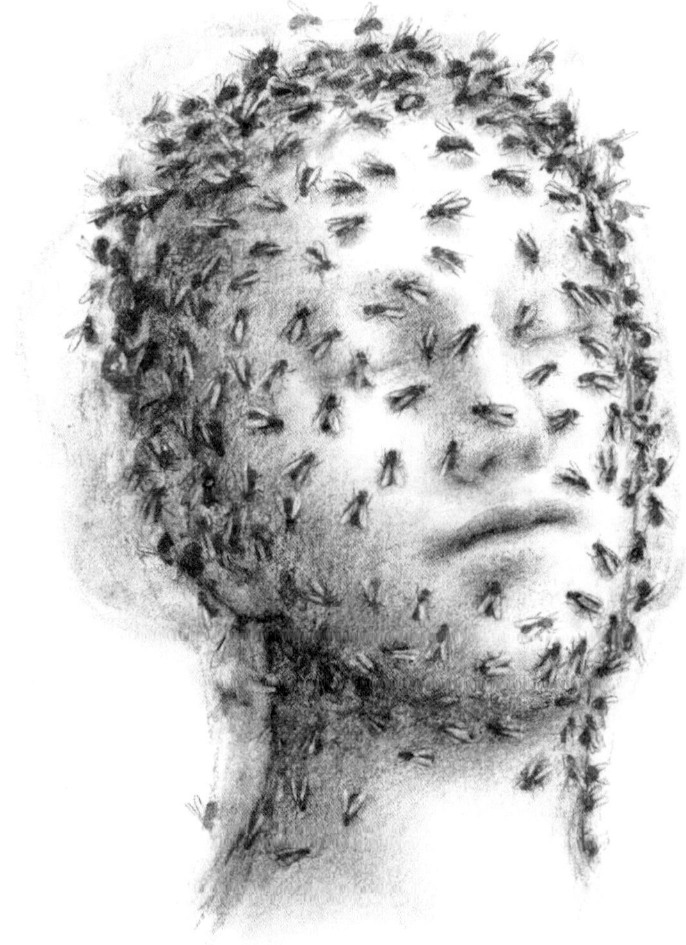

< Untitled, 2005
Charcoal and red ink on paper
184.7 × 95.4 cm (72 ¾ × 37 ½ in.)

Untitled, 2009
Charcoal on paper
54 × 46.5 cm (21 ¼ × 18 ¼ in.)

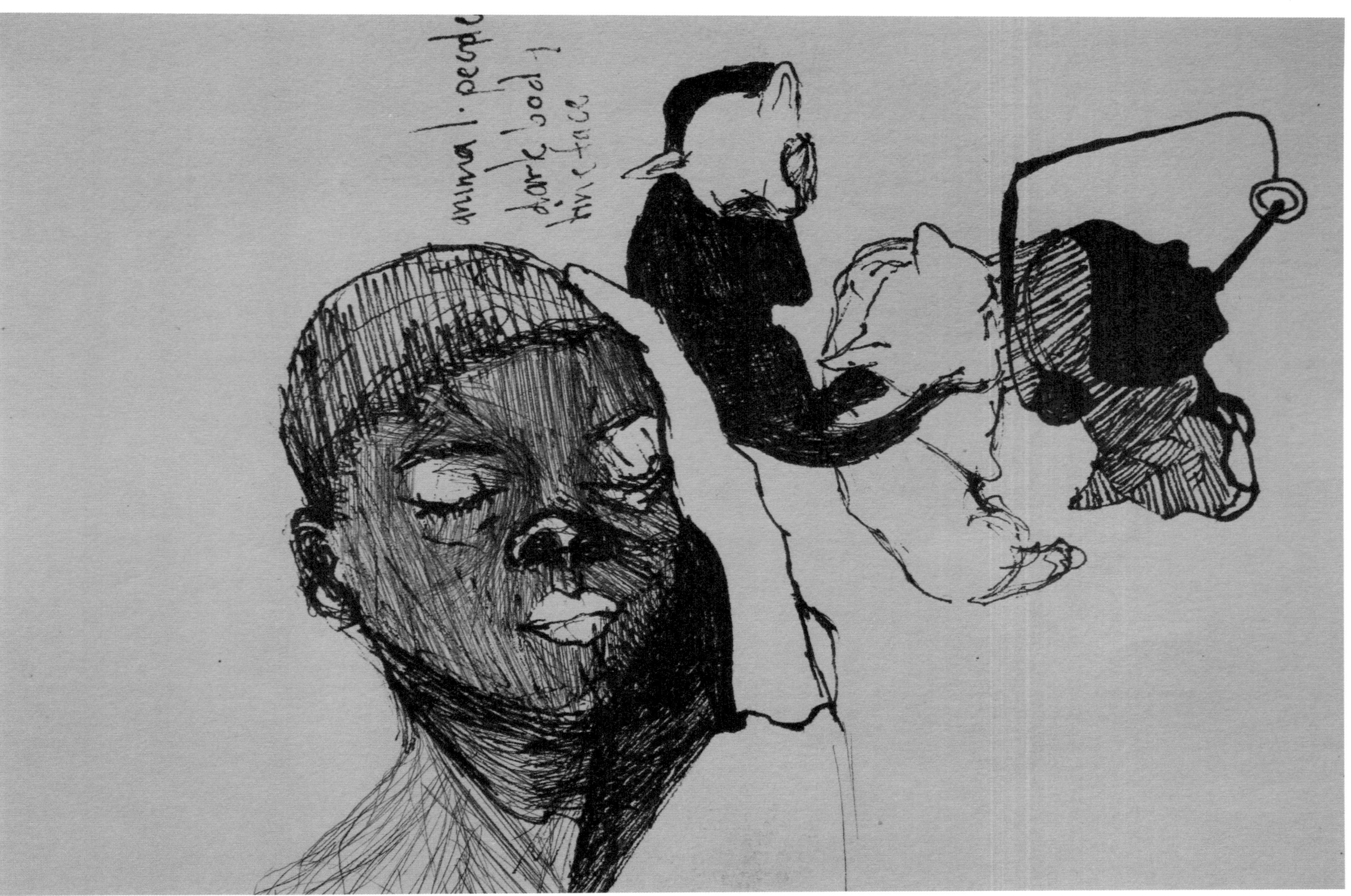
animal people
dark body
fine face

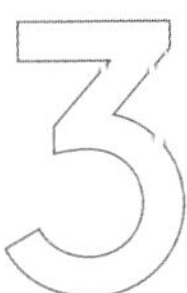

personal lives

Universal assent is already a quite miraculous and incomprehensible prejudice. Why should anyone claim that the shape of a watch is round – a manifestly false proposition – since it appears in profile as a narrow rectangular construction, elliptic on three sides; and why the devil should one only notice its shape at the moment of looking at the time? Perhaps under the pretext of utility. But a child who draws a watch as a circle will also draw a house as a square, as a facade, without any justification, of course; because, except perhaps in the country, he will rarely see an isolated building, and even in a street the facades have the appearance of very oblique trapezoids.

ALFRED JARRY, *Exploits and Opinions of Doctor Faustroll, Pataphysician*, 2006

We tend to think of the face as an intimate expression of the self – although everyone knows that looks can deceive, that a smile can mask malevolent intent, make-up can disguise blemishes and that the simple addition of a beard or glasses can transform a person's appearance. We assume too that facial characteristics are preserved over a lifetime – albeit with a degree of deterioration as we age – so that it is often possible to recognize the 'same' person at twelve, twenty and fifty. If we look back now at an image of ourselves as a child, for instance in a school photograph, where our own tiny face looks out at us from a sea of similarly distant faces, what is it that convinces us that this is indeed the child we were? Can we be sure that we have not mixed up one person with another, and that on closer inspection we will not discover ourselves several rows further back, squinting distractedly away from the camera and betraying none of the alertness, sensitivity or good humour that we imagine ourselves

possessing at that age? The face is unmistakably our own; the gestalt, even on that miniature scale, adds up exactly to someone, the person we were and continue to be. But while the photograph may supplant memory as the one sure piece of evidence that we were there, it cannot retain the traces of our inner lives and the way that we relate to the world around us.

Our personal lives – our daily experiences, thoughts and encounters – constitute what we consider to be our essential condition of being-in-the-world, and artistic representations of the face and body often bear the key to this inner existence. Photographs can offer a superficial substitute, albeit one that endures. What happens, though, when the face is expunged from the photographic record? The Saudi artist Jowhara AlSaud makes subversive play with the conventions of image censorship prevalent in her country by eliminating all features in her snapshots of young people, friends and acquaintances

< VIRGINIA CHIHOTA *hama dzangu (my relatives)*, 2011
Pen and ink drawing on paper, 21 × 15 cm (8 ¼ × 5 ⅞ in.)

socializing. 'I tried to apply the language of the censors to my personal photographs. I began by making line drawings, omitting faces and skin. Keeping only the essentials allowed me to circumvent, and comment on, some of the cultural taboos associated with photography. Namely the stigma attached to bringing the "personal portrait", commonly reserved for the private domestic space, into the public sphere. It became a game of how much you can tell with how little. When reduced to sketches, the images achieved enough distance from the original photographs that neither subjects nor censors could find them objectionable. For me, they became autonomous, relatable, pared down narratives.'

We might say that these images are drained of emotion, of the inner lives of their subjects. Few signs remain in these animated but anonymous figures of the exuberance and conviviality, sadness and passion that were evidently experienced at the time. Without smiling faces, telling glances, affectionate kisses or tearful embraces, the gestures speak only of an absence, a moment that has been wiped from the records. The images are frozen as if under an officious and all-seeing eye, one that denies personal (and especially sexual) liberty in the name of moral rectitude – a rectitude enforced in Saudi Arabia through the Committee for the Propagation of Virtue and the Prevention of Vice. The thought is paralyzing. It bears on the activity of drawing, which we hold to be a free zone, and which is deployed by AlSaud to parody government prohibitions. Tracing in outline these intimate personal encounters, the artist celebrates forbidden pleasures just as artists have done throughout history. There is irony in the fact that the censor also draws, emphatically with a black fibre pen, thereby signifying at the same time as erasing. And there is further irony in the fact that her images are likely more graphically vivacious and luxuriously evocative with the faces removed than were the relatively banal originals. What is taken away also adds to their poetic resonance, conveying both a sense of loss and the universality of the poses.

The early modernists often omitted or abbreviated facial features in their paintings, regarding such particularities as an irrelevant distraction from the formal unity of the artwork as a whole. This might also apply to Amy Sillman's series of wash drawings of couples lying around together on sofas, with arms and legs affectionately intertwined. These final pieces were not drawn directly from life, but abstracted later from more literal sketches made at the time. They are vigorous analytical drawings in which space is organized and shapes defined as if in preparation for a painting. There is no trace of nostalgia or

sentimentality, yet we have a strong impression of the sitters' personal lives, and when one considers Sillman's practice as a whole, including her cartoons, it is evident that personality is at the forefront of her attention. 'My work is always psychological, whether I want it to be or not. The shapes that I am interested in looking at and drawing always turn into forms that have some kind of psychological narrative. Even if it's in the sense of formal predicament, that a shape is at the edge of another.… There is some kind of discomfort or complexity that makes the object troubled in a way. The object is endangered, its stability is imperilled in some way; it's tipping over, or you can see through it. Or it is abject.'

Emma Talbot's characters are similarly anonymous, their faces blank or averted. As a formal device, this enables the artist to summarize figures briefly in space without becoming enmeshed in incidental detail. But it surely serves another purpose: Talbot describes her comic-strip sequences as 'psychological stories'. Her emphasis is on the everyday events that might happen to anyone, and it seems natural that the facial features are omitted because the figures are depicted subjectively, from within, as though they are dreaming or remembering a dream. When Talbot presents two or more individuals interacting in the same image they are all equivalently abstracted. With this technique, she touches on how the mind actually operates when we recall a situation, or when we dream about someone known and loved. Certainly, in recalling our own past we are familiar with the protagonists and there is no necessity for us to fill in every detail, and we likewise feel no need to visualize ourselves as we would appear to an onlooker. The faces of those closest to us may be a blur, their presence felt emotionally without being precisely pictured.

Disappearance, self-effacement and invisibility are themes in many artists' work, a counter-current to the seemingly universal compulsion to self-publicize that the internet inspires. Reasons for withdrawing from the public gaze and into personal life may be psychological, political or socio-theological. The specific conditions in Saudi Arabia may not necessarily be replicated elsewhere – except of course that they are, wherever repressive societies lay down the law about personal relations, and especially for certain groups such as gay people, who are harassed and oppressed in half the world. Hiding from the eye of the authorities is bound to induce a state of mind that is instinctively averse to the camera and to other potentially incriminating forms of documentary evidence. Illegal immigration is, in moral terms, a mild offence.

Who could blame someone for wanting to get away from impossible circumstances at any cost? The artist Julio César Morales grew up in a Mexican border town, and based his series of drawings *Undocumented Interventions* (2007–ongoing) on US Government Immigration website photographs of unsuccessful attempts to smuggle people across the border. These are poignant memorials to individuals who are heroes, in a sense: they have taken a risk, and the fact of their failure somehow makes them all the more worthy of sympathy.

Morales is an activist as well as an artist, and these drawings are intended to raise awareness and contribute to the debate about illegal immigration and the marginalized status of Latino communities in the US. By translating the official x-ray photos exposing the immigrants' subterfuge into the gentle, timeless medium of watercolour, the artist softens the images, just as a traditional war artist might humanize the image of soldiers, conveying their vulnerability and dignity. The intimacy of a drawing can thus subvert the meaning of what was intended to be a harshly factual piece of documentary evidence. This helps to explain why certain artists devote long hours to painstakingly rendering and altering pre-existing photographs (or, in AlSaud's case, negatives) by hand. It is a minor act of personal resistance to the ruthless hegemony of the machine, a declaration of independence from definitions imposed from above.

Richard Forster addresses what he calls the 'persuasive power' of the photograph as an index to the real. How to unsettle that authority, that implicit claim to an unambiguous and stable meaning? Forster's drawings are based on photographs from his extensive archive of visual documents and reflect his 'experience of site/place and my research into particular social/political contexts and histories'. His initial photographic exercises are buttressed by second-hand research involving images from the internet, books and magazines. 'These "ethnographic studies" I begin to internalize through the slow, concentrated effort of drawing.' One instance of his preoccupation with ethnography – specifically modernist design and social experiment – can be seen in the work *Two Girls Dancing, East Germany* (2012), for which he uses a photograph of two girls dancing in East Germany in the 1980s. The German Democratic Republic was a totalitarian state with one of the most extensive secret police networks in the world, equivalent to contemporary Saudi Arabia in the extent that it reached into the personal lives of its citizens – although this was an intrusion based on altogether different principles. Like AlSaud's images of young people socializing and Talbot's

remembrances of her early life, Forster's image is drenched in nostalgic detail: hairstyles and clothes that evoke a moment in history. And like AlSaud he intervenes – by cropping out the boys with whom these girls were dancing. 'Somehow the image became purer with only the two girls dancing, and this was an informed but ultimately subjective personal response to the notion of *ostalgie* [the German term for nostalgia for aspects of life in the former DDR].' Through this subjective act, Forster destroys the documentary validity of the image but simultaneously reminds us that it was already subjectively cropped by the photographer: it was never a neutral record of an objectively perceived event.

An artist who draws with equally astonishing verisimilitude but with quite different motives is David Haines, who constructs his compositions from multiple photographic sources, some found on the internet and others taken himself. In his recent drawings, Haines has been less interested in the fetish subcultures that have been his subject in the past, and more in the possibility of private spiritual epiphany. In the 2013 work *Boy with a Laptop*, for instance, the religious symbols surrounding the boy lend a metaphysical significance to the light emanating from the computer screen. Perhaps this quasi-mystical dimension was always implicit in this artist's work: earthly degradation aspiring to transcendence, being-in-the-world as a drop-off point for heaven. Nonetheless, as a fellow perfectionist Haines would doubtless agree with Forster's observation that 'the digital age has consolidated the interiority of the obsessive and intimate bedroom practice' of slow, extended-time drawing. The recluse can now access the world electronically without the inconvenience and embarrassment of having to go out and meet other people. The social sphere, the very ground of the encounter between self and other, is in flux and possibly shrinking, leaving increased space for the personal sphere. And this personal sphere – by no means a new subject in art – is the constant preoccupation of many contemporary figurative artists as it shifts and is constantly redefined in the modern age.

While fasting in Tibet, when the hardship, transience and fragility of earthly life dawned on him, Li Jin discovered his creative subjects: food and sex – the good life – depicted with humour and relish and a skill worthy of the Chinese masters of brush and ink. In the 1980s Li Jin became associated with the New Literati, a group in Tianjin made up of artists seeking to revive the tradition of scholar–painters working in South China in the fifteenth and sixteenth centuries, who had valued personal expression and spontaneity over truth to nature. Li Jin is more irreverent and playful than his peers, however, confining himself to the light-hearted indulgences of everyday life. He subverts erotic ideals with gentle satire, portraying imperfect bodies in their plump reality enjoying the sensual pleasures of eating, drinking, making love and lounging in hot tubs. The men are loosely modelled on the artist himself, while the women may resemble his ideal: sweet and voluptuous. Yet Li Jin reserves the majority of his creative attention for the epicurean pleasures of the table. He has painted a banqueting table 23 metres long and once inscribed onto one of his works the entire menu of a feast he experienced when on an 'Art & Gourmet' tour of ten cities across China, Europe and the United States.

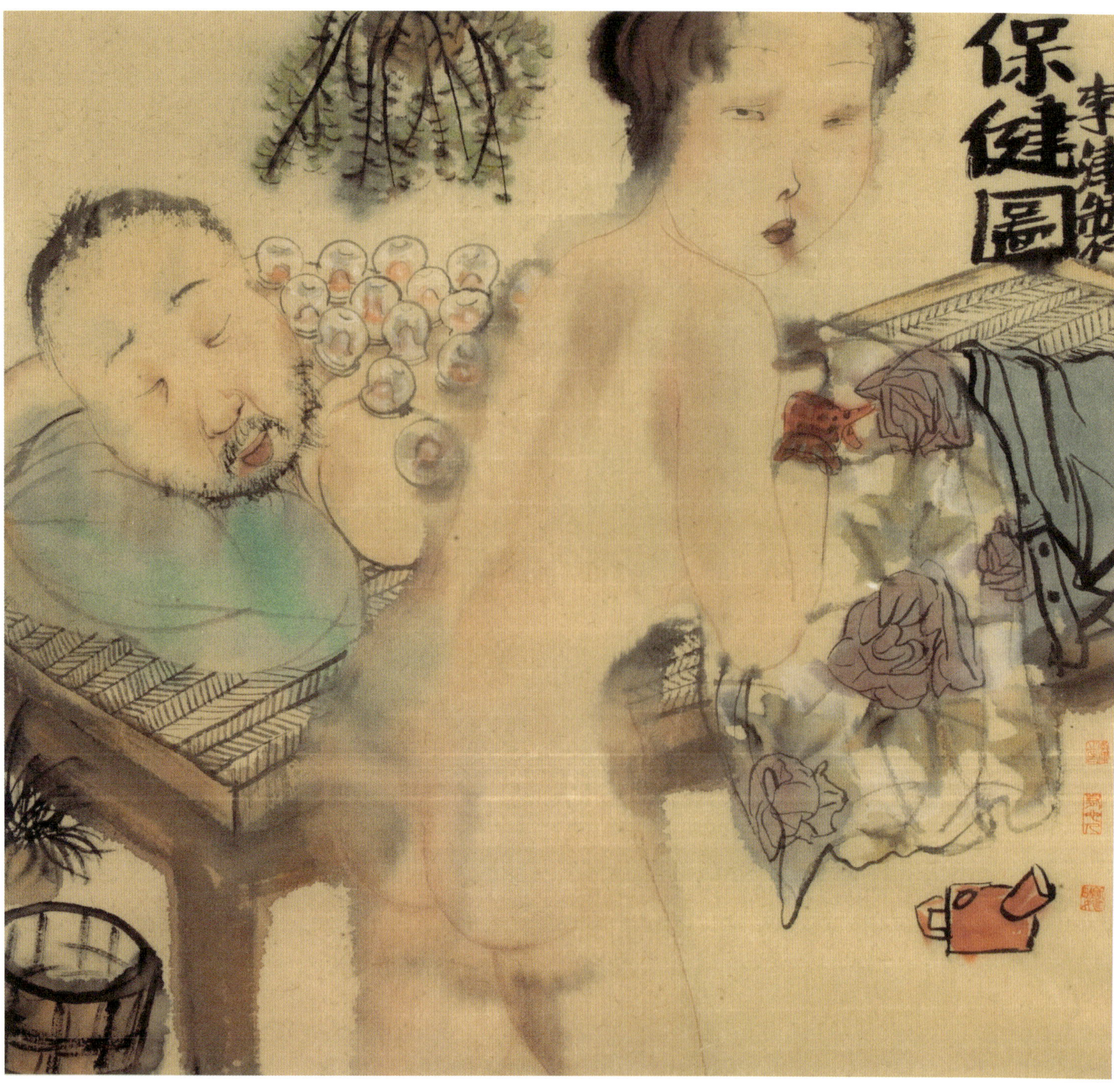

Keeping Healthy, 2006
Ink and colour on paper
39.5 x 42 cm (15 ½ x 16 ½ in.)

Picture of a Pink Lady, 2006 >
Ink and colour on paper
38 × 41 cm (15 × 16 ⅛ in.)

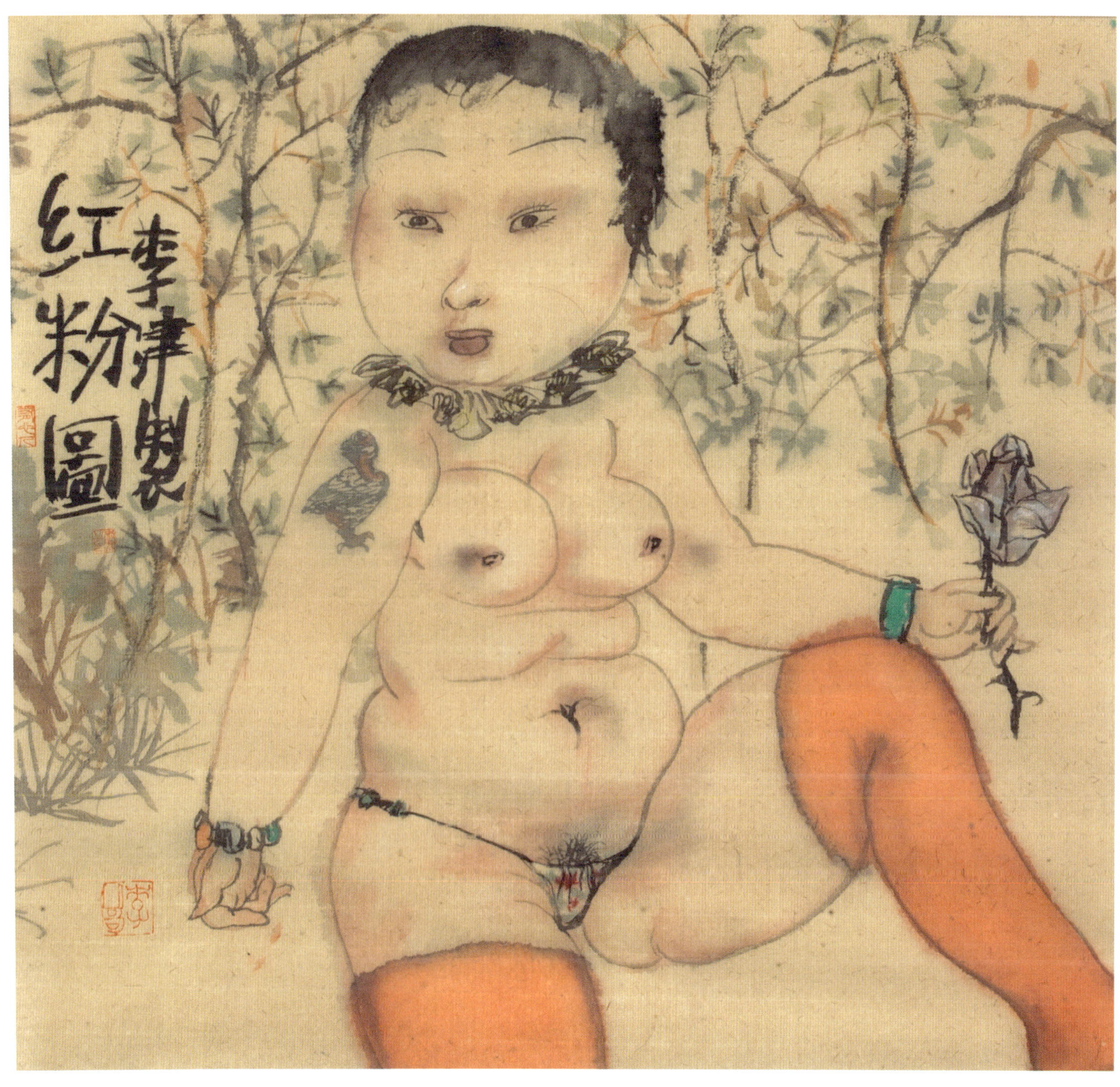

紅粉圖
李津製

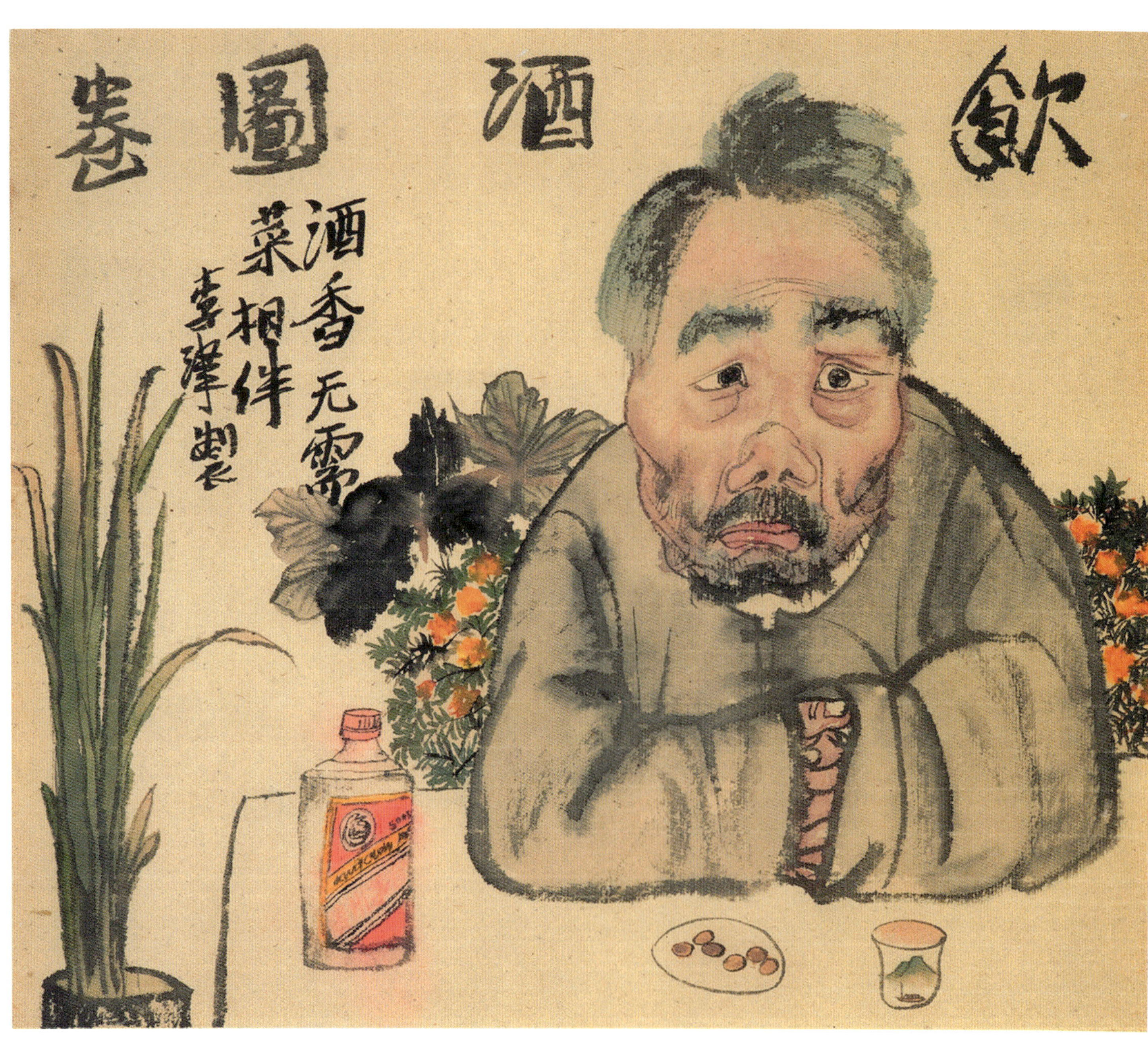

Liquor, 2011
Ink and colour on paper
38 × 44 cm (15 × 17 ⅜ in.)

A Family Portrait, 2003 >
Ink and colour on paper
43 × 45 cm (16 ⅞ × 17 ¾ in.)

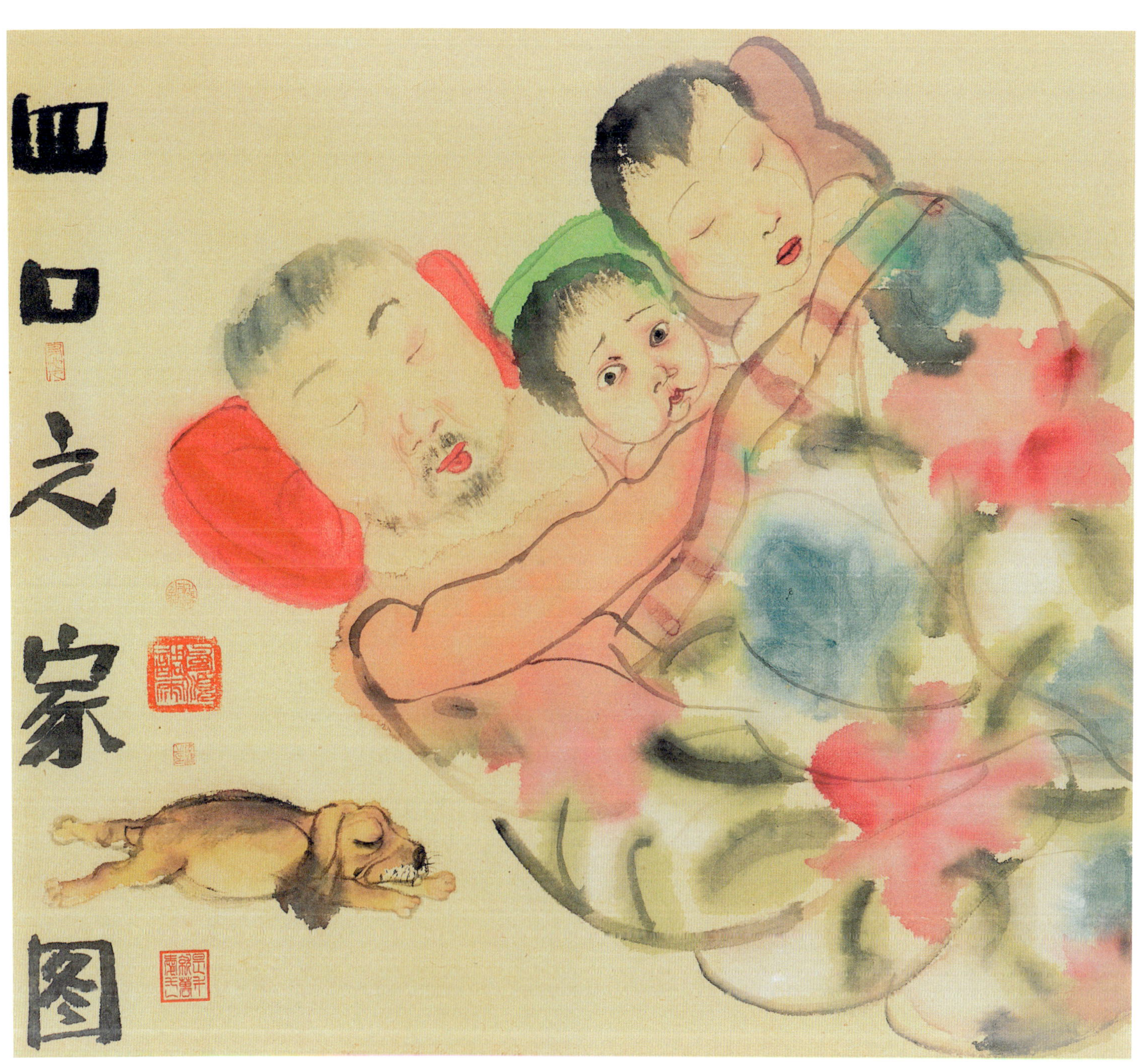

四口之家图

Emma Talbot's watercolour drawings have the unselfconscious intimacy of a personal journal, with private thoughts, memories and imaginings recorded in a looping girlish hand, as though intended to be seen by no one but herself. There is a consistency to her style that allows her to incorporate whichever phenomena happen to occur to her – mundane details and emotionally charged moments – and translate them fluently into her own visual language. One has the sense of seeing a world through Talbot's eyes, exactly as she experienced it. Her subdued palette of secondary colours filters and unifies the imagery, suggesting that these are scenes recalled from across a void of time rather than an immediate, diaristic recapitulation of the day's events.

In fact, each frame of Talbot's loosely assembled narratives illustrates a scene recalled from her past. They are drawn spontaneously, without preparatory sketches, thus becoming exercises in the power of recollection. She includes a plethora of local detail – the Victorian bricks and tiles, the period lampshades, wallpaper and bedspreads, handbags, sweaters and coats – that together evoke a distinctly British atmosphere of claustrophobia and constraint. The space is tightly enclosed and the heavy dark lines suggest an underlying shadow of menace or loneliness.

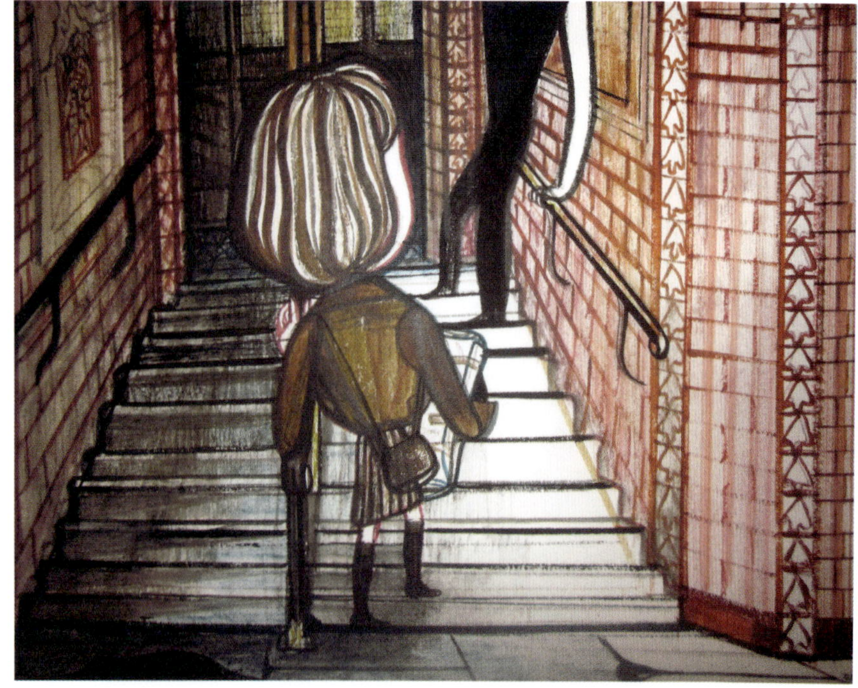

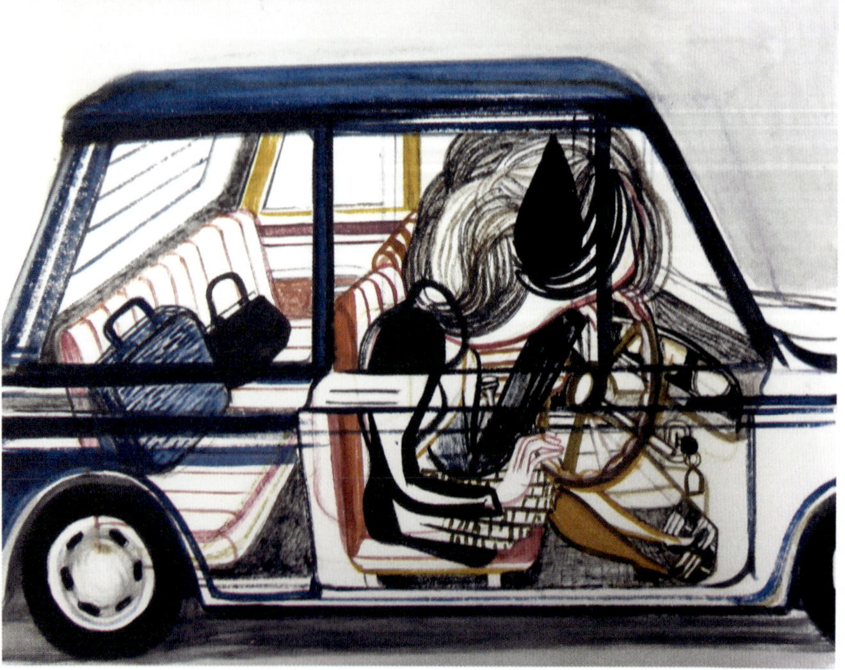

(this page, top) *First Day Birmingham,* 2013
Watercolour on paper
24 × 30 cm (9 ½ × 11 ¾ in.)

(this page, below) *Leaving Harrow,* 2012
Watercolour on paper
24 × 30 cm (9 ½ × 11 ¾ in.)

(opposite, top) *Midnight Running Under,* 2013
Watercolour on paper
24 × 30 cm (9 ½ × 11 ¾ in.)

(opposite, centre) *Candlewick,* 2012
Watercolour on paper
24 × 30 cm (9 ½ × 11 ¾ in.)

(opposite, below) *Novel Olivetti Flower of Strood,* 2013
Watercolour on paper
24 × 30 cm (9 ½ × 11 ¾ in.)

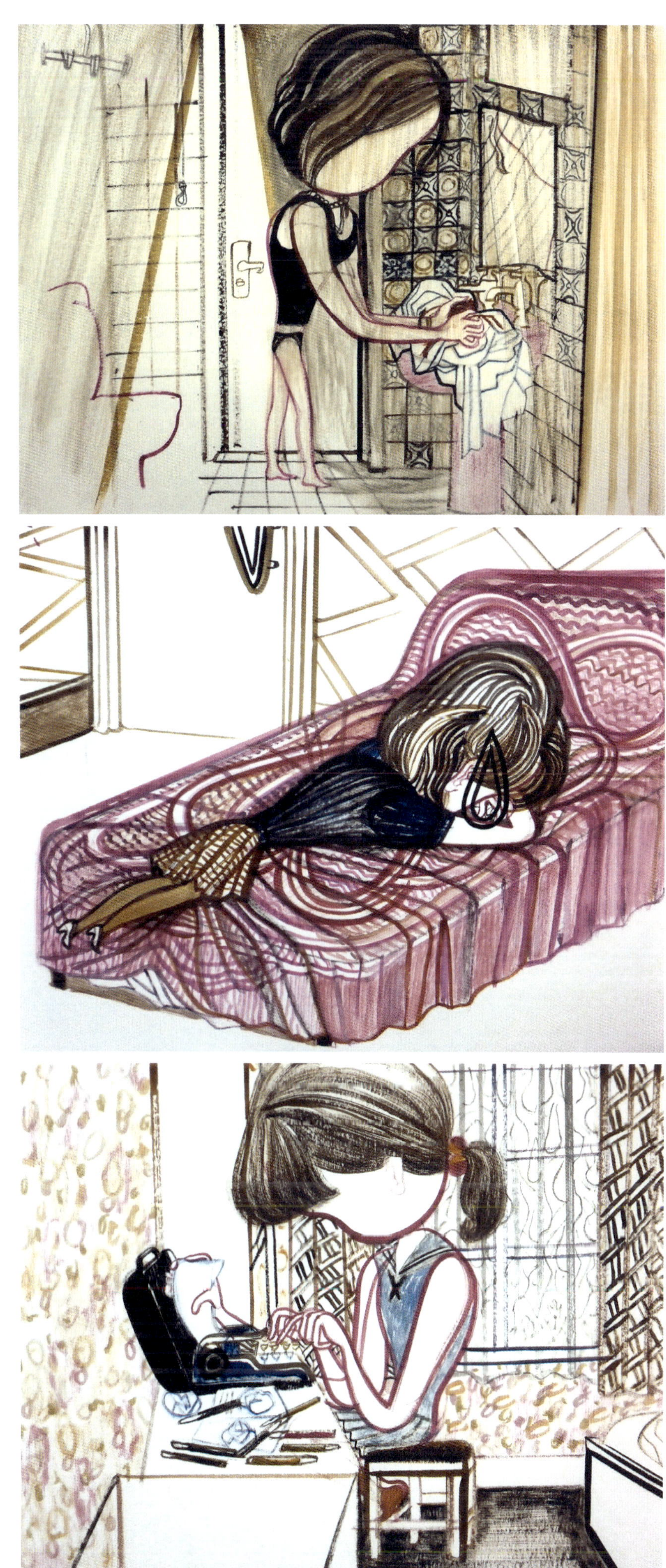

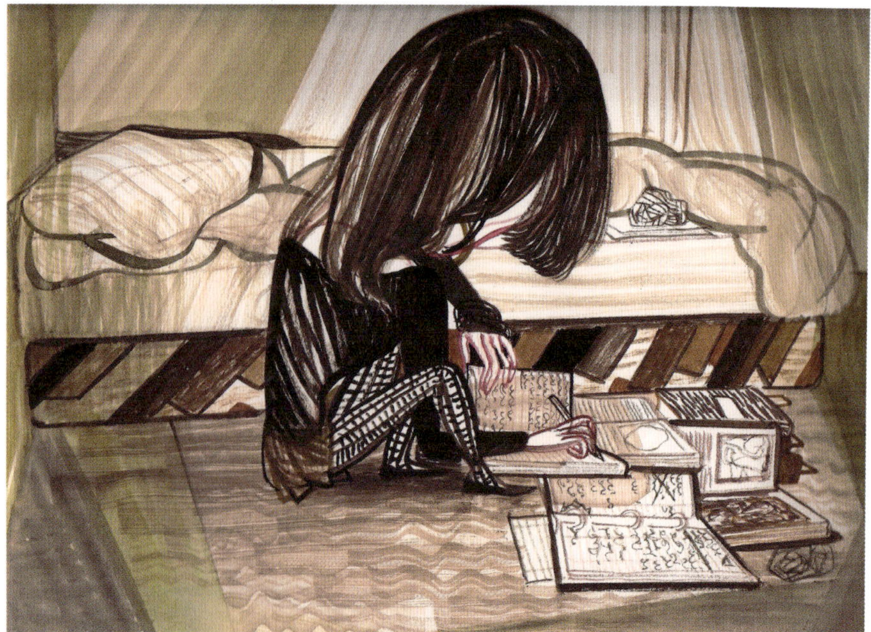

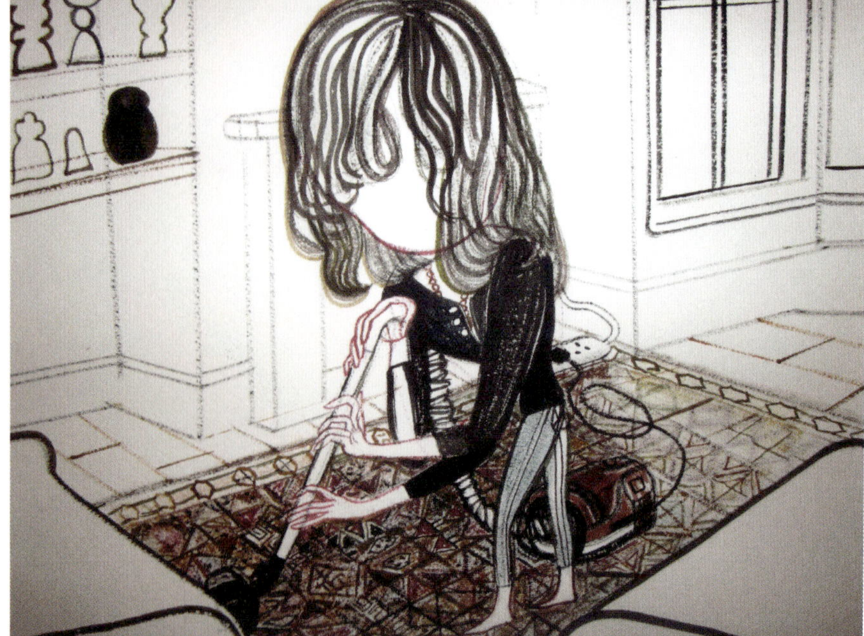

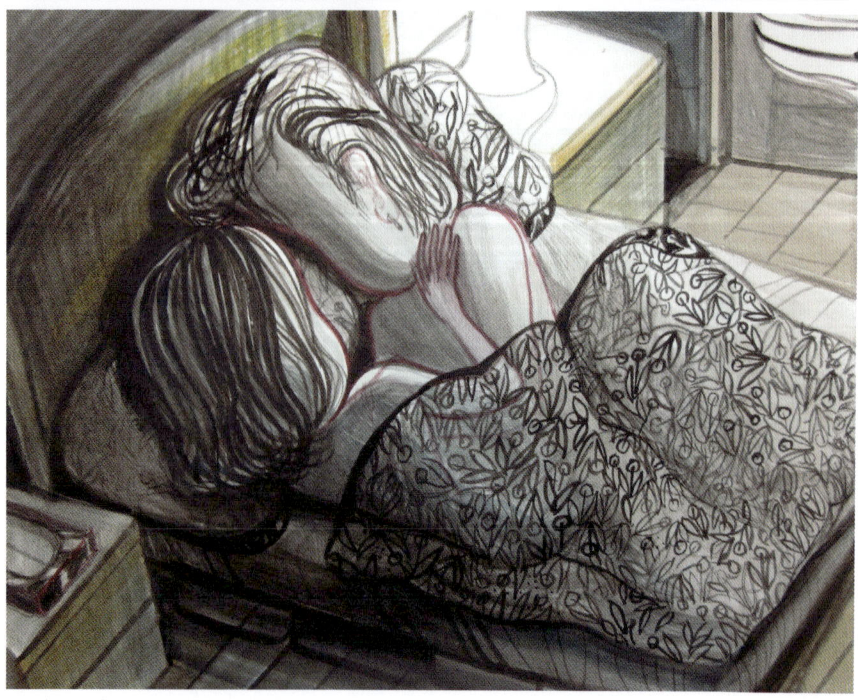

(this page, top) *Writing,* 2011
Watercolour on paper
24 × 30 cm (9 ½ × 11 ¾ in.)

(this page, centre) *The House the Black Book Hoovering,* 2013
Watercolour on paper
24 × 30 cm (9 ½ × 11 ¾ in.)

(this page, bottom) *Lovers,* 2010
Watercolour on paper
24 × 30 cm (9 ½ × 11 ¾ in.)

(opposite, top) *Second Hand,* 2011
Watercolour on paper
24 × 30 cm (9 ½ × 11 ¾ in.)

(opposite, centre) *The Hill (Flower of Strood),* 2013
Watercolour on paper
24 × 30 cm (9 ½ × 11 ¾ in.)

(opposite, below) *Wedding Ring,* 2011
Watercolour on paper
24 × 30 cm (9 ½ × 11 ¾ in.)

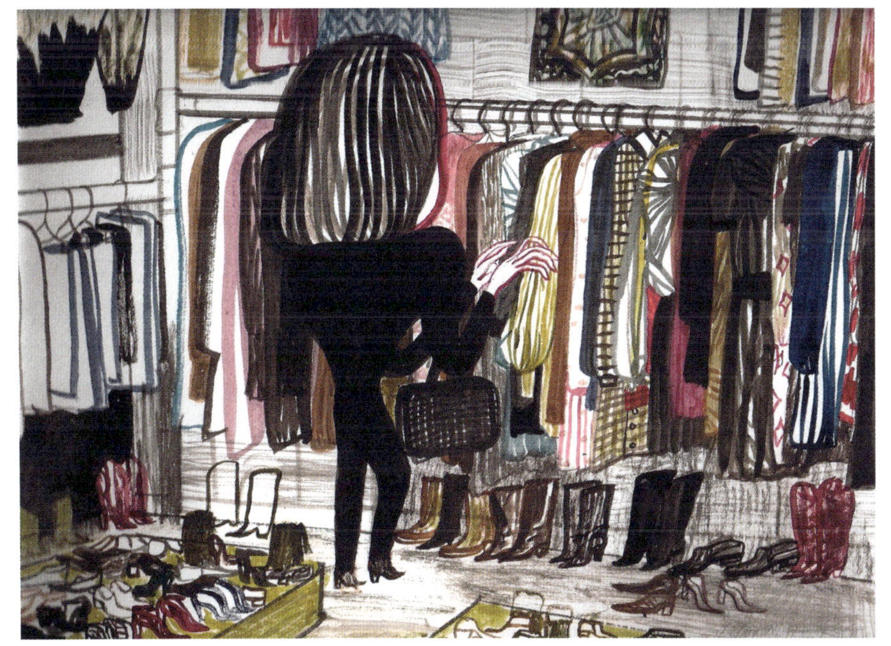

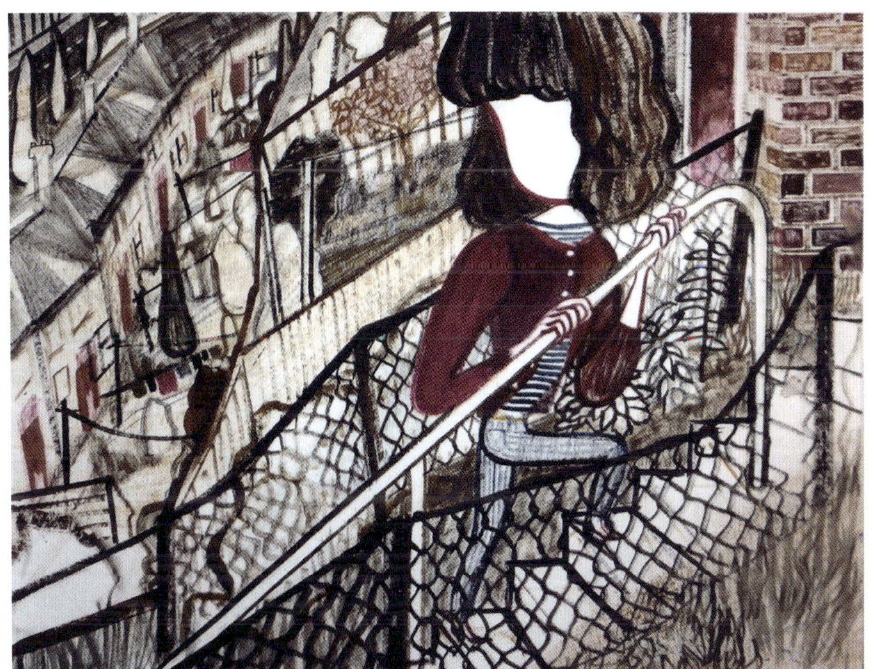

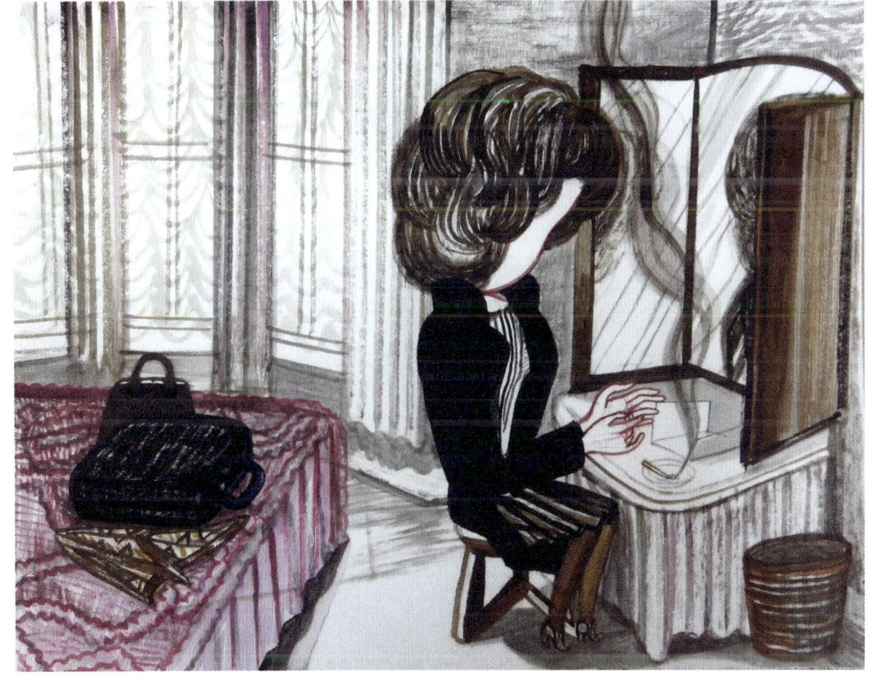

As a painter and draughtswoman, Amy Sillman explores an imaginative space between abstraction and figuration. The human form is invariably present; even in her most abstract images it can be discerned in the awkward entanglements and clusters of lines. Sillman is also a cartoonist and a satirical commentator on art and the art world, and humour is an important ingredient in all of her work. Yet it is her way of looking at people, observing them in relation to one another, and representing them abstractly while holding onto the emotional significance that distinguishes them as subjects, that gives her work its psychological charge.

Third Person Singular is an ongoing series of ink drawings of couples who are personal friends of the artist. She asks them to pose for her *as couples*, assuming their characteristic ways of being around one another, whether sprawling and leaning cosily against each other or lying comfortably entwined. She draws them from life, and then makes further drawings from memory, until four or five generations away from the initial drawing the shapes of faces and limbs have become abstracted, packed into the rectangular space of the paper in a tightly knotted composition. The 'third person' of the title is the artist herself, who observes this intimacy but is ultimately excluded from it.

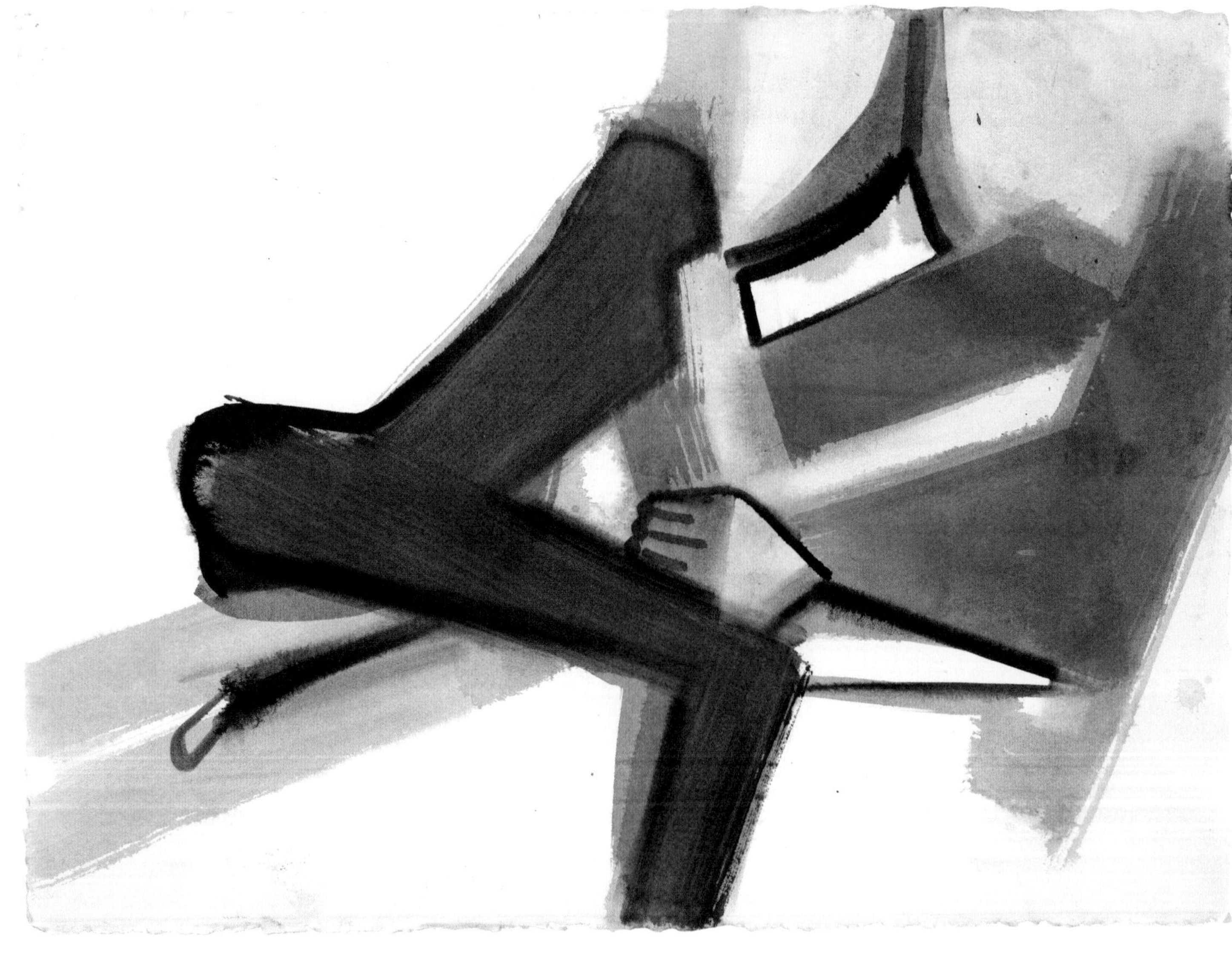

S&E, 2007
Ink on paper
57.8 × 76.2 cm (22 ¾ × 30 in.)

B&P, 2007 >
Ink on paper
57.8 × 76.2 cm (22 ¾ × 30 in.)

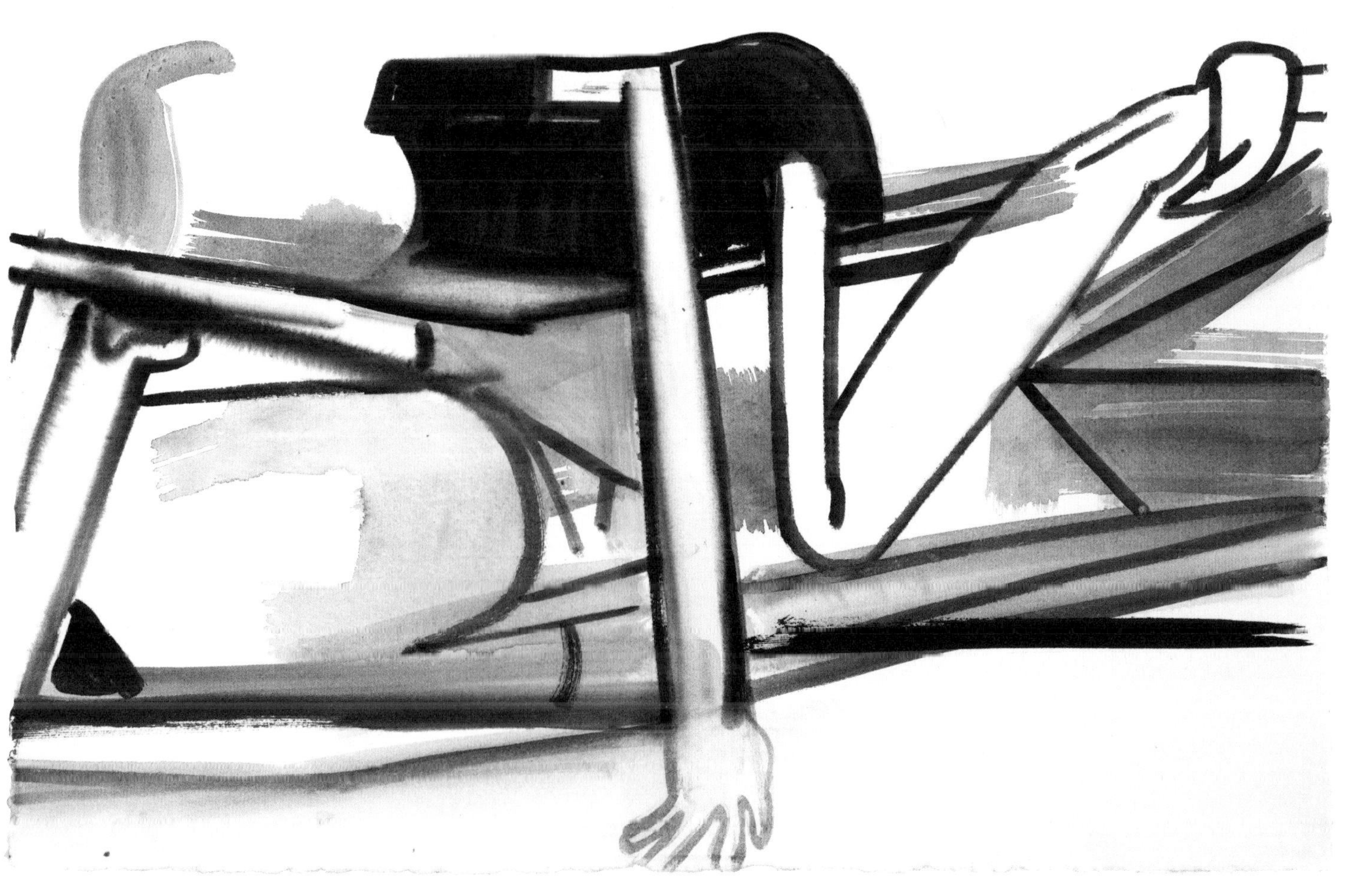

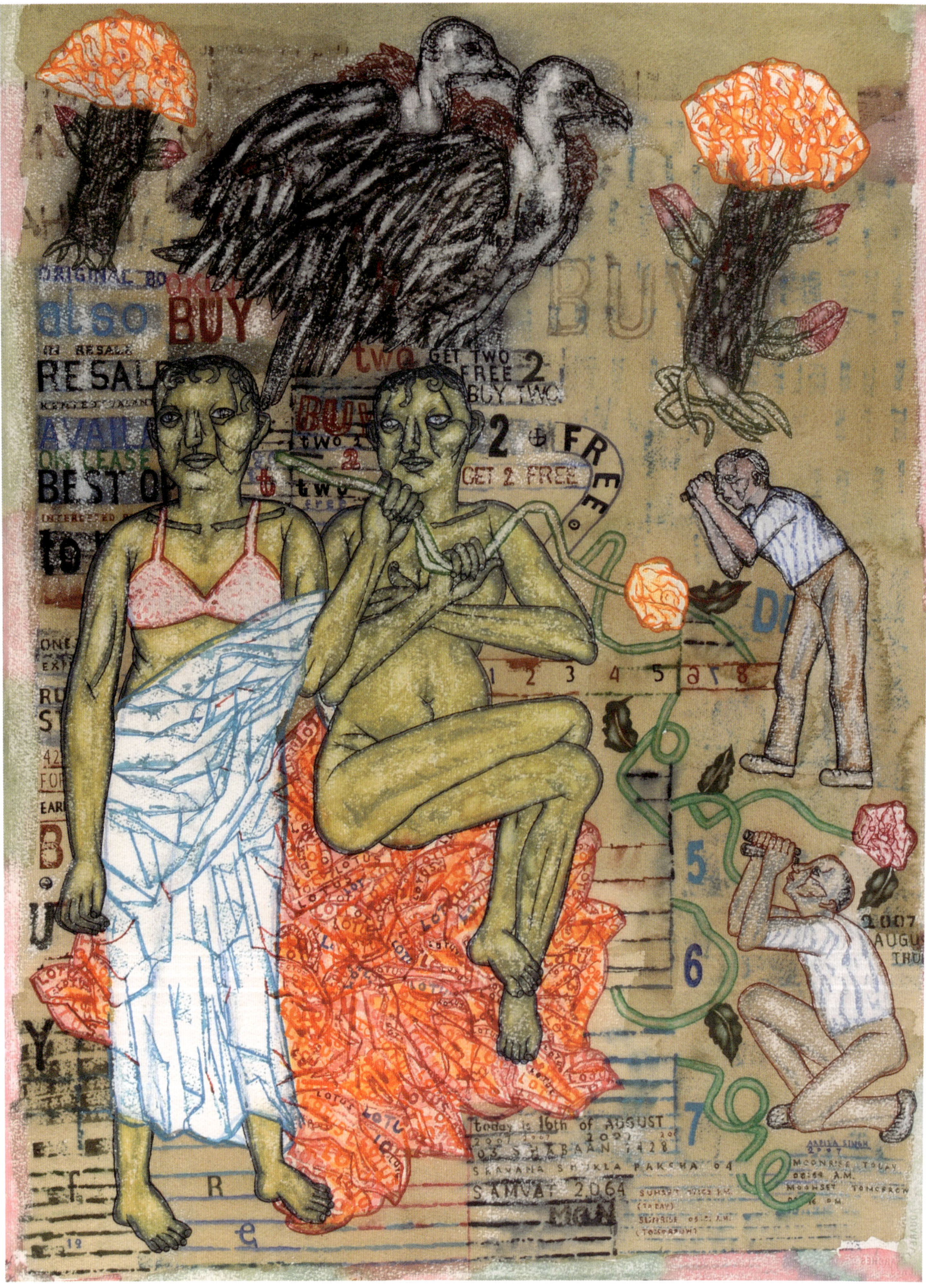

ARPITA SINGH *Born 1937, West Bengal, India. Lives and works in New Delhi, India*

During the 1960s and '70s Arpita Singh made abstract paintings and designed fabrics for the Weavers' Service Centre, the base for the traditional handloom industry in rural Bengal. Like many Indian artists of her generation, her loyalties were divided between a commitment to the 'universalist' values of international modernism on the one hand, and an allegiance to indigenous traditions on the other. As a consequence, the distinctive visual language that has evolved in her oil paintings and ink and watercolour drawings combines the whimsical poetics of her favourite Western painters, Marc Chagall and Paul Klee, with the formal directness and simplicity of textile design and Indian folk art traditions such as Kalighat painting.

Personal biography, social commentary and fantasy coexist in Singh's dreamlike narratives. In her watercolours, the surface is layered and translucent; the flattened picture plane is scattered with repeatedly stencilled figures, words and numbers, road maps, town plans and ornamental motifs. The imagery contains a distinctly autobiographical element: in recent years, Singh's work has featured poignant allusions to ageing – the female body exposed, its internal organs revealed. The underlying threat of violence and social catastrophe is also a recurring theme, frequently signalled in Singh's work by the depiction of men in uniform, pistols in hand.

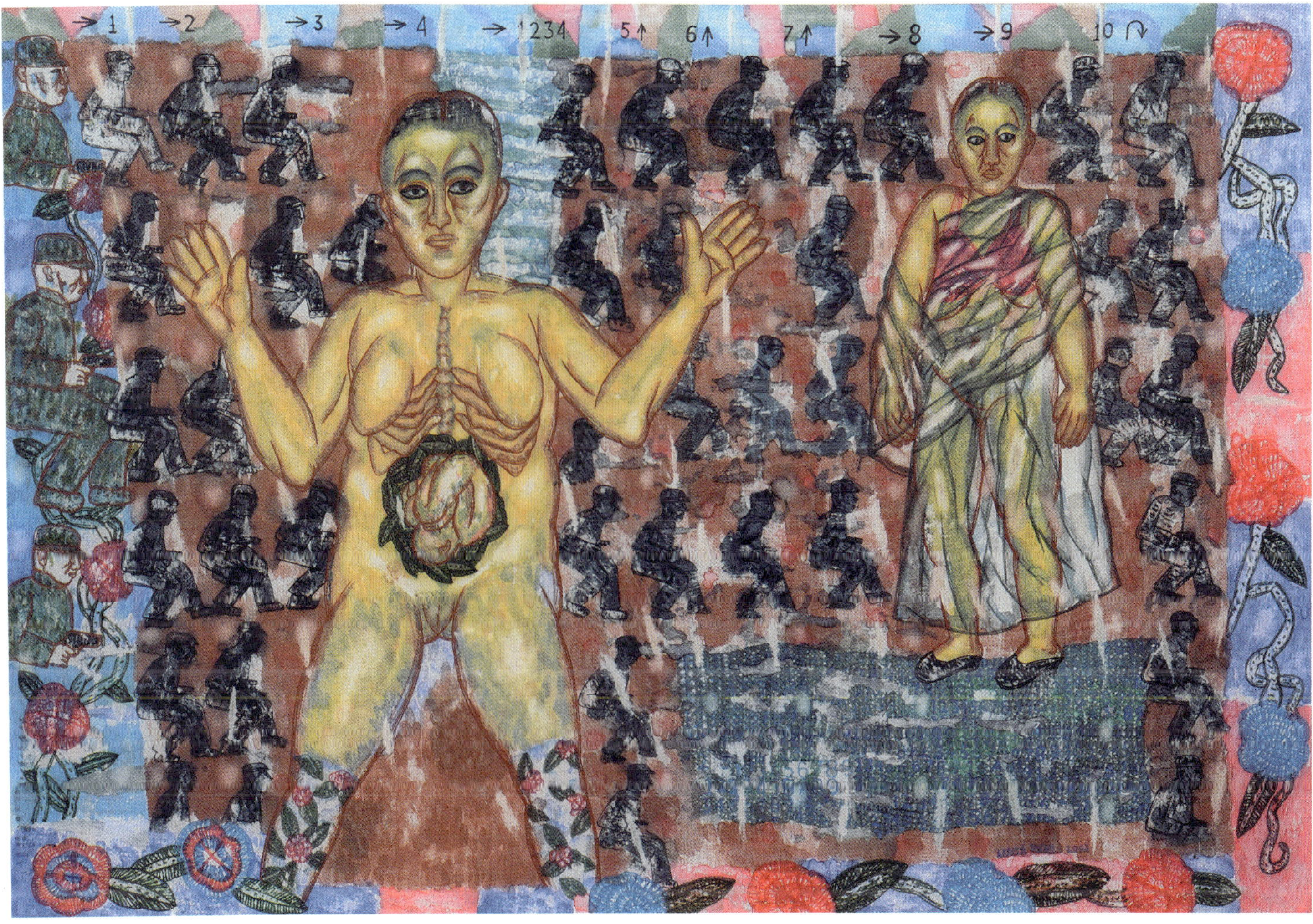

< *Buy 2 get two free*, 2007
Watercolour on paper
80 × 59.7 cm (31 ½ × 23 ½ in.)

Security Check, 2003
Watercolour on board
55.9 × 81.3 cm (22 × 32 in.)

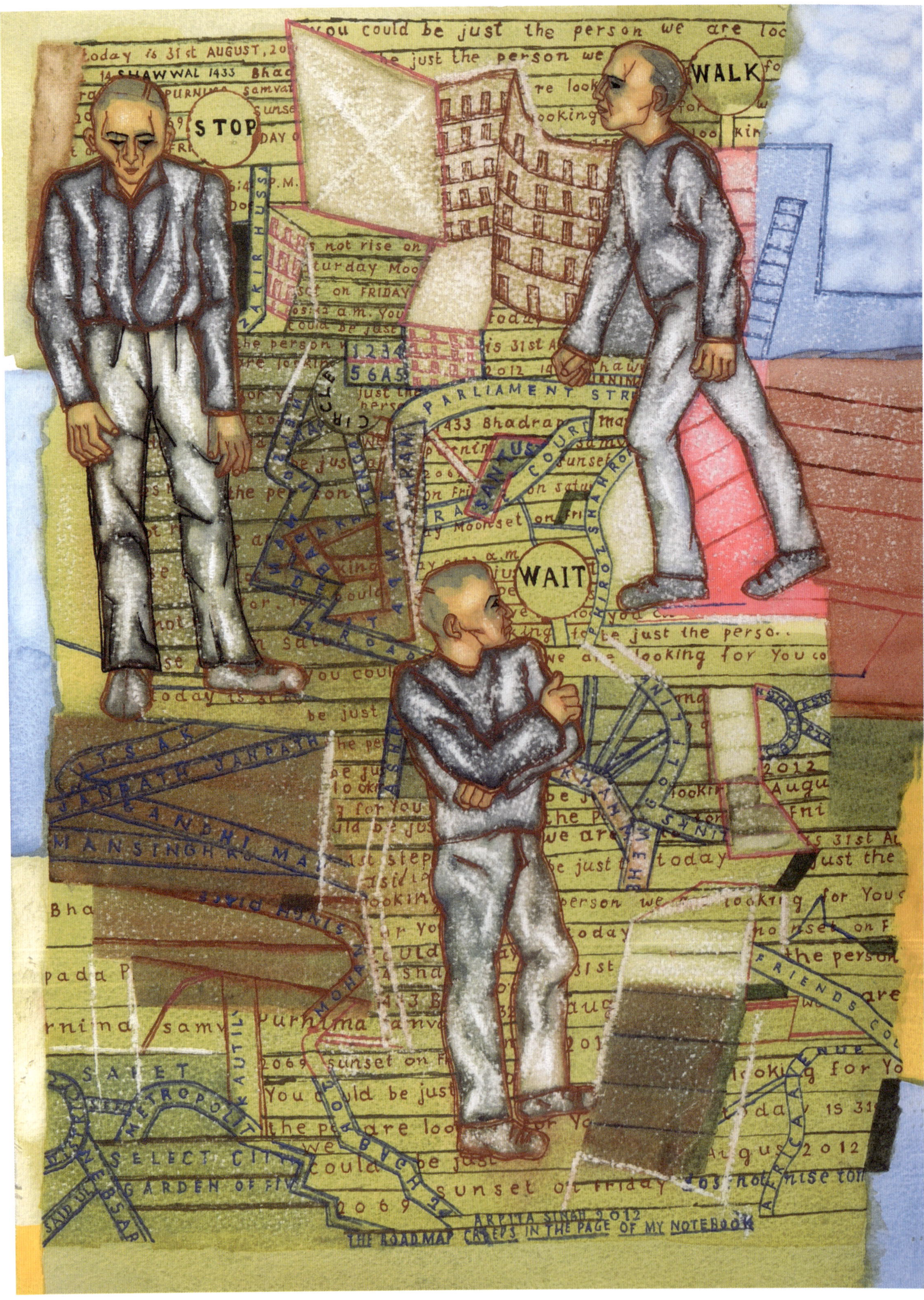

The Roadmap Creeps in the Page of My Notebook, 2012
Watercolour on paper
40.6 × 29.2 cm (16 × 11 ½ in.)

B for Boxes, 2007 >
Watercolour on paper
76.2 × 57 cm (30 × 22 ½ in.)

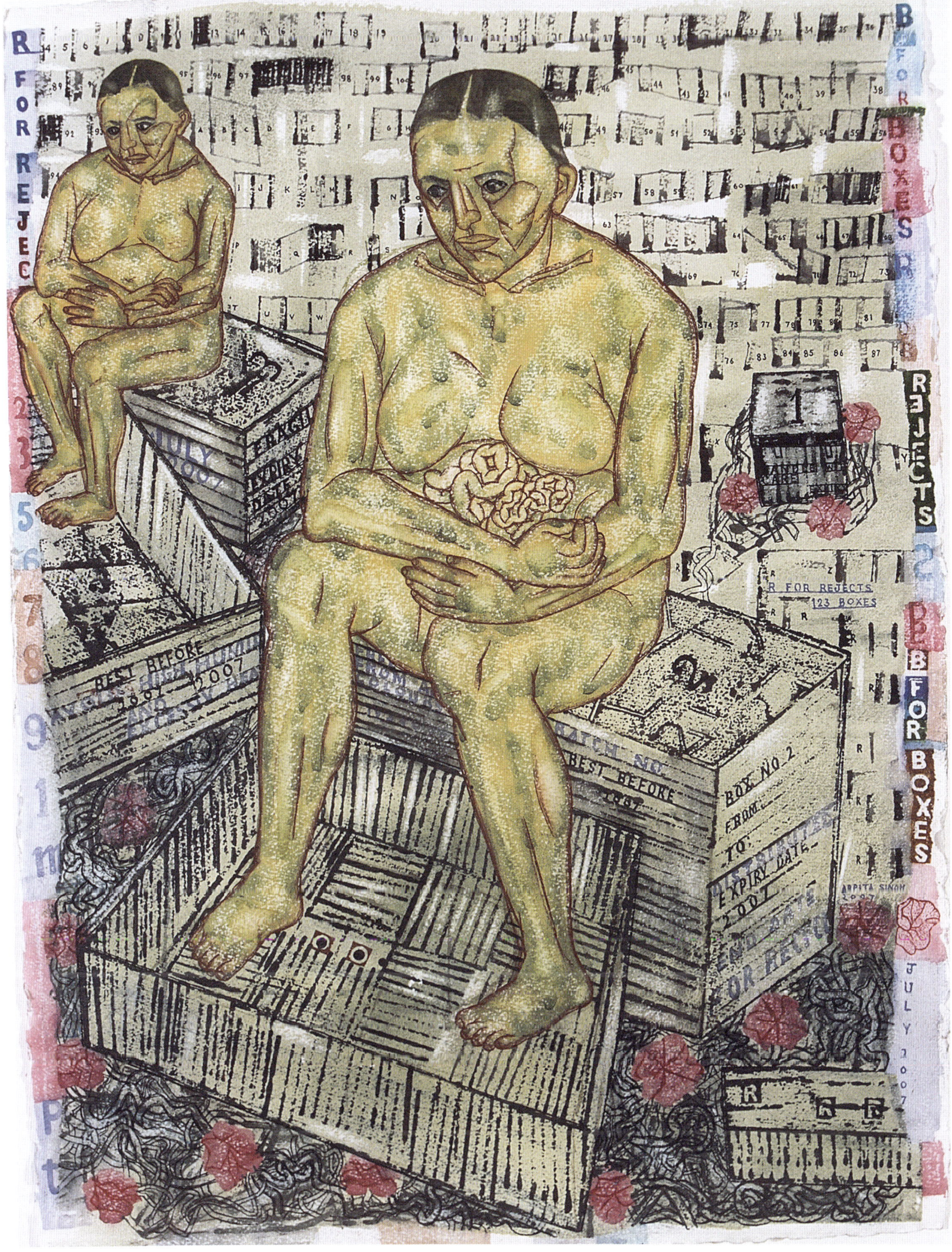

R FOR REJECT
R FOR REJECTS
B FOR BOXES
R FOR REJECTS
R FOR BOXES
REJECTS
R FOR REJECTS
123 BOXES
R FOR REJECTS
B FOR BOXES
JULY 2007
BEST BEFORE
2007
EXPIRY DATE
2007
BEST BEFORE
2007
BOX NO. 2
FROM
TO
EXPIRY DATE
2007
ARPITA SINGH
2007
JULY 2007

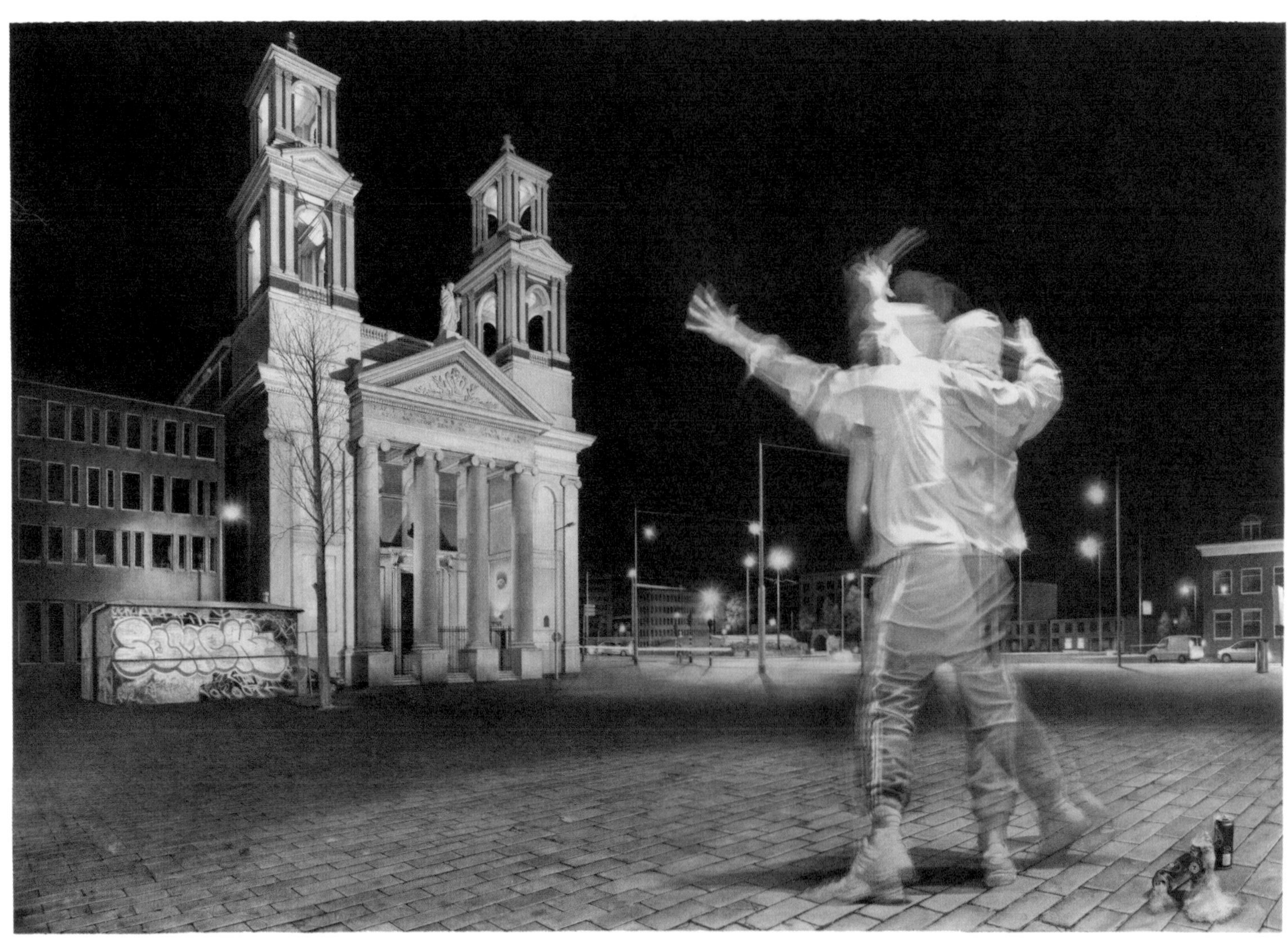

David Haines's immaculately executed fine pencil drawings are usually composed from photographic imagery sourced from gay websites, particularly the previously hermetic fetishist subcultures that became increasingly visible in the late 1990s when these groups began to share imagery online. Haines is fascinated by the way that certain gay groups imitate the straight world in their style of dress, such as the 'chav' sportswear look of heterosexual working class culture, which then becomes a private coded language. The inherent 'timelessness' of sportswear (which, Haines remarks, has changed relatively little since the 1930s) appealed to the artist as a costume for human dramas with more universal – and even metaphysical – significance.

Haines's drawings have a complicated relationship with photography. They are composed from a 'patchwork' of found images and staged scenarios. The marks are small, light and fine, but clearly discernible. Rather than photo-realism, his painstaking labours hark back to the obsessive rendering of the visible world by the Flemish masters. The drawing remains, in Haines's words, 'a true, direct and honest index of the presence and time of the artist who made it'.

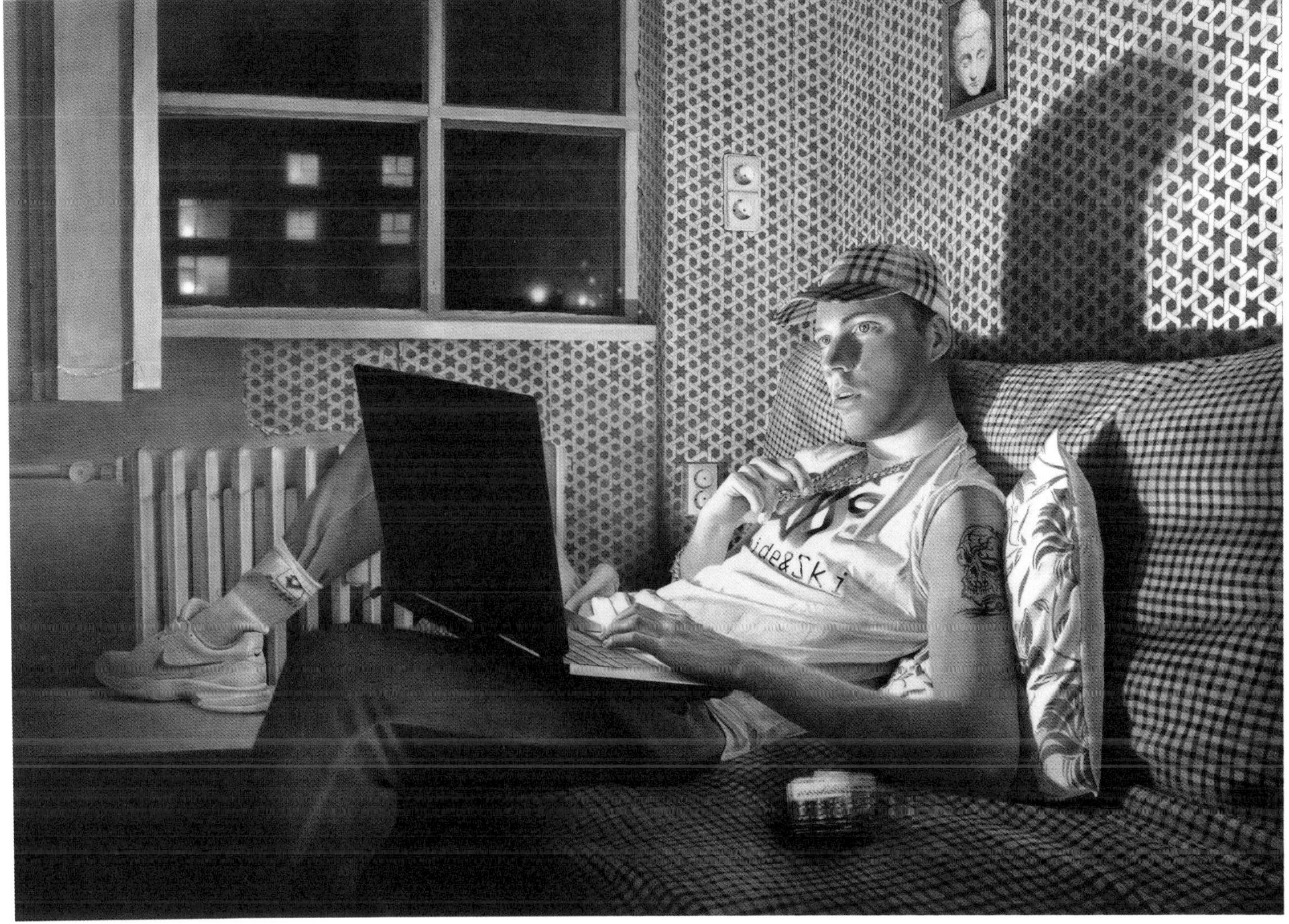

< *Radiant Bodies*, 2013
Graphite on paper
140.5 × 202 cm (55 ⅜ × 79 ½ in.)

Boy with a Laptop, 2013
Graphite on paper
99.5 × 140.5 cm (39 ⅛ × 55 ⅜ in.)

Tal R is a painter with a passion for drawing. 'The only thing I was really good at in primary school was drawing. But it was never called art – it was just what I did when the teacher was talking.' Tal R is a prolific image-maker, sampling from the vast visual output of mass culture and the street. He has stated that he always wanted to make art from his surroundings, and as a flâneur, roaming the city of Copenhagen, he has discovered the figures and motifs that serve his creative practice. The drawings here, executed in a fluid, intuitive line, relate to recent paintings, yet they do not feel like studies. The figure of the wanderer, an aimless, deadpan individual, recurs frequently – the artist's alter ego, with a stove-pipe hat and a vacant air, eating a banana on a bench or drifting past a strip club. The wanderer's name, 'S', is also the title of one of the drawings, and refers to Shlomo, the artist's own middle name and a Hebrew derivative of Solomon, 'the wise one'. Yet 'S' is ever the secondary character, Tal R explains, and never the hero. He is the archetypal singular self, banana in hand, reflecting on his own existence.

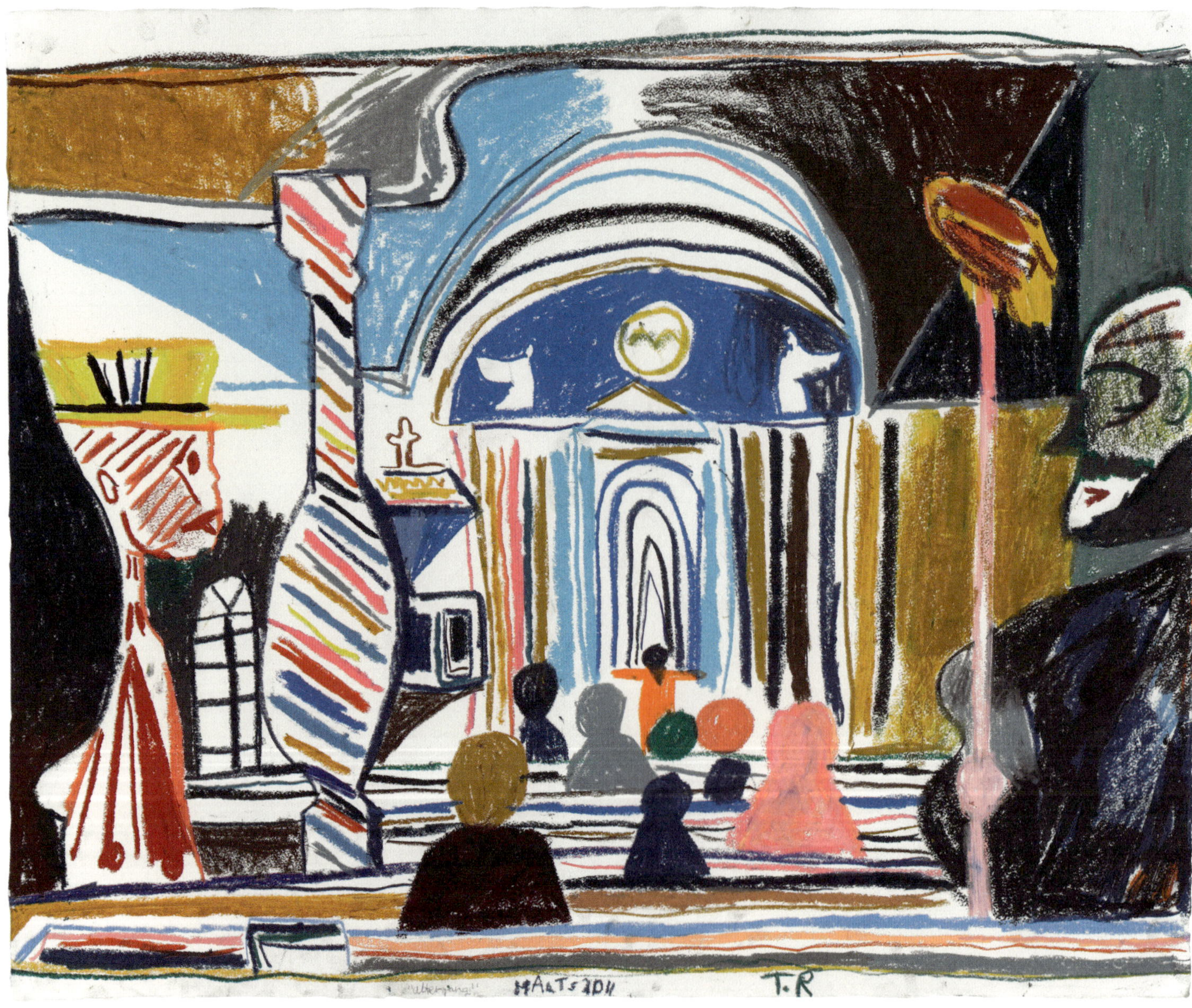

Altergang, 2011
Oil crayon on paper
77 × 94 cm (30 ⅜ × 37 in.)

Invisible Chair Little Version, 2013 >
Crayon, oil pastel, pigment and rabbit glue on paper
31 × 21 cm (12 ¼ × 8 ¼ in.)

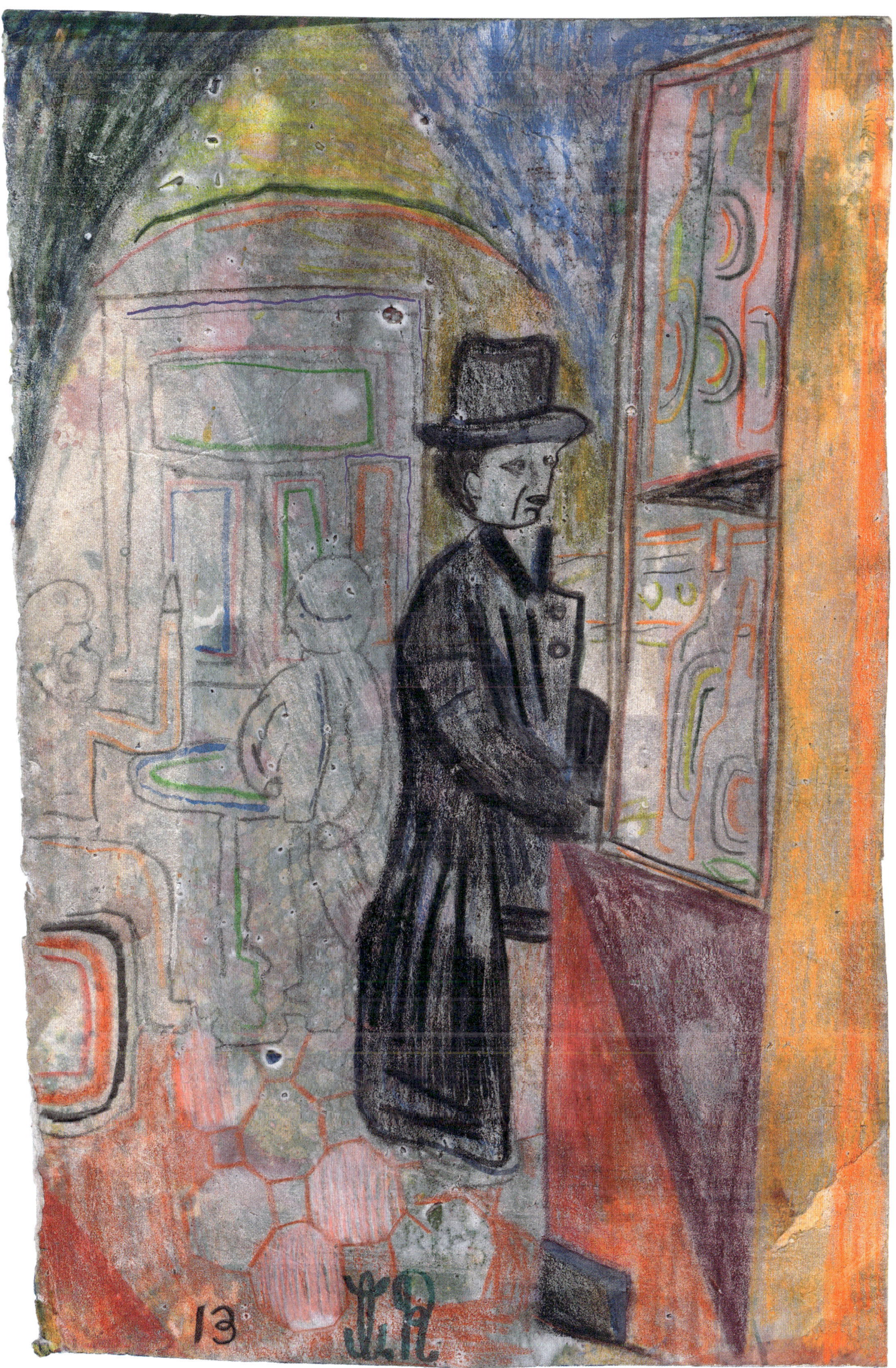
13

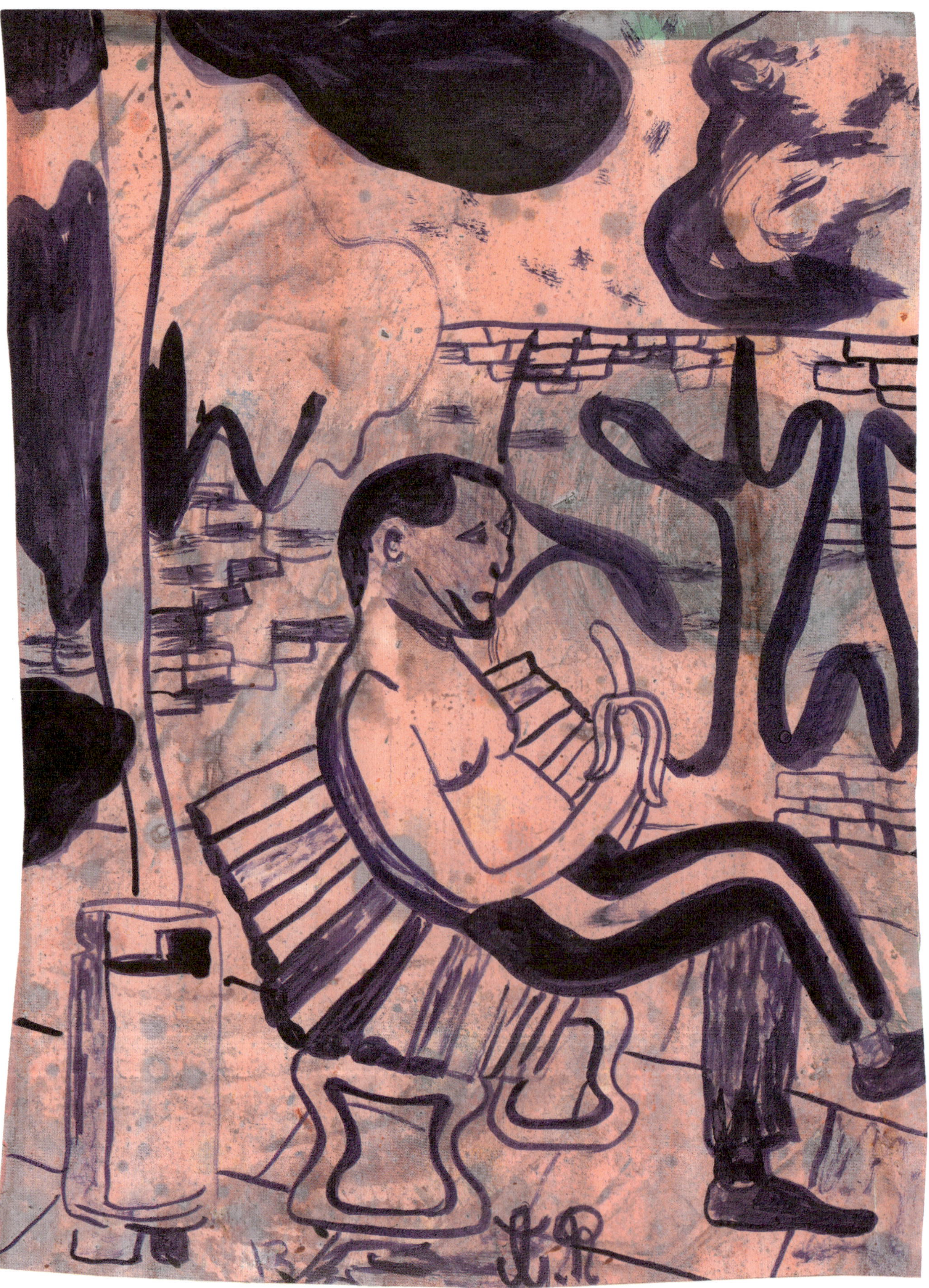

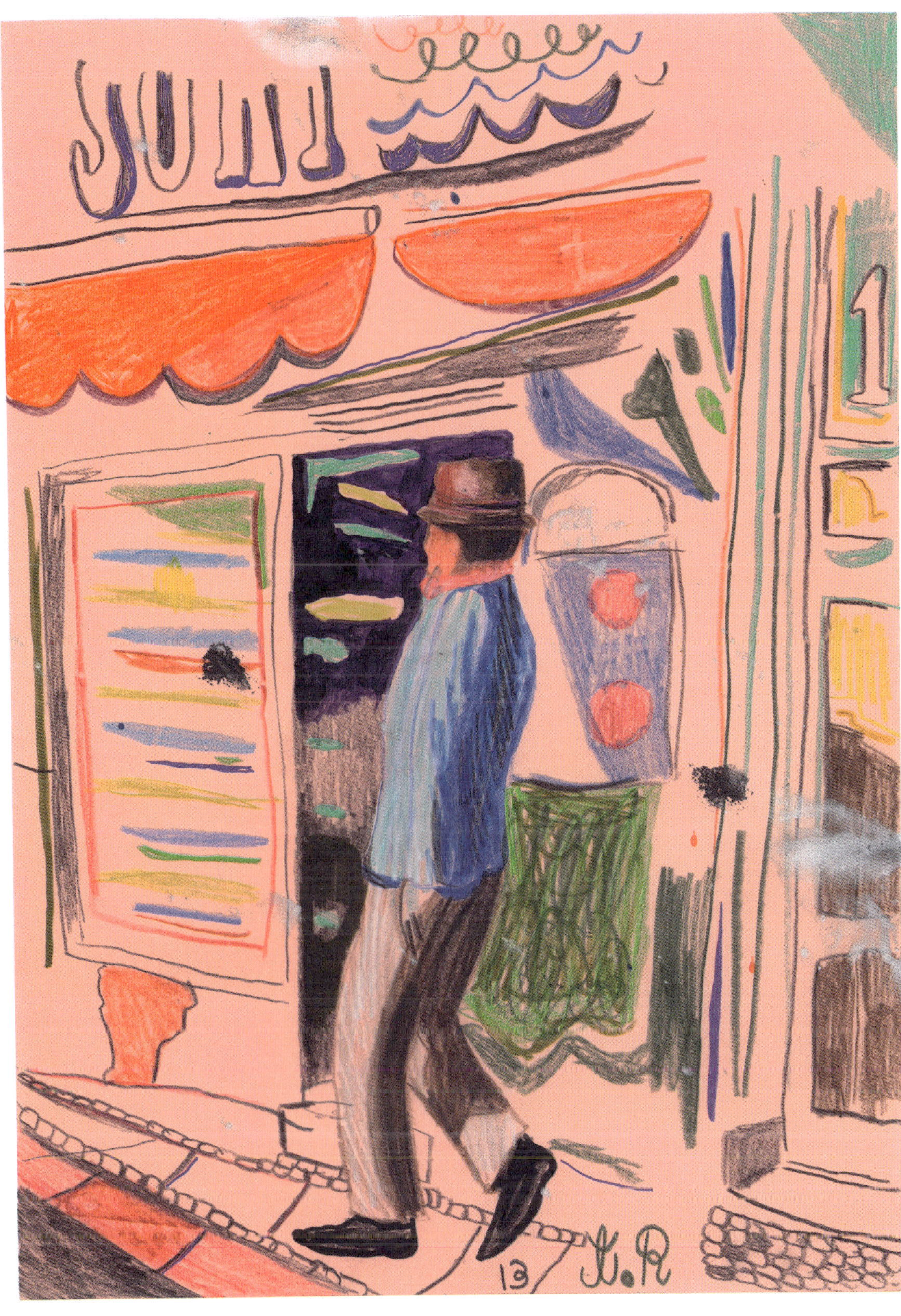

< *Bananen,* 2013
Pigment and rabbit glue on paper
32 × 24 cm (12 ⅝ × 9 ½ in.)

S, 2013
Crayon, ink, pigment and rabbit glue on paper
30 × 21 cm (11 ¾ × 8 ¼ in.)

124

Jowhara AlSaud studied film theory and photography in the US, and her series *Out of Line* (2008–10) began as an exploration of censorship in her native Saudi Arabia, where a small army of official censors is employed to black out parts of the body considered indecent in photographs published daily in magazines and newspapers. 'Skirts [are] lengthened and sleeves crudely added with black markers in magazines or faces blurred out on billboards', AlSaud observes. In *Out of Line*, she applies the black-marker language of the censors to her personal photographs – snapshots showing intimate fleeting moments with her friends and family – by making line drawings based on these images in which she omits the faces and skin. As well as parodying the erasure of identity through censorship, this has allowed her to subvert the taboo against bringing the 'personal portrait, commonly reserved for the private domestic space, into the public sphere'.

AlSaud's technique involves drawing directly onto her 4-inch by 5-inch negatives with a sharp etching tool, tracing the outlines of the figures and faces. Where the emulsion is scratched away, the light enters and it prints as black. She then photographs backgrounds with a large-format camera, and prints her snapshots onto the results. 'I've always felt that a photograph functions more like a memory,' she says, 'in that it's a singular perspective of a split second in time, entirely subjective and hence impressionable.'

(this page, top) *Halos,* 2008
C-print
76.2 × 101.6 cm (30 × 40 in.)

(this page, below) *Sway,* 2009
C-print
127 × 152.4 cm (50 × 60 in.)

(opposite, top) *Bed,* 2008
C-print
76.2 × 101.6 cm (30 × 40 in.)

(opposite, centre) *Airmail,* 2008
C-print
76.2 × 101.6 cm (30 × 40 in.)

(opposite, below) *Fan,* 2010
C-print
127 × 152.4 cm (50 × 60 in.)

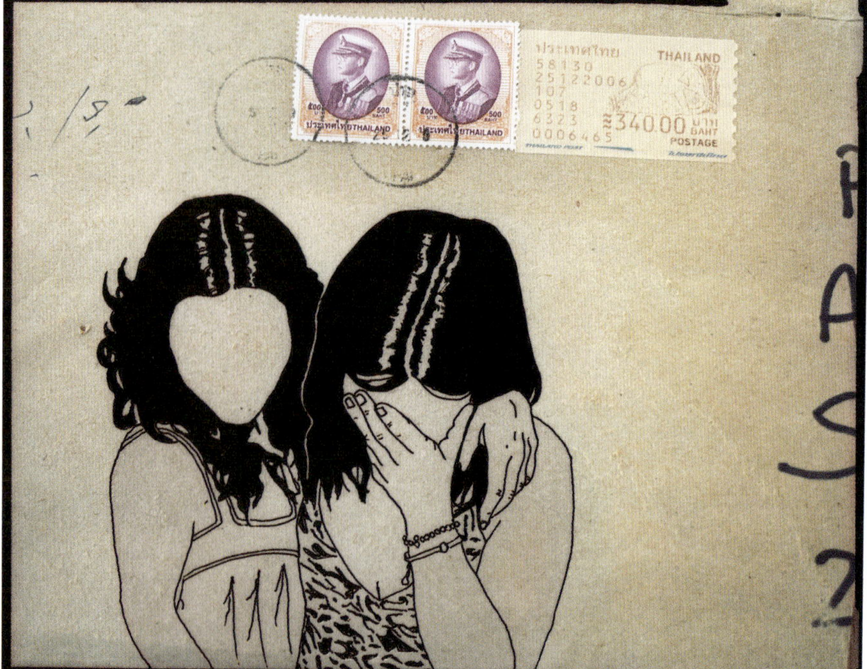

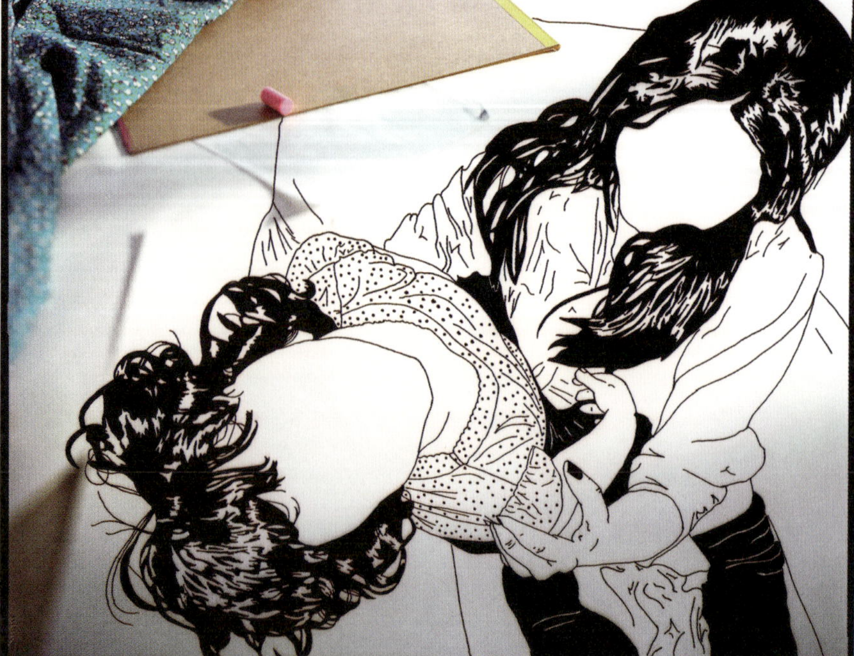

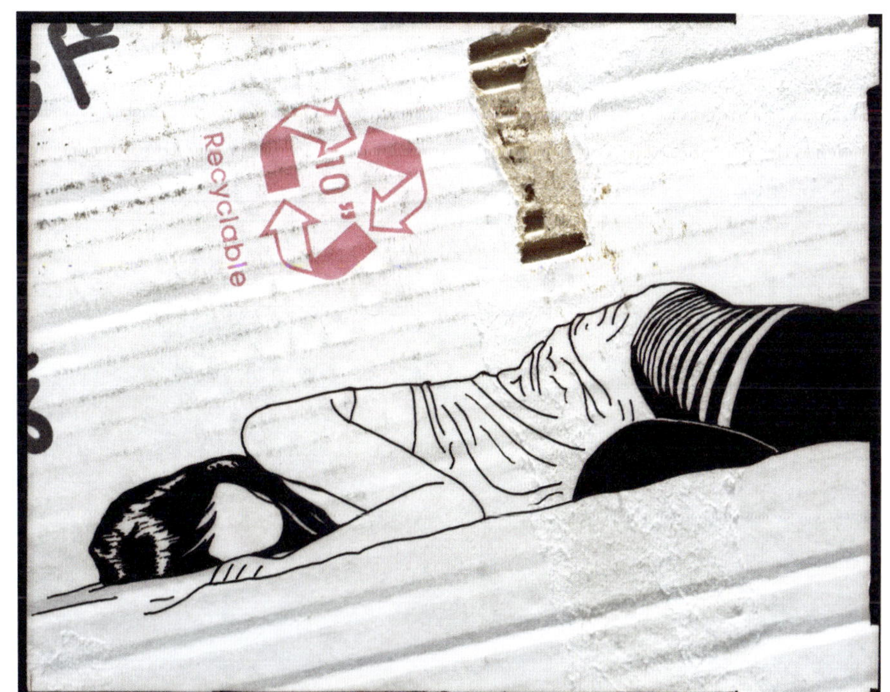
10"
Recyclable

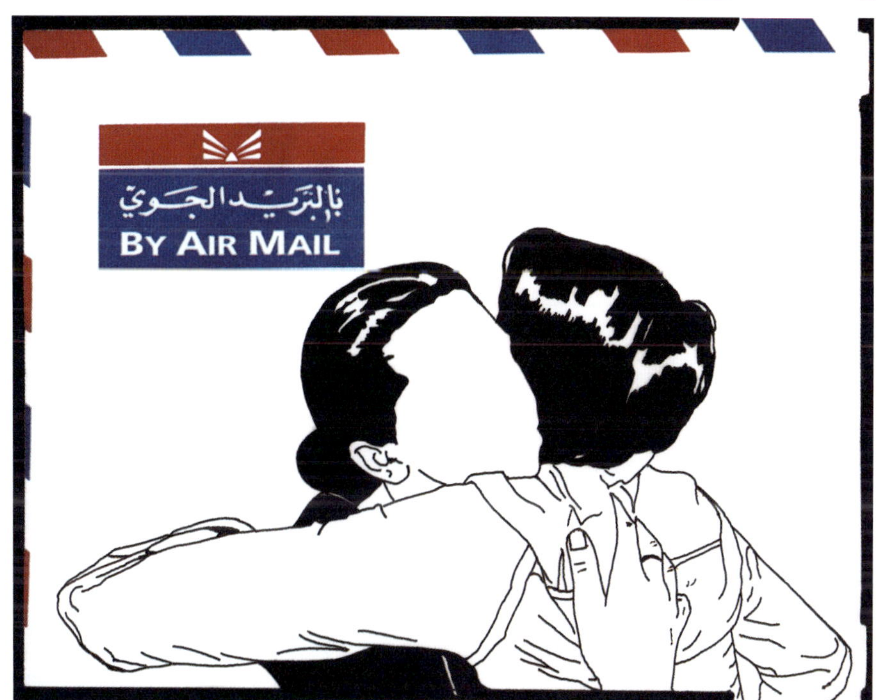
بالبريد الجوي
BY AIR MAIL

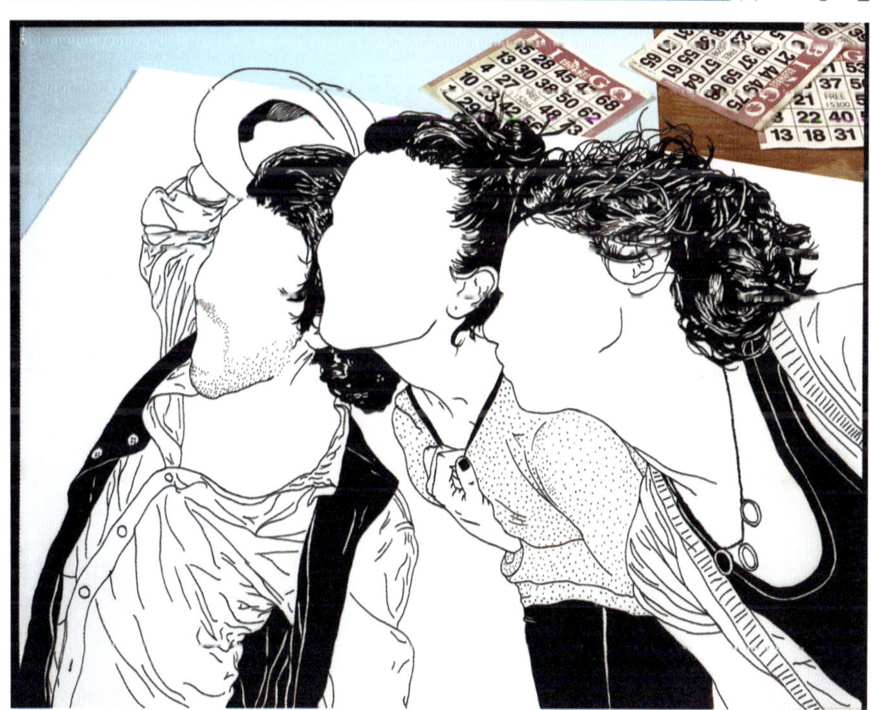

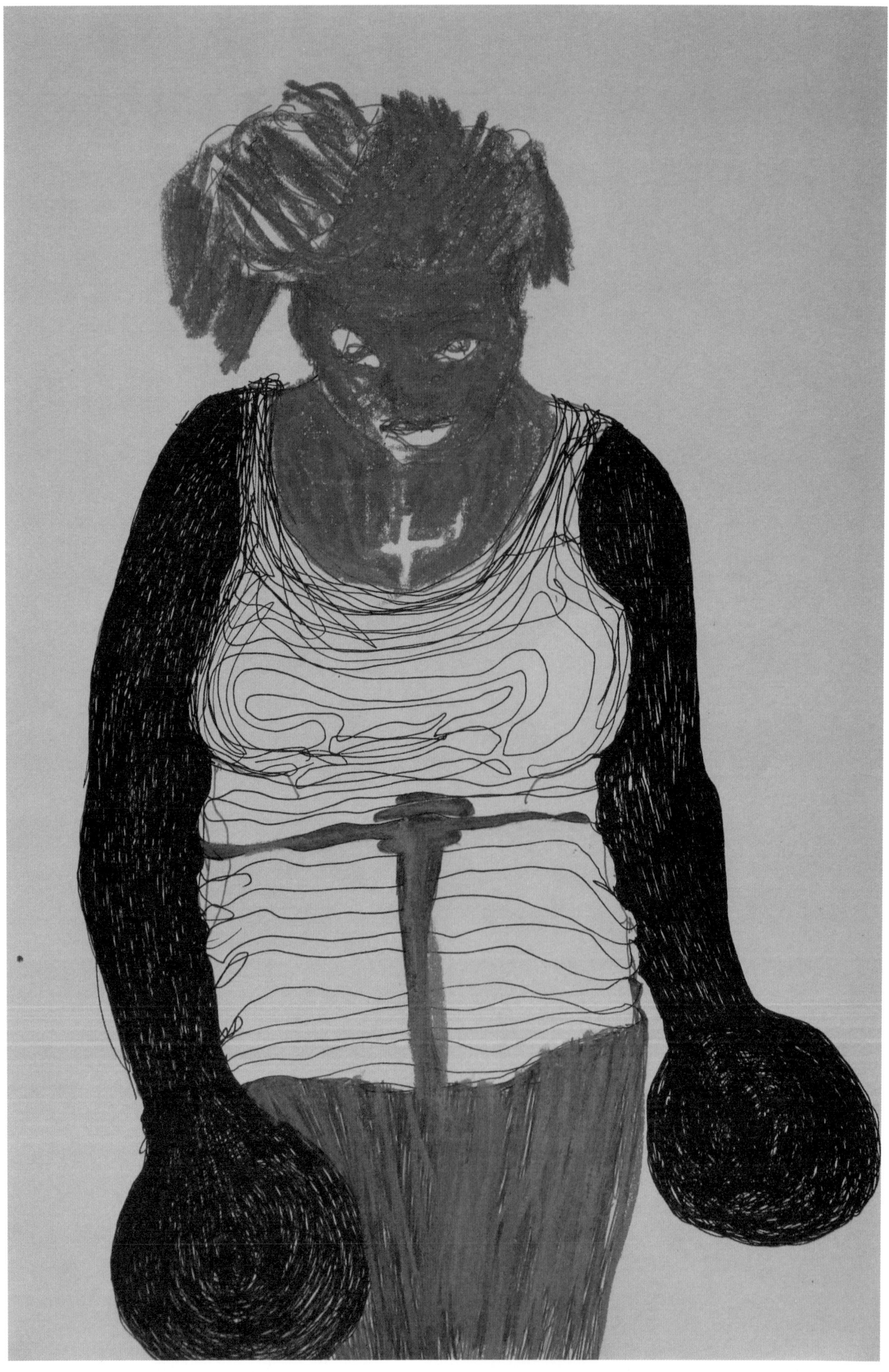

VIRGINIA CHIHOTA *Born 1983, Chitungwiza, Zimbabwe. Lives and works in Tripoli, Libya*

Virginia Chihota uses drawing as a tool for self-analysis as well as the observation of the people around her. The subjugation of women has always been a strong theme in her work. She trained as a printmaker specializing in serigraphy, and her drawings are informed by her confident, highly original sense of design and pattern. She draws people with delicate lines or emphatically silhouetted, often sleeping or vulnerably reclined. She has often deployed the motif of a rag doll to represent the self: defenceless but indestructible.

Having moved from Zimbabwe to Libya in 2012 to live with her husband, Chihota was prompted by her experience of isolation and social dislocation to explore more broadly the personal, political, religious and social foundations of human relationships, and to discover 'where we have gone wrong'. 'As an artist I am keen to retain my identity and continue expressing myself from a distance', says Chihota. 'It is in my work that I have the space and freedom to… ask questions, give suggestions or offer solutions to life's tribulations…. All I want is to nurture the love and respect which seems to have frozen within ourselves and to free the massive tension that holds us.'

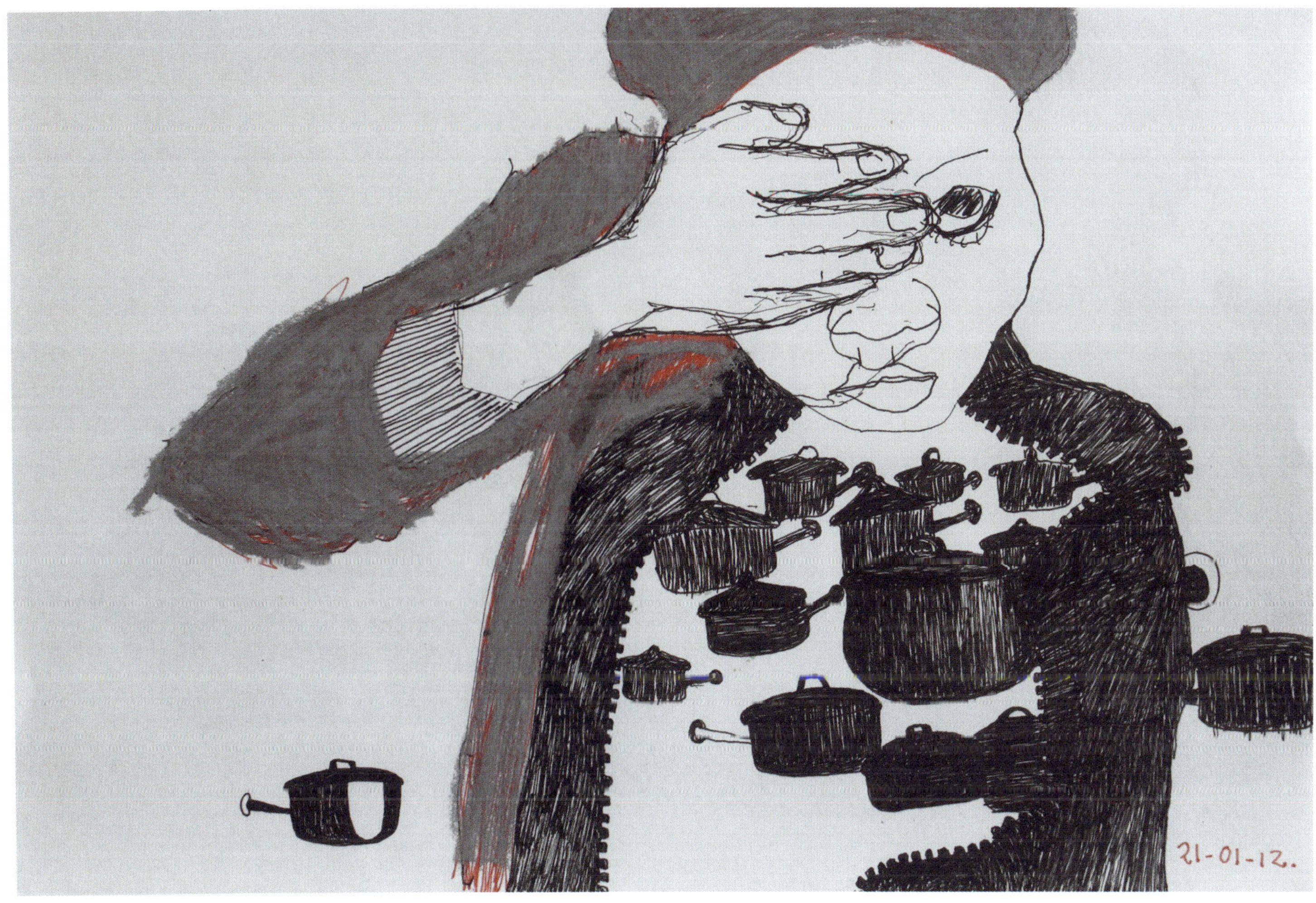

< *handichazvirwira (no longer fight for self)*, 2012
Pen and ink and oil pastel drawing on paper
25 × 17 cm (9 ⅞ × 6 ¾ in.)

handi mapoto chete akakumirira (not only pots await you), 2012
Pen and ink and oil pastel drawing on paper
17 × 25 cm (6 ¾ × 9 ⅞ in.)

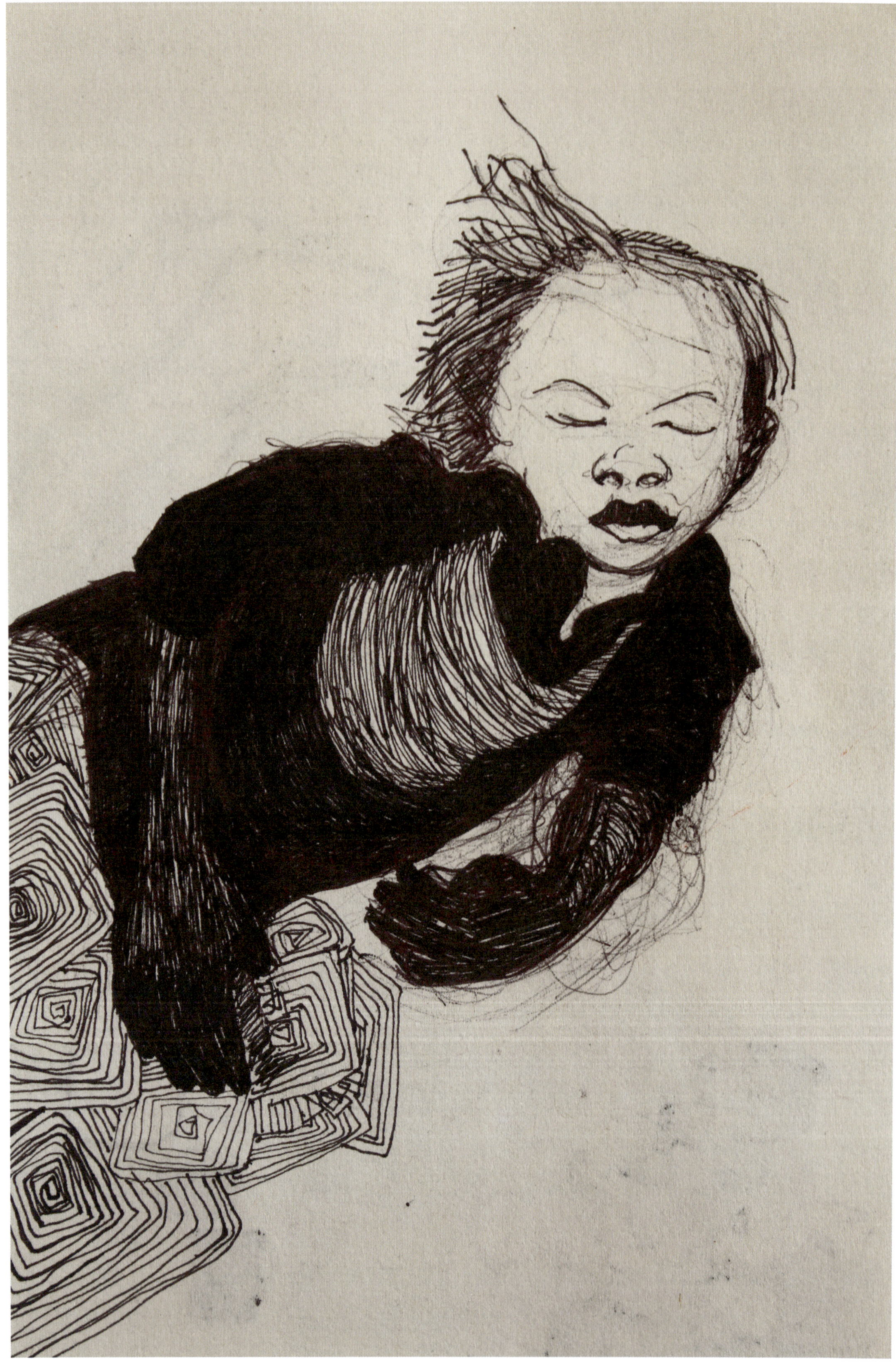

128

VIRGINIA CHIHOTA

sarudzo (choice), 2011
Pen and ink drawing on paper
21 × 15 cm (8 ¼ × 5 ⅞ in.)

ndombundira chokwadi chandinoziva (I embrace the truth I know) 2011 >
Pen and ink drawing on paper
21 × 15 cm (8 ¼ × 5 ⅞ in.)

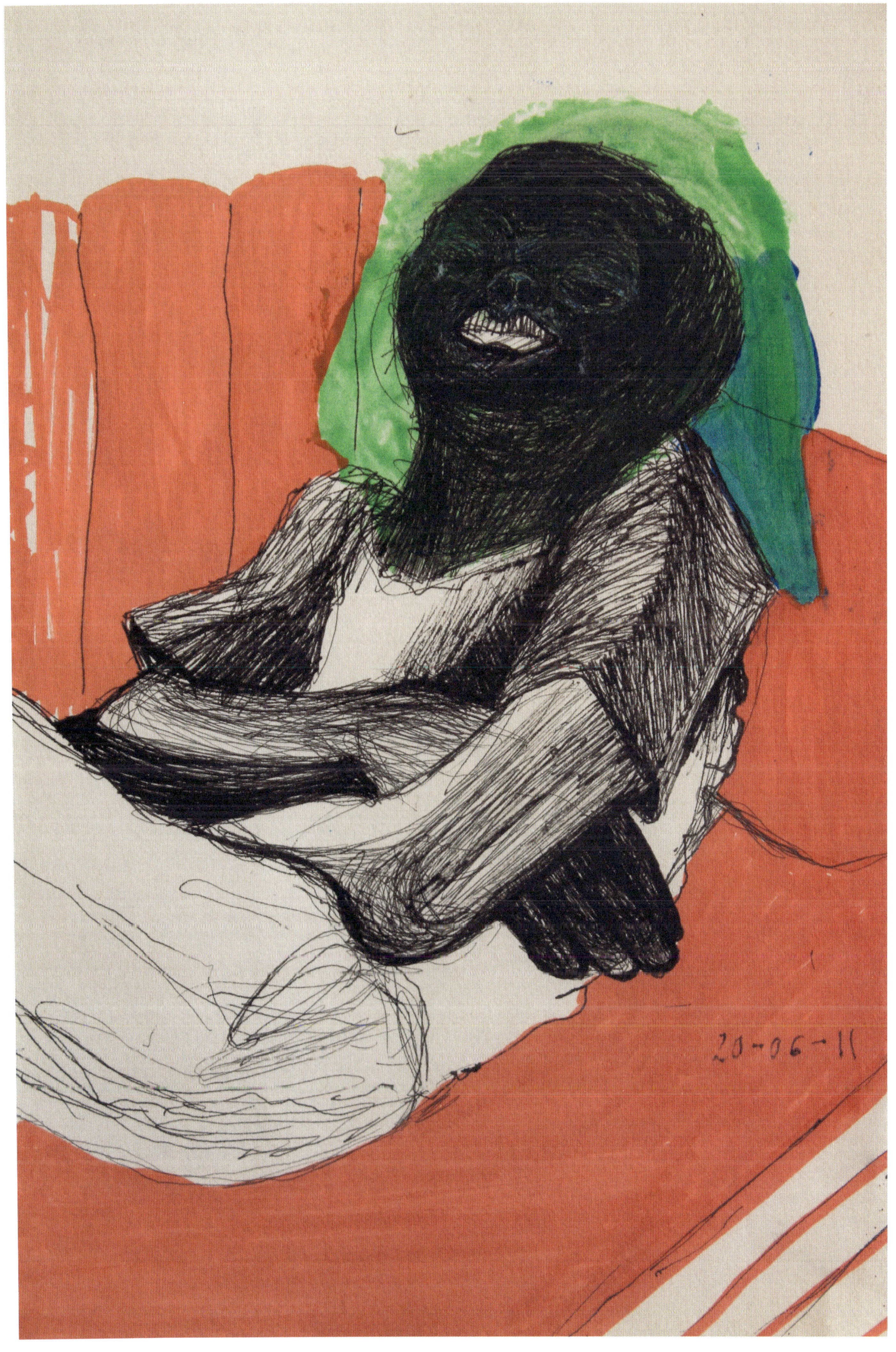
20-06-11

Julio César Morales is an artist, curator and educator. He was born in Tijuana and grew up in the Mexican border town of San Ysidro. As a child he crossed between Mexico and the United States daily, and much of his work stems from his resulting bicultural identity. Morales works in many media, including photography, video and performance, and has collaborated with architects, sound artists and food anthropologists. His strategic use of watercolour and ink for this particular series, *Undocumented Interventions* (2007-ongoing), is conceptually outstanding and exemplifies how the personal touch of a drawing in what the artist calls 'the softest medium' can subtly communicate something more than can the same image in its original photographic form. In this series, Morales translates into drawings real photographs sourced from a US immigration website that document Mexican citizens' failed attempts at entry to the US. These people hide themselves in vehicles, washing machines, wheels and fuel tanks, and children are concealed inside dolls and other toys. Morales's quiet line and gentle colours enact the self-effacement of the subjects, who are literally pretending not to exist, keeping still, silent and hopefully invisible.

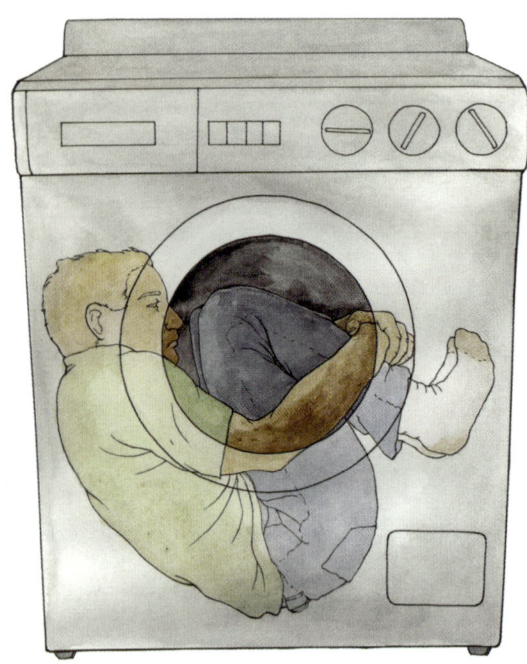

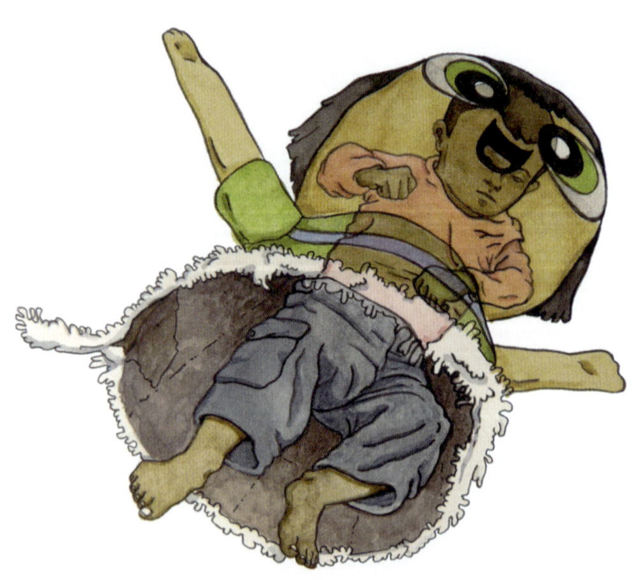

(this page and opposite) *Undocumented Interventions,* 2007–ongoing
Watercolour and ink on paper
Each: 22.9 × 30.5 cm (9 × 12 in.)

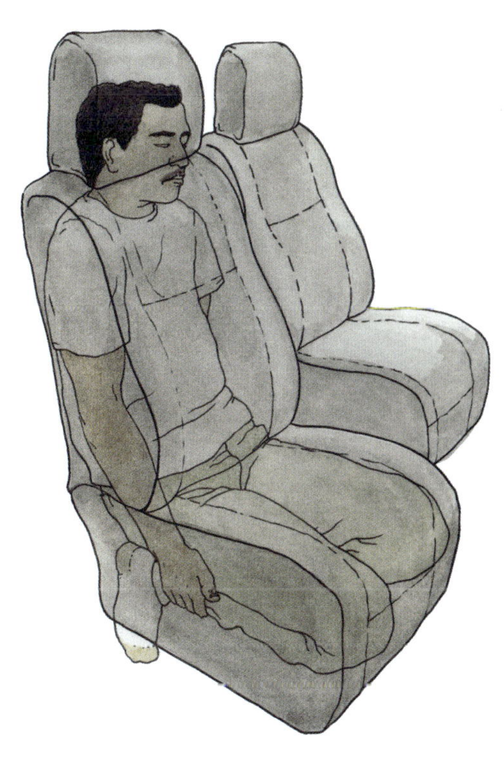

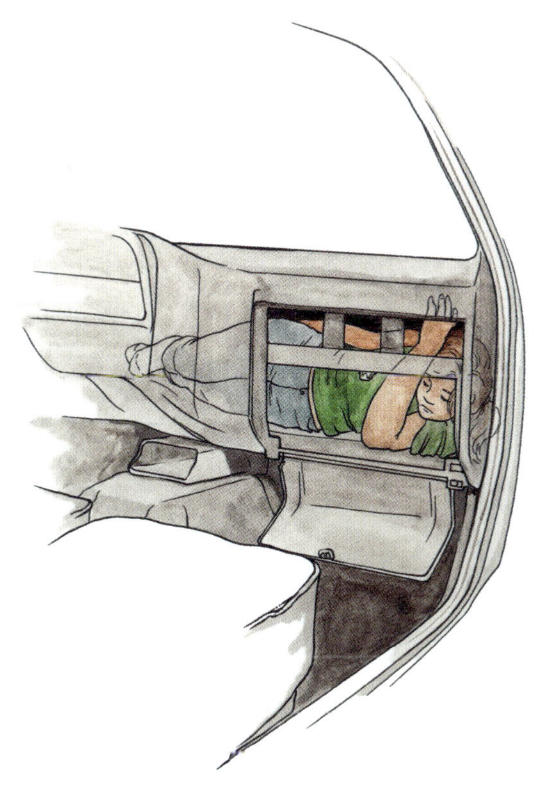

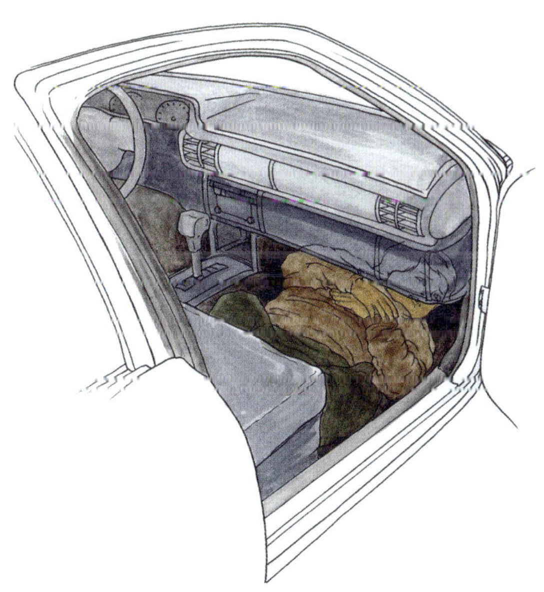

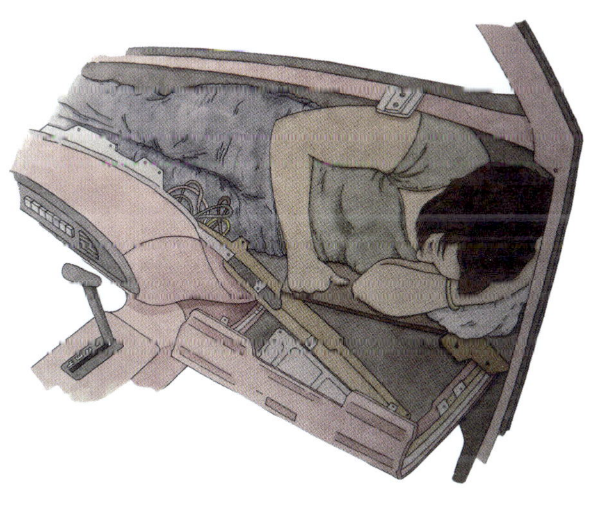

RICHARD FORSTER *Born 1970, Saltburn-by-the-Sea, UK. Lives and works in Darlington, UK*

Richard Forster first began to draw during his formative years, as 'an anxious teenager alienated in an English suburban bedroom'. With hindsight, Forster regards his introverted and seemingly powerless condition as a youth as the breeding ground for his concerns as an artist. Out of this upbringing developed an interest in the history of modernist experiments such as social housing projects and the Bauhaus, along with Forster's penchant for experimenting with graphic media, both abstract and figurative, culminating in the meticulous documentary style that he employs today.

Forster's painstakingly detailed graphite drawings have an almost hallucinatory intensity. The slow, concentrated effort of drawing allows him to internalize the atmosphere of his sources, which may be his own photographs or material from his archive of 'image-documents'. He often tends towards 'simple pictorial structures' and patterns, and explores the indexical relationship between the drawing and the original – for example the watercolour-painted masking tape in the collaged image *Two Girls Dancing, East Germany*, which introduces another level of pictorial illusion. In the other drawing reproduced here, a nude from an American camera magazine of the 1920s – a period of social experiment – is juxtaposed with a 1970s East German wallpaper pattern, the flat geometry offsetting the introspective depth of watery reflections of the female form.

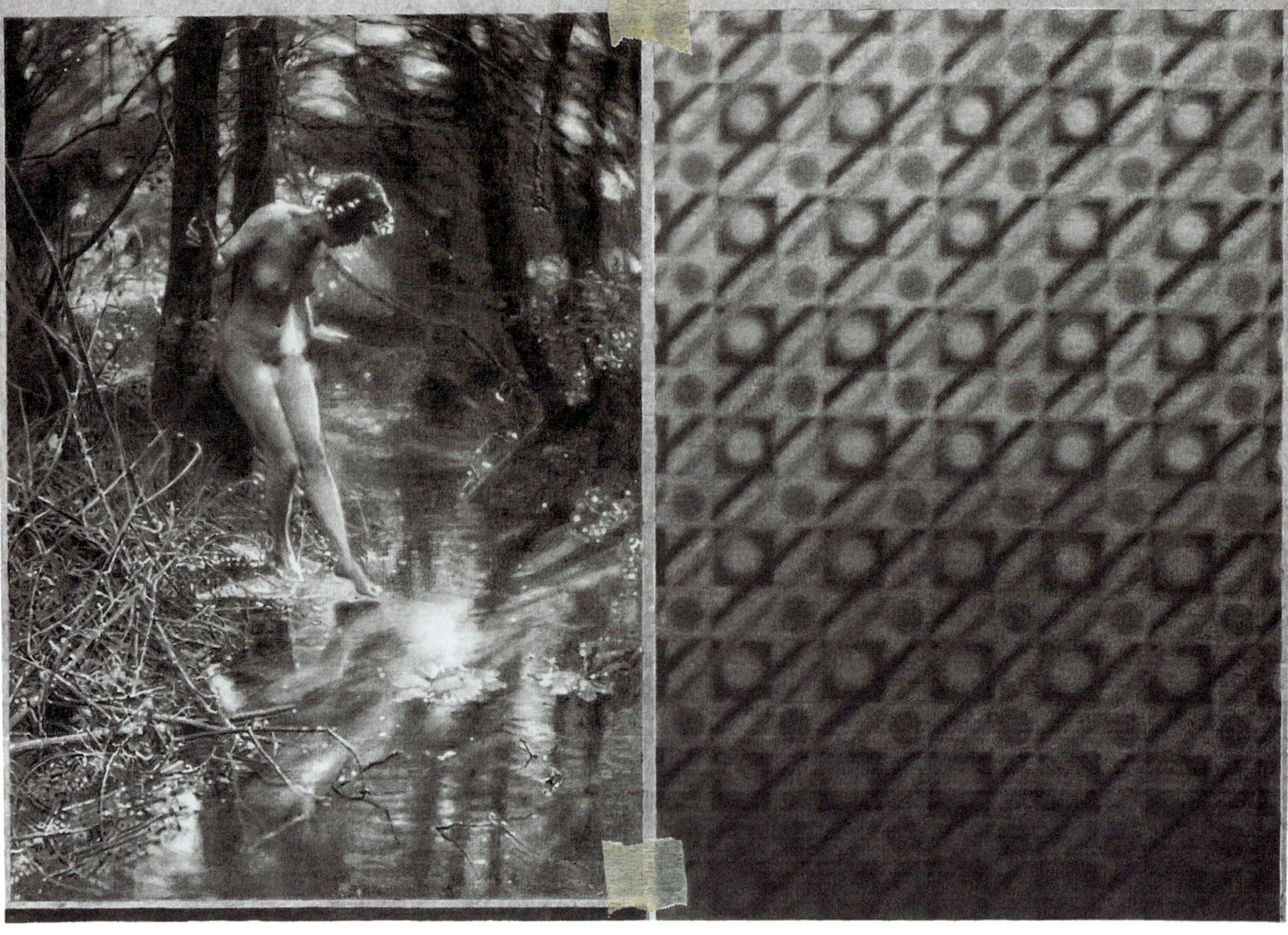

American Pastoral / Ostalgie Pattern with Tape, 2011
Graphite, acrylic medium and watercolour on Bristol Board
Page size: 30 × 42.5 cm (11 ¾ × 16 ¾ in.)

Two Girls Dancing, East Germany, 2012 >
Graphite and acrylic medium on card
Page size: 21 × 23 cm (8 ¼ × 9 in.)

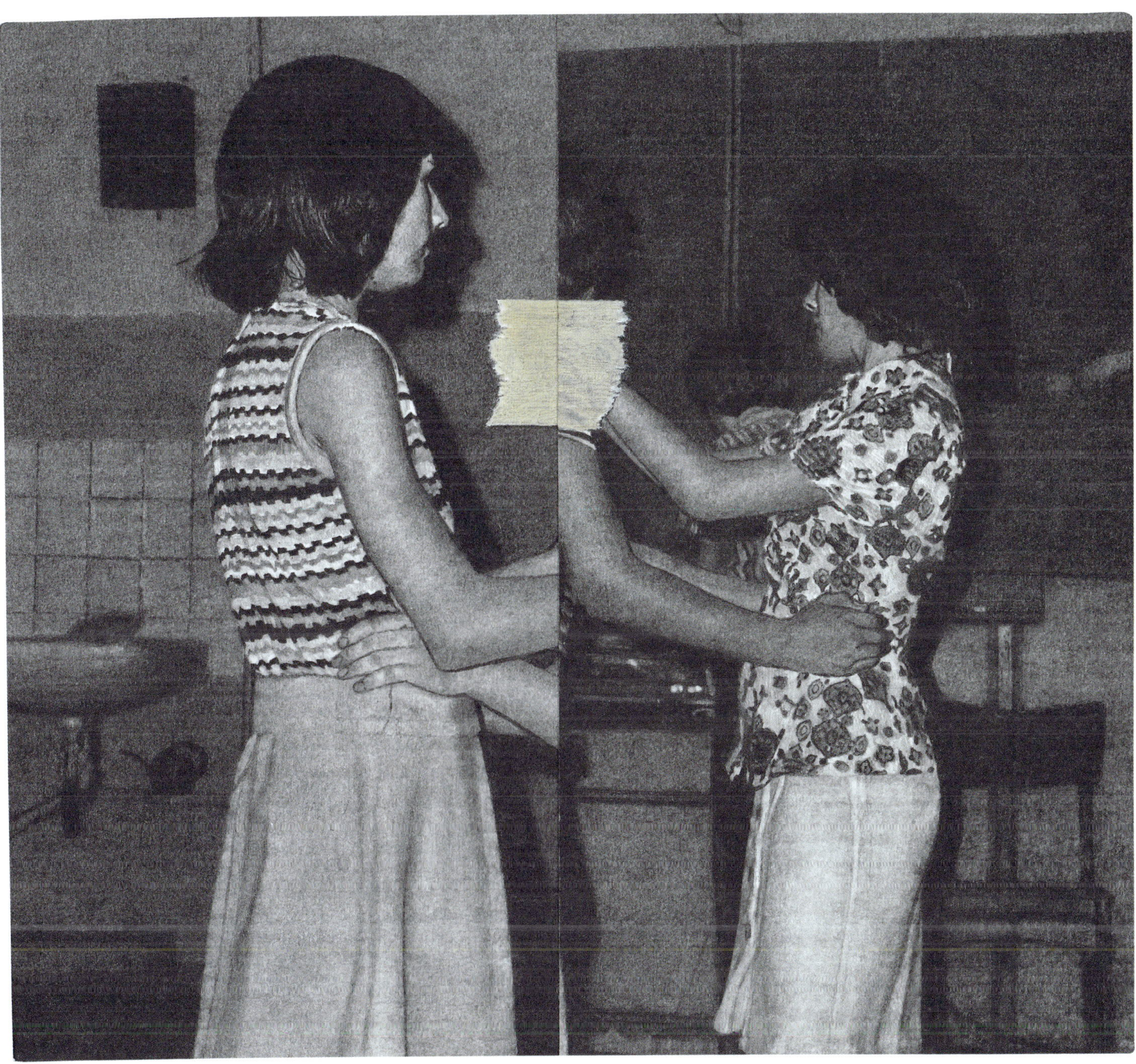

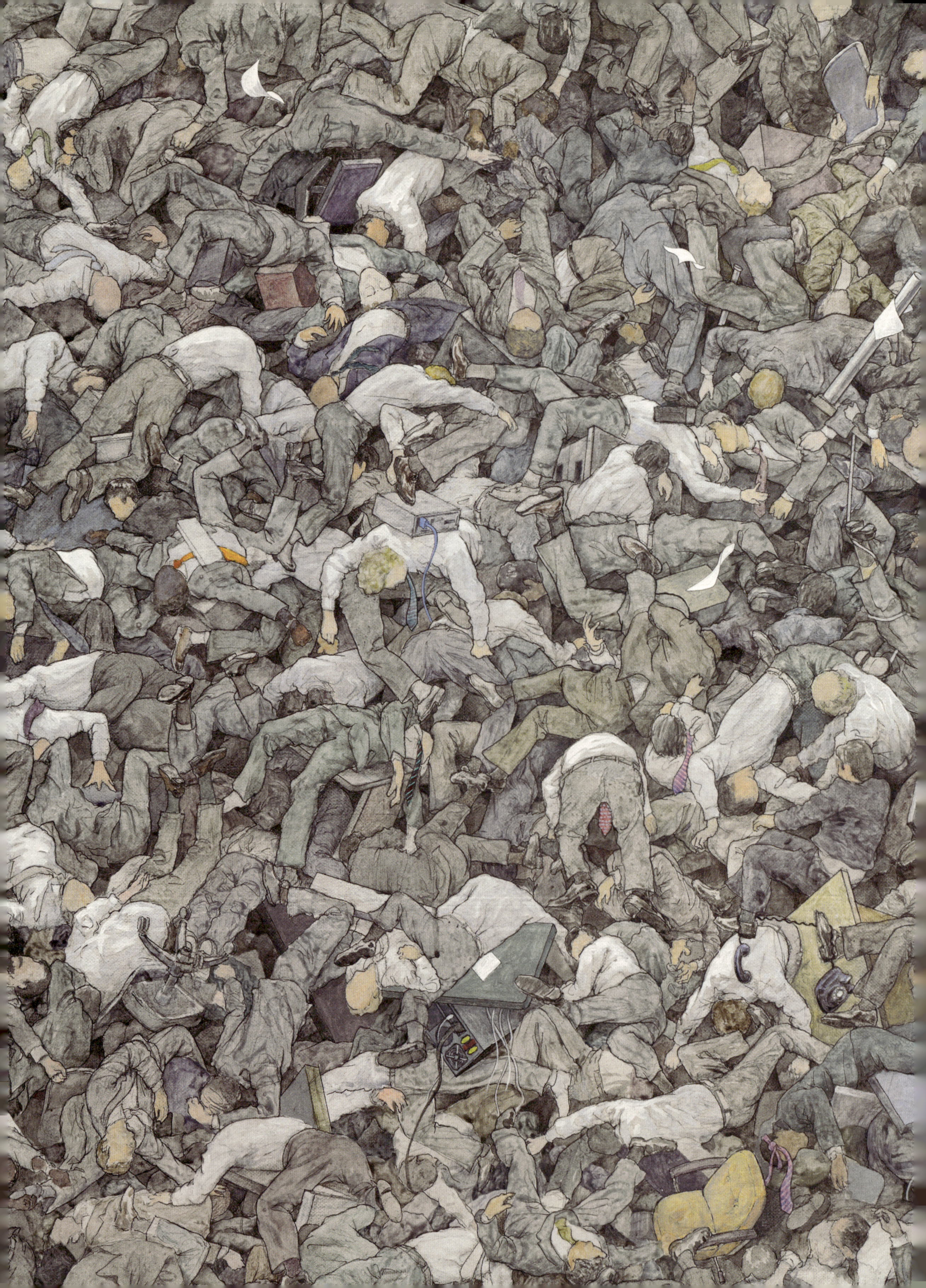

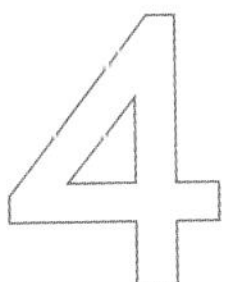

social reality

People do not want anything to disturb the order of the current system. The artist and poet are not obliged to co-operate in this respect, their function is exactly the opposite. It is to put the finger on the contradiction and enlarge the conflict.

MATTA *The Logic of Hallucination*, 1984

In our imaginations we may roam freely, but our physical being is ineluctably positioned in time and place. The instant of our birth pins us into circumstances which will in crucial ways determine our lives forever; however wilful we are, whether we are by nature more active or passive, we will never escape our own time, just as we cannot, through the power of thought, add one centimetre to our stature. For certain artists, a sense of time — of timing and timeliness – is vital to their practice: exactly judged, it could make a decisive difference to the look and the meaning of a work, the difference between today and yesterday. For others, the times in which they happen to live seem hardly relevant. Artists may refuse history, regarding it, as Joyce's Stephen Dedalus did, as the nightmare from which they are trying to awake, or they may embrace it as the essential condition of their work and its principal subject. There are artists in this book whose drawings could have been made at any time in the last hundred years; others who are totally engaged with the here and now.

Figurative artists are especially entangled in history because their art has been subject to the vicissitudes of politics so often, especially over the past century. Not only have artists and art theorists held strong views on the rights and wrongs of figuration, but politicians themselves – fascists and communists with no claims to artistic talent – have dictated to artists what and how they should paint and draw. Depressing as this is, it still has consequences today. One is the persistence of figurative training in former Communist countries, such as China, Russia and Romania, during a period when those traditions have been neglected or rejected in the West. Many contemporary artists in China have a complex relationship with realism, having been taught by instructors who were themselves trained in the Stalinist era in the Soviet Union. These artists frequently put the technical skills they have learned to use in unexpected ways: they regard society's problems as a proper subject for art, and the political history

< AIDA MAKOTO *Ash Color Mountains* (detail), 2009–11
Acrylic on canvas, 300 × 700 cm (118 ½ × 275 ⅝ in.)

of China as something they are compelled by their conscience to address. The iconography of twentieth-century Chinese political history is their frame of reference, as palpable an influence as the architecture and decor that surrounds them, and since it is commonly understood within China, it can be used as a tool for deconstructing the residual political ideology. Appropriating photographic imagery and subverting it through drawing requires a technique that displaces the authoritative linear narrative, substituting for the familiar 'story of the nation' one that is altogether more ambiguous and open-ended.

For Chen Shaoxiong, who in fact was not trained in the realist manner, that technique is animation. His work is structured as a rapid sequence of hand-drawn stills without captions or rationalizing commentary. Shown in this way, history does indeed become 'one damned thing after another', with no sense of teleology or culmination. The technique of animation is also used by Sun Xun, whose narratives allegorize the moral vacuum, the deception, venality and abuses of power that he considers prevalent in contemporary Chinese society. Significantly, both artists' reflections on China's ordeals under the dictatorship of the proletariat were originally inspired by the stop-frame animations of William Kentridge, whose own allegories of misrule were first conceived under the repressive apartheid regime in South Africa. (Kentridge's character Ubu is a precursor of Sun Xun's devious Magician.) The simple medium of charcoal has given Kentridge scope to create a homogeneous world that incorporated as much or as little of the actual environment as he chose. Kentridge's skills as a draughtsman are not inhibited by the conventions of an inherited style. His version of realism is largely self-taught; it is his own invention. In fact, it is 'out of time' and quite remote from the preoccupations of mainstream North American and European art of the period. He is free to draw whatever he likes, just as Chen Shaoxiong can draw the history of the twentieth century in ink, unimpeded by any of the stylistic mannerisms he would have acquired had he undergone classical training.

The question of style is paramount for those artists who want to draw and comment critically on social reality and history. What language to adopt, to speak of the world 'as it is'? There is no established mode of realism that can be played straight – none that has currency, unexamined, in the digital age. Drawing's intimacy gives it an indisputable value in relation to personal subjects and private fantasies, but in representing the social sphere it is difficult to find ground for originality, to escape the freight of art-historical associations – Social

Realism or Ashcan or Neue Sachlichkeit – or from the more pluralist or vernacular languages of graffiti and graphic novels.

Parody and pastiche are two viable strategies as alternatives to the methodical hand-drawn reproduction of the photograph or straight drawing from life. Two of the most original and sophisticated exponents of subversive appropriation, artists who have perfected styles that are uniquely their own and who are also lucid enough to allow us to see and comprehend the reality of the world they represent, are Yun-Fei Ji and Fernando Bryce. Ji adopts the traditional techniques and style of Song Dynasty landscape painting 'to explore the utopian dreams of Chinese history, from past collectivization to new consumerism'. His work is subtle but the message is clear. In the art of the Song Dynasty, the landscape was conceived to be emblematic of a moral order, yet Ji depicts distinctively contemporary figures in his mountain scenes: displaced peasants struggling with their possessions as they are forced to move from their homes; seven intellectuals undergoing re-education during the Cultural Revolution (an allusion to the classical theme of the 'seven sages', who retreat from the public realm, with its corruption and hypocrisy, to the countryside to drink wine and recite poetry); a loudspeaker in the sky blasting Maoist propaganda to a motley collection of crows and frogs. In fusing a thousand-year-old art form with imagery from recent history, Ji creates a moral universe to be read like a parable or poem: a quiet but eloquent satire.

Peruvian artist Fernando Bryce's drawings do not so much appropriate an artistic style; rather they translate an encoded world of printed ephemera, usually from periods of colonial or fascist history, into the artist's own fluent but staunchly inexpressive graphic language. His immaculate ink-and-wash renderings of Nazi magazines, newspapers and posters and their sequential arrangement reflect this material's provenance as the product of an oppressive ideology. There is a shameless air of innocence and homeliness about the originals. Yet in Bryce's remaking of them, they seem eerily remote: extracted from their archival context as paper items with the material characteristics (page size, smell, texture, patina and discolouration) evocative of their period, they seem disinfected, tranquilized, fictionalized. Obsolete totalitarian systems of government encapsulated in a period style, old-fashioned typefaces and haircuts, vintage cars and all the trappings of military and civilian life, smiling young women and children in warm coats, soldiers with a confident, straight-ahead look: all of this, when we examine it at one remove through the veil of Bryce's ink and wash drawings, seems almost as if it might never have existed anywhere but on the printed page. It is as though his neat brush, like a cat's tongue, has licked clean each line and letter. As Bryce observes, 'things calm down with drawing'. History can be put back in its archival box, safe from the harmful rays of the sun.

Imaginary worlds can be represented as convincingly, with as much consistency and apparent conviction, as those that actually exist or have existed. We can fleetingly indulge the notion that the Nazi regime was nothing more than a gruesome horror story in a cheap comic book. Reduced to drawings, this world is no more credible than the one represented in Chad McCail's storyboard sequence, *Food Shelter Clothing Fuel* (1999–2003). McCail's utopian vision is poised somewhere between revolutionary communist propaganda for young children and a gentle satire on the distance of the present capitalist system from our youthful ideals. Is McCail offering a blueprint for a new social order, featuring prototypical citizens performing their exemplary tasks? Or have these scenes been staged for some theatrical purpose, a sequence of tableaux with actors moving mechanically from one to the next? The underlying principle is clearly the achievement of happiness, but through his depiction of anonymous figures that resemble those in an instruction manual, McCail suggests that this must be the happiness of society at large rather than of the individual. McCail's actors don't entice us to join them; the pictures simply show their way of life as a matter of fact. The captions are descriptive, not hortatory. But there is something unsettling about this anarchist dream; it seems to have come about effortlessly, by a collective awakening, without a fight.

Schematic drawings of social interaction are not always so fanciful or so evidently fabricated as those presented by McCail. The basic elements of life – land, homes, sustenance – are at issue in all societies, and to represent them in pictorial form is a challenge that every artist must face on their own terms, if they wish to avoid the ready-made languages of social engagement. History painting and documentary photography are two conventional poles of representation – one allegorical, the other realist – that an artist can borrow from, refer to or manipulate, but there are many other codes available for visualizing the world, from maps, charts and diagrams to children's book illustrations and Constructivist graphics. The Nigerian artist Otobong Nkanga invents a system similar to McCail's, but without the latter's undercutting irony. The world that Nkanga wants to show is the 'real' one, where land has been carved up arbitrarily and people segregated as a result of the imposition of colonial rule, for example, and where resources are spirited away over the heads of

local inhabitants by multinational corporations. There is no need for a naively conceived version of 'realism' to illustrate actual relations of power and wealth. Nkanga finds a way to do it abstractly through diagrams and emblematic drawings, whose less hectoring style may be more effective as a means of communicating these ideas, as well as resulting in better works of art. Nkanga's images are not didactic, but illustrate a way of thinking visually, through drawing. Parts stand for the whole: disembodied arms and hands holding instruments and tools represent men and women at work, for example, and a single plant symbolizes the environment. Rope, string and barbed wire link people together, or entangle them, or forbid them access. The point is not that these pictorial devices are new. There is nothing startlingly original about representing the unseen forces controlling people's lives by puppets and strings; political cartoonists have been using such metaphors for centuries. What makes Nkanga's work unusual is its clarity and formal economy, and her allusions to modernist art history – De Chirico, Léger and Russian Constructivism – combined with an elementary, and therefore all the more salutary, humanist message. It is a mark of her good judgment that the message is delivered wordlessly; while McCail's images necessarily make use of captions for their meaning, the opposite is true of Nkanga's. Words would undermine them.

Word and image flow from the same pen with a facility and grace that appear peculiarly timeless in the work of Pavel Pepperstein. His drawings hark back to a pre-technological age when handwriting was cultivated as the primary expression of the self, and great illustrators such as Saul Steinberg could invoke a multiplicity of styles with a few lines. In Pepperstein's universe, political allegory is couched in the symbolic language of Russian Suprematism of the early twentieth century, an avant-garde so far ahead of its time that a century after its manifestation it still appears to foresee a future at which we may never arrive. Paradoxically, for a figurative artist like Pepperstein, with one foot in children's book illustration and the other in political cartoons, it is Malevich's *Black Square* (1915), the absolute negation of figurative imagery, that heralds the new order. This would be the mystical 'end of history', when all conflicts are resolved, gangsters no longer rule the roost and justice prevails. It may look rather like Chad McCail's utopia, however: a world where 'no one is born no one dies'. Meanwhile, in the imperfect present, artists who draw will seek ways to depict the conditions of life as they experience them, a practice impossible without reference to the art of the past as well as their immediate social and political environs.

CHO DUCK HYUN   *Born 1957, Cheong Il, South Korea. Lives and works in Seoul, South Korea*

Cho Duck Hyun's investigations into memory and the construction of history have taken many different forms over the past two decades, including installation, performance, film, photography and drawing. He has made many meticulously executed, large-scale charcoal and graphite drawings on canvas from vintage photographs and has incorporated them, framed, into installations. His early drawings were created from images from the Korean War (1950–53), but Cho has since concentrated mainly on family album photographs, drawing them with illusionistic refinement and presenting them in ornate frames as ceremonial portraits. In his series *A History of Korean Women* (1991) he has taken a fabric worn by the woman in the original photograph and had it spill out of the frame across the floor. Cho used a similar historical mirroring technique in *The Sir Peter Wakefield Collection* (2006), for which he collaborated with a British former diplomat who had spent twenty years in the Far East, working with him to excavate his personal history and then mixing it with other stories. For instance, in one image he places Sir Peter alongside a young Korean diplomat from the early twentieth century. Cho has also staged performances of fictional archaeological digs carried out in reverse, burying rows of life-sized fibreglass dogs in pits and later excavating them with pseudo-scientific fanfare.

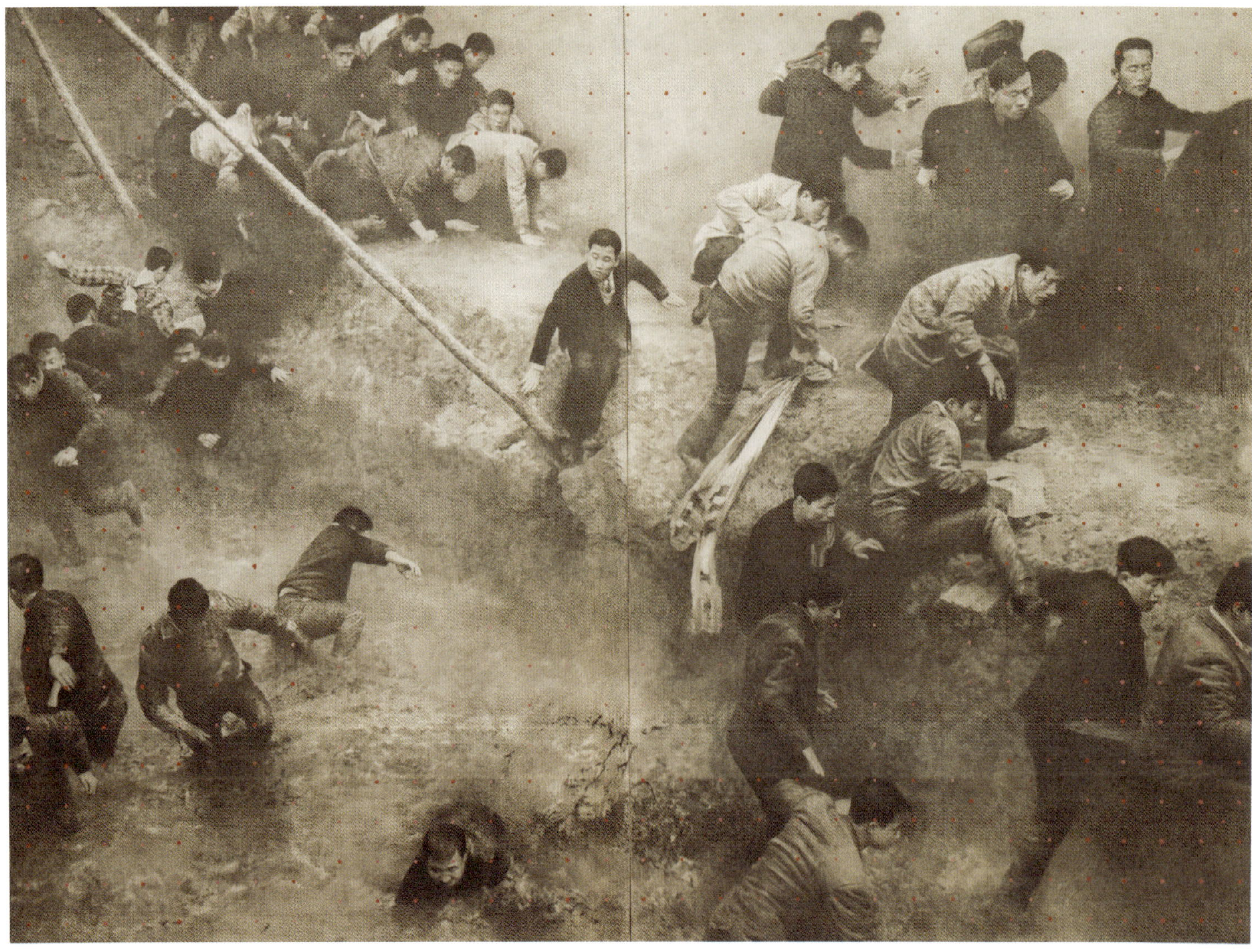

April 19th, main part, 1997
Graphite, charcoal and acrylic on canvas
158 × 272 cm (62 ¼ × 107 ⅛ in.)

Motherhood, main part, 2012 >
Graphite and charcoal on canvas
175 × 285 cm (68 ⅞ × 112 ¼ in.)

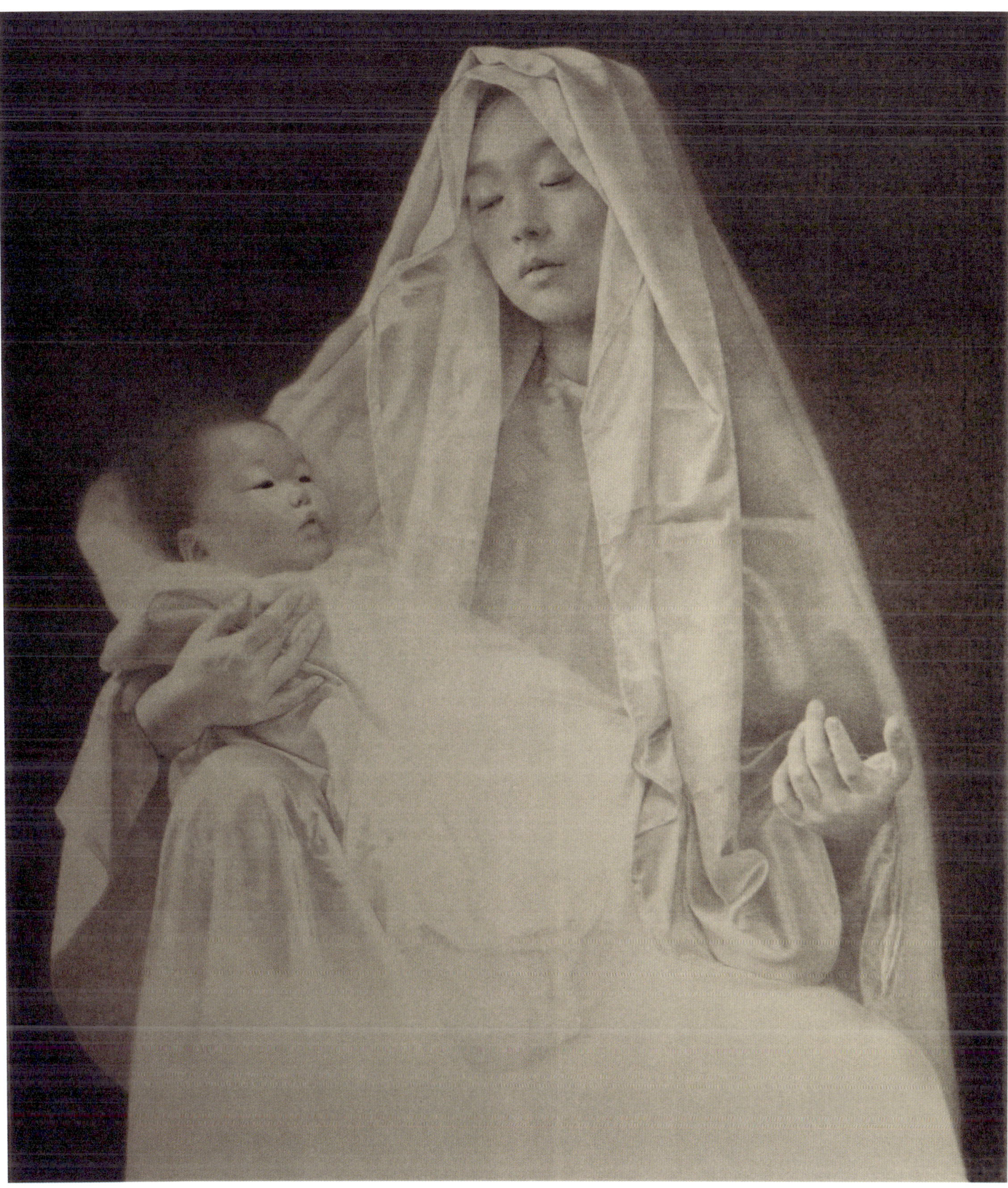

Fernando Bryce goes about his task of reproducing archival printed material by hand with the methodical dedication of a medieval copyist. His project is subtly rationalized and exquisitely executed. He has made many monumental series of drawings from ephemeral publications, invariably displayed in tight formations, storyboard-style. Each group pertains to a particular historical epoch and usually reflects a single ideology: most belong to the colonial or fascist eras and reveal the parochialism and condescension of those cultures with regard to the exotic 'Other'.

Bryce begins with exhaustive research, immersing himself in archival documents, newspapers, magazines, film posters, tourist brochures and propaganda. He describes the process of selecting and copying the pages and photographs in brush and ink as 'mimetic analysis', an active reflection on the 'construction and mediated condition of these images'. Rendered in his meticulous hand, the essence of his drawings' ideological message seems to be extracted and exposed more lucidly than it would be in a mechanical reproduction accompanied by deconstructive text, despite the fact that his style, with its fluent brush strokes and shadow effects, is so distinctive and personal. The Nazi period magazines and posters in the drawings here show the everyday, homely side of fascism – the banality of evil.

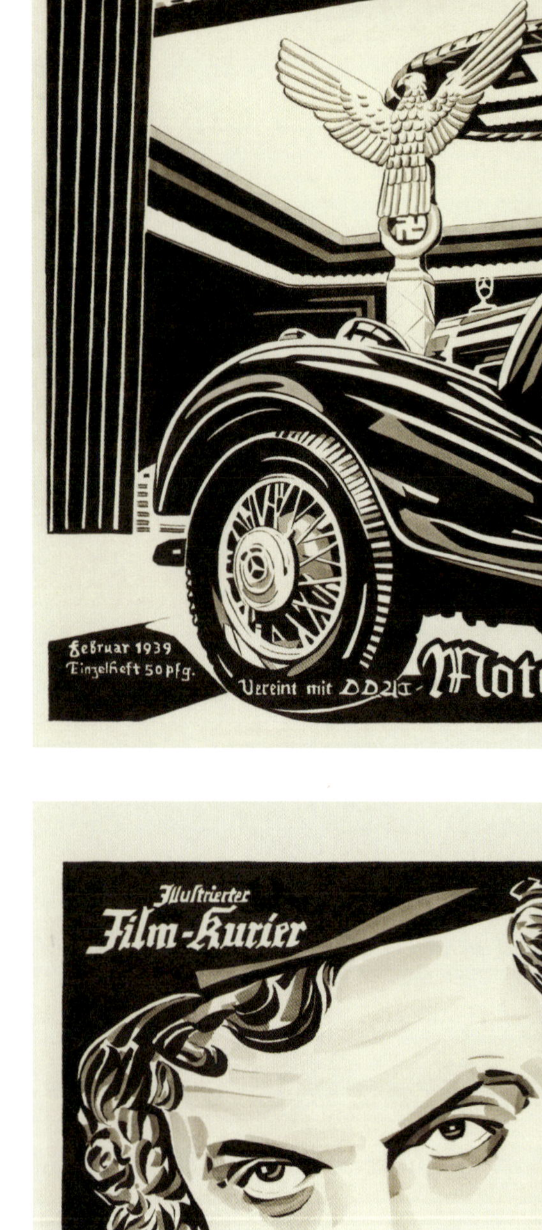

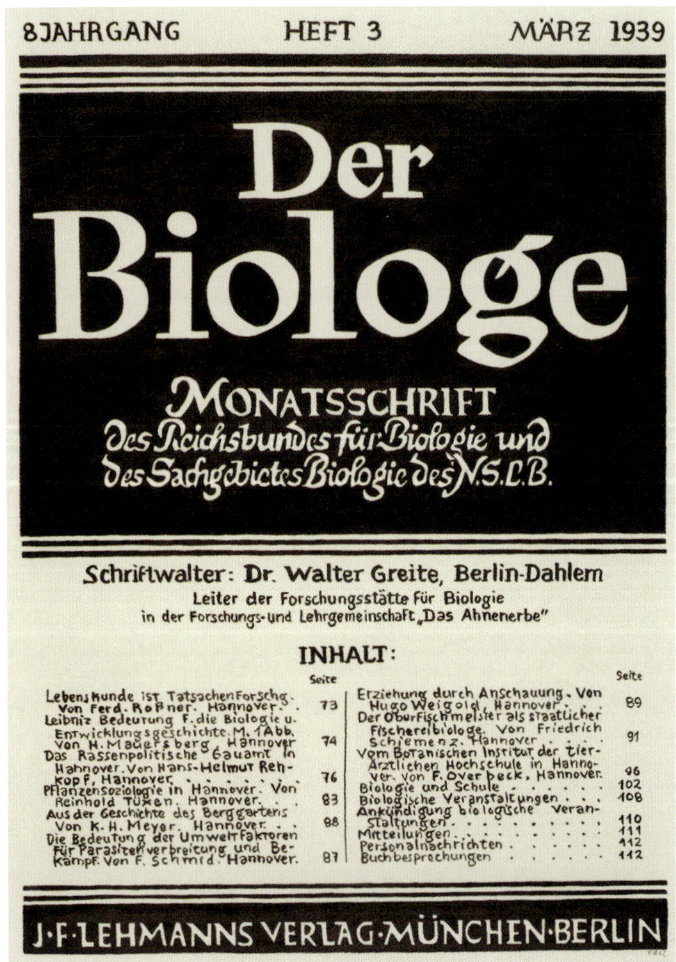

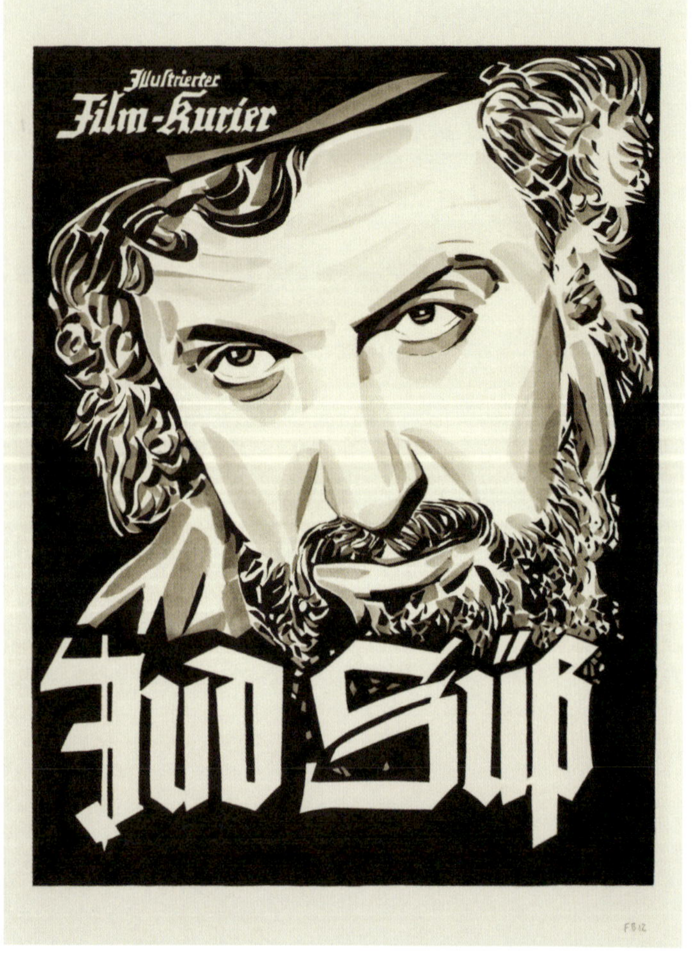

(this page, opposite and pp. 142–43) *Der Biologe,* 2012
Ink on paper
Series of 22 drawings, each: 42 × 30 cm (16 ½ × 11 ¾ in.)

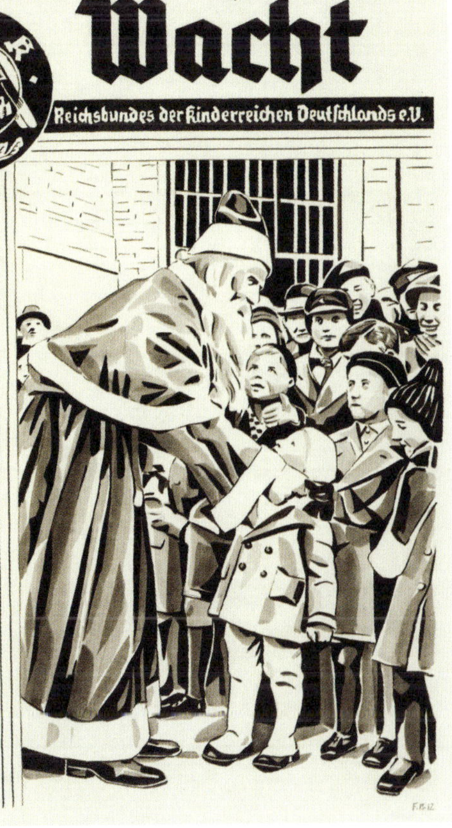

Angeschlossen dem Rassenpolitischen Amt der NSDAP.
Mitglied des Reichsausschusses für Volksgesundheitsdienst beim Reichs und Preußischen Ministerium des Innern
Völkische Wacht
17 Jahrgang
12 Folge
Dezember 1937
Organ des
R.D.K.
Reichsbundes der Kinderreichen Deutschlands e.V.
Weihnacht 1937
Von drauß', vom Walde komm' ich her;
ich muß auch fagen,
es weihnachtet sehr...
Aus dem Inhalt:
Frohe Weihnacht! — In der Weihnachtsbäckerei - Bücher für den Weihnachtstisch — Trommeln, Pfeifen und Gewehr... — Weihnacht in der Kinderreichen Familie - Kinder Spielen Theater.

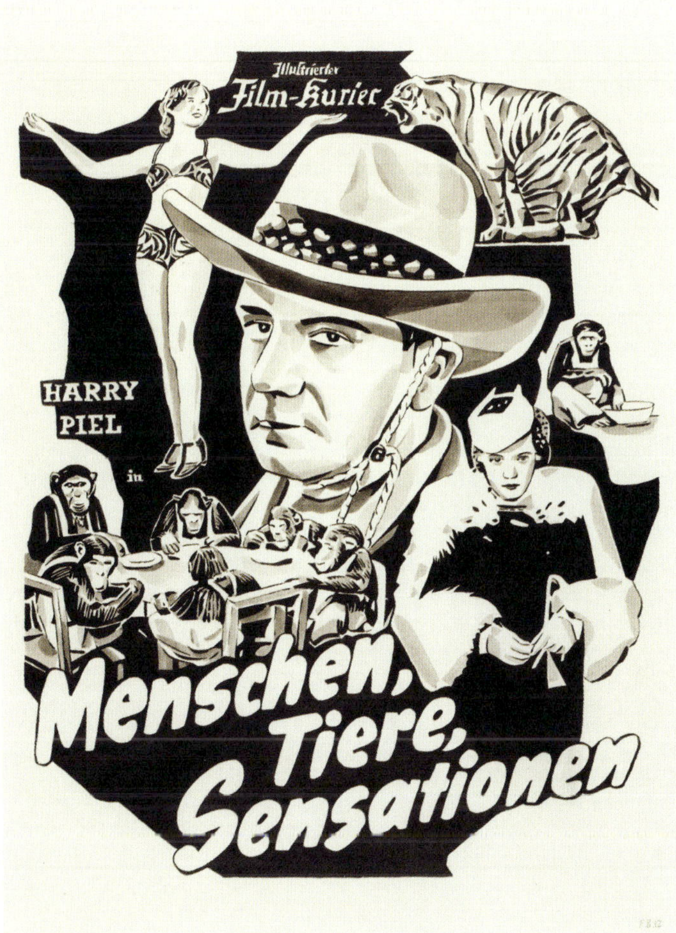

Illustrierter Film-Kurier
HARRY PIEL
in
Menschen, Tiere, Sensationen

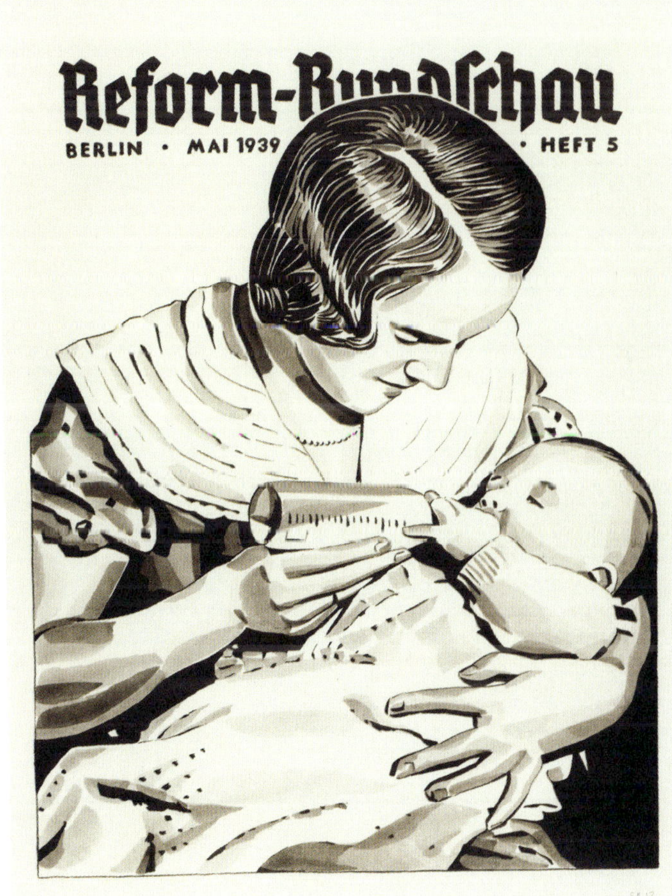

Reform-Rundschau
BERLIN · MAI 1939 · HEFT 5

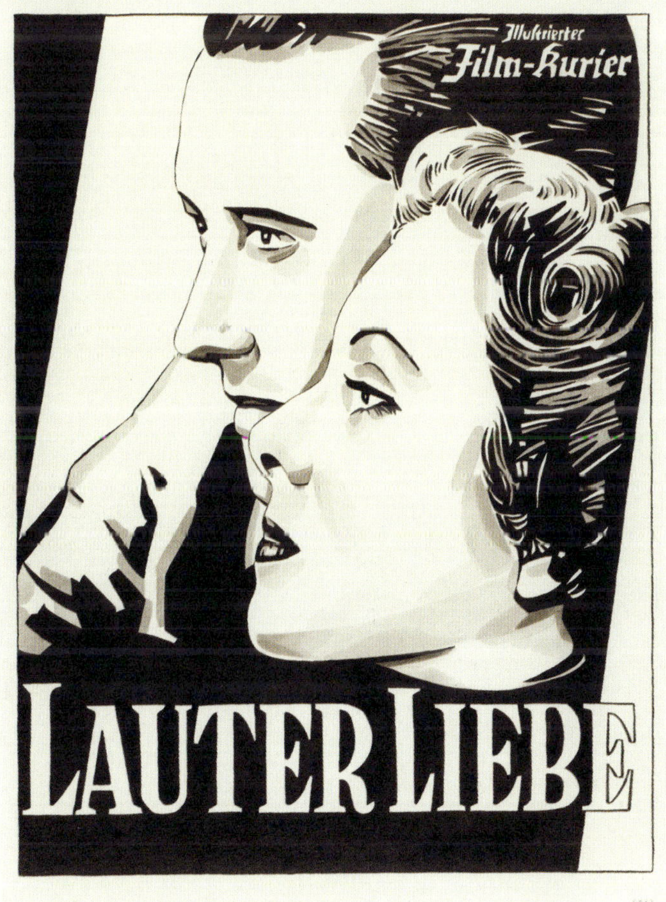

Illustrierter Film-Kurier
LAUTER LIEBE

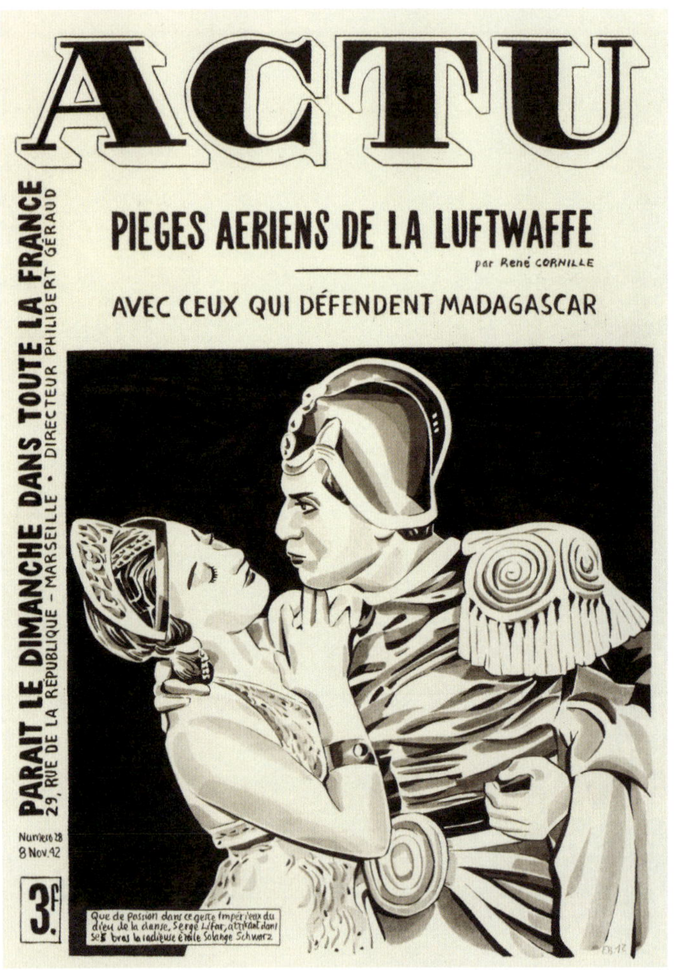
ACTU
PIEGES AERIENS DE LA LUFTWAFFE
par René CORNILLE
AVEC CEUX QUI DÉFENDENT MADAGASCAR
PARAIT LE DIMANCHE DANS TOUTE LA FRANCE
29, RUE DE LA REPUBLIQUE - MARSEILLE • DIRECTEUR PHILIBERT GÉRAUD
Numéro 28
8 Nov. 42
3f.

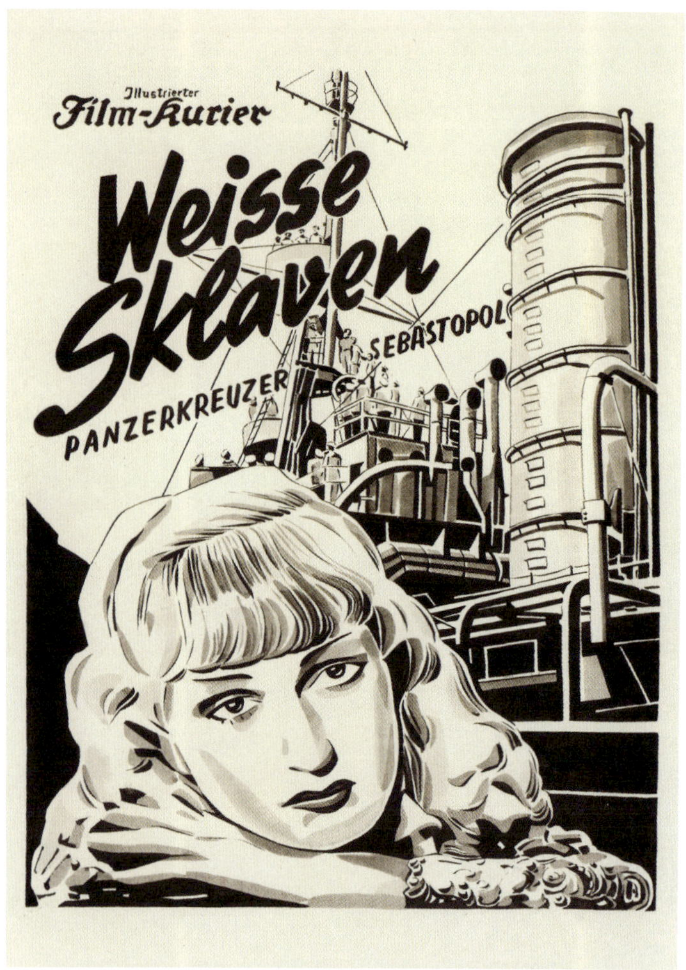
Illustrierter
Film-Kurier
Weisse
Sklaven
PANZERKREUZER SEBASTOPOL

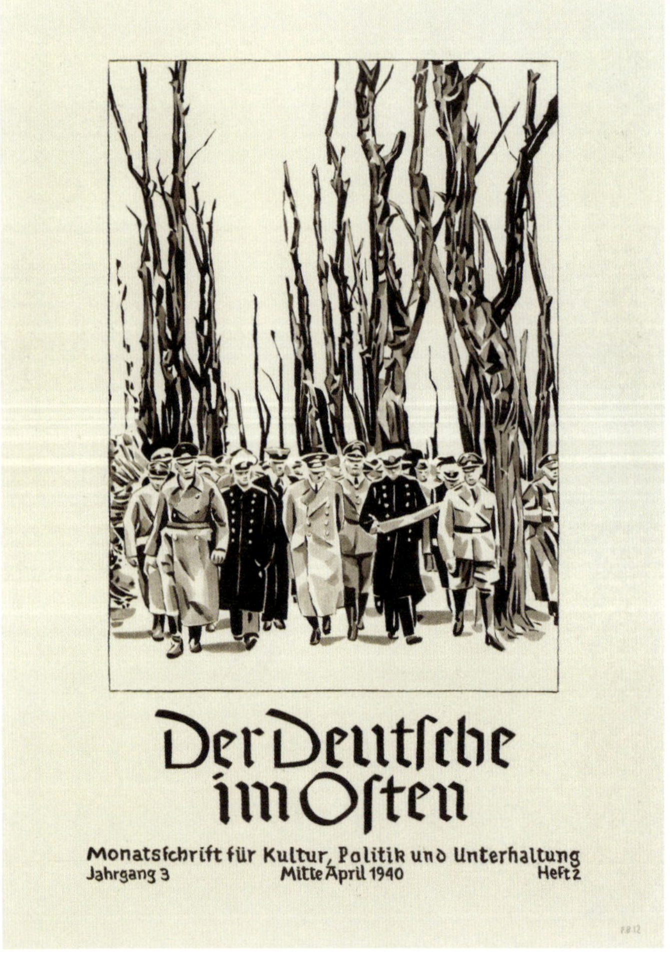
Der Deutsche
im Osten
Monatsschrift für Kultur, Politik und Unterhaltung
Jahrgang 3   Mitte April 1940   Heft 2

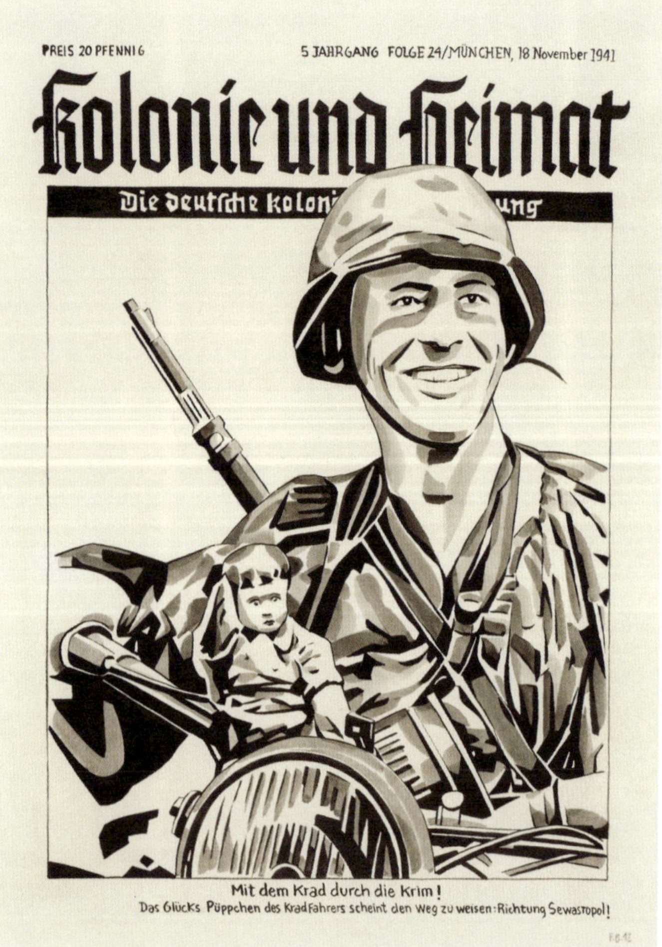
PREIS 20 PFENNIG   5 JAHRGANG FOLGE 24/MÜNCHEN, 18 November 1941
Kolonie und Heimat
Die Deutsche koloniale Zeitung
Mit dem Krad durch die Krim!
Das Glücks-Püppchen des Kradfahrers scheint den Weg zu weisen: Richtung Sewastopol!

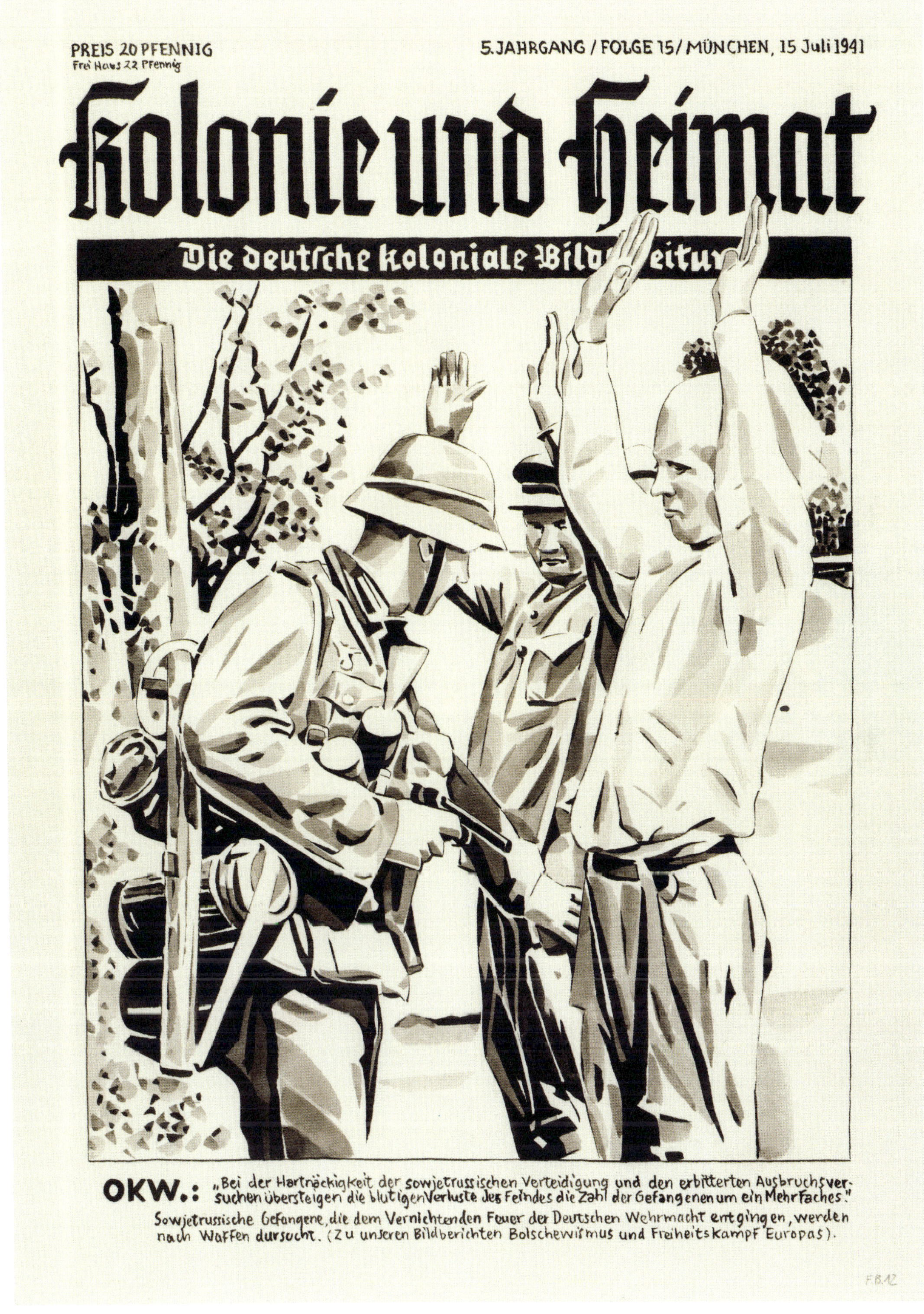

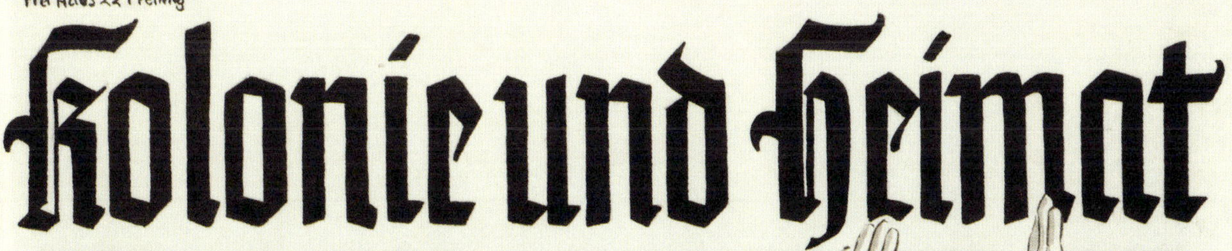

OKW.: „Bei der Hartnäckigkeit der sowjetrussischen Verteidigung und den erbitterten Ausbruchsversuchen übersteigen die blutigen Verluste des Feindes die Zahl der Gefangenen um ein Mehrfaches."

Sowjetrussische Gefangene, die dem vernichtenden Feuer der Deutschen Wehrmacht entgingen, werden nach Waffen durchsucht. (Zu unseren Bildberichten Bolschewismus und Freiheitskampf Europas).

F.B.12

Francis Alÿs's interdisciplinary practice includes painting and drawing, performance, video and animation. He occasionally orchestrates events involving crowds of volunteers and produces related artwork: enigmatic pale line drawings on pieces of vellum stuck together with masking tape in a workmanlike manner. Alÿs has said of his practice: 'Drawings are my way of thinking about a project without thinking – of thinking about it in a different way, from another angle…. It's really a way of generating ideas.'

When Faith Moves Mountains was a large-scale event that took place in the sand dunes near Lima, Peru. It involved 500 student volunteers, armed with shovels, forming a line and digging in unison to 'move' the dune forward by ten centimetres. Many of Alÿs's projects entail a heroic but futile circularity; he recently filmed two small children in Kabul unravelling and simultaneously re-ravelling a reel of 35mm film. *The Modern Procession* was a more upbeat event in New York that marked the temporary relocation of the Museum of Modern Art from Manhattan to Queens. A brass band accompanied the procession as it carried replicas of famous works from the collection and also bore aloft, like a model of the Virgin or a saint in a Catholic procession, the enthroned, real-life form of the artist Kiki Smith.

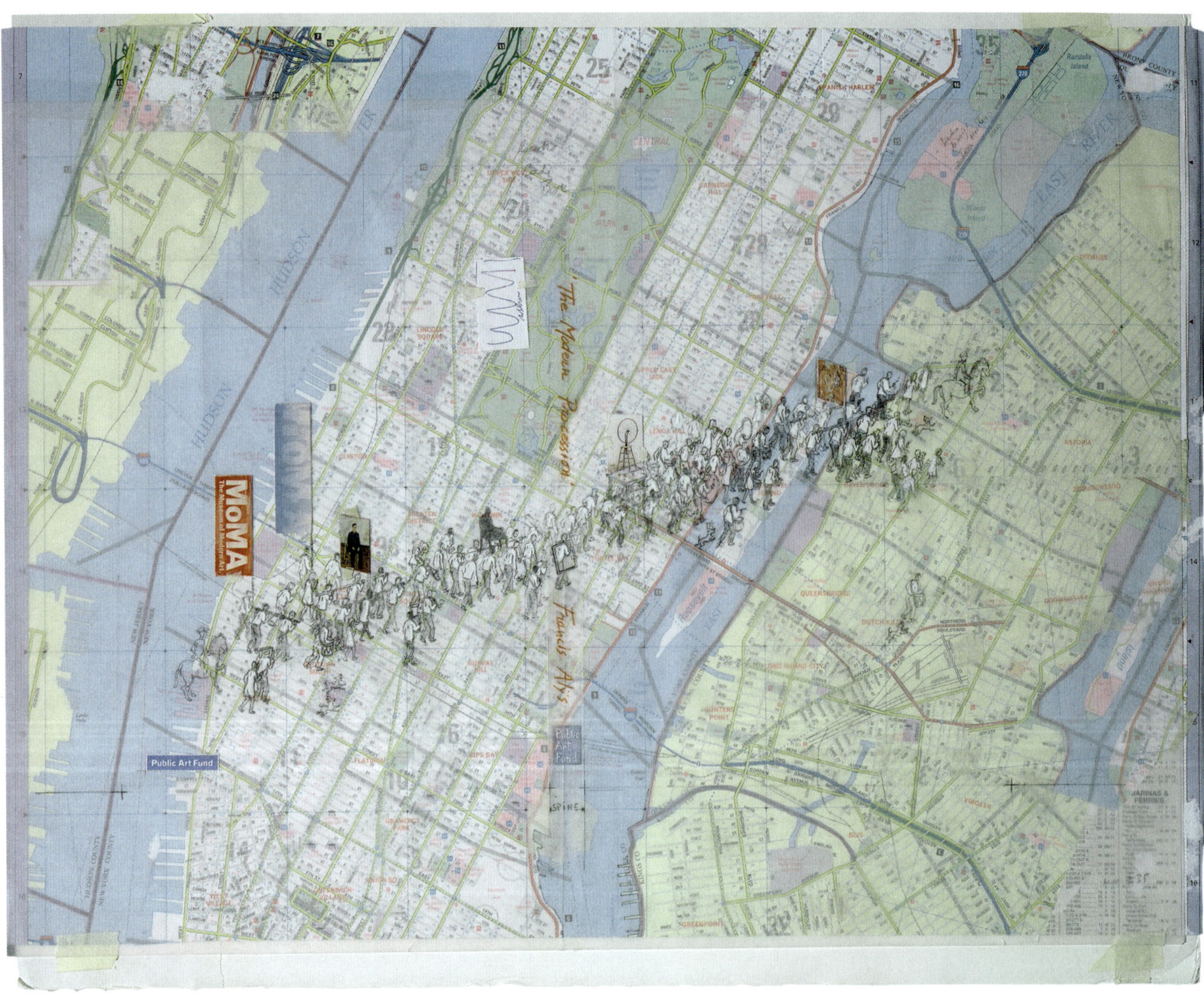

Study for The Modern Procession, 2002
Pencil, paint and collage on map
16 × 21.45 cm (6 ¼ × 8 ½ in.)

WFMM Viñeta 2, Untitled, Study for When Faith Moves Mountains, 2001–2 >
Oil and pencil on tracing paper
26.4 × 35.4 cm (10 ⅜ × 13 ⅞ in.)

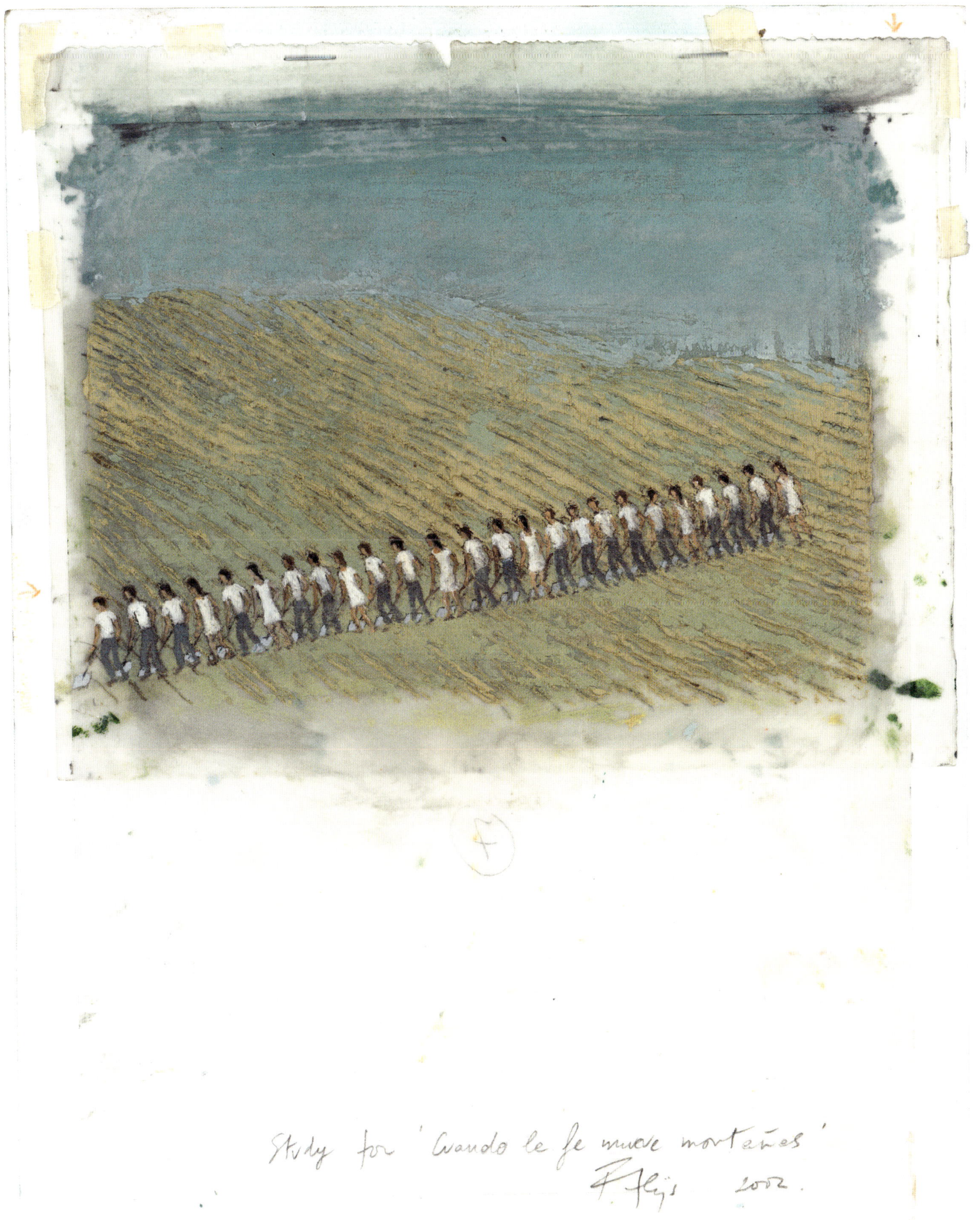

Study for 'Cuando le fe mueve montañes'

F. Alÿs 2002.

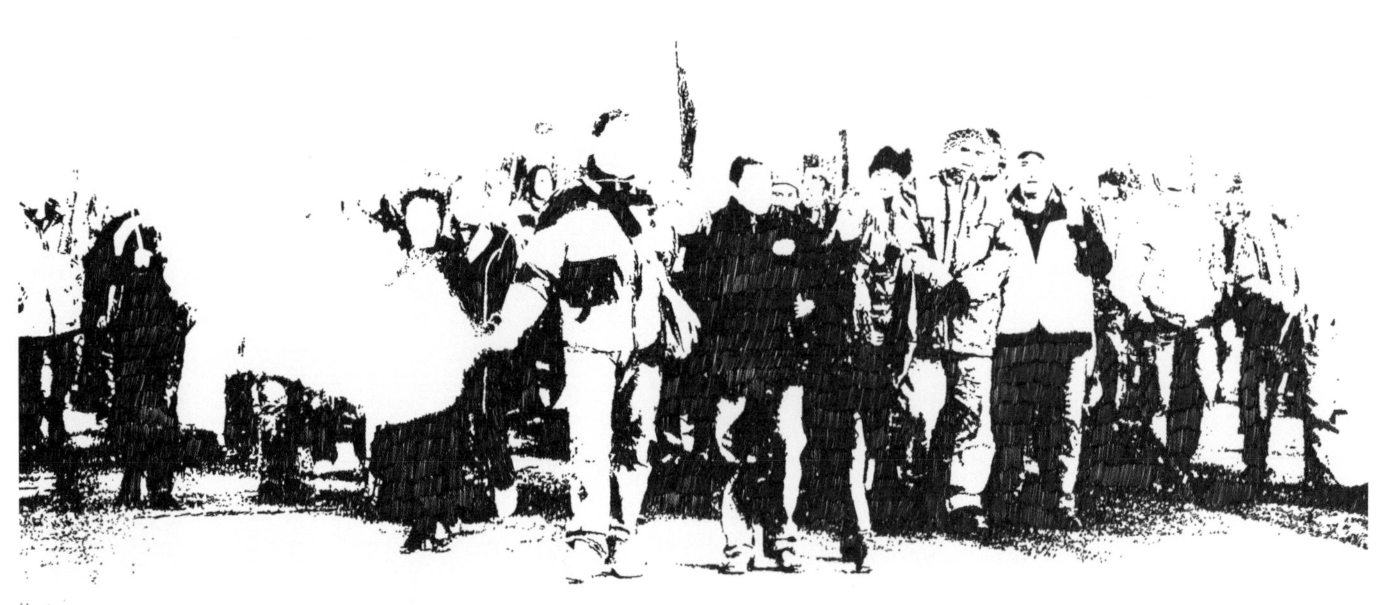

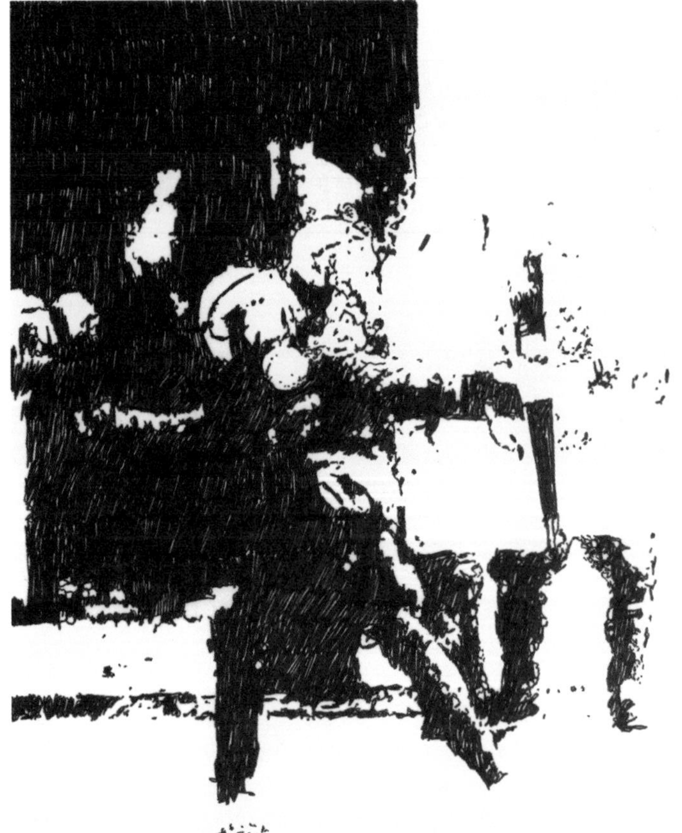

Emmanuel Régent's method of painting mimics in reverse the effect he creates in his drawings. For the paintings, he applies numerous layers of monochrome paint to canvas and then sands them back to achieve a diffused luminosity, like the flare of a comet in the night sky. By contrast, the drawings begin with the whiteness of the paper on which the progressive accretion of fine black lines builds up shadowy forms that set off positive against negative, thus resembling an over-exposed photograph in which the substance of its subjects is dissolved. Régent describes his way of drawing as a 'eulogy for slowness'. He draws ruins and monuments, people waiting in queues and flickering light on tranquil water surrounding rocks, as well as more active scenes in which flat white surfaces such as protest banners and riot shields catch the light. Régent is interested in 'naively contemplating the necessity to draw by hand still today, to link the ancestral gesture of a single stroke of charcoal to the extra-sensitive PAD of my new Mac. To take the time to "do" something, to use hundreds of markers, to fill in with ink, to conserve paper…. Drawing is an autonomous language that doesn't need any explanation. I like its economy of "no matter where, no matter when, with almost nothing".'

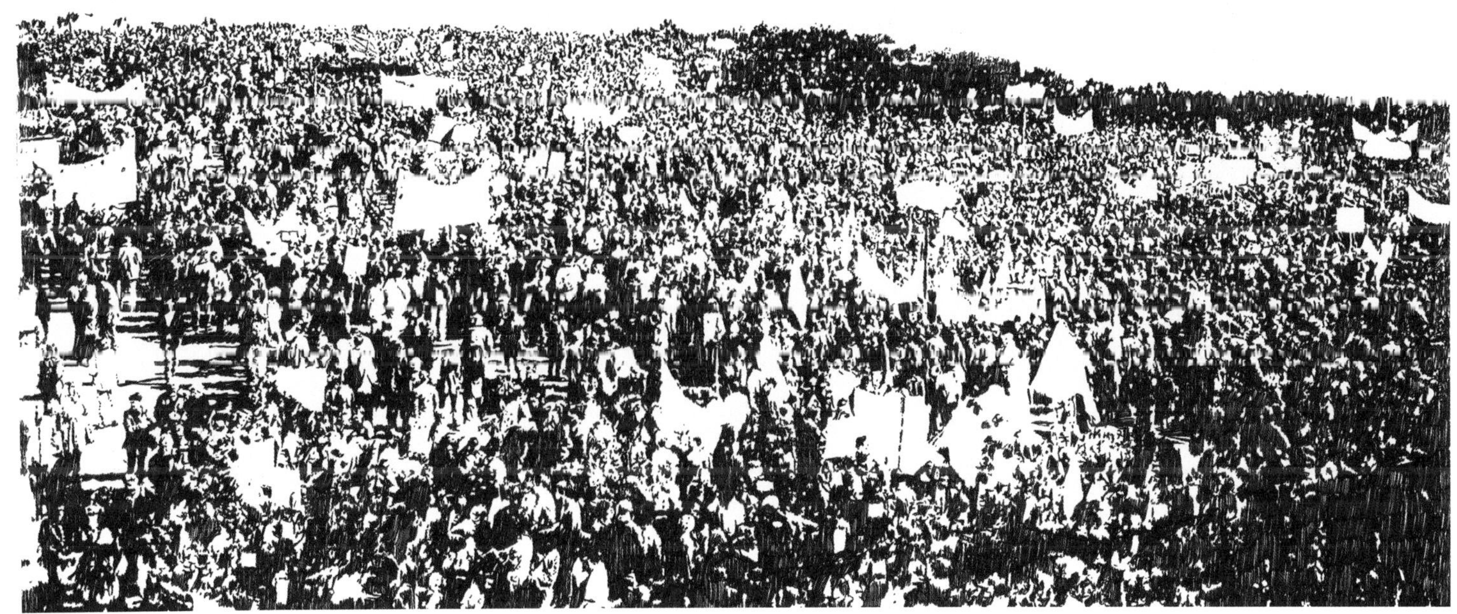

< (top) *Manifestations 5*, 2009
Felt tip ink on paper
56 × 76 cm (22 × 29 ⅞ in.)

< (below) *L'angle noir (Antiquités grecques)*, 2008
Felt tip ink on paper
30 × 40 cm (11 ¾ × 15 ¾ in.)

Sortir de son lit…, 2010
Diptych, felt tip ink on paper
230 × 130 cm (90 ½ × 51 ⅛ in.)

The diverse strands of Otobong Nkanga's practice in performance, photography, installation and drawing are connected thematically through her interest in the politics and poetics of geography. In her drawings she visualizes our complex relationship to the land as a personal and cultural space, a resource and a location. Her graphic language is a lively combination of the surreal and the diagrammatic, illustrating abstract concepts such as ownership, interdependence, exploitation and protection through combinations of simple schematic elements: silhouetted body parts, disembodied arms and hands holding tools, topographical sections, ropes, buildings and plants. Surprisingly un-didactic considering the literal nature of the subject matter, each drawing reads like a rebus, a playful way of thinking without words. A community of hands is linked by threads, suggesting a controlling puppeteer: the corporate 'decider'. Threads of rope, string or barbed wire define space, enclosing, entangling or defending it or, in a colonial tug of war, pulling it apart. In the top left corner of each panel a cluster of colours represents Nkanga's palette. The artist also thinks of the issues she addresses as a palette of ideas to be combined or juxtaposed, which helps to explain why her treatment of them is so original and engaging. The issues are interrelated, and the same metaphors apply in the domestic, economic and political spheres.

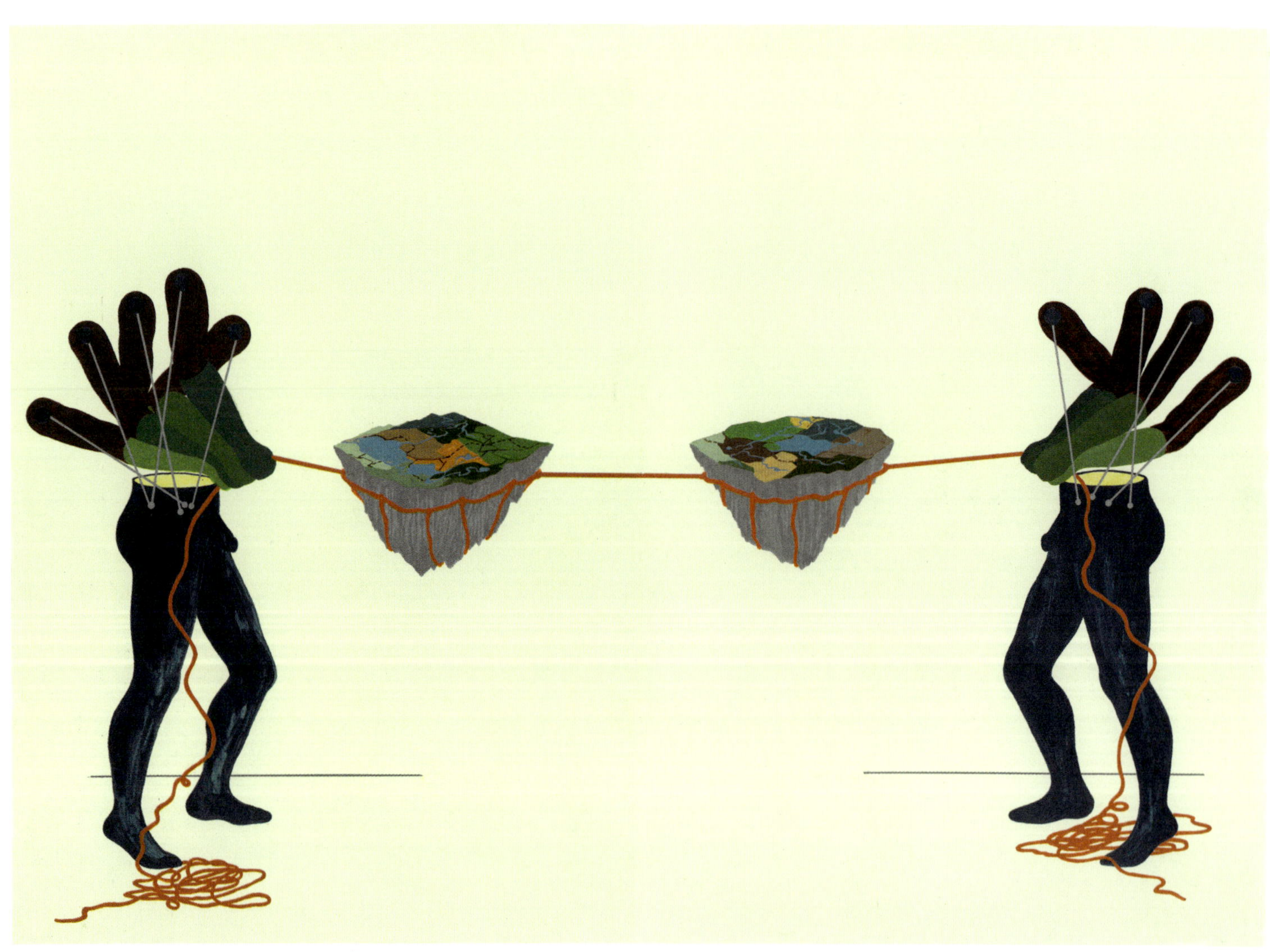

Social Consequences I: Crisis, 2009
Drawing, round stickers and acrylic on paper
2 parts, each 29 × 42 cm (11 ⅜ × 16 ½ in.)

Social Consequences II: Constructivism, 2009 >
Drawing, round stickers and acrylic on paper
29 × 42 cm (11 ⅜ × 16 ½ in.)

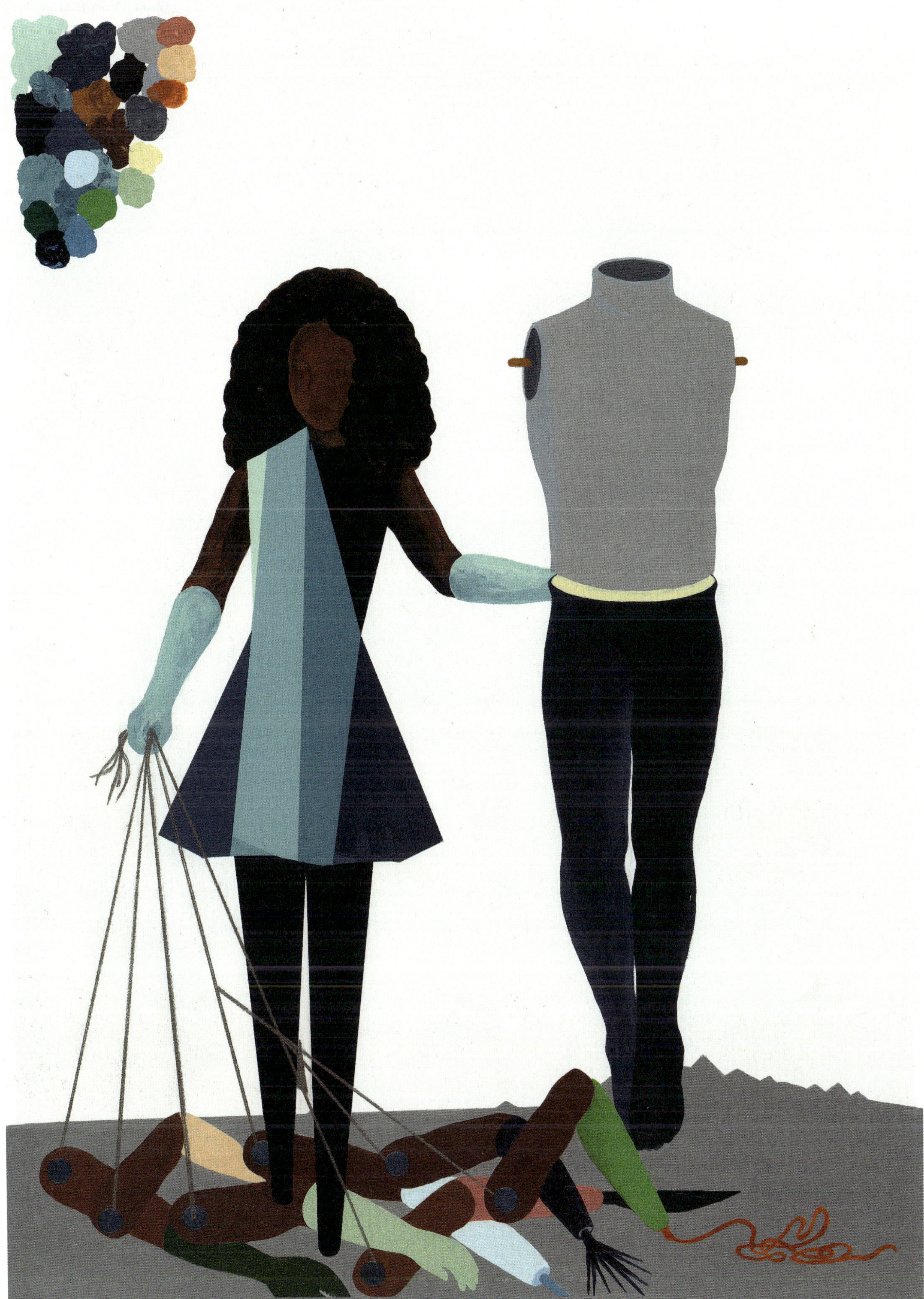

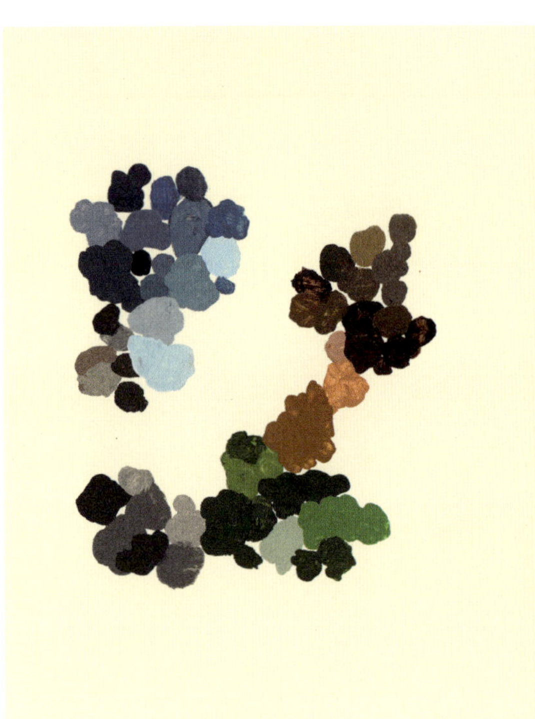
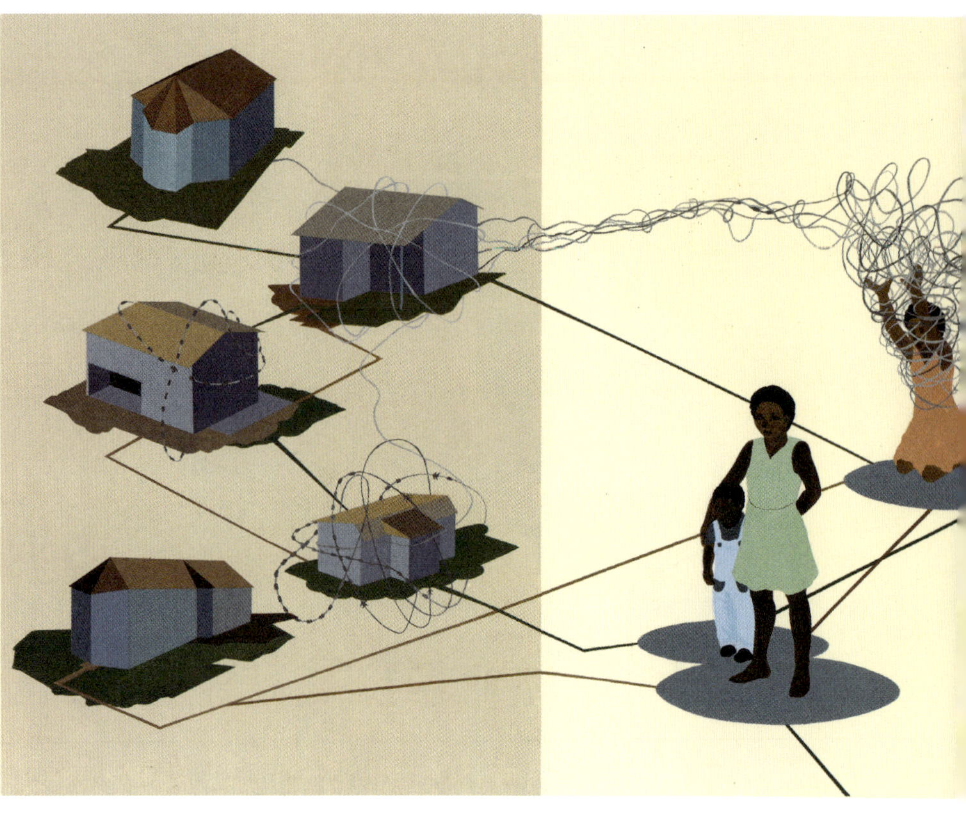

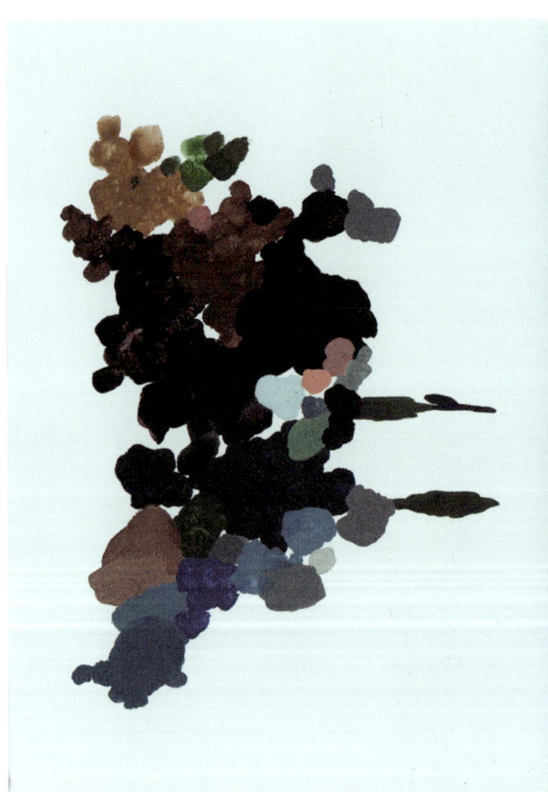
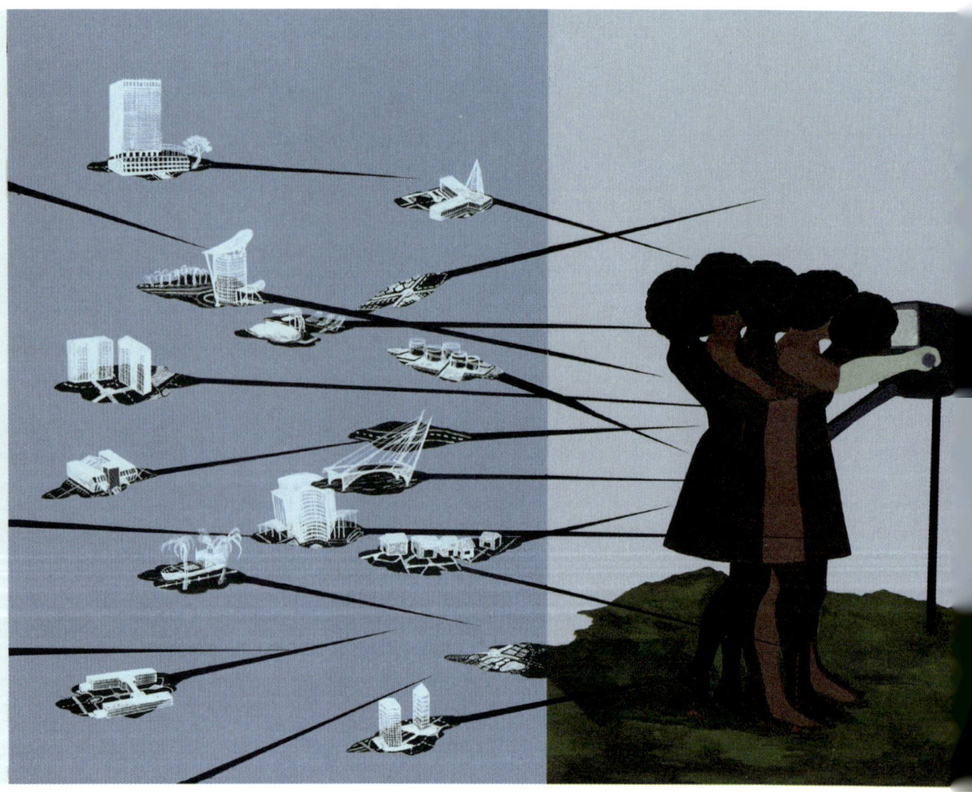

(top) *Social Consequences I: Segregation – Encroaching Barricade – Entangled – Endangered Species – Rationed Measures – Intertwined,* 2009
Drawing, round stickers and acrylic on paper
6 parts, each 29 × 42 cm (11 ⅜ × 16 ½ in.)

(below) *Social Consequences II: The Overload – Projectiles – Piercing Pressure – Hostage – Wastescape – The Overflow,* 2009
Drawing, round stickers and acrylic on paper
6 parts, each 29 × 42 cm (11 ⅜ × 16 ½ in.)

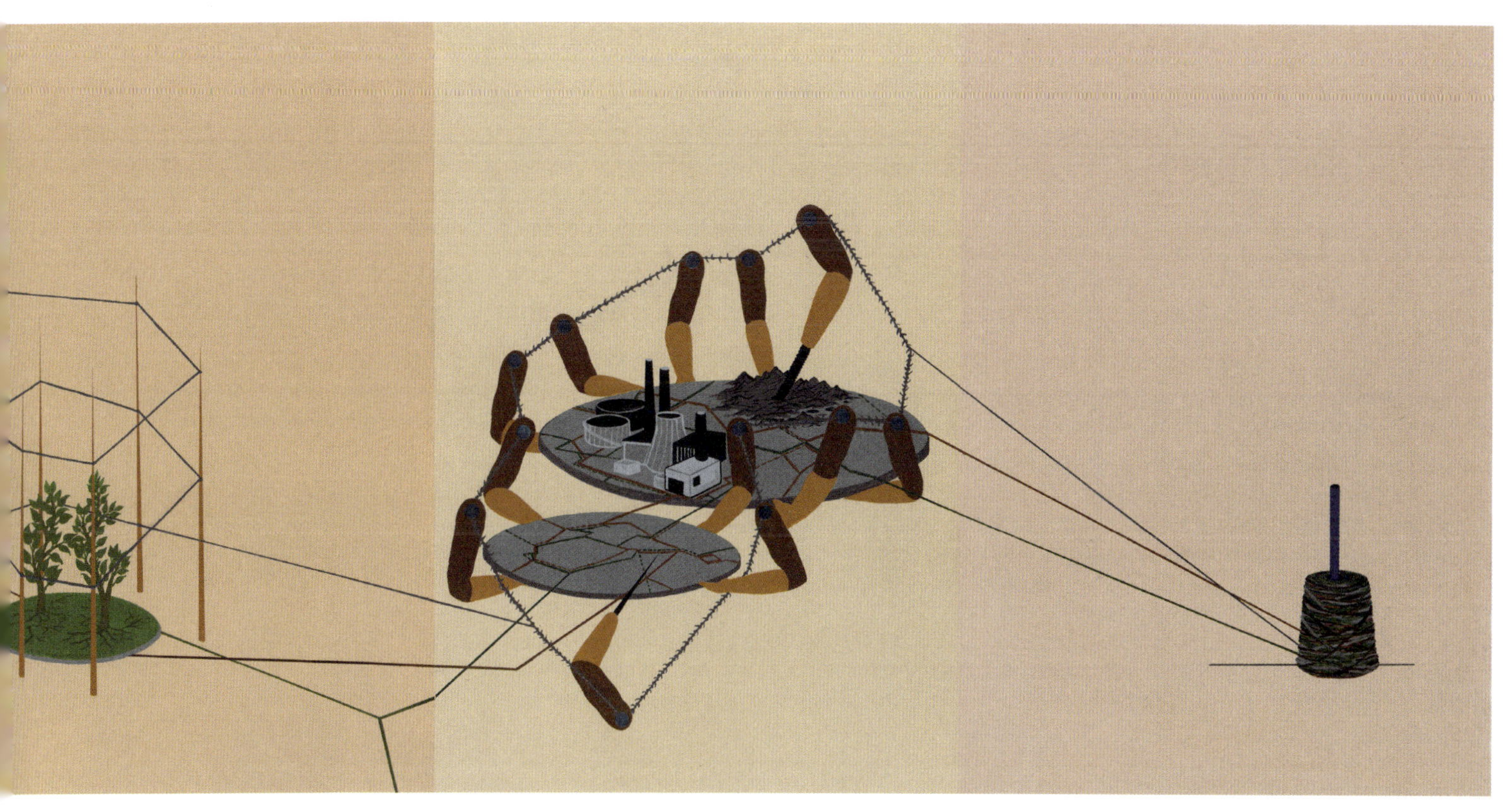

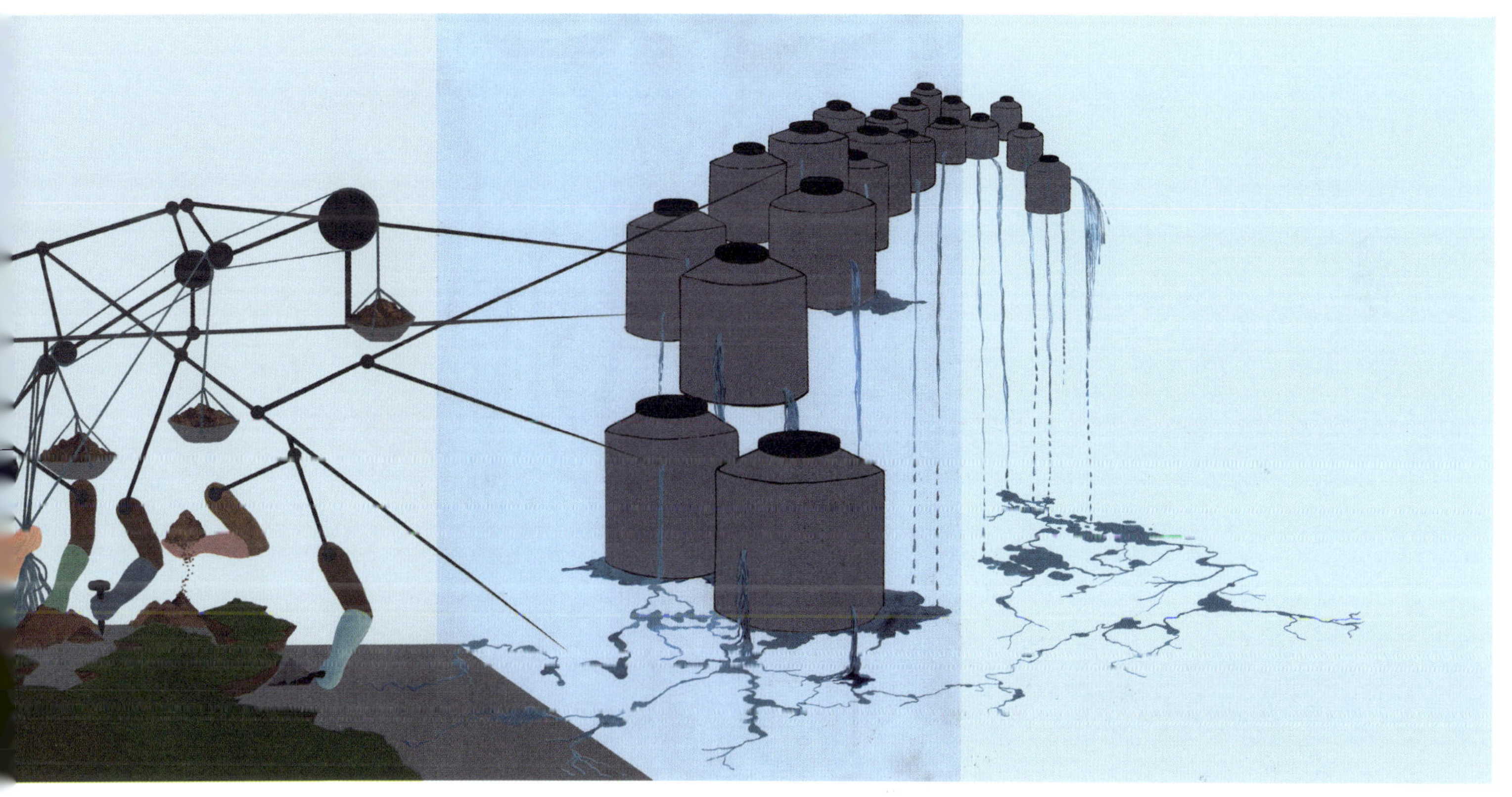

William Kentridge is internationally renowned for his animated films, video installations, drawings, prints and theatre and opera productions, many of which address the contemporary state of his hometown Johannesburg and the still palpable legacy of South African apartheid. He describes himself foremost as 'an artist who makes drawings', and it is significant that when he gave the prestigious Charles Eliot Norton lectures at Harvard University in 2012, he entitled the series 'Drawing Lessons'. Drawing is the primary impulse propelling Kentridge's extraordinary range of activities: it is the medium in which he thinks. He uses charcoal for his animations, he says, because

of its tonal range, which is good for film, and because of the speed and ease with which it can be changed. His procedure for making an animated film is to draw with charcoal, walk across the studio to photograph the drawing, cross back to the paper to erase or alter it, then back to the camera and so on, hundreds of times a day. The traces of erasure and change remain, giving a rippling fluidity to the narrative that helps him to present history and social experience in innovative ways. Preconceived ideas are kept to the minimum, and there is no storyboard; thinking evolves through activity.

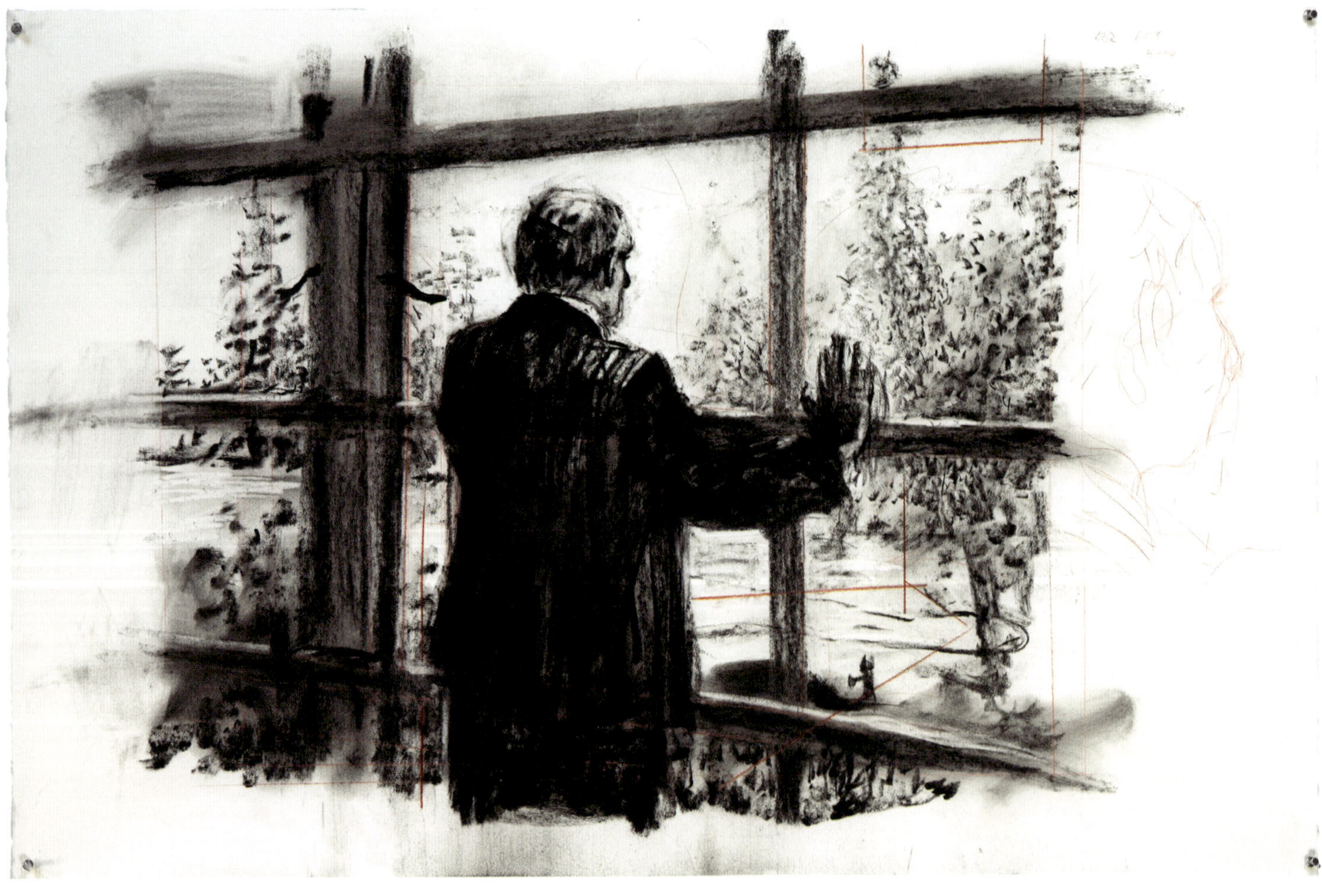

Drawing for the film *Other Faces,* 2011
Charcoal and coloured pencil on paper
80 × 121 cm (31 ½ × 47 ⅝ in.)

(opposite, top) Drawing for the film *Other Faces,* 2011 >
Charcoal and coloured pencil on paper
92 × 114 cm (36 ¼ × 44 ⅞ in.)

(opposite, below) Drawing for the film *Other Faces,* 2011 >
Charcoal and coloured pencil on paper
78.5 × 121 cm (30 ⅞ × 47 ⅝ in.)

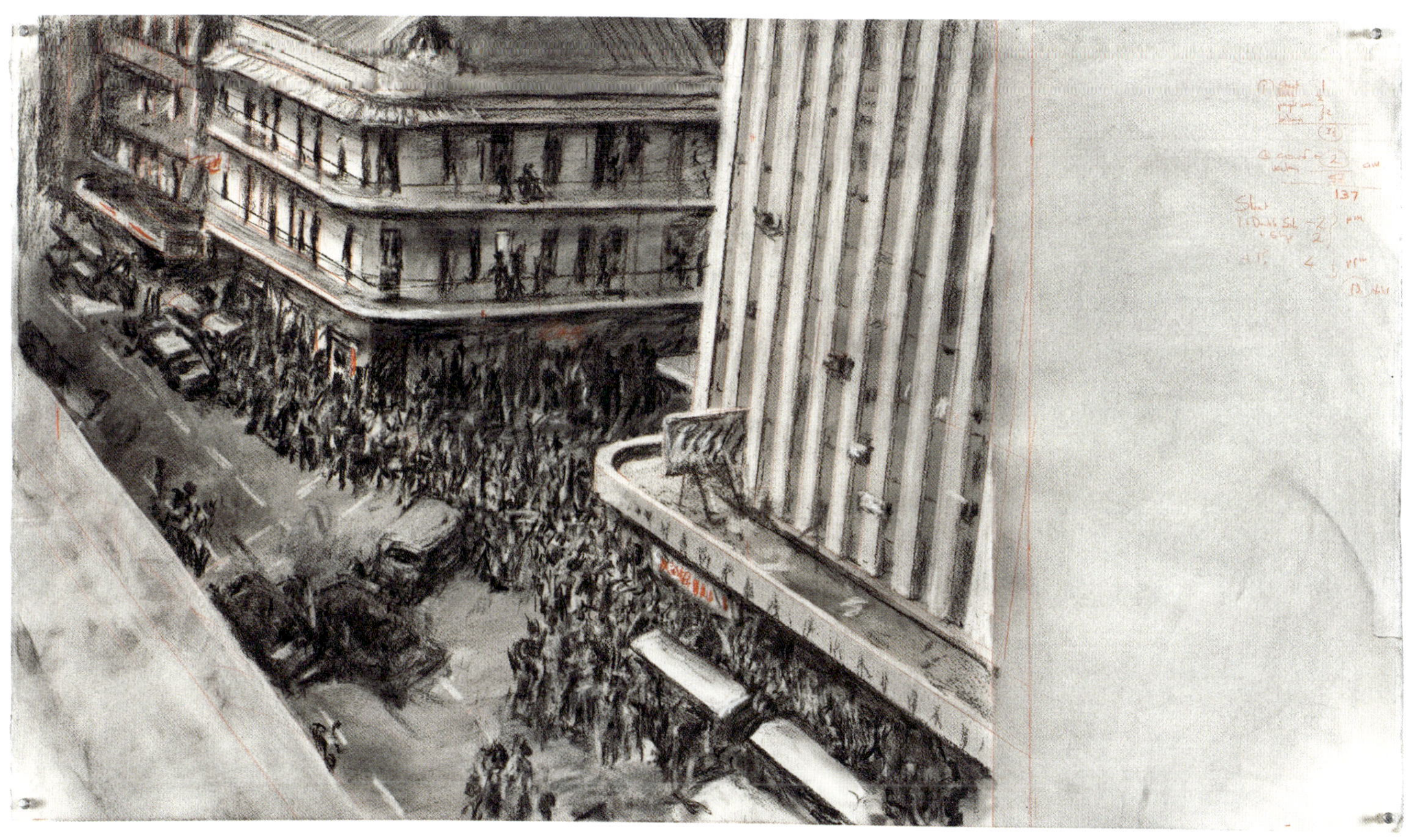
HORN
OF AFRICA
NO. 238A
JEPPE ST

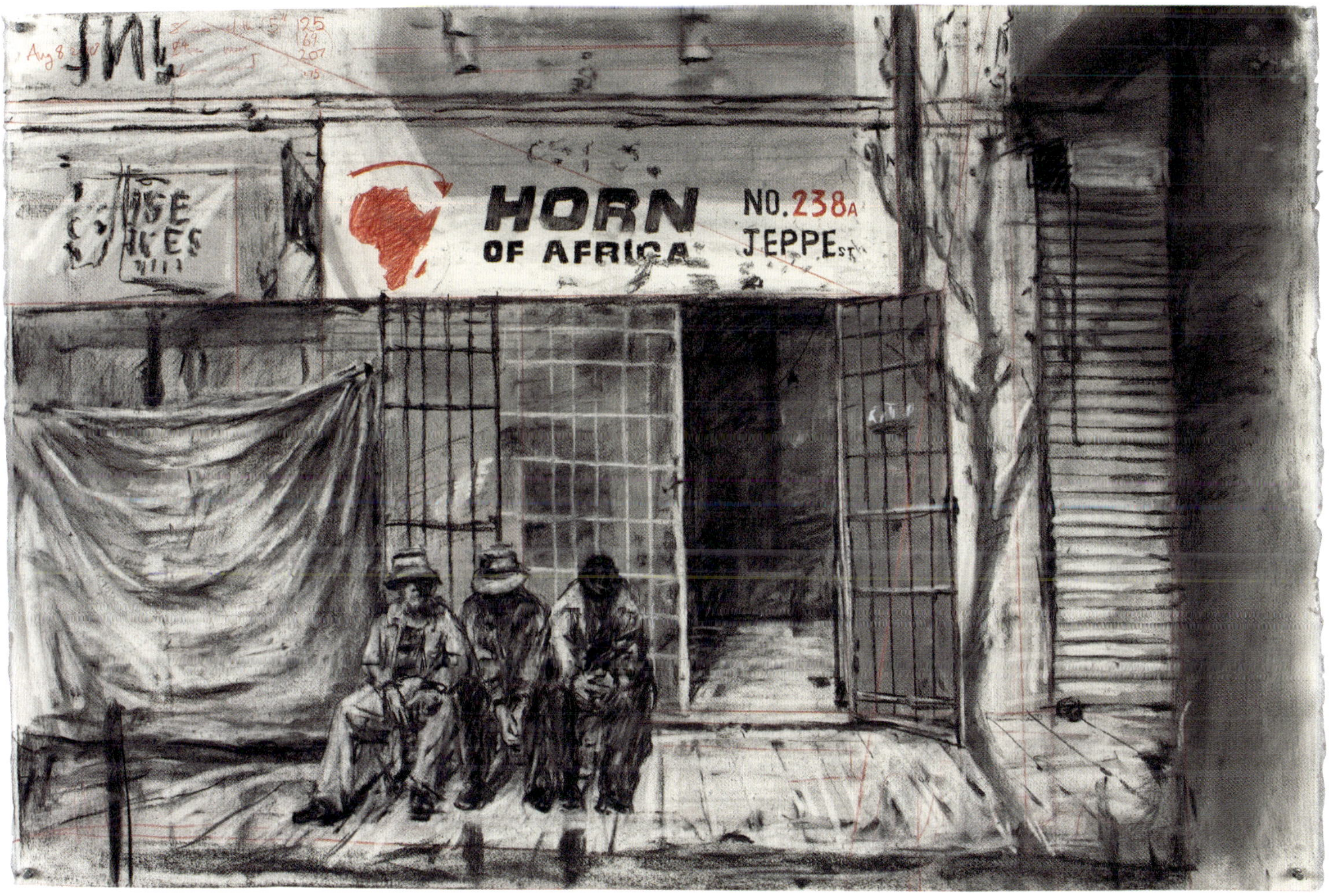

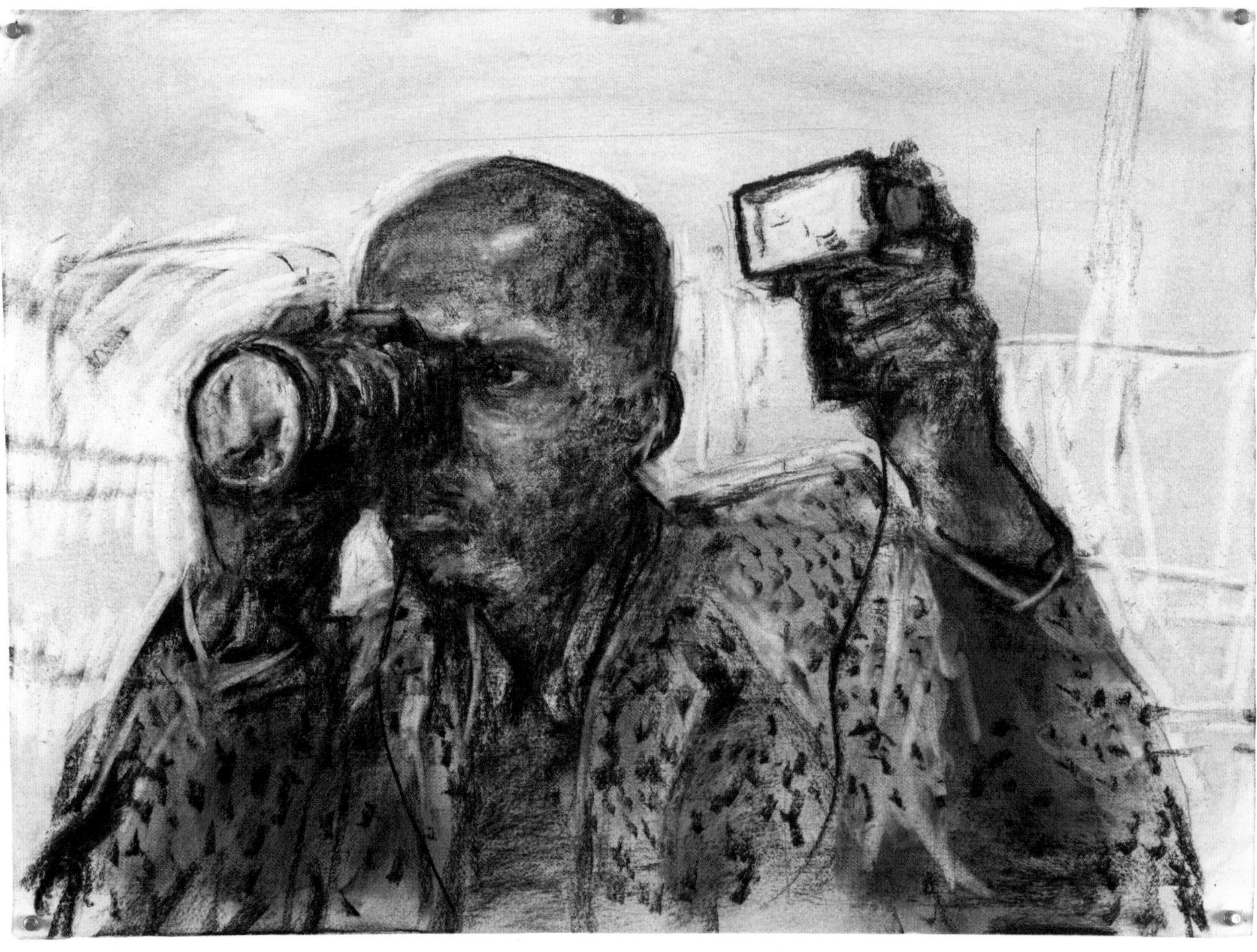

Drawing for the film *Other Faces,* 2011
Charcoal and coloured pencil on paper
57 × 78 cm (22 ½ × 30 ¾ in.)

Drawing for the film *Other Faces,* 2011 >
Charcoal, pastel and coloured pencil on page from mine ledger book
47 × 67 cm (18 ½ × 26 ⅜ in.)

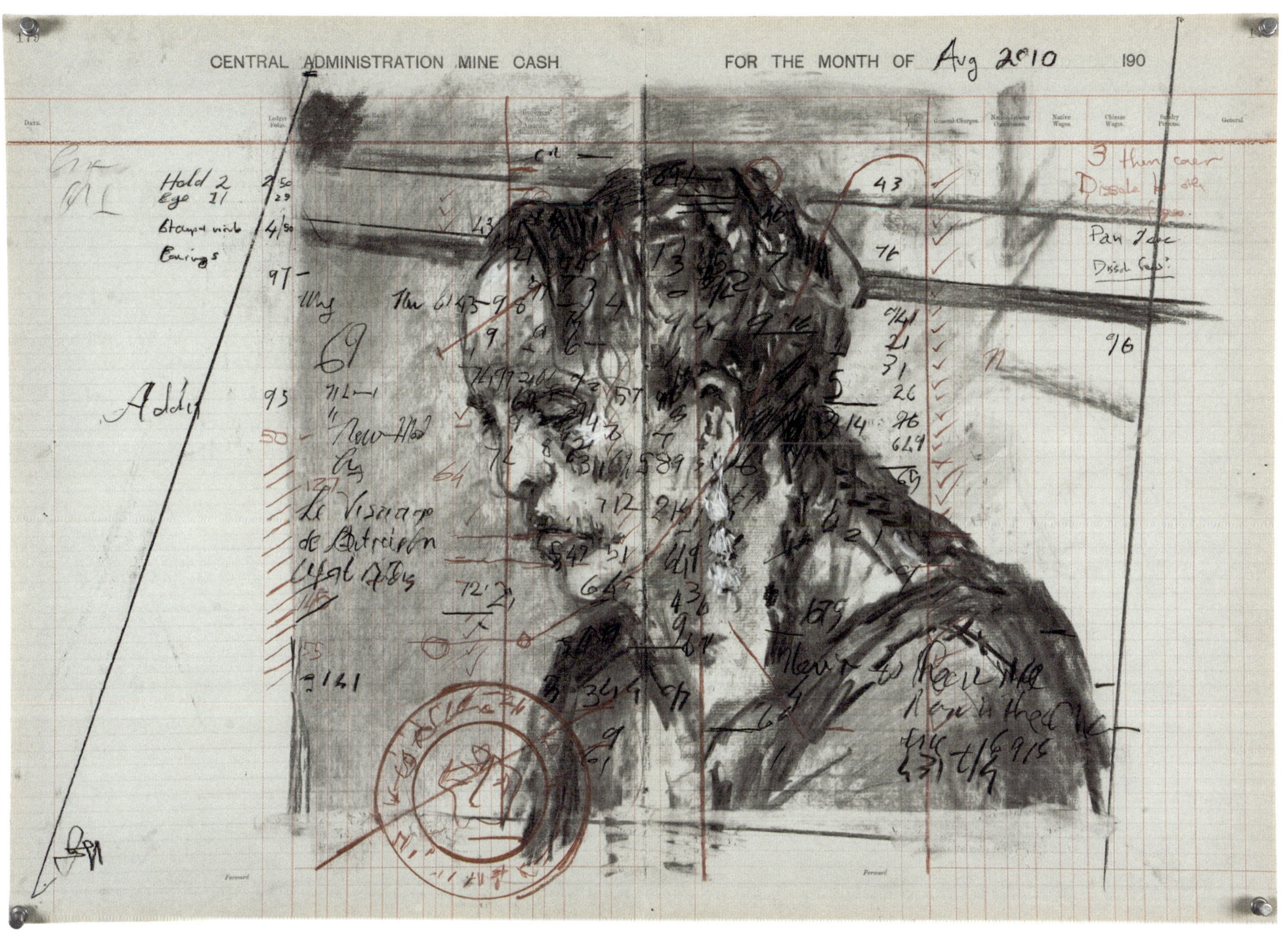

Michaël Borremans conceives of his drawings and his paintings as 'two very different bodies of work, with very different means, for very different purposes'. He originally trained as an etcher and this has clearly had a bearing on the intimacy of his drawings – his tendency to play with scale and his imagery of figures looming over and manipulating miniature worlds. These figures are often generic mid-twentieth-century workers who seem to be conducting or overseeing social experiments. Individuals are boxed in or compartmentalized; decapitated heads are arranged on trays or shelves, or placed on pedestals. There is an air of impending doom: or perhaps one of a disaster that has already occurred.

Borremans describes his experience of the world in ominous terms: 'It's a cold and strange place. I don't know, I find it in everything: in contact with other people, in politics, in economics, I feel like we're living on a time bomb. I'm always surprised nothing worse happens, as if I'm anticipating it, and eventually it will happen…. That's why I'm into drawing…. I've made drawings all my life. I can't live without drawing. It's my way of dealing with reality. It is a kind of escape: when I feel uncomfortable in certain situations, I create my own reality.'

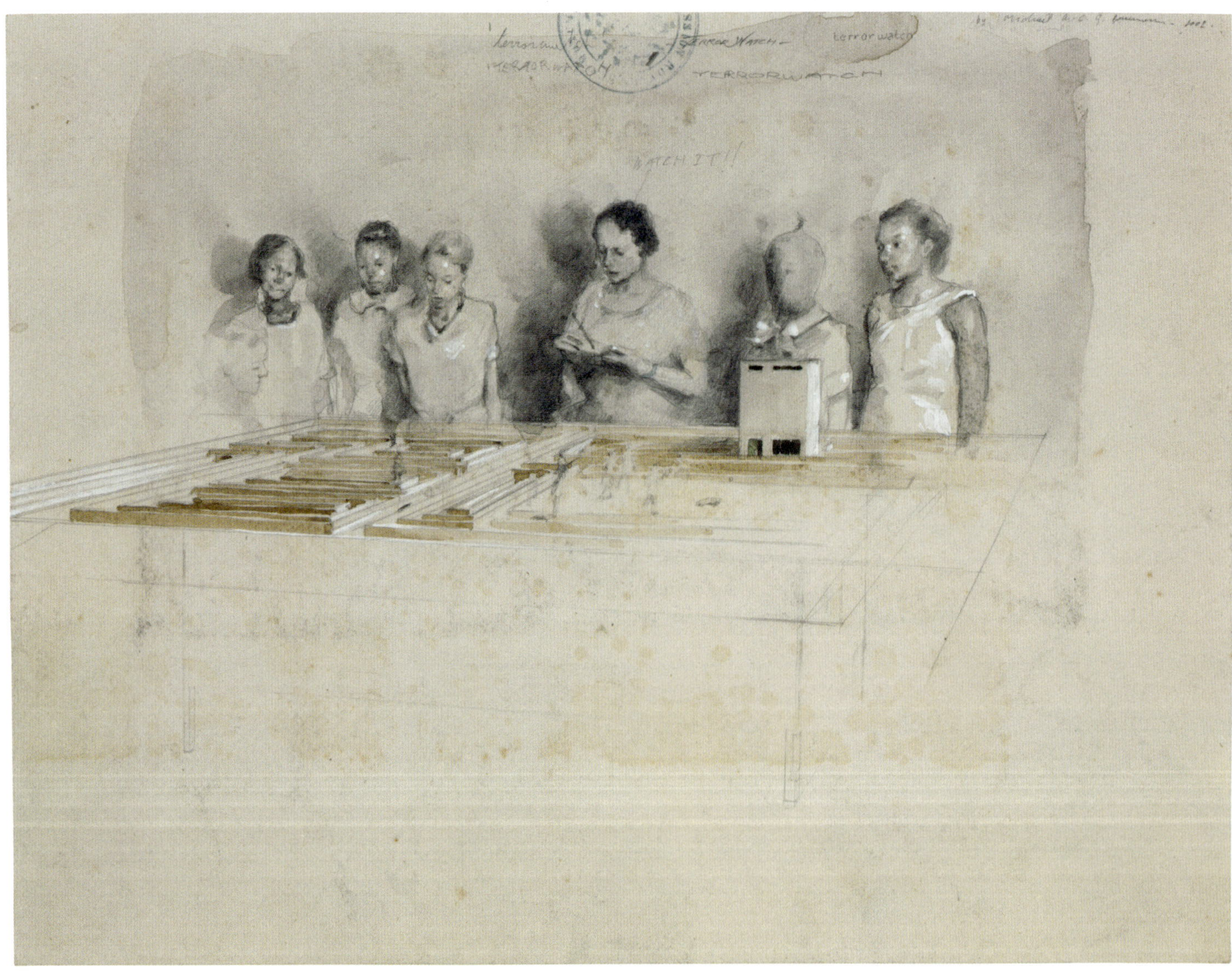

Terror Watch, 2002
Pencil and watercolour on paper
23 × 30 cm (9 × 11 ¾ in.)

In the Louvre: The House of Opportunity, 2003 >
Watercolour, pencil and oil on paper
26.6 × 27.9 cm (10 ½ × 11 in.)

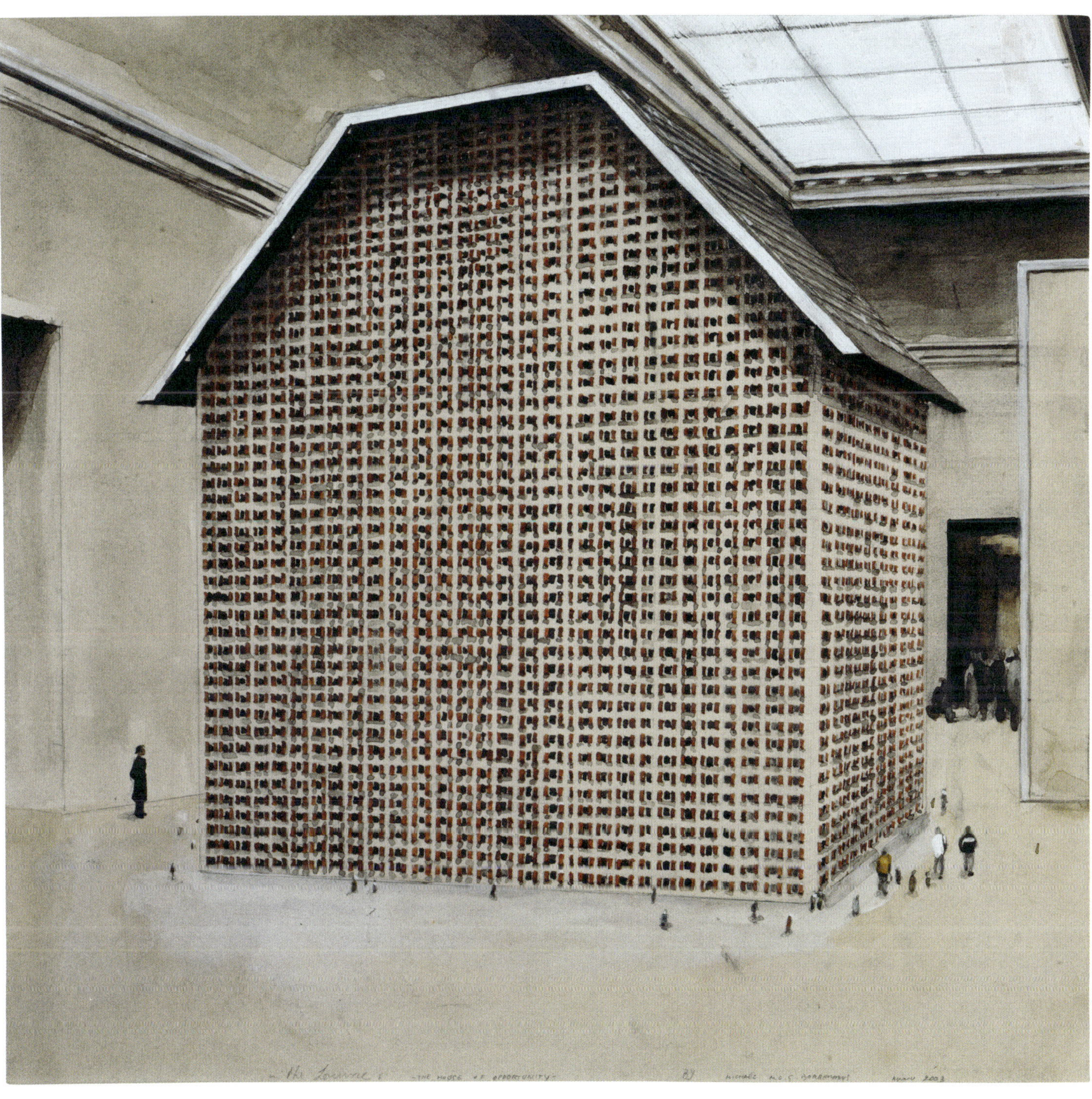
"THE HOUSE OF OPPORTUNITY"

AIDA MAKOTO *Born 1965, Niigata, Japan. Lives and works in Kanagawa, Japan*

158

Aida Makoto's apocalyptic images that parody the fantasies of Japanese consumer culture are double-edged, sometimes appearing to exemplify the vices they purport to satirize. The excesses of manga and anime-style kitsch are magnified and carried to outrageous, occasionally revolting extremes, delivered with bravado and nihilistic humour. Aida's 2012–13 retrospective at Tokyo's Mori Art Museum was entitled 'Monument to Nothing', reflecting an artistic vision that is uncompromising and pitiless. His subjects are evidently those that he most enjoys drawing, whether nubile schoolgirls mangled to a pulp or a mountain of corpses of Japanese salary men – famous for their conformism and retarded sexuality – in suits and ties, piled high among briefcases, laptops and office equipment. The sheer scale and detail of *Ash Color Mountains* (2009–11) are awe-inspiring: painted in acrylic on canvas, this work is considered here as a drawing for the way in which it displays the artist's distinctly graphic technique. Every figure is carefully delineated in a comic-book illustrative style, yet the effect of the whole scene – a traditional vista of mountains in the mist – is somehow sublime.

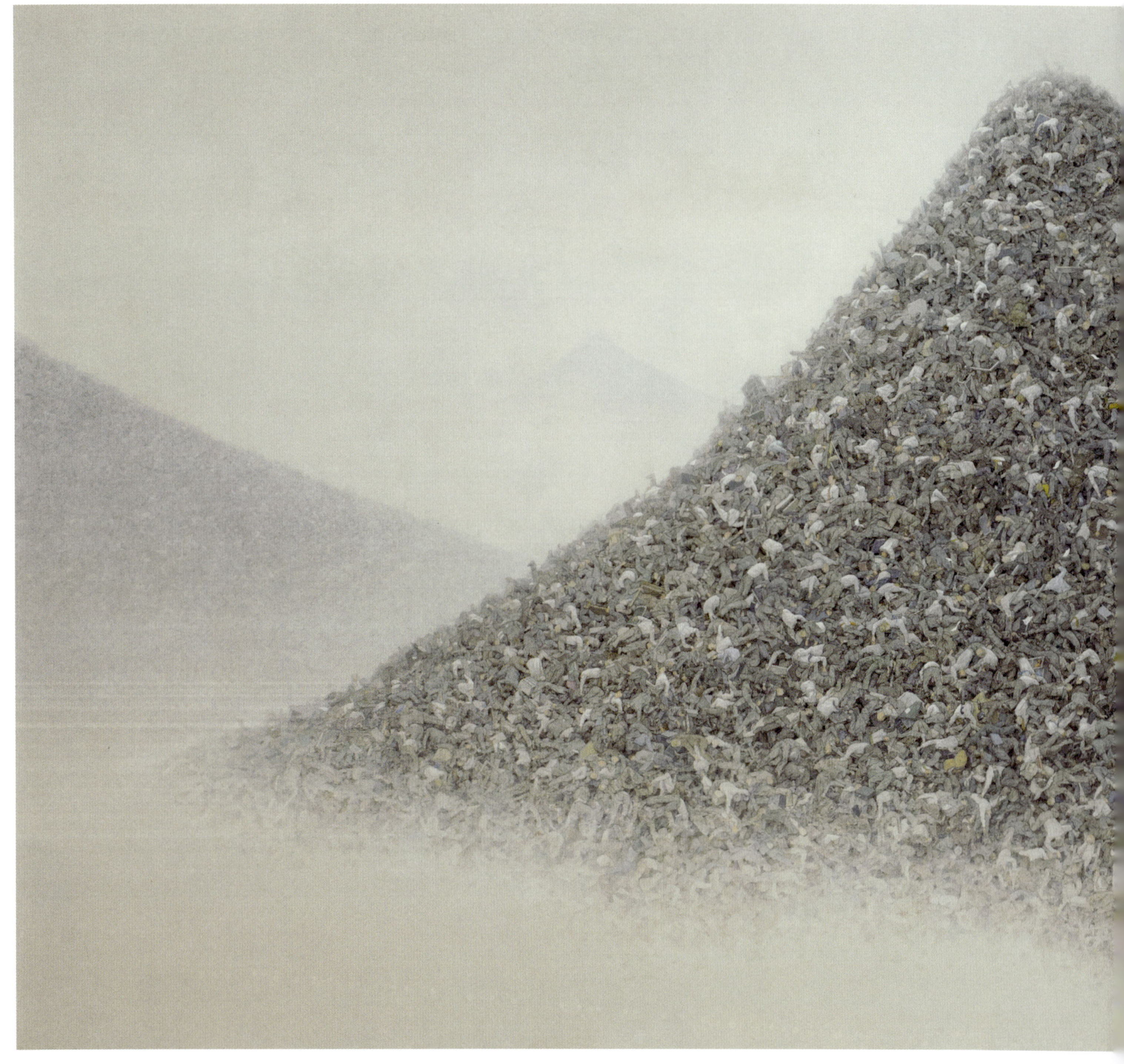

Ash Color Mountains, 2009–11
Acrylic on canvas
300 × 700 cm (118 ⅛ × 275 ⅝ in.)

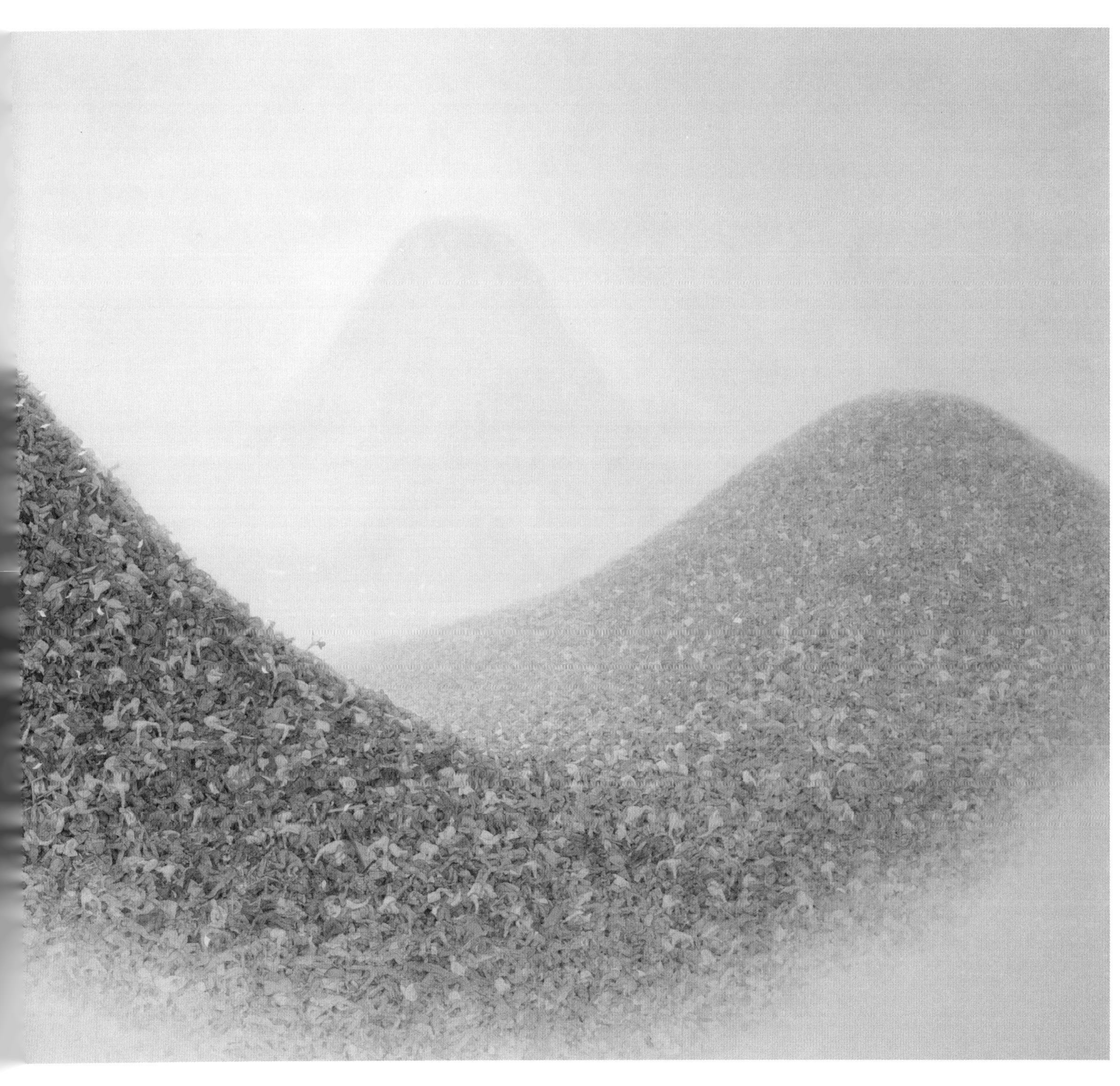

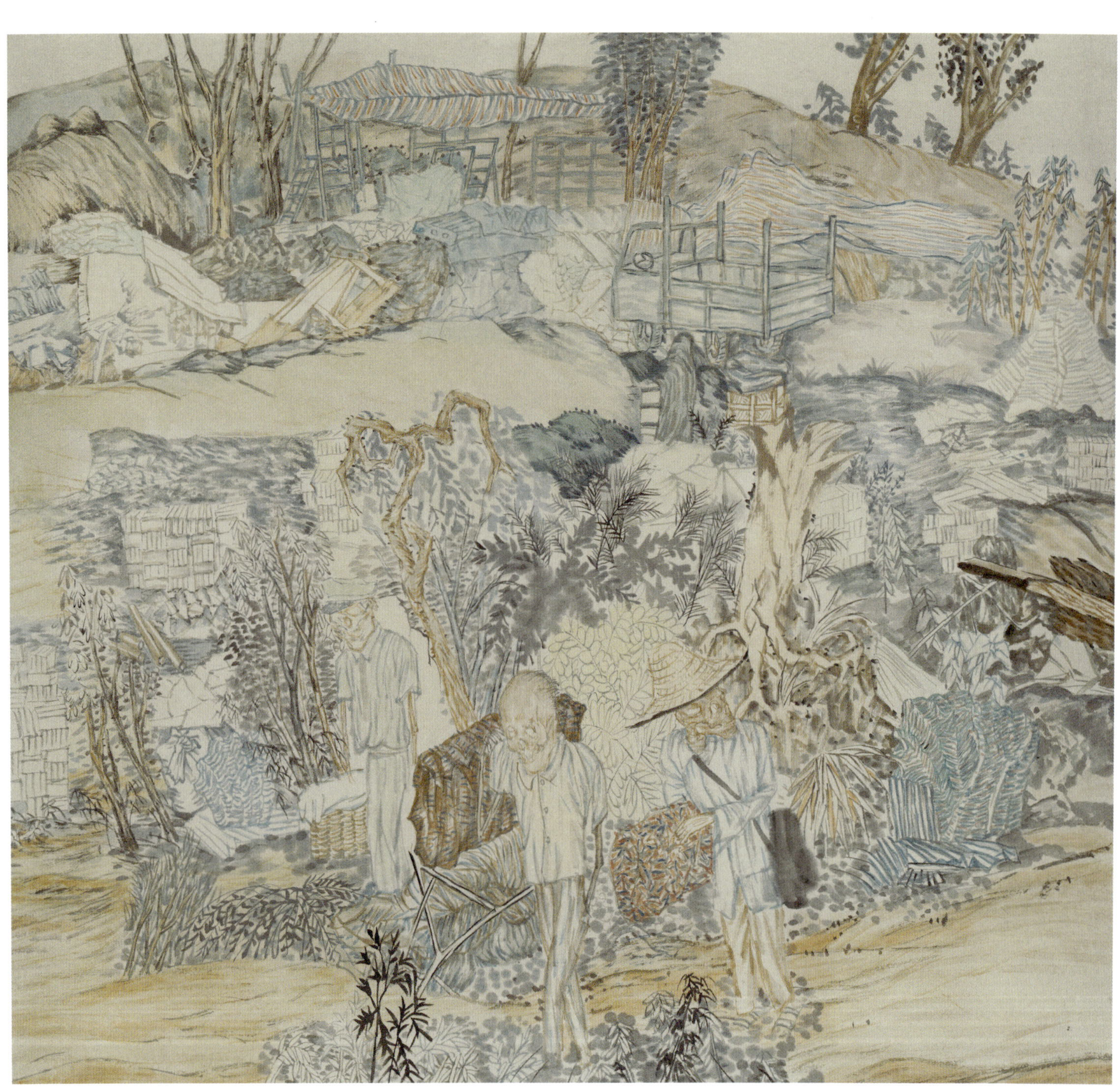

YUN-FEI JI *Born 1963, Beijing, China. Lives and works in New York, USA*

Yun-Fei Ji was born during the Cultural Revolution in China, and his mother was sent away for seven years' re-education when the artist was two years old. He studied at the Central Academy of Art in Beijing, where the aesthetic regime at the time was Socialist Realism. It was the discovery of ancient Buddhist narrative frescoes that inspired Ji to revive the 'abandoned' tradition of landscape painting in watercolour and ink and to use it to depict contemporary scenes of social injustice. Since 1990 Ji has lived in New York, but he visits China frequently and has made work that represents such manmade disasters as the massive destruction caused by the Three Gorges Dam project, which has displaced up to two million people.

Ji's landscapes are populated with grotesque figures reminiscent of the work of twentieth century artists George Grosz and Otto Dix. He uses ghosts as metaphors to address human problems: the plight of the villagers displaced by the Dam, for instance, who literally had to dig up their ancestors' bones and take them with them. In *Seven Intellectuals* (2007), which alludes to a traditional theme in Chinese art of artist-scholars living in the countryside, the seven individuals are overseen by a loudmouthed Maoist official, visible in the lower right corner. Ji declares his belief in the power of observation – 'I am putting all my faith in looking and describing' – a power that is clearly seen in his relentless, unflinching visions of his country's social and cultural problems.

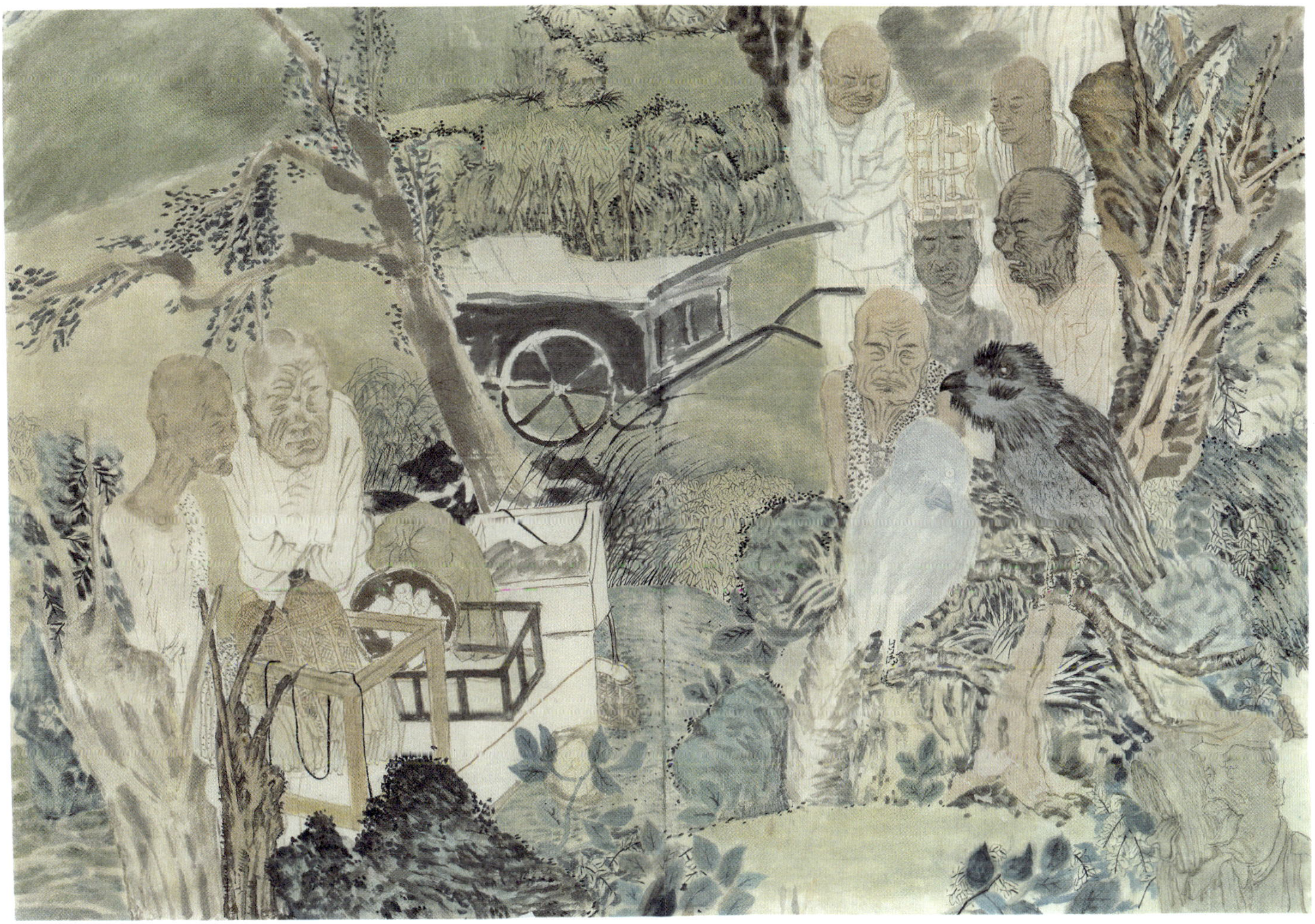

< *The died are also moving,* 2007
Mineral pigments and ink on rice paper
89.5 × 97 cm (35 ¼ × 38 ¼ in.)

Seven Intellectuals, 2007
Mineral pigments and ink on Xuan paper
132.1 × 193 cm (52 × 76 in.)

PAVEL PEPPERSTEIN *Born 1966, Moscow, Russia. Lives and works in Moscow, Russia*

Artist, writer, political rapper, film-maker and mystic Pavel Pepperstein was a founding member of the neo-conceptualist collective Inspection Medical Hermeneutics in Moscow in 1987, a group whose goal was 'investigating social consciousness and applying gentle therapeutic measures to calm it down'. Their tools included psychoanalysis, Buddhism, semiotics, Russian Orthodox theology and pharmacology. Pepperstein later called himself a 'psychedelic realist', and tried to steer artists away from an 'excessive interest in social and political problematics' and towards an investigation of 'the consciousness of the solitary individual who is entirely isolated from society'.

Following in the footsteps of his father Viktor Pivovarov and his father's friend Ilya Kabakov, both conceptual artists who had supported themselves in their early years by illustrating children's books, Pepperstein is a prodigious draughtsman. His *nom de plume* is adapted from a character in Thomas Mann's 1924 novel *The Magic Mountain* whose philosophical ruminations on the meaning of life are drowned out by the roar of a nearby waterfall. Pepperstein's philosophical illustrations are infused with political satire, surrealistic free-association, Russian fairy tale and avant-garde iconography, and futuristic fantasy.

162

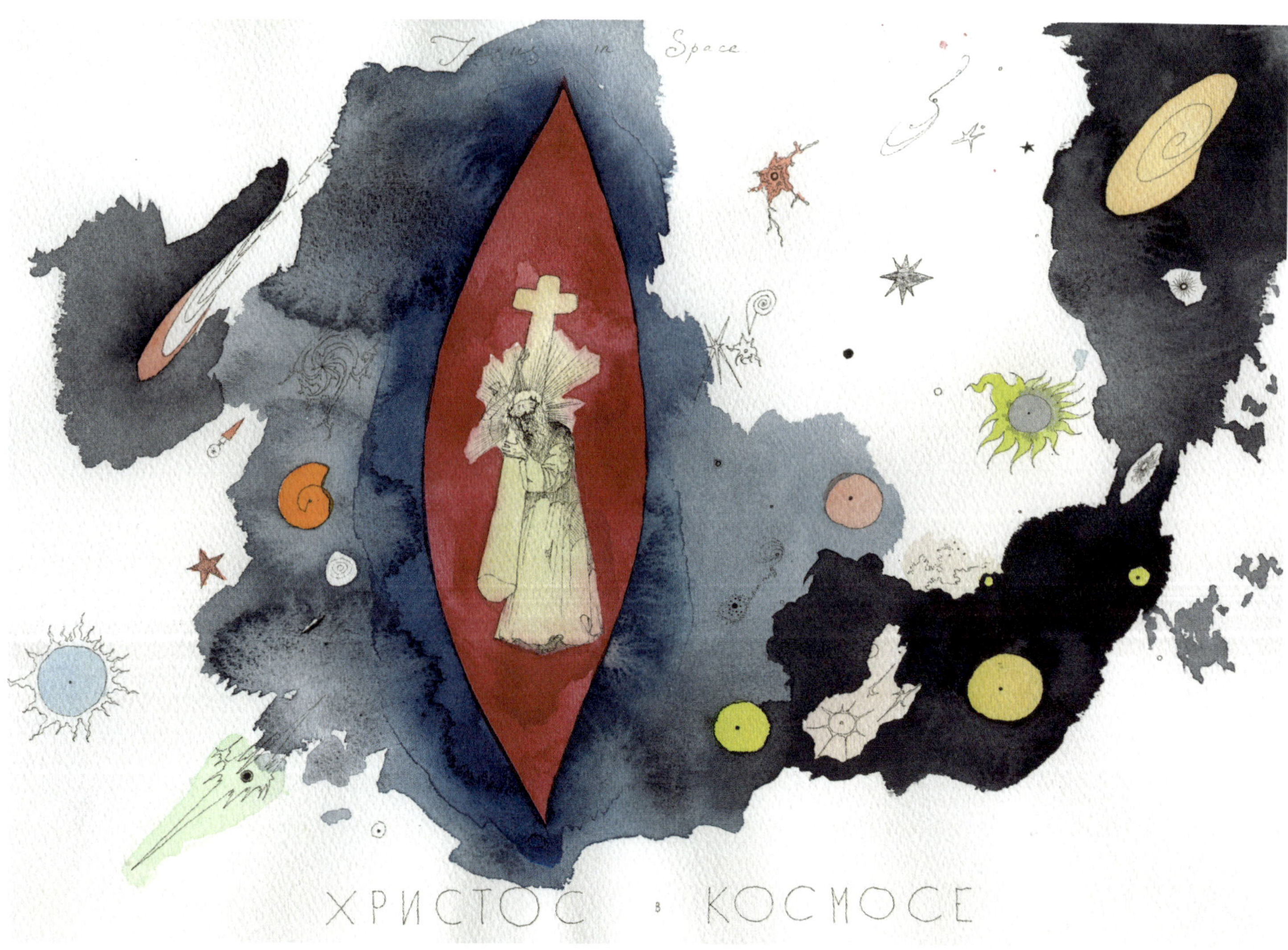

Jesus in Space, 2011
Watercolour on paper
29.6 × 42 cm (11 ⅝ × 16 ½ in.)

(opposite, top) *Dirty Johnny,* 2009 >
Watercolour on paper
62 × 85 cm (24 ⅜ × 33 ½ in.)

(opposite, below) *Human being as a frame of a landscape,* 2013 >
Watercolour on paper
50 × 70 cm (19 ⅝ × 27 ½ in.)

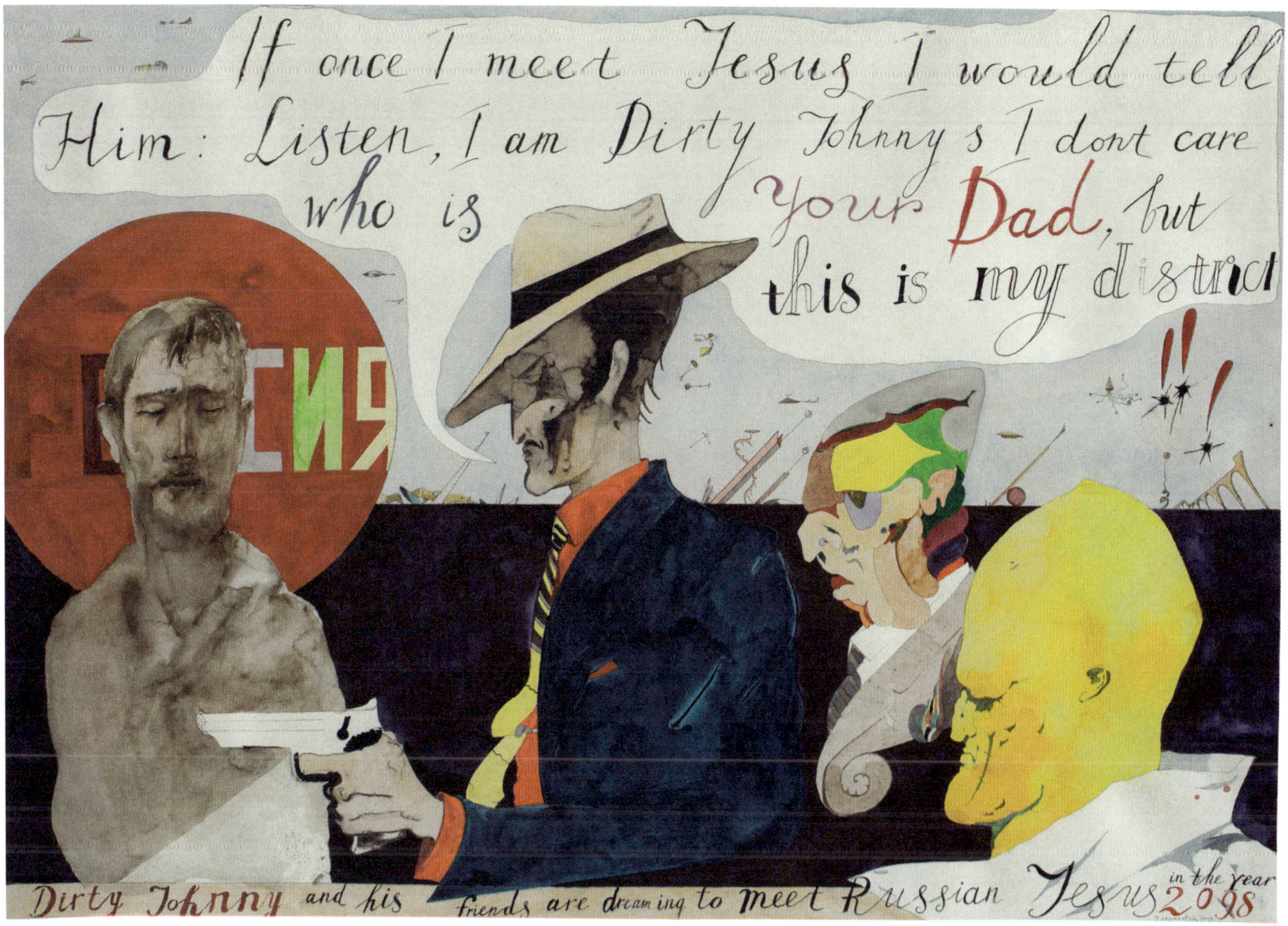

If once I meet Jesus I would tell
Him: Listen, I am Dirty Johnny's I dont care
who is Your Dad, but
this is my district
Dirty Johnny and his friends are dreaming to meet Russian Jesus in the year 2098

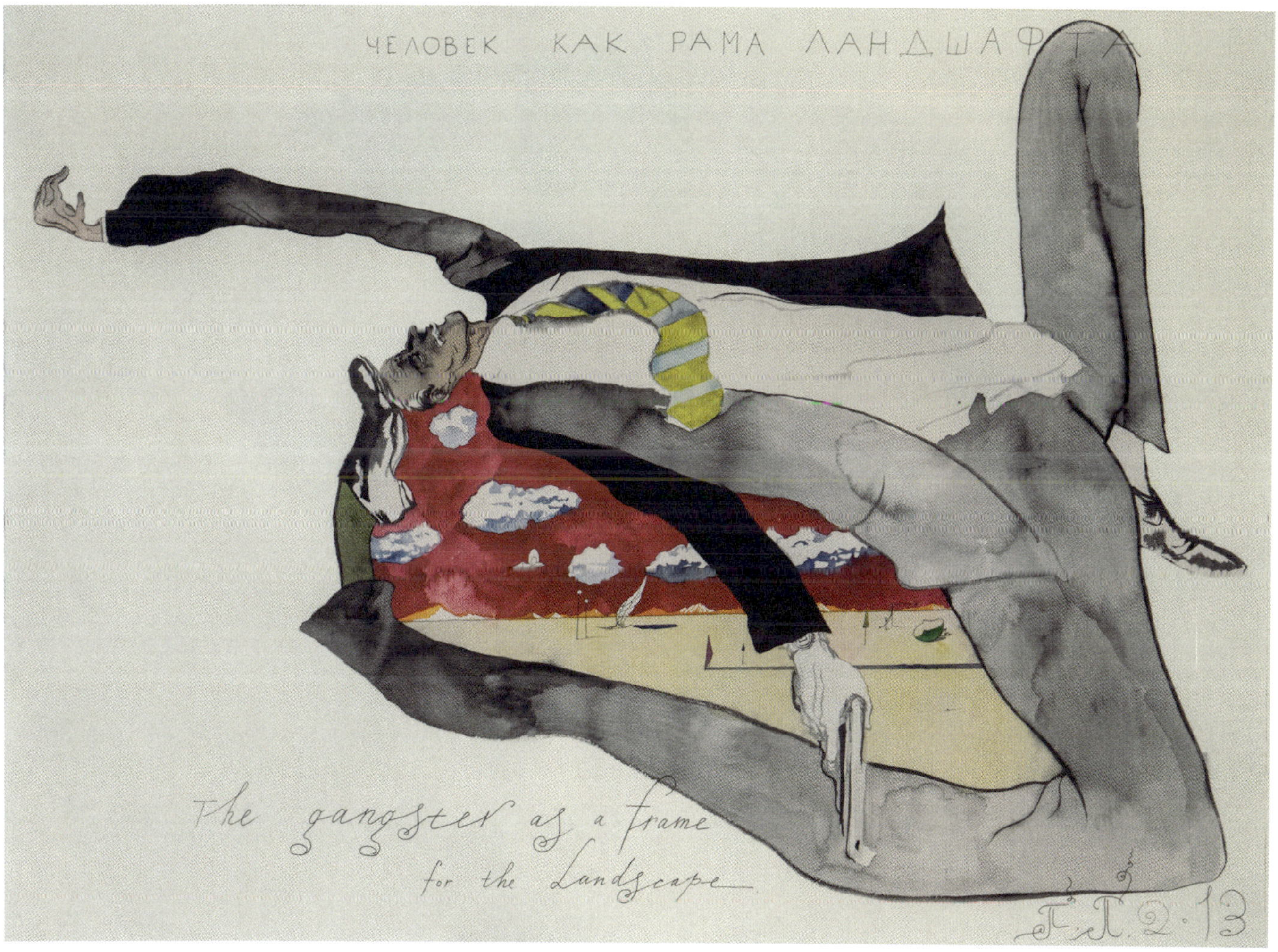

ЧЕЛОВЕК КАК РАМА ЛАНДШАФТА
The gangster as a frame
for the landscape

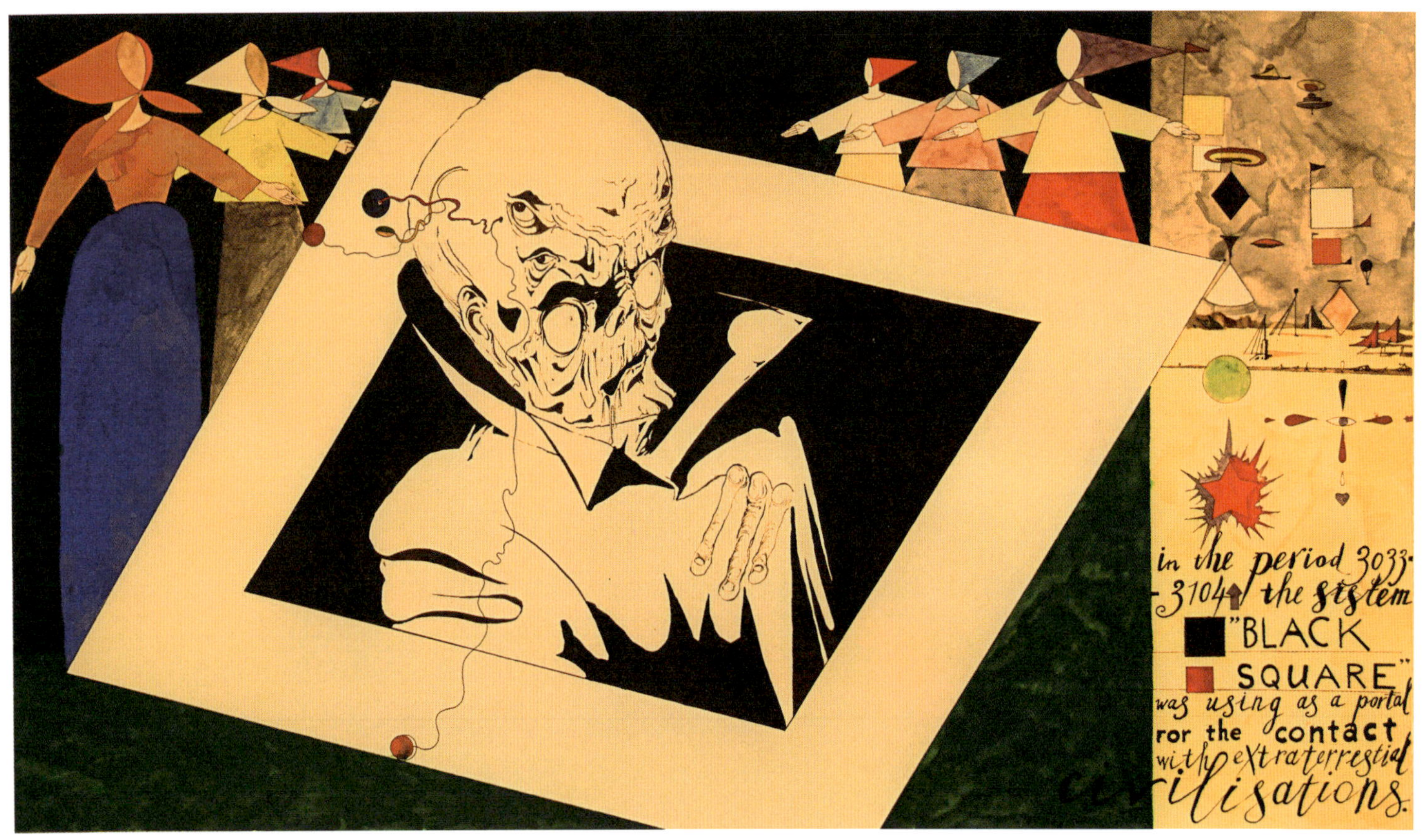

in the period 3033-3104 the system
"BLACK
SQUARE"
was using as a portal
ror the contact
with extraterrestial
civilisations.

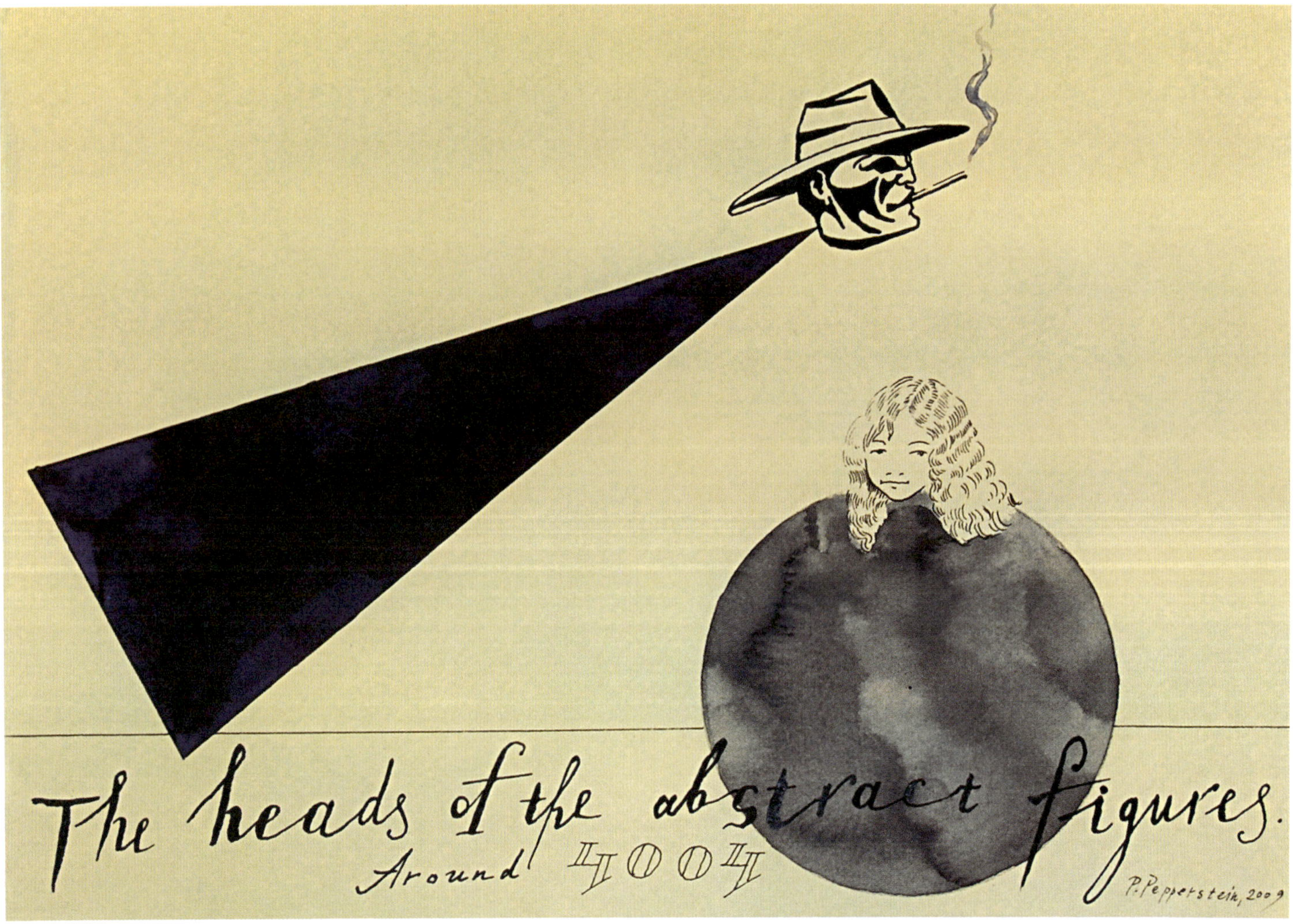

The heads of the abstract figures.
Around 4004
P. Pepperstein, 2009

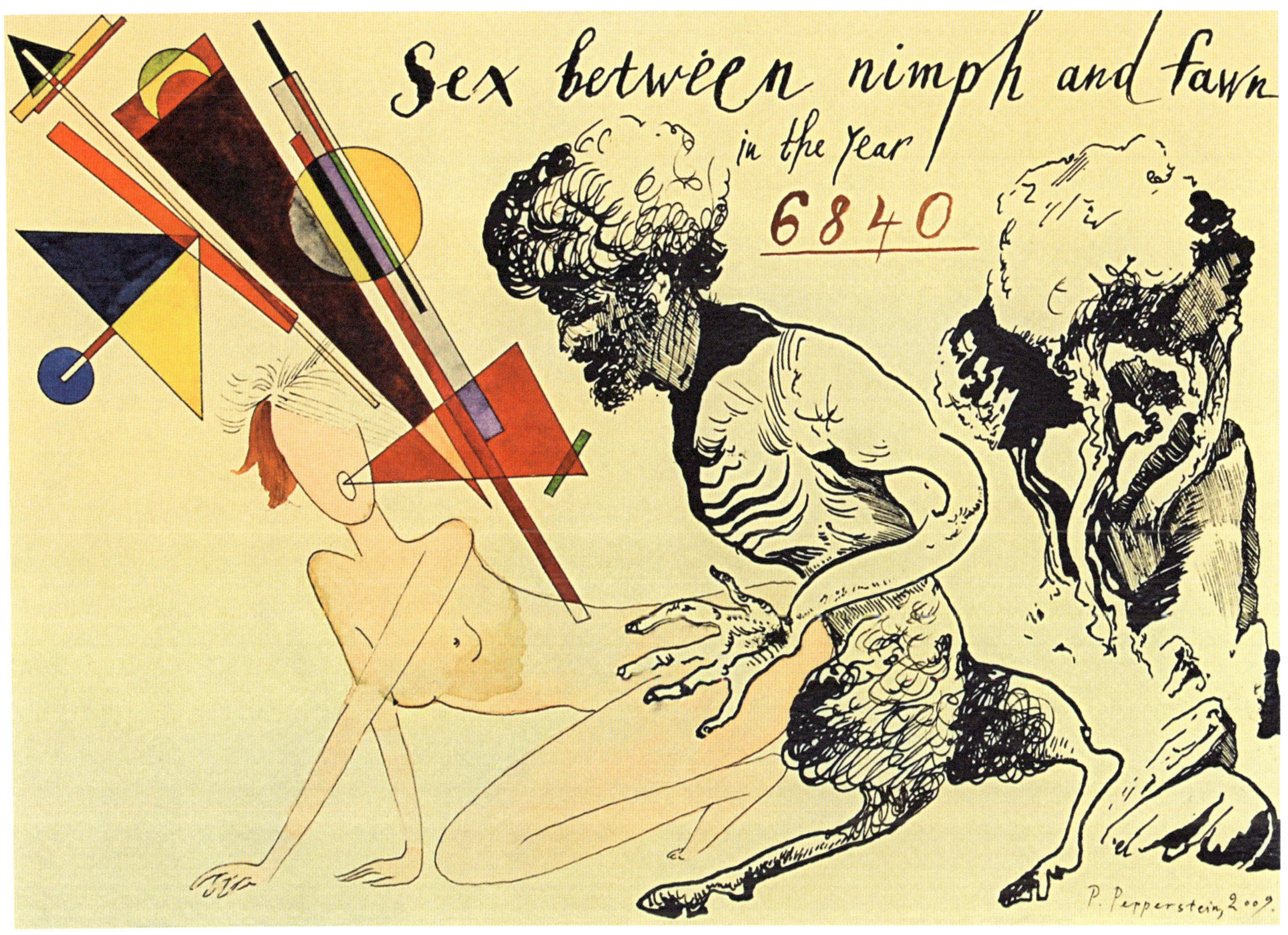

< (opposite, top) *Black square as a portal in 3033–3104*, 2009
Watercolour on paper
44 × 76 cm (17 ⅜ × 29 ⅞ in.)

< (opposite, below) *The heads of the abstract figures. Around 4004*,
2009
Watercolour on paper
17.5 × 24.9 cm (6 ⅞ × 9 ¾ in.)

Sex between Nymph and Fawn in the year 6840, 2009
Watercolour on paper
17.5 × 24.9 cm (6 ⅞ × 9 ¾ in.)

Having grown up in a mining town in which the workers were awoken every morning by loudspeakers blaring propaganda, and public spaces were strewn with Communist party newspapers celebrating the 'New China', Sun Xun is 'infatuated with imagined history…. I want to know what is invented, and what is true in the past that I imagine.' Sun's medium is stop-motion animation, which entails hand-drawing scenes frame-by-frame onto silk, canvas and sheets of paper (the latter often taken from communist-era newspapers). He established his own animation studio in 2006. Sun's dystopian vision mixes fantasy and reality, past and present: 'The world has no specific time; we live in vanity… there is no law, no rule, and the lie dominates everything. There is only lying and being lied to.' A recurring figure in the artist's work is the Magician, who rules by lies: 'when people feel lost, they mortgage their souls, and pin their hopes on magicians.' Sun's 2010 film *21KE* derives its title from American physicist Duncan MacDougall's estimation in 1907 that the weight of a human soul was precisely 21 grams. The surreal blend of poetry and politics in Sun's films presses the viewer to locate 'the boundary between the present and the past', only to find that 'in fact history has no such boundary'.

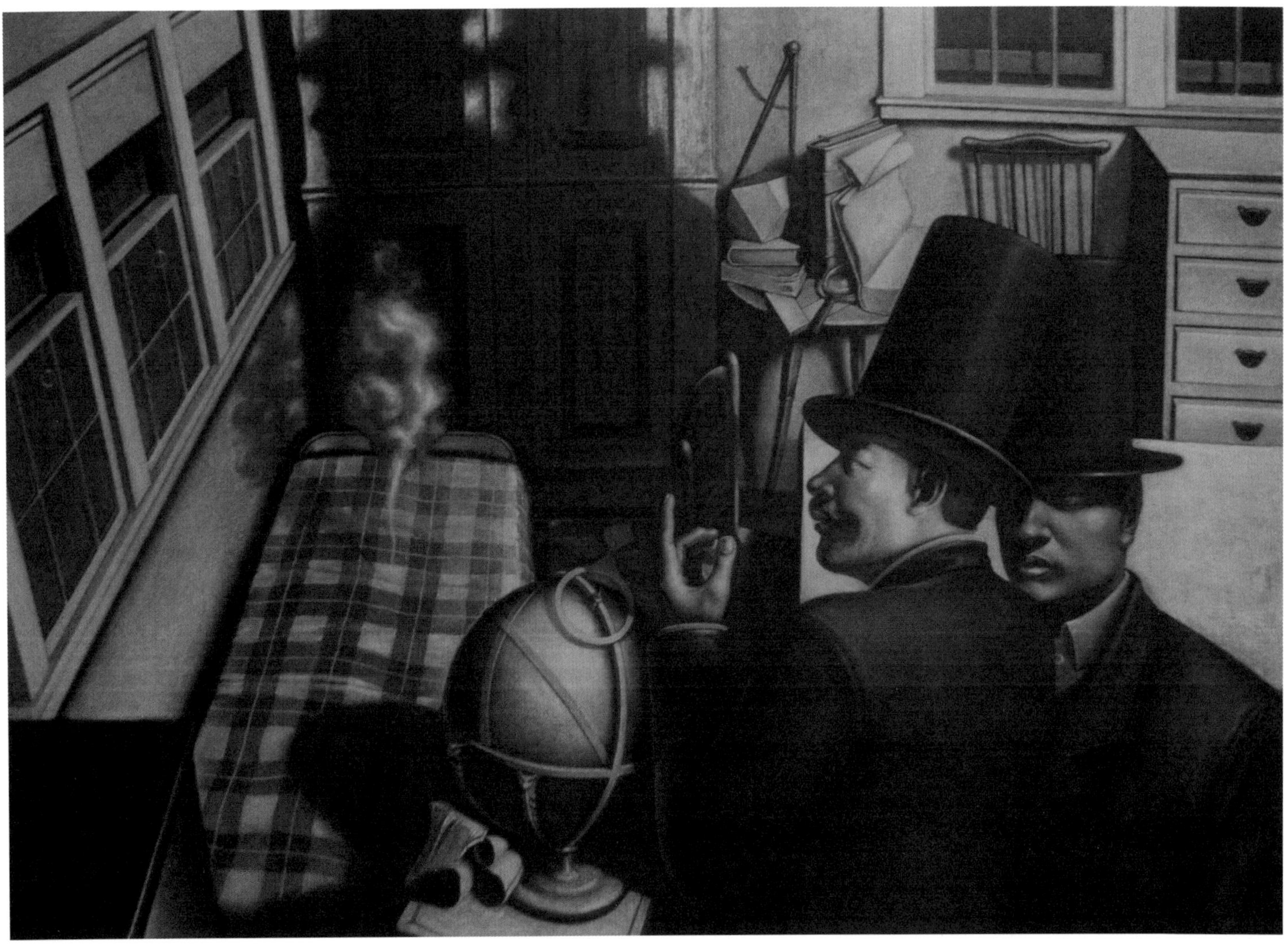

21KE-18, 2010
Pastel on canvas
100 × 140 cm (39 × 55 in.)

(opposite, top) *21KE-1,* 2010 >
Pastel on canvas
100 × 140 cm (39 × 55 in.)

(opposite, below) *21KE-11,* 2010 >
Pastel on canvas
100 × 140 cm (39 × 55 in.)

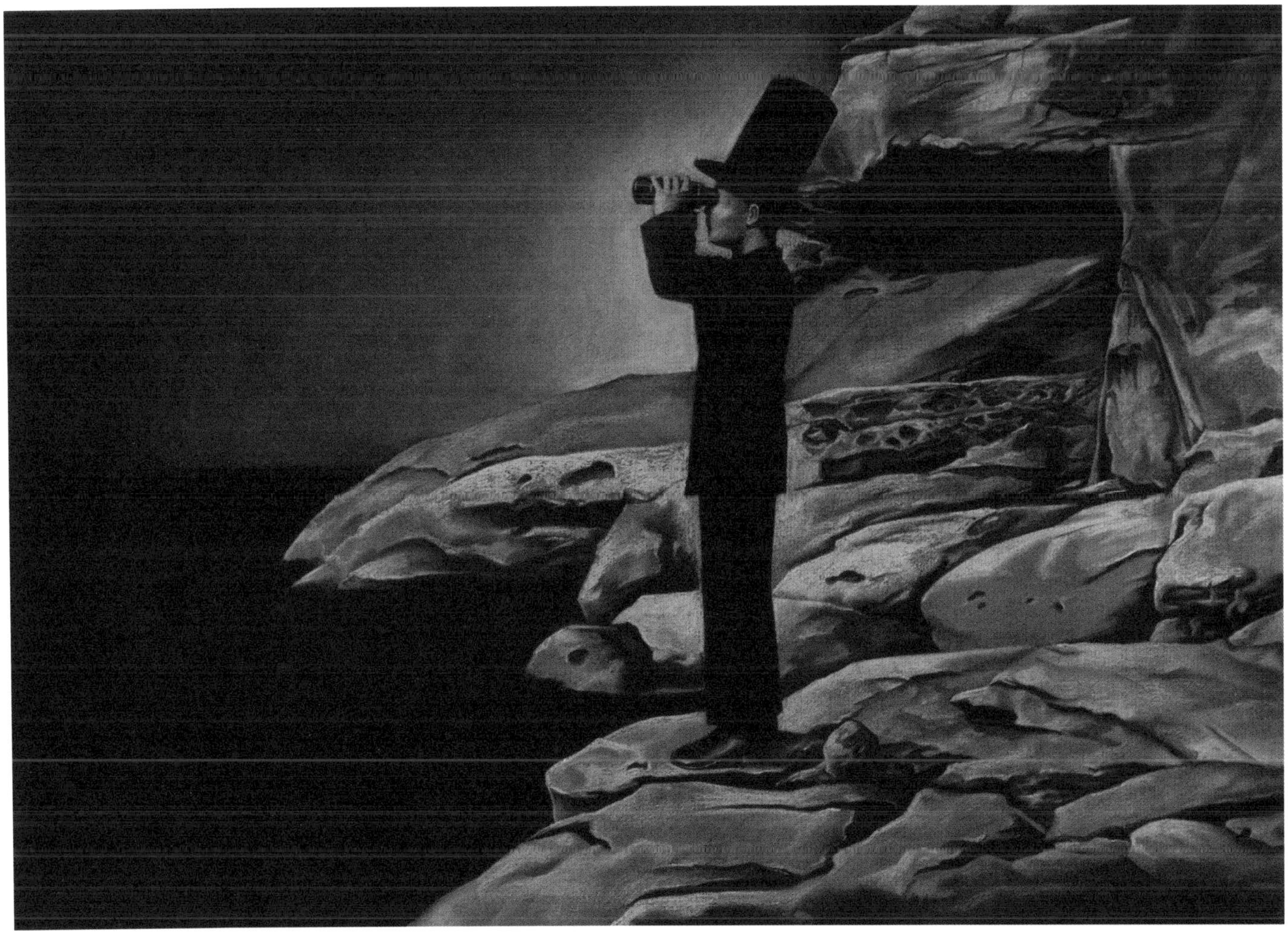

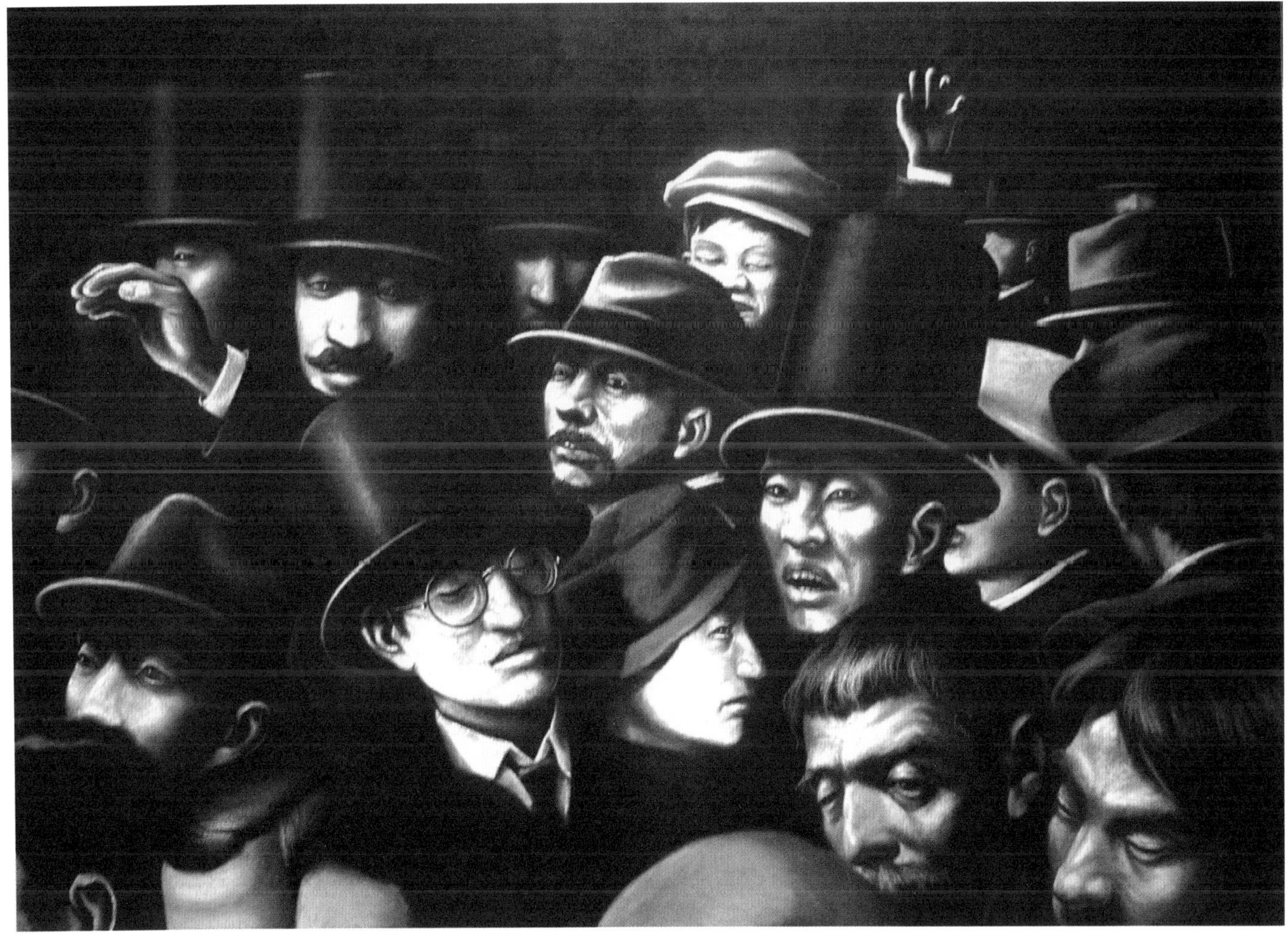

Chad McCail's *Food Shelter Clothing Fuel,* a series originally made as gouache drawings that were later transformed into ink-jet prints and even enlarged and shown on billboards, is a storyboard illustrating a post-revolutionary utopia in which all conflict is resolved and people live in perfect harmony. The built-in captions, written in the elementary style of a children's first reading book, describe in a bland, matter-of-fact tone the way that this ideal society operates. These images could be intended as propaganda for children in a communist state, one that had been arrived at without violence or coercion but in a spirit of calm, enlightened cooperation. But the figures are anonymous, faceless, like prototypical humans in a corporate instructional manual, and there is an uncanny twist to some of the captions ('Obedience doesn't relieve pain'), while others display a certain nihilistic absurdity ('People stop using things'). If this is a critique of real social relations, then the irony renders this message elusive. One of McCail's sources of inspiration is the revolutionary psychoanalyst Wilhelm Reich (1897–1957), who proposed a society free from sexual neurosis under the assumption that 'Mental and sexual hygiene presuppose a regulated, economically secure existence'. Perhaps the 'relaxing orgasms' enjoyed in this earthly paradise are dependent on the well-being provided by a benign superior power, one with a distinctly totalitarian vision.

(this page and opposite) *Food Shelter Clothing Fuel Series,* 2003
Digital illustration
Dimensions variable

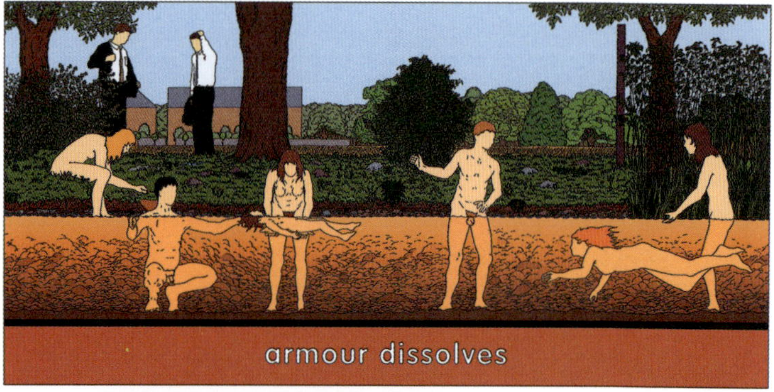

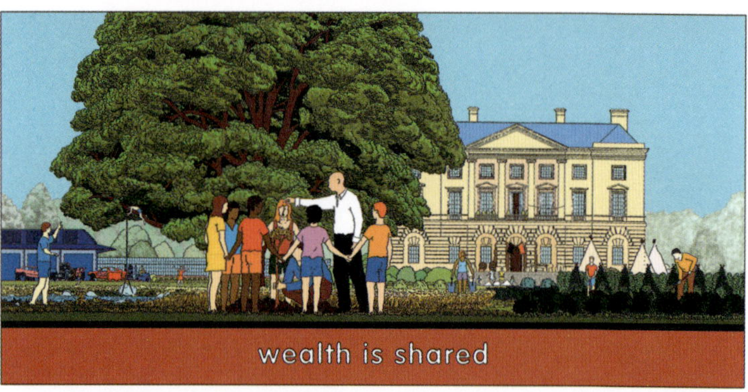

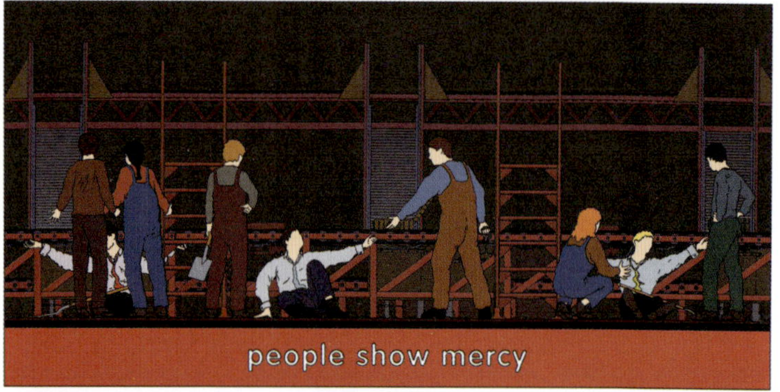

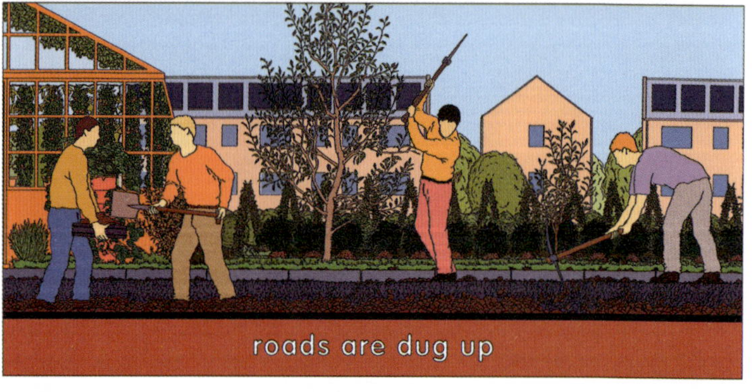

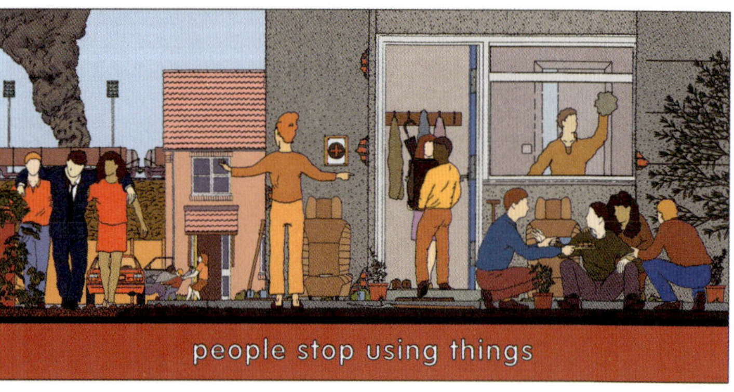

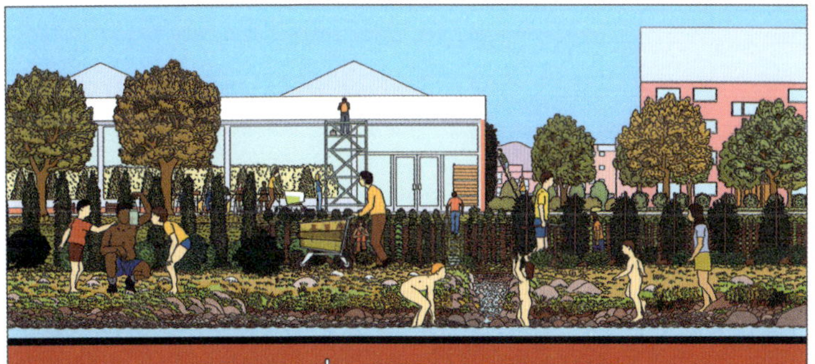

no one charges no one pays

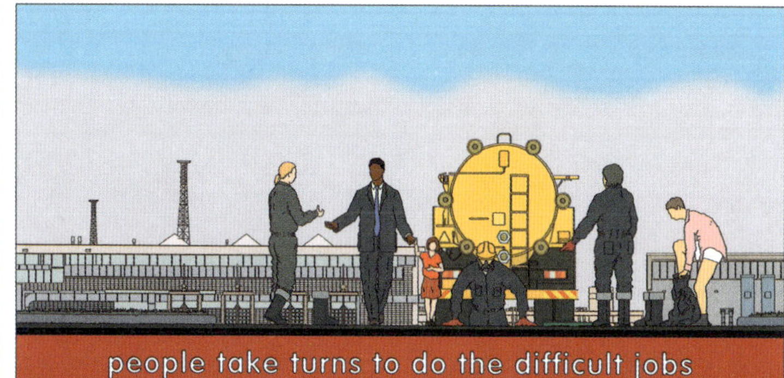

people take turns to do the difficult jobs

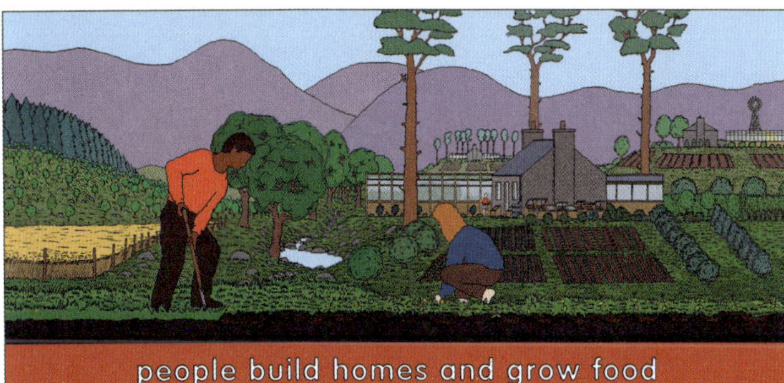

people build homes and grow food

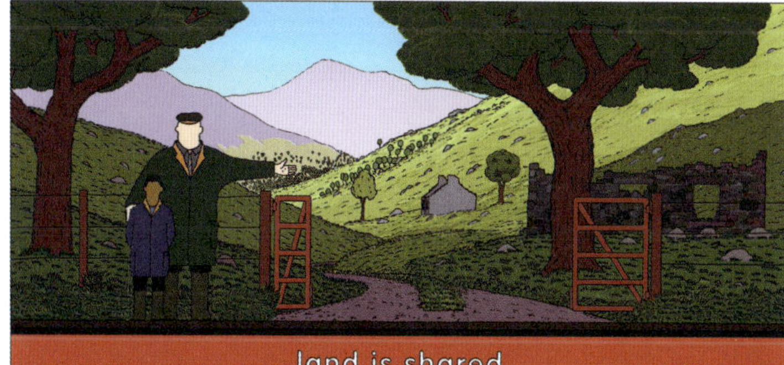

land is shared

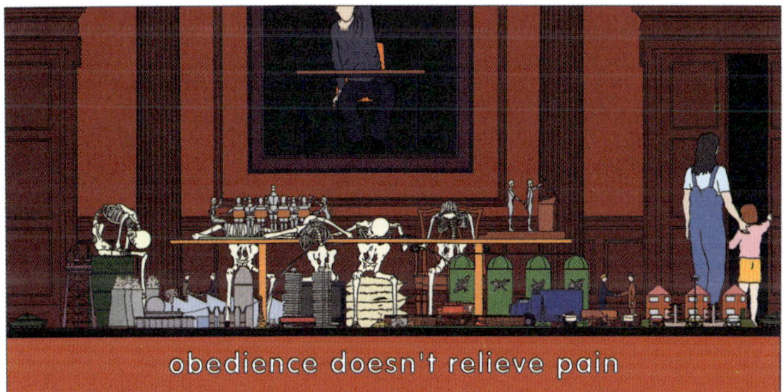

obedience doesn't relieve pain

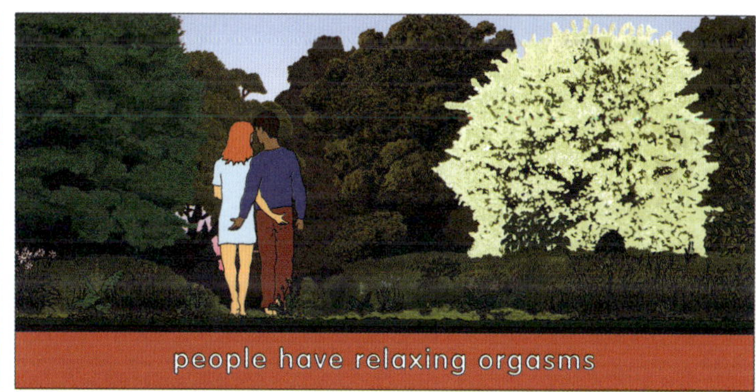

people have relaxing orgasms

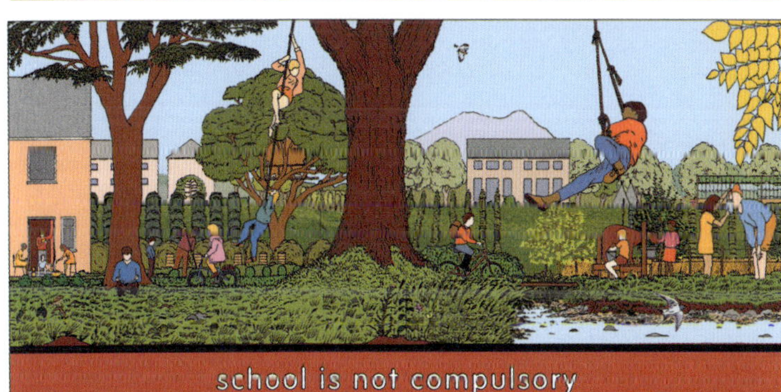

school is not compulsory

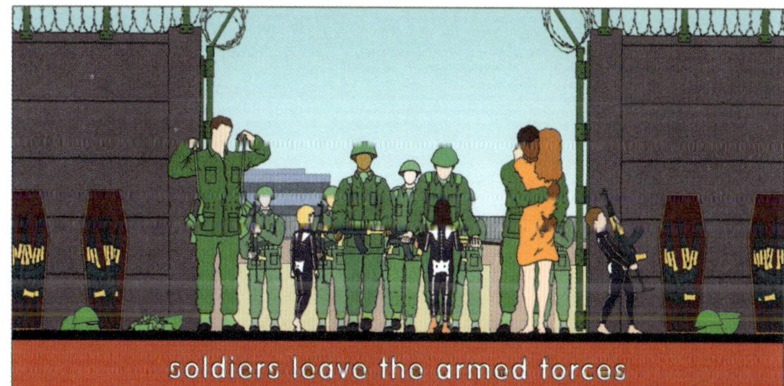

soldiers leave the armed forces

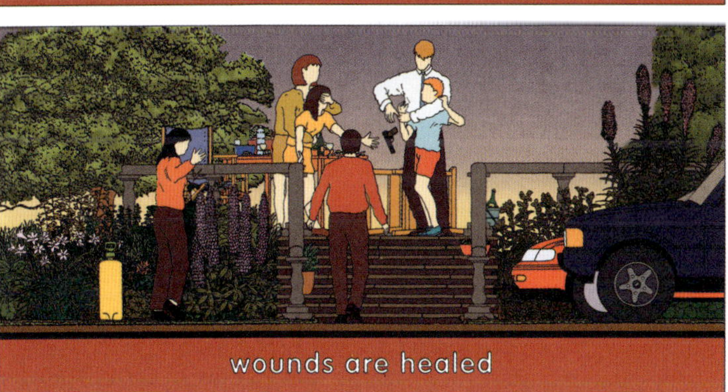

wounds are healed

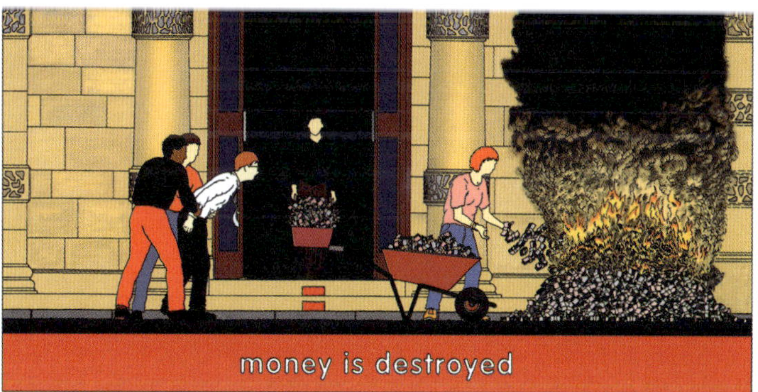

money is destroyed

Francesc Ruiz uses the graphic language of comics and their modes of dissemination to investigate urban geographies and subcultures. He creates his own comic books and playfully invites the viewer to interact with their narratives while simultaneously exploring the cities in which they are set. In his Cairo drawings, for example, he created a series of comics that brought together a cast of international characters from comic book history for an adventure in that city. The reader was required to follow the narrative trail to collect the next instalment from a physical distribution point which had featured in the closing scene of the previous episode. In this expanded, self-reflexive form, the comic book combines social commentary with psycho-geography.

The project illustrated here, *Yaoi*, grew out of a residency at the Gasworks artists' studios in London's Vauxhall, an area long known for its gay nightlife. Ruiz transformed the gallery at Gasworks into a fictitious 'women only' comics shop specializing in *yaoi* ('boys' love') comic books, a Japanese genre depicting male homoerotic narratives created by and for women. The comics were drawn by Ruiz but sold as the work of fictional female amateur illustrators, and portray the encounters of a group of gay men in Vauxhall. The drawings feature the gallery in which the exhibition is staged, thus bringing the real into the space of the represented.

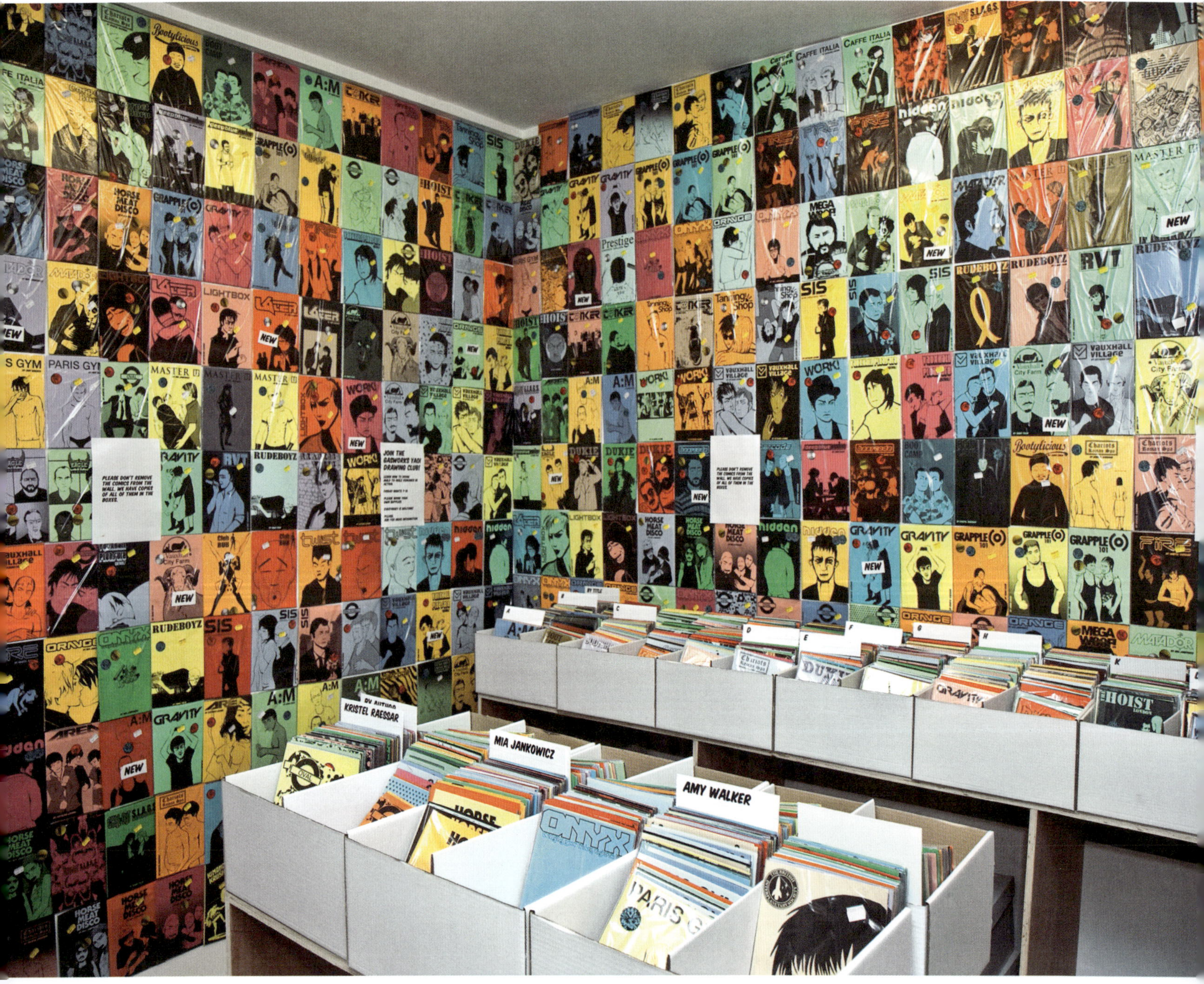

Gasworks Yaoi, 2010
Installation consisting of 5000 copies of comic books, simulating a bookshop. Installation view at Gasworks, London, UK.

(opposite, top) *Gasworks Yaoi*, 2010 >
Excerpt from comic book, pages 2–3

(opposite, below) *Gasworks Yaoi*, 2010 >
Excerpt from comic book, pages 6–7

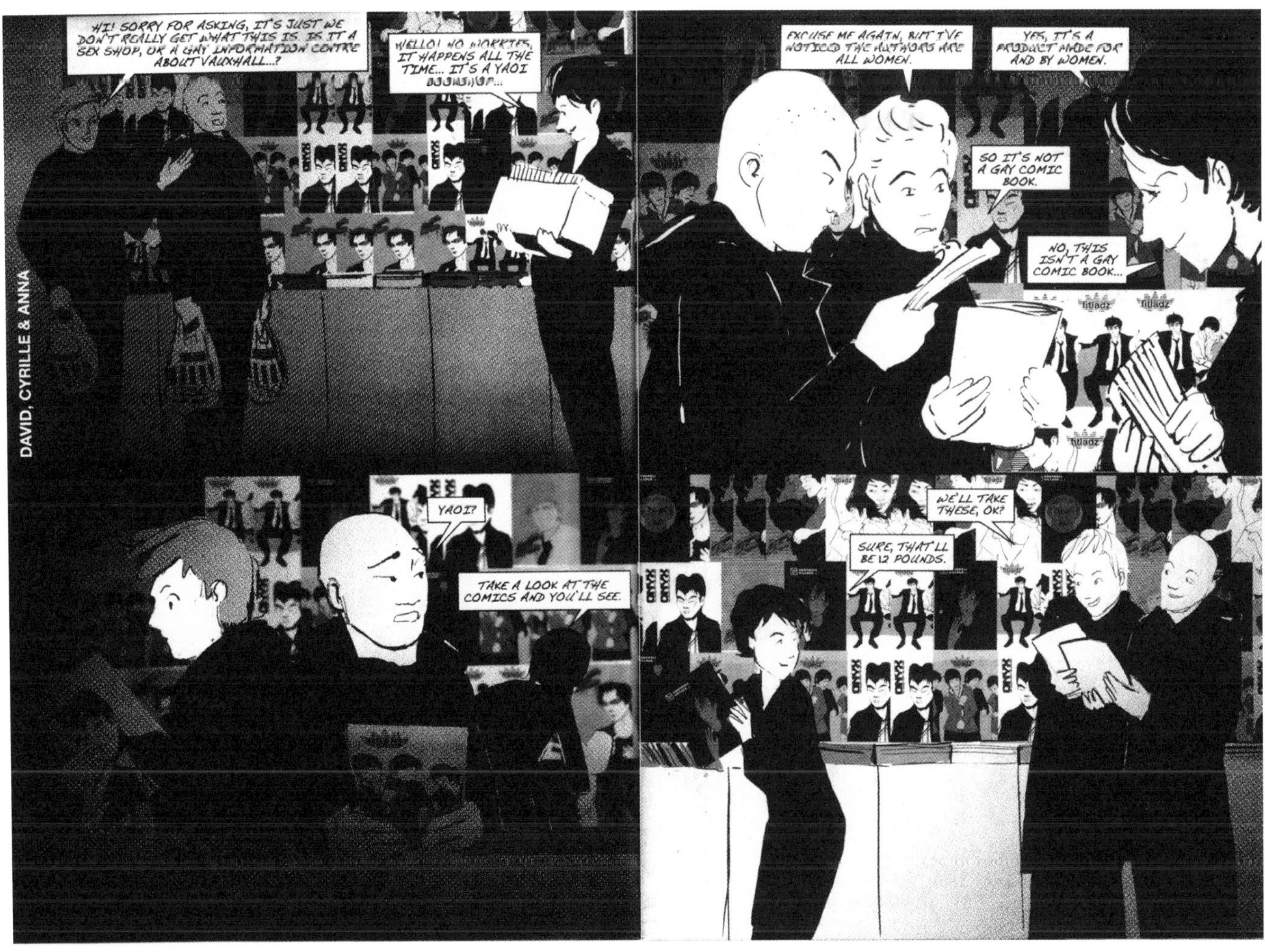

DAVID, CYRILLE & ANNA
HI! SORRY FOR ASKING, IT'S JUST WE DON'T REALLY GET WHAT THIS IS. IS IT A SEX SHOP, OR A GAY INFORMATION CENTRE ABOUT VAUXHALL...?
HELLO! NO WORRIES, IT HAPPENS ALL THE TIME... IT'S A YAOI BOOKSHOP...
EXCUSE ME AGAIN, BUT I'VE NOTICED THE AUTHORS ARE ALL WOMEN.
YES, IT'S A PRODUCT MADE FOR AND BY WOMEN.
SO IT'S NOT A GAY COMIC BOOK.
NO, THIS ISN'T A GAY COMIC BOOK...
YAOI?
TAKE A LOOK AT THE COMICS AND YOU'LL SEE.
WE'LL TAKE THESE, OK?
SURE, THAT'LL BE 12 POUNDS.

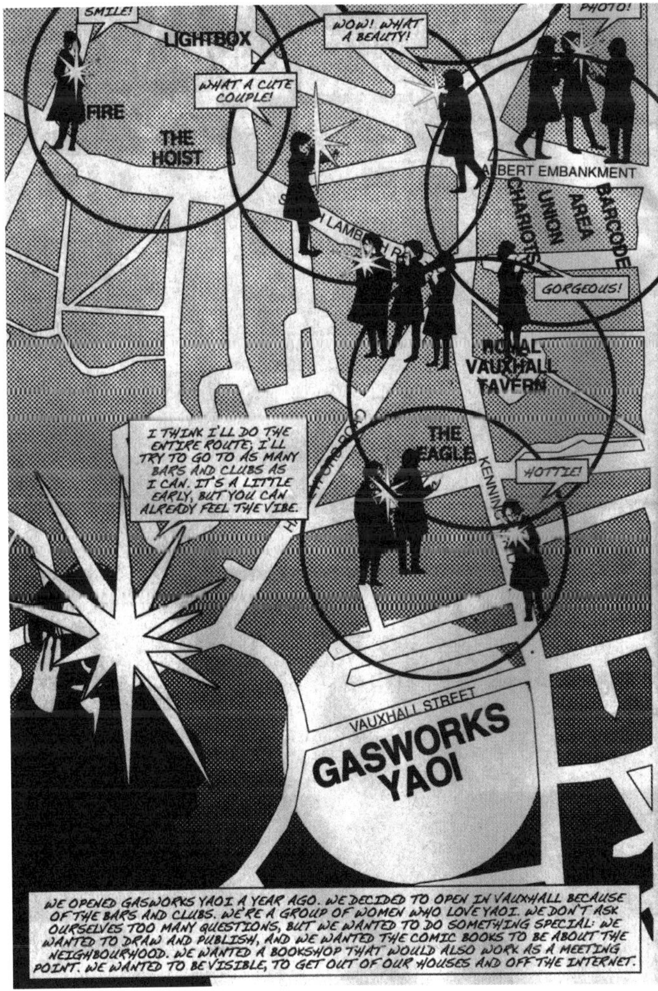

SMILE!
LIGHTBOX
WOW! WHAT A BEAUTY!
PHOTO!
WHAT A CUTE COUPLE!
FIRE
THE HOIST
ALBERT EMBANKMENT
LAMBETH
UNION
CHARIOTS
BARCODE
AREA
GORGEOUS!
ROYAL VAUXHALL TAVERN
I THINK I'LL DO THE ENTIRE ROUTE, I'LL TRY TO GO TO AS MANY BARS AND CLUBS AS I CAN. IT'S A LITTLE EARLY, BUT YOU CAN ALREADY FEEL THE VIBE.
THE EAGLE
KENNINGTON
HOTTIE!
VAUXHALL STREET
GASWORKS YAOI
WE OPENED GASWORKS YAOI A YEAR AGO. WE DECIDED TO OPEN IN VAUXHALL BECAUSE OF THE BARS AND CLUBS. WE'RE A GROUP OF WOMEN WHO LOVE YAOI. WE DON'T ASK OURSELVES TOO MANY QUESTIONS, BUT WE WANTED TO DO SOMETHING SPECIAL: WE WANTED TO DRAW AND PUBLISH, AND WE WANTED THE COMIC BOOKS TO BE ABOUT THE NEIGHBOURHOOD. WE WANTED A BOOKSHOP THAT WOULD ALSO WORK AS A MEETING POINT. WE WANTED TO BE VISIBLE, TO GET OUT OF OUR HOUSES AND OFF THE INTERNET.

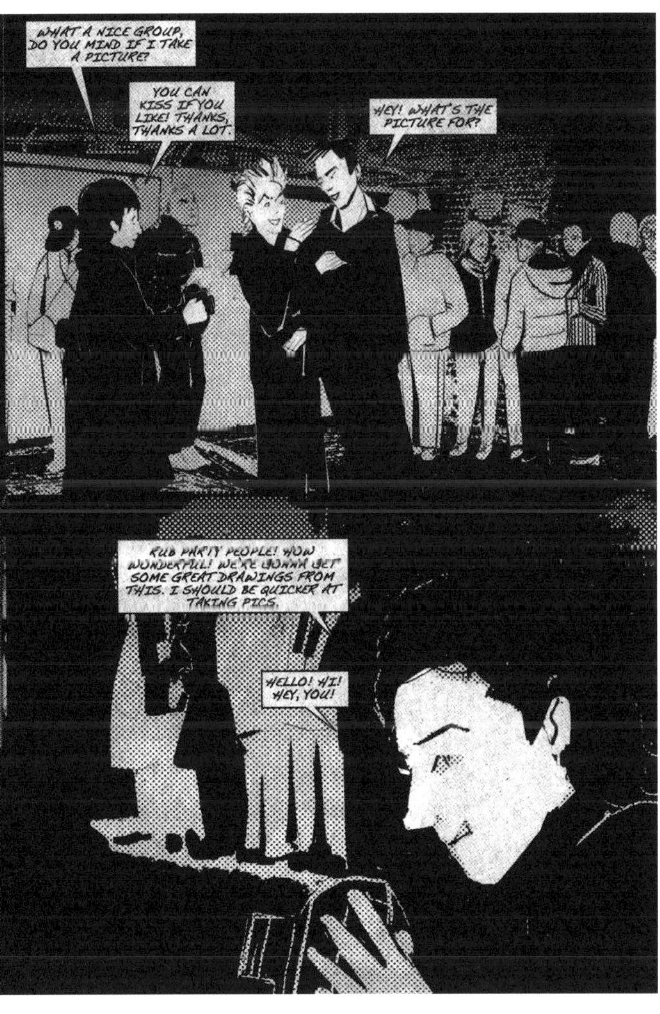

WHAT A NICE GROUP, DO YOU MIND IF I TAKE A PICTURE?
YOU CAN KISS IF YOU LIKE! THANKS, THANKS A LOT.
HEY! WHAT'S THE PICTURE FOR?
RUB PARTY PEOPLE! HOW WONDERFUL! WE'RE GONNA GET SOME GREAT DRAWINGS FROM THIS. I SHOULD BE QUICKER AT TAKING PICS.
HELLO! HI! HEY, YOU!

Chen Shaoxiong is an artist whose wide-ranging practice incorporates video, photography, installation and animation. Since 2005 he has produced a series of animated films each consisting of a rapid sequence of black-and-white ink drawings derived from photographs. The first was *Ink City* (2005), a montage of urban scenes that cuts and weaves across the city. *Ink Media: Air-Dry History* (2011–12) featured images of political protest from across the world, taken from the internet and presented without context or interpretation, thus dislocating them from time and place.

Chen uses ink to 'warm up' the images that he uses for his films. His drawing style makes no concessions to Chinese tradition; his brushstrokes are loose and uninflected, flattening his subject matter. Chen is suspicious, too, of the single-frame photograph – 'intrigued by what's left outside the frame and the moments leading up to as well as after the framed one' – and sceptical about the way in which certain photographs of political events are absorbed into the collective consciousness of a society and come to define its past. *Ink History* (2008–10) is a condensed history of modern China, from the fall of the Qing dynasty in 1911 to today, presented in a rapid-fire succession of 300 iconic images accompanied by a soundtrack of rousing patriotic music and the ticking of a clock. 'It would take a century to show a film of a century depicting every detail', he says (recalling Jorge Luis Borges' short story about a 1:1 scale map of a city). Chen's version takes three minutes.

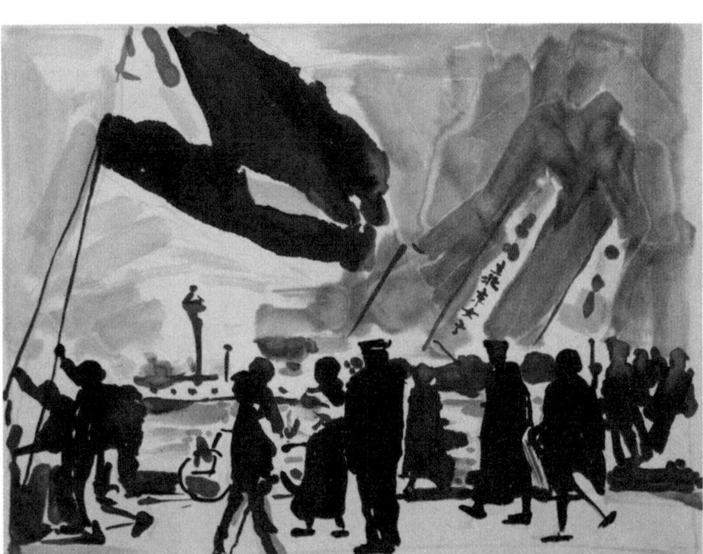

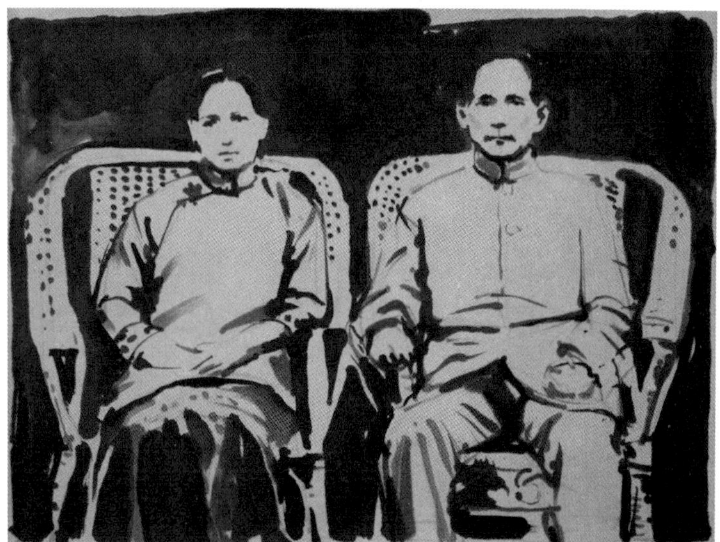

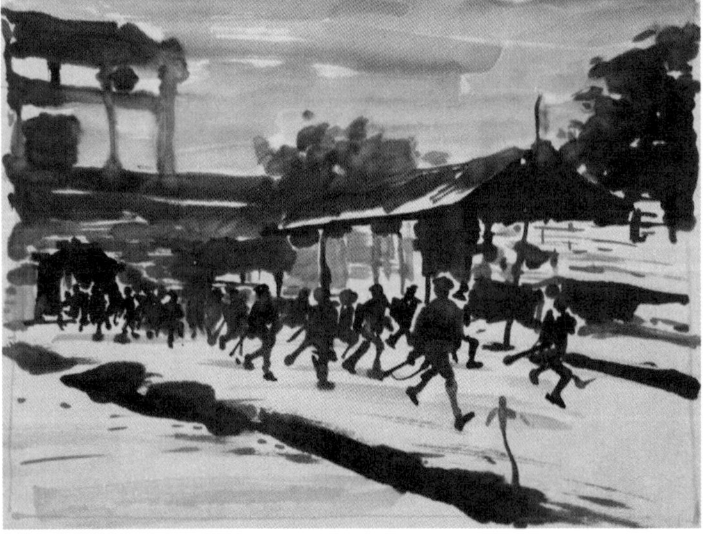

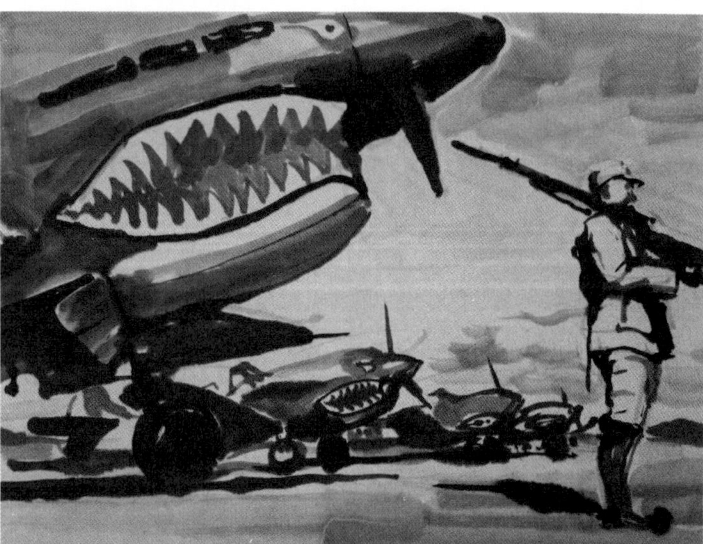

(this page, opposite and pp. 174–75) *Ink History,* 2008–10
Ink on paper, each: 35 × 46 cm (13 ¾ × 18 ⅛ in.)
Video, duration 3 min.

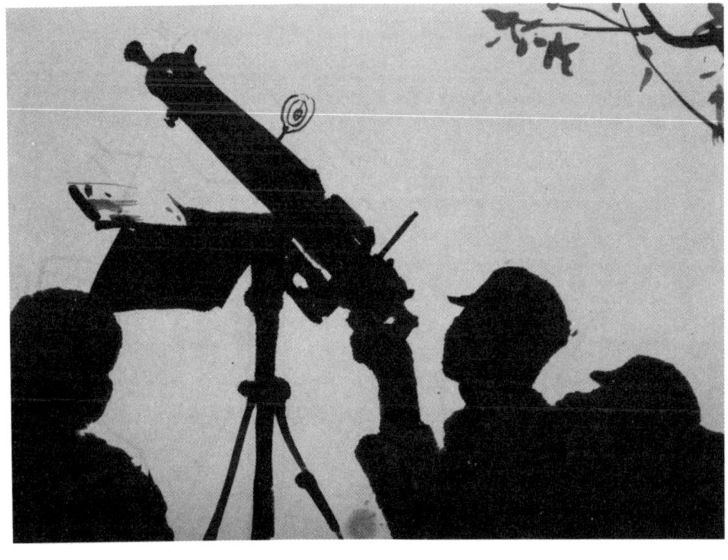
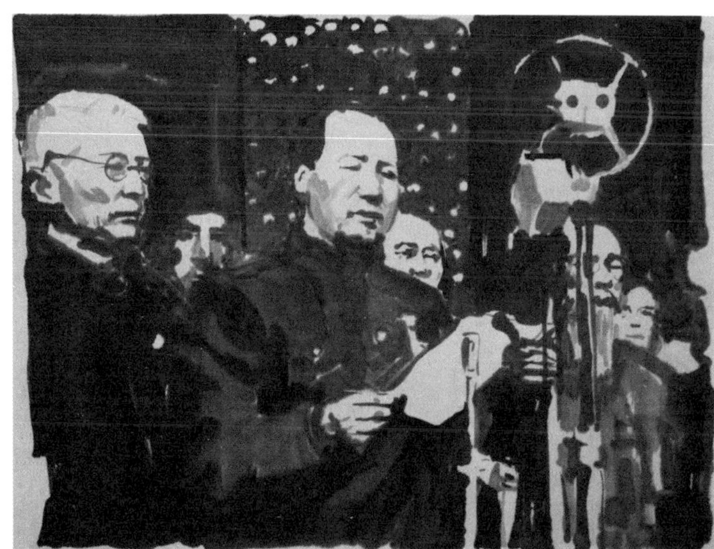
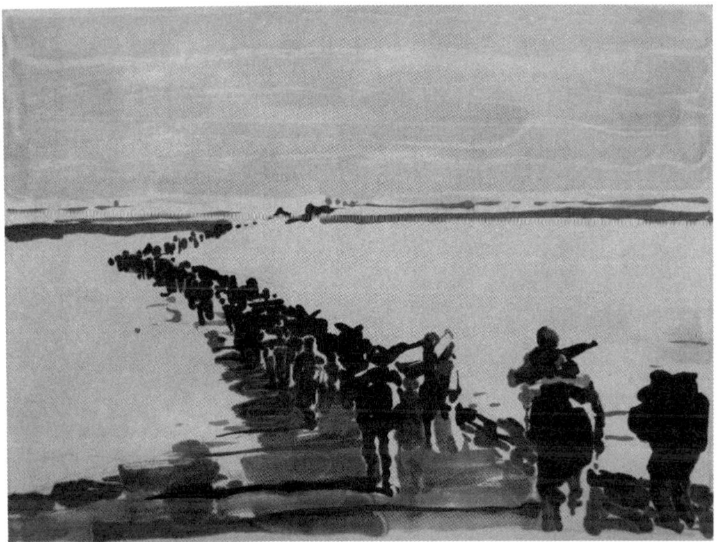
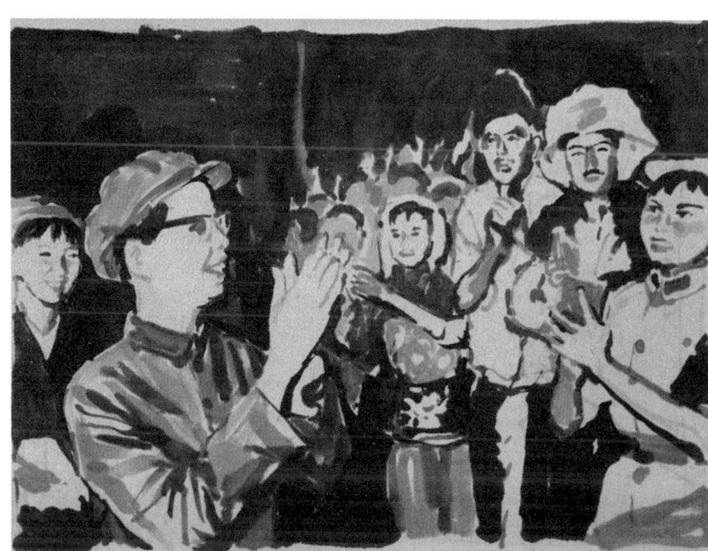
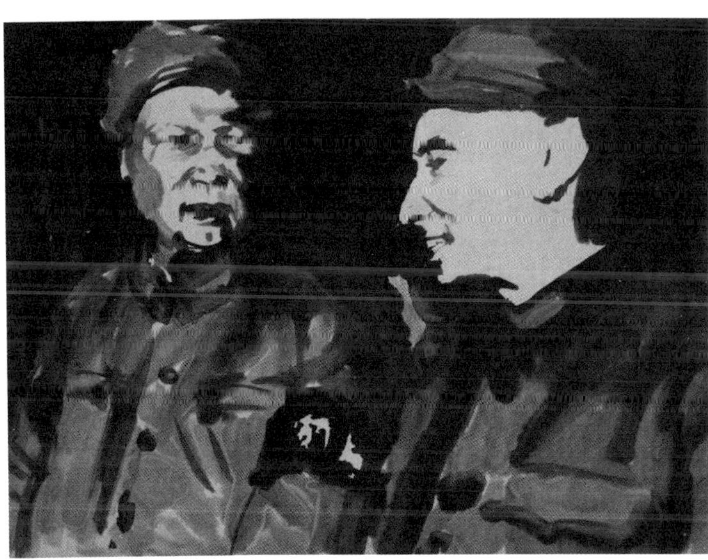
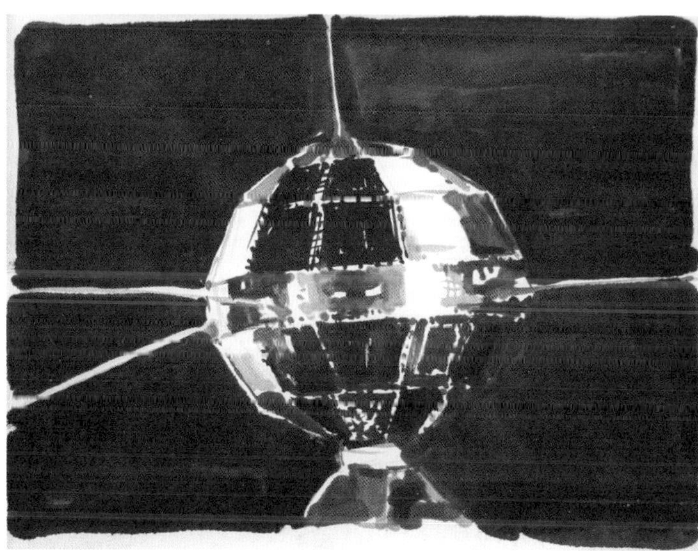

174

CHEN SHAOXIONG

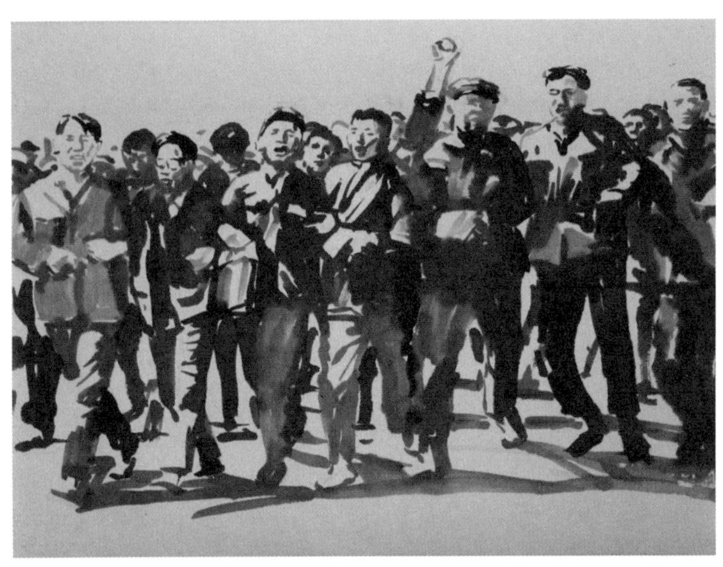
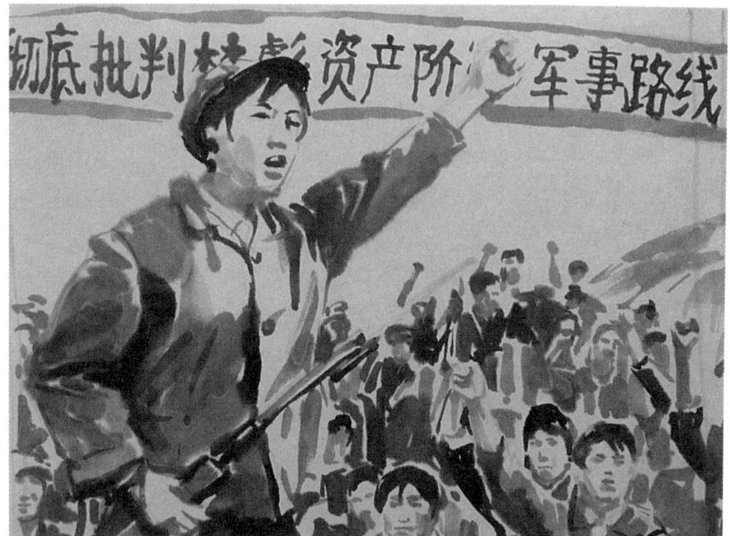

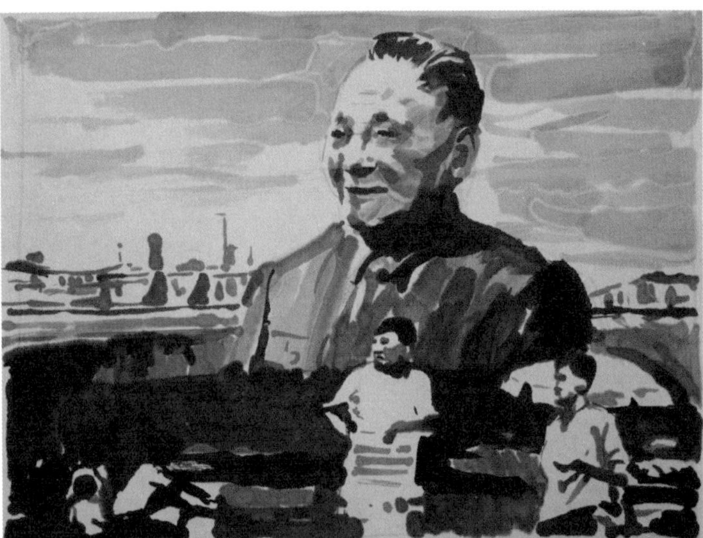
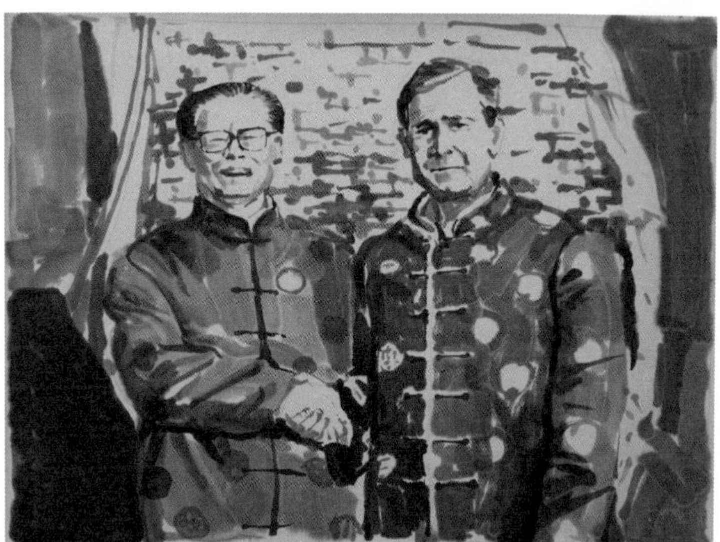
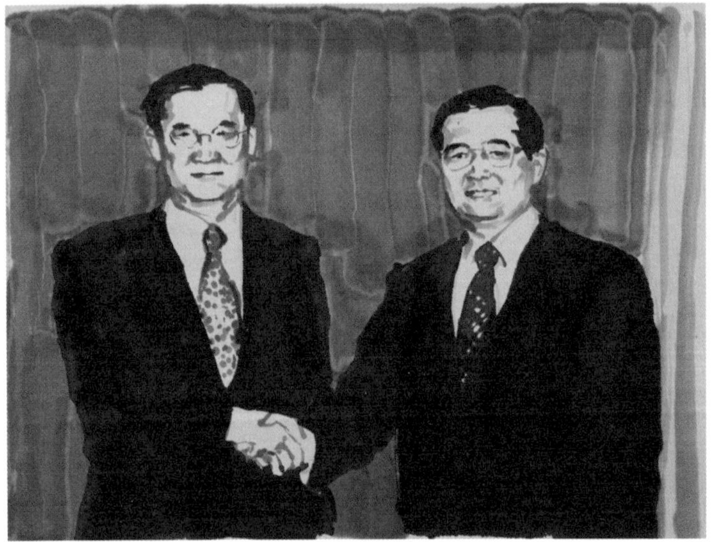
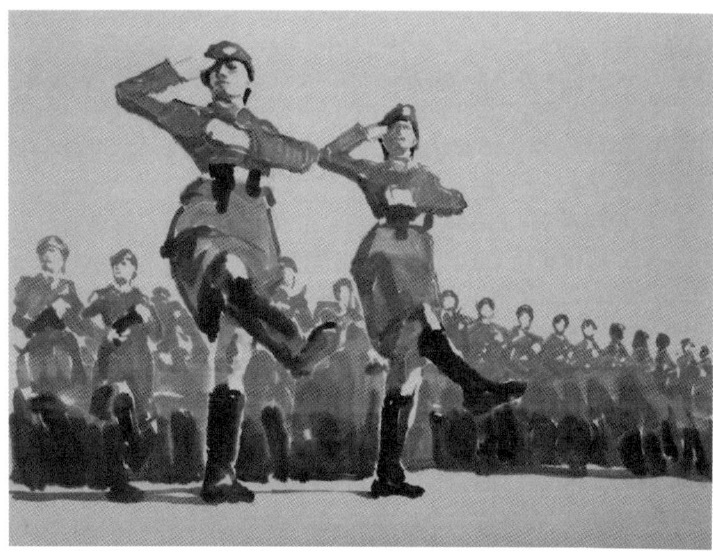

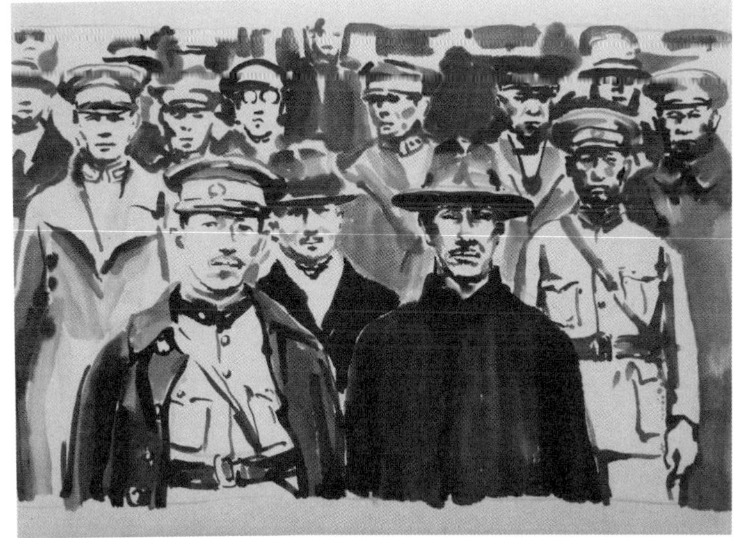
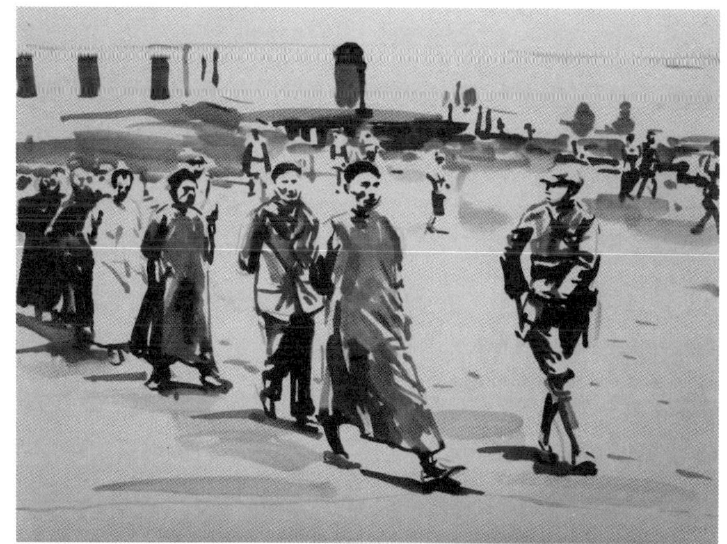
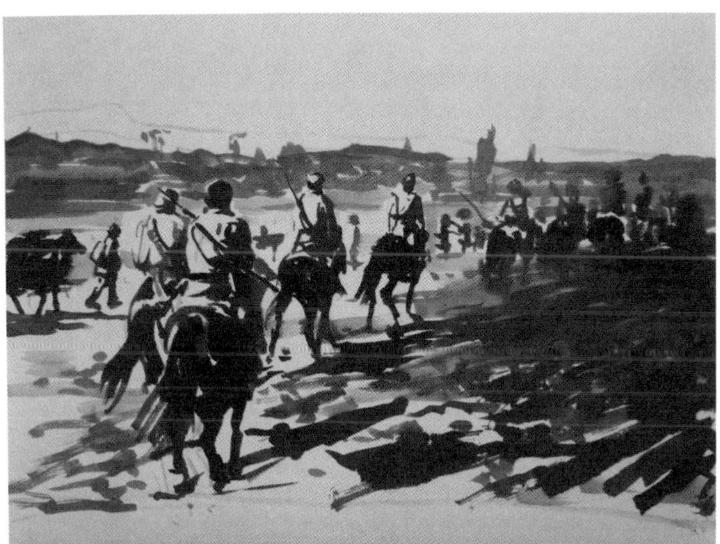
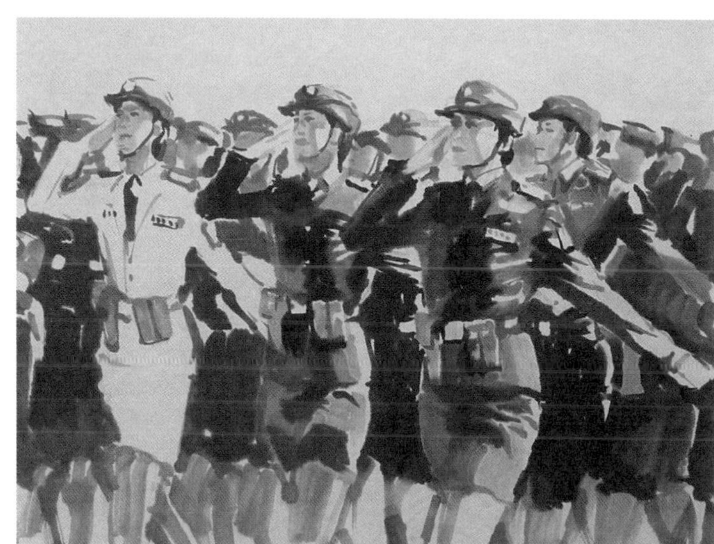
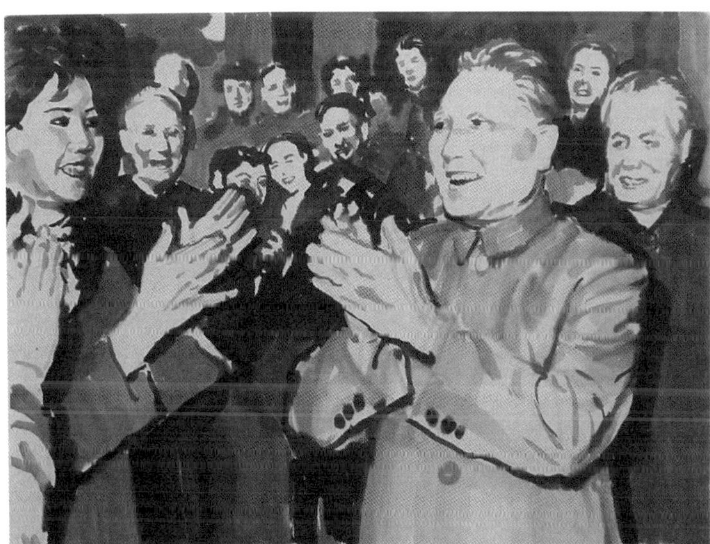
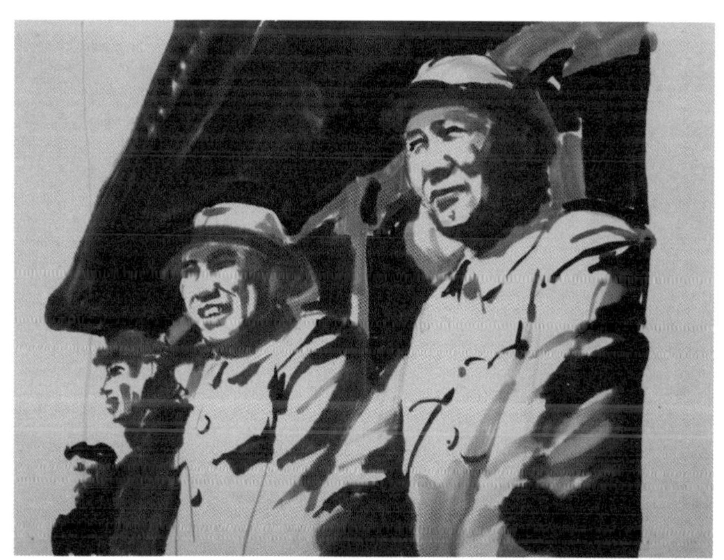

Having been brought up in a family of official Soviet artists, Ivan Razumov is particularly attuned to the iconography of Socialist Realism. He parodies these tropes in his series *Pioneers*, which focuses on members of the Soviet youth movement, the Young Pioneer Organization of the Soviet Union (Razumov was himself a 'pioneer'). According to Razumov, Soviet illustrations of the 1930s to the 1950s were 'fixed in the collective consciousness by the patriotic song, in which the rhetorical question, "What does the homeland start with?" is answered with assurance: "It starts with a picture in your primer."'

Razumov has spoken of a moment in the early 1990s that is key to the artistic practices of his generation. 'The Soviet symbolic order collapsed so unexpectedly that a relatively long period of time had passed before the unveiled chasm of chaos and freedom started to form into an order of a new type. This thrill of finding yourself suspended in a clear space between the departing world of our totalitarian childhood and the arriving adult world of consumerism and high-tech recreational activities coincided with a period of our having a realization that we were actually part of culture.' By returning to what Razumov calls the 'phantasms' of Socialist Realism, the artist aims not to revive them but to gain insight into the limits of their influence on the visual language of the present.

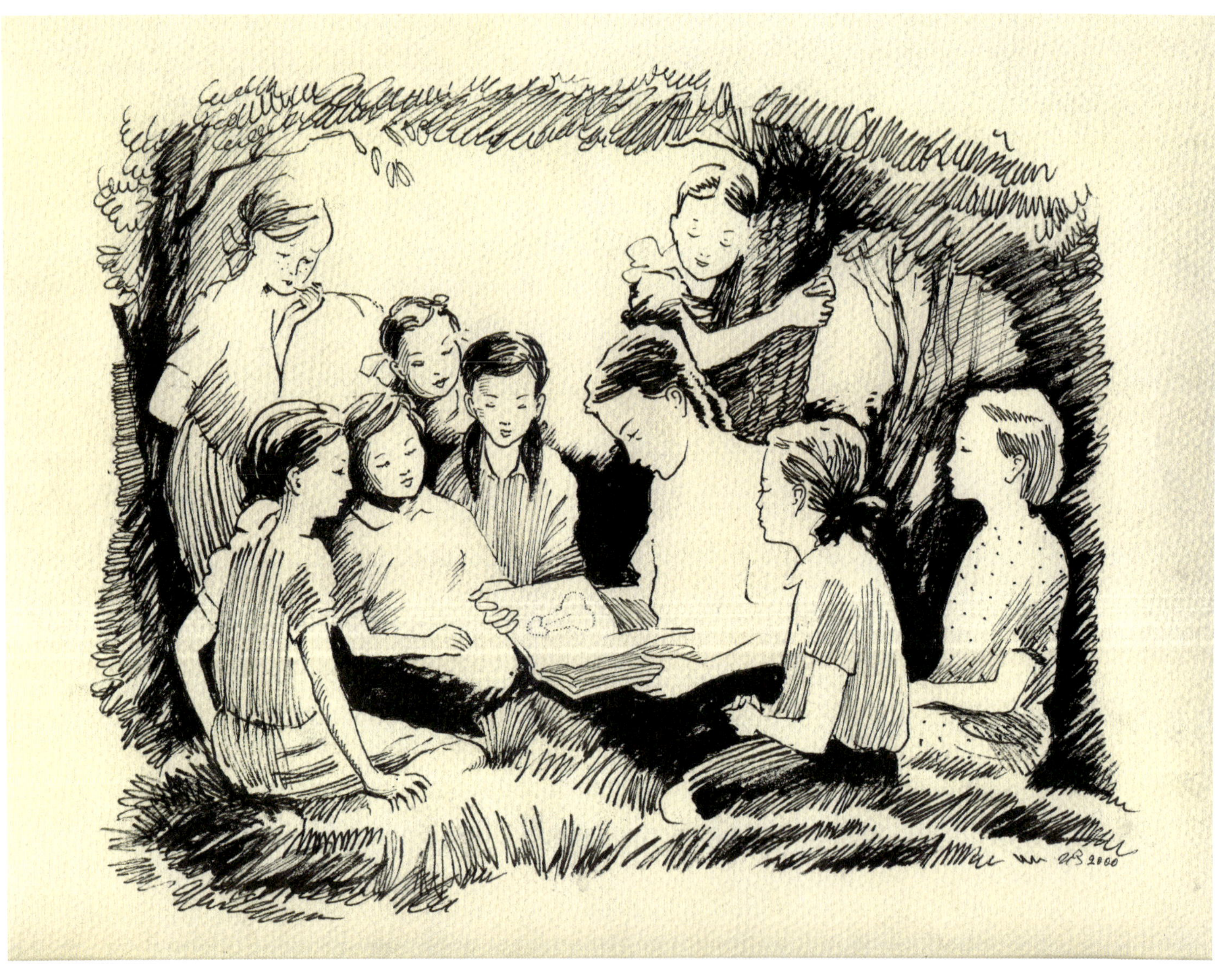

Imaged Away, 1999
Ink on paper
21 × 29 cm (8 ¼ × 11 ⅜ in.)

(opposite, top) *Marianna*, 2012 >
Ink and watercolour on paper
73 × 102 cm (28 ¾ × 40 ⅛ in.)

(opposite, below) *Honour of the Comrade*, 2010 >
Ink on paper
21 × 29 cm (8 ¼ × 11 ⅜ in.)

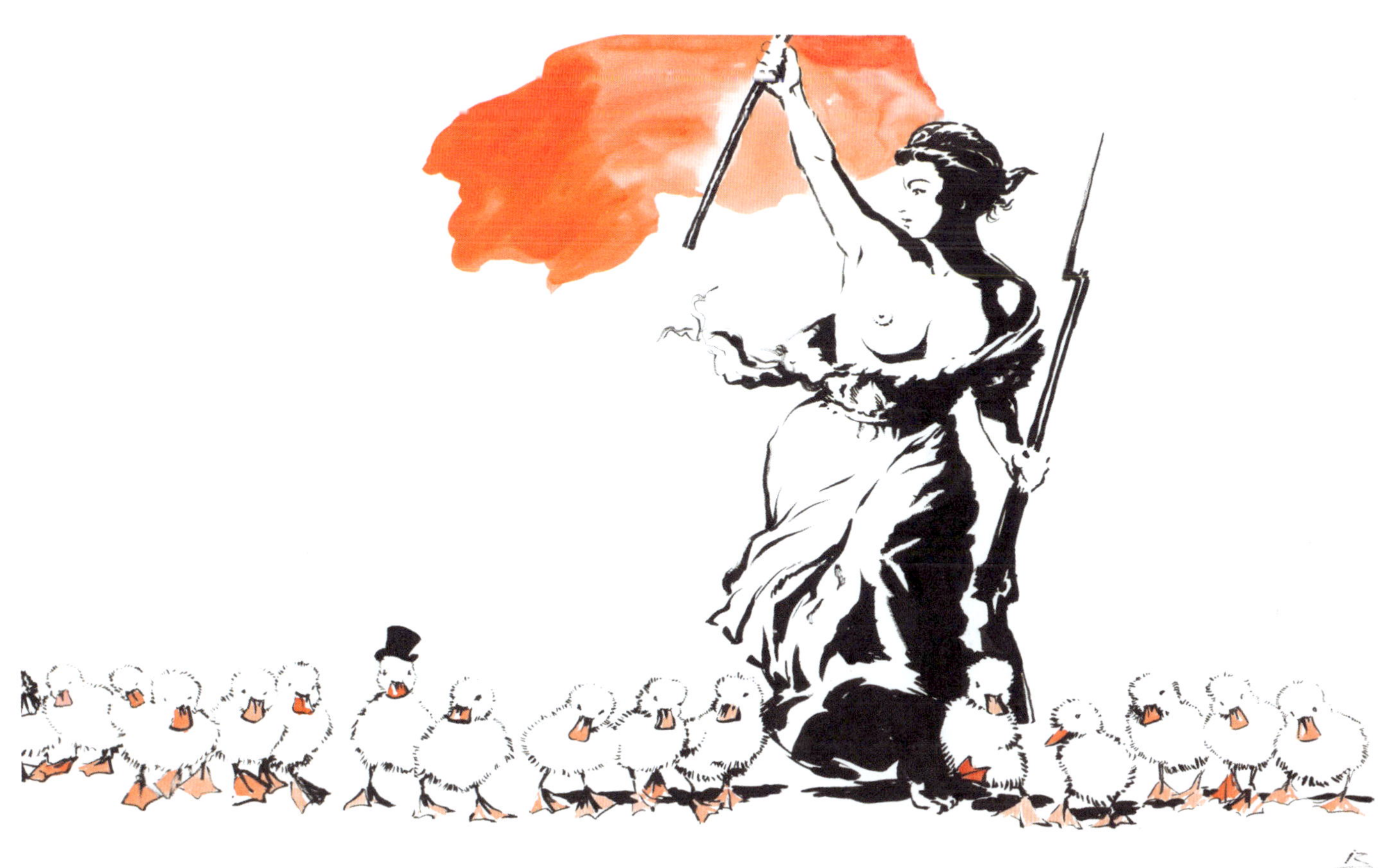

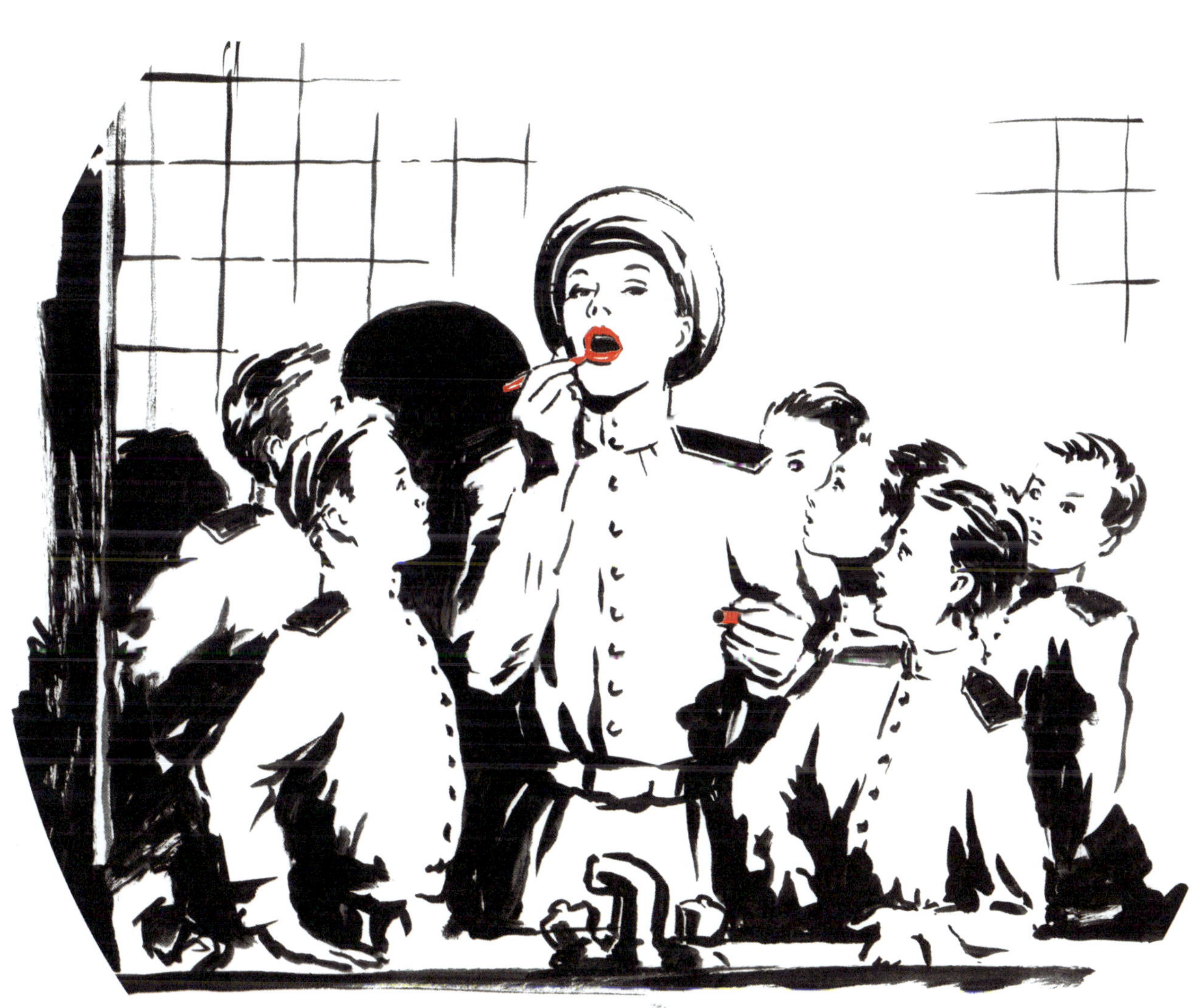

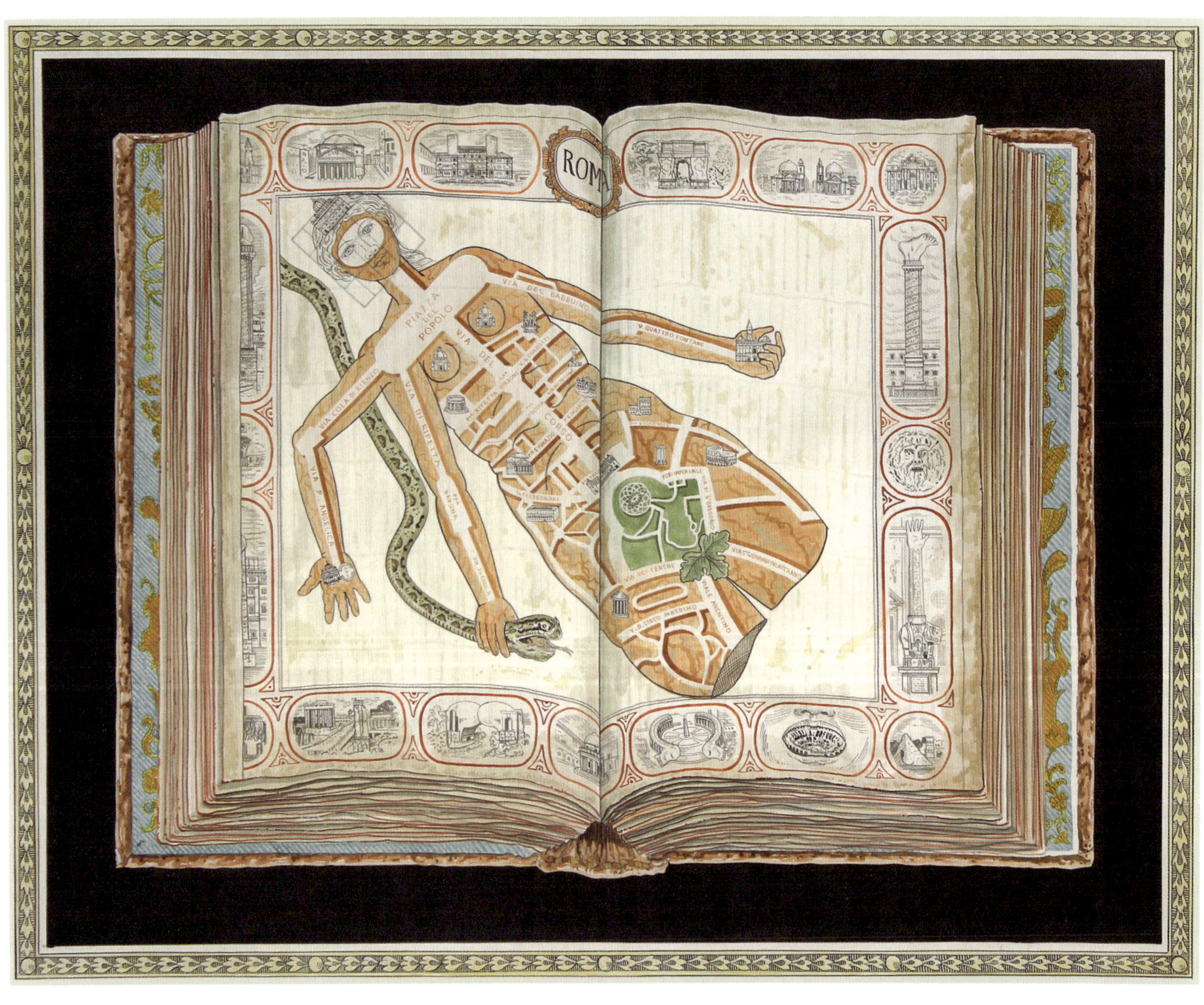

ROMA
PIAZZA DEL POPOLO
VIA DEL BABBUINO
VIA DEL CORSO
VIA DI RIPETTA
VIA COLA DI RIENZO
VIA P. ANGELICA
V. QUATTRO FONTANE
P.ZA NAVONA
VIA TUSCOLANA
VIALE AVENTINO
FORI IMPERIALI

Adam Dant is best known for his humorous panoramic drawings that chronicle and satirize London life, yet he is also interested more broadly in 'strange alternative perspectives' on social experience. A member of The London Institute of 'Pataphysics – a group devoted to the 'science of imaginary solutions' – Dant has worked on conceptual projects that have included revealing 'subliminal' images in Old Master paintings and mapping unexpected psycho-historical routes around famous museums.

The 2012 series *From the Library of Dr London* consists of *trompe l'oeil* drawings of antique volumes containing maps of cities re-imagined in the form of the human body. The work *Shunga Metro* shows Tokyo, in Dant's words, 'personified in a "subconscious" and literally "subterranean" fashion through wrestling figures intertwined to form the lines of the subway map.' The style parodies Japanese Shunga woodcut prints, in which writhing figures drawn with heavy black outlines are tangled up in erotic poses, here a reference to the overcrowding on rush hour trains and Tokyo's troubling subway 'groping' culture, both of which occur literally under the surface of everyday life. The Via del Corso runs down the spine of the figure of Rome in the drawing *Roma and the Tiber*, which embodies Pope Alexander VII's rationalizing of Rome's street plan in the mid-seventeenth century. The body's two arms appear naturally either side as Via Ripetta and Via dei Babuino, and a third arm links the body to St Peter's and Vatican City – a 'spiritual arm' that sets Vatican City apart from Rome. The River Tiber is represented as a snake and the symmetrical order of the human body in the fashion of the Vitruvian Man is rendered as a piece of red-marble classical statuary.

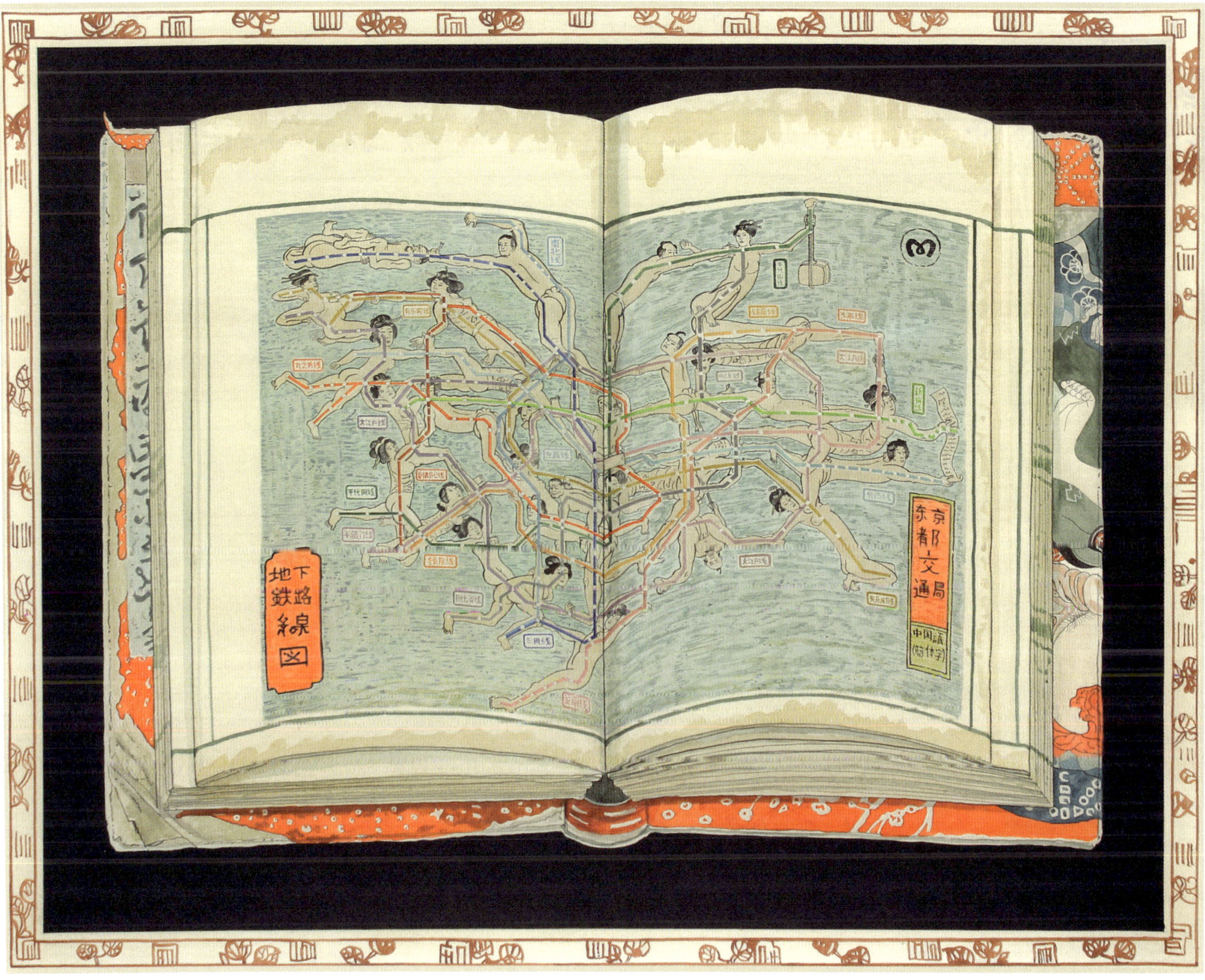

< *Roma and the Tiber*, 2012
Ink on paper
132.5 × 163 cm (52 ⅛ × 64 ⅛ in.)

Shunga Metro, 2012
Ink on paper
132.5 × 163 cm (52 ⅛ × 64 ⅛ in.)

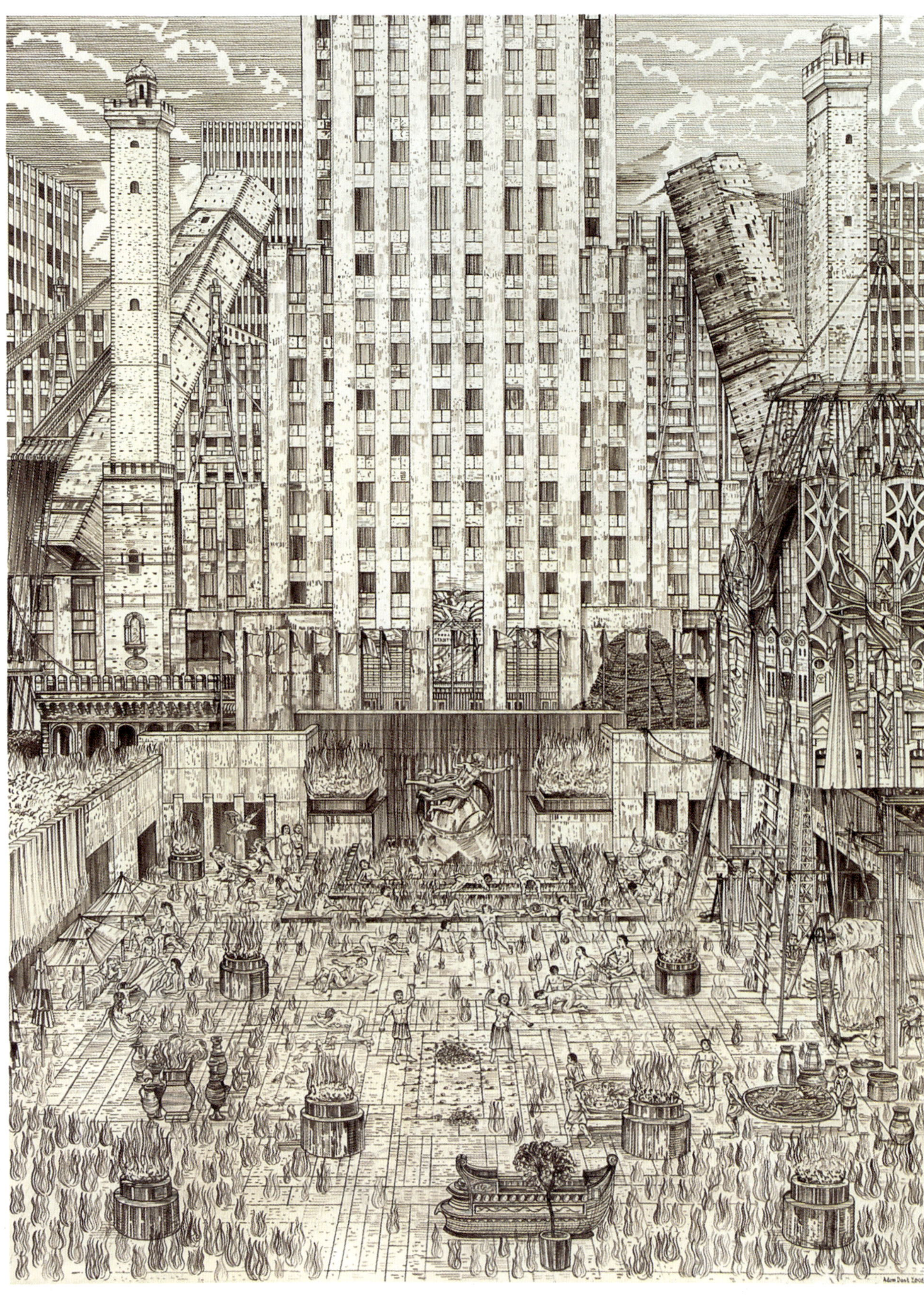

The Rockefeller Center (Myth of Prometheus), 2008
Ink on paper
205 × 153 cm (80 ¾ × 60 ¼ in.)

St Paul's Slave Market, 2006 >
Ink on paper
261 × 170 cm (102 ¾ × 66 ⅞ in.)

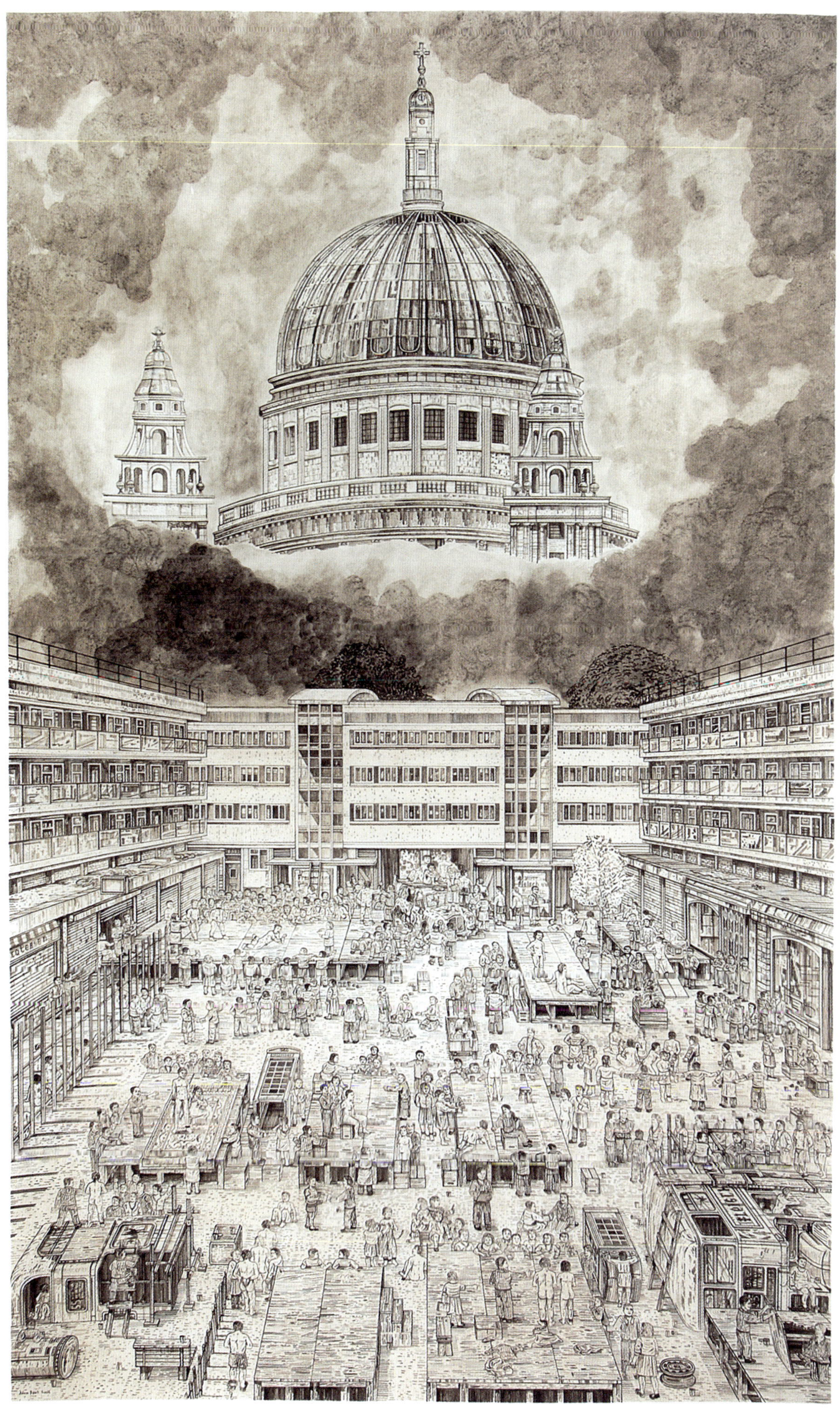

African American artist Kara Walker is renowned for her black-and-white silhouette wall drawings and animated films exploring themes of racial and sexual oppression and violence in the United States. She depicts fantastical parodies of life among slaves and slave owners in the antebellum South with a mischievous, transgressive humour that has occasionally caused controversy. Walker subverts the old-fashioned amateur craft of the paper cut-out, and deploys the anachronistic term 'negro' satirically by adopting the persona of a 'negress' for herself in her polemical writings.

The graphite drawings reproduced here belong to a series Walker made in 2011 entitled *Dust Jackets for the Niggerati –*

and Supporting Dissertations; Drawings Submitted Ruefully by Dr. Kara E. Walker. The title is an allusion to the Harlem Renaissance writer Wallace Thurman's ironic characterization of the group of black intelligentsia that gathered in New York during the 1920s. Walker's drawings are illustrations for an 'unwritten collection' of New Negro literature, invoking the lost talent of generations who lacked the education and means to fulfil the African American cultural writer Alain Locke's dream of a thriving black culture. Here, Walker's 'muckraking prophet' of the twenty-first century, who could be either a stripper or a slave for sale, angrily harangues a crowd of miscellaneous rural types, one bearing a pitchfork, while a girl taps at her iPhone.

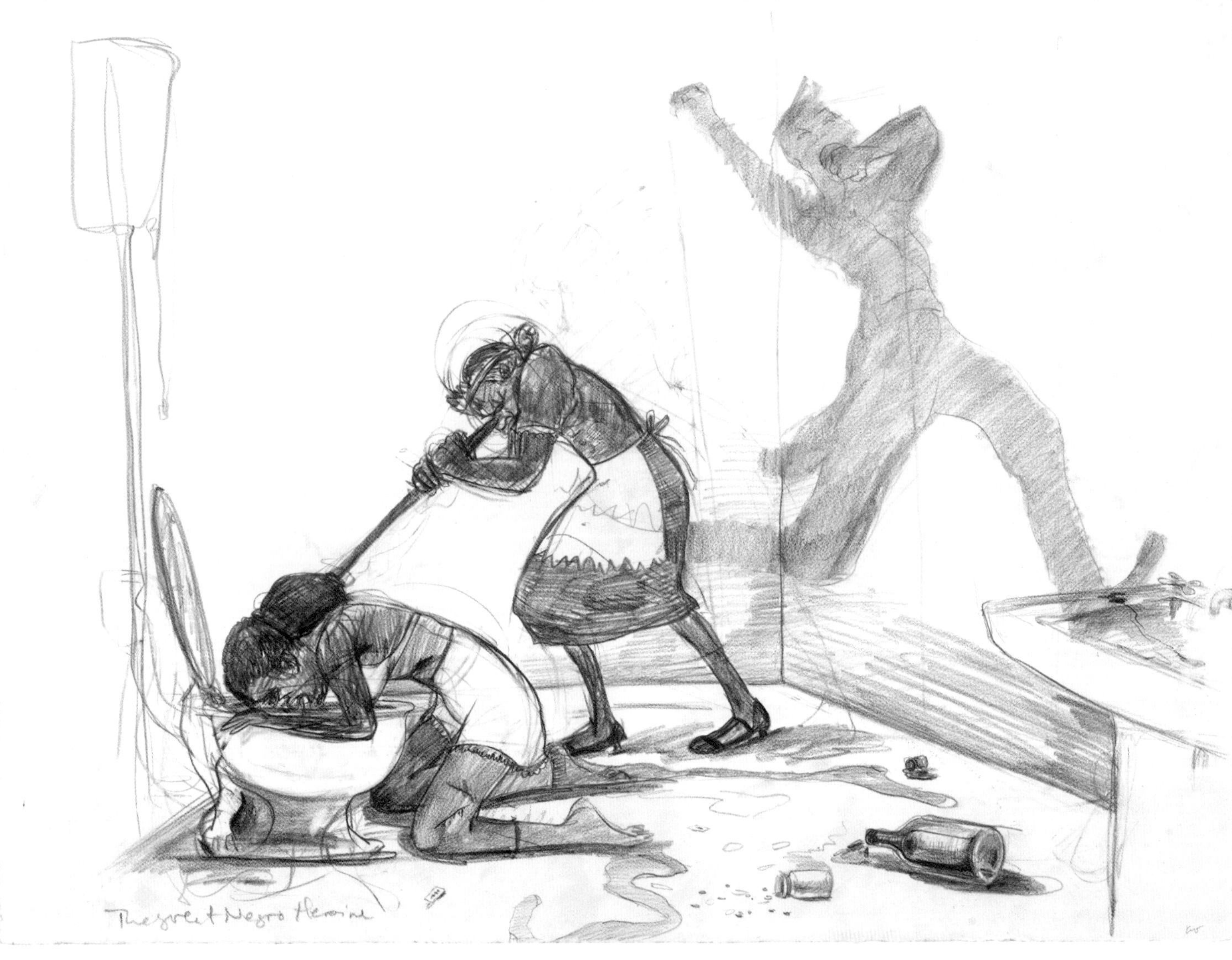

The Great Negro Heroine, 2011
Graphite on paper
57.2 × 76.2 cm (22 ½ × 30 in.)

Muckraking Prophet from the 21st c. Foretells Coming Doom and Encourages the Youth (left part), 2011 >
One of two drawings, graphite and pastel on paper
182.9 × 212.7 cm (72 × 83 ¾ in.)

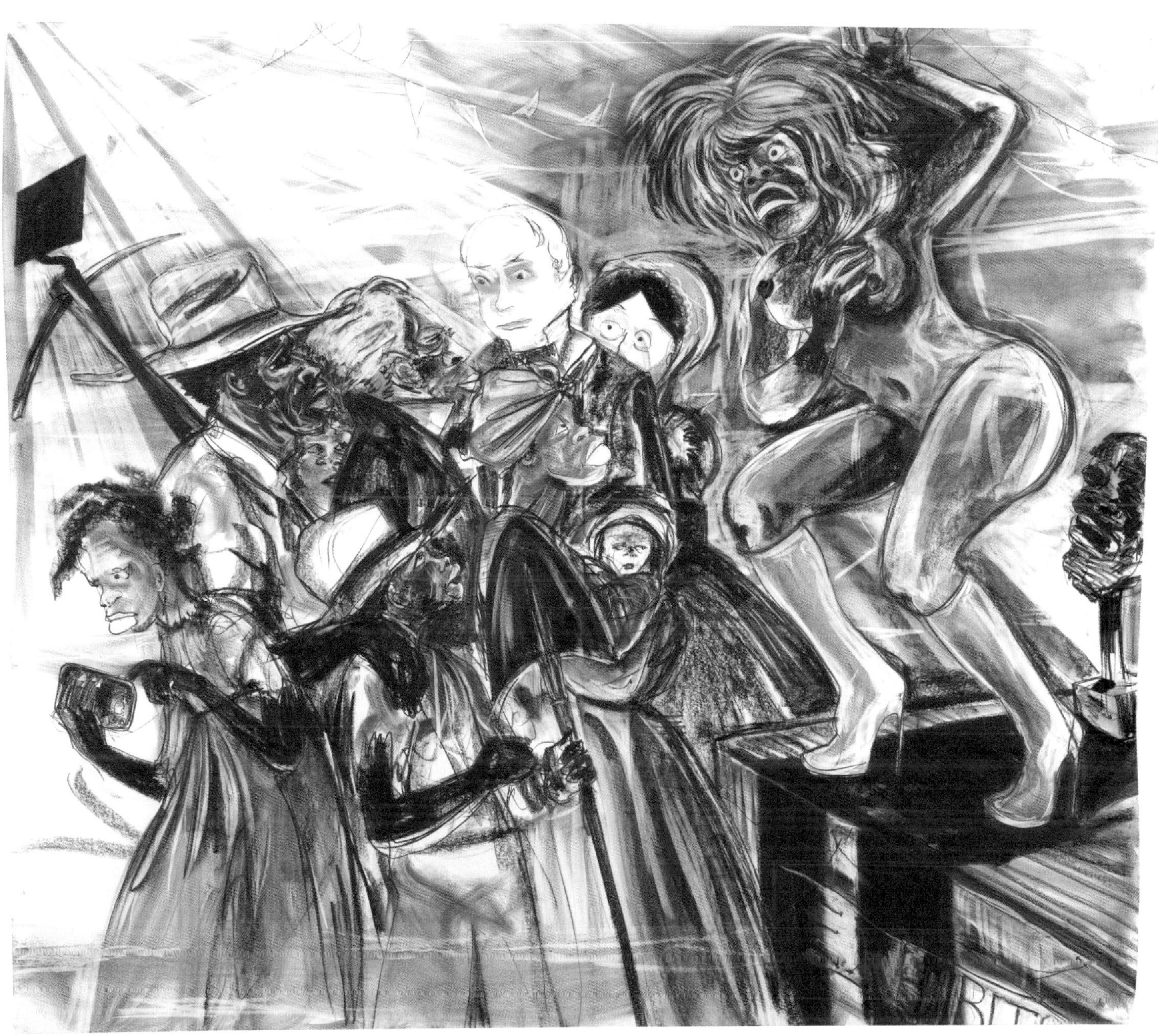

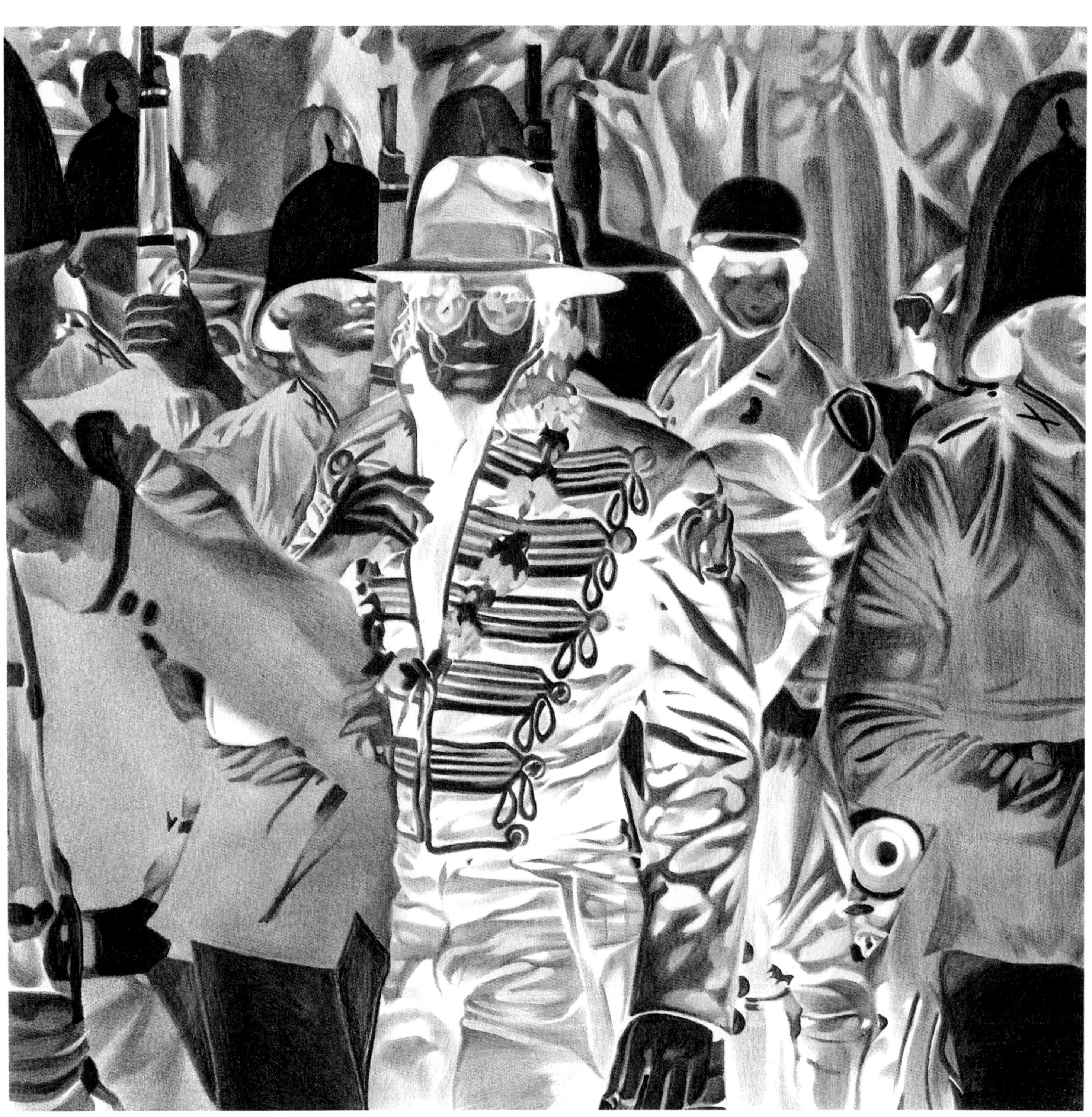

'It's important to my work to attract attention to the surface, to the texture of things', Marc Brandenburg has said, 'and to make clear that it's a representation of something. I'm more interested in the structures of things than in meanings and stories contained in the motif. This emptiness at the heart of the images, this white shining through is important.' In his meticulous drawings of photographic imagery turned inside-out – made by reversing the black-and-white photographs from which he works so that they read as negatives – Brandenburg pushes documentary literalism into abstraction. He draws mostly from his own photographs: freeze-frame shots of street life, fairgrounds, music and club scenes and a cast of marginal male characters, including street people, football fans, vendors, clowns and masquerading revellers. Reversed and digitally manipulated, the images take on a faintly sinister, hallucinatory atmosphere of perpetual night, where light is dark and dark light, and solid forms are rendered insubstantial. Brandenburg reproduces these effects in graphite with painstaking precision, declaring that he wants his work to be 'almost completely determined by technology and not by taste or romance'.

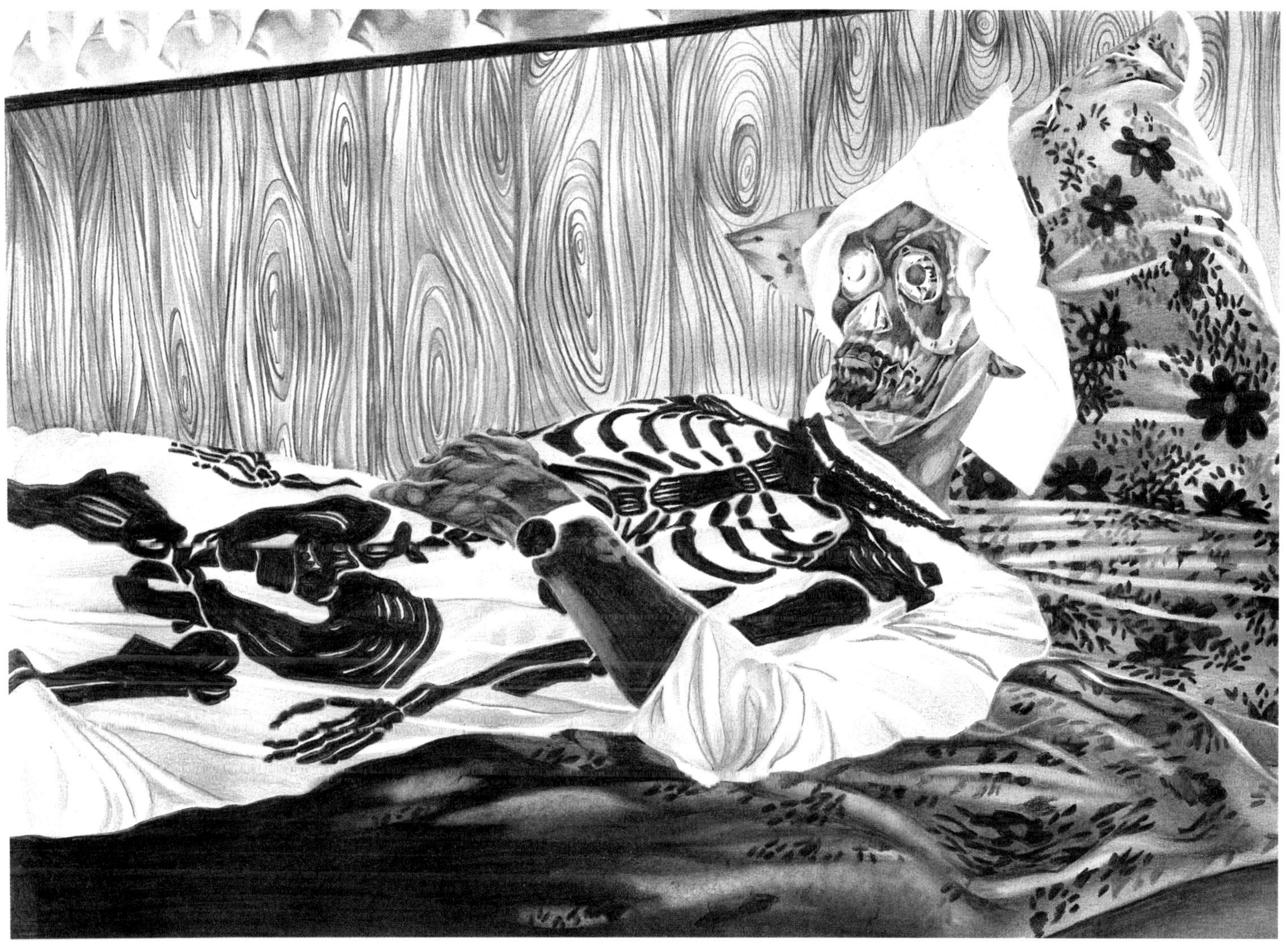

< *Untitled*, 2004
Pencil on paper
20 × 22 cm (7 ⅞ × 8 ⅝ in.)

Untitled, 2000
Pencil on paper
21 × 30 cm (8 ¼ × 11 ¾ in.)

As a student at the School of Art in Cluj a decade after the fall of Communism, Mircea Suciu acquired the skills associated with a figurative tradition reaching back far beyond Socialist Realism. He identifies with the masters of *chiaroscuro*, Caravaggio and Rembrandt, although he is philosophically and temperamentally closer to Goya. The darkness of Suciu's melancholy realism is unrelieved by spiritual illumination; the mood is predominantly one of existential despair. In his subdued, almost monochrome paintings and large charcoal drawings, the people are usually anonymous, their faces averted or obscured, their gestures limp and ambiguous. The late 1950s Theatre of the Absurd and the Surrealism of Magritte are evident influences on Suciu's work, as are the American adverts of the 1940s and '50s, the latter specifically for the figures, which Suciu strips from their glossy contexts and subjects to a newer, darker existence. In *It All Ends with a Laugh* (2012), the uniformed audience is convulsed by involuntary laughter at an unexpected joke – a momentary release from what Suciu refers to as the 'horrible historical events' that lie behind many of his scenes. The flare of smoke in the study of the worker, *Dust to Dust* (2013), is a brilliant example of the artist's illusionistic powers with charcoal – an image conjured out of nothing but dust.

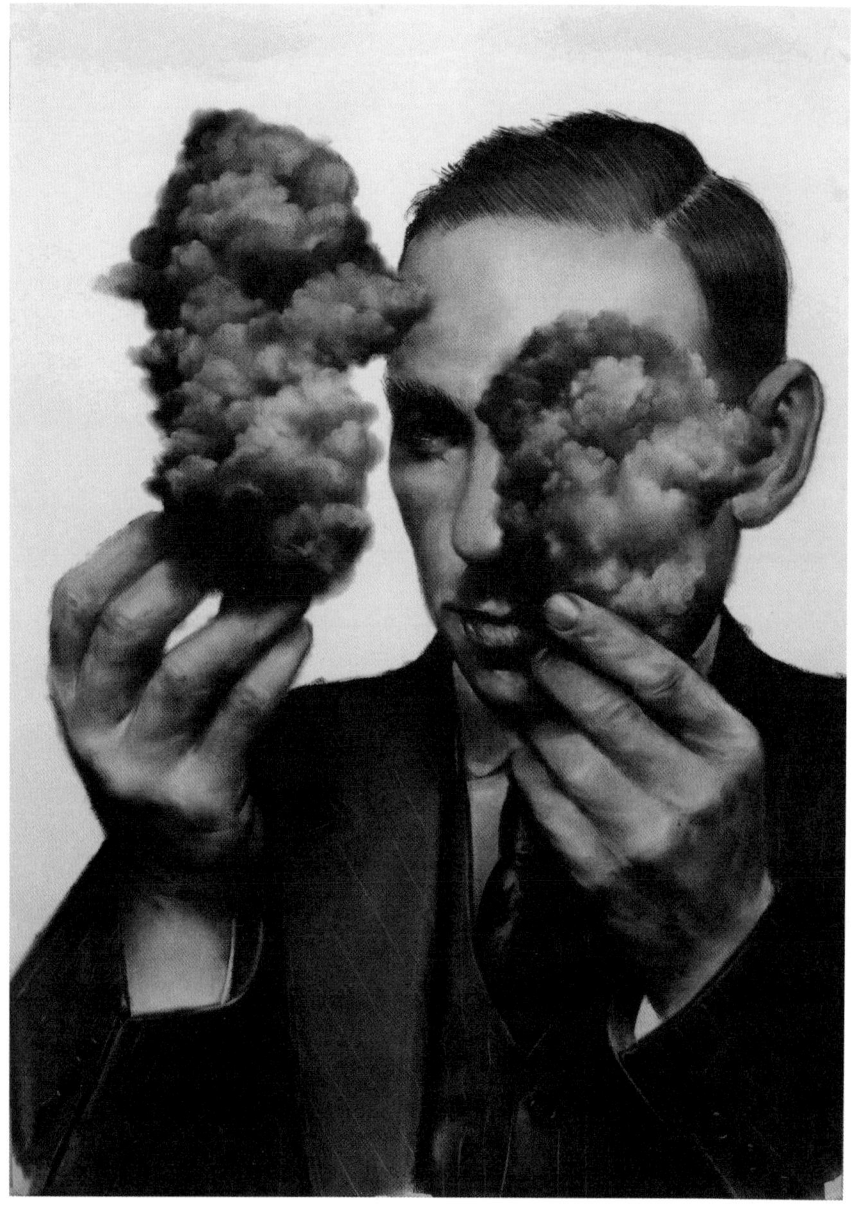

The Deceiver, 2012
Charcoal on paper
100 × 70 cm (39 ⅜ × 27 ½ in.)

Dust to Dust, 2013 >
Charcoal on paper
150 × 151 cm (59 × 59 ½ in.)

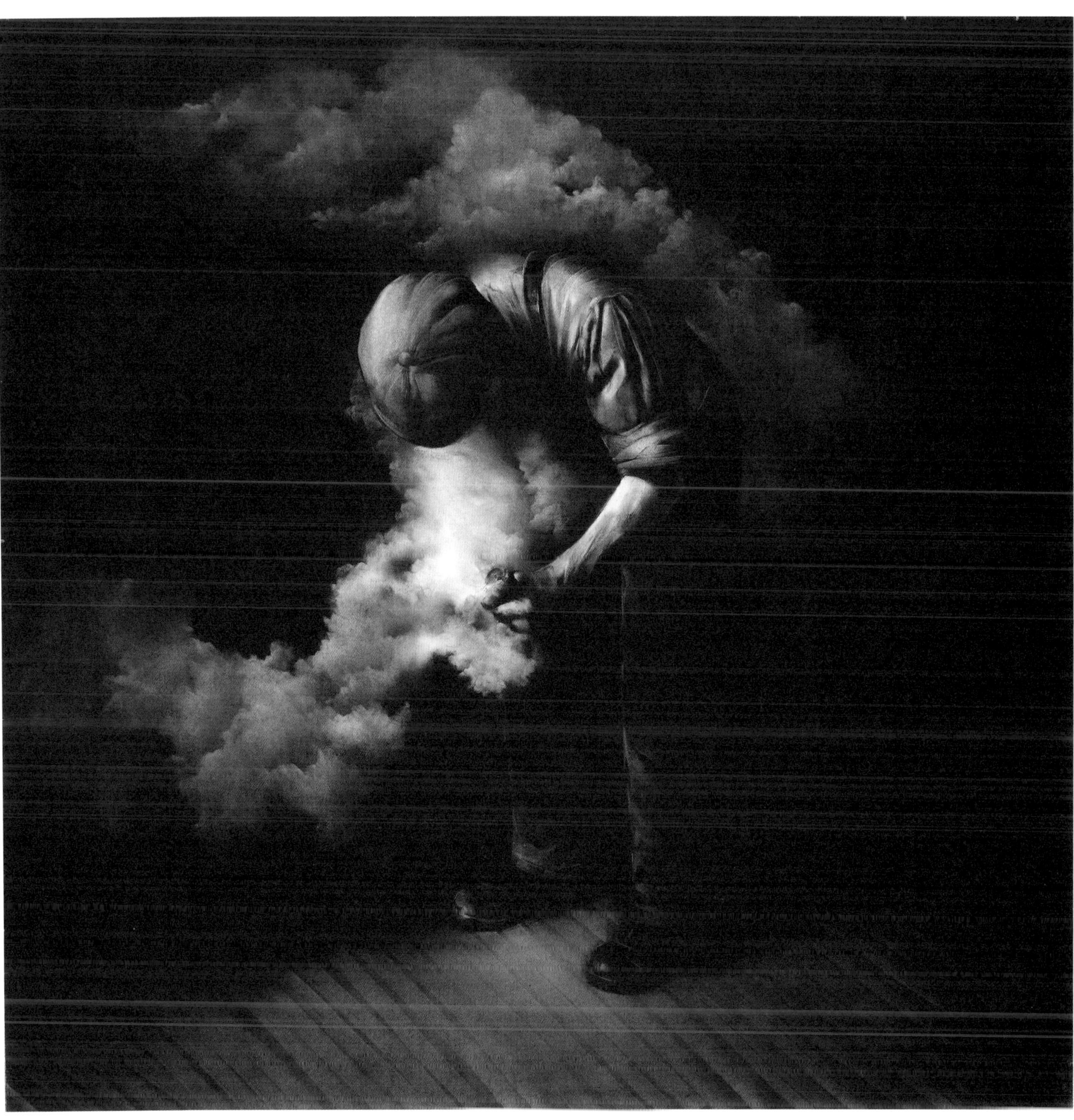

188

MIRCEA SUCIU

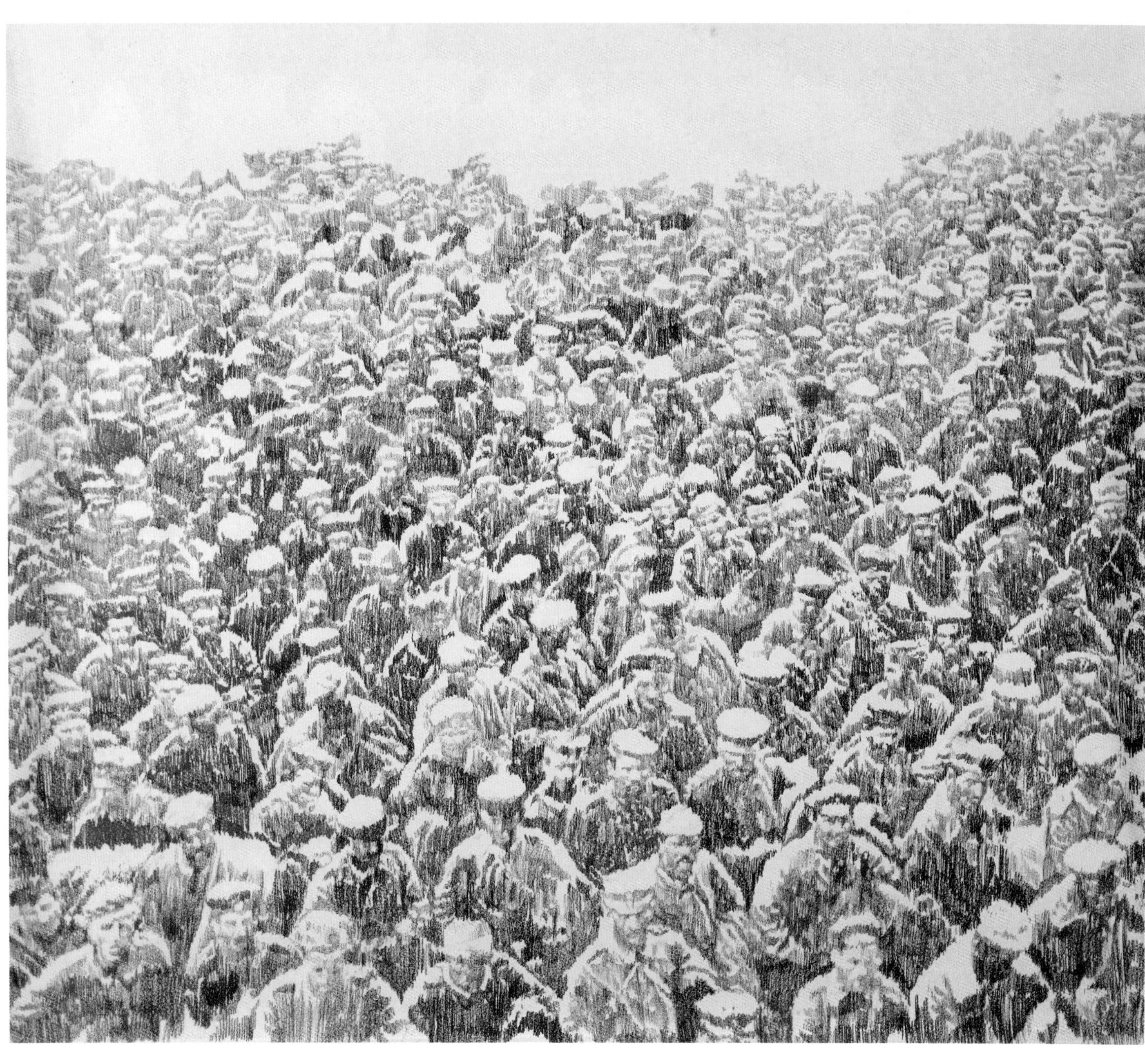

In Line, 2011
Charcoal on paper
167 × 150 cm (65 ¾ × 59 in.)

It All Ends with a Laugh, 2012 >
Charcoal on paper
101 × 150 cm (39 ¾ × 59 in.)

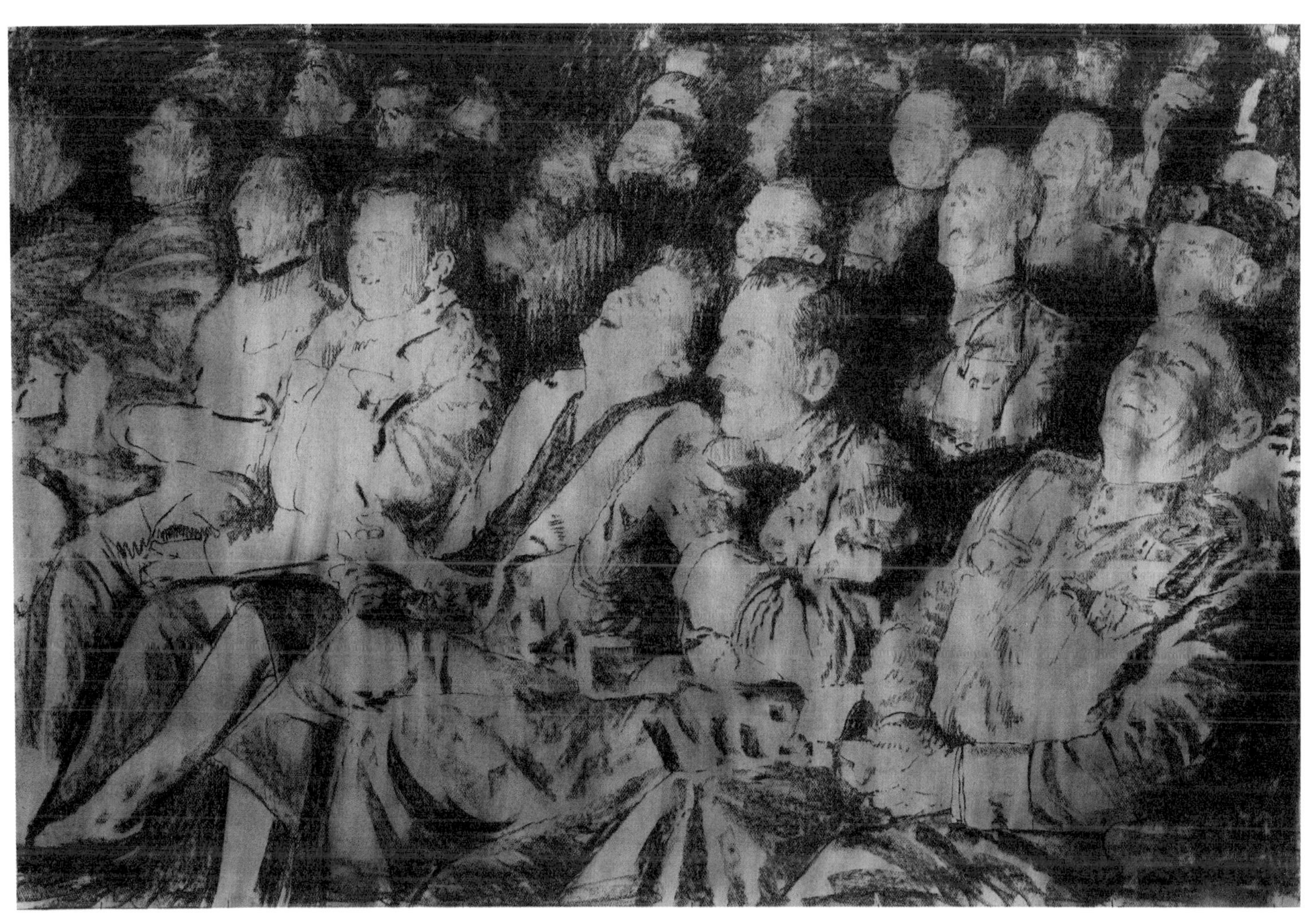

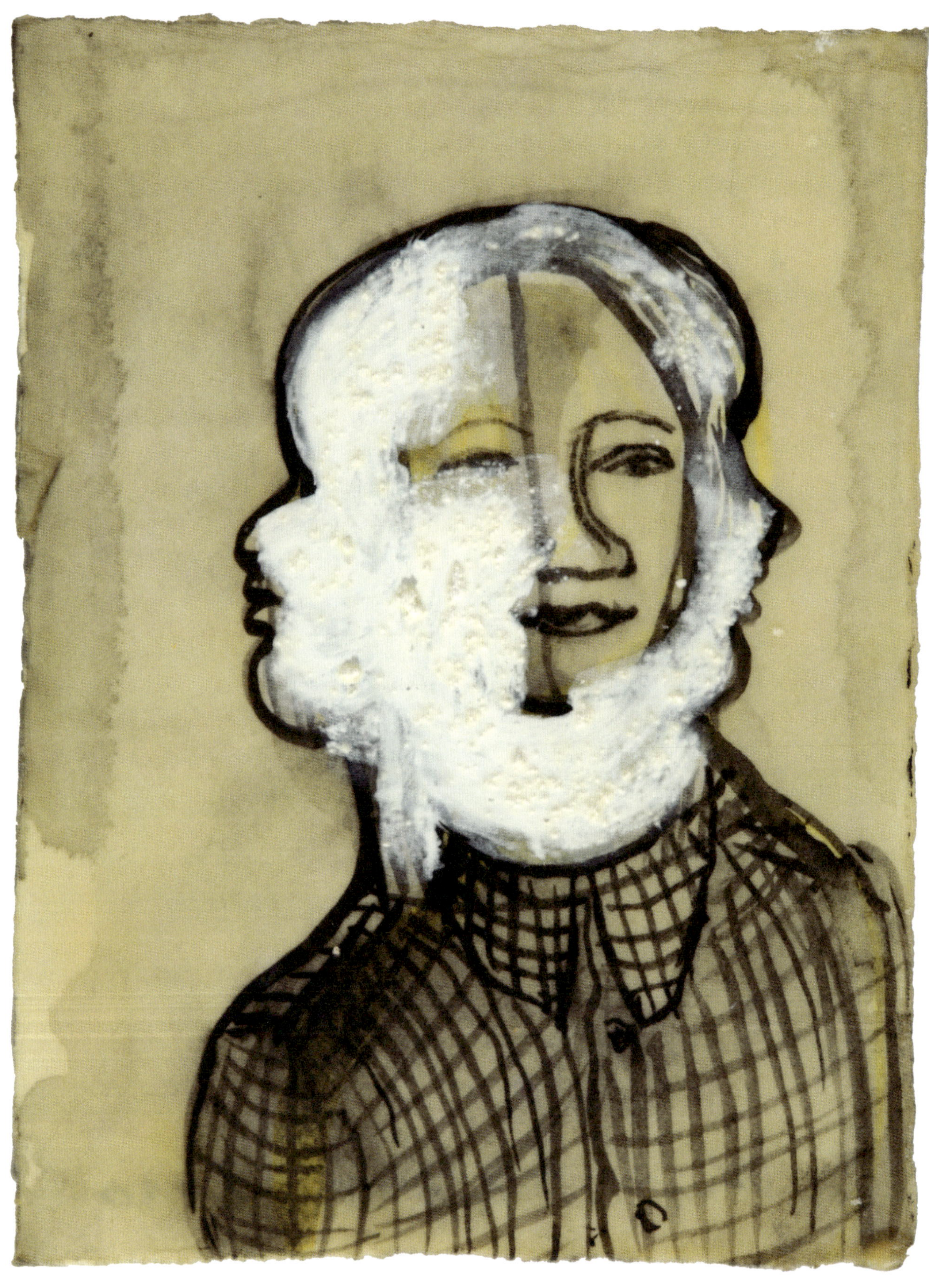

5

fictions

The artist begs the public to be indulgent with him, because he has neither imitated other works, nor even used studies from nature. The imitation of nature is as difficult as it is admirable, if it is really perfect. But an artist may also, surely, remove himself entirely from nature and depict forms of movements which to this day have only existed in the imagination.... Painting, like poetry, selects from the universe whatever it considers most suitable for its purposes. It unites qualities and characters which nature has scattered among different individuals and concentrates them in a single fantastic being. Thanks to this creative combination, the artist ceases to be a mere copyist and acquires the title of an inventor.

FRANCISCO GOYA Draft prospectus for the the album *Los Caprichos*, 1799.
Translation published in Francis Klingender, *Goya in the Democratic Tradition*, 1948

The artist as witness can often be the artist with the wildest and most outlandish imagination. Both a realist and a fantasist, he or she can be an observer and critic of reality on the one hand, and an inventor of bizarre and possibly nightmarish visions on the other. In such cases realism and fiction do not exist in separate compartments; the same mind is responsible for both. Images of the observed world may be infused with a sense of absurdity and irrationality, and fantastical scenes made credible by the artist's practised powers of observation. Artists who have studied the human form and know what people look like in daily life – walking, embracing, talking aloofly to a stranger or laughing intimately with a friend, marching to war or curling up asleep – will have the necessary resources, a repertoire of characters and poses available for imaginative compositions. This is not to say that every worthwhile fantasy needs a dose of realism to give it weight and depth, but rather that the most powerful and memorable often do contain that vital ingredient. In the post-Surrealist age when fantastical imagery is so easy to come by, representations of the imaginary that bear an authentic relation to lived experience may have greater intensity. The best artist–fabulists have a wide visual vocabulary which stems from looking closely at the external world. Their inner vision is grounded in observation. And no two artists see alike.

Several artists in this chapter whose work revolves around a fictional narrative evidently do draw from life in the course of composing images with multiple figures. *Untitled (View of the Port of Onomatopoeia)* (2009–10), Charles Avery's delicate study of young people balancing on a beam under a dock, gives an idea of how complex the process of composition must have been, with its many individualized characters, each with carefully defined peculiarities – a gait, stoop and expression – that distinguish them from their neighbours. Whether or

< SANDRA VÁSQUEZ DE LA HORRA *El Niño Janus*, 2011
Watercolour, wax and oil on paper, 17 × 13 cm (6 ¾ × 5 ⅛ in.)

192

not a particular figure was the result of preparatory drawings or arose straight from the artist's imagination, there is a strong sense of his enjoyment of the power to create these individuals, and his ability to enter into each person in order to bring them to life. Nowhere in the drawing does that enthusiasm for precise characterization wane; no figure has been vaguely sketched with casual indifference; no one escapes the artist's fanatical attention.

A similar delight in the power to invent characters and confound reality with fiction is apparent in the fiercely comic drawings of Paula Rego, an artist often aptly described as a magical realist. The two reproduced in this book belong to a group of twenty, created during a year in which the artist abandoned colour and drew in nothing but Conté, charcoal and graphite. These are as large as her major pastels, making the figures almost life-sized. As is often her practice, Rego has based these on three-dimensional tableaux set up in her studio, incorporating real-life models along with sculpted dummies, mannequins and other props. Those incongruous combinations create an absurd, fantastical world before the drawing even begins. Rego draws directly from her assemblages, carving out a fictional space and rendering the figures with vigorous, literal-minded diligence, hatching and shading until each has a solid and convincing presence. Live models and dummies are drawn with equal conviction and coexist on the same stage on equal terms. The strength of Rego's emotions and her passionate identification with the scenarios she creates – whether inspired by literature, folk and fairy tales, or stories of her own invention – give her images immense psychological force. Yet she is by no means a self-obsessed fantasist living in a world of her own. Her involvement with the real world is demonstrated by the formidable pastels and etchings she made of girls suffering illegal abortions, which she created in outrage at the failure of the Portuguese to vote for the liberalization of abortion law in a 1998 referendum. (Rego's artistic protest is credited with helping to reverse that decision in a second referendum in 2007.) Rego has spoken of being particularly 'intrigued and horrified by the tradition of cruelty of women towards women', and has made outspoken works about female genital mutilation, honour killings and human trafficking. It is clear that the cruelty Rego finds in the folk stories that so fascinate her, she also finds in reality.

An artist who shares Rego's passion for fairy tales and her love of black humour is Sandra Vásquez de la Horra, who also happens to have grown up, like Rego, in a staunchly Catholic society under a fascist military dictatorship (Rego in Portugal under Salazar, Vásquez de la Horra in Chile under Pinochet). Intimations of violence, sexual repression and patriarchal domination pervade both artists' drawings, undercut by a mischievous impulse to mock authority and overturn idols; subversive laughter and erotic perversity redeem the spirit from the mirthless, sanctimonious and hypocritical bourgeois regime, at least in the artists' imaginations. If this absurdist, grotesquely comic strain is attributable to the paranoia induced by living under tyranny, Ricardo Lanzarini's imagery can be regarded in a similar light: it bears the imprint, as he says, of 'the oppressive experience lived through during the Uruguayan military dictatorship in the 1970s and '80s'. Much like Vásquez de la Horra's hooded, cloaked or uniformed apparitions, beak-nosed faces, death's heads and animal–human hybrids, Lanzarini's tumultuous outpouring of tiny military officers ludicrously cavorting in endless costumed parades may be satire, but could perhaps more accurately be described as a form of revenge: banishing demons through ridicule. Rego has spoken of her pleasure in using her drawings to 'punish' people who have wronged her in the past, such as harsh schoolteachers or bigoted critics; in this limited arena, the artist is in total command, although admittedly she or he may become a victim once more, at the mercy of the repressed memories and fearful emotions that come flooding back when the censoring mechanisms of the conscious mind are relaxed.

No such disturbing associations with brutal reality taint Marcel Dzama's capricious inventions; or if they do, they are at a certain remove – less the result of direct experience than of an innocent imagination run riot. There is plenty of violence, but it is staged for amusement, not catharsis. Evocations of war are quaintly historicized or miniaturized as in a board game, or theatricalized as in dance. Conflict is a constant theme, but it might be sublimated into chess, or eroticized as girl soldiers skipping into battle without underwear, or diverted into hunting, pageantry and acrobatics. Dzama's ever-expanding repertoire of characters and costumes is choreographed in increasingly complex and extravagant spectacles, yet his fantasy is kept in check by skilful adherence to self-imposed rules, including consistency of scale, anatomical feasibility (more or less) and a strictly limited palette. The instinct of the illustrator or narrator with a story to tell, whose aim is to hold the viewer or reader in thrall, guards him against exceeding the boundaries of fiction. Dzama's drawings might be storyboards showing scenes meant for enaction or animation, and indeed his expansion into actual performances and video could be what makes the graphic constraints tolerable for him; drawing is not his only means of escape.

That Dzama can draw so well and sustain himself imaginatively in a world of his own invention links him to the great traditions of illustration, to the children's books and comics that inspired him in his childhood and youth, and to dreamers like Henry Darger and Joseph Cornell. It could be argued that Dzama has quietly subverted the very concept of illustration, by holding faithfully to its values as an art form while declaring independence from text and the contingencies of reproduction. The drawings are autonomous; they produce their own narrative by virtue of the repetition of figures and motifs, but that narrative is non-linear and arcane, and anyway may turn out to be only a rehearsal for eventual realization in another medium.

Dzama's nostalgia for the 1920s, an age of innocence in popular entertainment and avant-garde art alike (and also his hometown Winnipeg's heyday), may be a metaphor for another level of nostalgia, for the innocent self-absorption of childhood. Like his friend and fellow artist Jockum Nordström, Dzama seems unusually connected with his childhood self. Both artists' adult practice is contiguous with the way they might have drawn in adolescence: the minor transgressions of nakedness and sex occupy a similar vein, and they are fuelled by memories of early enthusiasms for model boats or soldiers and imaginary adventures with animals in the wilderness. Nordström distinguishes his work as an illustrator of children's books from his practice as an artist: 'When I illustrate, I always have an audience somewhere in mind. I am ready for compromises. It is a collaboration. When I make my artwork, I never think about the observers, I'm working inwards. It's more like a current.' But the intimate and unpretentious activity of drawing at a table or cutting up paper on the floor can never quite become professionalized or streamlined into 'artistic production'. It retains the aura of art made on the margins, purely for personal satisfaction.

By contrast to Dzama and Nordström's approaches, the imaginative drawings of Marcel van Eeden and Rinus Van de Velde are propelled not solely by inner currents but also by systems and procedures set up in imitation of the conventions governing sequential imagery in comics and graphic novels. Van de Velde's energetic charcoal drawings envelop or confront the viewer cinematically and his handwritten narrative spills off the canvas onto the gallery walls. Excess,

pictorial and verbal, characterizes his work. His drawings illustrate his own words, a meta-fiction in which the artist's alter ego features as protagonist and narrator of a stream-of-consciousness reflecting narcissistically on his own precarious existence within the story he is telling. There is no question of separating the images from the accompanying texts, although the individual drawings (with their texts) could be extracted from the narrative and stand alone, strangely but impressively, as single instances of the artist's idiosyncratic practice. Marcel van Eeden's method of story-telling is, by contrast, impersonal and cryptic; there are captions and a nominal protagonist, but the sequence of images can be shuffled and rearranged without impairing or improving the sense. That they belong in a serial format is more important than their actual order. The atmosphere of period and locale is convincing because they are drawn from found, not invented, archival images from an inexhaustible supply, fuelling a narrative without beginning or end.

A stock of ready-made images may also lie behind Raymond Pettibon's vast oeuvre of drawings, or they may simply spew from his brush in the manner of one of the many genres he has internalized and can imitate at will. This is another means of fictionalizing: always mimicking, never speaking in one's own voice – a world away from the passionate subjectivity of Paula Rego. Yet both Rego and Pettibon cite the same artist as their greatest inspiration: Goya, the presiding spirit of the capricious imagination, satirist, social critic, realist and fantasist in one. There is surely hardly an artist here who would not bow to Goya with love and respect, and who would not acknowledge him as an influence on their own fictionalizing practices.

CHARLES AVERY *Born 1973, Oban, Scotland, UK. Lives and works in London, UK*

Having grown up on the Scottish island of Mull, Charles Avery adapted himself to metropolitan life by inventing an imaginary island whose topography, wildlife, population, social structure and belief systems he has elaborated in an ambitious series of drawings, sculptures and writings. The artist describes this ongoing narrative project, begun in 2004, as 'a philosophical meditation on art-making and the impossibility of finding truth'. The metaphysical dimension of the series is conveyed through ingenious conceits in the naming of things such as the elusive wild beast, the Noumenon, a being which is held by some to dwell in the Eternal Forest, and over whose existence the Islanders constantly argue.

Yet it is the Islanders' physical appearance, shown in great detail in the drawings, that gives the fiction its depth and verisimilitude. These individuals often have the dour, weather-beaten, steely-eyed look of Highland folk. Recently, however,

194

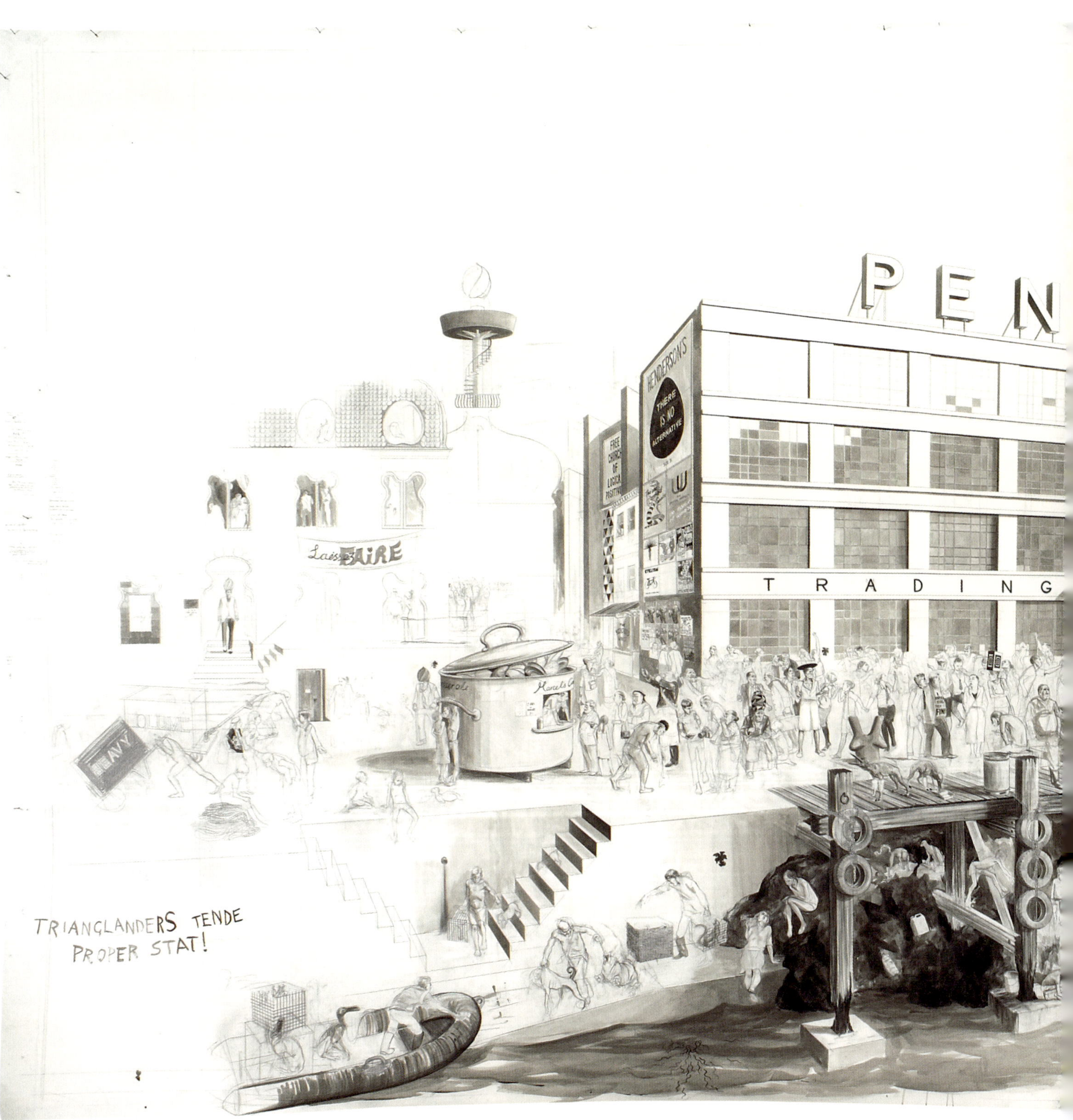

Untitled (View of the Port of Onomatopoeia), 2009–10
Pencil, ink and gouache on paper
240 × 510 cm (94 ½ × 200 ¾ in.)

they have come to seem like Londoners: skinny, hard-living, impoverished East Enders. Even the art world gets its equivalent in Avery's world via the opening of a museum on the island.

Avery's eye for character, type and gesture is instinctive and sharp – not, he insists, satirical or even cynical. As a fabulist, he filters observation through the screen of his own literary inventions. Perhaps it would bore him to draw the prosaic reality that surrounds him; yet his parallel world is full of incident that exactly corresponds with our own. The most spectacular drawings, such as *The Port of Onomatopoeia*, are masterpieces of observation and invention: the children in the study shown here, for instance, balancing on the beams under the pier, who reappear in the final composition, are just one detail among many.

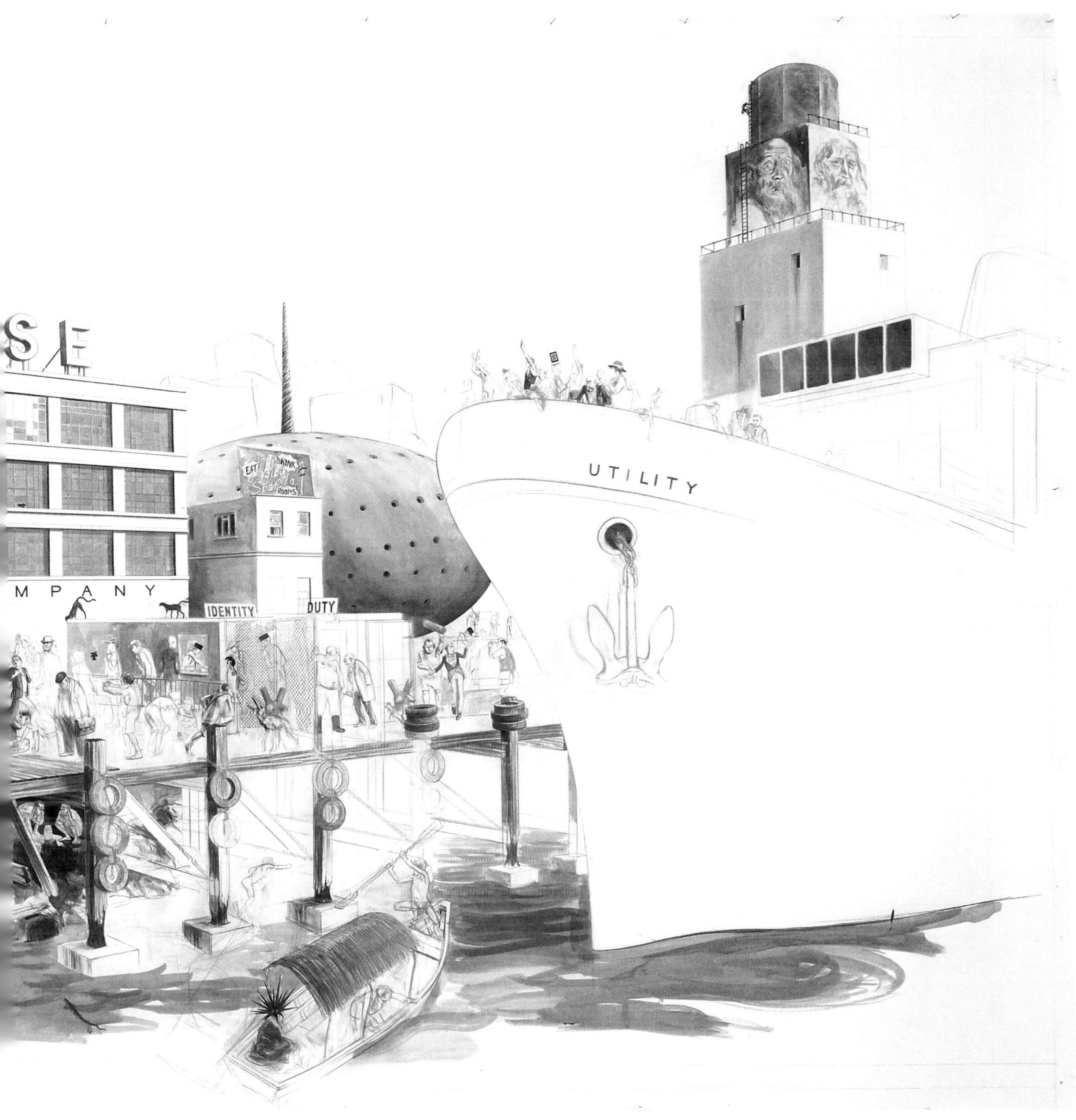

196

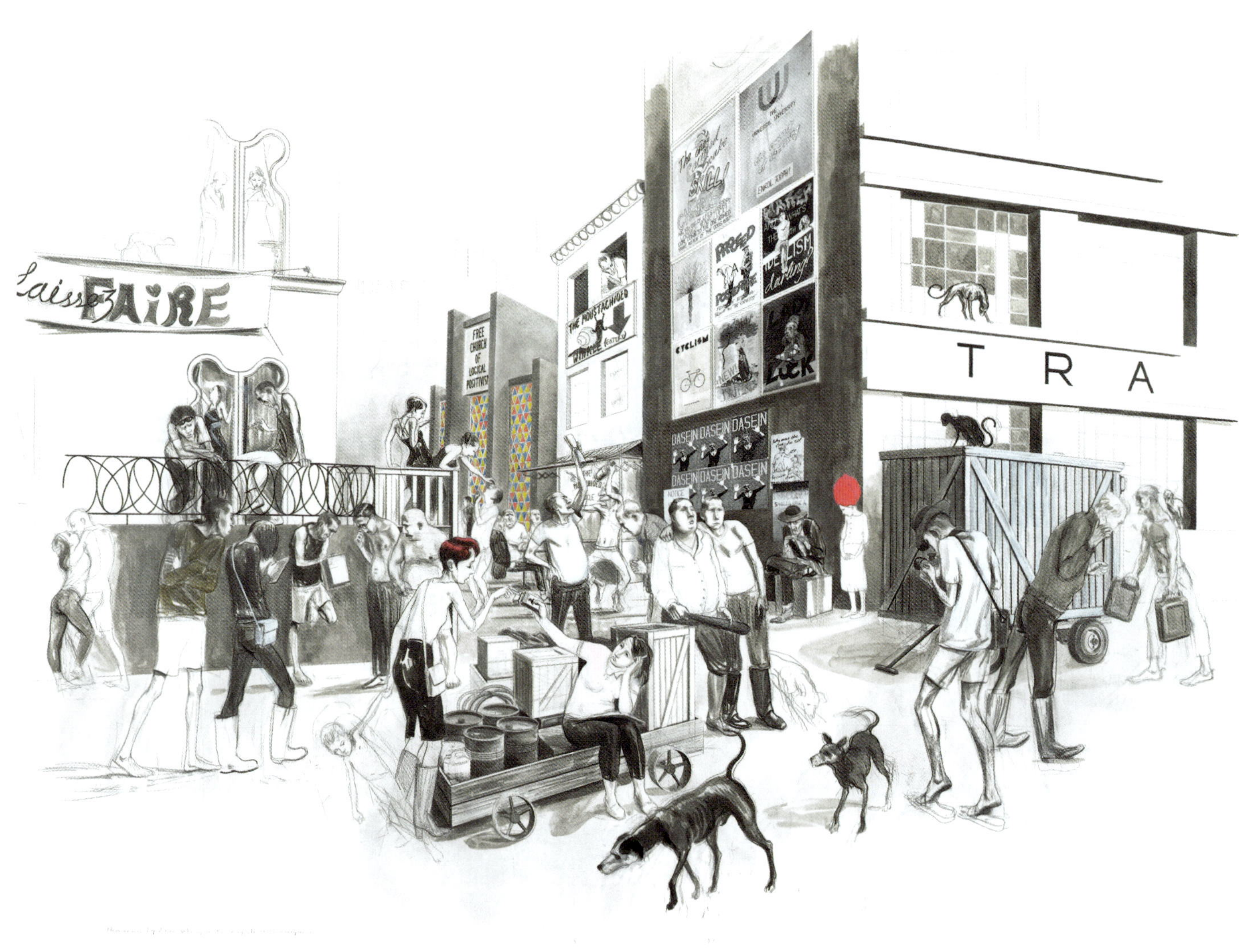

Untitled (Expedition), 2012
Pencil, ink, acrylic on paper
140.8 × 201.5 cm (55 ⅜ × 79 ⅜ in.)

Untitled (Children Playing Under the Pier at Onomatopoeia), 2010 >
Pencil, ink and gouache on paper
66.5 × 50.5 cm (26 ⅛ × 19 ⅞ in.)

children playing under the pier at Onomatopoeia

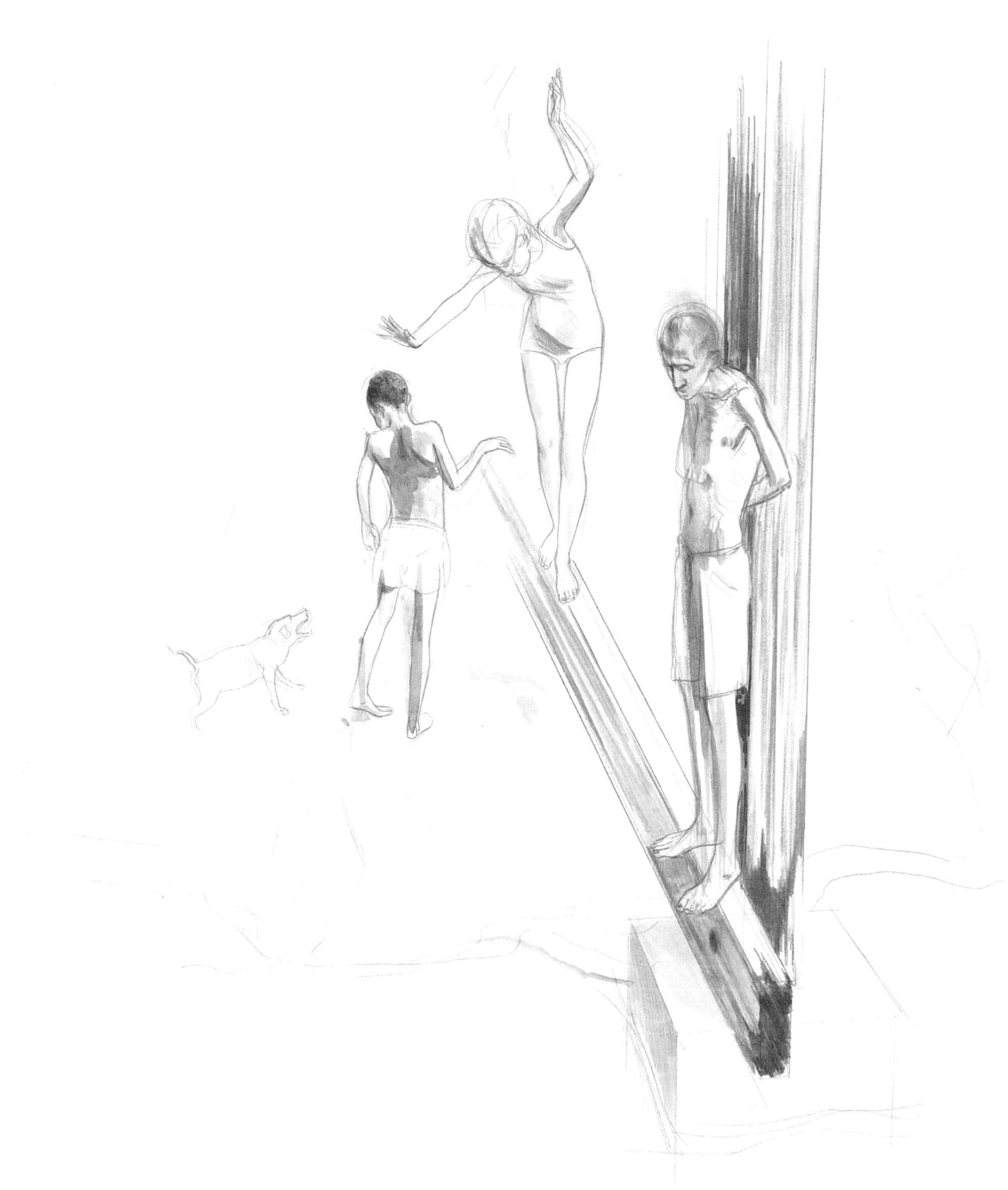

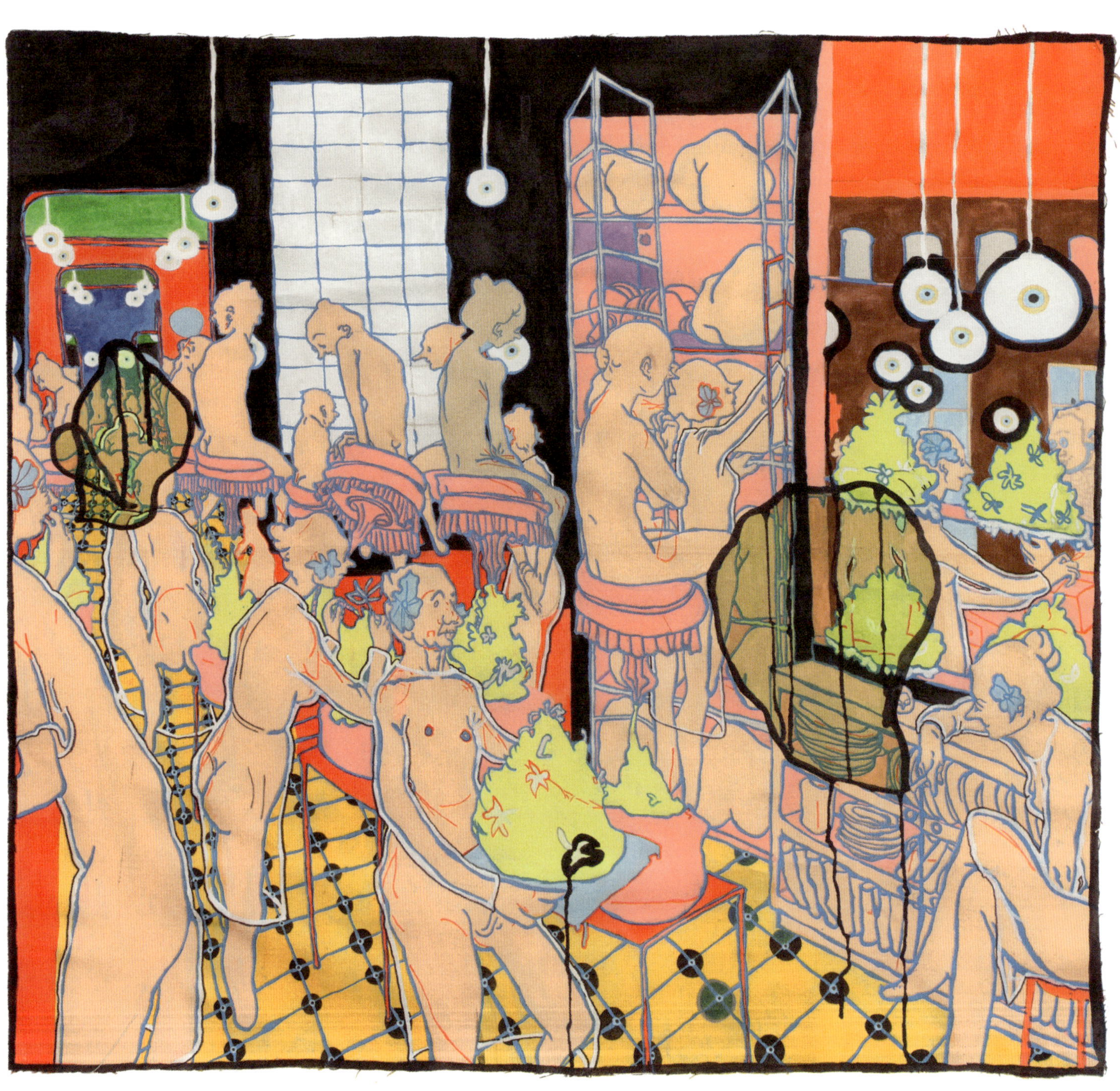

DASHA SHISHKIN *Born 1977, Moscow, Russia. Lives and works in New York, USA*

Dasha Shishkin's loose, splashy technique lends itself to a surrealistic stream of wildly perverse imagery, a febrile blend of Toulouse Lautrec and Henry Darger, executed with the spontaneous energy of the Surrealist Matta. Shishkin's father was a puppeteer, and the figure of the puppet Pinocchio is a frequent leitmotif in her phantasmagorical scenes of decadent society women partying in brilliantly lit, lavish interiors, their noses and nipples sprouting phallic extensions as they feast on dishes of dismembered body parts.

Although she uses colour emphatically, Shishkin defines her mixed media works as drawings: 'I think why I remove myself from the painters' milieu is because I make drawings and not paintings. I am still attached to line and the eloquent silhouettes that line creates, leaving paint and colours to be fillers and not definers. I am thinking of Picasso's quote about painting as an act of participation and drawing as an act of voyeurism. I like being a voyeur for now.'

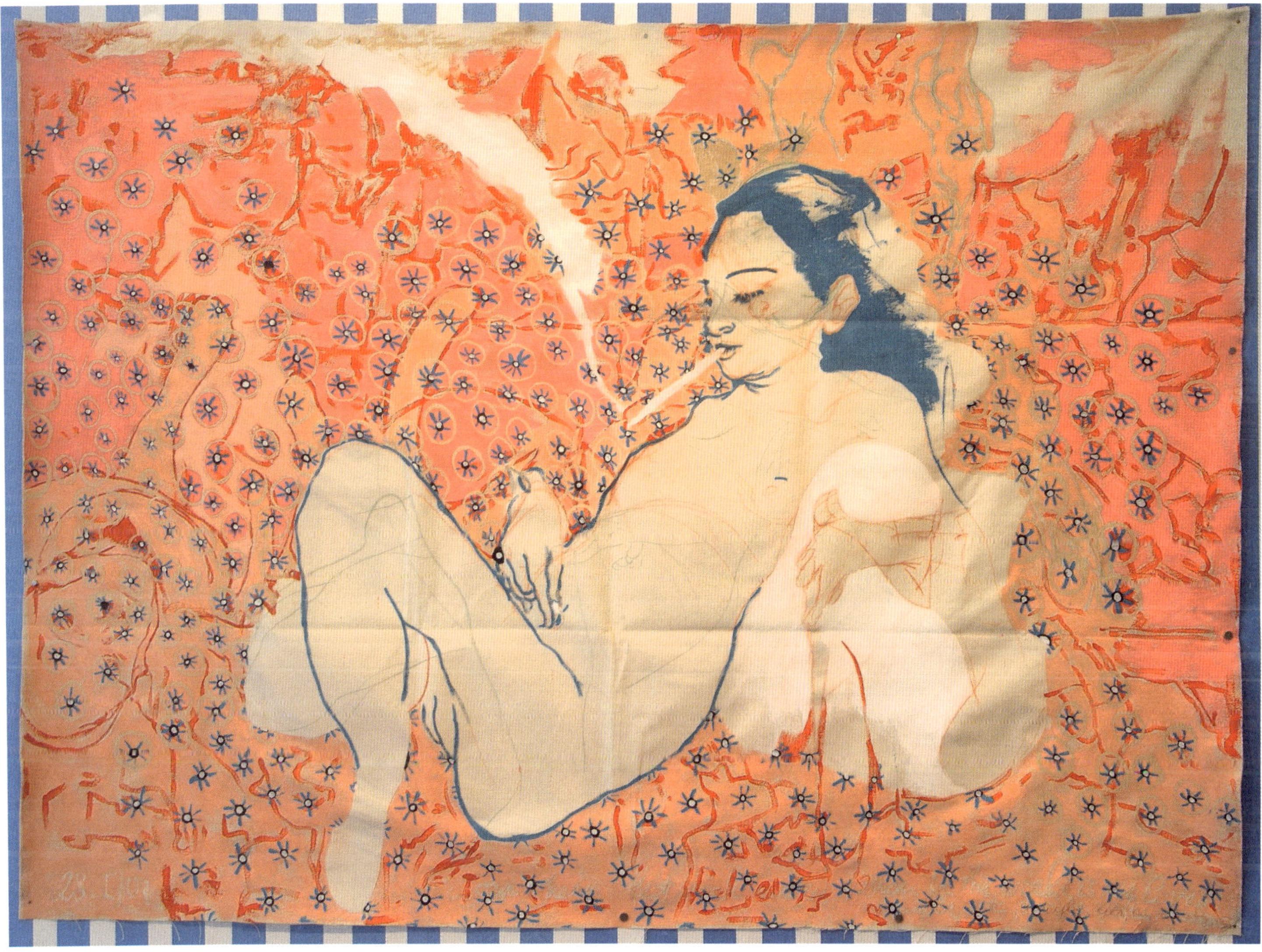

< *We Are Not Afraid for Comparable Lives,* 2011
Mixed media on canvas
102.24 × 96.52 cm (40 ¼ × 38 in.)

I Don't Want Any Problems, None What So Ever, 2007
Pastel and acrylic on canvas
134.62 × 182.88 cm (53 × 72 in.)

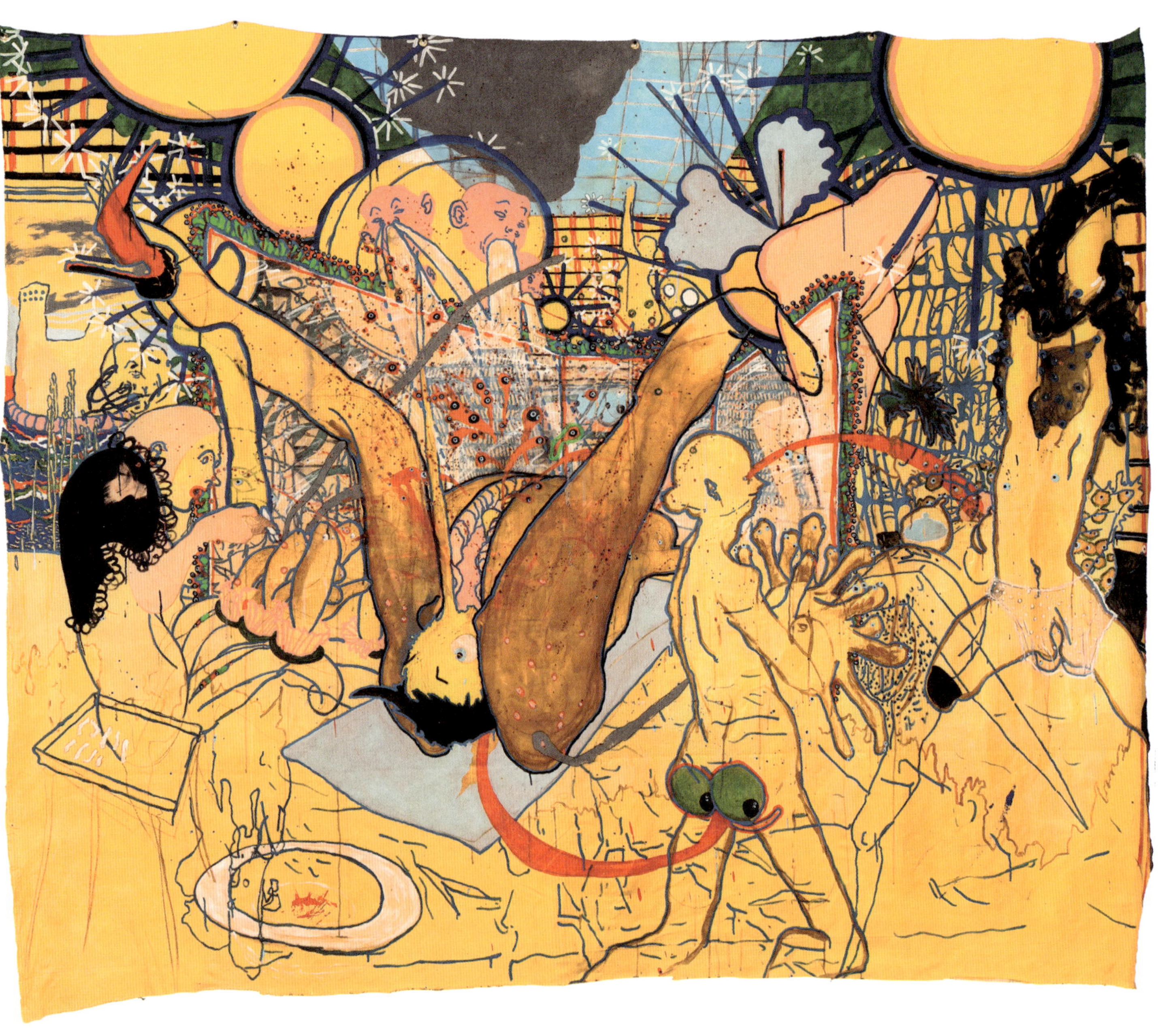

Geppetto Makes Another One, 2009
Acrylic, ink and Conté on canvas
242.57 × 304.8 cm (95 ½ × 120 in.)

Afraid of Certainty, 2009 >
Acrylic, ink and graphite on canvas
180.98 × 147.96 cm (71 ¼ × 58 ¼ in.)

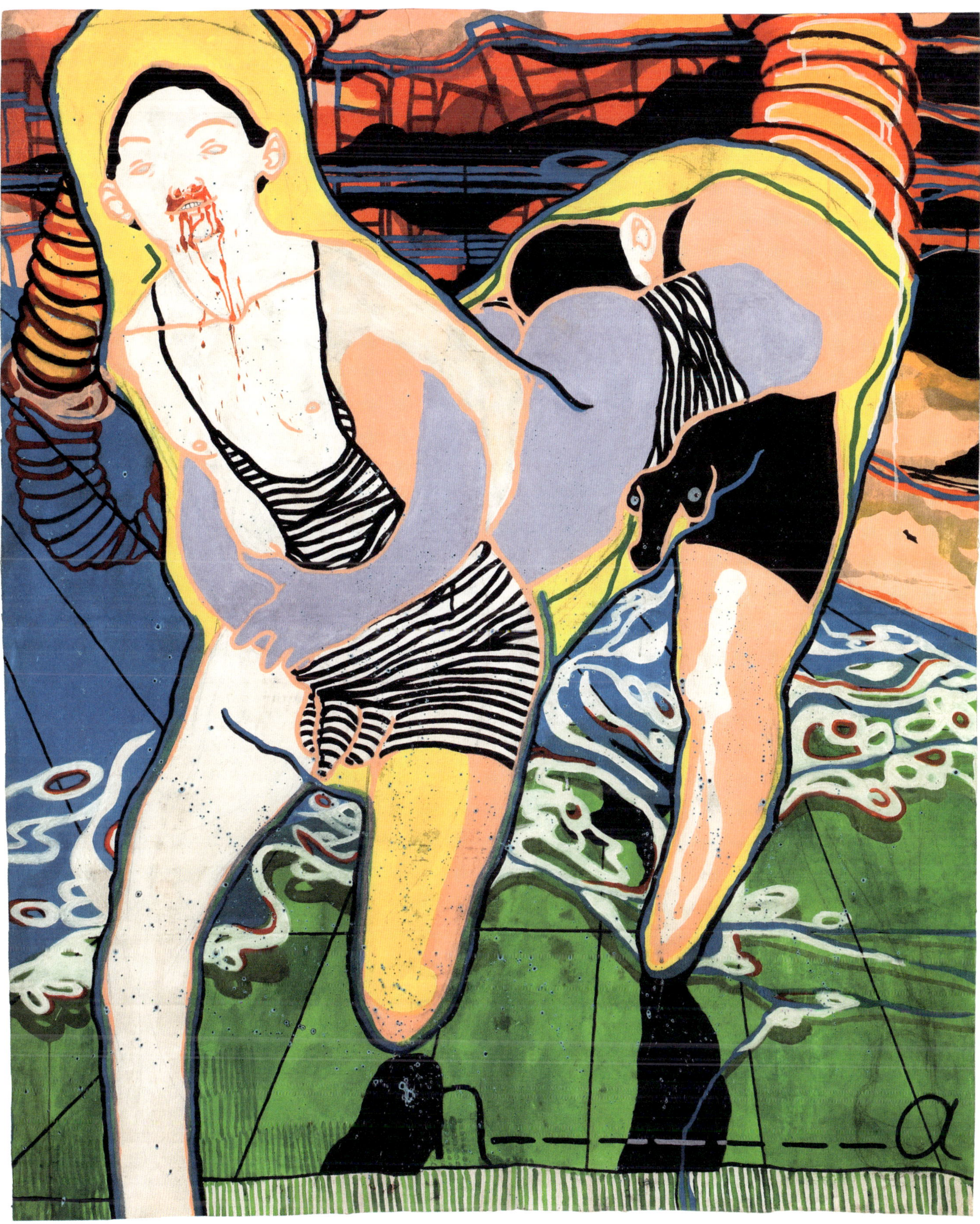

RICARDO LANZARINI *Born 1963, Montevideo, Uruguay. Lives and works in Montevideo, Uruguay*

A multitude of tiny figures swarms across the page in an 'endless pilgrimage'. In his work, Ricardo Lanzarini's stream of consciousness takes the shape of characters that seem as light and delicate as petals or insects. The plump, naked little men with moustaches, military caps and furious expressions, cavorting on tiny feet, seem more absurd than threatening, but there is a darker meaning behind such scenes. 'The oppressive experience of the military dictatorship in Uruguay in the 1980s and '90s has left an imprint on my work', says Lanzarini. He explores the human condition through these miniscule figures on their endless pilgrimage: 'enraged men abusing one another, violence and sex mixed, conflict between packs struggling to demarcate their territory; insecurity and insanity have taken over the houses.'

Originally a conceptual artist working in installation and 'urban intervention', it was in the 1990s that Lanzarini began drawing his tiny figures onto JOB cigarette rolling papers, creating miniature books. He called them 'clandestine' drawings; they could be mistaken for prisoners' art. Since then he has enlarged his imagery to the scale of murals painted onto the walls of a disused jail cell, for instance, and the rusting exterior of an abandoned ship. Lanzarini describes his practice as a product of confinement, reflection and writing. The restless, unstoppable drama of daily political and social life is his raw material. He immerses himself in it and then extracts his narratives: 'I need to live the work until it becomes unbearable for me.'

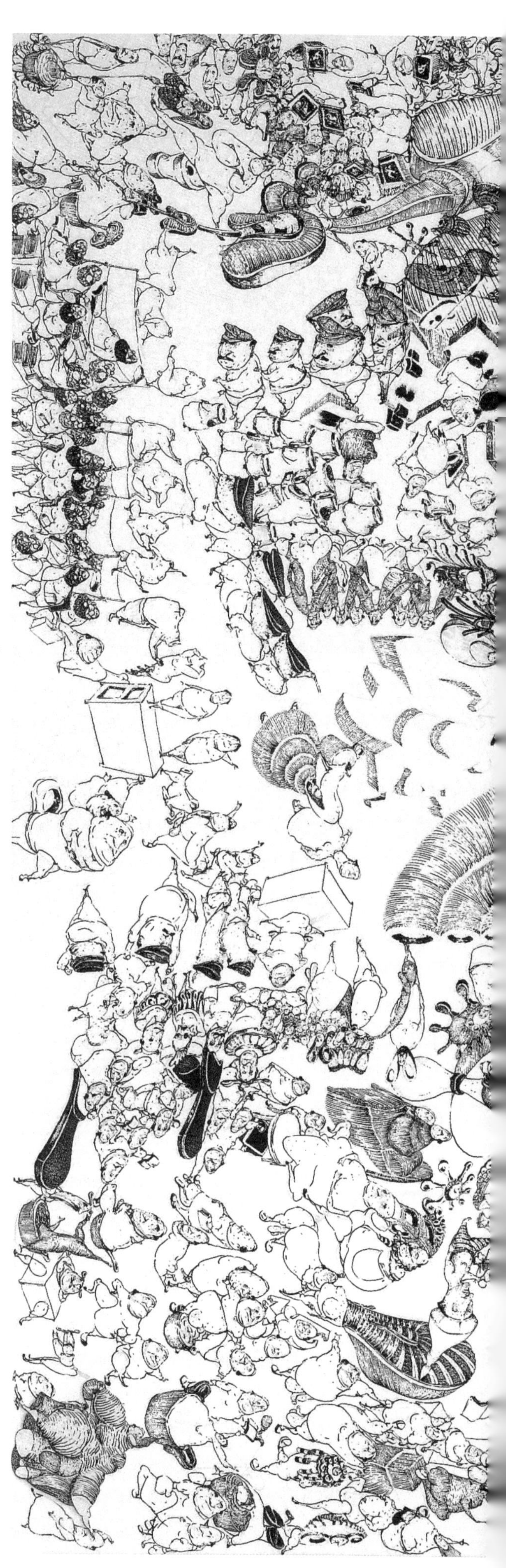

Delirio abstracto contagioso, 2013
Ink on paper
36 × 43 cm (14 ⅛ × 16 ⅞ in.)

(pp. 204–5) *Delirio abstracto contagioso* (detail), 2013
Ink on paper
36 × 43 cm (14 ⅛ × 16 ⅞ in.)

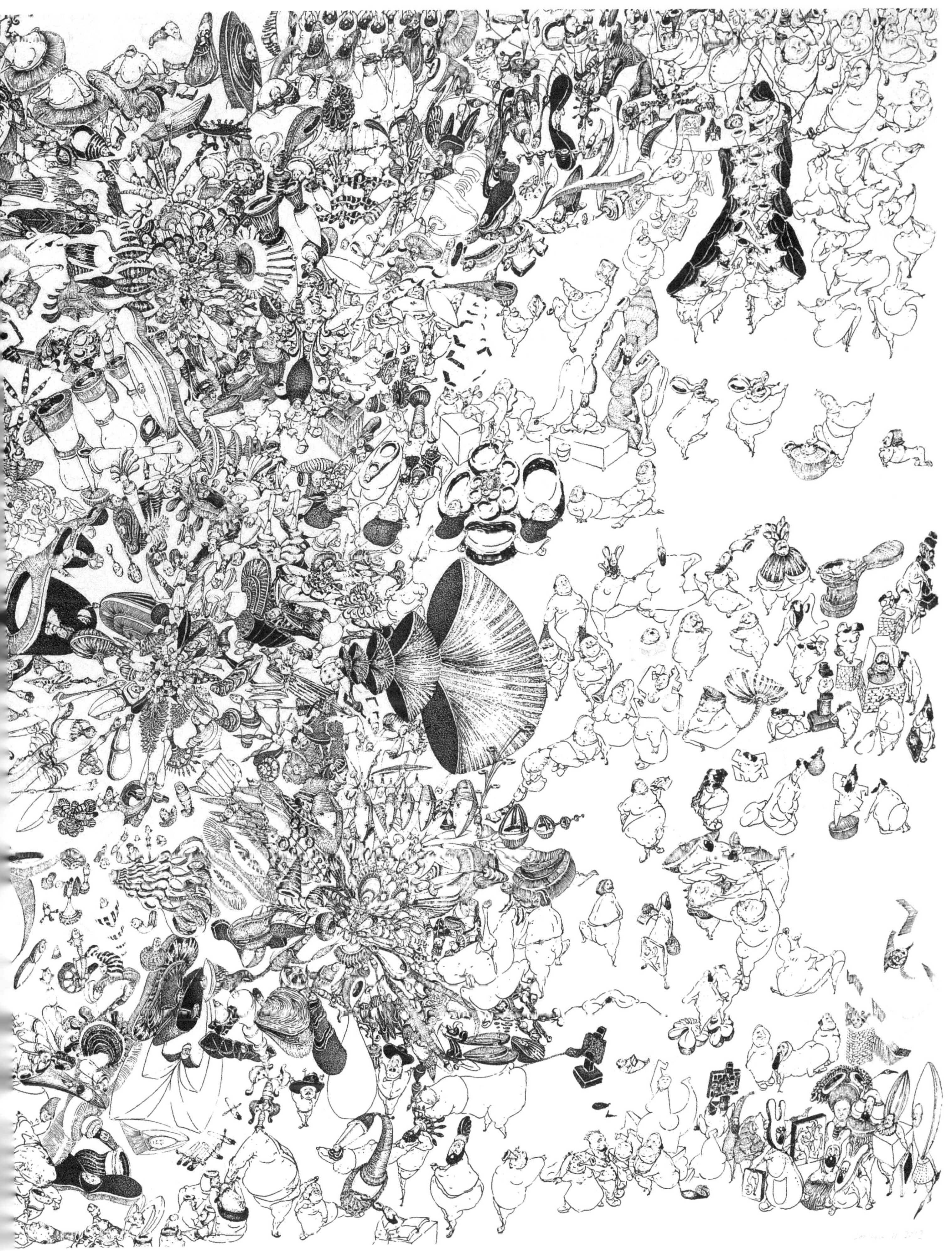

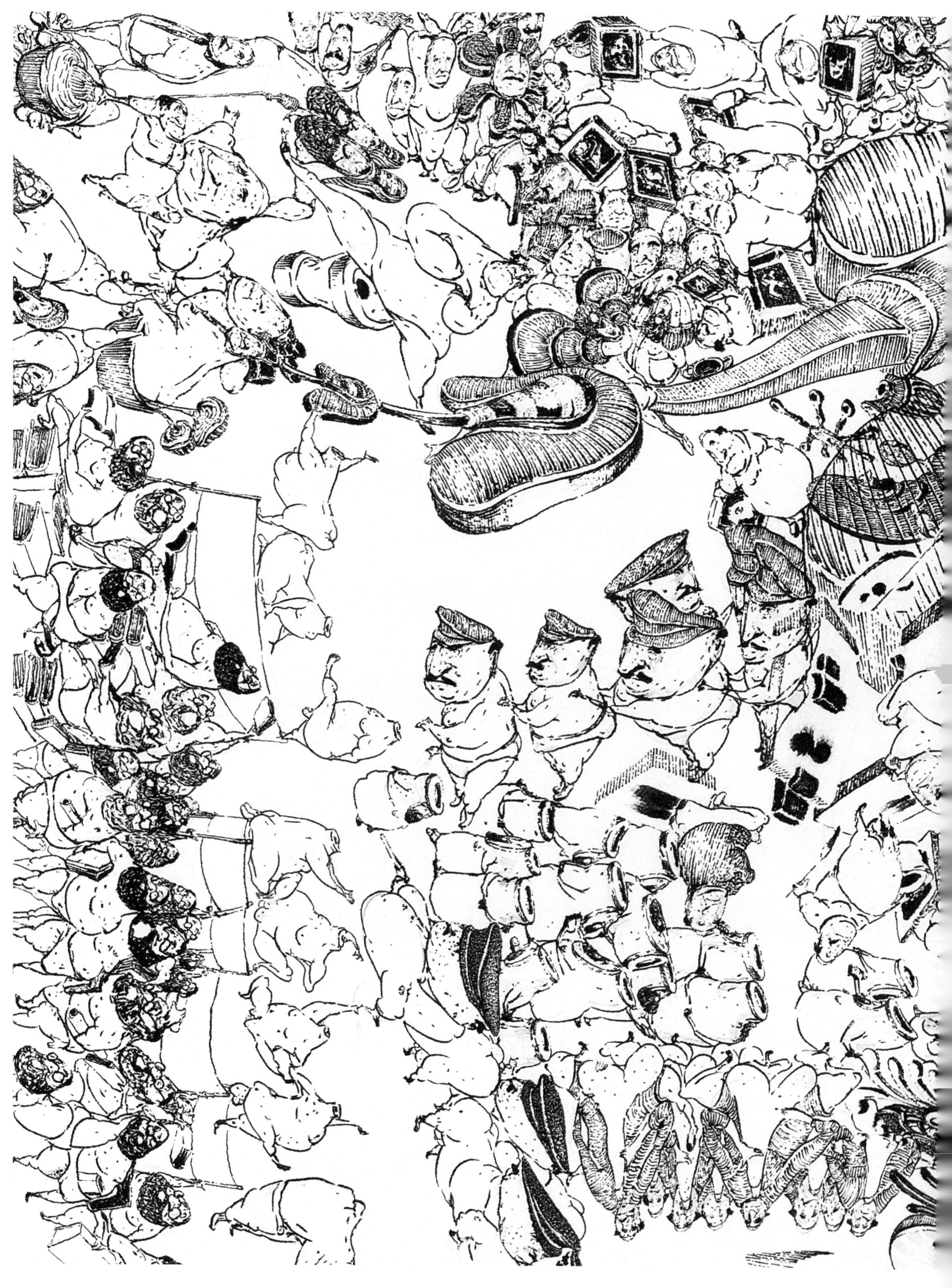

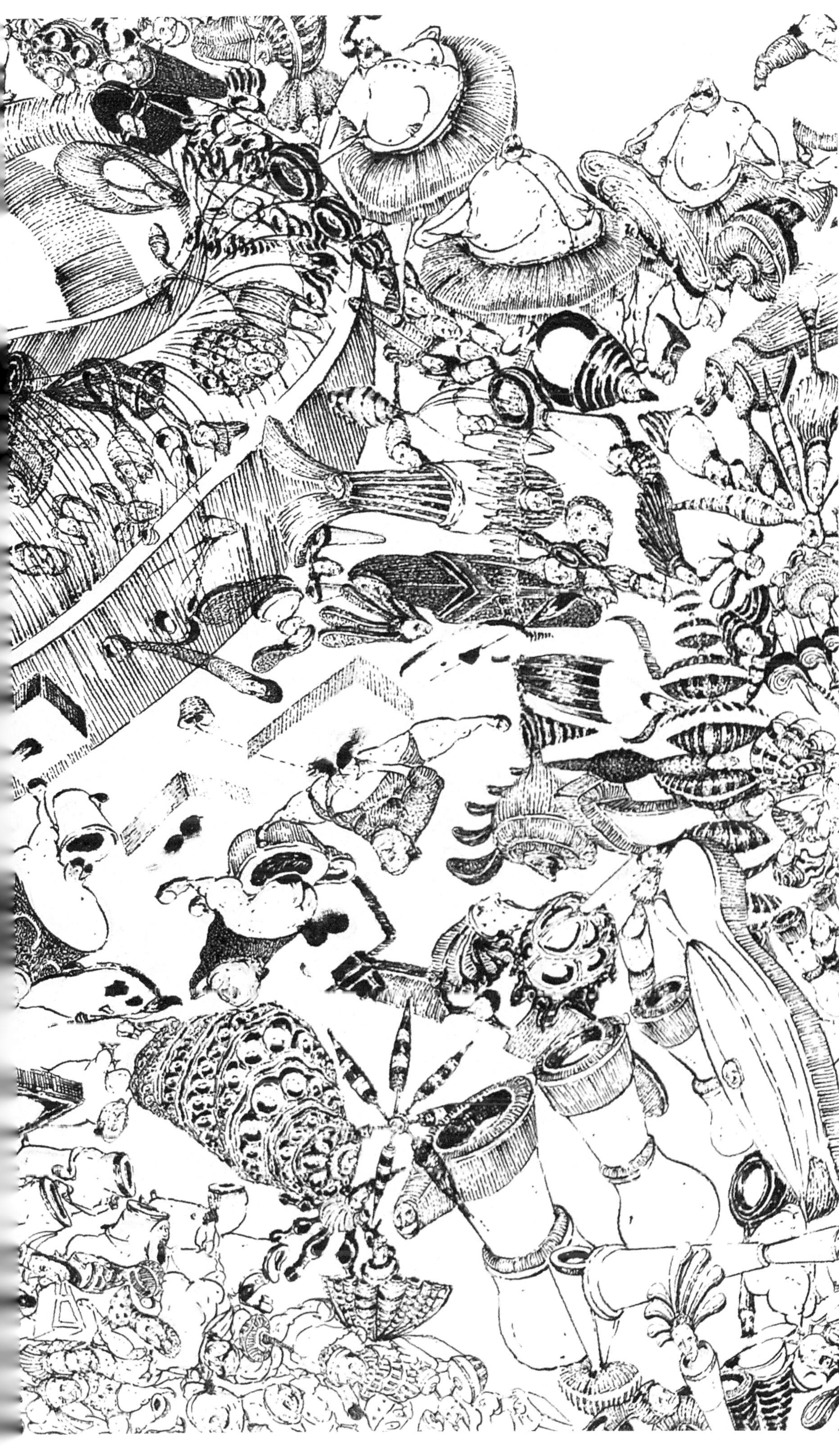

Since leaving the Canadian prairie town of Winnipeg and the artist's collective The Royal Art Lodge (founded in 1996 and disbanded in 2008), Marcel Dzama has flourished in New York, developing further an artistic vision that remains faithful to The Royal Art Lodge's surreal humour, collaborative spirit and passion for drawing. Today his collaborators are the dancers in his films and the artists from the past who inspire him – notably Marcel Duchamp, Francis Picabia and Oskar Schlemmer (especially the latter's *Triadic Ballet* of 1922). Drawing remains central to Dzama's work, and having perfected his inimitable style, he has set about creating an expanding troupe of costumed and masked performers, as well as ever more elaborate, epic scenarios. The drawings are extremely distinctive, their earth tones – root-beer browns and greys – evoking a 1920s atmosphere: part-circus, part-Busby Berkeley spectacle, part-military (possibly revolutionary) training camp and part-country house fancy dress party. Balletic girl guides and trim women soldiers commingle with uniformed, hooded men with rifles; chorus girls in polka dot outfits dance and pose in formation; sex is everywhere and occasionally a man hangs himself from a tree. There is too much incident to enumerate, all drawn with the same delicate skill and taken together seemingly nostalgic for another time, possibly the early twentieth-century avant-garde period of boundless invention.

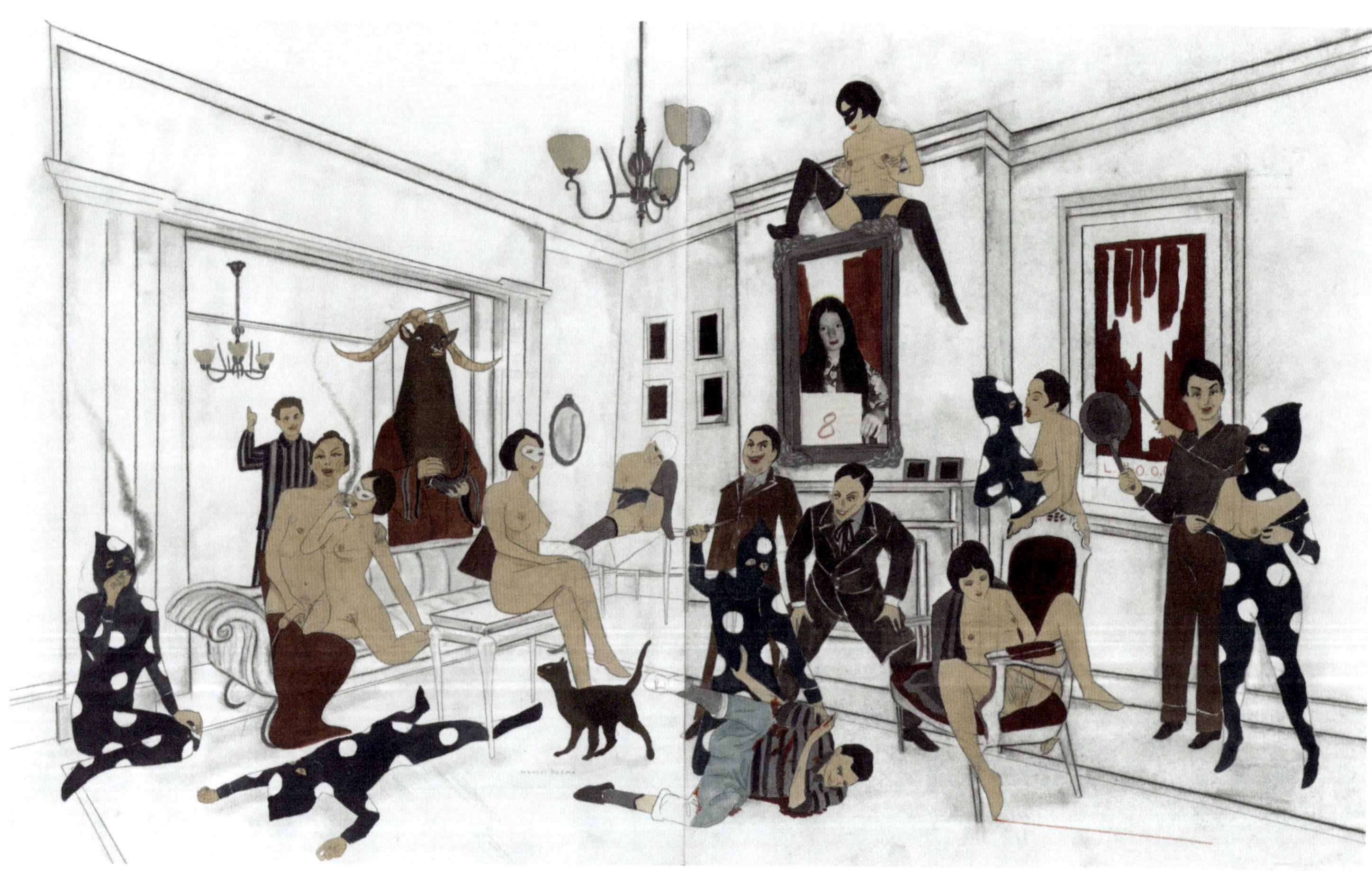

The After Party, 2012
Ink, gouache and graphite on paper
2 parts, overall: 43.2 × 71.1 cm (17 × 28 in.),
each: 43.2 × 35.6 cm (17 × 14 in.)

Descending Pawns, 2012 >
Ink and gouache on paper
4 parts, overall: 55.9 × 43.2 cm (22 × 17 in.),
each: 27.9 × 21.6 cm (11 × 8 ½ in.)

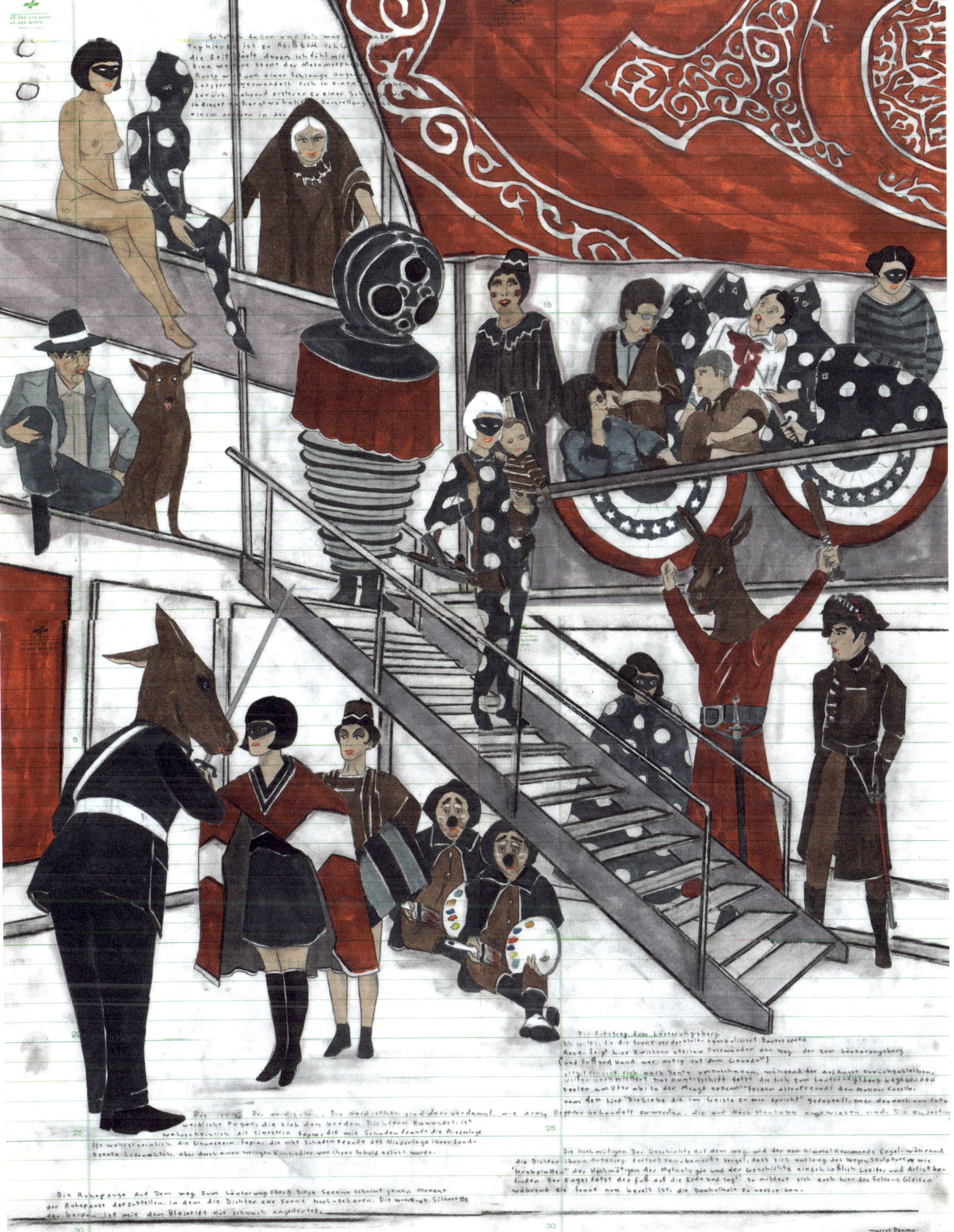

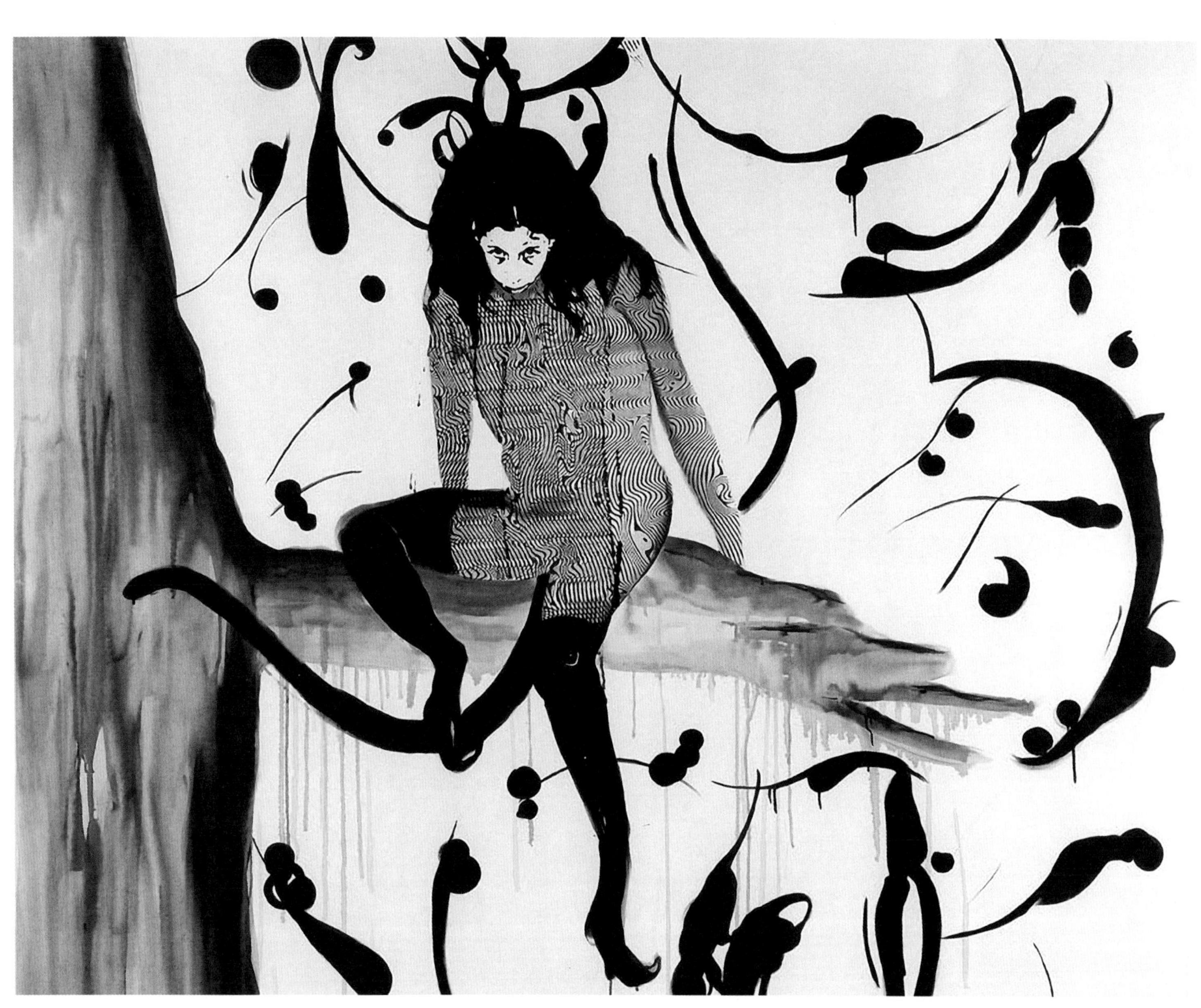

 Born 1956, Ankara, Turkey. Lives and works in Istanbul, Turkey

Inci Eviner's multi-faceted practice is grounded in drawing: 'I draw, and have been drawing for so long, that the act is an extension of my body and the womb of all my works.' In hundreds of Chinese ink-and-brush drawings Eviner generates imagery in a quasi-surrealistic automatist fashion: animal–human hybrids that are then redeployed on a larger scale in monochrome paintings and silk-screen prints on canvas, or incorporated into wall drawings, or intermingled with stencilled figures, projected animations and texts. Like the artist Nancy Spero, whom she admires, Eviner has gathered a lexicon of mainly female figures that populate her wall drawings in frieze-like formations. 'I produce ready-made images, ideograms and symbols together with the broken allegories. So, the anonymous and the very personal are juxtaposed.... I am suspicious of personal expression. Of course this suspicion came from, and got heavier, with the symbolic burden of being a woman.'

Eviner's aesthetic approach took a turn from convention when as a student she would escape from classical drawing classes to visit homes for the physically handicapped. There she made hundreds of drawings, and realized that it was real-life people in motion, not models in statuesque poses, that truly interested her as an artist. Eviner's wariness of subjectivity, her wish to qualify pure personal expression with references to a mediated realm of social imagery, is related to her broader concern for 'in between' states. This connects to her own experience as a woman educated in Western philosophy, psychoanalysis and feminist theory yet living in Turkish society, which, situated on the edge of Europe, still partially adheres to conservative values of female modesty and chastity, such that ideas of the body and sexuality are complicated there, at best. As a result, Eviner considers the body 'not only as a site for liberation, but also as a site for working and researching, or even as a site which is in conflict with the symbols and meanings it is charged with'.

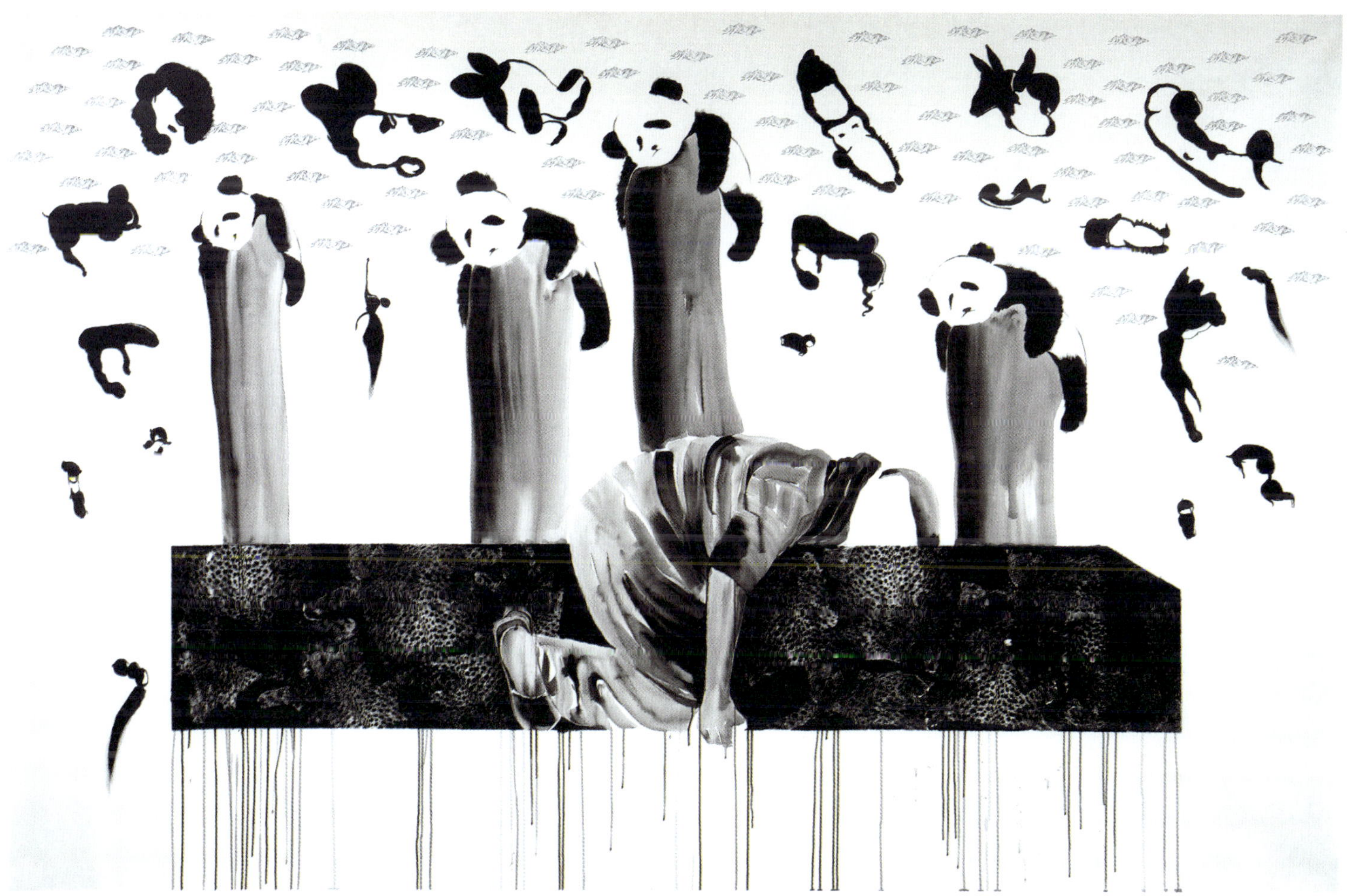

< *Monkey on a Branch*, 2010
Acrylic and silk screen on canvas
190 × 205 cm (74 ¾ × 80 ¾ in.)

Pandas: Smashed Empathy, 2007
Acrylic and silk screen on canvas
200 × 317 cm (78 ¾ × 124 ¾ in.)

SANDRA VÁSQUEZ DE LA HORRA *Born 1966, Viña del Mar, Chile. Lives and works in Berlin, Germany*

Sandra Vásquez de la Horra grew up in Chile under the violent dictatorship of General Pinochet, and her imagery is haunted by shadowy figures harbouring cruel or perverse intent. Yet these figures are usually more absurd than genuinely menacing, and form part of a company of grotesque characters whose human frailties are apparent beneath their capes, hoods and masks. In drawings that each feature a single figure, or at the most a pair, torture and execution are confused with the mischievous antics of clowns and acrobats, often accompanied by a cryptic or sardonic caption. The carnivalesque humour of these scenes is reminiscent of Goya, though the style is decidedly her own.

De la Horra draws on small sheets of old discoloured paper, sometimes taken from ledgers. Perhaps it is this that permits her imagination to run more freely, uninhibited by the aura of preciousness that comes with high quality drawing paper. Her work reflects a fascination for popular culture, folk stories, comic illustration and Mexican Day of the Dead imagery. To preserve her poor materials, she dips each drawing in beeswax, a process that gives them an antique feel and a solid presence as sculptural objects. As an alternative to framing, the drawings are arranged in ad hoc (sometimes fixed, sometimes variable) formations, and simply pinned onto the wall.

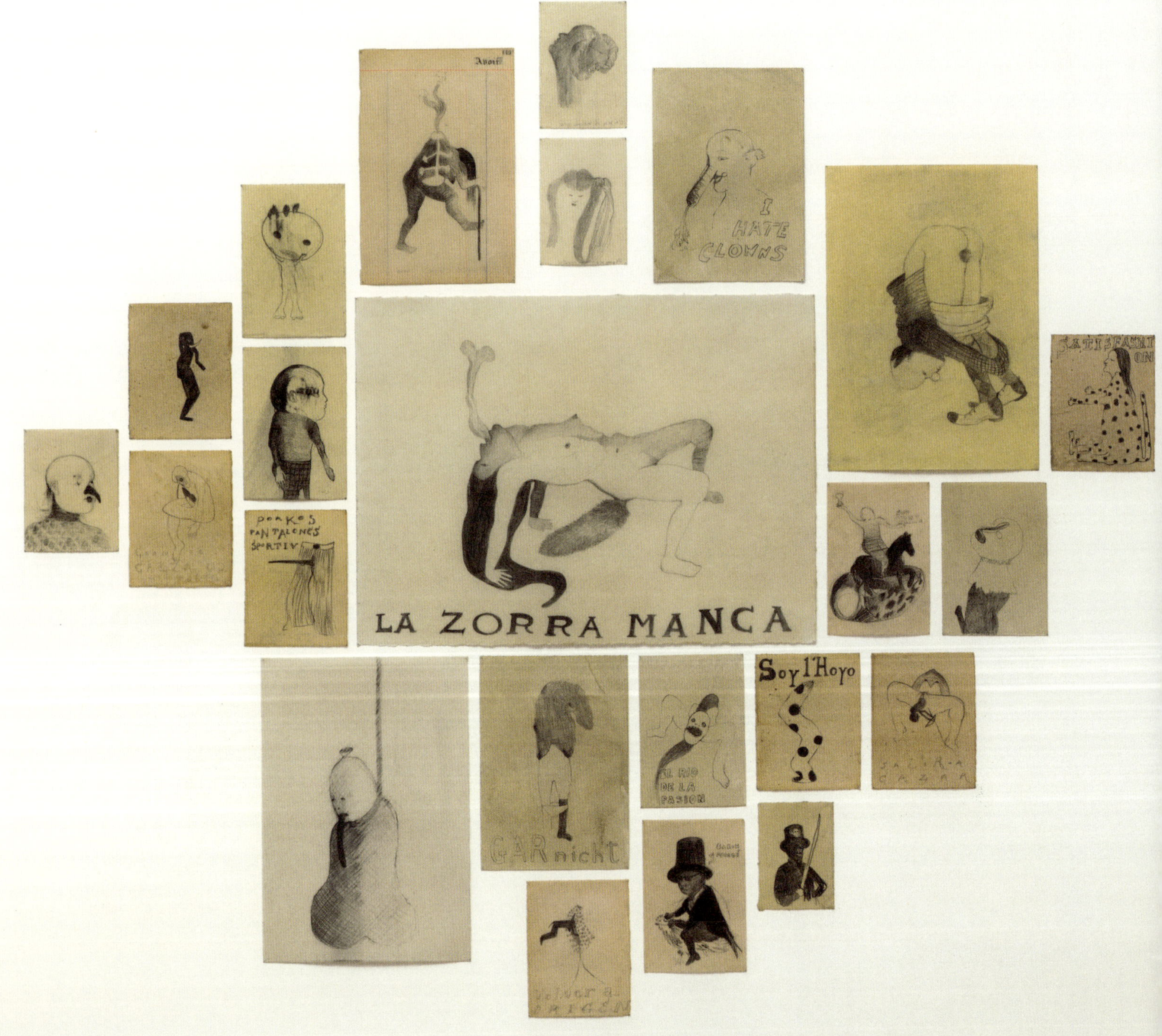

Installation view of De La Horra's works on display
at the Bonnefantenmuseum, Maastricht, The Netherlands

El Susurro Del Egun, 2011 >
Graphite on paper, waxed
38.5 × 26 cm (15 ⅛ × 10 ¼ in.)

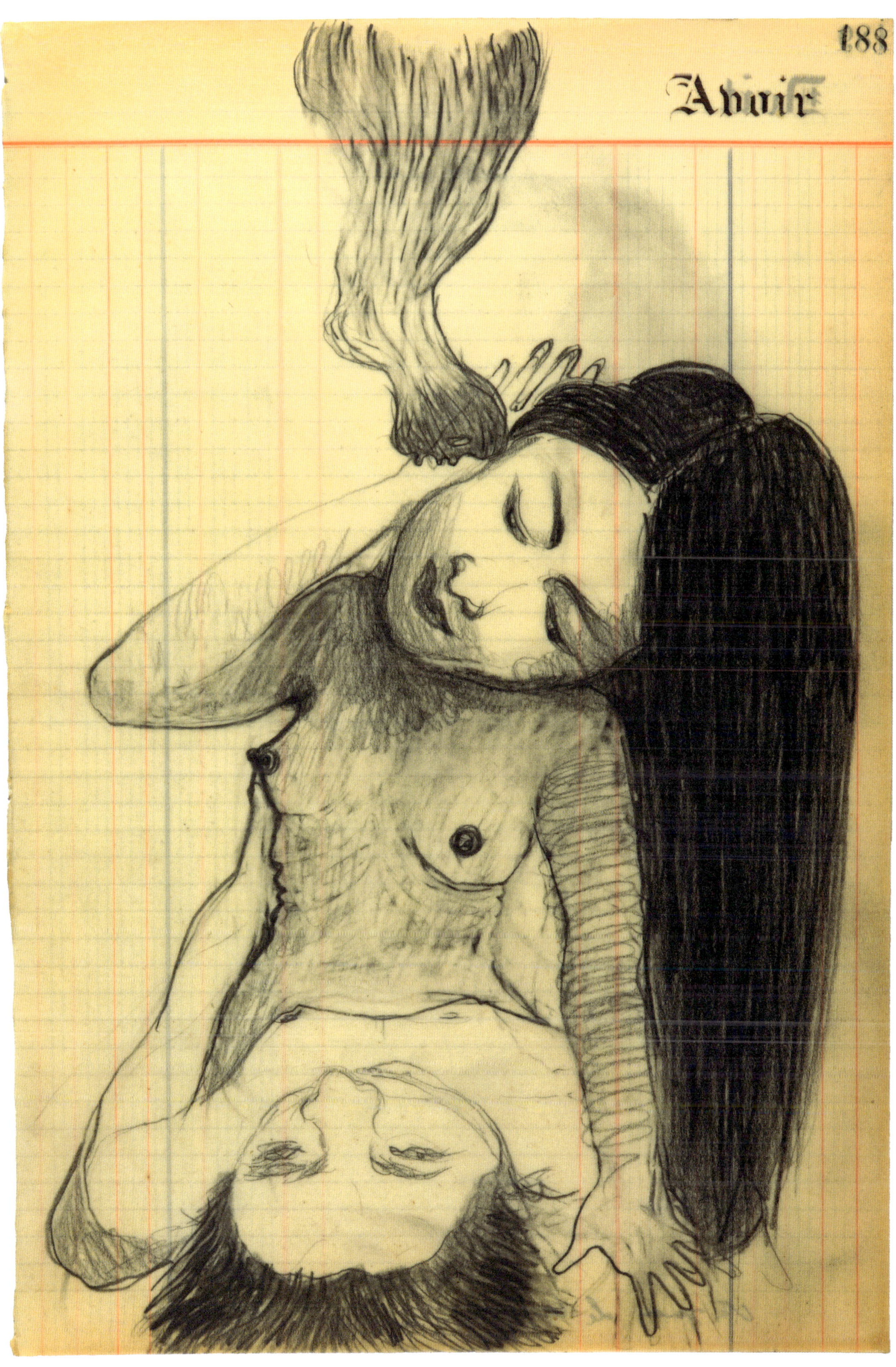
Avoir

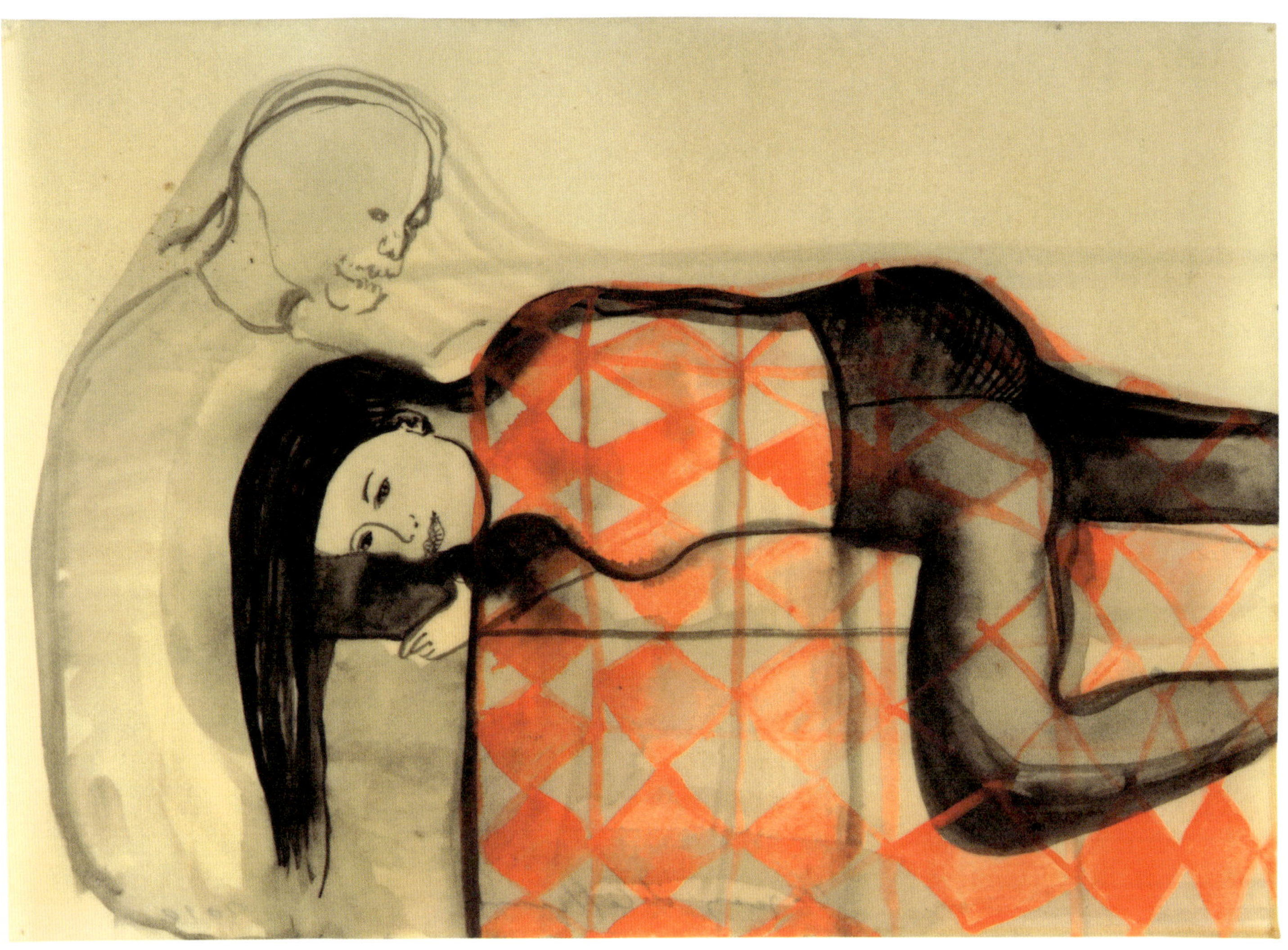

La Durmiente, 2011
Watercolour on paper, waxed
29.5 × 42 cm (11 ⅝ × 16 ½ in.)

Die Exotik Nutte, 2003 >
Graphite on paper, waxed
35 × 25 cm (13 ¾ × 9 ⅞ in.)

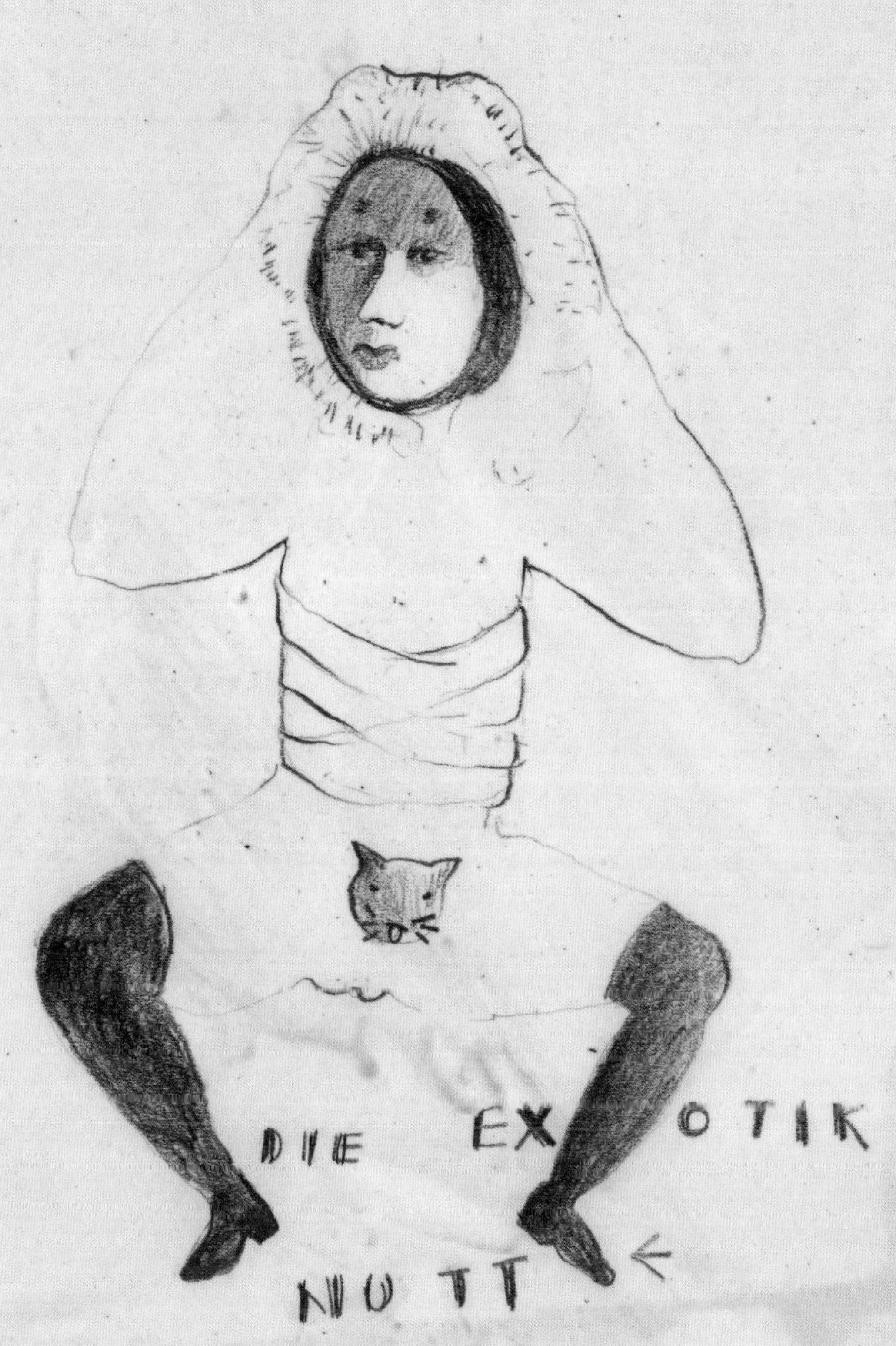
DIE EX OTIK
NUTT

Marcel van Eeden makes drawings from images
that pre-date the year of his birth, extracting them
from an archive of old photographs, film stills,
newspaper clippings, magazines, postcards and book
illustrations. They are rendered in his distinctive
style, mostly in black and white using Nero
pencil, and dramatically shaded so they have the
atmosphere of film noir or illustrated crime stories
from the 1950s. The drawings are presented in quasi-
narrative sequences with running captions, but they
rarely add up as coherent stories – although his
more recent series do show a single fictional persona
and reflect real events in the artist's life.

214

Van Eeden is obsessed by the idea of his own
exclusion from the historical period he depicts.
'If you draw a photo like this, you are, as it were,
in the photo and can walk around in it… you get
close to the moment in which the photo was taken.
You can almost hear the people in it talk to one
another, but not to you. You remain an outsider.'
As in the past, so in the future: 'When you were not
yet around, it did not affect anyone, and when you
will no longer be there, everything will, in fact, be the
same. That's a strange thought that fascinates me.'

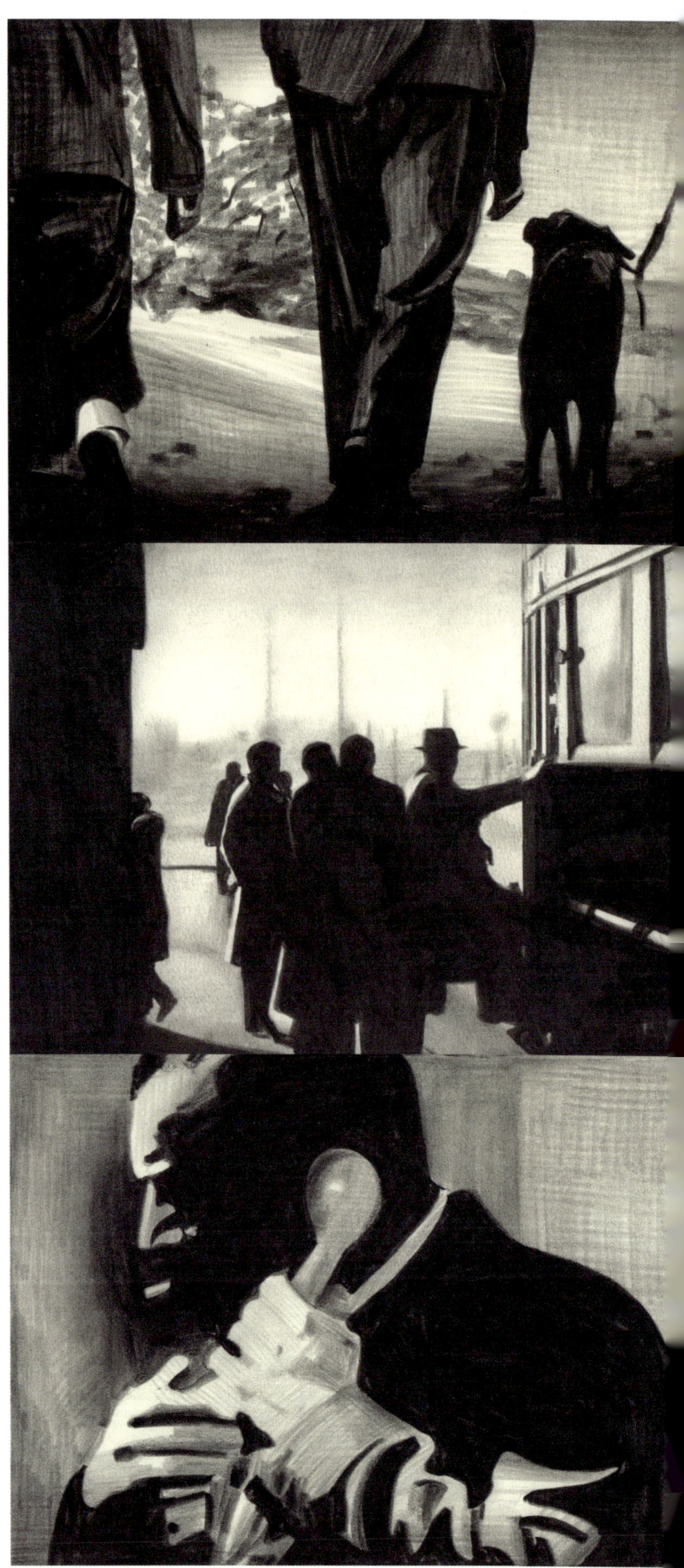

(top) *Untitled*, from the series
The Death of Matheus Boryna, 2006
Nero pencil on paper
19 × 28 cm (7 ½ × 11 in.)

(centre) *Untitled*, 2005
Nero pencil on paper
19 × 28 cm (7 ½ × 11 in.)

(below) *Untitled*, 2011
Nero pencil on paper
19 × 28 cm (7 ½ × 11 in.)

(opposite, top left) *Untitled*, 2006
Nero pencil on paper
19 × 28 cm (7 ½ × 11 in.)

(opposite, top right) *Untitled*, 2005
Nero pencil on paper
19 × 28 cm (7 ½ × 11 in.)

(opposite, below) *Untitled*, from the
series *Dizengoff's Commission*, 2014
Nero pencil on paper
19 × 28 cm (7 ½ × 11 in.)

(overleaf, top left) *Untitled*, from the series
K.M. Wiegand, Life and Work, 2005–6
Nero pencil on paper
19 × 28 cm (7 ½ × 11 in.)

(overleaf, top right) *Untitled*, from the series
November 22, 1948, 2011
Nero pencil on paper
19 × 28 cm (7 ½ × 11 in.)

(overleaf, centre left) *Untitled*, from the
series *K.M. Wiegand, Life and Work*, 2005–6
Nero pencil on paper
19 × 28 cm (7 ½ × 11 in.)

(overleaf, centre right) *Untitled*, from the
series *The Death of Matheus Boryna*, 2006
Nero pencil on paper
19 × 28 cm (7 ½ × 11 in.)

(overleaf, below) *Untitled*, from the series
K.M. Wiegand, Life and Work, 2005–6
Nero pencil on paper
19 × 28 cm (7 ½ × 11 in.)

(page 217, top left) *Untitled*, 2010
Nero pencil on paper
28 × 38 cm (11 × 15 in.)

(page 217, top right) *Untitled*, 2006
Nero pencil on paper
19 × 28 cm (7 ½ × 11 in.)

(page 217, centre) *Untitled*, from the series
K.M. Wiegand, Life and Work, 2005–6
Nero pencil on paper
19 × 28 cm (7 ½ × 11 in.)

(page 217, below left) *Untitled*, from
the series *Gladbeck 1928*, 2013
Nero pencil on paper
19 × 28 cm (7 ½ × 11 in.)

(page 217, below right) *Untitled*, from
the series *Gladbeck 1928*, 2013
Nero pencil on paper

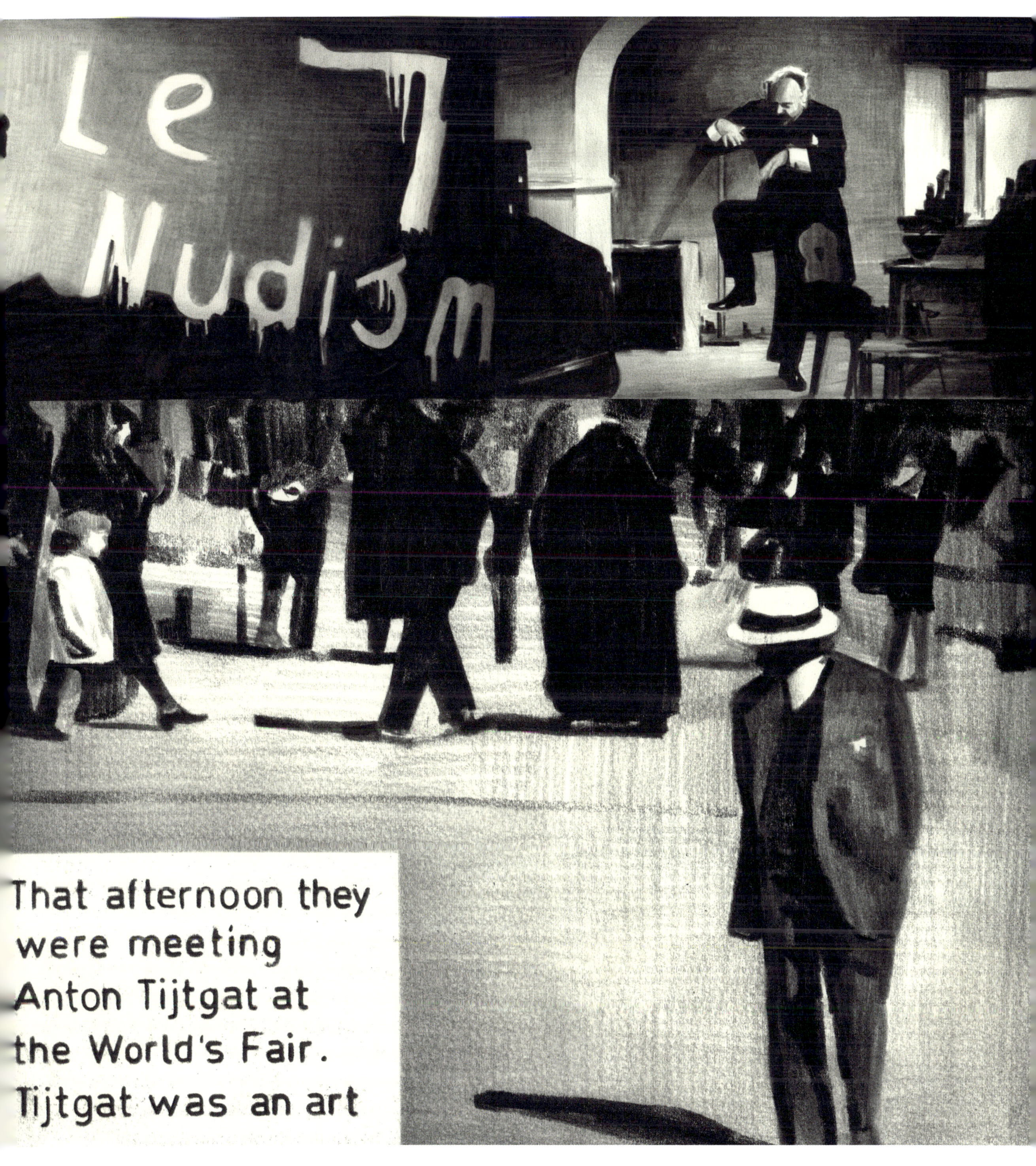
LE NUDISM
That afternoon they
were meeting
Anton Tijtgat at
the World's Fair.
Tijtgat was an art

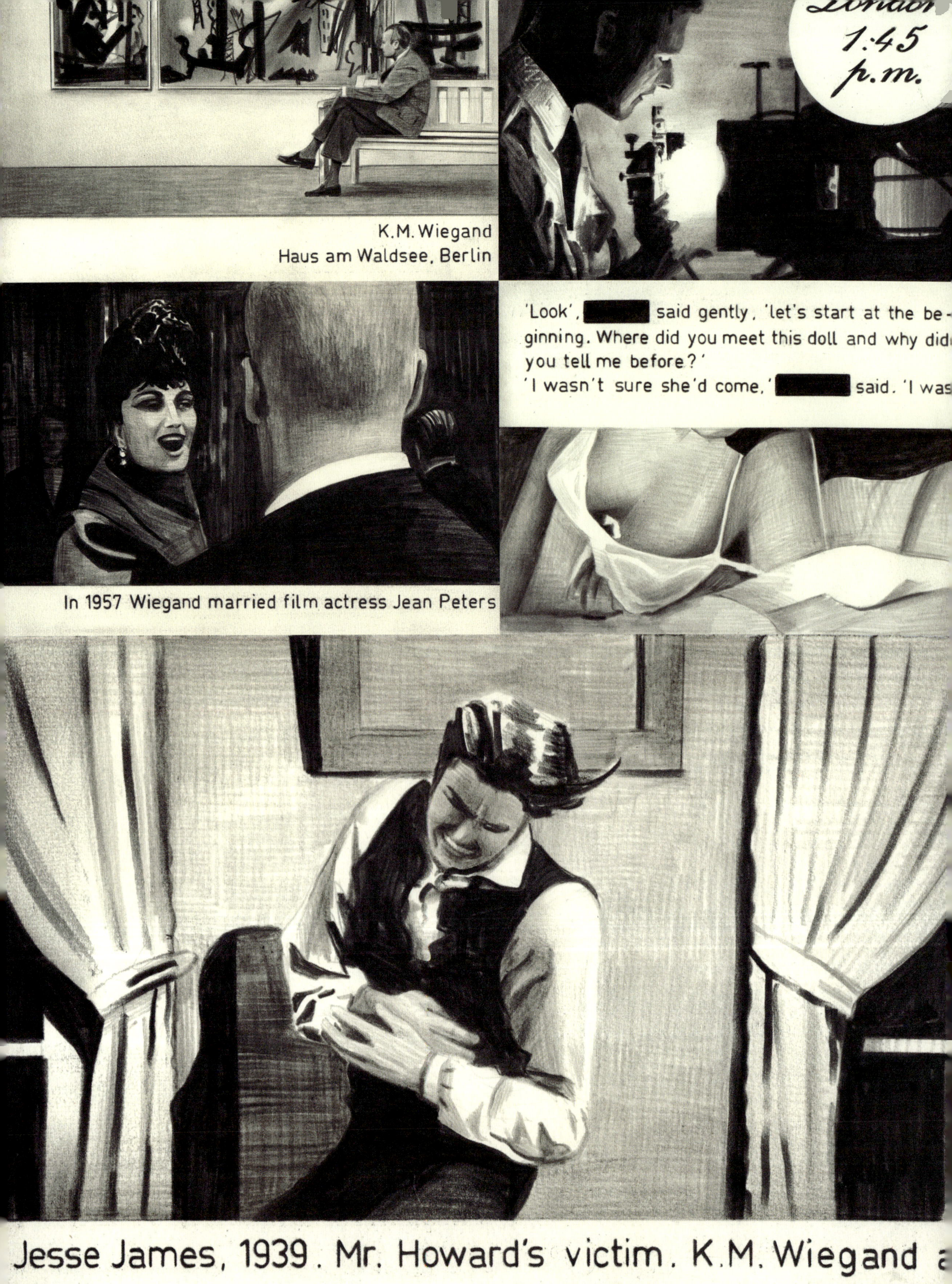
London
1:45
p.m.
K.M. Wiegand
Haus am Waldsee, Berlin
In 1957 Wiegand married film actress Jean Peters
'Look', ███ said gently, 'let's start at the be-
ginning. Where did you meet this doll and why did
you tell me before?'
'I wasn't sure she'd come,' ███ said. 'I was
Jesse James, 1939. Mr. Howard's victim. K.M. Wiegand a
Jesse James is shot as he nails "God Bless Our Home" to

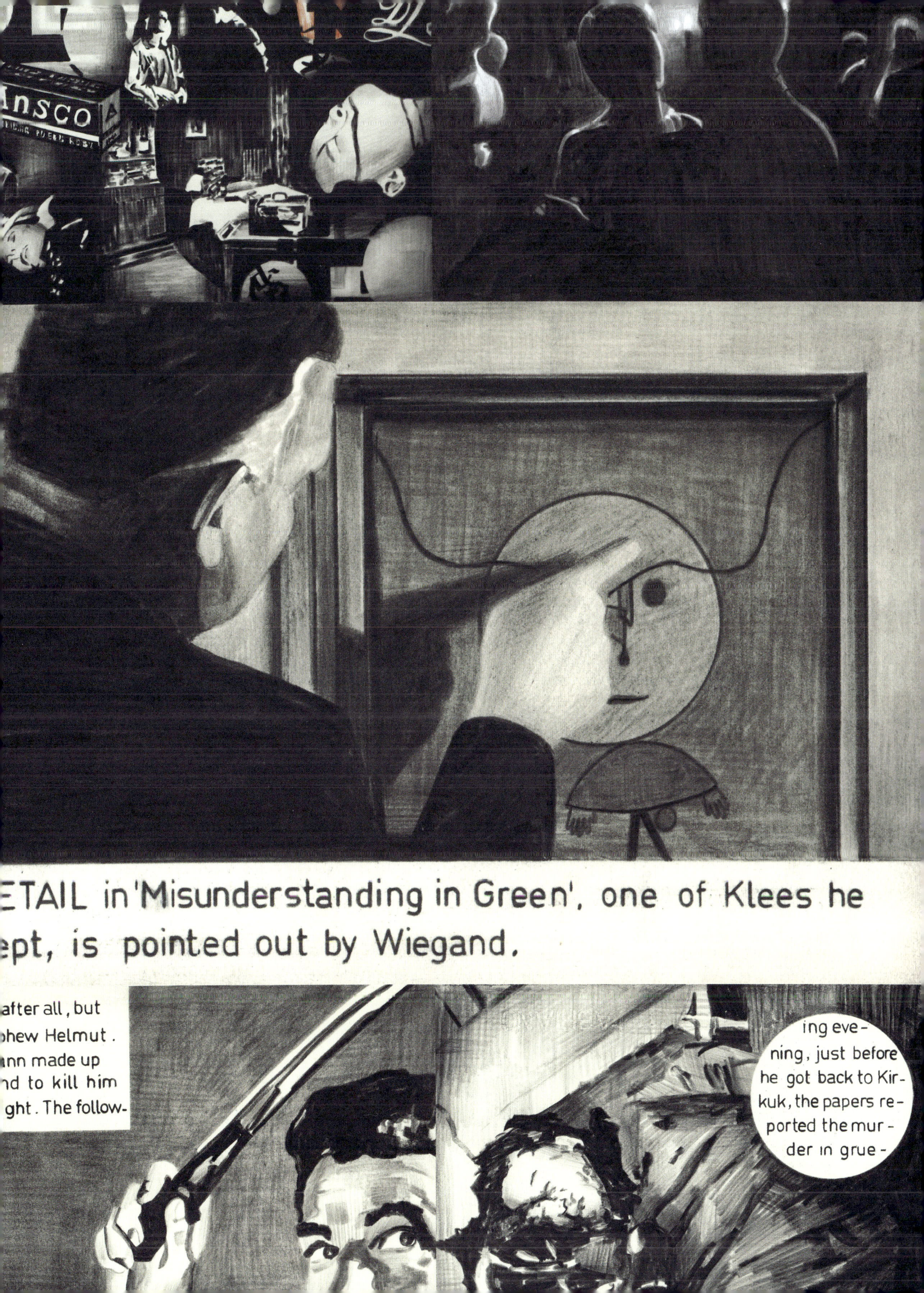

DETAIL in 'Misunderstanding in Green', one of Klees he kept, is pointed out by Wiegand.

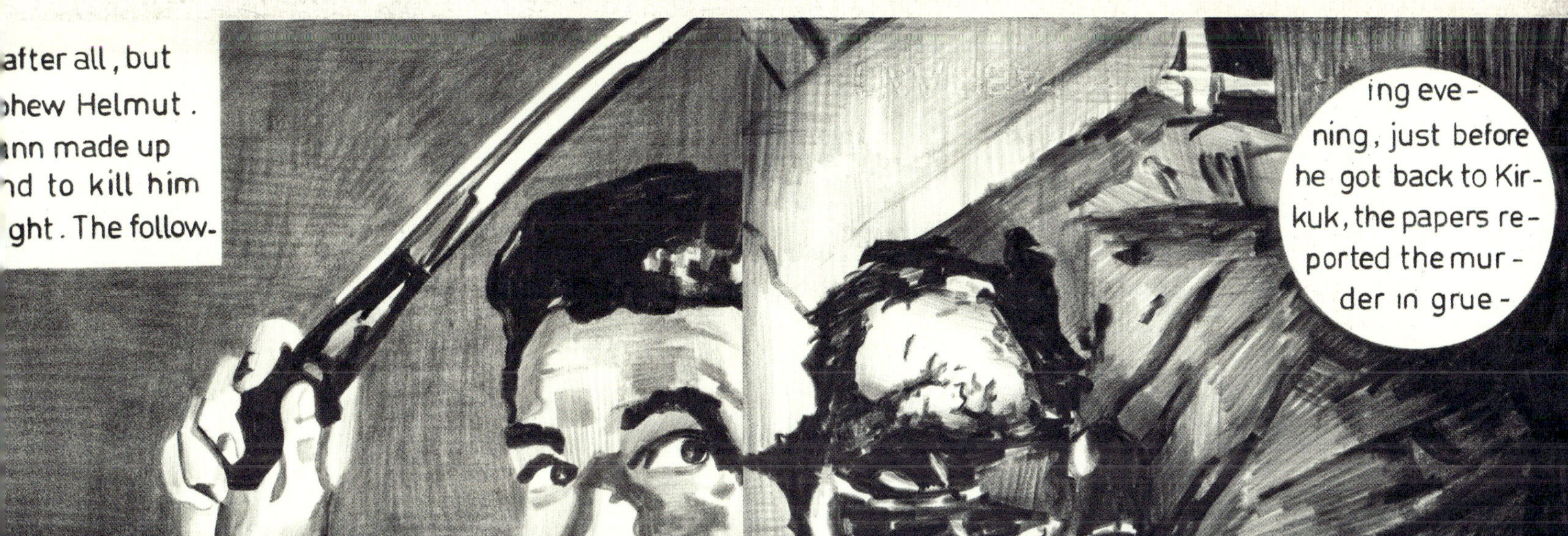

ERINÇ SEYMEN *Born 1980, Istanbul, Turkey. Lives and works in Istanbul, Turkey*

It is perhaps reassuring to learn that Erinç Seymen is an artist who works in performance and installation as well as drawing, and that he is politically vocal, writing in magazines about militarism, nationalism, colonialism and gender issues – in other words, that he is engaged with the world and not permanently isolated in a subterranean interior of his own invention such as those depicted here. One drawing in his meticulous pen-and-ink style, entitled *Daddy*, portrays a surrealistic military man with a swarm of eyes embedded in the centre of his face, in contrast to the Hansel and Gretel-type children in the *Surprise Witness* drawings, whose eyes are darkly shadowed and apparently unseeing. The overripe compositions they have

stumbled into look as though they have never previously been disturbed, and have possibly been manufactured by the image-making machines that dominate the composition, rather than by a human imagination. Mushrooms, probably poisonous or hallucinogenic, stalactites, sea anemones and other bulbous excrescences clog the space, and every surface is embroidered with microscopic detail. The absence of colour heightens the atmosphere, rendering more sinister what might be merely a spooky Hieronymous Bosch-inspired fantasy. In other works, the artist introduces overtly sado-masochistic themes of punishment and bondage, themes that in these drawings may be conveyed implicitly through the exactitude and restraint of their creation.

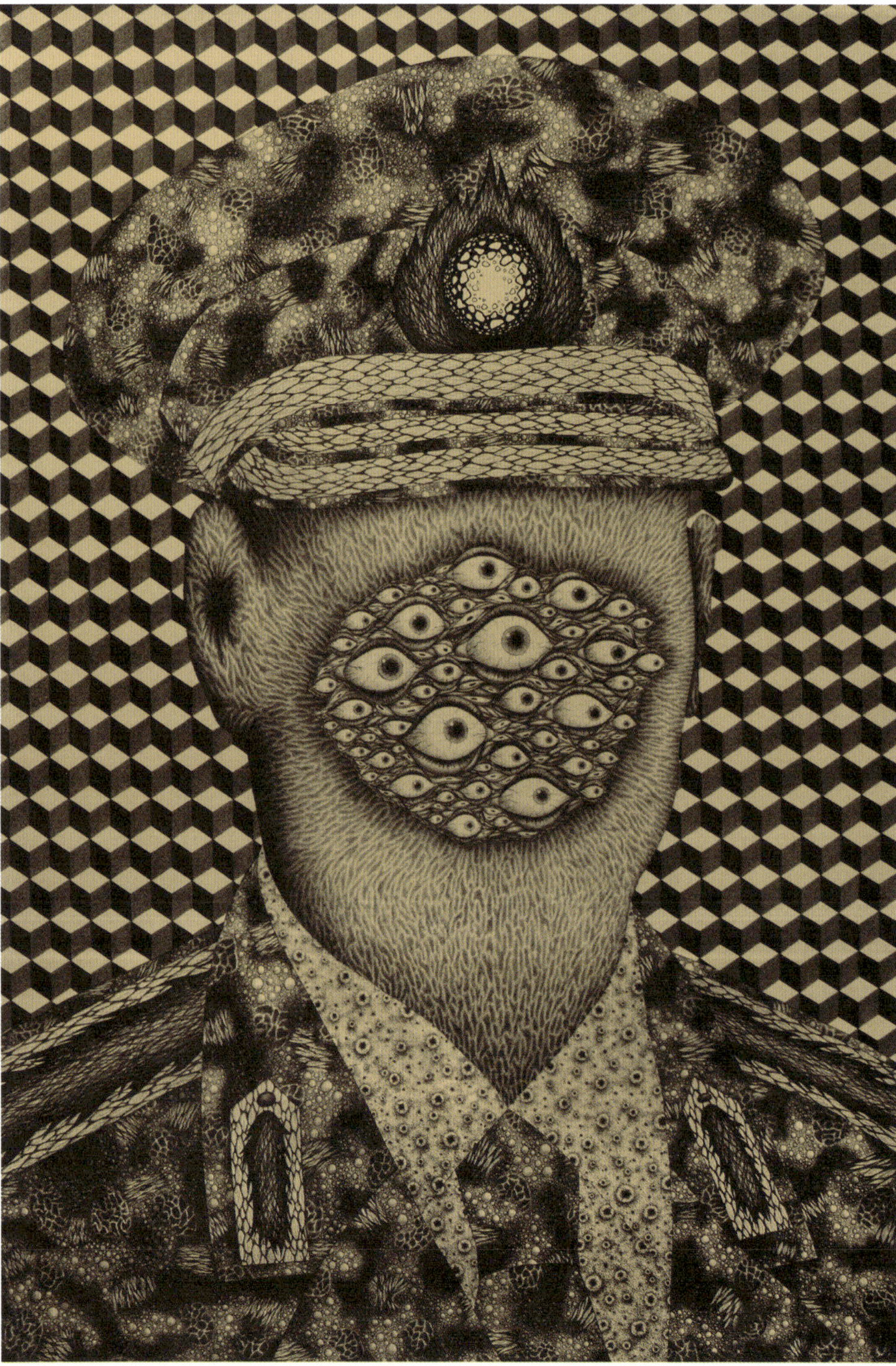

< *Daddy,* 2011
Ink pen on paper
100 × 70 cm (39 ⅜ × 27 ½ in.)

(opposite, top) *Surprise Witness II,* 2012 >
Ink pen on paper
70 × 100 cm (27 ½ × 39 ⅜ in.)

(opposite, below) *Surprise Witness I,* 2011 >
Ink pen on paper
70 × 100 cm (27 ½ × 39 ⅜ in.)

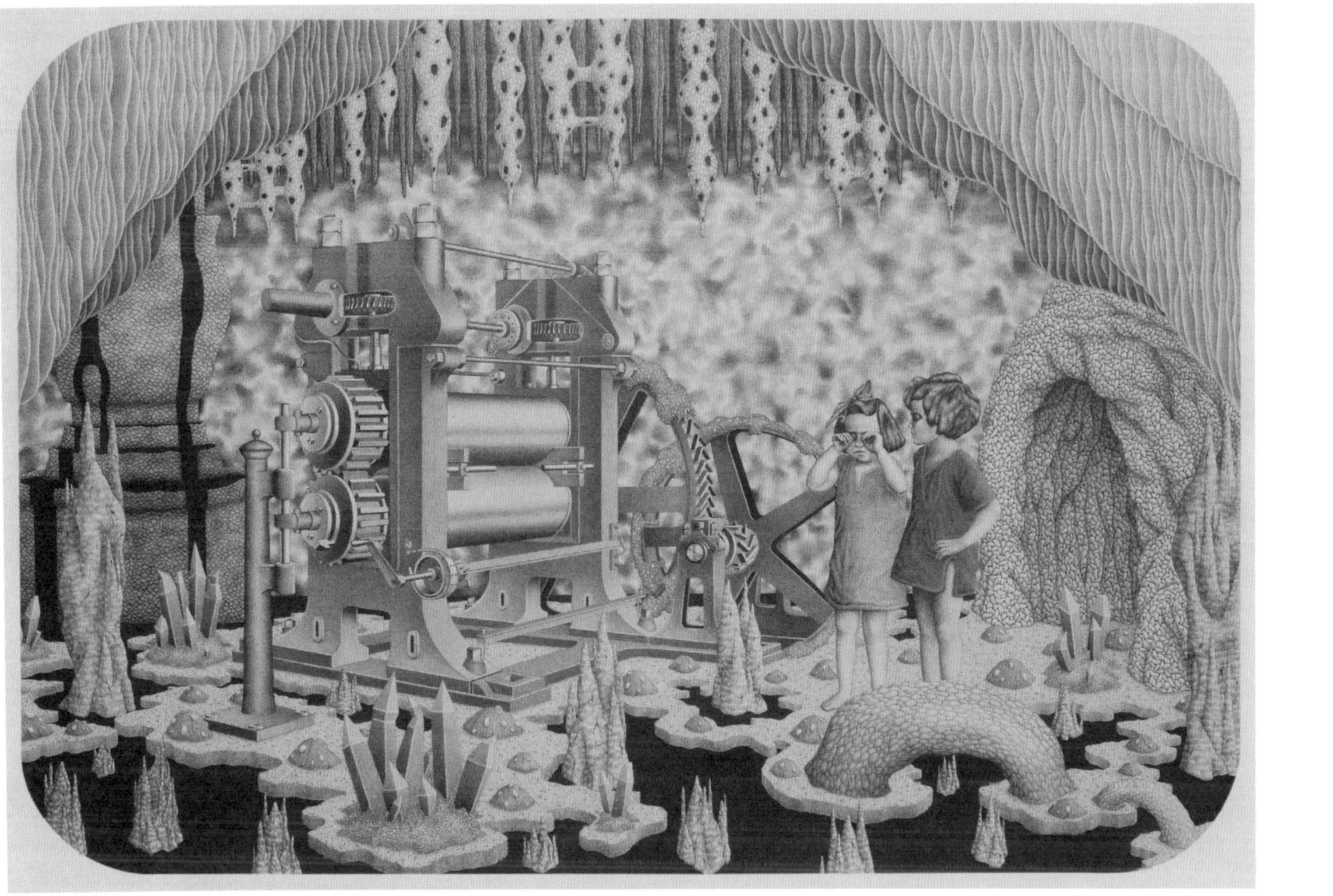

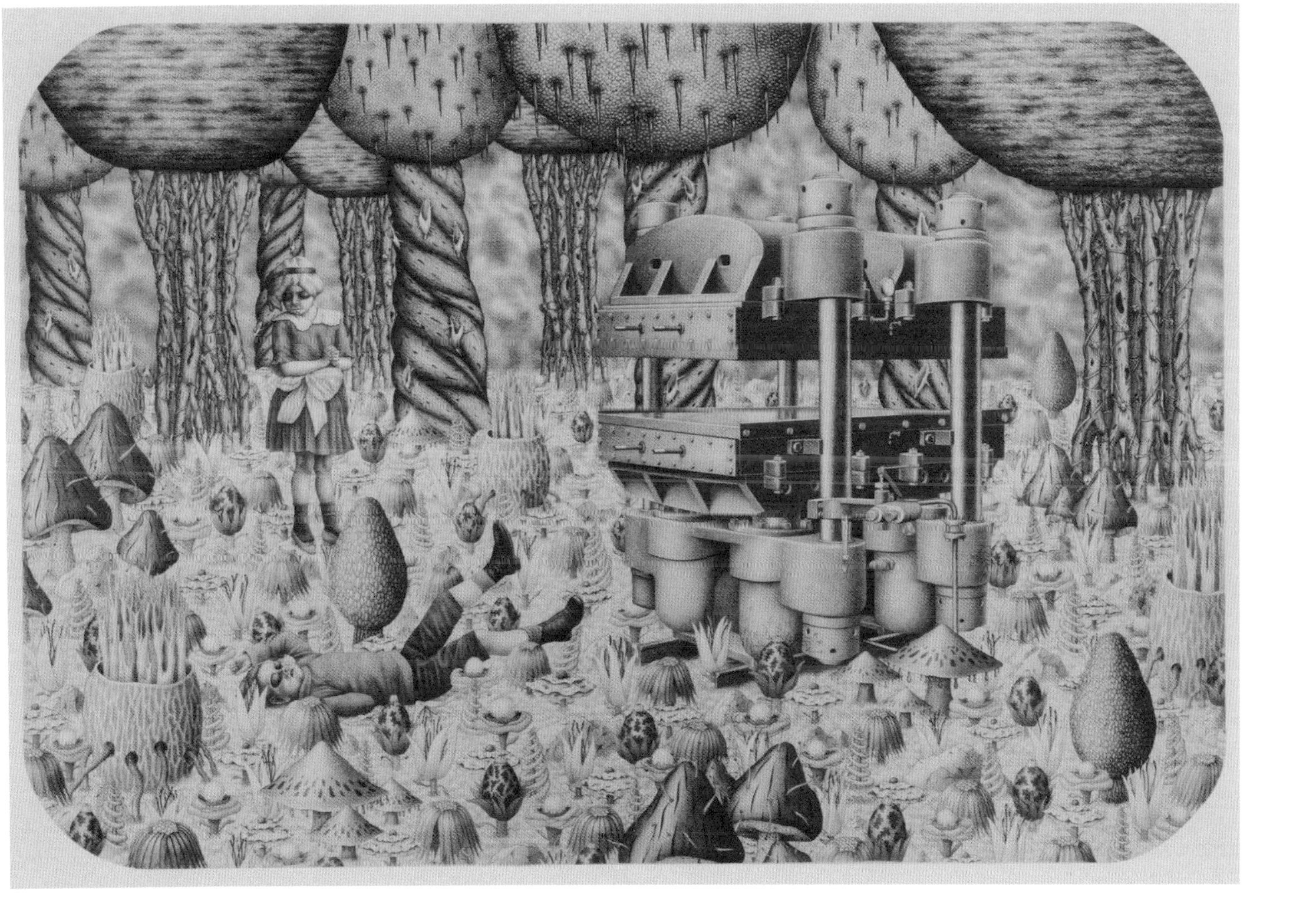

 Born 1957, Los Angeles, California, USA. Lives and works in New York, USA

220

The double-edged sword of image and word has been Raymond Pettibon's weapon since he started designing flyers for the Los Angeles punk rock band Black Flag in the late 1970s. Pettibon's funky black-and-white graphics combine crudely drawn parodies of comic-style heroes and anti-heroes with satirical and sacrilegious handwritten captions. He has proved to be an inexhaustible fountain of subversive wit, never losing the menacing tone of youthful anarchy or the violent disjunction of sense and nonsense; he is so brilliantly prolific that his drawings are included in nearly every major museum collection in the Western world. The key to Pettibon's success seems to be his marriage of high and low: a montage of quotations from literature, pulp fiction and low-grade graphic genres. There is no narrative thread between images, yet they are arranged on the wall in groups according to the artist's elusive criterion of 'affinity' that is neither logical nor aesthetic. With his limitless capacity for improvisation and ventriloquism, Pettibon is believable when he claims that he is still trying to teach himself to draw every time he picks up a brush or pen. There is never a single style to polish or to become stale. The voice is never his own.

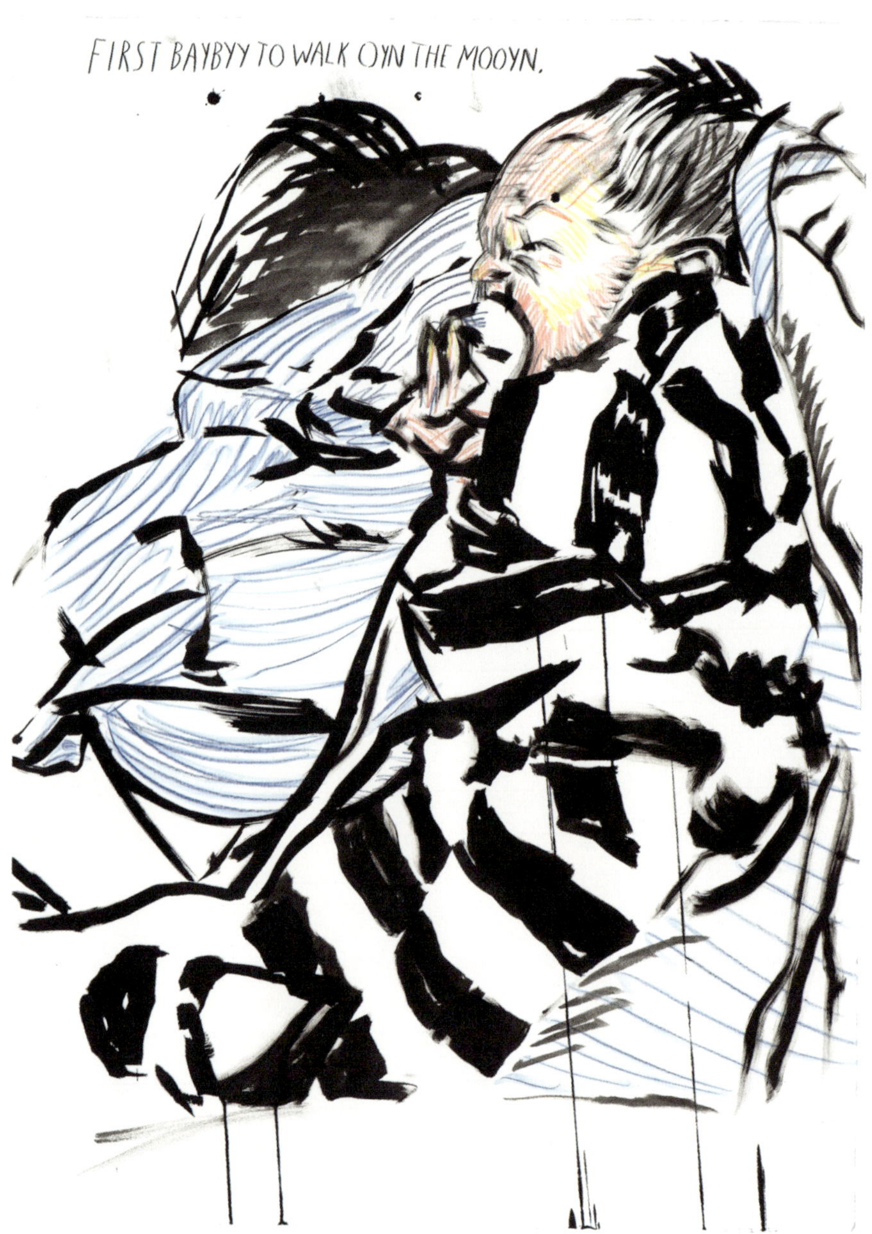

No Title (First baybyy to), 2012
Pen, ink and coloured pencil on paper
106.7 × 75.6 cm (42 × 29 ¾ in.)

No Title (Once the judge), 2006 >
Pen and ink on paper
76.2 × 55.9 cm (30 × 22 in.)

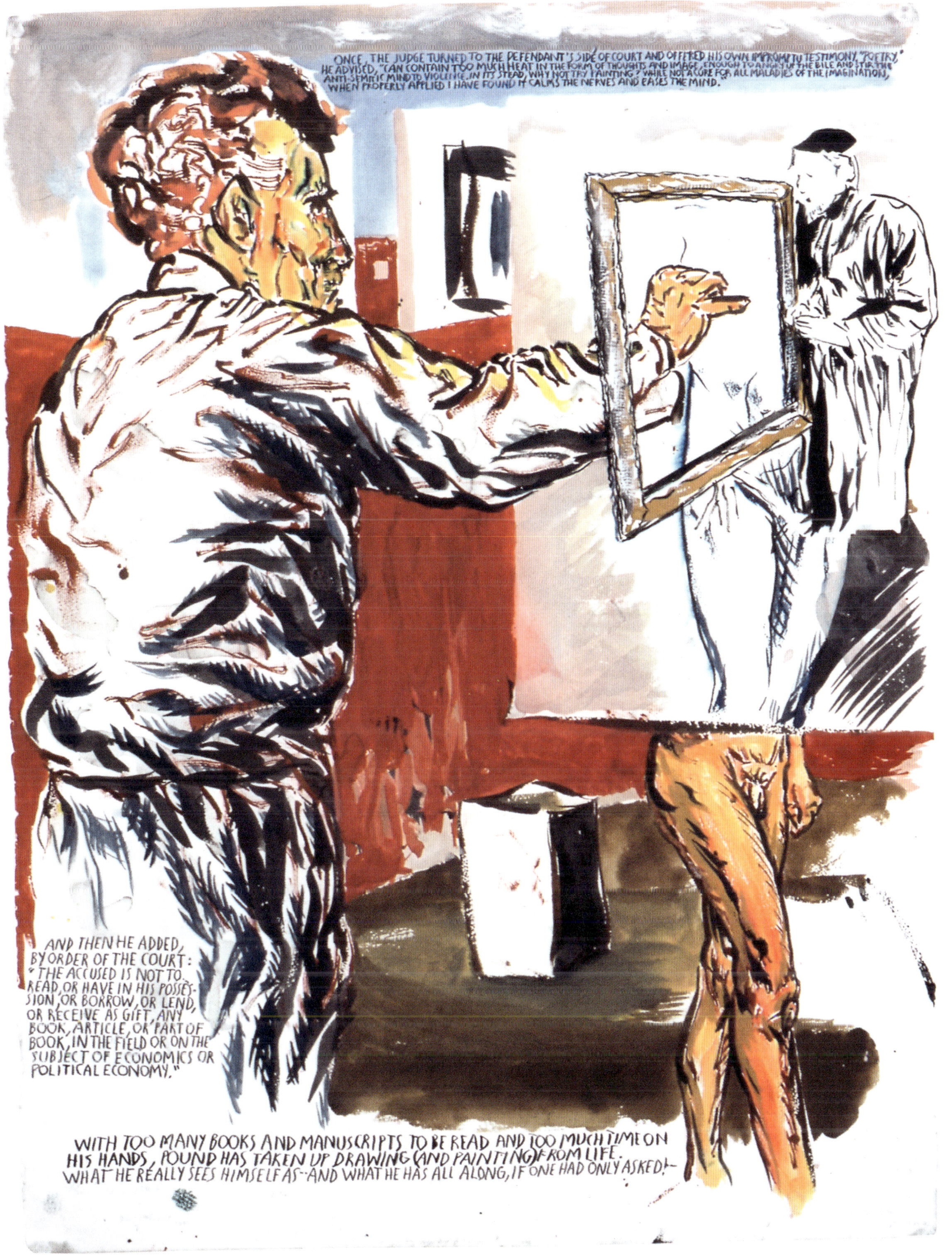

ONCE, THE JUDGE TURNED TO THE DEFENDANT'S SIDE OF COURT AND OFFERED HIS OWN IMPROMPTU TESTIMONY. "POETRY," HE ADVISED, "CAN CONTAIN TOO MUCH HEAT IN THE FORM OF THOUGHTS AND IMAGE, ENOUGH TO ANGRY UP THE BILE AND STIR THE ANTI-SEMITIC MIND TO VIOLENCE. IN ITS STEAD, WHY NOT TRY PAINTING? WHILE NOT A CURE FOR ALL MALADIES OF THE IMAGINATION, WHEN PROPERLY APPLIED I HAVE FOUND IT CALMS THE NERVES AND EASES THE MIND."

AND THEN HE ADDED, BY ORDER OF THE COURT: "THE ACCUSED IS NOT TO READ, OR HAVE IN HIS POSSESSION, OR BORROW, OR LEND, OR RECEIVE AS GIFT, ANY BOOK, ARTICLE, OR PART OF BOOK, IN THE FIELD OR ON THE SUBJECT OF ECONOMICS OR POLITICAL ECONOMY."

WITH TOO MANY BOOKS AND MANUSCRIPTS TO BE READ AND TOO MUCH TIME ON HIS HANDS, POUND HAS TAKEN UP DRAWING (AND PAINTING) FROM LIFE. WHAT HE REALLY SEES HIMSELF AS—AND WHAT HE HAS ALL ALONG, IF ONE HAD ONLY ASKED!—

'I'm not a painter, really. I'm a drawer. I draw a lot. I don't like it when you paint and the brush bends. When you draw you can push your pencil or your pastel – everything is much more violent.'

Although she has lived in London for most of her adult life, Paula Rego is deeply connected to her childhood memories and the folk stories of Portugal. The narrative impulse is always primary, whether she is illustrating existing stories and fairy tales or fabricating her own wildly outlandish costumed fantasies. (The Portuguese museum founded in her honour is called the House of Stories.) Rego began to take her inspiration partly from the American outsider artist Henry Darger in the 1970s, and since then has given her imagination free rein, finding beauty in the grotesque and delighting in transgression. The apparently harsh and cruel world she has invented is also largely feminine: 'I can turn the tables and make women stronger than men. I can make them obedient and murderous at the same time.' For the *Human Cargo Series* (2007–8), she drew from tableaux set up in her studio using a combination of dummies and live models. Unusually, Rego has dispensed with pastel colours for this series, stripping the imagery down to the rawness of black and white.

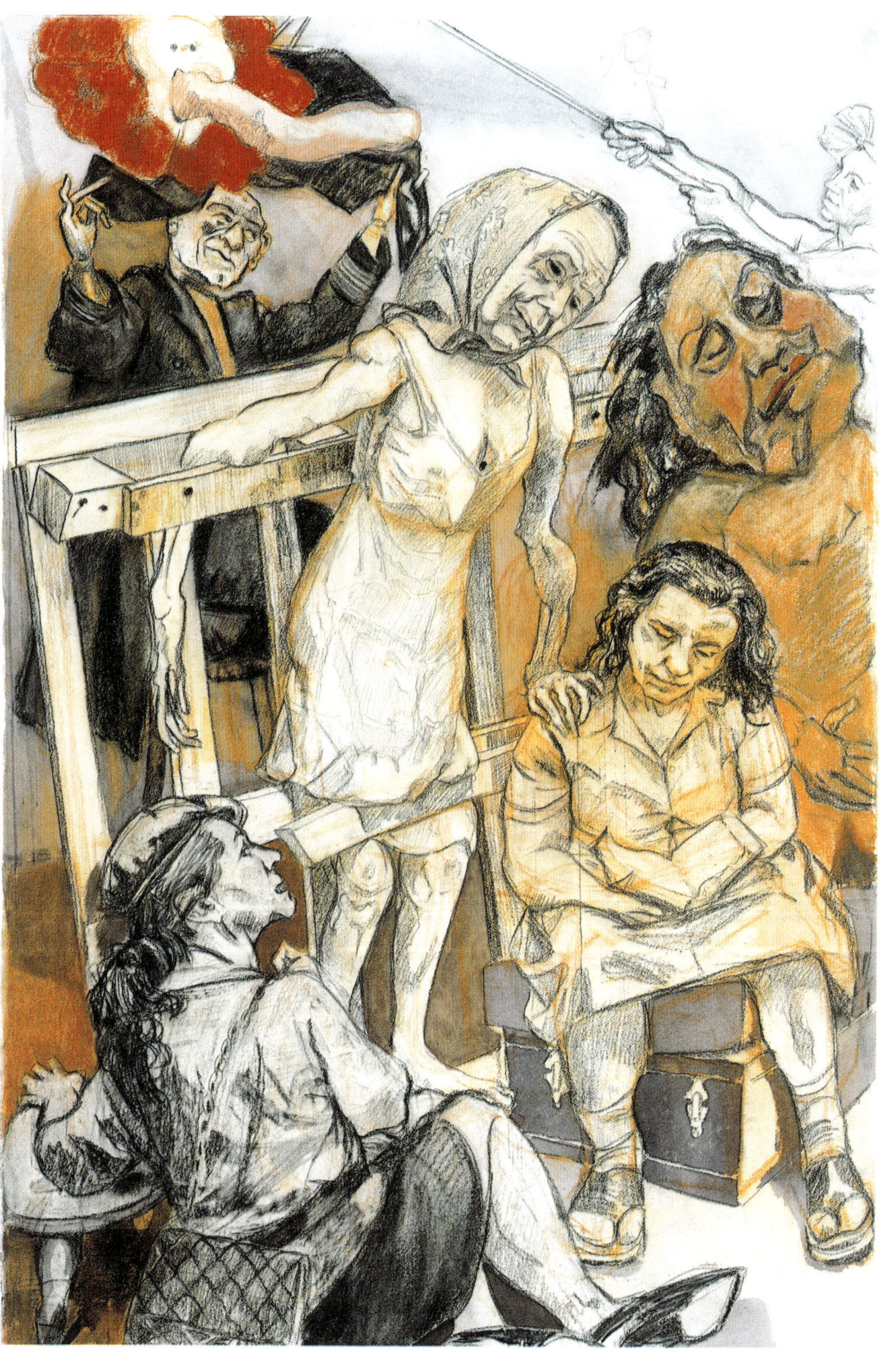

Human Cargo Series (Crate), 2008
Conté pencil, charcoal, colour wash and Conté on paper
149.9 × 122.9 cm (59 × 48 ⅜ in.)

Human Cargo Series (Discarded Muses), 2007 >
Graphite and Conté pencil on paper
137.2 × 101.9 cm (54 × 40 ⅛ in.)

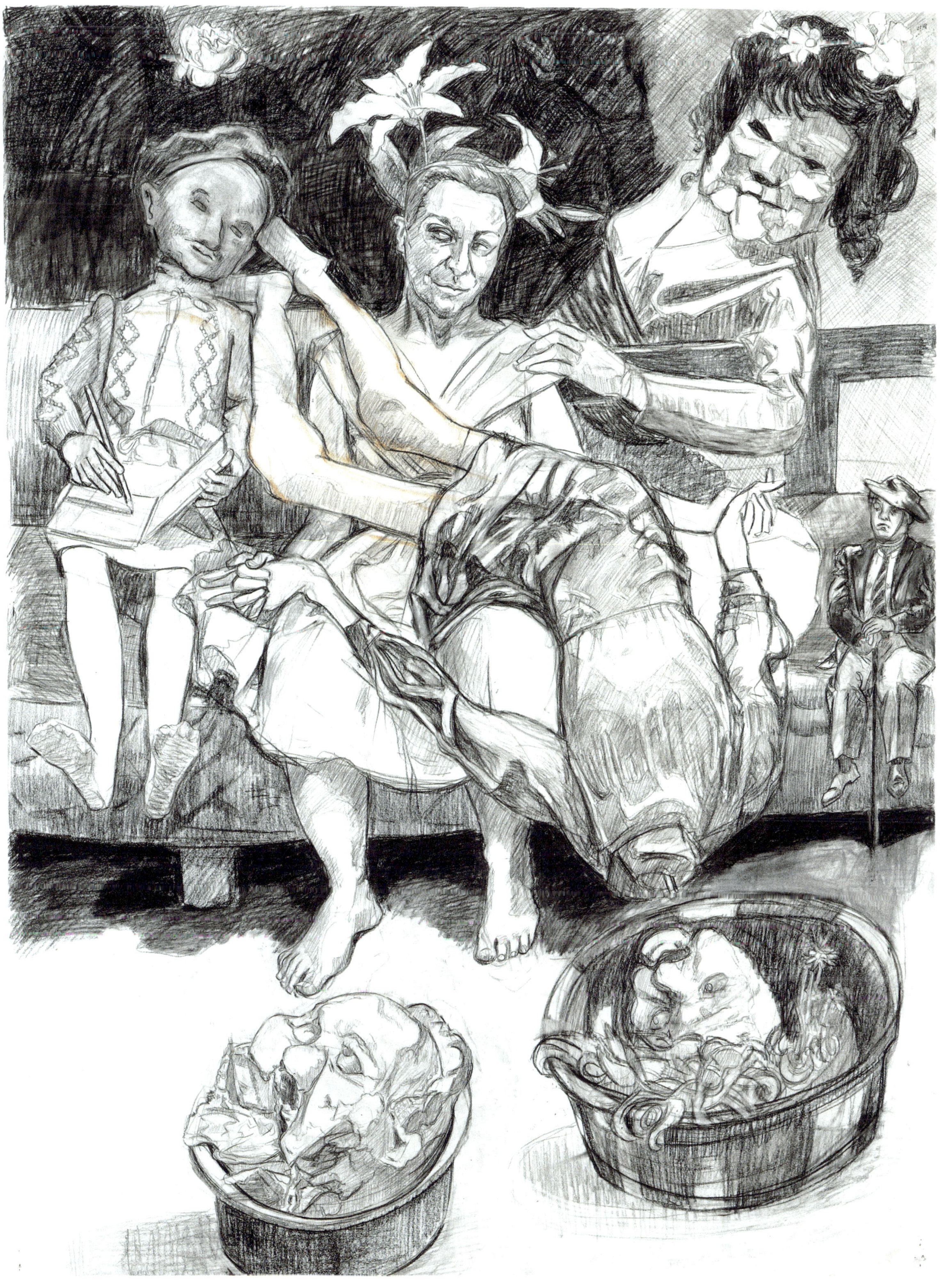

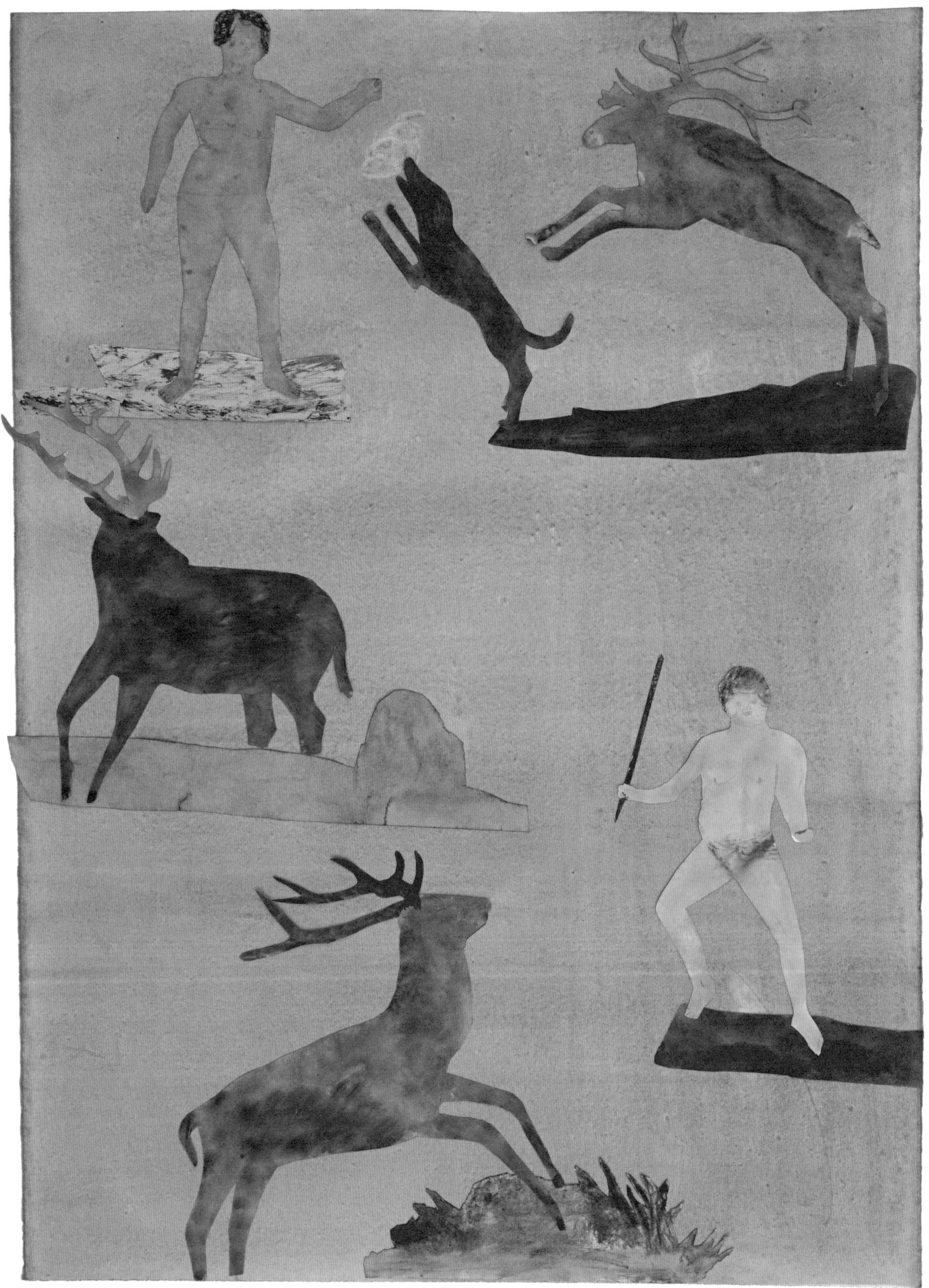

JOCKUM NORDSTRÖM *Born 1963, Stockholm, Sweden. Lives and works in Stockholm, Sweden*

The two parallel avenues of activity in Jockum Nordström's works on paper – his watercolour collages and his drawings in pencil and graphite – are symbiotically related. The collages, made from cut-out shapes including human figures and animals painted in delicate earth and ochre colours, have the apparent simplicity of naive or folk art or children's book illustration, yet they are quietly sophisticated. The casual disposition of the cut-out figures, scattered across the shallow space, implies the presence of narratives that never quite declare themselves. The pencil and graphite drawings, however, are more explicitly loaded with meaning while remaining ambiguous. Architectural structures – stately homes, suburban houses and low-rise blocks of flats – are carefully drawn in hard-leaded pencil with a ruler, while objects, people and animals are drawn in different styles, with various degrees of hard and soft graphite, sharply defined or smudged. Sex, music and class are among the recurring themes, and the individuals depicted look like the kind of people Nordström might know – moneyed and cultured, they could easily be art collectors. Yet these figures are often naked and surreptitiously engaged in sexual acts, a detail that may hold the key to Nordström's particular fiction: a lament for lost innocence and nostalgia for the carefree dreams of childhood.

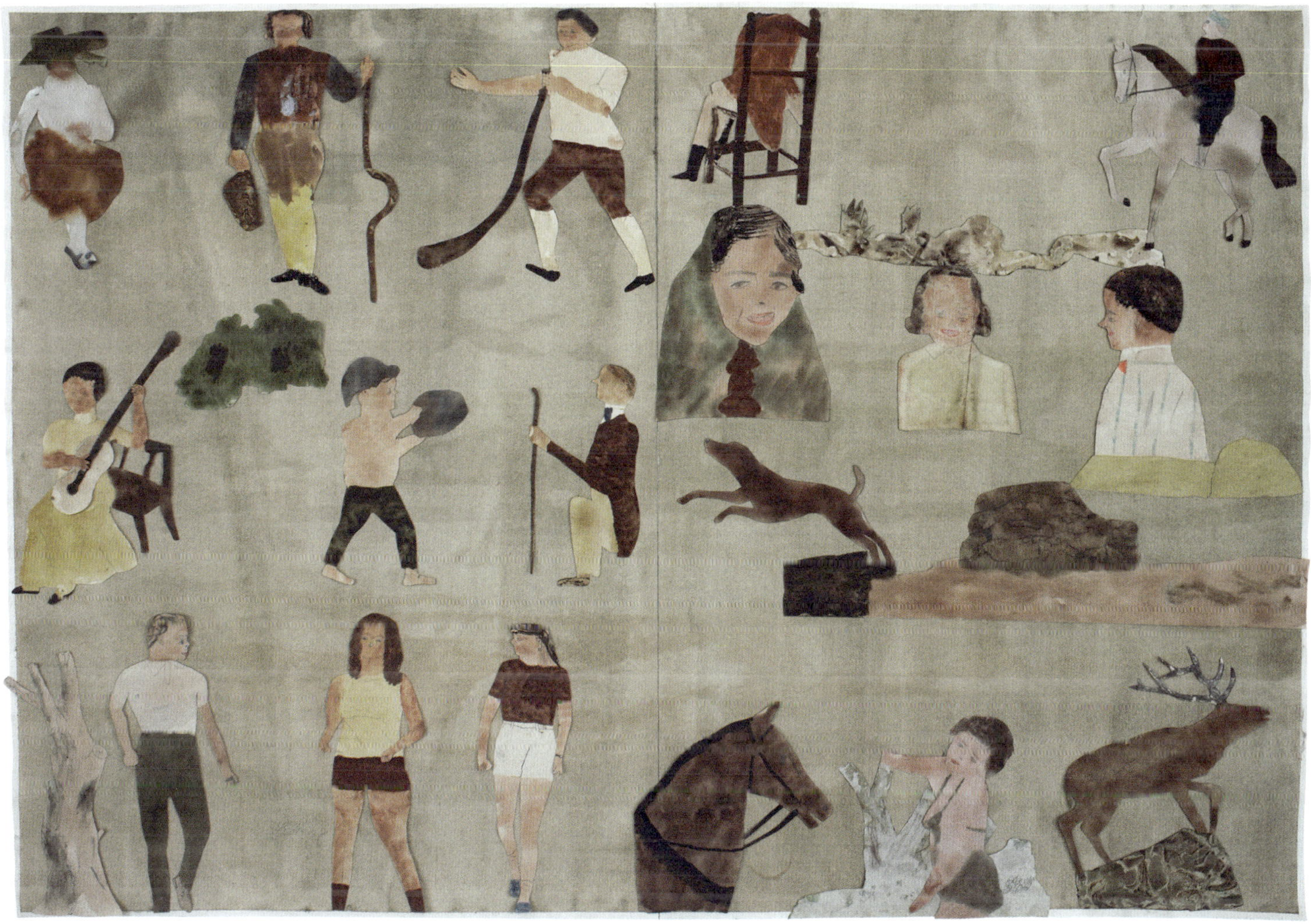

< *Child of Nature*, 2010
Watercolour, graphite and collage on paper
75.9 × 57.2 cm (29 ⅞ × 22 ½ in.)

Europa, 2010
Collage on paper
83.5 × 118.5 cm (32 ⅞ × 46 ⅝ in.)

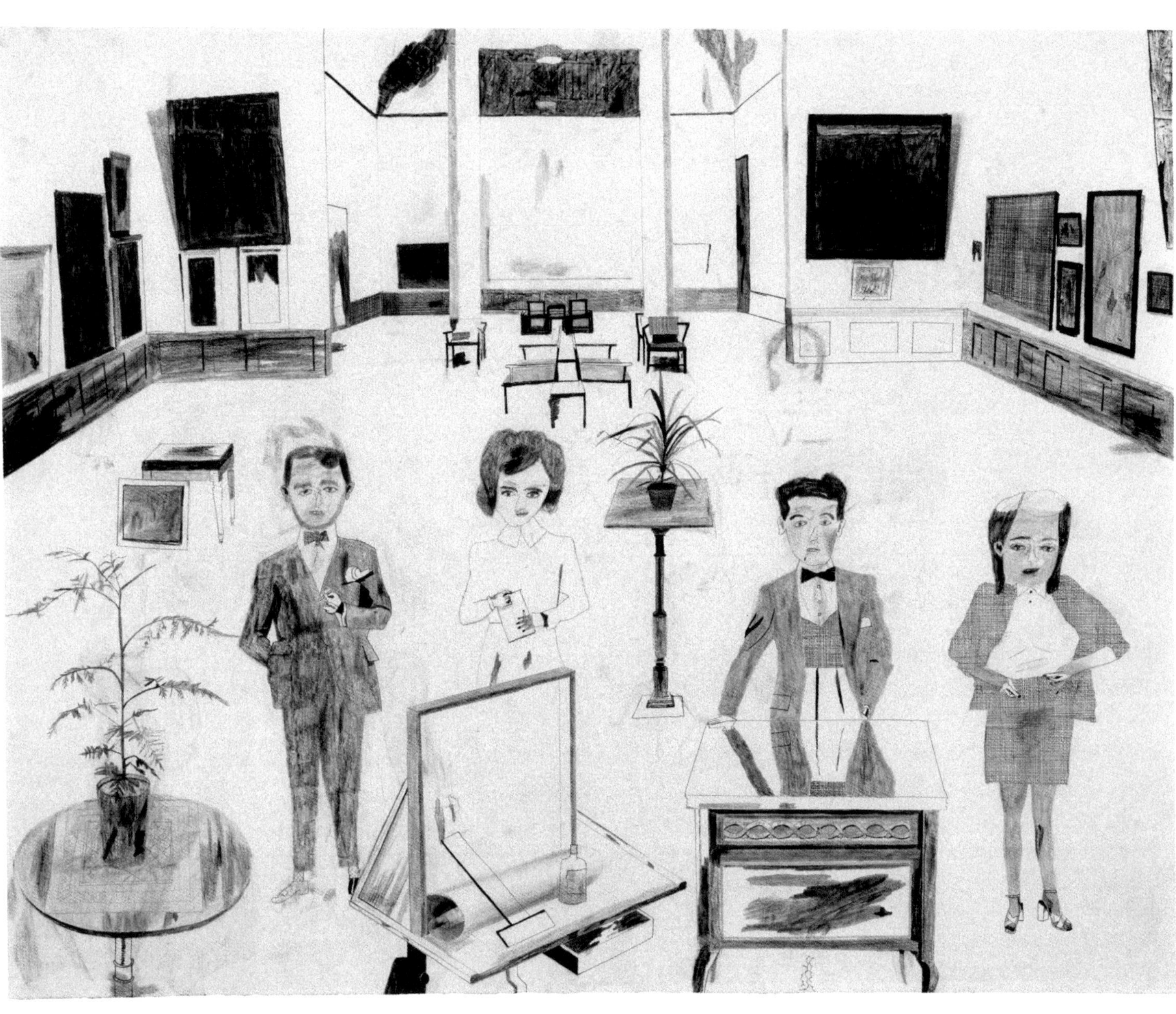

Back at Work, 2003
Graphite on paper
56 × 69 cm (22 × 27 ⅛ in.)

The Pot Boilers, 2003 >
Mixed media on paper
75 × 57 cm (29 ½ × 22 ½ in.)

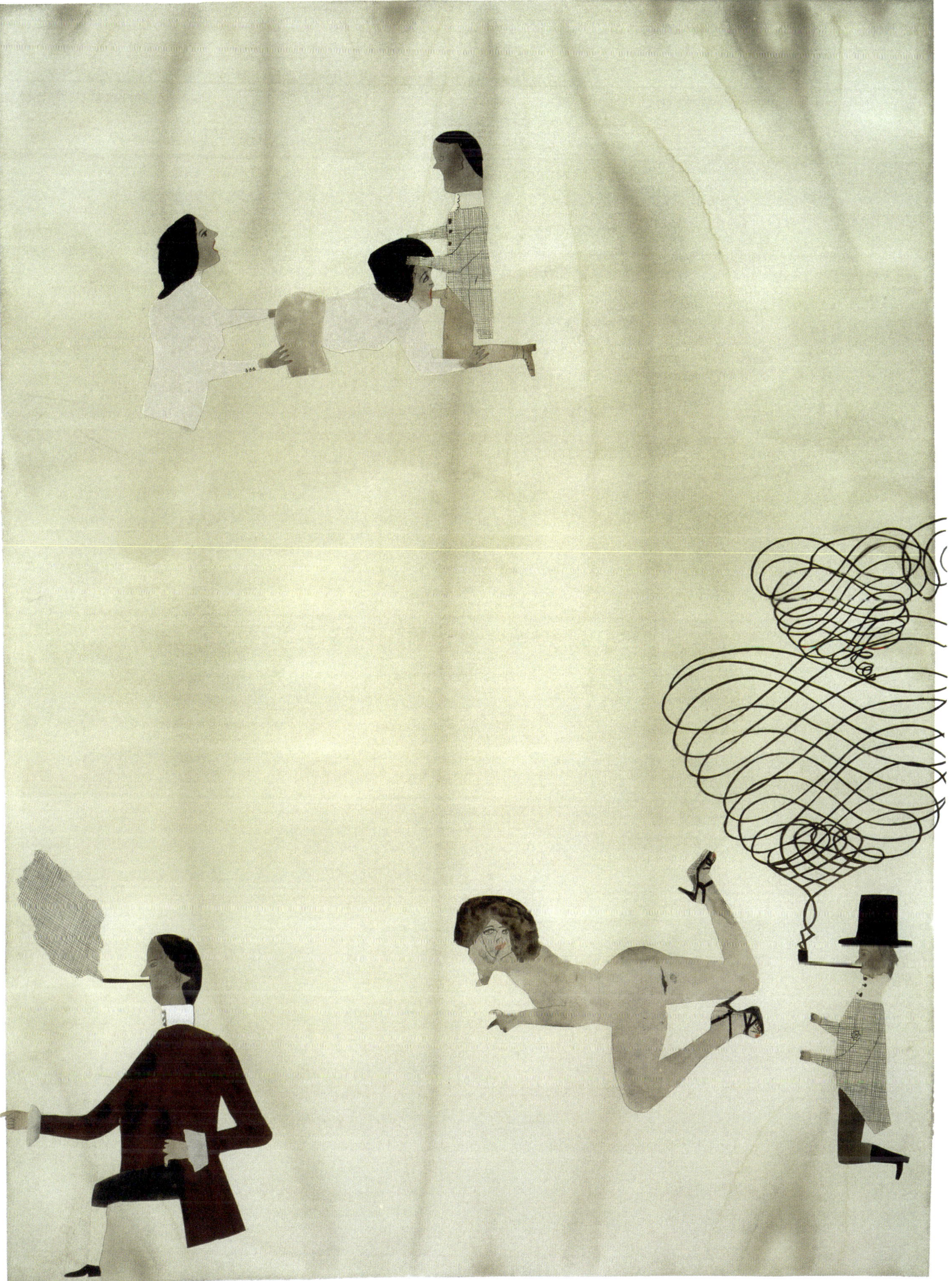

DR LAKRA   *Born 1972, Mexico City, Mexico. Lives and works in Oaxaca, Mexico*

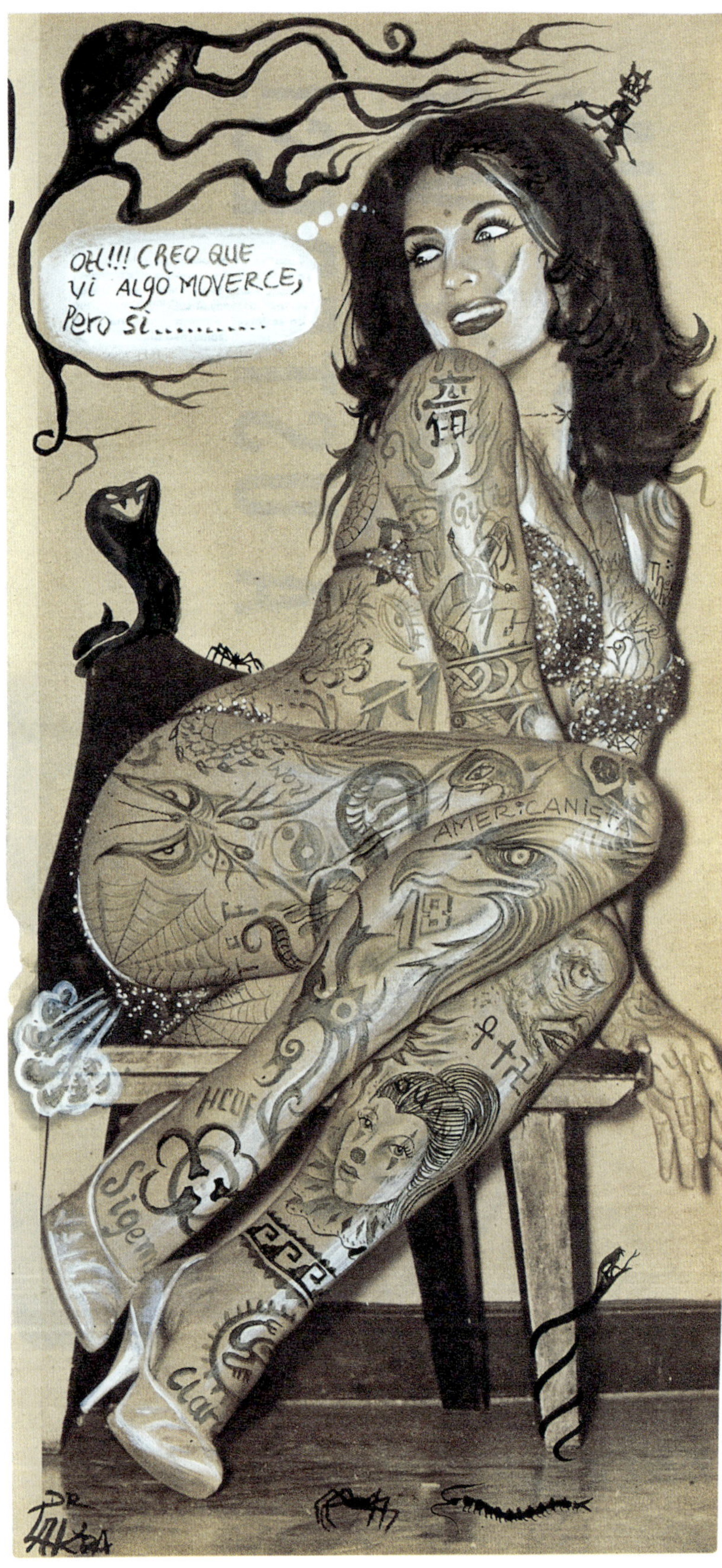

Dr Lakra (Jerónimo López Ramirez) straddles high and low culture with unique aplomb. His father is an eminent Mexican painter and his mother a poet and anthropologist. He took up tattooing at the age of sixteen and acquired his pseudonym from the doctor's briefcase in which he carried his equipment; 'Lacra' means scar or blemish in Spanish and is also slang for delinquent. Dr Lakra continues to practise as a tattooist while also exhibiting his work in museums and galleries across the world. The content and style of his drawings in both spheres are more or less identical: 'I've always drawn,' he says, 'sometimes on skin, sometimes on paper.' His best-known works on paper are his ink-drawn interventions on vintage postcards and photographs from popular Mexican magazines – pin-ups and wrestlers he embellishes with spiders, skulls and demons, redolent of the imagery of the Mexican Day of the Dead. These diabolical and carnivalesque visions occasionally spill out onto the gallery wall in Dr Lakra's more complex compositions.

Pedorra (She Who Farts), 2003
Ink and paint on vintage magazine
36 × 17 cm (14 ⅛ × 6 ¾ in.)

Puños (Punch), 2003 >
Ink and paint on vintage magazine
26 × 19 cm (10 ¼ × 7 ½ in.)

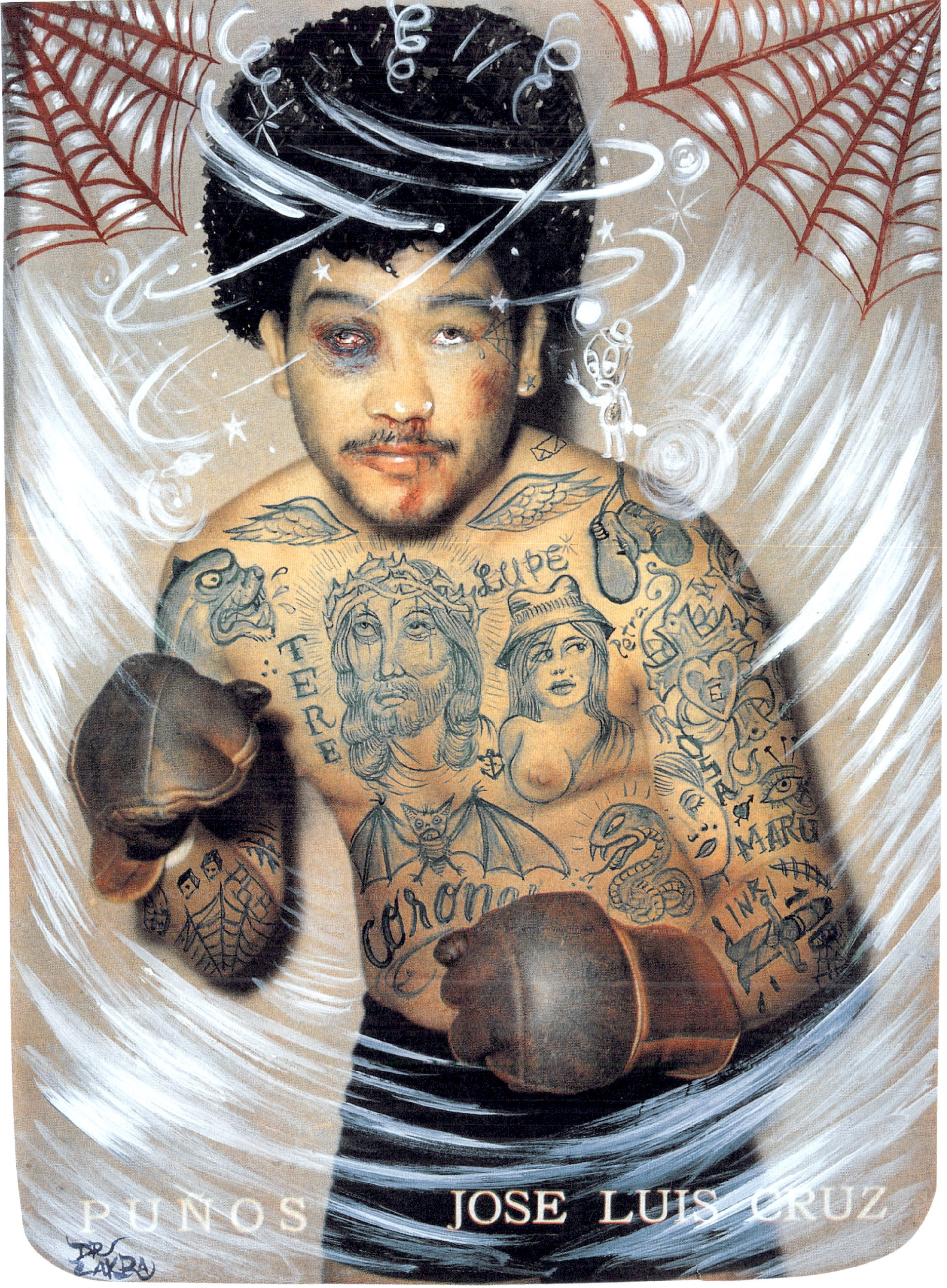
PUÑOS
JOSE LUIS CRUZ

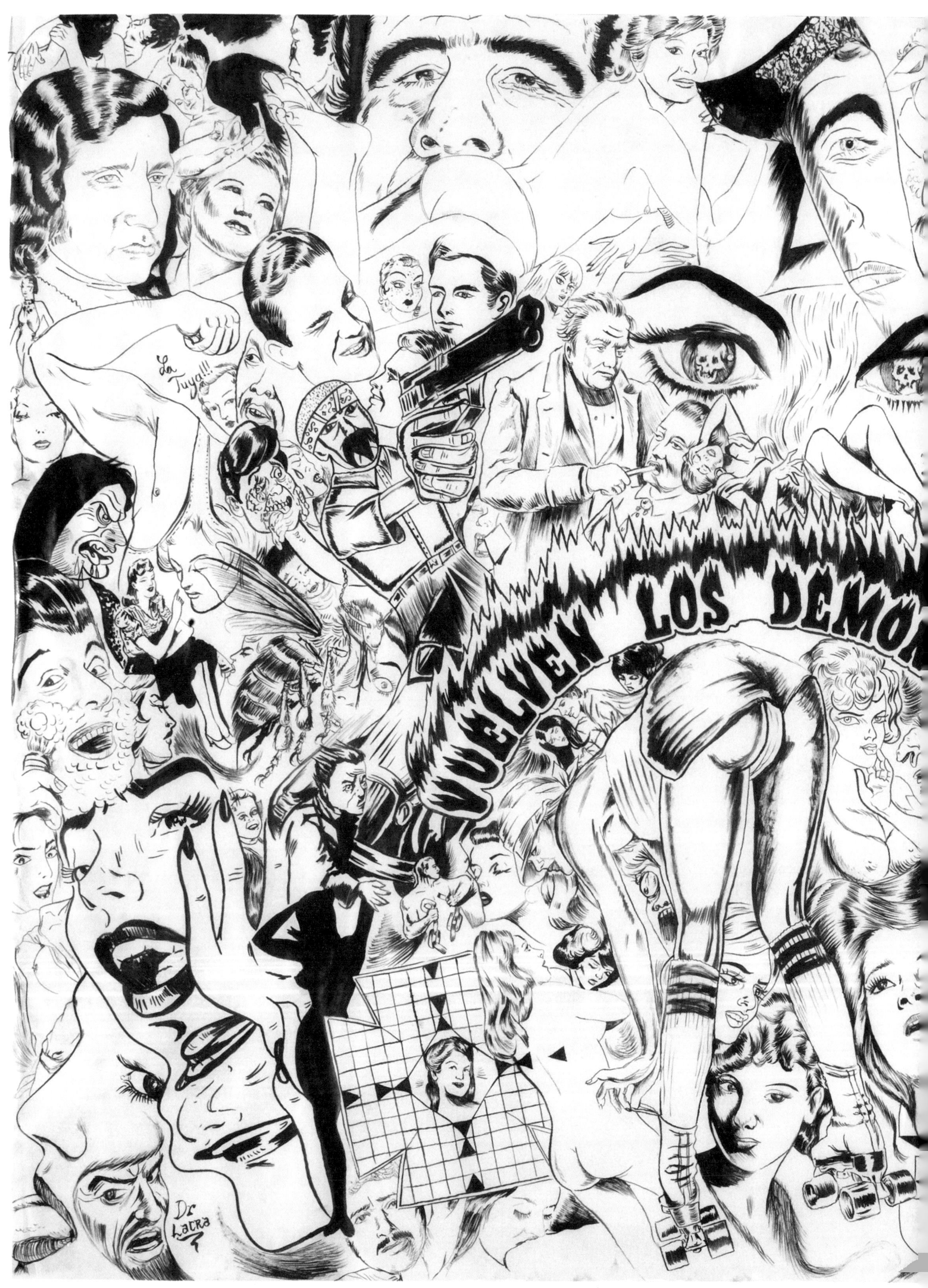

Sin título / Untitled (vuelven los demonios), 2006
Ink on tracing paper
90 × 61 cm (35 ⅜ × 24 in.)

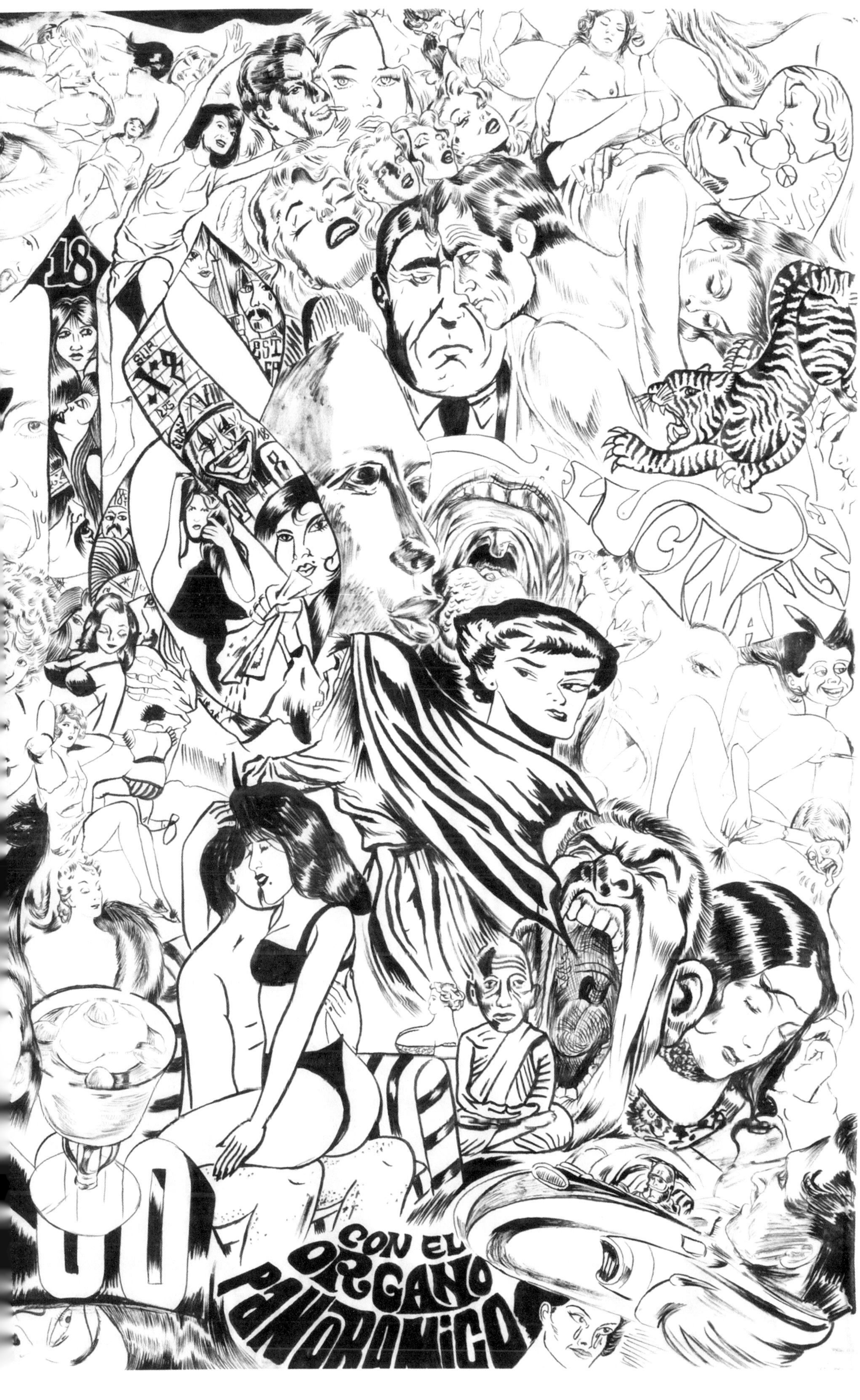
18
CON EL
ORGANO
PANORAMICO

The normality of bourgeois family life is unsettled and given a twist of strangeness in Marijn Akkermans's drawings. Faces are masks, and conventionally reassuring figures – mother, father, nurse – become weirdly threatening. The atmosphere is claustrophobic; things are out of scale; hands or feet are too large; space closes in. There is no point of reference or explanation. Adults and children seem unhealthily intermingled, and in any case it is difficult to distinguish real people from toys – Daddy is being repaired by the little girl with a needle and thread. The meaning remains opaque, for ambiguity is the artist's intention: 'The subject in my drawings (the whole scene) is floating like an idea, which can come close and yet drift away', he says. 'I am interested in the phenomenon of fear, the feeling that you cannot ascribe clear meaning to things and that you have no control. We think we are adults, but how true is that?'

234

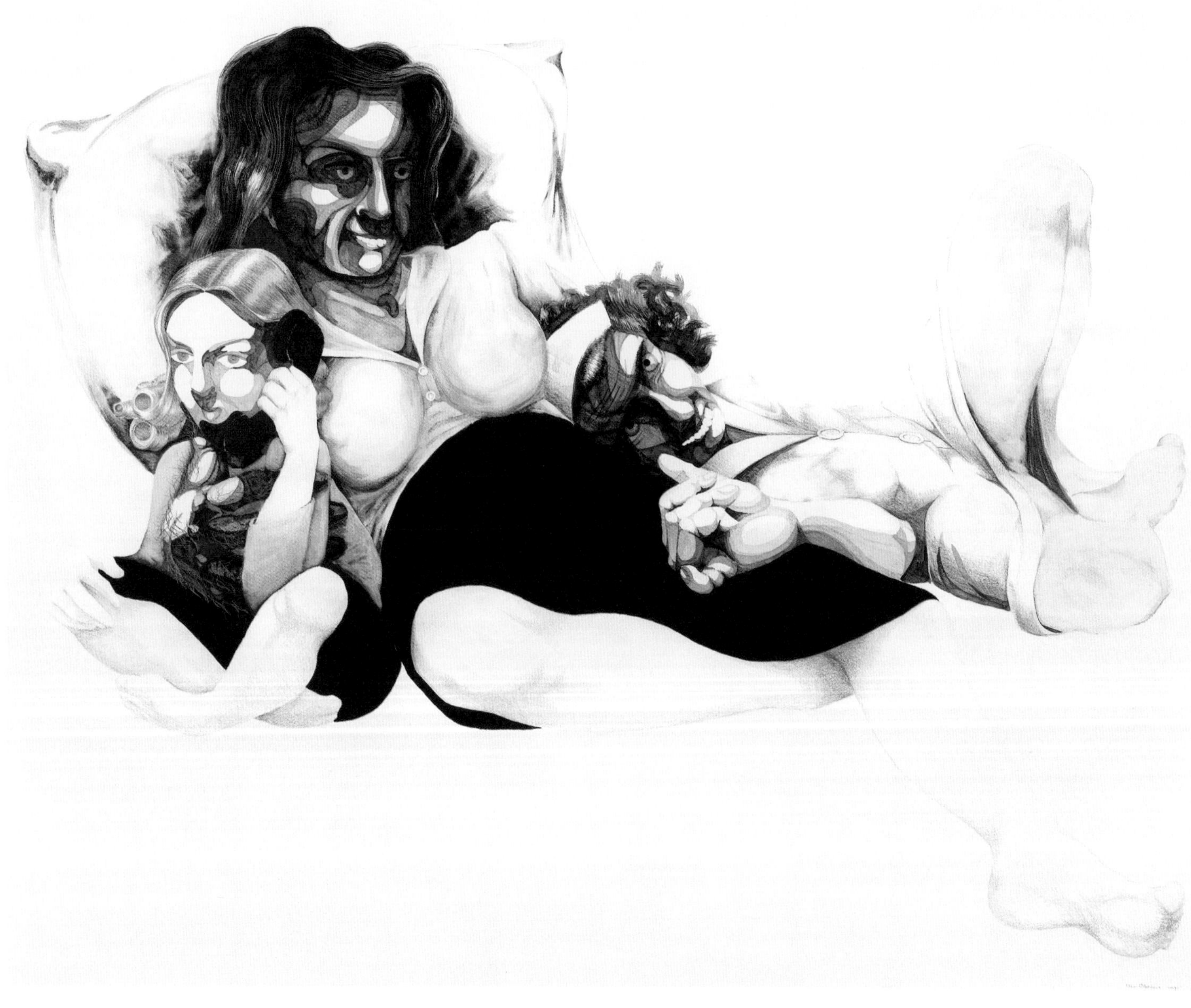

A Company of Three, 2007
Poster paint, acrylic paint, gesso, coloured pencil, ink
and collage on paper
150 × 177.5 cm (59 × 69 ⅞ in.)

(opposite, top) *Untitled 9 – The Teddy-bear Conventions,* 2005 >
Coloured pencil, acrylic, ink, collage and enamel on paper
150 × 253 cm (59 × 99 ⅝ in.)

(opposite, below) *Untitled 11 – The Teddy-bear Conventions,* 2005 >
Coloured pencil, acrylic, ink, collage and enamel on paper
150 cm × 279.5 cm (59 × 110 in.)

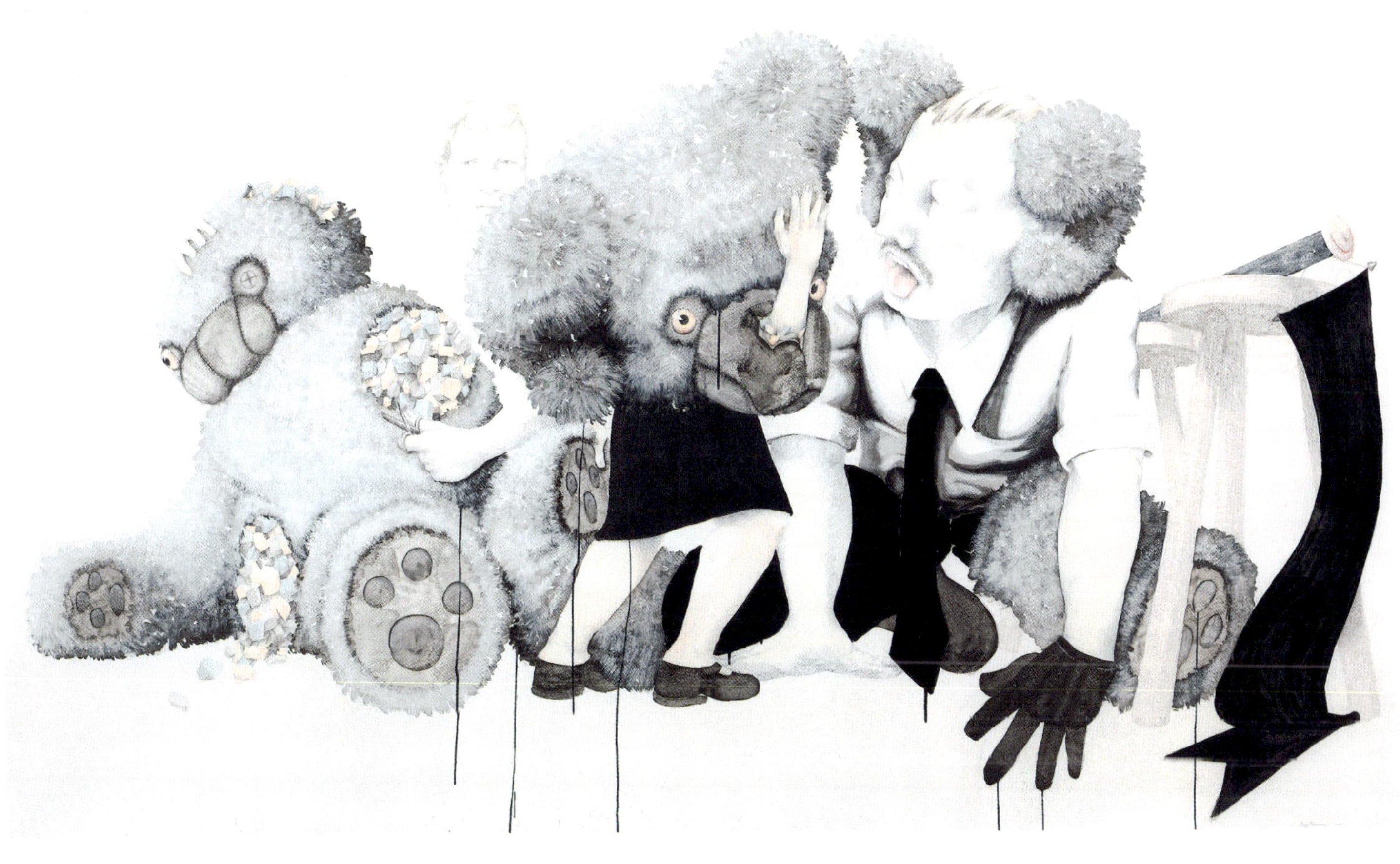

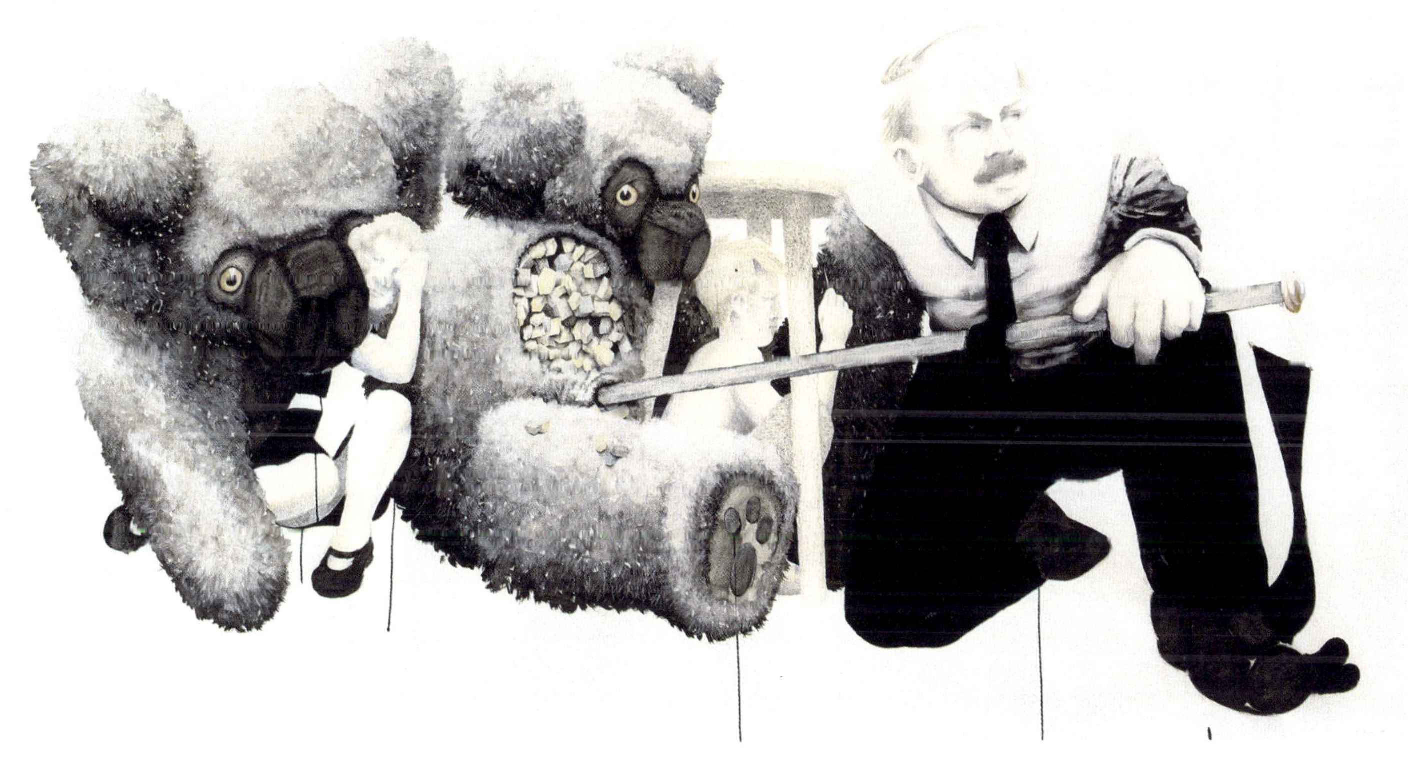

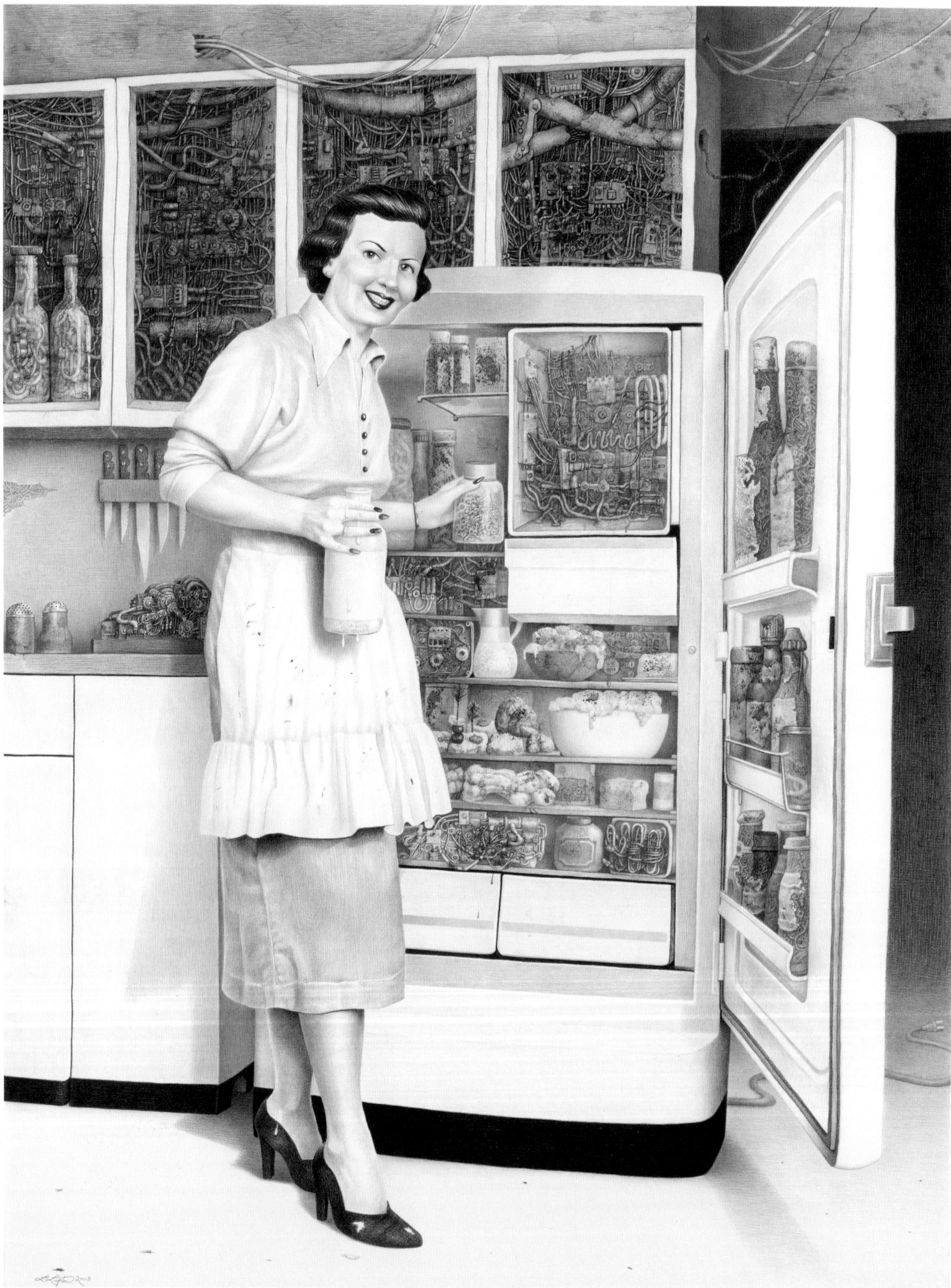

LAURIE LIPTON *Born 1953, New York, USA. Lives and works in West Hollywood, California, USA*

Although Laurie Lipton graduated from the Carnegie Mellon University in Pennsylvania with a Fine Art degree in drawing, she considers herself to be essentially self-taught. Rebelling against the dominant ethos of North American art in the 1970s, when figurative drawing was largely proscribed, Lipton escaped to Europe and developed her own minutely detailed technique using fine crosshatched charcoal lines. With this technique she achieves a luminosity akin to that of the Flemish Masters of the sixteenth century whom she so admires. Her meticulously executed large-format drawings are created with such

painstaking care that she has been described as a 'borderline fanatic'. Her subject matter is relentlessly dark and she is a cult figure in the marginal world of Gothic illustration. Lipton's principle themes are death – often represented in the manner of Mexican Day of the Dead imagery – and cool satires on consumerism. She is entirely wedded to black and white, which she describes as 'the colour of ancient photographs and old TV shows… the colour of ghosts, longing, time passing, memory and madness'.

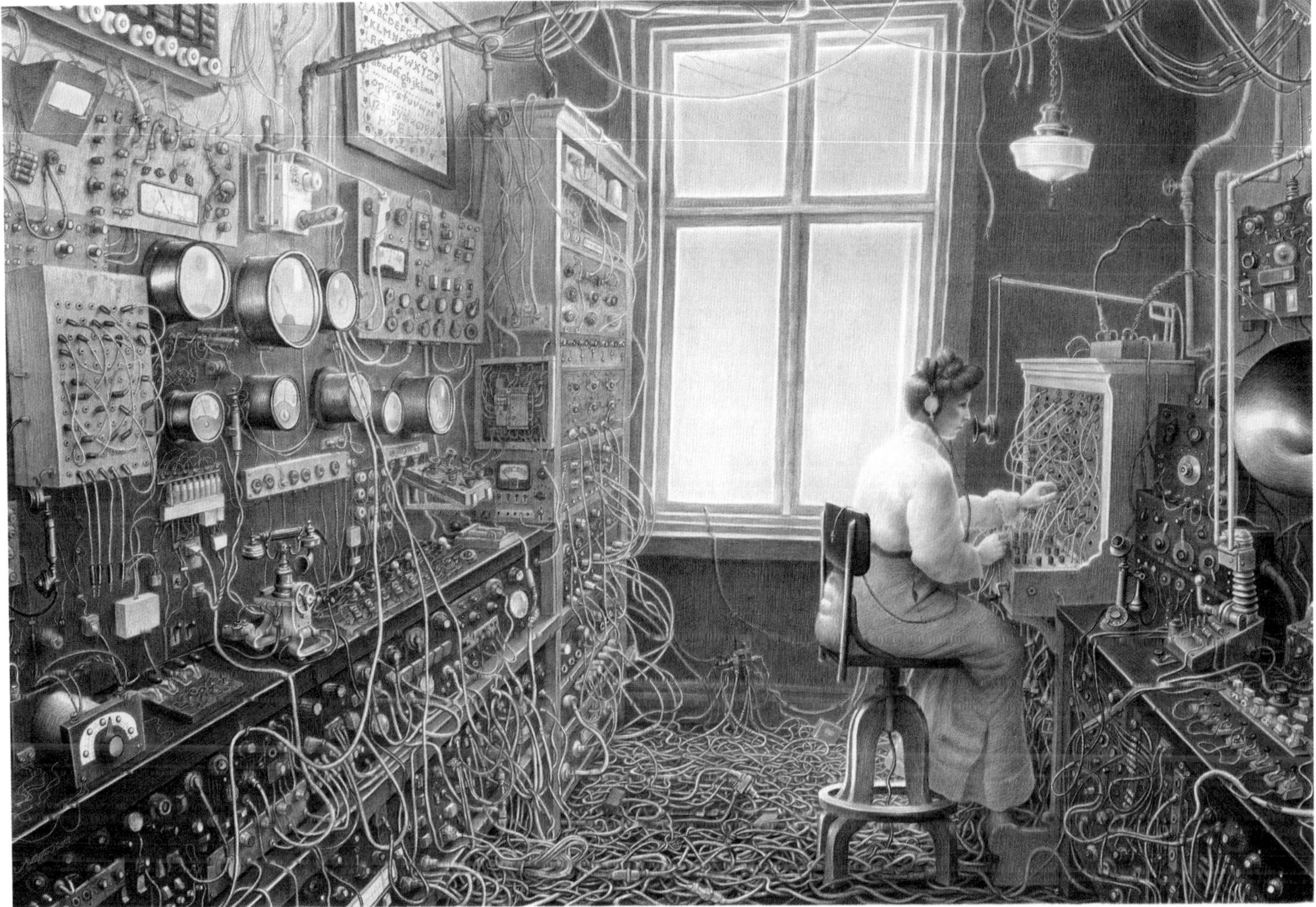

< *Off*, 2008
Pencil and charcoal on paper
124 × 93.5 cm (48 ⅞ × 36 ¾ in.)

Communication, 2009
Pencil and charcoal on paper
67 × 98 cm (26 ⅜ × 38 ⅝ in.)

Akayo Tabata – known internationally as Tabaimo, a nickname meaning 'younger Tabata sister' – trained as a graphic artist before turning to the multi-screen video animations for which she is now famous. She scans hundreds of pen-and-brush ink drawings into a computer to make these animations, which resemble in style the classic Japanese *ukiyo-e* ('Floating World') woodblock prints. Tabaimo's surreal imagination gives a disquieting tone to the themes of everyday life and social problems in Japan that she addresses in her work. She takes familiar settings, such as a kitchen, public toilet or commuter train, and explodes them into shocking allegories of isolation, anxiety and desperation: a housewife cooks with 'human' ingredients, and watches schoolgirls dropping from the sky past her window while a radio news report talks of teenage suicides. A woman gives birth through her nostril in a public toilet. A body's nervous system runs between the floors of a doll's house.

In 2009, Tabaimo collaborated with Japanese novelist Shūichi Yoshida on a serialized story in a daily newspaper. The resulting drawings, reproduced here, picked out key words in Yoshida's story, since Tabaimo refused to illustrate it literally. Yoshida, meanwhile, described a feeling of 'having to apply the brakes to myself to avoid being pulled along too much' by Tabaimo's images.

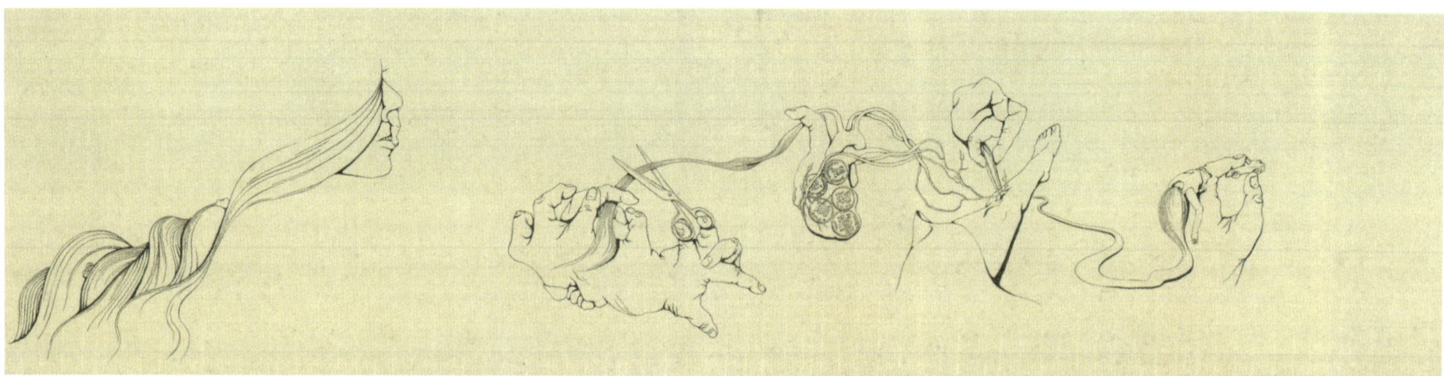

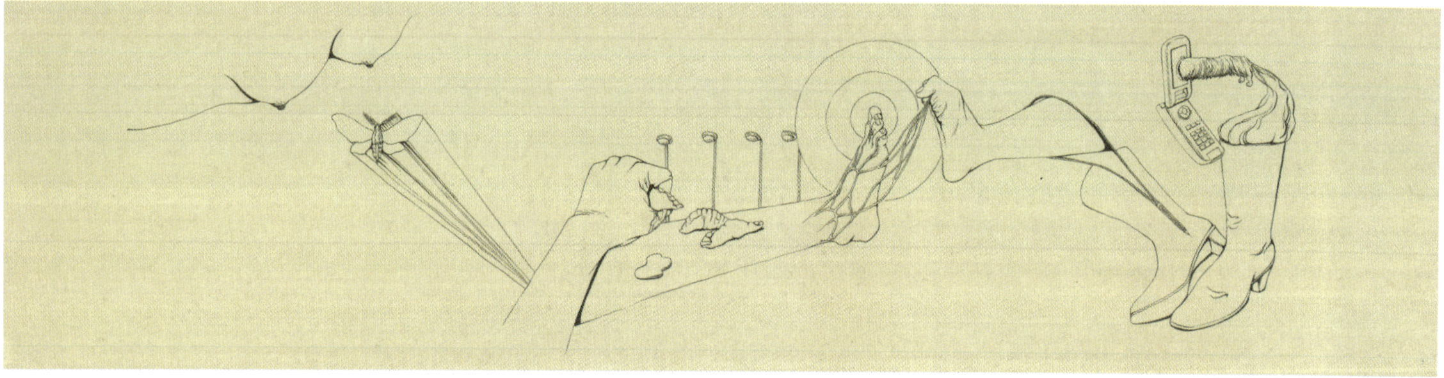

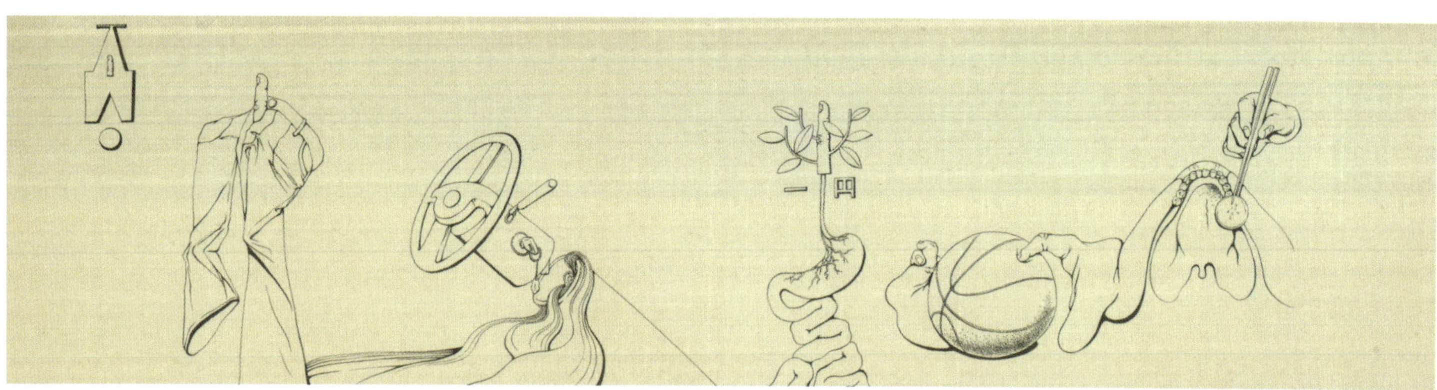

(this page and opposite) From *Akunin,* 2006
Illustrations originally published in Shuichi Yoshida's novel
Akunin (Villain), Asahi Shimbun newspaper, 2006–7

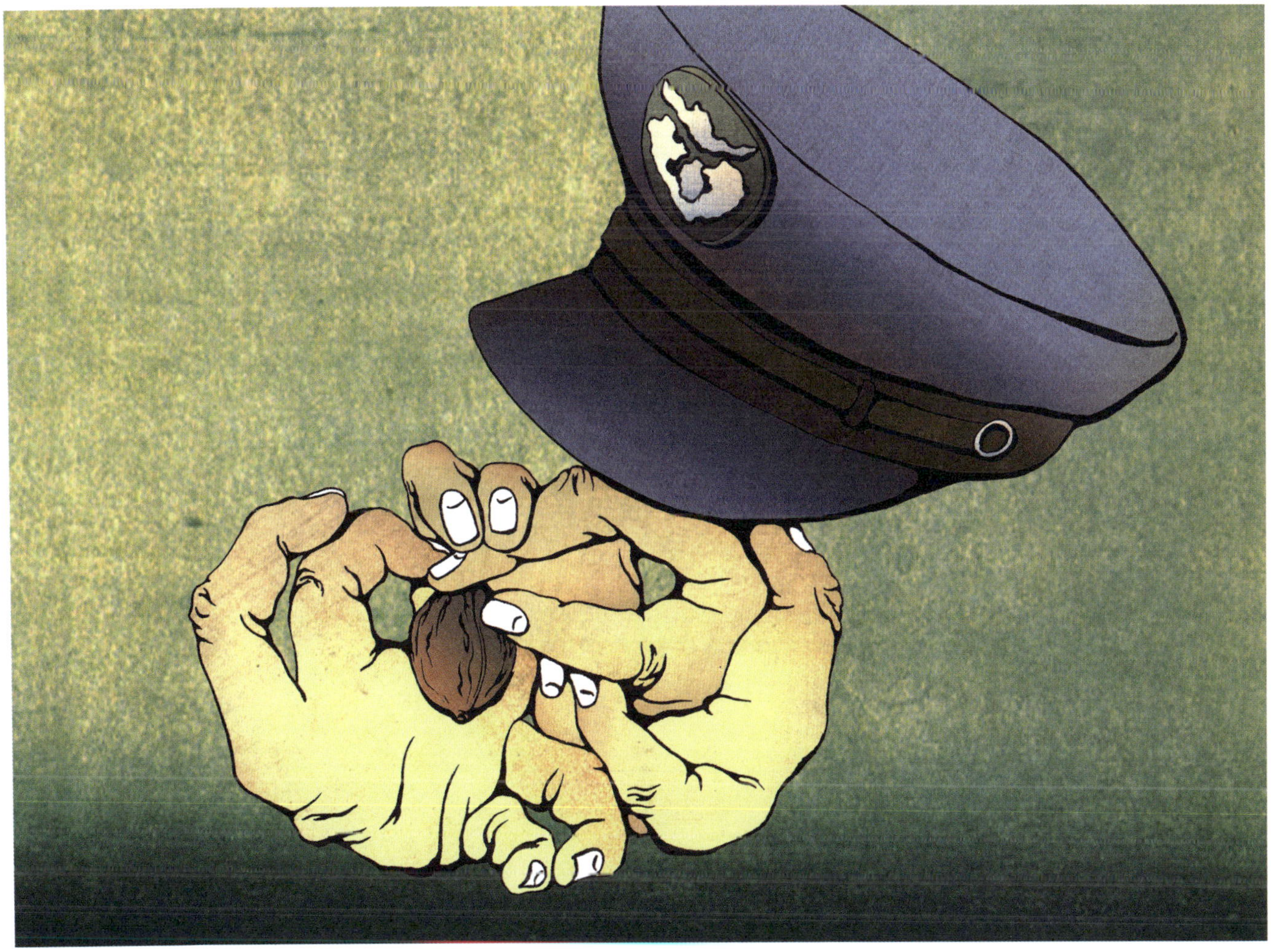

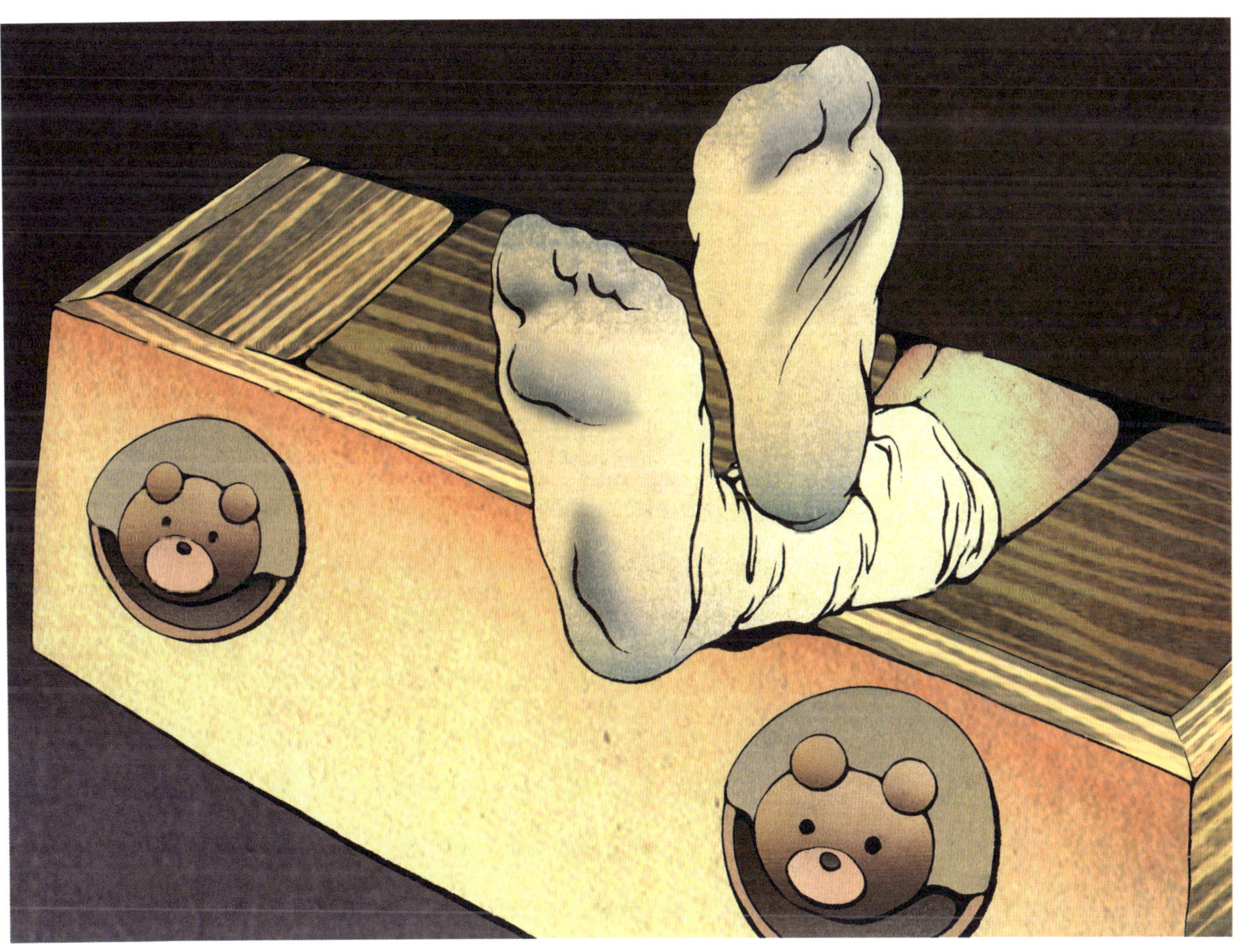

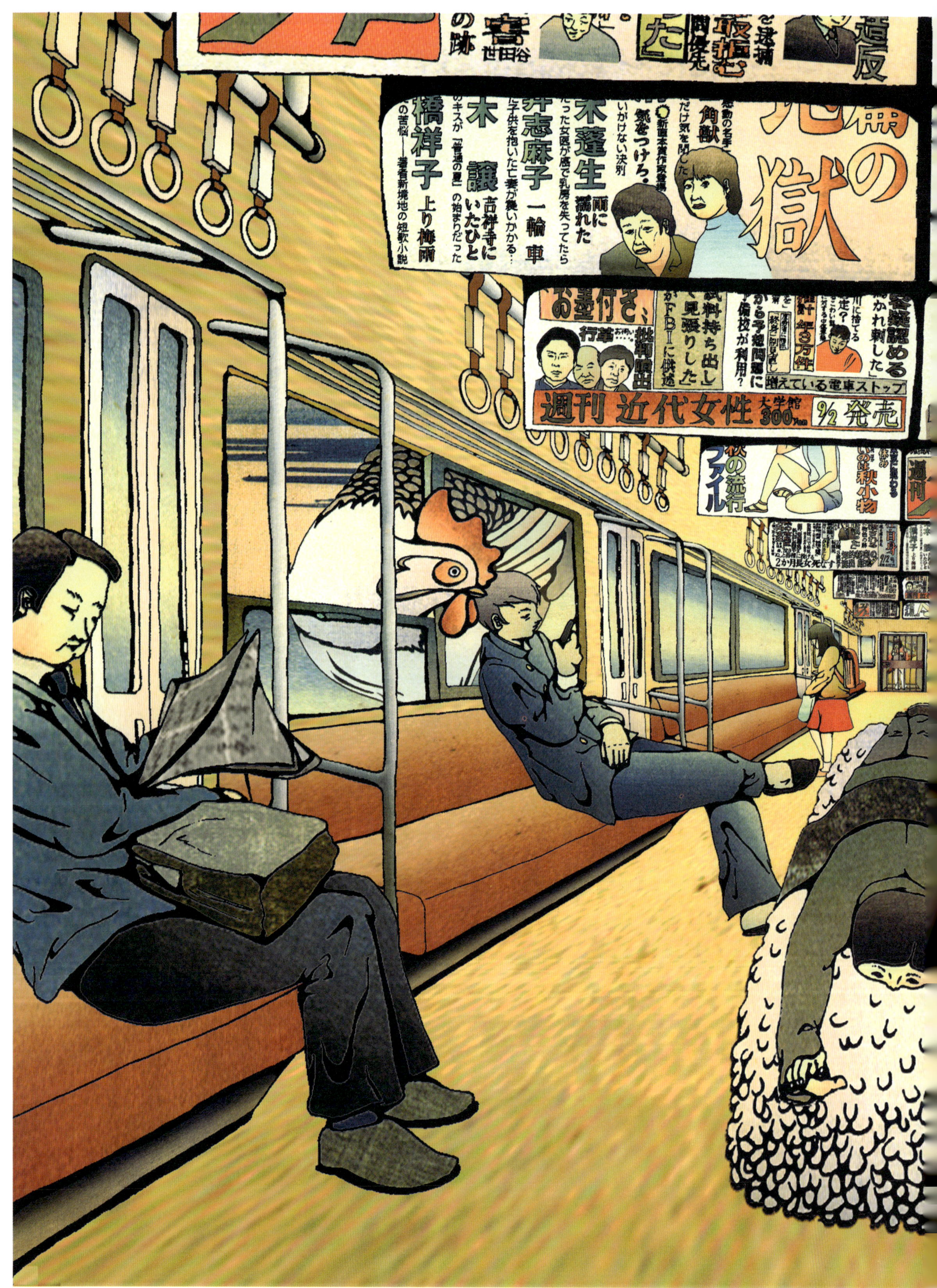

Japanese Commuter Train, 2001
Video still
Video installation, duration 8 min.

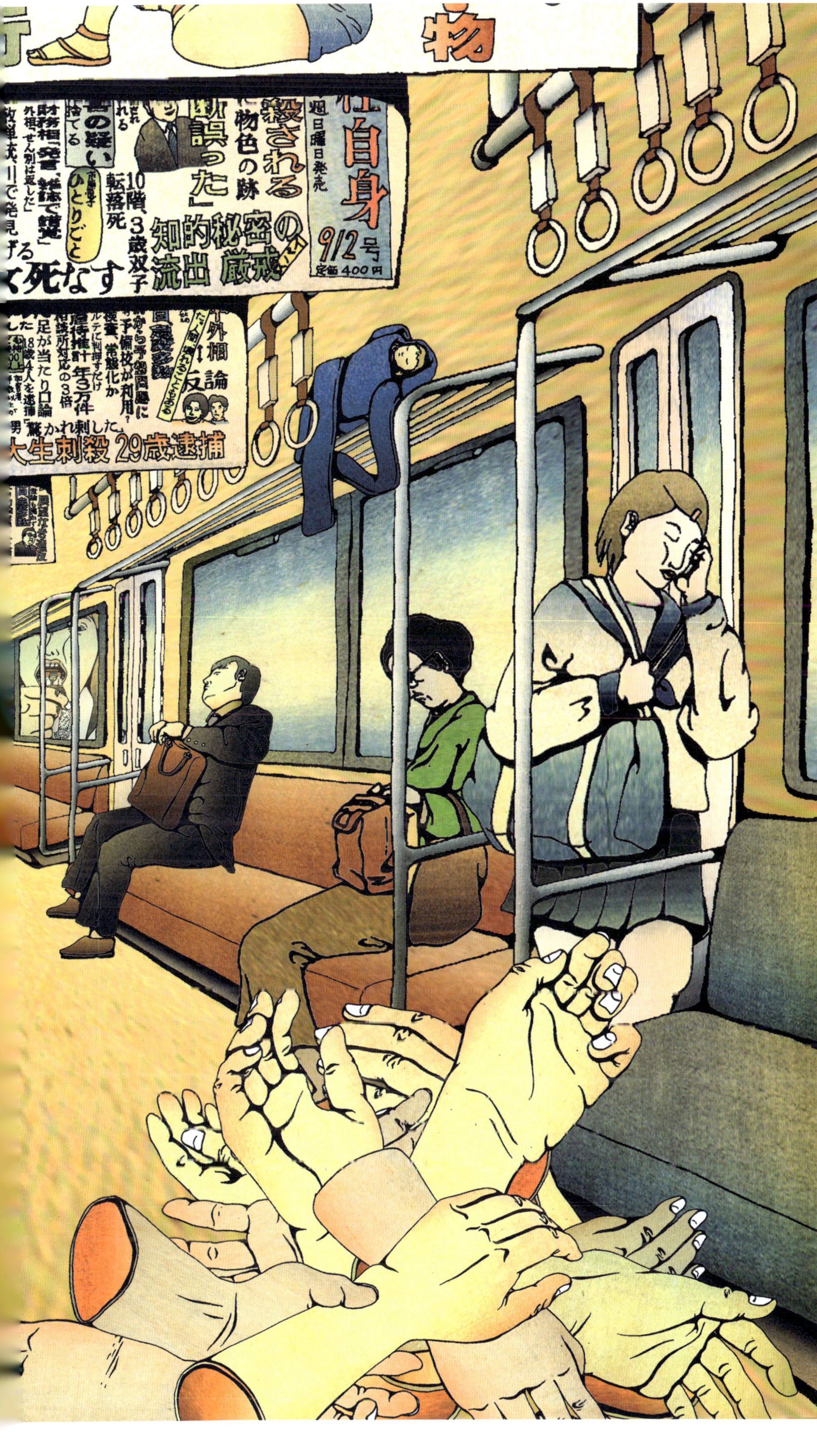
週刊誌
物
紅白身
9/2号
定価400円
日曜日発売
殺される
物色の跡
誤った
知的秘密の
流出厳戒
10階
3歳双子
転落死
反論
大生刺殺 29歳逮捕
て死なす

242

'Drawing is a way of navigating the imagination and it remains the fundamental vehicle of my practice. Drawing allows me to connect various formats and mediums while keeping the urgency of thought transparent throughout the process.' Shahzia Sikander originally studied traditional Indo-Persian miniature painting at the National College of Arts in Lahore during the late 1980s, submitting herself to this rigorous discipline in order to use it to challenge and subvert the techniques and narratives associated with the miniature. Her work since has grown to encompass large-scale digital animations, projections and murals, but is always grounded in an intimate relationship with materials – 'how ink sits on paper, how mark-making can give birth to various forms' – and always begins with drawing. Her 2010 video animation *The Last Post* deals with British colonial history through the figure of an East India Company officer who travels across India and into China and becomes involved in the Opium Wars. In this animation, the imagery is rendered in the style of Company Painting, a documentary form of miniature painting that used to be commissioned by British colonialists in India in the nineteenth century.

In her ink-and-gouache drawings exploring these themes, Sikander borrows from Goya as well as the Hamzanama (the enormous sixteenth-century illustrated manuscript that documents the exploits of the prophet Mohammad's uncle), especially in her depictions of military men, monks and traders; here she shows an officer with his tuba metamorphosing into a pipe and eventually dissolving into myriad fragments. The other drawing shows composite forms in which the human and the mechanical, the violent and the comical come together. The frequent appearance of the overweight man acts as a stand-in for power relations and hierarchies.

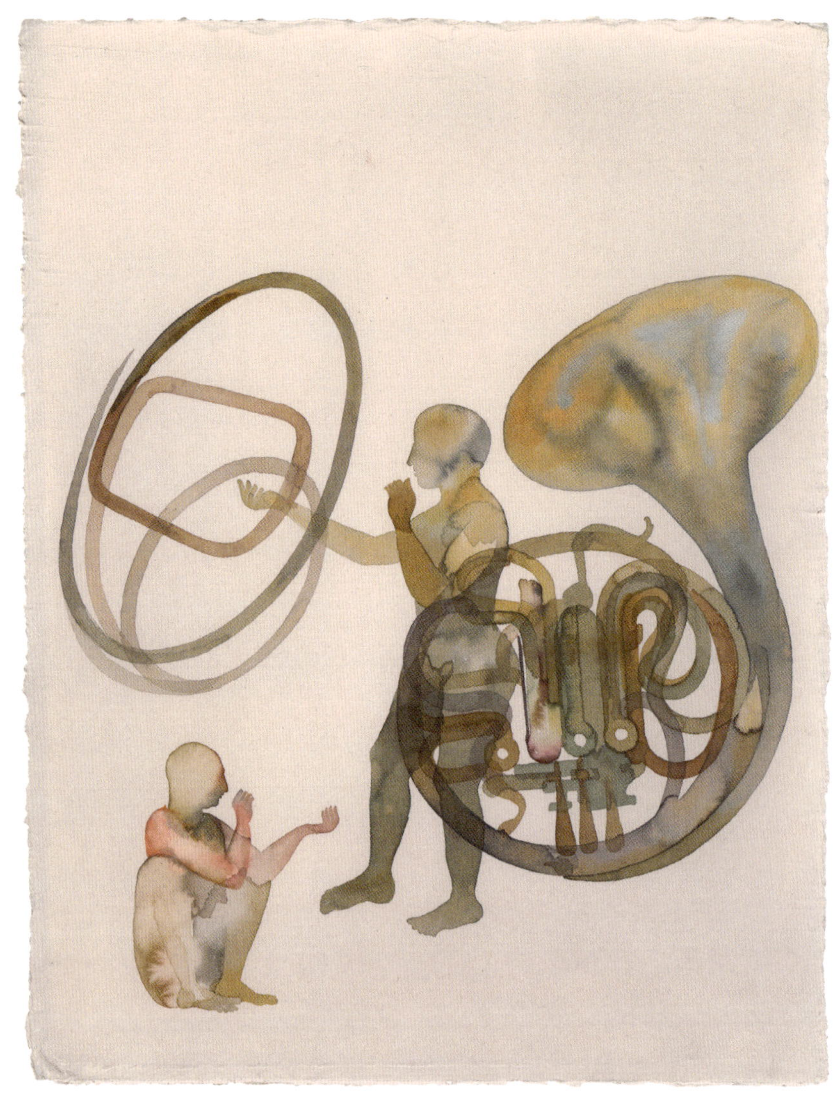

In Our DNA II, 2009
Ink and gouache on prepared paper
38 × 28.5 cm (15 × 11 ¼ in.)

The Little Boys Club II, 2009 >
Ink and gouache on prepared paper
38 × 29 cm (15 × 11 ⅜ in.)

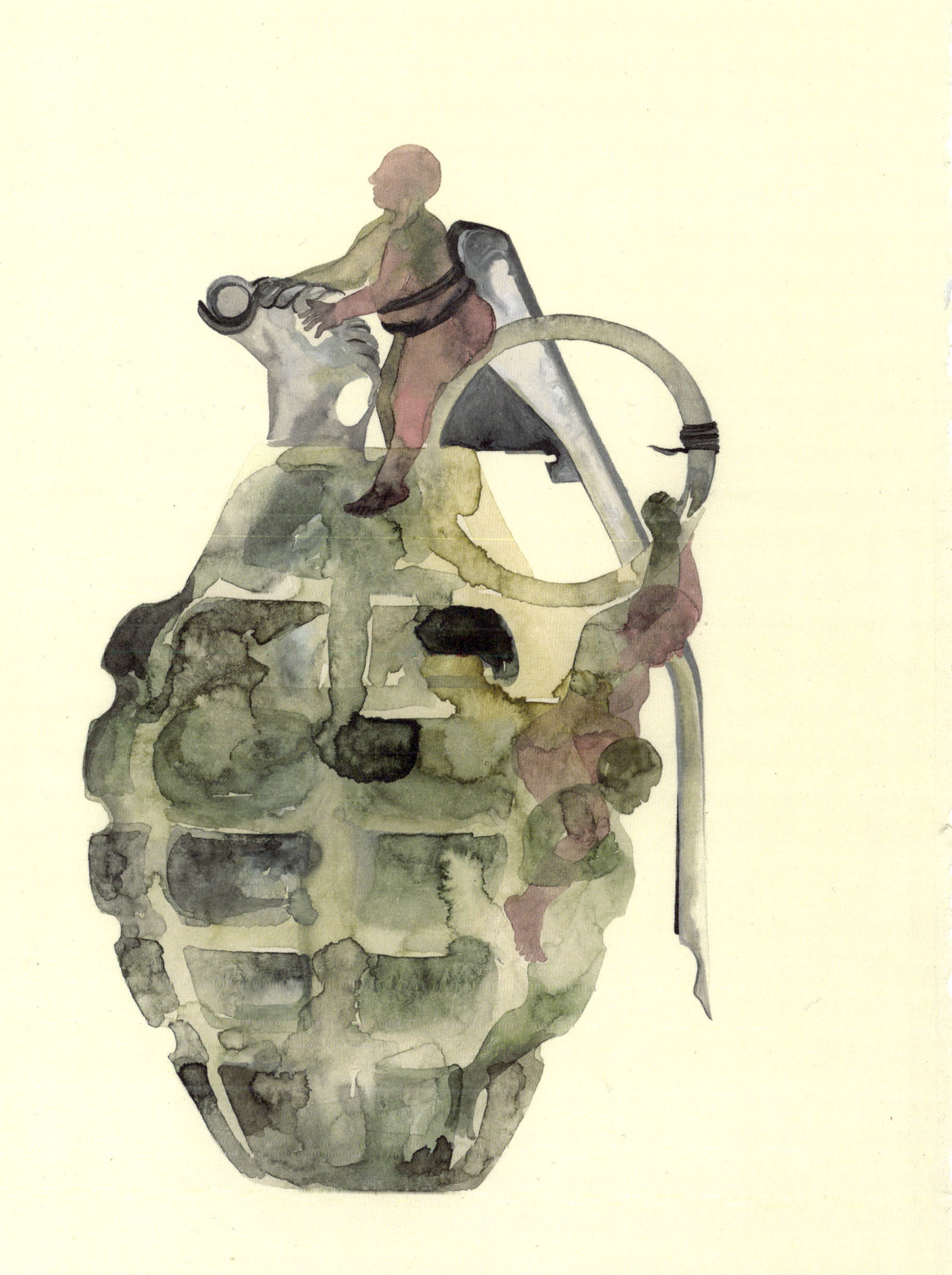

Rinus Van de Velde trained as a sculptor and his large charcoal drawings have a physical impact, a muscular energy that is magnified by his practice of hanging them in dense groups with lengthy hand-written captions spilling onto the wall space between them. In these drawings he weaves elaborate meta-narratives featuring a cast of masculine characters, one of whom is himself in the guise of a – usually fictitious but sometimes real – hero of modern art. The other figures are variously chess champions, sportsmen, scientists, musicians and hard-drinking adventurers. Van de Velde's studio, cluttered and blackened with charcoal dust, often appears in these

scenes, showing the artist at work on a figurative or abstract work. *The Story of Frederic, Conrad, Jim and Rinus* is a cabin-fever tale of four friends living in isolation in a wood (Van de Velde built an actual set for this piece in his studio). The character Conrad is Rinus's doppelgänger, a writer of fiction in whose imagination the artist stages his own biography. Van de Velde has a mania for drawing in charcoal – his world is resolutely black and white – and he chooses adventurous figures to draw, he says, to add colour to an otherwise monotonous life consisting of protracted periods spent in his studio.

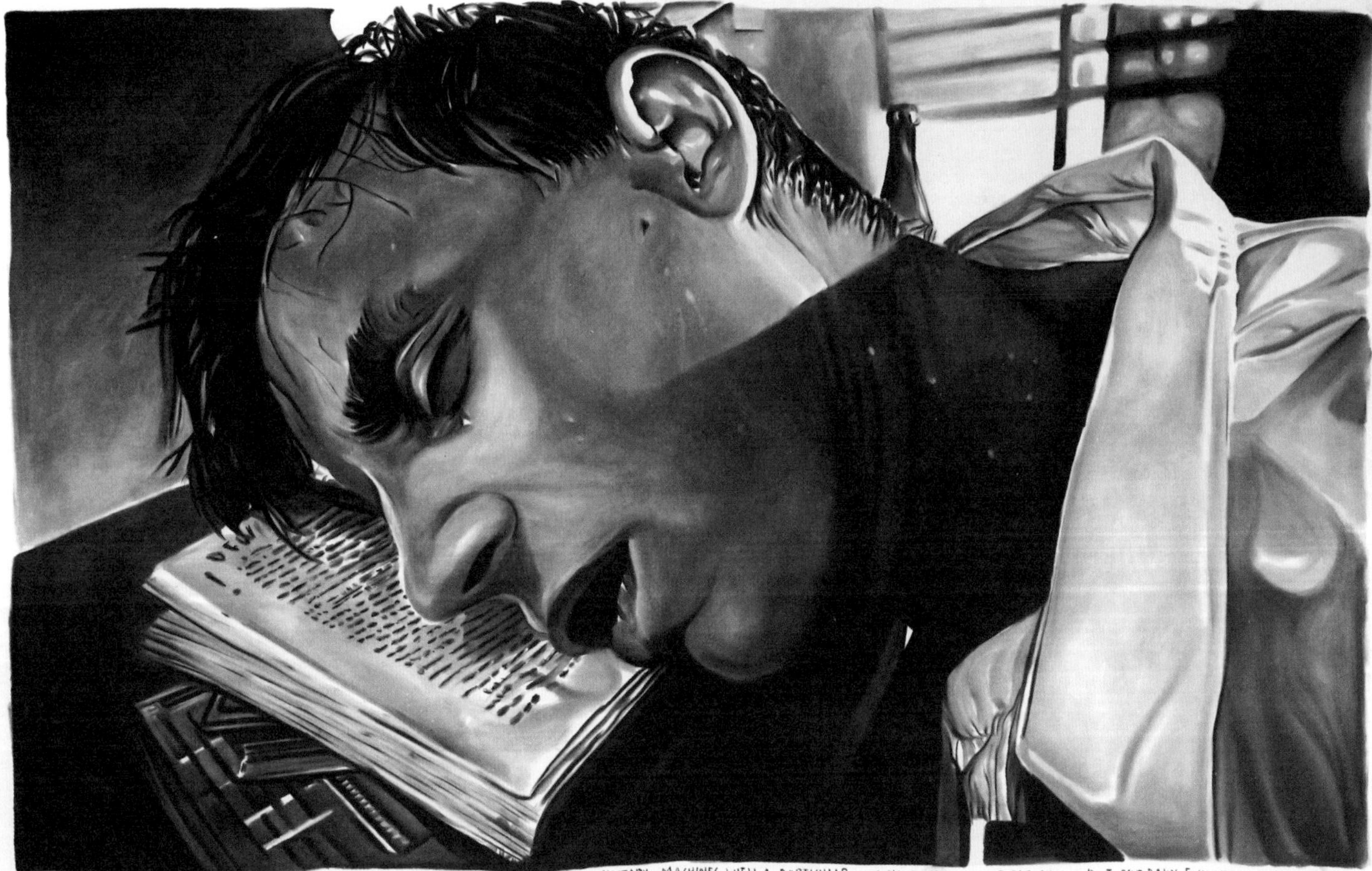

We suffer from a strange kind of amnesia. Yes, we are individuals with a personal history, machines with a particular wiring that generate meanings..., 2013
Charcoal on canvas
Framed: 130 × 200 cm (51 ⅛ × 78 ¾ in.)

I enter another dimension, Rinus, tighten all my muscles and try to look at everything at the same time..., 2013 >
Charcoal on canvas
Framed: 190 × 170 cm (74 ¾ × 66 ⅞ in.)

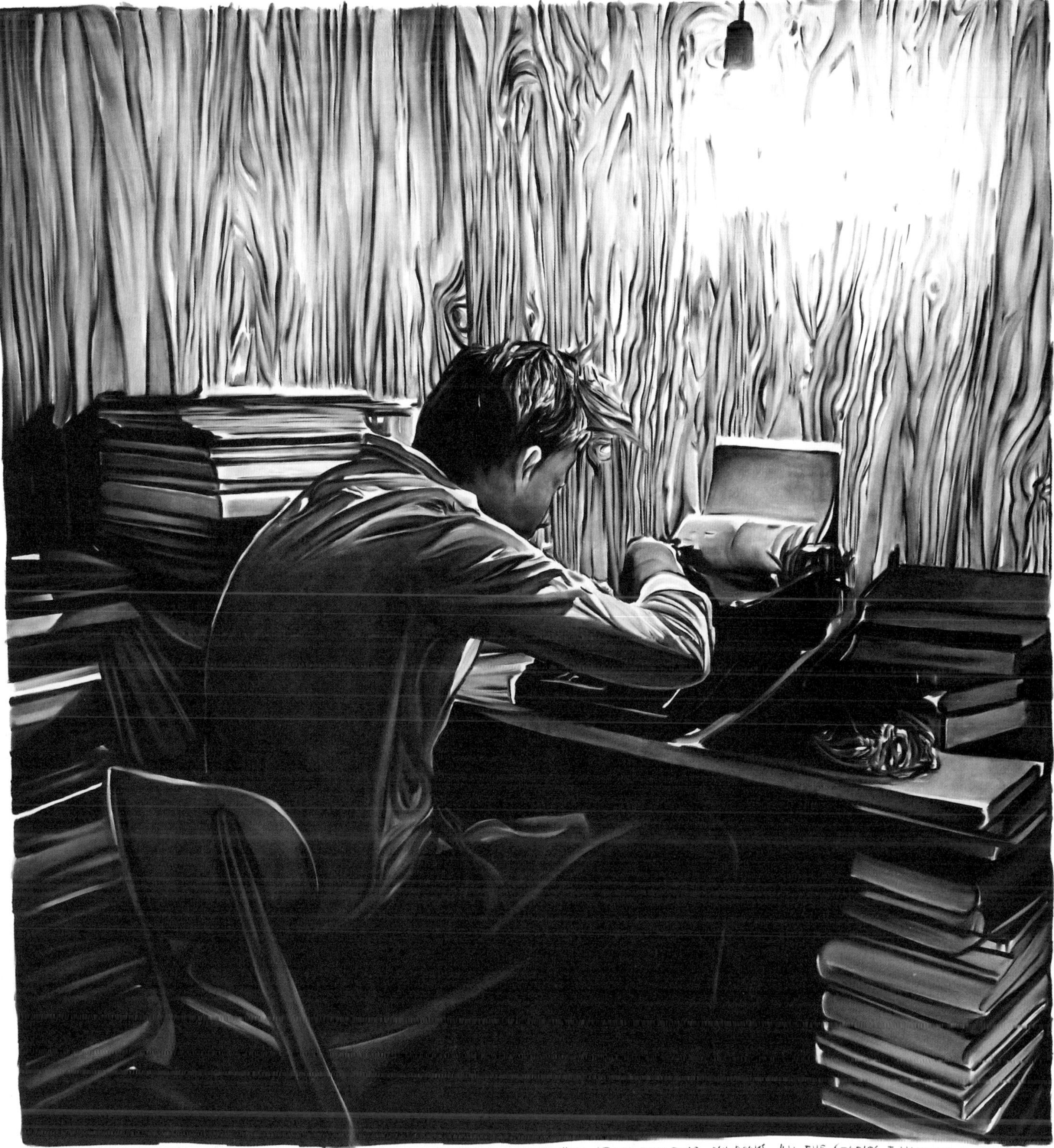

"I ENTER ANOTHER DIMENSION, RINUS, TIGHTEN ALL MY MUSCLES AND TRY TO LOOK AT EVERYTHING AT THE SAME TIME. MY BOOKS, ALL THE STORIES I HAVE HEARD, MY CONTRASTING FEELINGS, THE WORDS I KNOW, EVERYTHING THAT HAPPENS IN HERE. IT'S ALL PART OF A BIGGER THING. AS LONG AS SOMETHING KEEPS CHANGING, I WILL NEVER BE ABLE TO FINISH ANYTHING. IT IS AN IMPOSSIBLE PUZZLE." "YOU ARE NOT A MARTYR, CONRAD. YOU ARE A CLOWN."

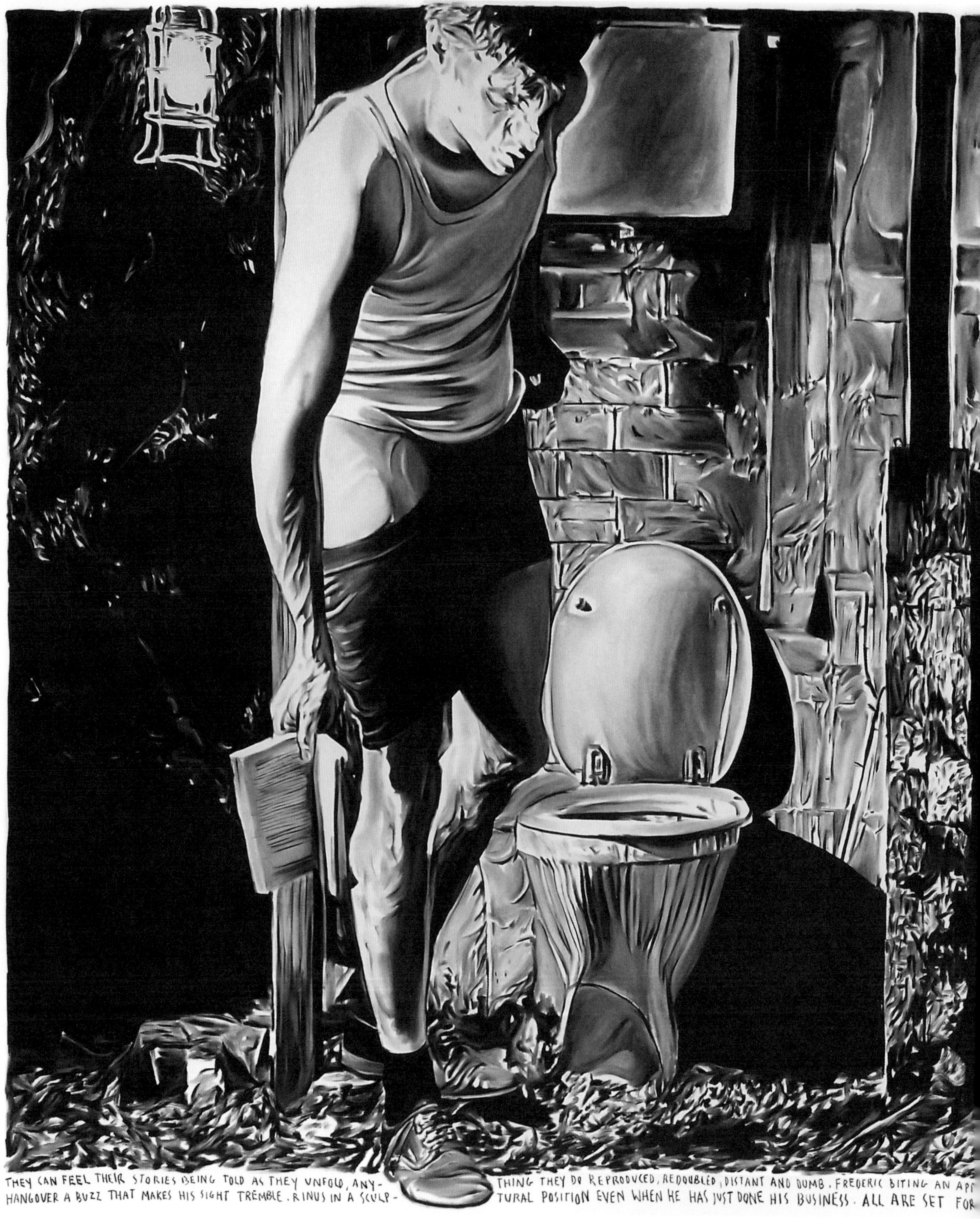

They can feel their stories being told as they unfold, anything
they do reproduced, redoubled, distant and dumb..., 2013
Charcoal on canvas
Framed: 225 × 400 cm (88 ⅝ × 157 ½ in.)

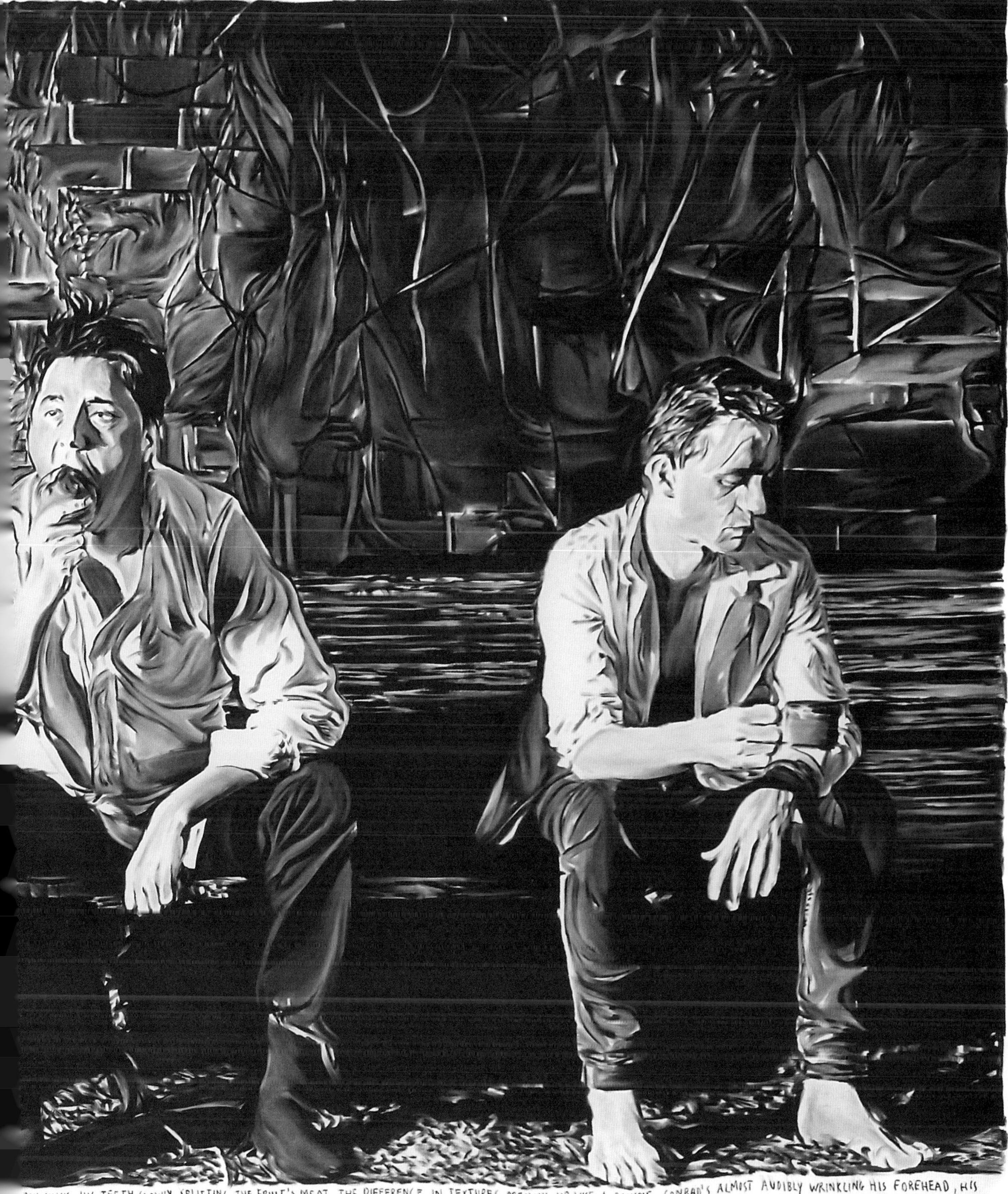

...BLY JUICY, HIS TEETH SLOWLY SPLITTING THE FRUIT'S MEAT. THE DIFFERENCE IN TEXTURES OPENING UP LIKE A RAVINE. CONRAD'S ALMOST AUDIBLY WRINKLING HIS FOREHEAD, HIS
...ND OF THE IMAGE. THEY HARDLY DO ANYTHING ANYMORE.

Barry McGee studied printmaking at the San Francisco Art Institute and achieved fame as a graffiti artist in San Francisco's Mission District in the early 1990s. He has maintained a balance between street and gallery ever since, inevitably tending towards the latter with age and increased international acclaim. In the process, he has gravitated towards a more abstract, geometric or Op Art decorative style and away from the sad-sack cartoon faces that were once his trademark – those portraits of down-at-heel middle-aged men on Mission Street with drink problems that were emblematic of the street artist's identification with the depressed, the poor and homeless. They return, however, in complex gallery installations where he has painted them onto multiple empty liquor bottles, printed them on T-shirts and drawn them on the wall in out-of-register green and orange or blue and red.

Another aspect of the artist's practice that signifies his populist orientation is the massing of images in densely packed clusters, as in the framed portrait drawings and other pictures, reminiscent of the ex-voto images in Catholic churches: a junk shop aesthetic, realized with the panache of a consummate professional. Ballpoint pen drawings of hairy hoboes, eyes peering out of matted beards, are strange enough to suggest not just another street tag motif but the obsessive intensity of a genuine outsider artist, reclusive and angry.

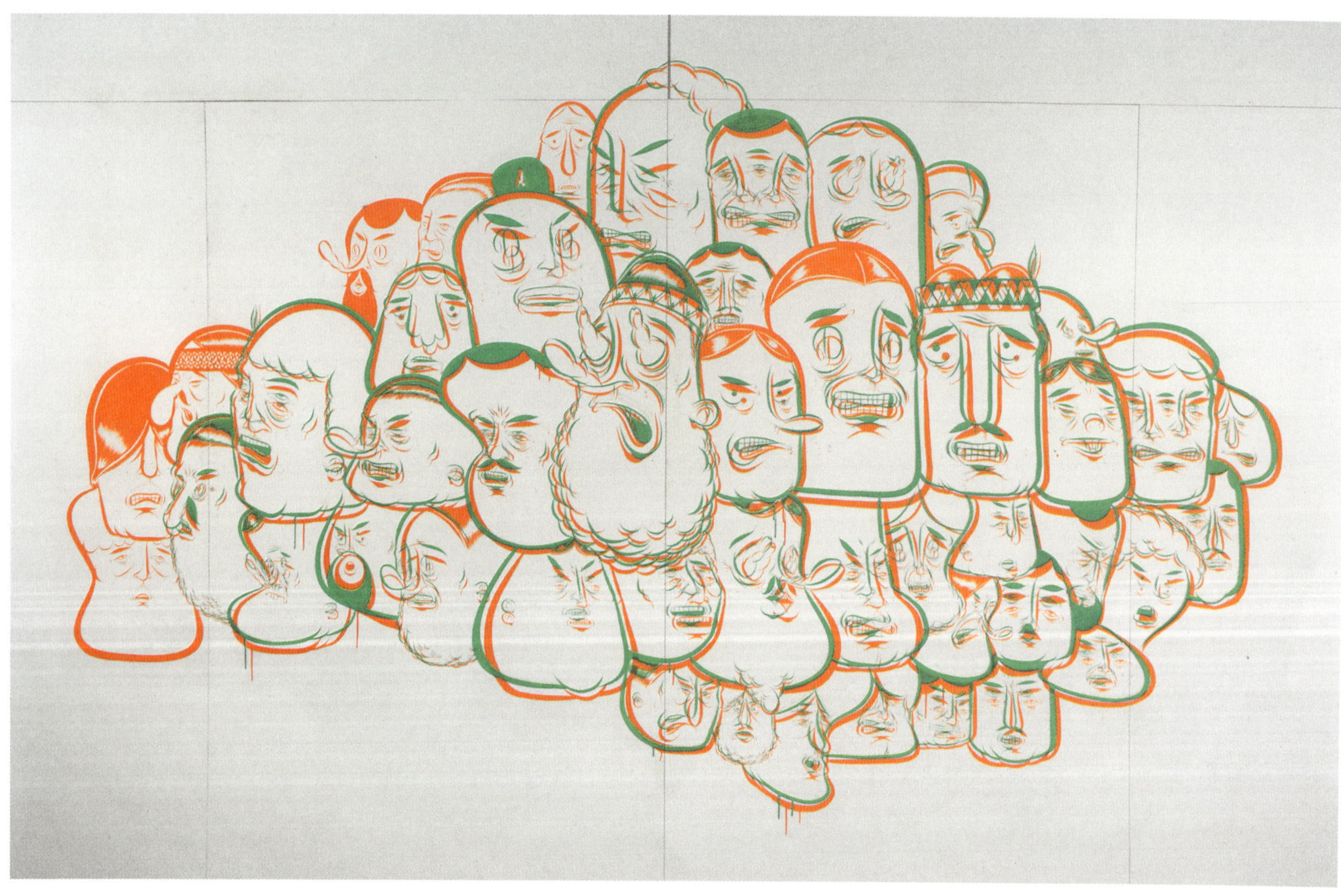

One More Thing, 2005
Installation view

Untitled, 2008 >
Ballpoint pen and acrylic on paper
13 elements, overall: 118.1 × 123.2 cm (46 ½ × 48 ½ in.)

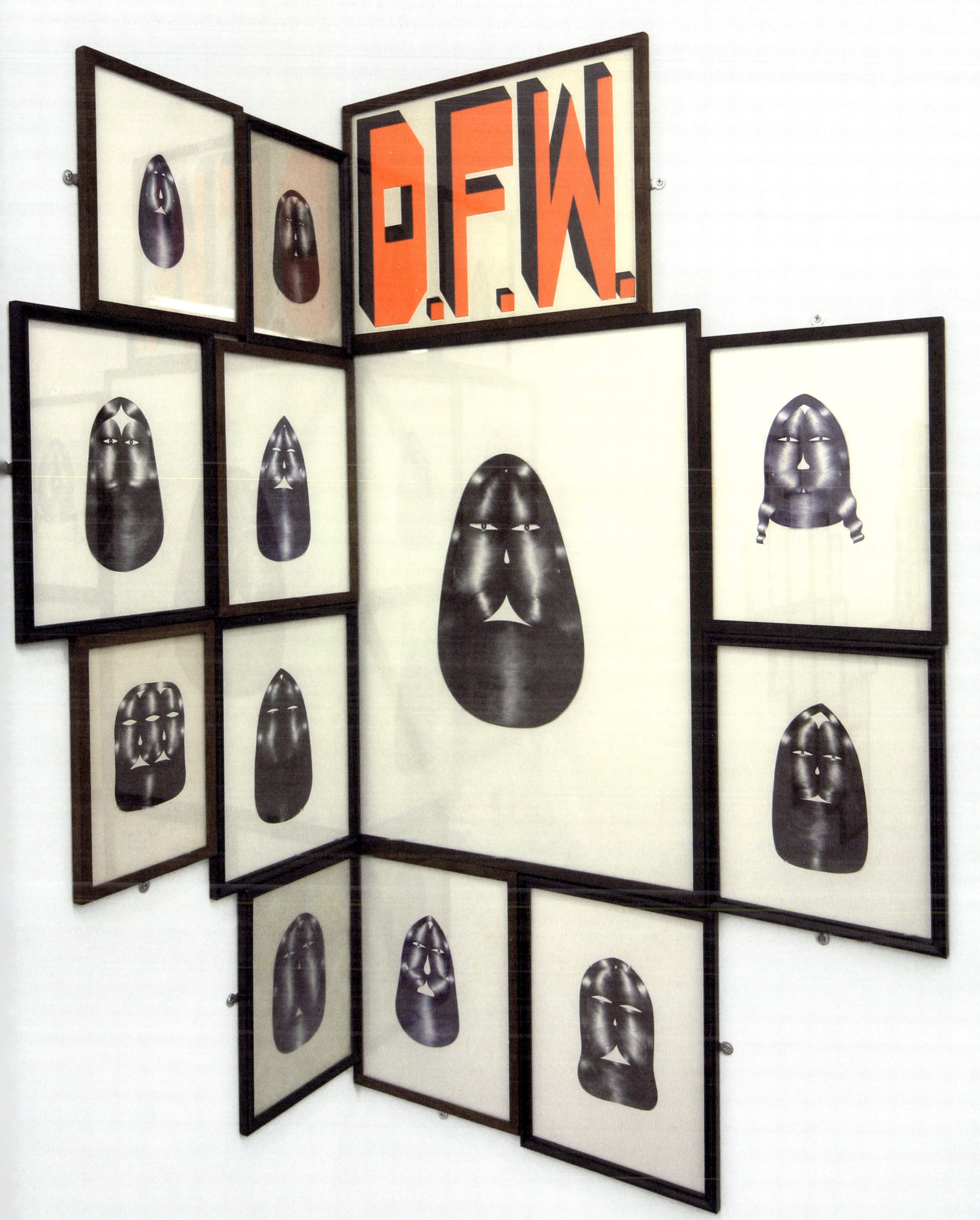

D.F.W.

Roger Malbert is head of Hayward Touring at the Hayward Gallery, Southbank Centre, London. He has organized and co-curated many exhibitions, including 'Rhapsodies in Black: The Art of the Harlem Renaissance' (1997), 'CoBrA' (2003), 'The End of the Line: Attitudes in Drawing' (2009), and 'Curiosity: Art and the Pleasures of Knowing' (2013), and is responsible for an innovative series of artist-curated exhibitions. He has written catalogue essays on the work of Matta, Francisco Goya, Richard Wentworth, Marco Valdivia, Tacita Dean and others, and on a range of themes in contemporary art including the still life, graphic satire, fetishism and the carnivalesque. Malbert's writing has also appeared in the *Independent, Times Literary Supplement, The Art Newspaper* and *Modern Painters.*

acknowledgments

I am grateful to friends and colleagues for help, advice and suggestions, especially: Emanuel von Baeyer, Cécile Bourne-Farrell, Izumi Chiaraluce, Raphael Chikukwa, Ann Demeester, Duygu Demir, Mary Doyle, David Elliott, Caroline Hancock, Isobel Harbison, Timothy Hyman, Mami Kataoka, David Krut, Ying Kwok, Catherine Lampert, Jiyoon Lee, Herman Lelie, Kate Macfarlane, Kate McCrickard, Jean Matthee, Ling Min, Deanna Petherbridge, Sarah Pickstone, Stephanie Rosenthal, Bisi Silva, Janis Tomlinson, Alister Warman, Marina Warner and Juliet Wilson-Bareau.

Thanks are also due to Kyung An, Michael Asbury, Lara Asole, Maeve Butler, Sadie Coles, Andrew Dempsey, Hope Dickens, Andreas Gegner, Zanna Gilberte, Hanna Hewins, Pippy Houldsworth, Rose Issa, Meirian Jump, Sandra Lee, Jessica Lin Cox, Sara MacKillop, Kate McGarry, Erin Manns, Julia Mechtler, Miriam Metliss, Hindenori Ota, Irina Popova, Poppy Pulitzer, Yamuna Ravindran, Corinne Isabelle Rinaldis, Fabio Rossi, Frederike Schuler, Nicolas Smirnoff, Irina Stark, Ferah Tuna and Yelena Walker.

Jessica Cerasi has worked closely with me on the book, provided vital assistance on many levels, organizationally and conceptually, and has been an astute reader of draft texts. At Thames & Hudson my thanks are due firstly to Commissioning Editor Jacky Klein, for giving me the opportunity and freedom to pursue a subject so close to my heart, and for her generous critical guidance. Editors Celia White and Edward Pearce, designer Sarah Praill and Picture Researcher Alexandra Boalch have all been exemplary and a pleasure to work with. My wife Pauline de Souza has given me all the moral support and encouragement I could have wished for. Finally, this book is dedicated to my sons, Emeka and Ikenna.

general bibliography

Fedja Anjelewsky, *Dürer: His Art and Life,* trans. Heide Grieve, London: Gordon Fraser Gallery, 1982.

Mikhail Bakhtin, *Rabelais and His World,* trans. Héléne Iswolsky, Bloomington, Indiana: Indiana University Press, 1984.

Roland Barthes, *A Roland Barthes Reader,* Susan Sontag (ed.), London: Vintage, 2000.

Roland Barthes, *Image Music Text,* trans. Stephen Heath, New York: Hill and Wang, 1977.

John Berger, *Bento's Sketchbook,* London and New York: Verso, 2011.

John Berger, *Berger on Drawing,* Jim Savage (ed.), Cork: Occasional Press, 2007.

Bill Berkson, 'Pyramid and Shoe: Philip Guston and the Funnies', in Michael Auping, *Philip Guston Retrospective* (exh. cat.), London, New York and Fort Worth, Texas: Thames & Hudson and Modern Art Museum of Fort Worth, 2003.

Stephanie Buck and Stephanie Porras (eds), *The Young Dürer: Drawing the Figure* (exh. cat.), London: The Courtauld Gallery/Paul Hoberton Publishing, 2013.

Hugo Chapman and Marzia Faietti, *Fra Angelico to Leonardo: Italian Renaissance Drawings* (exh. cat.), London: British Museum Press, 2010.

Jacques Derrida, *Memoirs of the Blind: The Self-Portrait and Other Ruins,* trans. Pascale-Anne Brault and Michael Nass, Chicago, Illinois: University of Chicago Press, 1993.

Emma Dexter (ed.), *Vitamin D: New Perspectives in Drawing,* London: Phaidon, 2005.

John Elderfield, *The Drawings of Henri Matisse* (exh. cat.), London: Arts Council of Great Britain and Thames & Hudson, 1985.

David Elliott, *Bye Bye Kitty!!! Between Heaven and Hell in Contemporary Japanese Art* (exh. cat.), New York and New Haven: Japan Society and Yale University Press, 2011.

Jack Flam (ed.), *Matisse on Art,* Berkeley and Los Angeles: University of California Press, 1995.

Carl Goldstein, *Teaching Art: Academies and Schools from Vasari to Albers,* Cambridge, UK: Cambridge University Press, 1988.

Robert Gordon and Andrew Forge, *Degas,* London and New York: Thames & Hudson, 1988.

Jerzy Grotowski, *Towards a Poor Theatre,* London and New York: Simon and Schuster, 1968.

Philip Guston, *Collected Writings, Lectures, and Conversations,* Clark Coolidge (ed.), Berkeley and Los Angeles: University of California Press, 2011.

Laura Hoptman, *Drawing Now: Eight Propositions* (exh. cat), New York: Museum of Modern Art, 2003.

Timothy Hyman and Roger Malbert, *Carnivalesque* (exh. cat.), London: Hayward Gallery Publishing, 2000.

Tania Kovats (ed.), *The Drawing Book: A Survey of Drawing – The Primary Means of Expression,* London: Black Dog Publishing, 2005.

Jean-Luc Nancy, *The Pleasure in Drawing,* trans. Philip Armstrong, New York: Fordham University Press, 2013.

Deanna Petherbridge, *The Primacy of Drawing,* New Haven: Yale University Press, 2010.

Pablo Picasso, *Les Demoiselles d'Avignon: A Sketchbook,* essay by Brigitte Leal, London and New York: Thames & Hudson, 1988.

Christian Rattemeyer, *Compass in Hand: Selections from the Judith Rothschild Foundation* (exh. cat.), New York: Museum of Modern Art, 2009.

Christian Rattemeyer, *The Judith Rothschild Foundation Catalogue Raisonné,* New York: Museum of Modern Art, 2009.

Christian Rattemeyer, *Vitamin D2: New Perspectives in Drawing,* London: Phaidon, 2013.

Susan Stewart, *On Longing: Narratives of the Miniature, the Gigantic, the Souvenir, the Collection,* Durham, North Carolina: Duke University Press, 1993.

David Sylvester, *Looking at Giacometti,* London: Chatto & Windus, 1994.

Marc Valli and Ana Ibarra, *Walk the Line: The Art of Drawing,* London: Laurence King, 2013.

Peter Weiermair, *Head to Toe: Drawing the Body from Louise Bourgeois to Andy Warhol,* Zurich: Edition Stemmle, 2001.

Ludwig Wittgenstein, *Last Writings on the Philosophy of Psychology, Vol. 1,* trans. C.G. Luckhardt and Maximilian A.E. Aue, Berkeley and Los Angeles: University of Chicago Press, 1982.

Catherine de Zegher (ed.), *The Stage of Drawing: Gesture and Act* (exh. cat.), London and New York: Tate Publishing and The Drawing Center, 2003.

artist bibliographies

MARIJN AKKERMANS

www.marijnakkermanns.nl

JOWHARA ALSAUD

www.jowharaalsaud.com

FRANCIS ALŸS

www.francisalys.com

Mark Godfrey and Klaus Biesenbach, *Francis Alÿs: A Story of Deception* (exh. cat.), New York: Museum of Modern Art, 2010.

Catherine Lampert (ed.), *Francis Alÿs: The Prophet and the Fly*, Madrid: Turner Ediciones, 2003.

Cuauhtémoc Medina (ed.), *Francis Alÿs: When Faith Can Move Mountains*, Madrid: Turner Ediciones, 2005.

Anne Wehr (ed.), *Francis Alÿs: The Modern Procession*, New York: Public Art Fund, 2003.

MARTIN ASSIG

Martin Assig: Polka, Paris: Vidal St Phalle Editeur, 2002.

Martin Assig, Zeichnungen 1989–92, Mering: Rainer Hampp Verlag, 1992.

Martin Assig: Zeichnungen 1993–99, München: Schirmer/Mosel, 1999.

Mark Gisbourne, *Martin Assig: Vases, Summits, Humans*, München: Schirmer/Mosel, 2010.

CHARLES AVERY

www.charlesavery.com

Charles Avery: The Islanders: An Introduction, essays by Ziba Ardalan and Nicolas Bourriaud, London: Parasol Unit Foundation for Contemporary Art and Walther König, 2008.

Charles Avery and René Zechlin, *Charles Avery: Onomatopoeia. The Port*, Cologne: Walther König, 2010.

MICHAËL BORREMANS

Michaël Borremans: Drawings, interview by Peter Doroshenko and essays by Jeffrey Grove and Anita Haldemann, Cologne: Walther König, 2005.

Michaël Borremans: Whistling a Happy Tune – Drawings, Antwerp: Ludion, 2008.

Jeffrey Grove (ed.), *Michaël Borremans: As Sweet as It Gets*, Ostfildern: Hatje Cantz, 2014.

LOUISE BOURGEOIS

Marie-Laure Bernadac and Elisabeth Bronfen (eds), *Louise Bourgeois: The Insomnia Drawings*, Zurich: Daros, 2000.

Lionel Bovier (ed.), *Louise Bourgeois*, text by Hans Ulrich Obrist, Zurich: JRP Ringier, 2008.

Philip Larratt-Smith (ed.), *Louise Bourgeois: The Return of the Repressed*, London: Violette Editions, 2012.

Philip Larratt-Smith and Paul Nesbitt, *Louise Bourgeois and John Hutton Balfour: Nature Study* (exh. cat.), Edinburgh: Inverleith House, Royal Botanic Garden, 2008.

MARC BRANDENBURG

www.ropac.net/artist/marc-brandenburg

FERNANDO BRYCE

Fernando Bryce: Americas, Barcelona: Ediciones Polígrafa, 2009.

Fernando Bryce, Gustavo Buntinx, Kevin Power and Rodrigo Quijano, *Fernando Bryce* (exh. cat.), Barcelona: Fundació Antoni Tàpies, 2005.

CHEN SHAOXIONG

www.chenshaoxiong.net

Chen Shaoxiong, essays by Pauline J. Yao and Hou Hanru, Hong Kong: Blue Kingfisher, 2010.

VIRGINIA CHIHOTA

www.1-54.com/artist/virginia-chihota

SEVDA CHKOUTOVA

www.chkoutova.com

Sevda Chkoutova, Vienna: Basis, 2010.

FRANCESCO CLEMENTE

www.francescoclemente.net

Francesco Clemente: A History of the Heart in Three Rainbows (exh. cat.), text by Derek Walcott, New York and Milan: Dietch Projects/Charta, 2009.

Francesco Clemente: Self Portraits (exh. cat.), text by Salman Rushdie, London: Gagosian Gallery, 2006.

Francesco Clemente and Arthur Danto, *Francesco Clemente: A Private Geography* (exh. cat.), Milan and New York: Charta/Mary Boone Gallery, 2011.

Max Hollein (ed.), *Francesco Clemente: Palimpsest*, Nürnberg: Moderne Kunst Nürnberg, 2012.

Joytindra Jain, *Francesco Clemente: Made in India*, Milan: Charta, 2011.

ADAM DANT

Adam Dant, Dant on Drink (exh. cat.), Walsall: New Art Gallery, 2010.

Adam Dant, Have a Nice Day! How Modern Life Drives You Mad, London: Redstone Press, 2008.

Adam Dant, The People Who Live on the Plank, London: Drawing Room, 2003.

MARLENE DUMAS

www.marlenedumas.nl

Marlene Dumas, Miss Interpreted (exh. cat.), Eindhoven: Van Abbemuseum, 1992.

Tronies: Marlene Dumas and the Old Masters (exh. cat.), essays by Leon Krempel and Chris Dercon, Munich: Richter Verlag, 2010.

Lisa Gabrielle Mark (ed.), *Marlene Dumas: Measuring Your Own Grave* (exh. cat.), New York and Los Angeles: DAP/Museum of Contemporary Art, Los Angeles, 2008.

Leontine Coelewij (ed.). *Marlene Dumas: The Image as Burden* (exh. cat.), London and New York: Tate Publishing/DAP, 2014.

MARCEL DZAMA

www.davidzwirner.com/artists/marcel-dzama

Marcel Dzama. The Never Known into the Forgotten (exh. cat.), Kunstverein Braunschweig: Kettler, 2012.

Marcel Dzama: Sower of Discord, foreword by Raymond Pettibon, essay by Bradley Bailey, short stories by David Eggers, interview by Spike Jonze, New York: Abrams, 2013.

Deborah Solomon, *Marcel Dzama: Puppets, Pawns, and Prophets* (exh. cat.), Ostfildern and London: Hatje Cantz/David Zwirner, 2013.

INCI EVINER

www.incieviner.net

Haldun Dostoğlu (ed.), *Inci Eviner*, Istanbul: GalleriNev, 2010.

Nasli Gürlek (ed.), *Inci Eviner*, Berlin: Revolver Publishing, 2011.

RICHARD FORSTER

www.richardforster.com

Richard Forster: Modern (exh. cat.), Edinburgh: Ingleby Gallery, 2014.

Richard Forster and Colm Tóibín, *Fast Time & Slow Time* (exh. cat.), Middlesbrough and Edinburgh: Middlesbrough Institute of Modern Art/Ingleby Gallery, 2011.

ANTHONY GORMLEY

www.antonygormley.com

Anna Moszynska, *Antony Gormley: Drawing*, London: British Museum Press, 2002.

Anna Moszynska, *Antony Gormley: Drawing Space* (exh. cat.), Milan and Rome: Mondadori Electa/Museo d'Arte Contemporanea Roma (MACRO), 2010.

DAVID HAINES

www.davidhaines.org

David Haines: Selected Works, 2008–2014, Amsterdam: Upstream Gallery, 2014.

CHO DUCK HYUN

www.chodukhyun.com

Cho Duck Hyun, From an Alien Past. A Contemporary Art Project (exh. cat.), Paris: Éditions du Jeu de Paume, 2000.

Cho Duck Hyun, Genealogy: On My Father (exh. cat.), Seoul: Kukje Gallery, 1996.

Cho Duck Hyun, The History of Korean Woman (exh. cat.), Seoul: Gallery Meegun, 1992.

YUN-FEI JI

Yun-Fei Ji: The Empty City (exh. cat.), texts by Melissa Chiu, Tan Lin and Gregory Volk, St Louis: Contemporary Art Museum St Louis, 2005.

Jessica Lin Cox (ed.), *Yun-Fei Ji: Mistaking Each Other for Ghosts* (exh. cat.), New York and Shanghai: James Cohan Gallery, 2010.

Paula Tsai (ed.), *Yun-Fei Ji: Water Work* (exh. cat.), texts by Zhu Zhu and Jonathan Spence, Beijing: UCCA Books, 2013.

LI JIN

www.li-jin.com

Li Jin: Today Banquet (exh. cat.), Beijing: Today Art Museum, 2012.

Meg Maggio (ed.), *Li Jin* (exh. cat.), Hong Kong: Timezone 8, 2004.

TOMOKO KASHIKI

Tomoko Kashiki (exh. cat.), essay by David Elliott, Tokyo: Ota Fine Arts, 2014.

WILLIAM KENTRIDGE

A Universal Archive: William Kentridge as Printmaker (exh. cat.), text by Rosalind Krauss and Kate McCrickard, London: Hayward Publishing, 2013.

William Kentridge: No, It Is (exh. cat.), Johannesburg: Fourthwall Books, 2013.

William Kentridge: The Refusal of Time (exh. cat.), introduction by Peter Galison, Paris: Editions Xavier Barral, 2013.

William Kentridge: Secondhand Reading (exh. cat.), Johannesburg: Fourthwall Books, 2014.

Lilian Tone (ed.), *William Kentridge: Fortuna*, London and New York: Thames & Hudson, 2013.

JUUL KRAIJER

www.juulkraijer.com

Juul Kraijer, texts by Wilma Sütö and Véronique Baar, Rotterdam: Freem Foundation, 2009.

Juul Kraijer, text by Giorgio Verzotti, Milan: Galleria Monica De Cardenas, 2007.

Juul Kraijer: Drawings, Bergen op Zoom: Philip Morris Holland, 2004.

DR LAKRA

www.katemacgarry.com/artists/dr-lakra

Dr Lakra, text by Dr Lakra and Gabriel Orozco, Barcelona: RM Verlag, 2010.

Dr Lakra: Health & Efficiency, Barcelona: RM Verlag, 2011.

RICARDO LANZARINI

www.xippas.com/en/i/artiste/ricardo_lanzarini

JINJU LEE

www.artistjinju.com

ULRIKE LIENBACHER

www.ulrikelienbacher.com

Ulrike Lienbacher, Catalogue: Drawing/Object/Photography/Video (exh. cat.), Vienna: Comet Books, 2007.

Ulrike Lienbacher: Nude, Pensive, Salzburg: Fotohof, 2012.

Ulrike Lienbacher: Rapunzel, Rapunzel, Vienna: Comet Books, 2005.

LAURIE LIPTON

www.laurielipton.com

The Drawings of Laurie Lipton, San Francisco: Last Gasp, 2013.

The Extraordinary Drawings of Laurie Lipton, San Francisco: beinArt Publishing, 2010.

CHAD McCAIL

www.chadmccail.co.uk

PAUL McCARTHY

Stacen Berg and Jens Hoffmann (eds), *Paul McCarthy's Low Life Slow Life: Tidebox Tidebook* (exh. cat.), Ostfildern and San Francisco: Hatje Cantz/CCA Wattis Institute for Contemporary Arts, 2010.

Joachim Jäger (ed.), *Paul McCarthy: The Box*, Ostfildern: Hatje Cantz, 2014.

Paul McCarthy and Damon McCarthy, *Rebel Dabble Babble* (artist's book), Zurich: JRP Ringier 2013.

Ralph Rugoff and Robert Storr, *Paul McCarthy: Piccadilly Circus* (exh. cat.), Zurich: Scalo, 2004.

BARRY McGEE

Lawrence Rinder and Dena Beard (eds), *Barry McGee* (exh. cat.), New York and Los Angeles: DAP and University of California, Berkeley Art Museum and Pacific Film Archive, 2012.

Aaron Rose (ed.), *Barry McGee: T.H.R.U.*, Bologna: Damiani, 2010.

KUMI MACHIDA

Kumi Machida, texts by Eveline Bernasconi and Satoru Nagoya, Cologne: Walther König, 2008.

David Elliott, *Kumi Machida*, Tokyo: Seigensha Art Publishing, 2012.

AIDA MAKOTO

Aida Makoto: Monument for Nothing (exh. cat.), Tokyo: Mori Art Museum, 2013.

NALINI MALANI

www.nalinimalani.com

Nalini Malani (exh. cat.), Dublin: Irish Museum of Modern Art, 2007.

Nalini Malani: In Search of Vanished Blood (exh. cat.), Ostfildern: Hatje Cantz, 2012.

Andreas Huyssen, *William Kentridge and Nalini Malani: The Shadow Play as Medium of Memory*, Milan: Charta, 2013.

JULIO CÉSAR MORALES

Julio César Morales: Contrabando (exh. cat.), text by Josh Kun, San Francisco: Gallery Wendi Norris, 2010.

WANGECHI MUTU

www.wangechimutu.com

Okwui Enwezor, *Wangechi Mutu: My Dirty Little Heaven*, Ostfildern: Hatje Cantz, 2010.

Trevor Schoonmaker (ed.), *Wangechi Mutu: A Fantastic Journey* (exh. cat.), Durham, North Carolina: Nasher Museum of Art at Duke University, 2013.

OTOBONG NKANGA

www.otobongnkanga.com

JOCKUM NORDSTRÖM

Jockum Nordström: A Stick in the Wood (exh. cat.), Stockholm: Moderna Museet, 2005.

Jockum Nordström: All That I Learned and Then Forgot (exh. cat.), text by Marc Donnadieu and John Hutchinson, Ostfildern: Hatje Cantz, 2013.

CHRIS OFILI

Chris Ofili: Ovid – Diana & Actaeon, text by Catherine Lampert, London: Victoria Miro Gallery, 2013.

Chris Ofili: Within Reach (exh. cat.), London: British Council, 2003.

David Adjaye and Thelma Golden, *Chris Ofili*, Milan: Rizzoli, 2009.

Judith Nesbitt (ed.), *Chris Ofili* (exh. cat.), London: Tate Publishing, 2010.

ODUN ORIMOLADE

www.contemporaryand.com/fr/exhibition/odun-orimolade-being-becoming

PAVEL PEPPERSTEIN

Matthias Haldemann (ed.), *Pavel Pepperstein and Guests*, essays Boris Groys, Matthias Haldemann, Ilya Kabakov, Viktor Mazin and Pavel Pepperstein, Ostfildern: Hatje Cantz, 2004.

RAYMOND PETTIBON

Raymond Pettibon: To Wit, text by Lucas Zwirner, New York and London: David Zwirner, 2013.

Benjamin H.D. Buchloh, *Raymond Pettibon: Here's Your Irony Back: Political Works, 1975–2013*, Ostfildern, London, New York and Los Angeles: Hatje Cantz/David Zwirner/Regen Projects, 2013.

Lynn Kost (ed.), *Raymond Pettibon: Whuytuyp* (exh. cat.), Zurich: JRP Ringier, 2012.

Ralph Rugoff, *Raymond Pettibon*, Milan: Rizzoli, 2013.

Ann Temkin and Hamza Walker (eds), *Raymond Pettibon: A Reader*, Philadelphia and Chicago: Philadelphia Museum of Art/The Renaissance Society at the University of Chicago.

ELIZABETH PEYTON

Elizabeth Peyton, texts by Steve Lafreniere, Dave Hickey and Roberta Smith, New York: Rizzoli, 2005.

Elizabeth Peyton: Here She Comes Now (exh. cat.), Cologne: Walther König, 2013.

ED PIEN

www.edpien.com

Ed Pien: Imaginings (exh. cat.), texts by Cate Rimmer, Oliver Girling and Lydia Kwa, Vancouver: Charles Scott Gallery, 2000.

Ed Pien: Tangled Garden (exh. cat.), text by Mark Laliberte, Banff: Canada House Gallery, 2007.

CHLOE PIENE

www.chloepiene.com

Barry Schwabsky, *Chloe Piene* (exh. cat.), Nîmes: Carré d'Art – Musée d'art contemporain de Nîmes, 2008.

IVAN RAZUMOV

www.iragui.com/en/Artists/Bio/13

EMMANUEL RÉGENT

Emmanuel Régent: Le temps du territoire, texts
by Théodore Wilson and Claude Parent, Dijon:
Les Presses du réel, 2011.

*Emmanuel Régent: Mes plans sur la comète / Drifting
Away* (exh. cat.), texts by Daria de Beauvais and
Caroline Smulders, Blou: Monographik, 2010.

PAULA REGO

Paula Rego: Human Cargo (exh. cat.), London:
Marlborough Fine Art, 2008.

Paula Rego: Oratorio (exh. cat.), London:
Marlborough Fine Art, 2010.

Marco Livingstone (ed.), *Paula Rego* (exh. cat.),
Madrid: Museo Nacional Centro de Arte Reina
Sofía/Ministerio de Cultura, 2007.

T.G. Rosenthal, *Paula Rego: The Complete Graphic
Works*, London and New York: Thames & Hudson,
2012.

FRANCESC RUIZ

Francesc Ruiz: Untitled (Magazine & Newspaper)
(exh. cat.), Philadelphia: Philagrafika Editions, 2010.

JORGE SATORRE

Modelling Standard: Jorge Satorre and Erick Beltrán
(exh. cat.), Amsterdam: Roma Publications, 2011.

MITHU SEN

www.mithusen.com

Mithu Sen: It's Good to be Queen (exh. cat.), texts
by Irina Aristarkhova, Olu Oguibe, David A. Ross
and Elaine Ng, New York: Bose Pacia Gallery, 2008.

Mithu Sen: Nothing Lost in Translation (exh. cat.),
Berlin: Nature Morte, 2010.

Andrew Maerkle, *Mithu Sen: Half Full* (exh. cat.),
New York: Bose Pacia Gallery, 2007.

ERINÇ SEYMEN

Erinç Seymen (exh. cat.), text by Erden Kosova,
Istanbul: Rampa, 2012.

DASHA SHISHKIN

www.dashashishkin.com

SHAHZIA SIKANDER

Shahzia Sikander (exh. cat.), texts by Sean Kissane
and Homi K. Bhabha, Dublin: Irish Museum
of Modern Art, 2007.

Shahzia Sikander: Nemesis (exh. cat.), texts by
Ian Berry and Jessica Hough, New York: Tang
Teaching Museum and Art Museum, 2005.

AMY SILLMAN

www.amysillman.com

Wayne Koestenbaum, *Amy Sillman: Works on Paper*
(exh. cat.), New York: Gregory R. Miller & Company,
2006.

Helen Molesworth (ed.), *Amy Sillman: One Lump
or Two* (exh. cat.), Boston, New York and London:
The Institute of Contemporary Art Boston/Prestel
Verlag, 2014.

ARPITA SINGH

Arpita Singh: Memory Jars (exh. cat.), text by
Nilima Sheikh, Peter Nagy and Deepak Ananth,
New York: Bose Pacia Gallery, 2003.

Arpita Singh: Picture Postcard 2003–2006 (exh. cat.),
London and New Delhi: Vadehra Art Gallery, 2006.

KIKI SMITH

Estrella de Diego and Martin Hentschel, *Kiki Smith:
Her Memory* (exh. cat.), Barcelona: Fundació Joan
Miró, 2009.

Siri Engberg, Linda Nochlin and Marina Warner,
Kiki Smith: A Gathering 1980–2005 (exh. cat.),
Minneapolis: Walker Art Center, 2005.

Helaine Posner, *Kiki Smith*, New York:
The Monacelli Press, 2005.

Wendy Weitman, *Kiki Smith: Prints, Books & Things*
(exh. cat.), New York: Museum of Modern Art, 2003.

MIRCEA SUCIU

www.suciumircea.blogspot.co.uk

Mircea Suciu: Black Milk (exh. cat.), Brussels:
Aeroplastics, 2012.

SUN XUN

www.sunxun.com

Sun Xun, Hong Kong: Blue Kingfisher, 2012.

Mathieu Borysevicz, *Sun Xun* (exh. cat.),
Los Angeles: Hammer Museum, 2008.

TABAIMO

Tabaimo: Boundary Layer (exh. cat.), text by Ziba
Ardalan de Week and J.J. Charlesworth, London:
Parasol Unit Foundation for Contemporary Art and
Walther König, 2010.

Tabaimo: Works: Akunin, Osaka: Asahi Shimbun, 2010.

TAL R

Tal R: The Egyptian Boy, Nürnberg: Moderne Kunst
Nürnberg, 2013.

Tal R: The Virgin, Cologne: Walther König, 2013.

Beate Ermacora and Gregor Jansen (eds), *Tal R:
Man Overboard*, Cologne: Walther König, 2013.

EMMA TALBOT

www.emmatalbot.org.uk

Emma Talbot: Untitled, Zurich: Nieves, 2009.

BARTHÉLÉMY TOGUO

www.barthelemytoguo.com

Barthélémy Toguo: Coexistence on the Earth (exh. cat.),
Dacgu; Wooson Gallery, 2013.

Barthélémy Toguo: Talking to the Moon (exh. cat.),
Saint-Priest-en-Jarez: Musée d'Art Moderne de
Saint-Etienne Métropole, 2013.

ROSEMARIE TROCKEL

Rosemarie Trockel: Post-Menopause, Cologne:
Walther König, 2006.

Anita Haldemann and Christoph Schreier (eds),
Rosemarie Trockel: Drawings, Collages, and Book Drafts
(exh. cat.), Ostfildern: Hatje Cantz, 2010.

RINUS VAN DE VELDE

www.rinusvandevelde.com

MRinus Van de Velde (exh. cat.), Berline and Nürnberg:
Galerie Zink/Moderne Kunst Nürnberg, 2011.

MARCEL VAN EEDEN

www.marcelvaneeden.nl

Marcel van Eeden: Tales of Murder and Violence,
The Hague: Stroom Den Haag, 2014.

Katja Blomberg and Konrad Bitterli, *Marcel van Eeden*,
Cologne: Walther König, 2011.

Michael Zink (ed.), *Marcel van Eeden: Drawings and
Paintings, 1992–2009*, Cologne: DuMont, 2009.

SANDRA VÁSQUEZ DE LA HORRA

www.vasquezdelahorra.de

Juerg Judin (ed.), *Sandra Vásquez de la Horra*,
Ostfildern: Hatje Cantz, 2010.

KARA WALKER

Kara Walker (exh. cat.), Chicago: The Renaissance
Society at the University of Chicago, 1997.

Kara Walker: Bureau of Refugees, Milan and New York:
Charta/Sikkema Jenkins, 2008.

Kara Walker: Dust Jackets for the Niggerati, New York:
Gregory R. Miller & Company, 2013.

*Kara Walker: My Complement, My Enemy,
My Oppressor, My Love* (exh. cat.), text by
Thomas McEvilley and Philippe Vergne, Minneapolis:
Walker Art Center, 2007.

Kara Walker: A Negress of Noteworthy Talent
(exh. cat.), texts by Olga Gambari, Luca Morena and
Rebecca Walker, Turin: Fondazione Merz, 2012.

picture credits

p.1 Photo Peter Cox. Courtesy Zeno X Gallery, Antwerp; pp.2–3 Beth Rudin DeWoody. Courtesy the artist and Hauser & Wirth; p.5 Photo Peter Cox. Courtesy the artist; p.8 Fogg Art Museum, Harvard University Art Museums/ Bequest of Meta and Paul J. Sachs/Bridgeman Images; p.11 Kupferstichkabinett, Staatliche Museen zu Berlin. Photo Scala, Florence/BPK, Bildagentur für Kunst, Kultur und Geschichte, Berlin; p.12 Royal Collection Trust, Her Majesty Queen Elizabeth II, 2014/Bridgeman Images; p.15 Archives H. Matisse. © Succession H. Matisse/ DACS 2014; p.17 British Museum, London. © Succession Picasso/DACS, London 2014; p.18 Katherine S. Dreier Bequest. Inv. no. 177.1953. Digital image 2014, Museum of Modern Art, New York/Scala, Florence. © ADAGP, Paris and DACS, London 2014; p.19 Gift of Lee Krasner Pollock, 1982 (1982.147.30). Image 2014, Metropolitan Museum of Art/Art Resource/Scala, Florence. © The Pollock-Krasner Foundation ARS, NY and DACS, London 2014; p.20 Private collection. Courtesy McKee Gallery, New York. © The Estate of Philip Guston; p.24 Photo Kunihiro Shikata. Courtesy of Parasophia Office. © William Kentridge; p.26 Collection the Museum of Modern Art, New York. Photo Christopher Burke. © The Easton Foundation/DACS 2014; pp.30–31 Courtesy the artist; p.32 Collection Hauser & Wirth, London; p.33 Private collection, Mumbai; pp.34–35 Courtesy the artist. © Wangechi Mutu; p.36 Courtesy Galerie Lelong, New York and Bandjoun Station, Cameroon. © Barthélémy Toguo; p.37 Photo Fabrice Gibert. Courtesy Galerie Lelong, New York and Bandjoun Station, Cameroon. © Barthélémy Toguo; pp.38–39 Photo Ed Pien; pp.40–41 Photo Toni Hafkenscheid. Courtesy the National Art Gallery of Canada, Ottawa; pp.42–43 Photo Christopher Burke. Courtesy Hauser & Wirth and Cheim & Read, New York. © The Easton Foundation/DACS 2014; p.44 Collection The Easton Foundation. Photo Christopher Burke. © The Easton Foundation/DACS 2014; p.45 Collection Tate, London. Photo Christopher Burke. © The Easton Foundation/DACS 2014; pp.46–49 Courtesy Galerie Krinzinger, Vienna. © Ulrike Lienbacher, VBK; pp.50–51 Odun Orimolade; pp.52–53 © Antony Gormley; pp.54–55 Courtesy the artist and Chemould Prescott Road, Mumbai; p.56 Courtesy Artist's Trust Fund, New York; p.57 Courtesy Museum of Contemporary Art, Los Angeles; p.58 Alain Celhay, private collection. Courtesy the artist and Hauser & Wirth; p.59 Friedrich Christian Flick Collection. Courtesy the artist and Hauser & Wirth; p.60 Private collection, New York. Courtesy the artist and Hauser & Wirth; p.61 Gift of Michael Lynne. Acc. no.: 146.2003.2. Digital image 2014, Museum of Modern Art, New York/Scala, Florence; p.62 Private Collection. Courtesy of Nishimura Gallery, Tokyo. © Kumi Machida; pp.66 and 69 Collection Museum of Old and New Art (MONA), Tasmania, Australia. Courtesy Ota Fine Arts. Copyright Tomoko Kashiki; pp.67–68 Courtesy Ota Fine Arts. Copyright Tomoko Kashiki; pp.70–71 Private collection; pp.72–73 Photo Kerry Ryan McFate. Courtesy Pace Gallery. © Kiki Smith; p.74 Photo G.R. Christmas. Courtesy Pace Gallery. © Kiki Smith; p.75 Photo courtesy the artist and Pace Gallery. © Kiki Smith; pp.76–79 Photo Peter Cox. Collection Stedelijk Museum, Amsterdam. © the artist; p.80 Collection Walker Art Center, Minneapolis. Miriam and Erwin Kelen Acquisition Fund for Drawings, 2001. Photo Bernhard Schaub Studio, Cologne. Courtesy Sprüth Magers, Berlin/London. Copyright Rosemarie Trockel, VG Bild-Kunst, Bonn 2014. © DACS 2014; p.81 Photo Photostudio Schaub (Bernhard Schaub/Ralf Höffner). Courtesy Sprüth Magers, Berlin/ London and Skarstedt, New York. Copyright Rosemarie Trockel, VG Bild-Kunst, Bonn 2014. © DACS 2014; pp.82– 83 Photo Reinhard Muxel; pp.84–87 Diehl, Berlin; p.88 Photo Stephen White. Courtesy the artist and Victoria Miro, London. © Chris Ofili; p.89 Collection Victoria

and Warren Miro. Courtesy the artist and Victoria Miro, London. © Chris Ofili; pp.90–91 Courtesy Sadie Coles HQ, London. © the artist; p.92 Takahashi Collection. Courtesy of Nishimura Gallery, Tokyo. © Kumi Machida; p.93 Private Collection. Courtesy of Nishimura Gallery, Tokyo. © Kumi Machida; pp.94–97 © Jinju Lee; p.98 Words by Shilpa Paralkar. Private collection, Princeton, NJ. Photo T. Haartsen; p.99 Photo Peter Cox. Courtesy the artist; p.100 Courtesy the artist; pp.104–7 Courtesy the artist and Dubner Moderne, Lausanne; pp.108–11 Courtesy the artist; pp.112–13 © 2007 Amy Sillman; pp.114–17 Courtesy the artist and Vadehra Art Gallery, New Delhi; pp.118–19 Courtesy Upstream Gallery, Amsterdam; p.120 Collection ARoS Aarhus Kunstmuseum. Photo Anders Sune Berg. Courtesy the artist and Victoria Miro, London. © Tal R; pp.121–23 Photo Anders Sune Berg. Courtesy the artist and Victoria Miro, London. © Tal R; pp.124–25 Courtesy the artist and Rose Issa Projects, London; pp.126–29 Courtesy the artist; pp.130–31 Courtesy the artist and Gallery Wendi Norris, San Francisco, CA; p.132 Collection Glenn and Amanda Fuhrman, courtesy The FLAG Art Foundation, New York. Photo John McKenzie. Courtesy the artist and Ingleby Gallery, Edinburgh; p.133 Collection Whitworth Art Gallery, The University of Manchester. Photo John McKenzie. Courtesy the artist and Ingleby Gallery, Edinburgh; p.134 Cooperation Watanabe Atsushi. Taguchi Art Collection. Photo Watanabe Osamu. © AIDA Makoto/Courtesy Mizuma Art Gallery, Tokyo; p.138 Collection The Hirshhorn Museum and Sculpture Garden, Washington, DC. Courtesy the artist; p.139 Courtesy the artist; pp.140–43 Courtesy the artist, Gallery Barbara Thumm, Berlin and Galeria Joan Prats, Barcelona; p.144 In collaboration with Rafael Ortega, The Public Art Fund and the Museum of Modern Art, New York. Courtesy the artist; p.145 Courtesy the artist; pp.146–47 Courtesy Bertrand Baraudou Gallery, Paris, Caroline Smulders/I love my job, Paris and Analix Forever Gallery, Geneva. © Emmanuel Régent; pp.148–51 Courtesy the artist, Lumen Travo Gallery, Amsterdam and In Situ Fabienne Leclerc Gallery, Paris; pp.152–55 Photo John Hodgkiss. Courtesy the artist; pp.156–57 Courtesy David Zwirner, New York/London and Zeno X Gallery, Antwerp; pp.158–59 Cooperation Watanabe Atsushi. Taguchi Art Collection. Photo Watanabe Osamu. © AIDA Makoto/Courtesy Mizuma Art Gallery, Tokyo; p.160 Photo Peter Cox. Courtesy Zeno X Gallery, Antwerp; p.161 Photo Peter Cox. Courtesy James Cohan Gallery, New York/Shanghai. © the artist; pp.162–65 Courtesy Nahodka Arts Ltd, London. © Pavel Pepperstein; pp.166–67 Courtesy the artist; pp.168–69 *Food Shelter Clothing Fuel*, 2003, digitally re-coloured by Polly Verity; p.170 Photo Kristel Raesaar. Courtesy Galeria Estrany de la Mota, Barcelona; p.171a and b Courtesy Galeria Estrany de la Mota; pp.172–75 Courtesy the artist and Pékin Fine Arts; pp.176–77 Courtesy Regina Gallery, Moscow; pp.178–79 Photo Charles Robinson. Courtesy of Hales Gallery, London. © Adam Dant; pp.180–81 Courtesy of Hales Gallery, London. © Adam Dant; pp.182–83 © 2011 Kara Walker; p.184 Museum of Modern Art, New York. Courtesy Marc Brandenburg; p.185 Private collection. Courtesy CFA/Marc Brandenburg; pp.186–88 Private collection. Courtesy of Zeno X Gallery, Antwerp; p.189 Courtesy of Zeno X Gallery, Antwerp; p.190 Courtesy the artist; pp.194–95 Tate Collection 2014. Photo Andy Keate. Courtesy the artist and Pilar Corrias, London; p.196 Photo Andy Keate. Courtesy the artist and Pilar Corrias, London; p.197 Private collection. Courtesy the artist and Pilar Corrias, London; pp.198–201 Courtesy the artist and Susanne Vielmetter, Los Angeles Projects; pp.202–5 Courtesy the artist; pp.206–7 Courtesy David Zwirner, New York/London; pp.208–9 Courtesy of the artist and Galeri Nev, Istanbul; pp.210–13 Courtesy the artist;

p.214a Private collection, Germany. Courtesy the artist, Galerie Zink, Berlin and Sprüth Magers, Berlin/London; pp.214–15 Courtesy the artist, Galerie Zink, Berlin and Sprüth Magers, Berlin/London; p.216al, cl, b and p.217c Collection Goetz. Courtesy the artist, Galerie Zink, Berlin and Sprüth Magers, Berlin/London; p.216ar Collection Hausmaninger. Courtesy the artist, Galerie Zink, Berlin and Sprüth Magers, Berlin/London; p.216cr Private collection, Germany. Courtesy of the artist; Galerie Zink, Berlin; Sprüth Magers Berlin London; p.217al, ar, bl and br Courtesy the artist, Galerie Zink, Berlin and Sprüth Magers, Berlin/London; pp.218–19 Courtesy the artist. Photo © Can Akgümüş; pp.220–21 Courtesy Regen Projects, Los Angeles. © Raymond Pettibon; pp.222–23 Courtesy the Artist; pp.224–25 Courtesy of Marlborough Fine Art, London; pp.226–28 Courtesy David Zwirner, New York/London; p.229 Photo Per-Erik Adamsson. Courtesy Galleri Magnus Karlsson, David Zwirner and Zeno X; pp.230–31 Photo Andy Keate. Courtesy of Kate MacGarry, London; pp.232–33 Photo Estudio Michel Zabé. Courtesy the artist and kurimanzutto, Mexico City; p.234 Collection Henk van der Reijd, Amsterdam. Photo Peter Tijhuis. © the artist; p.235a Photo Peter Tijhuis. © the artist; p.235b Collection Gemeentemuseum, Den Haag. Photo Edo Kuipers. © the artist; pp.236–37 © Laurie Lipton; p.238a, c and b Courtesy of Gallery Koyanagi, Tokyo. © Tabaimo; pp.239–41 Courtesy the artist, Gallery Koyanagi, Tokyo and James Cohan Gallery, New York/ Shanghai; pp.242–43 Photo Andy Keate. Courtesy the artist and Pilar Corrias, London; p.244 Private collection, Antwerp. Courtesy Tim Van Laere Gallery, Antwerp; pp.245–47 Private collection, Belgium. Courtesy Tim Van Laere Gallery, Antwerp; p.248 Deitch Projects, New York. Courtesy the artist, Ratio 3, San Francisco and Cheim & Read, New York; p.249 University of California, Berkeley Art Museum and Pacific Film Archive, Museum purchase, bequest of Phoebe Apperson Hearst, by exchange. Courtesy the artist, Ratio 3, San Francisco and Cheim & Read, New York.

254

Published and distributed in North America by
arrangement with Thames & Hudson Ltd., London

D.A.P./Distributed Art Publishers, Inc.
155 6th Avenue, 2nd Floor
New York NY 10013
artbook.com

*Drawing People: The Human Figure in Contemporary
Art* © 2015 Thames & Hudson Ltd, London
Text © 2015 Roger Malbert

Designed by Sarah Praill

A CIP record for this book is available from the
Library of Congress

ISBN 978-1-938922-68-8

Printed and bound in China by C&C Offset Printing
Co. Ltd

On the cover: (front) Mircea Suciu, *The Deceiver*,
2012; private collection, courtesy of Zeno X Gallery,
Antwerp. (Back, clockwise from left) Raymond
Pettibon, *No Title (First baybyy to)*, 2012; courtesy
Regen Projects, Los Angeles; © Raymond Pettibon.
Paul McCarthy, *Dwarf Heads, Dwarf Mine*, 2008; Beth
Rudin DeWoody; courtesy the artist and Hauser &
Wirth. Tal R, *Altergang*, 2011; Collection ARoS Aarhus
Kunstmuseum; photo Anders Sune Berg; courtesy the
artist and Victoria Miro, London; © Tal R.